Hitler's Table Talk

The Complete Edition 1941–1944

Hitler's Table Talk

The Complete Edition 1941–1944

Compiled by Heinrich Heim, Henry Picker, and Martin Bormann

Introduced and Annotated by R. P. Tomlinson

With 618 new footnotes contextualizing references, events, and personalities mentioned in the text.

Scrawny Goat Books

Hitler's Table Talk

The Complete Edition 1941–1944

Compiled by Heinrich Heim, Henry Picker, and Martin Bormann

Introduced and annotated by R. P. Tomlinson

Scrawny Goat Books

152 City Road

London, EC1V 2PD

United Kingdom

scrawnygoatbooks.com

ISBN 978-1-915645-14-2

Contents

Introduction vii

PART ONE
July to December 1941 1

PART TWO
January to September 1942 143

PART THREE
June 1943 627

PART FOUR
March to November 1944 636

Index 644

Introduction

Hitler's Table Talk consists of the notes taken of the informal conversations in which the German leader participated around the lunch and dinner tables with his intimate staff and senior party or ideological colleagues.

They were recorded upon the instruction of the head of the Party Chancellery and private secretary to Hitler, Martin Bormann—with Hitler's express permission.

The first notes were taken by the lawyer and *Nationalsozialistische Deutsche Arbeiterparteiparty* (NSDAP, or National Socialist German Workers' Party) undersecretary Heinrich Heim, who started on July 5, 1941, and ended in mid-March 1942.

Henry Picker, a senior executive and legal staff member in the *Führer's* Headquarters, took over and prepared notes from March 21, 1942, until August 2, 1942.

After that date, Heim and Martin Bormann continued appending material at increasingly irregular dates until November 1944, when the records ended.

The documents survived in two versions: the combined Heim and Picker notes, and a more "complete" version kept by Bormann. This latter version was sent piecemeal to Bormann's wife, Gerda, in Munich.

Gerda fled to Italy at the end of the war but was arrested and died of natural causes while in detention in 1946. An Italian official acquired the manuscript from her and sold it to a Swiss national and NSDAP sympathizer, François Genoud.

It seems that Gerda lost at least one copy of the manuscript while still in Munich, as a fragment of a third copy, which consists of forty-two typed pages is in the *Adolf Hitler Collection* at the U.S. Library of Congress. This fragment has a handwritten note at the top of the first page, which reads: "Found by Mr. Jos. Shrasberger, Munich, Herzog Wilhelm Strasse 4."

Picker and Heim together published the first version, in the original German, of the notes in 1951, under the title "Adolf Hitler Monologe im Führerhauptquartier 1941–1944".

Genoud published a French translation in 1952, and an English edition was published with an introduction by Hugh Trevor Roper in 1953. Finally, the original German content of the Bormann manuscript was published in 1980 by Werner Jochmann, although that edition does not contain the 100 entries made by Picker between March 12 and September 1, 1942.

The topics under discussion varied greatly, as the reader will discover. Hitler's remarkable general knowledge serves as a testament to his self-education, and his ability to talk with authority on almost any topic was remarked upon by many observers.

The main recurring themes of the manuscript, can however be pinpointed:

1. Caustic comments on his prime enemies, the Russians; Americans, the English and of course, Jews;

2. His plans for Germany and the occupied territories after a German victory in the conflict; and

3. A pronounced dislike of Christianity and that religion's influence in Germany and elsewhere.

It is the first and third main themes which have aroused the most controversy and which has led to claims that the manuscript has either been forged or altered to misrepresent his true views on the matter.

The very first entry in the manuscript is highly derogative of Russians, and in the first part of the book, repeated reference is made to alleged Russian mental and racial inferiority. These references have led to the book being formally banned in 2008 Russia under that country's anti-extremism laws.

At first reading, there can be no doubt that initially Hitler viewed Russians as racially inferior.

However, as the war progressed, the derogatory remarks become fewer and fewer, and in one of the last entries, Hitler even praises Stalin as a "giant" and "successor of the Tsars."

It is clear that his earlier derogatory remarks, made the flush of early victories and rampant German nationalism, did not represent Hitler's ultimate position on Russia or Russians.

This was evidenced in Hitler's later actions as well, when, for example, hundreds of thousands of Russians were allowed to take up German arms and uniforms to join in the crusade against Communism in the "Russian National Liberation Army" under former Soviet General Vlassov.

The anti-Russian remarks should also be contextualized in the light of his equally vehement attacks on the nature of Americans and American culture. In one section, Hitler claims, for example, that the closure of an opera house in New York was evidence of the cultural degeneracy of Americans. There are also derogatory remarks about the English, the French, the Czechs, the Romanians, the Spaniards, the Hungarians and even the Finns. The latter four were, at the time the remarks were made, allies of Germany.

The insults which Hitler so liberally dished out were therefore, not limited to Russians, and by the end of the war, there can be little doubt that the German leader had acquired enough cause to revise his opinions on all of them.

The other section of the manuscript which has been the source of much controversy are the biting attacks upon Christianity.

The reason for the uproar lies in the fact that the comments attributed to Hitler about that religion in this book are far more vehement than anything he has to say about Jews and are directly contradictory to his public position on the matter and even what he wrote in *Mein Kampf.*

The controversy stems from differences in translation between the Genoud (French) version, its English translation, and the Heim and Picker version.

The French, English and German versions do contain subtle differences which might very well be interpreted differently, but which can most likely be attributed to figurative translations of difficult German phrases.

A good example is the use of the word "disease" to describe Christianity in the English and French versions of the entry for 27 February 1942. That particular word does not appear in the published German version and is clearly a figurative translation linked to the next sentence which calls for the "cleaning" of all life.

It has been claimed that Genoud has inserted words in the manuscript, an allegation which he denied, pointing out that the original manuscript was typewritten and is uniform, with the only insertions being handwritten notes by Bormann in the margin.

The quibbling over figurative and literal translations has therefore provided ammunition to those who object to the anti-Christian comments in the manuscript.

No-one, however, disputes the essential content and anti-Christian posturing contained in Hitler's private conversation.

This edition has followed the original Genoud version, but for the sake of historical relevancy, it is important for readers to be aware that there are translations which differ slightly in detail, but not in meaning or direction.

As to be expected, the topic of Jews and Jewish influence features heavily in this manuscript. The most interesting part of the conversations deal with the treatment of Jews during the war, and specifically how they would be "rooted out" of Europe and "dumped in Russia."

Significantly, Hitler dismisses allegations of mass extermination, remarking that it was "good that popular rumour" attributes such an action to the Germans, because, he says, "terror is a salutary thing."

The text is also often presented as Hitler's "monologues" as if he subjected his staff and guests to an endless solo haranguing on various topics.

In fact, as many observers (such as the Belgian Leon Degrelle) said, Hitler was a very polite dinner table host and was always an attentive listener.

The nature of the manuscript was however to capture Hitler's thoughts only, and this has created the impression that it was only he who spoke at these mealtimes.

The vast number of topics discussed, and the occasional inserted remarks by guests, indicate however that the conversations were the product of an animated discussion rather than a solo discourse.

This new edition contains for the first time over 600 footnotes explaining personalities, events, and other sometimes obscure references within the text to the present-day reader.

Hitler's Table Talk remains one of the most powerful insights into the mind of Adolf Hitler, and is required reading for anyone seeking to understand this tragic period of history.

R. P. Tomlinson
London
December 2022

PART ONE
July to December 1941

5th July 1941
Aryans and Russians—Necessity of the mailed fist in Russia—
Deterioration of soil

What we need is a collective view of people's wish to live and manner of living. We must distinguish between the Fascist popular movement and the popular movement in Russia. The Fascist movement is a spontaneous return to the traditions of ancient Rome. The Russian movement has an essential tendency towards anarchy.

By instinct, the Russian does not incline towards a higher form of society. Certain peoples can live in such a way that with them a collection of family units does not make a whole; and although Russia has set up a social system which, judged by Western standards, qualifies for the designation "State", it is not, in fact, a system which is either congenial or natural to her.

It is true that, in a sense, every product of human culture, every work gifted with beauty can be born only of the effect of the constraint which we call education. The Aryan peoples are peoples who are particularly active.

A man like Krümel[1] works from morning to night; such-and-such another person never stops thinking. In the same way, the Italian is as diligent as an ant. In the eyes of the Russian, the principal support of civilisation is vodka. His ideal consists in never doing anything but the indispensable. Our conception of work (work, and then more of it!) is one that he submits to as if it were a real curse.

It is doubtful whether anything at all can be done in Russia without the help of the Orthodox priest. It's the priest who has been able to reconcile the Russian to the fatal necessity of work—by promising him more happiness in another world.

The Russian will never make up his mind to work except under compulsion from outside, for he is incapable of organising himself. And if, despite everything, he is apt to have organisation thrust upon him, that is thanks to the drop of Aryan blood in his veins. It's only because of this drop that the Russian people has created something and possesses an organised State, It takes energy to rule Russia.

---

[1] Otto Günther, nicknamed "Krümel," ("crumb"), one of Hitler's cooks.

The corollary is that, the tougher a country's regime, the more appropriate it is that equity and justice should be practised there. The horse that is not kept constantly under control forgets in the wink of an eye the rudiments of training that have been inculcated into it. In the same way, with the Russian, there is an instinctive force that invariably leads him back to the state of nature.

People sometimes quote the case of the horses that escaped from a ranch in America, and by some ten years later had formed huge herds of wild horses. It is so easy for an animal to go back to its origins! For the Russian, the return to the state of nature is a return to primitive forms of life.

The family exists, the female looks after her children, like the female of the hare, with all the feelings of a mother. But the Russian doesn't want anything more. His reaction against the constraint of the organised State (which is always a constraint, since it limits the liberty of the individual) is brutal and savage, like all feminine reactions. When he collapses and should yield, the Russian bursts into lamentations. This will to return to the state of nature is exhibited in his revolutions.

For the Russian, the typical form of revolution is nihilism.

I think there's still petroleum in thousands of places. As for coal, we know we're reducing the natural reserves, and that in so doing we are creating gaps in the sub-soil. But as for petroleum, it may be that the lakes from which we are drawing are constantly renewed from invisible reservoirs.

Without doubt, man is the most dangerous microbe imaginable. He exploits the ground beneath his feet without ever asking whether he is disposing thus of products that would perhaps be indispensable to the life of other regions. If one examined the problem closely, one would probably find here the origin of the catastrophes that occur periodically in the earth's surface.

Night of 5th–6th July 1941
The shortening of space by roads—The Ural frontier—Moscow must disappear—The treasures of the Hermitage

The beauties of the Crimea, which we shall make accessible by means of an *autobahn*—for us Germans, that will be our Riviera. Crete is scorching and dry. Cyprus would be lovely, but we can reach the Crimea by road. Along that road lies Kiev! And Croatia, too, a tourists' paradise for us. I expect that after the war there will be a great upsurge of rejoicing.

Better than the railway, which has something impersonal about it, it's the road that will bring peoples together. What progress in the direction of the New Europe! Just as the *autobahn* has caused the inner frontiers of Germany to disappear, so it will abolish the frontiers of the countries of Europe.

To those who ask me whether it will be enough to reach the Urals as a frontier, I reply that for the present it is enough for the frontier to be drawn back as far as that. What matters is that Bolshevism must be exterminated. In case of necessity, we shall renew our advance wherever a new centre of resistance is formed.

Moscow, as the centre of the doctrine, must disappear from the earth's surface, as soon as its riches have been brought to shelter. There's no question of our collaborating with the Muscovite proletariat. Anyhow, St. Petersburg, as a city, is incomparably more beautiful than Moscow. Probably the treasures of the Hermitage[2] have not been stored at the Kremlin, as they were during the Great War, but in the country-houses—unless they've been shifted to the cities east of Moscow, or still further by river.

Night of 11th–12th July 1941
The natural piety of man—Russian atheists know how to die—No atheistical education

I think the man who contemplates the universe with his eyes wide open is the man with the greatest amount of natural piety: not in the religious sense, but in the sense of an intimate harmony with things.

At the end of the last century the progress of science and technique led liberalism astray into proclaiming man's mastery of nature, and announcing that he would soon have dominion over space. But a simple storm is enough—and everything collapses like a pack of cards!

In any case, we shall learn to become familiar with the laws by which life is governed, and acquaintance with the laws of nature will guide us on the path of progress. As for the *why* of these laws, we shall never know anything about it. A thing is so, and our understanding cannot conceive of other schemes.

Man has discovered in nature the wonderful notion of that all-mighty being whose law he worships. Fundamentally in everyone there

---

[2] The Hermitage is the name still given to a collection of Russian Imperial-era buildings used as a museum, of which the most famous is the "Winter Palace." These buildings contain a vast trove of treasure which date back to the time of Empress Catherine the Great, who reigned from 1762 to 1796.

is the feeling for this almighty, which we call God (that is to say, the dominion of natural laws throughout the whole universe). The priests, who have always succeeded in exploiting this feeling, threaten punishments for the man who refuses to accept the creed they impose.

When one provokes in a child a fear of the dark, one awakens in him a feeling of atavistic dread. Thus this child will be ruled all his life by this dread, whereas another child, who has been intelligently brought up, will be free of it.

It's said that every man needs a refuge where he can find consolation and help in unhappiness. I don't believe it! If humanity follows that path, it's solely a matter of tradition and habit. That's a lesson, by the way, that can be drawn from the Bolshevik front. The Russians have no God, and that doesn't prevent them from being able to face death. We don't want to educate anyone in atheism.

Night of 17th–18th July 1941

National Socialism and religion cannot exist together—No persecution of religions, let them wither of themselves—Bolshevism, the illegitimate child of Christianity—Origin of the Spartan gruel—The Latvian morons—Stalin, one of history's most remarkable figures

When National Socialism has ruled long enough, it will no longer be possible to conceive of a form of life different from ours. In the long run, National Socialism and religion will no longer be able to exist together.

On a question from C. S.,[3] *whether this antagonism might mean a war, the Führer continued:* No, it does not mean a war. The ideal solution would be to leave the religions to devour themselves, without persecutions. But in that case we must not replace the Church by something equivalent.

That would be terrifying! It goes without saying that the whole thing needs a lot of thought. Everything will occur in due time. It is a simple question of honesty, that's what it will finally boil down to. In England, the status of the individual in relation to the Church is governed by considerations of State. In America, it's all purely a matter of conformism.

The German people's especial quality is patience; and it's the only one of the peoples capable of undertaking a revolution in this sphere. It could do it, if only for the reason that only the German people have made moral law the governing principle of action.

[3] Christa Schroeder (1908–1984), one of Hitler's secretaries.

4

The heaviest blow that ever struck humanity was the coming of Christianity. Bolshevism is Christianity's illegitimate child. Both are inventions of the Jew. The deliberate lie in the matter of religion was introduced into the world by Christianity. Bolshevism practises a lie of the same nature, when it claims to bring liberty to men, whereas in reality it seeks only to enslave them. In the ancient world, the relations between men and gods were founded on an instinctive respect. It was a world enlightened by the idea of tolerance. Christianity was the first creed in the world to exterminate its adversaries in the name of love. Its key-note is intolerance.

Without Christianity, we should not have had Islam. The Roman Empire, under Germanic influence, would have developed in the direction of world-domination, and humanity would not have extinguished fifteen centuries of civilisation at a single stroke.

Let it not be said that Christianity brought man the life of the soul, for that evolution was in the natural order of things.

The result of the collapse of the Roman Empire was a night that lasted for centuries. The Romans had no dislike of the Germans. This is shown by the mere fact that blond hair was fashionable with them. Amongst the Goths there were many men with dark hair.

The Italian, Spanish, French and English dialects were created by mixtures of local languages with the linguistic elements imported by the migrant peoples. At first they were mere vernaculars, until a poet was found who forged the nation's language. It takes five or six centuries for a language to be born.

The conqueror of a country is forced to adapt himself to the local language. That is why language is not the immovable monument on which a people's characteristics are inscribed. A people's way of eating, for example, is racially more typical—for every man remains persuaded in his heart that his mother is the best cook.

When I tasted the soup of the people of Schleswig-Holstein, it occurred to me that the gruel of the Spartans cannot have been very different. In the time of the great migrations, the tribes were the product of ceaseless mixtures. The men who arrived in the South were not the same as those who went away. One can imagine two hundred young Friesians setting out for the South, like a tank setting out across country, and carrying with them men belonging to other tribes. The Croats are certainly more Germanic than Slav.

The Esthonians, too, have a lot of Germanic blood. The Esthonians are the elite of the Baltic peoples. Then come the Lithuanians, and lastly the Latvians. Stalin used Latvians for the executions which the Russians found disgusting. They're the same people who used to have the job of executioners in the old empire of the Tsars.

Stalin is one of the most extraordinary figures in world history. He began as a small clerk, and he has never stopped being a clerk. Stalin owes nothing to rhetoric. He governs from his office, thanks to a bureaucracy that obeys his every nod and gesture.

It's striking that Russian propaganda, in the criticisms it makes of us, always holds itself within certain limits. Stalin, that cunning Caucasian, is apparently quite ready to abandon European Russia, if he thinks that a failure to solve her problems would cause him to lose everything. Let nobody think Stalin might reconquer Europe from the Urals! It is as if I were installed in Slovakia, and could set out from there and reconquer the Reich. This is the catastrophe that will cause the loss of the Soviet Empire.

Night of 21st–22nd July 1941
Gratitude to the Jesuits—Protestant fanaticism—Similarities between Germany and Italy—Dante and Luther—The Duce is one of the Caesars—The march on Rome—a turning point in history—Delightful Italian towns—Rome and Paris

When all is said, we should be grateful to the Jesuits. Who knows if, but for them, we might have abandoned Gothic architecture for the light, airy, bright architecture of the Counter-Reformation? In the face of Luther's efforts to lead an upper clergy that had acquired profane habits back to mysticism, the Jesuits restored to the world the joy of the senses. It's certain that Luther had no desire to mould humanity to the letter of the Scriptures. He has a whole series of reflections in which he clearly sets himself against the Bible. He recognises that it contains a lot of bad things.

Fanaticism is a matter of climate—for Protestantism, too, has burnt its witches. Nothing of that sort in Italy, The Southerner has a lighter attitude towards matters of faith. The Frenchman has personally an easy way of behaving in his churches. With us, it's enough not to kneel to attract attention.

But Luther had the merit of rising against the Pope and the organisation of the Church. It was the first of the great revolutions. And thanks to his translation of the Bible, Luther replaced our dialects by the great German language! It's remarkable to observe the resemblances between the evolution of Germany and that of Italy. The creators of the language, Dante and Luther, rose against the ecumenical desires of the papacy. Each of the two nations was led to unity, against the dynastic interests, by *one* man. They achieved their unity against the will of the Pope.

I must say, I always enjoy meeting the Duce. He's a great personality. It's curious to think that, at the same period as myself, he was working in the building trade in Germany. Our programme was worked out in 1919, and at that time I knew nothing about him. Our doctrines are based on the foundations proper to each of them, but every man's way of thinking is a result.

Don't suppose that events in Italy had no influence on us. The brown shirt would probably not have existed without the black shirt. The march on Rome, in 1922, was one of the turning-points of history. The mere fact that anything of the sort could be attempted, and could succeed, gave us an impetus.

A few weeks after the march on Rome, I was received by the Minister Schweyer. That would never have happened otherwise. If Mussolini had been outdistanced by Marxism, I don't know whether we could have succeeded in holding out. At that period National Socialism was a very fragile growth.

If the Duce were to die, it would be a great misfortune for Italy. As I walked with him in the gardens of the Villa Borghese, I could easily compare his profile with that of the Roman busts, and I realised he was one of the Caesars. There's no doubt at all that Mussolini is the heir of the great men of that period.

Despite their weaknesses, the Italians have so many qualities that make us like them. Italy is the country where intelligence created the notion of the State. The Roman Empire is a great political creation, the greatest of all. The Italian people's musical sense, its liking for harmonious proportions, the beauty of its race! The Renaissance was the dawn of a new era, in which Aryan man found himself anew.

There's also our own past on Italian soil. A man who is indifferent to history is a man without hearing, without sight. Such a man can live, of course—but what a life? The magic of Florence and Rome, of Ravenna, Siena, Perugia! Tuscany and Umbria, how lovely they are! The smallest palazzo in Florence or Rome is worth more than all Windsor Castle. If the English destroy anything in Florence or Rome, it will be a crime.

In Moscow, it wouldn't do any great harm; nor in Berlin, unfortunately. I've seen Rome and Paris, and I must say that Paris, with the exception of the Arc de Triomphe, has nothing on the scale of the Coliseum, or the Castle of San Angelo, or St. Peter's.

These monuments, which are the product of a collective effort, have ceased to be on the scale of the individual. There's something queer about the Paris buildings, whether it's those bull's-eye windows, so badly proportioned, or those gables that obliterate whole façades. If I compare the Pantheon in Rome with the Pantheon in Paris, what a poor building—and what sculptures! What I saw in Paris has disappeared from my memory: Rome really seized hold of me.

When the Duce came to Berlin, we gave him a magnificent reception. But our journey in Italy, that was something else! The reception when we arrived, with all the ceremonial. The visit to the Quirinal!

Naples, apart from the castle, might be anywhere in South America. But there's always the courtyard of the royal palace. What nobility of proportions!

My dearest wish would be to be able to wander about in Italy as an unknown painter.

Night of the 22nd–23rd July 1941
British arrogance—The birth of German industry—Trade competition with Britain—Steps towards a durable understanding between Germany and Britain—Dearth of philosophic and artistic sense of the British—Germany and England

The Englishman is superior to the German in one respect—that of pride. Only the man who knows how to give orders has pride. Everywhere in the world, Germans are working without getting the wages they deserve. Their abilities are recognised, but the fact that they live solely by their work makes them an object of contempt to the people whom they enrich. That's the reason why, in the period just before the Great War, the German got so little sympathy in the Anglo-Saxon world.

Around 1870 we had a huge excess population, with the result that every year between two and three hundred thousand of our people had to make up their minds to emigrate. The remedy for this state of affairs would have been to incorporate them in the labour cycle. The only form of production that could be considered was that of the German primary materials—coal and steel. In this field, the needs of the market had until then been covered by England.

The English demanded the best, and paid high prices to get it. In these conditions, anyone who wants nevertheless to do business has only one solution—to ask lower prices.

Our desperation for work enabled us to produce cheap, mass produced articles that could nevertheless compete with English goods on the quality level. We were beginners, and did not know all the secrets of manufacture. Thus it was that during the 'eighties, at a World Exhibition in Philadelphia, German production was called "shoddy".

Nevertheless, with time, we were able to out-class English work in three sectors of production: the chemical industry (especially as regards pharmaceutical products, the manufacture of dyes and, just before the Great War, the extraction of nitrogen from the air); the production of electrical apparatus; and the production of optical instruments.

England felt this competition so keenly that she reacted with all her strength. But neither her attempts at tariff protection, nor certain international agreements, nor the compulsory use of the phrase "Made in Germany" as a label for our goods, made any difference at all.

For the English, the ideal existence was represented in the society of the Victorian age. At that time England had at her service the countless millions of her colonial Empire, together with her own thirty-five million inhabitants. On top of that, a million bourgeois—and, to crown the lot, thousands of gentlefolk who, without trouble to themselves, reaped the fruit of other people's toil. For this ruling caste, Germany's appearance on the scene was a disaster. As soon as we started our economic ascent, England's doom was sealed.

It is quite certain that in future England's Empire won't be able to exist without the support of Germany. I believe that the end of this war will mark the beginning of a durable friendship with England. But first we must give her the K.O.[4]—for only so can we live at peace with her, and the Englishman can only respect someone who has first knocked him out. The memory of 1918 must be obliterated.

E. D.[5] asked the Führer whether Germany was fortified against the dangers of over-easy living, which were threatening to be the ruin of England.

Yes, and that's why I pay attention to the arts. Amongst the English, culture, like sport, is a privilege of good society. Just imagine, in no country is Shakespeare so badly acted as in England. They love music,

4 "Knock out" blow, as in boxing.
5 Eduard Dietl (1890–1944), commander of the 20th Mountain Army.

but their love is not returned! Besides, they have no thinker of genius. What does the National Gallery mean there, to the mass of the people? It's like their social reform. It wasn't called for, like German reform, by the needs of conscience, but solely by reasons of State.

At Bayreuth[6] one meets more Frenchmen than Englishmen. Quote me the example of a single theatre in England where work is done that compares with the work we do in hundreds of theatres.

But I've met a lot of Englishmen and Englishwomen whom I respect. Let's not think too much about those whom we know, with whom we've had those deceptive official dealings—they're not men. Despite everything, it's only with the people that we can associate.

Night of 24th–25th July 1941
The qualities of the German soldier—SS losses pay dividends—
Weaknesses of the German High Command in 1914–18

I can say that I've never doubted the qualities of the German soldier—which is more than I can say even of some of the chiefs of the *Wehrmacht*. The German army is technically the most perfect in the world; and the German soldier, in a moment of crisis, is safer and sounder than any other soldier. I'm truly happy that it has been granted to me to see, in my lifetime, the German soldier rewarded by Providence.

For an elite force, like our SS, it's great luck to have suffered comparatively heavy losses. In this way, it's assured of the necessary prestige to intervene, if need be, on the home front—which, of course, won't be necessary. But it's good to know that one disposes of a force that could show itself capable of doing so, on occasion. It's marvellous to see how our *Gauleiters*[7] are everywhere in the breach. I cannot tell you how greatly I suffered, during the Great War, from the weaknesses of our command. In a military sense we were not at all clever, and in a political sense we were so clumsy that I had a constant longing to intervene. If I would been Reich Chancellor at the period, in three months' time I would have cut the throat of all obstruction, and I would have reasserted our power.

---

[6] Bayreuth: a town in Bavaria where Richard Wagner lived and where an operatic centre celebrating and performing his work was established.

[7] Under Nazi rule, the German federal states were abolished and replaced with regions called "*Gaus*." A "*Gauleiter*" was the leader of each *Gau*. This was a senior post, and the third highest rank in Nazi Germany, subordinate only to the *Reichsleiters* ("Reich Leaders") and to the Führer.

If I were twenty to twenty-five years younger, I would be in the front line. I passionately loved soldiering.

Friday, 25th July 1941, midday
Romania must become an agricultural country

Romania would do well to give up, as far as possible, the idea of having her own industry. She would direct the wealth of her soil, and especially her wheat, towards the German market. She would receive from us, in exchange, the manufactured goods she needs. Bessarabia is a real granary. Thus the Romanian proletariat, which is contaminated by Bolshevism, would disappear, and the country would never lack anything. I must admit that King Carol[8] has worked in that direction.

Friday, 25th July 1941, evening
Anglo-American rivalries

England and America will one day have a war with one another, which will be waged with the greatest hatred imaginable. One of the two countries will have to disappear.

10 Saturday, 26th July 1941, night
Monarchy is doomed

The people need a point upon which everybody's thoughts converge, an idol. A people that possess a sovereign of the stature of Frederick the Great can think itself happy; but if he's just an average monarch, it's better to have a republic. Notice that when the institution of monarchy has been abolished in a country—see France and Yugoslavia today!—thenceforward the institution is given over to ridicule, and can never again assert itself. I am tempted to believe that the same thing will happen with the Church. Both are institutions that naturally developed in the direction of ceremonial and solemnity. But all that apparatus no longer means anything when the power that lay beneath it has disappeared.

Sunday, 28th July 1941, evening
Old and young nations—Never again a military power in the East—
British domination in India—No education for illiterate Russians—
Colonisation of the Ukraine—The soldier-peasants

It is striking to observe to what a degree a people's place in the world is a function of its age. A young nation is compelled to constant successes. An old nation can allow itself continual set-backs. We must take

---

[8] Carol II (1893–1953), who served as King of Romania from 1930 until 1940, when he was forced to abdicate under a cloud of corruption.

care to prevent a military power from ever again establishing itself on this side of the Urals, for our neighbours to the West would always be allied with our neighbours to the East. That's how the French once made common cause with the Turks, and now the English are behaving in the same fashion with the Soviets. When I say, on this side of the Urals, I mean a line running two or three hundred kilometres east of the Urals.

It should be possible for us to control this region to the East with two hundred and fifty thousand men plus a cadre of good administrators. Let's learn from the English, who, with two hundred and fifty thousand men in all, including fifty thousand soldiers, govern four hundred million Indians. This space in Russia must always be dominated by Germans.

Nothing would be a worse mistake on our part than to seek to educate the masses there. It is to our interest that the people should know just enough to recognise the signs on the roads. At present they can't read, and they ought to stay like that. But they must be allowed to live decently, of course, and that's also to our interest. We'll take the southern part of the Ukraine, especially the Crimea, and make it an exclusively German colony. There'll be no harm in pushing out the population that's there now.

The German colonist will be the soldier-peasant, and for that I'll take professional soldiers, whatever their line may have been previously. In this way we shall dispose, moreover, of a body of courageous N.C.O.s, whenever we need them. In future we shall have a standing army of a million and a half to two million men.

With the discharge of soldiers after twelve years of service, we shall have thirty to forty thousand men to do what we like with every year. For those of them who are sons of peasants, the Reich will put at their disposal a completely equipped farm. The soil costs us nothing, we have only the house to build. The peasant's son will already have paid for it by his twelve years' service. During the last two years he will already be equipping himself for agriculture.

One single condition will be imposed upon him: that he may not marry a townswoman, but a countrywoman who, as far as possible, will not have begun to live in a town with him. These soldier peasants will be given arms, so that at the slightest danger they can be at their posts when we summon them. That's how the ancient Austria used to keep its Eastern peoples under control.

By the same token, the soldier-peasant will make a perfect school-teacher. The N.C.O. is an ideal teacher for the little country boy. In any case, this N.C.O. will make a better teacher than our present teacher will make an officer! Thus we shall again find in the countryside the blessing of numerous families.

Whereas the present law of rural inheritance dispossesses the younger sons, in future every peasant's son will be sure of having his patch of ground. And thirty to forty thousand peasants a year—that's enormous! In the Baltic States, we'll be able to accept as colonists some Dutch, some Norwegians—and even, by individual arrangement, some Swedes.

Night of 27th–28th July 1941

Primary importance of Eastern Europe—Use everything regardless of its origin—The role of the chosen

It's in man's nature to act through his descendants. Some people think only of their family and house. Others are more far-sighted. For my part, I must say that when I meet children, I think of them as if they were my own. They all belong to me. The reason why I'm not worrying about the struggle on the Eastern Front is that everything that happens there is developing in the way that I've always thought desirable.

At the outbreak of the Great War, many people thought we ought to look towards the mineral riches of the West, the raw materials of the colonies, and the gold. For my part, I always thought that having the sun in the East was the essential thing for us, and today I have no reason to modify my point of view.

At the beginning of our movement, I acted above all by intuition. During my imprisonment[9] I had time to provide my philosophy with a natural, historical foundation. From their own point of view, the rulers of the day made a miscalculation in locking me up. They would have been far wiser to let me make speeches all the time, without giving me any respite!

The National Socialist theory is to make use of all forces, wherever they may come from. I realise that the families that have dedicated themselves for generations to the service of the State contain good elements, and that the Bolsheviks made a mistake, in their over-eagerness, in exterminating the intelligentsia. But it is intolerable that the members of a class should suppose that they alone are competent to

---

[9] Hitler was sentenced to five years imprisonment for his role in the failed putsch of 1923. He only served eight months before being released for good behaviour.

hold certain functions. The work that everybody is called on to supply cannot be judged by its objective value. Everyone has only one duty: to take trouble. Whoever does this duty becomes, by doing so, indispensable to the community—whether it is something that only he can do, or that's within the capacities of anyone.

Otherwise the man who achieves something important, the effect of which can be felt for decades, or even for centuries, would have a right to puff himself up and despise the man who sweeps the streets.

The example set by the English aristocracy—in wishing the eldest son of a family to be the only heir to the title—is quite reasonable. Thus the younger sons go back to the people, and the family retains its economic power whilst at the same time keeping its bonds with the people.

When somebody remarks, with an air of sorrowful sympathy, that such-and-such an outcast from an ancient family is a useless creature, a tramp, a failure—very good! It's right that a healthy family should eject one of its members who have become unworthy of it. The error would be precisely to allow the failure to continue to be privileged. It goes without saying that only a planned economy can make intelligent use of *all* a people's strength. Darré[10] has done two good things: the law of agrarian inheritance, and the regulation of markets. If in future we obtain the primary materials that the shortage has compelled us to replace by synthetic products—a thing we could do, thanks to our scientific researches and our superior technique—that will be no reason to stop producing these synthetic products.

Night of 1st–2nd August 1941
Bureaucracy—The value of intelligent disobedience—A continent to be ruled—A dominant race

I am often urged to say something in praise of bureaucracy—I can't do it. It's certain that we have a clean, incorruptible administration, but it's also too punctilious. It's over-organised, and, at least in certain sectors, it's overloaded.

Its principal fault is that nobody in it is seeking for success, and that it includes too many people without responsibility. Our functionaries fear initiative worse than anything else—and what a way they have of behaving as if they were nailed to their office chairs! We have much

---

[10] Richard Walther Darré (1895–1953), Nazi Germany's Minister of Food and Agriculture. A revolutionary ecologist, he founded much of what is today regarded as the "Green" movement, advocating and implementing policies such as organic farming, nature conservation, animal protection and other measures.

more elasticity in the army, with the exception of one sector of the *Wehrmacht*, than in these civilian sectors. And that although the salaries are often inadequate!

Their fixed idea is that legislation should be the same for the whole Reich. Why not a different regulation for each part of the Reich? They imagine that it's better to have a regulation which is bad, but uniform, rather than a good regulation that would take account of particular circumstances. What matters for them is simply that the higher bosses should have a comprehensive view of the activity of the administration, and should pull all the strings.

The *Wehrmacht* gives its highest distinction to the man who, acting against orders, saves a situation by his discernment and decisiveness. In the administration, the fact of not carrying out an order makes a man liable to the most severe penalty. The administration ignores the exception. That is why it lacks the courage which is indispensable to those who are to assume responsibilities.

One favourable circumstance, in view of the changes of method that are called for, is that we are going to have a continent to rule. When that happens, the different positions of the sun will bar us from uniformity!

In many places, we shall have to control immense regions with a handful of men. Thus the police there will have to be constantly on the alert. What a chance for men from the Party!

We must pay the price for our experiences, of course. Mistakes are inevitable, but what difference do they make if in ten years I can be told that Danzig, Alsace and Lorraine are now German! What will it matter then if it can be added that three or four mistakes have been made at Colmar, and five or six in other places?

Let's take the responsibilities for these mistakes, and save the provinces! In ten years we'll have formed an elite, of whom we'll know that we can count on them whenever there are new difficulties to master. We'll produce from it all a new type of man, a race of rulers, a breed of viceroys. Of course, there'll be no question of using people like that in the West!

14th August 1941, midday
Plutocracy and the Saxon proletariat—An incredibly stupid bourgeoisie—The Kaiser and the working people—Bismarck was right—A strike at some Communists

There's nothing astonishing about the fact that Communism had its strongest bastion in Saxony, or that it took us time to win over the Saxon workers to our side. Nor is it astonishing that they are now counted amongst our most loyal supporters.

The Saxon bourgeoisie was incredibly narrow-minded. These people insisted that we were mere Communists. Anyone who proclaims the right to social equality for the masses is a Bolshevik! The way in which they exploited the home worker was unimaginable.

It's a real crime to have turned the Saxon workers into proletarians. There was a ruling plutocracy in those parts comparable to what still exists today in England. Recruiting for the *Wehrmacht* enabled us to observe the progressive lowering of the quality of the human material in this region. I don't blame the small man for turning Communist; but I blame the intellectual who did nothing but exploit other people's poverty for other ends. When one thinks of that riff-raff of a bourgeoisie, one sees red even today. The masses followed the only course possible. The worker took no part in national life. When a monument was unveiled to the memory of Bismarck, or when a ship was launched, no delegation of workers was ever invited—only the frock-coats and uniforms. For me, the top hat is the signature of the bourgeois.

I sometimes entertain myself by rummaging through old back numbers of the *Woche*.[11] I have a collection of them. It's truly instructive to plunge one's nose in them. At the launching of a ship, nothing but top-hats, even after the revolution! The people were invited to such festivities only as stage extras.

The Kaiser received a delegation of workers *just once*. He gave them a fine scolding, threatening simply to withdraw the Imperial favour from them!

At their local meetings, I suppose the delegates had plenty of time in which to draw their conclusions from the Imperial speech. When war came, the harm had been done, and it was too late to go into reverse. Moreover, people were too cowardly to crush Social Democracy. It's what Bismarck wanted to do, but with the corollary of good social legislation. If they'd followed that path systematically, it would have led us to our goal in less than twenty years. Thälmann[12] is the very type

---

[11] *Die Woche* ("The Week") was a weekly newspaper, first published in 1899. It was the equivalent of a present-day "tabloid" newspaper.
[12] Ernst Thälmann (1886–1944), leader of the Communist Party of Germany from 1925 to 1933. Closely linked to the Soviet Union and Stalin, Thälmann regarded the socialist Social Democratic Party (SDP) as his biggest opponent and fought them as much as he did the Nazis. His revolutionary organization, the paramil-

of those mediocrities who can't act otherwise than as they have acted. He's not as intelligent as Torgler, for example. He's a narrow-minded man. That's why I let Torgler[13] go free, whilst I had to keep Thälmann locked up, not in revenge, but to prevent him from being a nuisance. As soon as the danger in Russia has been removed, I'll let him go, too. I don't need to lock up the Social Democrats. Indeed, all I ever had to fear from them was that they might find some base abroad to support their attacks on us.

Our pact with Russia[14] never implied that we might be led to adopt a different attitude towards the danger within. Taken by themselves, I find our Communists a thousand times more sympathetic than Starhemberg,[15] say. They were sturdy fellows. Pity they didn't stay a little longer in Russia. They would have come back completely cured.

15th August 1941, during dinner
Lawyers and their potential prey—Corporal punishment—Simplification of deterrents

In the same way as owners of moors take care, a long time in advance, of the game they'll kill in the shooting-season, so lawyers take care of the criminal class. The greatest vice of our penal system is the exaggerated importance attached to a first sentence. Corporal punishment would often be much better than a term of imprisonment. In prison and in penitentiary establishments, the delinquent is at too good a school.

The old lags he meets there teach him, first that he was stupid to be caught, and secondly to do better next time. All that his stay in prison

---

itary *Roter Frontkämpferbund* ("Red Front Fighting Union") was banned by the SDP government in 1929 for its violent activities. Thälmann was arrested in 1933, and executed in 1944.

[13] Ernst Torgler (1893–1963), the chairman of the Communist Party of Germany (KPD) in the German Reichstag until 1933. Arrested after the Reichstag fire (set by a Dutch communist), Torgler was acquitted in the subsequent trial. In 1940 he took up a job in the Goebbels propaganda ministry, and worked on anti-Bolshevist propaganda until the end of the war. He lived in obscurity thereafter.

[14] The Treaty of Non-Aggression between Germany and the Union of Soviet Socialist Republics (the "Molotov-Ribbentrop Pact") was signed in August 1939.

[15] Prince Ernst Rüdiger Camillo von Starhemberg (1899–1956) was a right wing Austrian nationalist who opposed the *Anschluss*. He fled Austria in 1938, and later served with the British and Free French air forces during the opening years of World War II. However, when the Allies entered into an alliance with the Soviet Union, he resigned in disgust and left for Argentina, where he domiciled.

amounts to in the end is only an uninterrupted course of instruction in the art of doing wrong.

(A murder had just been committed in Berlin. There was much talk of it in the press, and Schaub[16] asked the Führer how long it would take for the case to come up for trial.) In such a case, I see no sense in a long trial, with all its formalities, to study the question of responsibility or *irresponsibility*. In my view, whether *irresponsible* or not, the author of that crime should disappear.

2nd August 1941, evening
Origin of the Iron Curtain—National Socialism not for export—Cattle, rubber and oil—Paris and Vichy in opposition—European task for the Norwegians

When Russia barricades herself within her frontiers, it's to prevent people from leaving the country and making certain comparisons. That's why Stalin was obliged to introduce Bolshevism into the Baltic countries, so that his army of occupation should be deprived of all means of comparison with another system.

At the beginning that wasn't Stalin's idea at all. It's important that we should shape Germany in such a way that whoever comes to visit us may be cured of his prejudices concerning us.

I don't want to force National Socialism on anybody. If I'm told that some countries want to remain democrats—very well, they must remain democrats at all costs! The French, for example, ought to retain their parties. The more social-revolutionary parties they have in their midst, the better it will be for us. The way we're behaving just now is exactly right.

Many Frenchmen won't want us to leave Paris, since their relations with us have made them suspect in the eyes of the Vichy French. Similarly, Vichy perhaps does not take too dim a view of our being installed in Paris, since, if we weren't there, they would have to beware of revolutionary movements.

Once the economy has been definitely organised, we shall have to see to increasing our livestock. We shall also have to devote 100,000 acres to the cultivation of rubber.

Because of the fault of capitalism, which considers only private interests, the exploitation of electricity generated by water-power is in Germany only in its infancy. The most important hydro-electric installations will have to be reserved, in the first place, for the most impor-

---

[16] Julius Schaub (1898–1967), chief aide and adjutant to Hitler.

tant consumers—for the chemical industry, for example. We shall have to use every method of encouraging whatever might ensure us the gain of a single kilowatt.

Let's not forget the old-style mills. If water flows, it's enough to build a dam to obtain energy. Coal will disappear one day, but there will always be water. It can all be exploited more rationally. One can build dams upon dams, and make use of the slightest slopes: thus one has a steady yield, and one can build beyond the reach of bombing. The new Fischer process[17] is one of the finest inventions ever discovered.

One day Norway will have to be the electrical centre of Northern Europe. In that way the Norwegians will at last find a European mission to fulfil. I haven't studied the problem as regards Sweden. In Finland, unfortunately, there is nothing to be done. If all our cities adopted the method used in Munich for producing lighting-gas by recovering it, that would be an enormous gain. In Munich 12 per cent of the gas for lighting is obtained in this fashion.

In the Weiserheide, the gas comes out of the earth. The town of Wels is heated in this way. I should not be surprised if petroleum were discovered there one day. But the future belongs, surely, to water—to the wind and the tides. As a means of heating, it's probably hydrogen that will be chosen.

Nights of 8th–9th and 9th–10th August; 10 a.m. to midday, 10 p.m. to midnight, and night of 10th–11th August 1941

Unpopularity of the German school-teacher—Organisation of the Eastern Territories—Let the Russian population live—Europe, a racial entity—Dangers of security—Evacuation of Germans and expulsion of Jews—A racial policy—The Swiss Innkeeper—Battles of attrition— Stalin's chosen tactics—Impertinence of the British—The arms of the future

The basic reason for English pride is India. Four hundred years ago the English didn't have this pride. The vast spaces over which they spread their rule obliged them to govern millions of people—and they kept these multitudes in order by granting a few men unlimited power. It would obviously have been impossible for them to keep great European areas supplied with foodstuffs and other articles of prime neces-

---

[17] The Fischer–Tropsch process was invented by the German scientists Franz Fischer (1877–1947) and Hans Tropsch (1889–1935) and is still used today to convert a mixture of carbon monoxide and hydrogen into liquid hydrocarbons— which are the main components of the world's current energy infrastructure.

sity. There was therefore no question for them, with a handful of men, to regulate life on these new continents. In any case, the Anglicans never sustained the slightest effort of a missionary description. Thus it was that the Indians never suffered any attack of this sort upon their spiritual integrity.

The German made himself detested everywhere in the world, because wherever he showed himself he began to play the teacher. It's not a good method of conquest. Every people has its customs, to which it clings, and nobody wants lessons from us.

The sense of duty, as we understand it, is not known amongst the Russians. Why should we try to inculcate this notion into them? The German colonist ought to live on handsome, spacious farms. The German services will be lodged in marvellous buildings, the governors in palaces. Beneath the shelter of the administrative services, we shall gradually organise all that is indispensable to the maintenance of a certain standard of living.

Around the city, to a depth of thirty to forty kilometres, we shall have a belt of handsome villages connected by the best roads. What exists beyond that will be another world, in which we mean to let the Russians live as they like. It is merely necessary that we should rule them. In the event of a revolution, we shall only have to drop a few bombs on their cities, and the affair will be liquidated.

Once a year we shall lead a troop of Kirghizes through the capital of the Reich, in order to strike their imaginations with the size of our monuments. What India was for England, the territories of Russia will be for us. If only I could make the German people understand what this space means for our future! Colonies are a precarious possession, but this ground is safely ours.

Europe is not a geographic entity, it's a racial entity. We understand now why the Chinese shut themselves up behind a wall to protect themselves against the eternal attacks of the Mongols. One could sometimes wish that a huge wall might protect the new territories of the East against the masses of Central Asia; but that's contrary to the teachings of history.

The fact is that a too great feeling of security provokes, in the long run, a relaxation of forces. I think the best wall will always be a wall of human breasts!

If any people has the right to proceed to evacuations, it is we, for we've often had to evacuate our own population. Eight hundred thousand men had to emigrate from East Prussia alone. How humanely sensitive we are is shown by the fact that we consider it a maximum of brutality to have liberated our country from six hundred thousand Jews. And yet we accepted, without recrimination, and as something inevitable, the evacuation of our own compatriots!

We must no longer allow Germans to emigrate to America. On the contrary, we must attract the Norwegians, the Swedes, the Danes and the Dutch into our Eastern territories. They'll become members of the German Reich. Our duty is methodically to pursue a racial policy. We're compelled to do so, if only to combat the degeneration which is beginning to threaten us by reason of unions that in a way are consanguineous.

As for the Swiss, we can use them, at the best, as hotel keepers.

We have no reason to dry up the marshes. We shall take only the best land, the best sites. In the marshy region, we shall install a gigantic plain for manoeuvres, three hundred and fifty kilometres by four hundred, making use of the rivers and the obstacles nature supplies.

It goes without saying that it would be a small thing for our war-trained divisions to get the upper hand over an English army. England is already in a state of inferiority by reason of the fact that she cannot train her troops on her own territory. If the English wanted to open up wide spaces within their own frontiers, they'd have to sacrifice too many country-houses.

World history knows three battles of annihilation: Cannae,[18] Sedan[19] and Tannenberg.[20] We can be proud that two of them were fought by German armies. Today we can add to them our battles in Poland and the West, and those which we're now fighting in the East. All the rest have been battles of pursuit, including Waterloo.

We have a false picture of the battle of the Teutoberg forest. The romanticism of our teachers of history has played its part in that. At that period, it was not in fact possible, any more than today, to fight a battle in a forest.

---

[18] The Battle of Cannae (216 BC) was Rome's greatest military defeat, inflicted by the Carthaginians and their allies, led by the famous General Hannibal.

[19] The Battle of Sedan, 1–2 September 1871, was the battle which effectively determined the outcome of the Franco-Prussian War.

[20] The Battle of Tannenberg, fought between Russia and Germany between 23 and 30 August 1914, resulted in the almost complete destruction of the Russian Second Army.

As regards the campaign in Russia, there were two conflicting views: one was that Stalin would choose the tactics of retreat, as in 1812; the other, that we must expect a desperate resistance. I was practically alone in believing this second eventuality. I told myself that to give up the industrial centres of St. Petersburg and Kharkov would be tantamount to a surrender, that retreat in these conditions meant annihilation, and that for these reasons Russia would endeavour to hold these positions at all costs. It was on this theory that we began the campaign, and the ensuing events have proved me right.

America, even if she were to set furiously to work for four years, would not succeed in replacing the material that the Russian army has lost up to the present. If America lends her help to England, it is with the secret thought of bringing the moment nearer when she will reap her inheritance.

I shall no longer be there to see it, but I rejoice on behalf of the German people at the idea that one day we will see England and Germany marching together against America. Germany and England will know what each of them can expect of her partner, and then we shall have found the ally whom we need. They have an unexampled cheek, these English! It doesn't prevent me from admiring them. In this sphere, they still have a lot to teach us.

If there is anyone who is praying for the success of our arms, it must be the Shah of Persia. As soon as we drop in on him, he'll have nothing more to fear from England. The first thing to do is to conclude a treaty of friendship with Turkey, and to leave it to her to guard the Dardanelles. No foreign power has any business in that part of the world.

As regards economic organisation, we are still only at the first fruits, and I can imagine how wonderful it will be to have the task of organising the economy of Europe. To give only one example, what couldn't we gain by successfully recovering the vapours produced by the manufacture of gas for lighting—vapours that at present are wasted? We could use them for warming green-houses, and all winter long we could keep our cities supplied with vegetables and fresh fruit.

Nothing is lovelier than horticulture. I believed until now that our army could not exist without meat. I've just learnt that the armies of ancient times had recourse to meat only in times of scarcity, that the feeding of the Roman armies was almost entirely based on cereals. If one considers all the creative forces dormant in the European space (Germany, England, the Nordic countries, Italy), what are the American potentialities by comparison? England is proud of the will shown by the Dominions to stand by the Empire.

Doubtless there is something fine about such an attitude, but this will holds good only in so far as the central power is capable of imposing it. The fact that in the new Reich there will be only one army, one SS, one administration, will produce an extraordinary effect of power.

In the same way as an old city, enclosed in its ancient walls, necessarily has a different structure from that of the new districts on the periphery, so we shall have to govern the new spaces by other methods than those current in the present Reich. It goes without saying that there should be no uniformity except in the essential matters. As regards Austria, it was the proper solution to destroy the centralised State, to the detriment of Vienna, and re-establish the provinces. In this way innumerable points of friction were removed. Each of the *Gaue* is happy to be its own master.

The arms of the future? In the first place, the land army, then aviation and, in the third place only, the navy. Aviation is the youngest arm. In a few years it has made remarkable progress, but one can't yet say it has reached the apogee of its possibilities.

The navy, on the contrary, has not changed, so to speak, since the Great War. There is something tragic in the fact that the battleship, that monument of human ingenuity, has lost its entire *raison d'être* because of the development of aviation. It reminds one of that marvel of technique and art which the armament of a knight and his horse—the cuirass[21] and the caparison[22]—used to be at the end of the Middle Ages.

What's more, the construction of a battleship represents the value of a thousand bombers—and what a huge amount of time! When the silent torpedo has been invented, a hundred aircraft will mean the death of a cruiser. Now already, no big warship can any longer remain in one harbour.

Night of 19th–20th August 1941
The virtues of war—Ten to fifteen million more Germans—War and human fecundity—Autocracy in Europe

For the good of the German people, we must wish for a war every fifteen or twenty years. An army whose sole purpose is to preserve peace leads only to playing at soldiers—compare Sweden and Switzerland. Or else it constitutes a revolutionary danger to its own country.

---

[21] Cuirass: An armor plate covering the upper torso.
[22] Caparison: An ornamental covering spread over a horse's saddle or harness.

If I am reproached with having sacrificed a hundred or two thousand men by reason of the war, I can answer that, thanks to what I have done, the German nation has gained, up to the present, more than two million five hundred thousand human beings.

If I demand a tenth of this as a sacrifice, nevertheless I have given 90 per cent. I hope that in ten years there will be from ten to fifteen millions more of us Germans in the world. Whether they are men or women, it matters little: I am creating conditions favourable to growth. Many great men were the sixth or seventh children of their family. When such-and-such a man, whom one knows, dies, one knows what one has lost. But does one know what one loses by the limitation of births? The man killed before he is born—that remains the enigma. Wars drive the people to proliferation, they teach us not to fall into the error of being content with a single child in each family.

It's not tolerable that the life of the peoples of the Continent should depend upon England. The Ukraine, and then the Volga basin, will one day be the granaries of Europe.

We shall reap much more than what actually grows from the soil. It must not be forgotten that, from the time of the Tsars, Russia, with her hundred and seventy million people, has never suffered from famine.

We shall also keep Europe supplied with iron. If one day Sweden declines to supply any more iron, that's all right. We'll get it from Russia.

The industry of Belgium will be able to exchange its products—cheap articles of current consumption—against the grain from those parts. As for the poor working-class families of Thuringia and the Harz mountains, for example, they'll find vast possibilities there.

In the regions we occupy in the Ukraine, the population is crowding into the churches. I would see no harm in that if, as is the case at present, the Masses were held by old Russian peasants. It would be different if they had priests, and as for those, we shall have to deliberate whether to let them come back. According to a report I've been reading, the Russian opposition thinks it can use the clergy as a base of departure for Pan-Slav activities.

Night of 14th–15th September 1941

Criminals in war-time—Attempted assassinations in the occupied territories—The habits of the Jurists—A path of extreme difficulty

The triumph of gangsterdom in 1918[23] can be explained. During four years of war great gaps were formed amongst the best of us. And

---

[23] The communist unrest in Germany which sparked the abdication of the Kaiser.

whilst we were at the front, criminality flourished at home. Death sentences were very rare, and in short all that needed to be done was to open the gates of the prisons when it was necessary to find leaders for the revolutionary masses.

I've ordered Himmler,[24] in the event of there someday being reason to fear troubles back at home, to liquidate everything he finds in the concentration camps. Thus at a stroke the revolution would be deprived of its leaders.

The old Reich knew already how to act with firmness in the occupied areas. That's how attempts at sabotage to the railways in Belgium were punished by Count von der Goltz.[25] He had all the villages burnt within a radius of several kilometres, after having had all the mayors shot, the men imprisoned and the women and children evacuated. There were three or four acts of violence in all, then nothing more happened.

It's true that in 1918 the population adopted a hostile attitude towards German troops going up into the line.

I remember a Town Major who urged us to continue on our way when we wanted to chastise some blighters who stuck out their tongues at us. The troops could easily have settled such incidents, but the lawyers always took the side of the population. I can't say how I hate that artificial notion of law.

Nowadays it's the same thing. During the campaign in Poland, the lawyers tried to blame the troops because the latter had shot sixty civilians in a region where wounded soldiers had been massacred. In such a case, a lawyer opens legal proceedings against X.

His enquiry leads nowhere, of course, for nobody has ever seen anything, and if anyone knows the guilty man, he'll take good care not to inform against a "member of the resistance". Lawyers cannot understand that in exceptional times, new laws become valid. I shall be interested to know whether they'll pass the death sentence on that madman who set fire to the *Bremen*—deliberately, it's said, from a liking for setting things alight. I've given instructions for the event of the man's not being condemned to death, that he is to be shot immediately.[26] The

---

[24] Heinrich Himmler (1900–1945), SS *Reichsführer* and for most of the war, one of the most powerful men in Germany.

[25] Count Rüdiger Graf von der Goltz (1865–1946), an army general who commanded divisions on the western and the eastern fronts in World War I.

[26] The SS *Bremen* was a luxury ocean liner set on fire on March 16, 1941, by a 15-year-old crew member, Walter Schmidt. The ship was completely gutted and

prosecutor usually demands the death penalty, but the judges, when in doubt, always find extenuating circumstances. Thus, when the law prescribes as penalty either death, imprisonment for life, penal servitude or a term of imprisonment, it's usually the last of these penalties that they select.

Nearly two thousand people in Germany disappear every year without trace—victims, for the most part, of maniacs or sadists. It's known that these latter are generally recidivists—but the lawyers take great care to inflict only very light penalties on them.

And yet these subhuman creatures are the ferment that undermines the State! I make no distinction between them and the brutes who populate our Russian P.O.W. camps.

The lawyers generally arrange to throw the responsibility for their mildness on the legislator. This time we've opened the road for them to extreme harshness. Nevertheless they pronounce sentences of imprisonment. Responsibility is what they fear, courage is what they lack.

The amazing thing is that those who do not wish to respect a country's laws should nevertheless be allowed to profit by the advantages of these laws.

17th September 1941, evening, and the night of 17th–18th

Hazard and the taking of decisions—The attack against Russia—The German soldier is the best in the world—Junior officers—Antonescu's tactics at Odessa—Success of our "mistakes"—No hegemony without possession of the Russian spaces—The birth of a world of slaves—No India without the British—Anarchy and the Slavs—The Germanic race and the conception of State—No University at Kiev—The importance of the Pripet Marshes—Germans must acquire a sense of Empire

The spirit of decision does not mean acting at all costs. The spirit of decision consists simply in not hesitating when an inner conviction commands you to act. Last year I needed great spiritual strength to take the decision to attack Bolshevism.

I had to foresee that Stalin might pass over to the attack in the course of 1941. It was therefore necessary to get started without delay, in order not to be forestalled—and that wasn't possible before June.

Even to make war, one must have luck on one's side. When I think of it, what luck we did have! I couldn't start a campaign of propaganda to create a climate favourable for the reverse situation; and innumera-

---

put permanently out of commission. Schmidt was motivated by a personal grudge against one of the ship's officers, and was subsequently executed.

ble lives were saved by the fact that no newspaper or magazine article ever contained a word that could have let anyone guess what we were preparing.

I decided to take into account the risk that in the ranks of the *Wehrmacht* there might still be some elements contaminated by Communism. If there were, I suppose that those of them who could see what happens in Russia have now been cured. But at the moment of our attack, we were entering upon a totally unknown world—and there were many people amongst us who might have reflected that we had, after all, a pact of friendship with the Russians!

The German soldier has again proved that he is the best soldier in the world. He was that in the time of Frederick the Great, and he has always been that. When it's a question of holding on, that's when he reveals his full effectiveness. On every level, every man does exactly what is expected of him. After the campaign in the West, people were still saying that the soldier of today hadn't the endurance of the infantryman of the Great War. Here, on the Eastern front, he has proved that he *has* this endurance.

At the time of the Great War, nobody paid any attention to the soldier's individual value in combat. Everything was done *en masse*. During the period of the war of movement, in 1914, compact units were thrown into the battle. In the war of position that followed, the posts were much too close together. Another mistake was to have as company-commanders elderly men of forty to fifty. For infantry, physical agility is everything. So one must have young officers leading these units. The factor of surprise is half the battle. That's why one cannot go on repeating an operation indefinitely, simply because it has been successful.

Antonescu[27] is using in front of Odessa the tactics of the Great War. Every day he advances a few kilometres, after using his artillery to pulverise the space he wishes to occupy. As regards artillery, he has a crushing superiority over his opponent. In view of the circumstances of the terrain, it's obviously possible to set about things in this fashion!

The operation now in progress, an encirclement with a radius of more than a thousand kilometres, has been regarded by many as impracticable.[28] I had to throw all my authority into the scales to force it

---

[27] Ion Antonescu (1882–1946), *Conducător* (Romanian for "Leader") and Prime Minister of Romania from 1940 to 1944.

[28] The encirclement action here being referred to is that which started on September 15 1941, when the Panzer armies of Generals Kleist and Guderian trapped

through. I note in passing that a great part of our successes have originated in "mistakes" we've had the audacity to commit.

The struggle for the hegemony of the world will be decided in favour of Europe by the possession of the Russian space. Thus Europe will be an impregnable fortress, safe from all threat of blockade. All this opens up economic vistas which, one may think, will incline the most liberal of the Western democrats towards the New Order. The essential thing, for the moment, is to conquer. After that everything will be simply a question of organisation.

When one contemplates this primitive world, one is convinced that nothing will drag it out of its indolence unless one compels the people to work. The Slavs are a mass of born slaves, who feel the need of a master. As far as we are concerned, we may think that the Bolsheviks did us a great service.

They began by distributing the land to the peasants, and we know what a frightful famine resulted. So they were obliged, of course, to re-establish a sort of feudal regime, to the benefit of the State. But there was this difference, that, whereas the old-style landlord knew something about farming, the political commissar, on the other hand, was entirely ignorant of such matters. So the Russians were just beginning to give their commissars appropriate instruction.

If the English were to be driven out of India, India would perish. Our role in Russia will be analogous to that of England in India.

Even in Hungary, National Socialism could not be exported. In the mass, the Hungarian is as lazy as the Russian. He's by nature a man of the steppe. From this point of view, Horthy[29] is right in thinking that if he abandoned the system of great estates, production would rapidly decline. It's the same in Spain. If the great domains disappeared there, famine would prevail.

The German peasant is moved by a liking for progress. He thinks of his children. The Ukrainian peasant has no notion of duty. There is a peasantry comparable to ours in Holland, and also in Italy, where every inch of ground is zealously exploited—also, to a certain extent, in France. The Russian space is our India. Like the English, we shall rule

---

four entire Soviet armies in the Kiev pocket. The action ended on September 27th with the surrender of 600,000 Soviet soldiers, 800 tanks and 3,000 artillery pieces.
[29] Miklós Horthy (1868–1957), the Hungarian naval officer and conservative leader who defeated the communist uprising after World War I and remained the country's head of state until 1944.

this empire with a handful of men. It would be a mistake to claim to educate the native. All that we could give him would be a half-knowledge—just what's needed to conduct a revolution! It's not a mere chance that the inventor of anarchism was a Russian.

Unless other peoples, beginning with the Vikings, had imported some rudiments of organisation into Russian humanity, the Russians would still be living like rabbits. One cannot change rabbits into bees or ants. These insects have the faculty of living in a state of society—but rabbits haven't. If left to himself, the Slav would never have emerged from the narrowest of family communities.

The Germanic race created the notion of the State. It incarnated this notion in reality, by compelling the individual to be a part of a whole. It's our duty continually to arouse the forces that slumber in our people's blood. The Slav peoples are not destined to live a cleanly life. They know it, and we would be wrong to persuade them of the contrary.

It was we who, in 1918, created the Baltic countries and the Ukraine. But nowadays we have no interest in maintaining Baltic States, any more than in creating an independent Ukraine. We must likewise prevent them from returning to Christianity. That would be a grave fault, for it would be giving them a form of organisation.

I am not a partisan, either, of a university at Kiev. It's better not to teach them to read. They won't love us for tormenting them with schools. Even to give them a locomotive to drive would be a mistake. And what stupidity it would be on our part to proceed to a distribution of land! In spite of that, we'll see to it that the natives live better than they've lived hitherto. We'll find amongst them the human material that's indispensable for tilling the soil.

We'll supply grain to all in Europe who need it. The Crimea will give us its citrus fruits, cotton and rubber (100,000 acres of plantation would be enough to ensure our independence). The Pripet marshes will keep us supplied with reeds. We'll supply the Ukrainians with scarves, glass beads and everything that colonial peoples like.

The Germans—this is essential—will have to constitute amongst themselves a closed society, like a fortress. The least of our stable-lads must be superior to any native.

For German youth, this will be a magnificent field of experiment. We'll attract to the Ukraine Danes, Dutch, Norwegians, Swedes. The army will find areas for manoeuvres there, and our aviation will have the space it needs.

Let's avoid repeating the mistakes committed in the colonies before 1914. Apart from the *Kolonialgesellschaft*,[30] which represented the interests of the State, only the silver interests[31] had any chance of raising their heads there. The Germans must acquire the feeling for the great, open spaces. We must arrange things so that every German can realise for himself what they mean. We'll take them on trips to the Crimea and the Caucasus. There's a big difference between seeing these countries on the map and actually having visited them. The railways will serve for the transport of goods, but the roads are what will open the country for us.

Today everybody is dreaming of a world peace conference. For my part, I prefer to wage war for another ten years rather than be cheated thus of the spoils of victory. In any case, my demands are not exorbitant. I'm only interested, when all is said, in territories where Germans have lived before. The German people will raise itself to the level of this empire.

1st September 1941, midday
The Czechs and Bolshevism—A Hohenzollern mistake—The Habsburgs,
a foreign dynasty—The generation of 1900

The Czechs are the people who will be most upset by the decline of Bolshevism, for it's they who have always looked with secret hope towards Mother Russia. When we learnt of the fall of Port Arthur,[32] the little Czechs in my class at school wept—while the rest of us exulted! It was then that my feeling for Japan was born.

It would have been the duty of the Hohenzollerns[33] to sacrifice the Habsburg monarchy to Russian aspirations in the Balkans. A dynasty's domination ceases to be justified when its ambitions are no longer adjusted to the nation's permanent interests. Once a dynasty adopts the safeguarding of peace at any price and the maintenance of undue consideration for the feelings of other foreign dynasties as its guiding principles, it is doomed. That's why I'm grateful to Social Democracy for having swept away all these royalties. Even supposing it had been indispensable, I don't know whether any of *us* would have so definitely set

---

[30] The *Deutsche Kolonialgesellschaft* (German Colonial Society), founded in 1887, was the driving force behind German colonial efforts.
[31] Capitalists.
[32] Port Arthur was the Russian Empire's naval base in Manchuria, and the scene of the concluding battle of the Russo-Japanese War (1904–1905).
[33] Wilhelm II was the last monarch of the House of Hohenzollern.

himself against the house of Hohenzollern. Against the Habsburgs,[34] yes! In my eyes, it was a foreign dynasty.

The injustice committed by the Kaiser at Bismarck's expense finally recoiled upon him.[35] How could the Kaiser demand loyalty from his subjects when he had treated the founder of the Reich with such ingratitude? The shameful thing is that the German people allowed such an injustice to be committed.

The generation of 1900 was lost—economically, politically and culturally. The men of the nationalist opposition exhausted themselves in being right. When one has preached in the desert for decades, it proves, when the time comes for action, that one has lost all contact with reality. These Germans of the old school were fine fellows, but their speciality was literature. Their audience was twenty thousand readers of their own stamp. None of them knew how to speak to the people.

Right from the beginning, I realised that one could not go far along that track. The man who means to act must find his support in faith, and faith is found only in the people. The great masses have no mercy, they go straight ahead with the simplicity of innocence. We have seen what a people is capable of, when it is led. All possibilities exist in it, for good as well as for evil.

The duty of National Socialism inevitably boils down to this: all that is best in the people should be allowed ceaselessly to develop.

Night of the 22nd–23rd September 1941
Social classes and means of transport—In the Army, the same meals for all—Ceremonial banquets and the cold buffet

It's terrifying to think that only a few years ago such discriminations could have existed, on our great transatlantic liners, in the treatment of passengers of different classes. It's inconceivable that nobody was embarrassed so to expose the differences between the various conditions of life. There we have a field in which the Labour Front[36] will find a chance to make itself useful.

In the East, on the railway, all Germans will have to travel first or second class, so as to distinguish themselves from the natives. The dif-

---

[34] The House of Habsburg included the Emperors of Austria.

[35] Otto von Bismarck (1815–1898), the Prussian foreign minister who created the united Germany of 1871 and became its first chancellor. He was dismissed from office after a clash with the new Kaiser Wilhelm II over workers' rights.

[36] The *Reichsarbeitsdienst* (Reich Labour Service), set up to regulate labor conditions in the Third Reich.

ference between first and second will be that one will have three places on each side, and the other four.

I think it's an excellent idea to have introduced a single style of messing throughout the army. Already during the Great War, the messing for the troops was much better when the officers used it too.

I don't see the point of an uninterrupted succession of dishes, such as used to be the rule. One is afflicted the whole evening with the same female neighbour, when one would have preferred to entertain oneself with other fellow-guests. It's impossible to eat enough of what one likes! And the other dishes are boring.

For Party receptions, the best notion is the cold buffet. Kindred spirits form groups. You can change places to chat, and move from one companion to another. This notion also puts an end to competition for the places of honour, such as is required by the classical method of arranging the table.

23rd September 1941, evening
The frontiers of Europe and Asia—Success justifies everything—Our right to fertile lands—The Russian flood must be dammed—Suicide candidates—National Socialism must not ape religion

It's absurd to try to suppose that the frontier between the two separate worlds of Europe and Asia is marked by a chain of not very high mountains—and the long chain of the Urals is no more than that. One might just as well decree that the frontier is marked by one of the great Russian rivers. No, geographically Asia penetrates into Europe without any sharp break. The real frontier is the one that separates the Germanic world from the Slav world. It's our duty to place it where we want it to be.

If anyone asks us where we obtain the right to extend the Germanic space to the East, we reply that, for a nation, her awareness of what she represents carries this right with it. It's success that justifies everything. The reply to such a question can only be of an empirical nature.

It's inconceivable that a higher people should painfully exist on a soil too narrow for it, whilst amorphous masses, which contribute nothing to civilisation, occupy infinite tracts of a soil that is one of the richest in the world. We painfully wrest a few metres from the sea, we torment ourselves cultivating marshes—and in the Ukraine an inexhaustibly fertile soil, with a thickness, in places, often metres of humus, lies waiting for us. We must create conditions for our people that favour its multiplication, and we must at the same time build a dike against the

Russian flood. If this war had not taken place, the Reich would scarcely have increased its population during the next ten years, but the Russian population would have grown vigorously. The earth continues to go round, whether it's the man who kills the tiger or the tiger who eats the man. The stronger asserts his will, it's the law of nature. The world doesn't change; its laws are eternal.

There are some who say the world is evil, and that they wish to depart from this life. For my part, I like the world! Unless the desire to die is due to a lover's quarrel, I advise the desperate man to have patience for a year. The consolations will come. But if a human being has any other reason to wish to die than this, then let him die, I'm not stopping him. I merely call attention to the fact that one cannot escape this world entirely.

The elements of which our body is made belong to the cycle of nature; and as for our soul, it's possible that it might return to limbo, until it gets an opportunity to reincarnate itself. But it would vex me if everybody wanted to have done with life.

To make death easier for people, the Church holds out to them the bait of a better world. We, for our part, confine ourselves to asking man to fashion his life worthily. For this, it is sufficient for him to conform to the laws of nature.

Let's seek inspiration in these principles, and in the long run we'll triumph over religion. But there will never be any possibility of National Socialism's setting out to ape religion by establishing a form of worship. Its one ambition must be scientifically to construct a doctrine that is nothing more than a homage to reason.

Our duty is to teach men to see whatever is lovely and truly wonderful in life, and not to become prematurely ill-tempered and spiteful. We wish fully to enjoy what is beautiful, to cling to it—and to avoid, as far as possible, anything that might do harm to people like ourselves.

If today you do harm to the Russians, it is so as to avoid giving them the opportunity of doing harm to us. God does not act differently. He suddenly hurls the masses of humanity on to the earth, and he leaves it to each one to work out his own salvation. Men dispossess one another, and one perceives that, at the end of it all, it is always the stronger who triumphs. Is that not the most reasonable order of things?

If it were otherwise, nothing good would ever have existed. If we did not respect the laws of nature, imposing our will by the right of the stronger, a day would come when the wild animals would once again devour us—then the insects would eat the wild animals, and finally nothing would exist on earth but the microbes.

25th September 1941, midday
Fanaticism of Russian leaders—Stupidity of the Russian soldier—The perpetual menace of Asia—A living wall—Justifiable claims

What is surprising about the Russian rulers is the fanaticism with which they adhere to a principle—perhaps a correct principle, in itself—even when it has become evident that the principle has ceased to be correct in fact. The explanation is their fear of having to accept responsibility for a failure. For they never suffer failure because of a weakness in their command, a shortage of ammunition or an irresistible German pressure. It's always because of "an act of treachery". They never produce any other explanation but treachery, and every commander of a unit who has not succeeded, in conformity with the orders he has received, runs the risk of having his head chopped off. So they prefer to be wiped out by us.

On the other hand, the offensive spirit that inspires the Russian, when he is advancing, does not surprise us. It was the same during the Great War, and the explanation for it is their bottomless stupidity. We've forgotten the bitter tenacity with which the Russians fought us during the Great War. In the same way, coming generations will see in the campaign now in progress only the magnificent operation that it will have been, without giving any more thought to the numerous crises that we had to overcome by reason of this tenacity.

We knew, during the Great War, a type of Russian combatant who was more good-natured than cruel. Nowadays, this type no longer exists. Bolshevism has completely wiped it out.

Asia, what a disquieting reservoir of men! The safety of Europe will not be assured until we have driven Asia back behind the Urals. No organised Russian State must be allowed to exist west of that line. They are brutes, and neither Bolshevism nor Tsarism makes any difference—they are brutes in a state of nature.

The danger would be still greater if this space were to be Mongolised. Suddenly a wave comes foaming down from Asia and surprises a Europe benumbed by civilisation and deceived by the illusion of collective security! Since there is no natural protection against such a flood, we must meet it with a living wall. A permanent state of war on the Eastern front will help to form a sound race of men, and will prevent us from relapsing into the softness of a Europe thrown back upon itself. The points we have reached are dotted along areas that have retained the memory of Germanic expansion. We've been before at the Iron Gates, at Belgrade, in the Russian space.

The German past, in its totality, constitutes our own patrimony, whatever may be the dynasty, whatever may be the stock from which we arise. It is important to bring together, in the German Pantheon, all the glories of Germany's pastas Ludwig I did in the eyes of the whole world. As regards myself, I shall never live to see it, but one day my successors must be in a position to bring out from a drawer every historical date that justifies a German claim.

Once our position is consolidated, we shall be able in this sphere to go back as far as the great invasions. Berlin must be the true centre of Europe, a capital that for everybody shall be *the* capital.

25th September 1941, evening

Time is on Germany's side—Problems to be solved—Success of the Four Year Plan—The white races have destroyed their world commerce— Export does not pay—Unemployed in Britain and America—The call of the East

The myth of our vulnerability, in the event of the war becoming prolonged, must be resolutely discarded. It's impermissible to believe that time is working against us. At present my mind is occupied by two important problems:

1. When I realise that a particular raw material is indispensable for the war, I shrink from no effort to make us independent in this field. We must be able to dispose freely of iron, coal, petroleum, grain, livestock and timber.

2. Economic life must be organised in terms of outlets situated in the territories we control.

I may say that Europe is today an autarky, but we have to prevent the existence of a gigantic State capable of using European civilisation against us. Our Four Year Plan was a very heavy blow to the English, for they felt that we had ceased to be vulnerable to blockade. They'd have offered me a loan in exchange for our giving up the plan! It's easy to import when one is in a favourable situation.

In the opposite event, one is hamstrung. The foreigner at once exploits the situation and blackmails one. How could we have paid for the wheat we would have imported from America? Even for foodstuffs, it wouldn't work! And much less so as regards industrial products. It would be a wise policy for Europe to give up the desire to export to the whole world. The white race has itself destroyed its world commerce. The European economy has lost its outlets in other continents. Our manufacturing costs prevent us from meeting foreign competition.

Wherever it may be, we are so handicapped that it's impossible to gain a footing anywhere. For the few articles that foreigners still need, there's a cut-throat struggle between the suppliers. To gain access to these markets, one must pay such premiums that it represents a disproportionate effort for our economy. Only new inventions sometimes enable one to do a little business.

To their misfortune, the English have industrialised India. Unemployment in England is increasing, and the English worker gets poorer. To think that there are millions of unemployed in America! What they should do there is to embark on a revolutionary new economic policy, abandon the gold standard and further increase the needs of their home market.

Germany is the only country that has no unemployment. And *that* hangs together with the fact that we are not slaves to the need to export.

The country we are engaged in conquering will be a source of raw materials for us, and a market for our products, but we shall take good care not to industrialise it.

The peasant is the being least of all accessible to ideologies. If I offer him land in Russia, a river of human beings will rush there headlong. For a man of the soil, the finest country is the one that yields the finest crops. In twenty years' time, European emigration will no longer be directed towards America, but eastwards.

The Black Sea will be for us a sea whose wealth our fishermen will never exhaust. Thanks to the cultivation of the soya bean, we'll increase our livestock. We'll win from that soil several times as much as the Ukrainian peasant is winning at present.

We'll be freed from the worry of having to seek outlets for our goods in the Far East. For our market is in Russia. We must make sure of it. We'll supply cotton goods, household utensils, all the articles of current consumption. The need for them is so great that we shan't succeed in ourselves producing all that will be necessary. I see there the greatest possibilities for the creation of an empire of world-wide importance. My plan is that we should take profits on whatever comes our way. But I insist on the fact that it's on our own soil that we must organise the production of whatever is vitally essential. The countries that work in harmony with us will be associated with all the positive contributions they can make. All deliveries of machines, even if they're made abroad, will have to pass through a German middleman, in such a way that Russia will be supplied with no means of production whatsoever, except of absolute necessities.

Two-thirds of American engineers are German. During our centuries of life under particularist conditions, a great number of our compatriots were thrust back in upon themselves, and although they had the souls of leaders, they vegetated. When we can offer great tasks to such men, we'll be surprised to discover their immense qualities. For the next centuries, we have at our disposal an unequalled field of action.

Night of 25th–26th September 1941
An unparalleled epoch—Talking to the soldiers—The individual does not count—Preservation of the species

I've been thrilled by our contemporary news-films. We are experiencing a heroic epic, without precedent in history. Perhaps it was like this during the Great War, but nobody was able to get a clear picture. I'm extremely happy to have witnessed such deeds.

I'm told that the reason why my speeches made such an impression is that I don't coin rhetorical phrases. I could never make the mistake of beginning a speech with the words: "There is no fairer death in the world . . ." For I know the reality, and I also know how the soldier feels about it.

The revelation that her encounter with her first man is for a young woman, can be compared with the revelation that a soldier knows when he faces war for the first time. In a few days, a youth becomes a man. If I weren't myself hardened by this experience, I would have been incapable of undertaking this Cyclopean[37] task which the building of an Empire means for a single man.

It was with feelings of pure idealism that I set out for the front in 1914. Then I saw men falling around me in thousands. Thus I learnt that life is a cruel struggle, and has no other object but the preservation of the species. The individual can disappear, provided there are other men to replace him. I suppose that some people are clutching their heads with both hands to find an answer to this question: "How can the Führer destroy a city like St. Petersburg?" Plainly I belong by nature to

---

[37] From Greek mythology: A Cyclops was a giant, and, according to the myths, the only ones capable of creating the massive stoneworks of many of the most famous ancient Greek sites such as the walls of Mycenae and Tiryns.

quite another species. I would prefer not to see anyone suffer, not to do harm to anyone. But when I realise that the species is in danger, then in my case sentiment gives way to the coldest reason. I become uniquely aware of the sacrifices that the future will demand, to make up for the sacrifices that one hesitates to allow today.

Night of 27th–28th September 1941
Misery—Social discrimination—Organisation of study—Christianity and the Spaniards

We must pursue two aims: 1. To hold our positions on the Eastern front at all costs. 2. To keep the war as far as possible from our frontiers.

By considering what Bolshevism has made of man, one realises that the foundation of all education should be respect—respect towards Providence (or the unknown, or Nature, or whatever name one chooses). Secondly, the respect that youth owes to maturity. If this respect is lacking, a man falls below the level of the animal. His intelligence, when it ceases to be controlled, turns him into a monster.

The Russian finds his place in human society only in its collectivist form—that is to say, he is tied to work by a horrible compulsion. The spirit of society, mutual consideration, etc., are to him things unknown.

Who knows? If my parents had been sufficiently well-to-do to send me to a School of Art, I should not have made the acquaintance of poverty, as I did. Whoever lives outside poverty cannot really become aware of it, unless by overthrowing a wall. The years of experience I owe to poverty—a poverty that I knew in my own flesh—are a blessing for the German nation. But for them, we would have Bolshevism today.

In one respect, the climate of want in which I lived left no mark on me. At that time, I lived in palaces of the imagination. And it was precisely at that time that I conceived the plans for the new Berlin.

We must pay attention to two things:

1. That all gifted adolescents are educated at the State's expense.

2. That no door is closed to them. Since I hadn't been able to finish my secondary studies, an officer's career would have been closed to me, even if by working I had learnt more about it than is proper for a boy who has matriculated to know. Only an officer could win the *Pour le Mérite*.[38] And at that, it was quite exceptional for an officer of middle-class origin to receive it. In that closed society, every man existed only by virtue of his origin. The man who lacked this origin,

---

[38] The *Pour le Mérite* (French for "For Merit") was an award established by King Frederick II of Prussia in 1740.

and university degrees into the bargain, could not dream of becoming a Minister, for example, except by the short-cut of Social Democracy. Until not long ago, we had four different styles of messing in the Navy, corresponding to the sailors' ranks or ratings. Very recently, that even cost us a ship.[39]

The view that suppression of these discriminations would be harmful to authority proved to be without foundation. A competent man always has the authority he needs. A man who is not superior by his talent invariably lacks authority, whatever his job may be.

It's a scandal to remember how household servants used to be lodged, particularly in apartments in Berlin. And the crews on ships, even luxury ships—what an insult!

I know that all that can't be changed by a single stroke of the pen, and everywhere at once. But the general attitude towards that sort of thing is very different today from what it used to be.

In future every worker will have his holidays—a few days in each year, which he can arrange as he likes. And everybody will be able to go on a sea-cruise once or twice in his life.

It's nonsense to fear that people will lose their modest ways of living. They *should* lose them—for that kind of modesty is the-enemy of all progress.

In this matter we see things like the Americans—and not like the Spaniard, who would content himself with a few olives a day rather than work to have more.

The Church has been able to profit by this conception of life. It proclaims that the poor in spirit—and the other poor, too—will go to heaven, whilst the rich will pay with eternal sufferings for the blessings of earthly existence.

The Church is moved to say this by the tacit contract between the priests and the possessors, who joyfully leave the Church a little money so that it may go on encouraging the poor to grovel. But what a queer sort of Christianity they practise down there!

We must recognise, of course, that, amongst us, Christianity is coloured by Germanism. All the same, its doctrine signifies: "Pray and work!"

28th–29th September 1941, midday
British reticence—Disadvantages of over-organisation—Nature wishes autocracy

---

[39] A reference perhaps to the arson on board the SS *Bremen*? See footnote 23.

The state of our relations with England is like that which existed between Prussia and Austria in 1866. The Austrians were shut up in the notion of their empire as the English are today in their Commonwealth.

When things go badly for his country, no Englishman lets anything of the sort appear before a foreigner. No Englishman ever leaves his country without knowing what he should reply to questions that might be asked him on thorny topics. They are an admirably trained people. They worked for three hundred years to assure themselves the domination of the world for two centuries.

The reason why they've kept it so long is that they were not interested in washing the dirty linen of their subject peoples. What *we* would like to do, on the other hand, would be to rub a negro until he becomes white—as if someone who feels no need to wash himself were to want to let himself be soaped by somebody else!

We must be careful not to push organisation too far, for the slightest accident can jam the whole machine. For example, it would be a mistake to decree that in the Ukraine the quality of the soil means that we should sow nothing but wheat. No, we must also leave room for pastures. Nature has made the various regions of the earth in such a way as to ensure a sort of autarky for each, and man must respect this modified kind of order. We shall therefore let the marshlands continue to exist, not only because they will be useful to us as fields for manoeuvres, but also in order to respect the local climatological conditions, and to prevent the desert from gradually encroaching on the fertile regions. The marshes play the role of a sponge. Without them, it might happen that a whole crop was wiped out by a wave of heat.

1st October 1941, evening

Characteristics of Vienna—Vienna and the Provinces—Vienna and Paris

What complicates things in Vienna is the racial diversity. It contains the descendants of all the races that the old Austria used to harbour, and thus it is that everyone receives on a different antenna and everyone transmits on his own wavelength. What's lacking in Austria, and what we have in Germany, is a series of towns of a high cultural level— and which therefore don't suffer either from an inferiority complex or from megalomania.

In the old Austria, Vienna had such a supremacy that one can understand the hatred the provinces felt against her. No such sentiment, in a similar form, was ever expressed against Berlin. Treasures of every kind were always accumulated in Vienna, like the Ambras collection.[40] Everything in Austria took its tune from Vienna, and jealous care was taken that this principle shouldn't be interfered with. Linz Cathedral, for example, couldn't be built to the pre-arranged height, simply so that the tower of St. Stephen's shouldn't cease to be the tallest in the country. The genuine Viennese turn green when they learn that a single painting can have ended up in Graz or somewhere else, instead of finding its way to Vienna. I hope, anyway, that Schirach[41] has not let himself be attacked by the Vienna bug. Vienna has such treasures that every German should nevertheless bear in mind that he shares in this wealth. I may say in passing that—other things being equal, of course—what there is in Vienna can bear comparison with what I saw in Paris.

Of course, the Concorde-Tuileries vista is magnificent. But what about the detail? We'll do still better. Vienna has a lot of monuments that ought to be classified. At the Museum, they should take away that canvas cloth that's covering the walls. That cloth is hiding a magnificent *stuccolustro.*[42]

Vienna ought to declare war on bugs and dirt. The city must be cleaned up. That's the one and only duty for the Vienna of the twentieth century. Let her but perform that, and she'll be one of the loveliest cities in the world.

Nights of 27th–28th September 1941 and 8th October 1941
The Duce's difficulties—When troops fail—Antonescu a born soldier— Romanian corruption

The Duce has his difficulties because his army thinks Royalist, because the *internationale* of the priests has its seat in Rome, and because the State, as distinguished from the people, is only half Fascist.

Give official praise to a unit that has suffered a reverse, and you attack its military honour. Such a unit must be clearly shown that its behaviour has been miserable. Any army can sometimes have a moment of weakness. It can happen that the troops in the line become subject to fleeting impressions of which the Command takes no account in its appreciation of the facts. But in such cases one must know how to be harsh. A unit that has fought badly must be sent back under fire as soon

---

[40] The *Kunst- und Wunderkammer* ("Chamber of Art and Wonders") at Ambras Castle, Innsbruck, was created by Archduke Ferdinand II (1578 1637).
[41] Baldur von Schirach (1907–1974), *Gauleiter* of Vienna.
[42] A lime based polished plaster.

as possible. One can triumph over death only through death: "If you retreat, you'll be shot! If you advance, you may save your skin!" It's only after the unit has redeemed itself that one can wipe the slate.

Of course, a Command has no right to act recklessly by sending men to death without purpose. It is not enough to try to obtain, by the employment of masses, what one couldn't obtain by more modest methods. One would simply be running the risk of increasing the number of victims without gaining anything.

There are cases in which it's important first of all to reflect, in order to discover the cause of the reverse. One must know how to have recourse to other methods, or else to change one's tactics. When all is said, one can likewise ask oneself whether one would not be doing better to give up a position that's difficult to hold, and consider a completely different operation. A few weeks ago Antonescu, in a communiqué, accused one of his units of being a disgrace to the nation. Antonescu is of Germanic origin, not Romanian; he's a born soldier. His misfortune is to have Romanians under his command.

But let's not forget that only a year ago these people were wildly fleeing from the Bolsheviks. It's wonderful how, in so short a time, Antonescu has been able to get what he has got out of his troops. Doubtless he will also succeed, with time, in obtaining administrators who aren't rotten with corruption.

Our own people hasn't always been as impeccable as it is nowadays. Remember the sabre-blows that Frederick William I used to administer to the Berliners with his own hand.[43] Moral cleanliness is the result of a long education, ceaselessly directed towards discipline.

Night of 9th–10th October 1941

Germany and the Asiatic Hordes—Balance of power—A Pyrrhic victory

We Germans are alone responsible that the tide of Huns, Avars, and Magyars[44] was halted in Central Europe. We were already a great empire when the English were only beginning to build up their maritime

---

[43] Frederick William I (1688–1740), known for his hatred of corruption.

[44] The Mongoloid Huns were defeated at the 451 AD Battle of the Catalaunian Plains by a combined Roman and Visigoth force under Aetius and Theodoric I. The Avars, a Turkic-Oghuri people, were defeated by the Frankish King Charlemagne and his son Pepin, in a series of wars waged from 791 to 796 A.D. The original Magyars were a Ugric people who invaded Eastern Europe following the fall of the Western Roman Empire. They were defeated by Otto I at the Battle of Lechfeld (955 A.D.) Hungarians still call themselves "Magyars" in their tongue, but have no actual genetic connection to the original Magyar tribes.

power. If we hadn't been such fools as to tear each other to pieces in order to find out whether we should consume God in the forms of bread and wine, or of bread only,[45] England would never have been able to have her say concerning the balance of power on the Continent. England is never a danger except when she can oppose a power who threatens her supremacy with other powers whom she induces to play her game. For England, the Great War was a Pyrrhic victory. To maintain their empire, they need a strong continental power at their side. Only Germany can be this power.

Night of 25th–26th September 1941
and night of 9th–10th October 1941
News-reels are valuable documents for the future

For the sake of the future, it's important to preserve the news-films of the war. They will be documents of incalculable value. New copies of these films will have to be constantly printed, and it would even be best to print them on strips of metal, so that they won't disappear.

I succeeded in getting my hands on some rare shots of the Great War. (They'd been collected for destruction.) But they were confiscated by the Bavarian State, at the same time as the Party's other possessions were confiscated. I could never find out what became of them, and they must be regarded as lost.

I hope that in future news-films will be made by our very best film experts. One can get extraordinary results in that field. They can confine themselves to twenty-minute one reelers, but these must be the result of intelligent work. The worst habit of all has been to restrict the films to thirty-foot strips, whatever the subject might be: an earthquake, a tennis match, a horse-race, the launching of a ship.

10th October 1941, midday
Fighting for open spaces—The flow back from West to East—Christianity and natural selection

War has returned to its primitive form. The war of people against people is giving place to another war—a war for the possession of the great spaces. Originally war was nothing but a struggle for pasture grounds. Today war is nothing but a struggle for the riches of nature. By virtue of an inherent law, these riches belong to him who conquers them. The great migrations set out from the East. With us begins the

---

[45] A reference to the religious wars between Protestant and Catholic, which ultimately (during the Thirty Years' War) saw half of Germany wiped out.

ebb, from West to East. That's in accordance with the laws of nature. By means of the struggle, the elites are continually renewed. The law of selection justifies this incessant struggle, by allowing the survival of the fittest.

Christianity is a rebellion against natural law, a protest against nature. Taken to its logical extreme, Christianity would mean the systematic cultivation of the human failure.

Night of 10th–11th October 1941
The Army High Command in the Great War—The Kaiser a bad Commander in war—Conrad von Hötzendorf

Apart from the great victories, like the battle of Tannenberg and the battle of the Masurian Marshes,[46] the Imperial High Command proved itself inadequate. The Kaiser put in an appearance on one single occasion, because he believed that all would go well. During the great offensive of 1918, it was trumpeted around that the Kaiser was commanding it in person. The truth was, the Kaiser had no notion of command.

The fact that there was no recognition on our side of the need for tanks, or at least for an anti-tank defence, is the explanation of our defeat. Bolshevism will collapse likewise for lack of anti-tank weapons.

On the other hand, the spring offensive in 1918 was premature. A month later the ground would have been dry and the meteorological conditions favourable. The terrain was likewise ill-chosen. How absurd, too, to have abandoned the agreed plan simply because, in the course of the operation, attention was incidentally drawn to Paris!

It's the same as if, instead of ordering the troops of the Smolensk sector to head southward, in view of the pre-arranged battles of encirclement and annihilation, I would made them march on Moscow to gain a prestige victory. It would have dangerously extended our front line, and I would have wasted the already realised profit of the operation on which I would decided.

The most intelligent commander in the Great War was very possibly Conrad von Hötzendorf.[47] He clearly recognised necessities that were

---

[46] The First Battle of the Masurian Lakes took place in September 1914, shortly after the Battle of Tannenberg, it resulted in all Russian forces being driven out of their territorial gains in eastern Germany, and pushed back to their own territory.
[47] Franz Conrad von Hötzendorf (1852–1925), Austrian Field Marshal and Chief of the General Staff of the military of the Austro-Hungarian Army and Navy from 1906 to 1917. After 1917, he commanded an army group on the Italian Front until he retired in 1918.

at once political and military. Only his tools failed him—he was commanding the Austrian Army.

13th October 1941, midday
SPECIAL GUEST: REICH MINISTER OF ECONOMIC AFFAIRS
FUNK[48]

*European collaboration in the Eastern Territories—Thirteen million
American unemployed—The Danube is the river of the future—Natural
wealth—Perpetual worries—Mentality of the émigrés*

The countries we invite to participate in our economic system should have their share in the natural riches of the Russian regions, and they should find an outlet there for their industrial production. It will be sufficient to give them a glimpse of the possibilities, and they'll at once attach themselves to our system. Once this region is organised for us, all threat of unemployment in Europe will be eliminated.

On the economic level, America could never be a partner for these countries. America can be paid only in gold. A commerce based on the exchange of products is not possible with America, for America suffers from a surplus of raw materials and a plethora of manufactured goods. This gold which the Americans receive in exchange for the labour they supply, they hide it away in their strong-rooms—and they imagine the world will yield to this policy born in the smoky brain of a Jewish thinker! The result is their thirteen million unemployed.

If I were in America, I shouldn't be afraid. It would be enough to set afoot a gigantic autarkic economy. With their nine and a half million square kilometres of territory, in five years the problem would be solved. South America cannot offer the United States anything but what they already have in superfluity.

The river of the future is the Danube. We'll connect it to the Dnieper and the Don by the Black Sea. The petroleum and grain will come flowing towards us. The canal from the Danube to the Main can never be built too big. Add to this the canal from the Danube to the Oder, and we'll have an economic circuit of unheard-of dimensions.

Europe will gain in importance, of herself. Europe, and no longer America, will be the country of boundless possibilities. If the Americans are intelligent, they'll realise how much it will be to their interest to take part in this work. There is no country that can be to a larger extent autarkic than Europe will be. Where is there a region capable of

---

[48] Walther Funk (1890–1960), Reich Minister for Economic Affairs (1938–1945) and president of Reichsbank (1939–1945).

supplying iron of the quality of Ukrainian iron? Where can one find more nickel, more coal, more manganese, more molybdenum?[49]

The Ukraine is the source of manganese to which even America goes for its supplies. And, on top of that, so many other possibilities! The vegetable oils, the plantations to be organised. With 100,000 acres devoted to the growing of rubber, our needs are covered. The side that wins this war will have to concern itself only with economic juggleries. Here, we're still fighting for the possession of the soil. Despite all its efforts, the side that hasn't got the natural riches must end by going under. The world's wealth is boundless, and only a quarter of the surface of the globe is at present at humanity's disposal. It's for this quarter that everyone's fighting. And it's all in the natural order of things—for it makes for the survival of the fittest.

When a man begets children without having previously enlarged the basis of his existence, it shows a lack of conscience on his part. But if he decides that he should therefore give up the idea of begetting children, he becomes doubly a sinner, by making himself life's debtor.

It's certain that worries never cease to trouble us. When I was a young man, I had worries to the extent of ten, twenty or thirty marks. The only period when I had no worries was the six years of my life as a soldier. Then one did not concern oneself with such matters. We were supplied with clothing, and although it was no great shakes, it was at least honourable. Lodging and board—or, in default of lodging, leave to sleep somewhere or other.

After that, the worries came back: worries about the Party—first to the extent of ten thousand marks, then of a few millions. After we took power, they were to the extent of thousands of millions.

Later still, I had new worries. First of all, how to find jobs for the unemployed? Then, when unemployment had disappeared, where to find enough workers? We must install machines! Continually new problems to settle. It's still the same today. We used to say: "Let's take prisoners!" Now we think: "What are we to do with all these prisoners?"

All refugees are alike. They fix their minds on a turning point in their own story, which they regard as a turning-point in the history of the world. They ignore everything that may have happened since that

---

[49] Molybdenum, which does not occur naturally as a free metal, was first isolated from the mineral salts of other metals by the Swedish chemist Petter Jacob Hjelm in 1781. As it has the sixth-highest melting point of any element, and is widely used to create hard, stable carbides in about 80 percent of the world's steel alloys.

moment, which for them is essential. Only a genius would be capable of transcending that private view of things. There are also psychological refugees. The Englishman is stranded on 9th November 1918!

13th October 1941, evening
Opportunities for all in the Eastern Territories

I've been wondering lately whether it wouldn't be best to collect the men responsible for the control of the economics of the following countries: Denmark, Norway, Holland, Belgium, Sweden and Finland. We would give them a notion of the vistas that present themselves nowadays. The majority of them are not at all aware of the immense field that opens up before us. And yet these are the men who have a positive interest in seeing to it that something should be done on behalf of their countries! If they clearly realise that an outlet can be found in Russia for their surplus population, and that their country can henceforward obtain all it requires, I think it not impossible that they may come over into our camp, with banners waving.

It would be a first step in a direction that would remind us of what the creation of the *Zollverein* once meant to us.[50] Today I laid my financial ideas before the Minister of Economic Affairs. He's enthusiastic. He foresees that in ten years Germany will have freed itself from the burden of the war without letting our purchasing-power at home be shaken.

13th October 1941, night
Decisions in lower military formations—Folly of the great offensives of the Great War—A people of artists and soldiers

The other day I called off an attack that was to procure us a territorial gain of four kilometres, because the practical benefit of the operation didn't seem to me to be worth the price it would have cost. I realise, in this connection, that it's more difficult to take a decision on a lower level than on the level of the High Command.

How could the man who carries out the orders, and has no comprehensive view of the situation, how could he make up his mind with full knowledge of the pros and cons? Is he to demand a sacrifice from his men, or is he to spare them this sacrifice? All that was done in that respect during the Great War was sheer madness. The offensive at Ver-

---

[50] The *Zollverein* ("Customs Union") was created in 1834 and set up a free-trade area in may of the then still independent German states. The economic growth it generated is widely regarded as a precursor to the political unification of Germany which followed 37 years later.

dun, for example, was an act of lunacy. From beginning to end, all the commanders responsible for that operation should have been put in strait-jackets. We've not yet completely got over those mistaken notions.

It's probable that, throughout the 1914–1918 war, some twenty thousand men were uselessly sacrificed by employing them as runners on missions that could have been equally well accomplished by night, with less danger.

How often I myself have had to face a powerful artillery barrage, in order to carry a simple post-card! It's true that later I had a commanding officer who completely put a stop to these practices. The spirit has changed since those days, and a day will come when such absurdities can no longer occur.

A war commander must have imagination and foresight. So it's not extraordinary that our people is at once a people of soldiers and of artists. My strength lies in the fact that I can imagine the situations that the troops are called upon to face. And I can do that because I've been an ordinary soldier myself. Thus one acquires the rapid understanding of the appropriate steps to take in every kind of circumstance.

Night of 13th–14th October 1941
How to expand—How to wait—How to meditate—How to recognise essentials

I've acquired the habit of avoiding every kind of vexation, once evening has come—otherwise I wouldn't be able to free myself from it all night. I likewise have the habit of allowing my despatch-rider to have a rest before I send him off. Some people are perhaps astonished not to get an answer to their letters. I dictate my mail, then I spend a dozen hours without bothering about it.

Next day I make a first set of corrections, and perhaps a second set the day after. In doing so, I'm being very prudent. Nobody can use a letter in my own hand against me.

Besides, it's my opinion that, in an age when we have facilities like the train, the motor-car and the aircraft, it's much better to meet than to write, at least when some matter of capital importance is at issue. You easily get your mind excited when you're writing to people. You want to show them your mettle. Your correspondent, of course, has the same wish. He answers you in the same tone, or else he rushes to see you in order to insult you. Not long ago one of my colleagues came to ask my advice on how to answer an offensive letter. I simply forbade him to reply. We have a ridiculous law by which, in matters of insult, a complaint must be lodged immediately, or else the right to bring suit lapses. It would be much more just to decide that complaints on such matters cannot be lodged until after a delay of three weeks.

In fact, as a rule the complainant's anger would have gone up in smoke, and the work of the courts would be lightened. I write drafts of letters only concerning matters of vital importance. It's what I did, for example, for the Four Year Plan—and last year, when I was contemplating the action against Russia.

At present, I spend about ten hours a day thinking about military matters. The resulting orders are a matter of half an hour, or three-quarters of an hour. But first of all every operation has to be studied and thought over at length. It sometimes takes up to six months for the thought to be elaborated and made precise.

Doubtless the time will come when I shall no longer have to concern myself with the war or the Eastern front, for it will be only a matter of carrying out what has been already foreseen and ordered. Thus, while these operations are being completed, I shall be able to devote my mind to other problems.

What is fortunate for me is that I know how to relax. Before going to bed, I spend some time on architecture, I look at pictures, I take an interest in things entirely different from those that have been occupying my mind throughout the day. Otherwise I wouldn't be able to sleep.

What would happen to me if I didn't have around me men whom I completely trust, to do the work for which I can't find time?

Hard men, who act as energetically as I would do myself. For me, the best man is the man who removes the most from my shoulders, the man who can take 95 per cent of the decisions in my place.

Of course, there are always cases in which I have to take the final decision myself. I couldn't say whether my feeling that I am indispensable has been strengthened during this war. One thing is certain, that without me the decisions to which we today owe our existence would not have been taken.

14th October 1941, midday
SPECIAL GUEST: REICHSFÜHRER HIMMLER
Disadvantages of a Concordat with the Churches—Difficulty of compromising with a lie—No truck with religion for the Party—Antagonism of dogma and science—Let Christianity die slowly—The metaphysical needs of the soul—No State religion—Freedom of belief.

It may be asked whether concluding a concordat with the churches wouldn't facilitate our exercise of power. On this subject one may make the following remarks: Firstly, in this way the authority of the State would be vitiated by the fact of the intervention of a third power concerning which it is impossible to say how long it would remain reliable. In the case of the Anglican Church, this objection does not arise, for England knows she can depend on her Church. But what about the Catholic Church? Wouldn't we be running the risk of her one day going into reverse after having put herself at the service of the State solely in order to safeguard her power? If one day the State's policy ceased to suit Rome or the clergy, the priests would turn against the State, as they are doing now. History provides examples that should make us careful.

Secondly, there is also a question of principle. Trying to take a long view of things, is it conceivable that one could found anything durable on falsehood? When I think of our people's future, I must look further than immediate advantages, even if these advantages were to last three hundred, five hundred years or more. I'm convinced that any pact with the Church can offer only a provisional benefit, for sooner or later the scientific spirit will disclose the harmful character of such a compromise. Thus the State will have based its existence on a foundation that one day will collapse.

An educated man retains the sense of the mysteries of nature and bows before the unknowable. An uneducated man, on the other hand, runs the risk of going over to atheism (which is a return to the state of the animal) as soon as he perceives that the State, in sheer opportunism, is making use of false ideas in the matter of religion, whilst in other fields it bases everything on pure science. That's why I've always kept the Party aloof from religious questions. I've thus prevented my Catholic and Protestant supporters from forming groups against one another, and inadvertently knocking each other out with the Bible and the sprinkler.[51] So we never became involved with these Churches' forms of worship. And if that has momentarily made my task a little more difficult, at least I've never run the risk of carrying grist to my opponents' mill. The help we would have provisionally obtained from a concordat would have quickly become a burden on us. In any case, the main thing is to be clever in this matter and not to look for a struggle where it can be avoided. Being weighed down by a superstitious past, men are afraid of things that can't, or can't yet, be explained—that is to

---

[51] The "sprinkler": a hand-held water dispenser used in Catholic services.

say, of the unknown. If anyone has needs of a metaphysical nature, I can't satisfy them with the Party's programme. Time will go by until the moment when science can answer all the questions.

So it's not opportune to hurl ourselves now into a struggle with the Churches. The best thing is to let Christianity die a natural death. A slow death has something comforting about it. The dogma of Christianity gets worn away before the advances of science. Religion will have to make more and more concessions.

Gradually the myths crumble. All that's left is to prove that in nature there is no frontier between the organic and the inorganic. When understanding of the universe has become widespread, when the majority of men know that the stars are not sources of light but worlds, perhaps inhabited worlds like ours, then the Christian doctrine will be convicted of absurdity.

Originally, religion was merely a prop for human communities. It was a means, not an end in itself. It's only gradually that it became transformed in this direction, with the object of maintaining the rule of the priests, who can live only to the detriment of society collectively.

The instructions of a hygienic nature that most religions gave, contributed to the foundation of organised communities. The precepts ordering people to wash, to avoid certain drinks, to fast at appointed dates, to take exercise, to rise with the sun, to climb to the top of the minaret—all these were obligations invented by intelligent people. The exhortation to fight courageously is also self-explanatory.

Observe, by the way, that, as a corollary, the Mussulman[52] was promised a paradise peopled with *houris*,[53] where wine flowed in streams—a real earthly paradise. The Christians, on the other hand, declare themselves satisfied if after their death they are allowed to sing *Hallelujahs!* All these elements contributed to form human communities. It is to these private customs that peoples owe their present characters.

Christianity, of course, has reached the peak of absurdity in this respect. And that's why one day its structure will collapse. Science has already impregnated humanity. Consequently, the more Christianity clings to its dogmas, the quicker it will decline.

But one must continue to pay attention to another aspect of the problem. It's possible to satisfy the needs of the inner life by an intimate

---

[52] An antiquated term for a Muslim.
[53] Beautiful young woman, especially one of the virgin companions of the faithful in the Muslim Paradise.

communion with nature, or by knowledge of the past. Only a minority, however, at the present stage of the mind's development, can feel the respect inspired by the unknown, and thus satisfy the metaphysical needs of the soul.

The average human being has the same needs, but can satisfy them only by elementary means. That's particularly true of women, as also of peasants who impotently watch the destruction of their crops. The person whose life tends to simplification is thirsty for belief, and he dimly clings to it with all his strength.

Nobody has the right to deprive simple people of their childish certainties until they've acquired others that are more reasonable. Indeed, it's most important that the higher belief should be well established in them before the lower belief has been removed. We must finally achieve this. But it would serve no purpose to replace an old belief by a new one that would merely fill the place left vacant by its predecessor.

It seems to me that nothing would be more foolish than to re-establish the worship of Wotan. Our old mythology had ceased to be viable when Christianity implanted itself. Nothing dies unless it is moribund. At that period the ancient world was divided between the systems of philosophy and the worship of idols. It's not desirable that the whole of humanity should be stultified—and the only way of getting rid of Christianity is to allow it to die little by little.

A movement like ours must not let itself be drawn into metaphysical digressions. It must stick to the spirit of exact science. It's not the Party's function to be a counterfeit for religion.

If, in the course of a thousand or two thousand years, science arrives at the necessity of renewing its points of view, that will not mean that science is a liar. Science cannot lie, for it's always striving, according to the momentary state of knowledge, to deduce what is true. When it makes a mistake, it does so in good faith. It's Christianity that's the liar. It's in perpetual conflict with itself.

One may ask whether the disappearance of Christianity would entail the disappearance of belief in God. That's not to be desired. The notion of divinity gives most men the opportunity to concretise the feeling they have of supernatural realities. Why should we destroy this wonderful power they have of incarnating the feeling for the divine that is within them? The man who lives in communion with nature necessarily finds himself in opposition to the Churches. And that's why they're heading for ruin—for science is bound to win.

I especially wouldn't want our movement to acquire a religious character and institute a form of worship. It would be appalling for me, and I would wish I would never lived, if I were to end up in the skin of a Buddha!

If at this moment we were to eliminate the religions by force, the people would unanimously beseech us for a new form of worship. You can imagine our *Gauleiters* giving up their pranks to play at being saints! As for our Minister for Religion, according to his own co-religionists, God himself would turn away from his family!

I envisage the future, therefore, as follows: First of all, to each man his private creed. Superstition shall not lose its rights. The Party is sheltered from the danger of competing with the religions. These latter must simply be forbidden from interfering in future with temporal matters. From the tenderest age, education will be imparted in such a way that each child will know all that is important to the maintenance of the State. As for the men close to me, who, like me, have escaped from the clutches of dogma, I've no reason to fear that the Church will get its hooks on them.

We'll see to it that the Churches cannot spread abroad teachings in conflict with the interests of the State. We shall continue to preach the doctrine of National Socialism, and the young will no longer be taught anything but the truth.

Night of 14th–15th October 1941
Meteorological forecasts—Reorganisation of the service

One can't put any trust in the met forecasts. The meteorological services ought to be separated from the Army.

Lufthansa had a first-class meteorological service. I was terribly sorry when that service was broken up. The present organisation is not nearly as good as the old one. Moreover, there are various improvements that could be made to meteorology generally.

Weather prediction is not a science that can be learnt mechanically. What we need are men gifted with a sixth sense, who live in nature and with nature—whether or not they know anything about isotherms and isobars. As a rule, obviously, these men are not particularly suited to the wearing of uniforms. One of them will have a humped back, another will be bandy-legged, a third paralytic.

Similarly, one doesn't expect them to live like bureaucrats. They won't run the risk of being transported from a region they know to another of which they know nothing—as regards climatological conditions, that's to say. They won't be answerable to superiors who necessarily know more about the subject than they do—in virtue of their pips and crowns—and who might be tempted to dictate to them the truths that are vested in a man by virtue of his superior rank.

Doubtless the best thing would be to form a civil organisation that would take over the existing installations.

This organisation would also use the information, communicated regularly by telephone and applicable to particular regions, which one would owe to these human barometers. It would cost very little.

A retired school-teacher, for example, would be happy to receive thirty marks a month as payment for his trouble.

A telephone would be installed in his home free of charge, and he'd be flattered to have people relying on his knowledge. The good fellow would be excused from making written reports, and he would even be authorised to express himself in his own dialect. He might be a man who has never set foot outside his own village, but who understands the flight of midges and swallows, who can read the signs, who feels the wind, to whom the movements of the sky are familiar.

Elements are involved in that kind of thing that are imponderable and beyond mathematics. There are bits of knowledge that are developed in the course of an existence intimately associated with the life of nature, which are often passed on from father to son. It's enough to look around one. It's known that in every region there are such beings, for whom the weather has no secrets. The central office will only have to compare these empirical pieces of information with those provided by the "scientific" methods, and make a synthesis. In this way, I imagine, we would finally again have an instrument on which one could depend, a meteorological service in which one could have confidence.

15th October 1941, evening
*The strong meat of National Socialism—Stresemann—If the French
. . . —Von Papen and the Young plan—Remedies against inflation—
The example of Frederick the Great—The economists make a mess of
everything*

Our conquest of power was not made without difficulty. The regime played all its cards, without forgetting a single one, to postpone the fatal event as long as possible. The National Socialist brew was a little strong for delicate stomachs! Amongst my predecessors, Stresemann[54]

---

[54] Gustav Stresemann (1878–1929), German chancellor in 1923, and then German foreign minister from 1923 to 1929.

was not the worst. But, in order to obtain partial gains, he forgot that to reduce a whole people to a state of slavery was to pay somewhat dearly.

At the time of the occupation of the Rhineland, a journey to the West was for me a troublesome and complicated matter. I had to avoid the occupied zones. One day, on leaving the Hotel Dreesen, in Godesberg, I intended to cross one of these zones. That same morning an unpleasant presentiment made me abandon the project. Two days later, I learnt in a letter from Dreesen that, contrary to the usual custom, the check at the frontier had been very strict.

If I would fallen into their hands on that occasion, the French would not have let me go! They had proofs concerning our activities, and they could have gone on from there to launch a whole machine against me. For the Reich Government, it would have been a deliverance. My former opponents would have disguised their joy and shed crocodile tears whilst raising, as a matter of form, a protest that would have been intended to fail.

Even men fairly close to us regarded the Young Plan[55] as a relief for Germany. I remember having come to Berlin for a meeting. Papen,[56] who was back from Lausanne, was explaining that he had scored a great success in reducing the total of reparations to a sum of five thousand eight hundred million marks. I commented that, if we succeeded in getting together such a sum, we ought to devote it to German rearmament. After the seizure of power, I immediately had all payments suspended—which we could already have done as far back as 1925. In 1933, the Reich had eighty-three million marks' worth of foreign currency. The day after the seizure of power, I was called upon to deliver immediately sixty-four millions. I pleaded that I knew nothing about the whole business, and asked time to reflect.

In the course of enquiring when this demand had been formulated, I was told: "Three months ago." I decided that, if people had been able to wait three months, they could easily wait another two. My advisers

---

[55] The Young Plan was a plan which hoped to settle the issue of German reparations for the Great War. Drawn up by American industrialist Owen D. Young. All reparation arrangements were rejected after Hitler's rise to power, but were resumed after 1945, with the last payment being made in 2010.

[56] Franz von Papen (1879–1969), the conservative politician who served briefly as chancellor in 1932, and then as the vice-chancellor under Hitler from 1933 to 1934. Later, Papen served as a German ambassador in Vienna from 1934 to 1938 and in Ankara from 1939 to 1944.

displayed a childish fear that this would cost us our reputation as good payers. My view was that German prestige would not be enhanced by our paying under threat of blackmail, but much more by our ceasing to pay.

The inflation could have been overcome. The decisive thing was our home war-debt; in other words, the yearly payment of ten thousand millions in interest on a debt of a hundred and sixty-six thousand millions. By way of comparison, I remember that before the war the total cost of imports paid for by the German people was five thousand million. To pay the interest, the people was compelled to walk the plank with paper money—hence the depreciation of the currency.

The just thing would have been: firstly, to suspend payment of interest on the debt; secondly, to put a very heavy tax on the scandalous war-profits. I would have forced the war-profiteers to buy, with good, clinking coin of the realm, various securities which I would have frozen for a period of twenty, thirty or forty years.

Weren't their dividends of 200 per cent and 300 per cent the reason why our war-debt had reached such a level? Inflation is not caused by increasing the fiduciary circulation. It begins on the day when the purchaser is obliged to pay, for the same goods, a higher sum than that asked the day before. At that point, one must intervene. Even to Schacht,[57] I had to begin by explaining this elementary truth: that the essential cause of the stability of our currency was to be sought for in our concentration camps. The currency remains stable when the speculators are put under lock and key. I also had to make Schacht understand that excess profits must be removed from economic circulation. I do not entertain the illusion that I can pay for everything out of my available funds. Simply, I've read a lot, and I've known how to profit by the experience of events in the past.

Frederick the Great, already, had gradually withdrawn his devaluated *thalers* from circulation, and had thus re-established the value of his currency.

All these things are simple and natural. The only thing is, one must not let the Jew stick his nose in. The basis of Jewish commercial policy is to make matters incomprehensible for a normal brain. People go into ecstasies of confidence before the science of the great economists.

---

[57] Hjalmar Schacht (1877–1970), an economist who served as Currency Commissioner and President of the Reichsbank from 1933–1939 and as Minister of Economics from 1934 to 1937.

Anyone who doesn't understand is taxed with ignorance! At bottom, the only object of all these notions is to throw everything into confusion. The very simple ideas that happen to be mine have nowadays penetrated into the flesh and blood of millions. Only the professors don't understand that the value of money depends on the goods behind that money.

One day I received some workers in the great hall at Obersalzberg, to give them an informal lecture on money. The good chaps understood me very well, and rewarded me with a storm of applause. To give people money is solely a problem of making paper.

The whole question is to know whether the workers are producing goods to match the paper that's made. If work does not increase, so that production remains at the same level, the extra money they get won't enable them to buy more things than they bought before with less money.

Obviously, that theory couldn't have provided the material for a learned dissertation. For a distinguished economist, the thing is, no matter what you're talking about, to pour out ideas in complicated meanderings and to use terms of Sibylline incomprehensibility.

17th October 1941, midday
The fall of Odessa—Antonescu's role—Necessary reforms in Romania—Rooting out of the Jew

With the fall of Odessa, the war will be practically over for Romania.

All that's left for the Romanians to do is to consolidate their position. In the face of Antonescu's success, the opposition will collapse. Peoples always give themselves to victorious commanders.

Reactionaries are like hollow nuts. They take a whisper uttered by one booby and transmitted to other boobies, they make a real rumour, and they end by persuading themselves that here is the true, thundering voice of the people.

In actual fact, what they hear is only the amplified echo of their own feeble voices. That's how, in some quarters, the people is credited with feelings that are utterly foreign to it. Antonescu has the merit of having intervened in favour of Codreanu.[58]

Apart from the Duce, amongst our allies Antonescu is the man who makes the strongest impression. He's a man on a big scale, who never

---

[58] Corneliu Zelea Codreanu (1899–1938), leader of the "The Legion of the Archangel Michael", also known as the Iron Guard, a pro-Nazi party. Arrested by order of the king and prime minister, Codreanu was executed without trial.

lets anything throw him out of his stride, and he's incorruptible, what's more—a man such as Romania has never had before.

I may say that there was nothing in Romania, including the officers, that couldn't be bought. I'm not even alluding to the venality of the women, who are always ready to prostitute themselves to gain promotion for a husband or father. It's true that the pay of all these servants of the State was ridiculously stingy. Antonescu now has the job of building up his State by basing it on agriculture. For industry, he'd need abilities that his peasant class (which is sober and honest) does not possess. On the other hand, a usable administration can be recruited amongst this class. But it must be small, and it must be adequately paid.

Whoever in Romania continues to abandon himself to corruption will have to be shot. There must be no shrinking from the death penalty when it's a question of strangling an epidemic.

The present type of official, when faced with such a threat, will prefer to give up his post—which can then be offered to somebody respectable. It goes without saying that the officers must be paid so that they will no longer be obliged to find subsidiary occupations in order to keep alive.

To bring decency into civil life, the first condition is to have an integral State: an incorruptible army, a police and administration reduced to a minimum. But the first thing, above all, is to get rid of the Jew. Without that, it will be useless to clean the Augean stables. If Antonescu sets about the job in this manner, he'll be the head of a thriving country, inwardly healthy and strong. For this purpose he has a good peasantry (Hungary has nothing like it) and natural riches. Moreover, Romania is a country with a thinly scattered population.

17th October 1941, evening
SPECIAL GUESTS: REICH MINISTER DR. TODT[59] AND GAULEITER SAUCKEL[60]

Expectations as regards the Eastern Territories—The Ukraine in twenty years' time—Bread is won by the sword—God only recognises power

In comparison with the beauties accumulated in Central Germany, the new territories in the East seem to us like a desert. Flanders, too, is only a plain—but of what beauty!

---

[59] Fritz Todt (1891–1942), Inspector General for German Roadways, and later as Reich Minister for Armaments and Ammunition.
[60] Ernst Sauckel (1894–1946), *Gauleiter* of Thuringia and General Plenipotentiary for Labour Deployment from 1942 to 1945.

This Russian desert, we shall populate it. The immense spaces of the Eastern Front will have been the field of the greatest battles in history. We'll give this country a past. We'll take away its character of an Asiatic steppe, we'll Europeanise it. With this object, we have undertaken the construction of roads that will lead to the southernmost point of the Crimea and to the Caucasus. These roads will be studded along their whole length with German towns, and around these towns our colonists will settle. As for the two or three million men whom we need to accomplish this task, we'll find them quicker than we think.

They'll come from Germany, Scandinavia, the Western countries and America. I shall no longer be here to see all that, but in twenty years, the Ukraine will already be a home for twenty million inhabitants besides the natives. In three hundred years, the country will be one of the loveliest gardens in the world.

As for the natives, we'll have to screen them carefully. The Jew, that destroyer, we shall drive out. As far as the population is concerned, I get a better impression in White Russia than in the Ukraine.

We shan't settle in the Russian towns, and we'll let them fall to pieces without intervening. And, above all, no remorse on this subject! We're not going to play at children's nurses; we're absolutely without obligations as far as these people are concerned. To struggle against the hovels, chase away the fleas, provide German teachers, bring out newspapers—very little of that for us! We'll confine ourselves, perhaps, to setting up a radio transmitter, under our control. For the rest, let them know just enough to understand our highway signs, so that they won't get themselves run over by our vehicles!

For them the word "liberty" means the right to wash on feast days. If we arrive bringing soft soap, we'll obtain no sympathy. These are views that will have to be completely readjusted. There's only one duty: to Germanise this country by the immigration of Germans, and to look upon the natives as Redskins.

If these people had defeated us, Heaven have mercy! But we don't hate them. That sentiment is unknown to us. We are guided only by reason. They, on the other hand, have an inferiority complex. They have a real hatred towards a conqueror whose crushing superiority they can feel. The *intelligentsia*? We have too many of them at home. All those who have the feeling for Europe can join in our work. In this business I shall go straight ahead, cold-bloodedly. What they may think about me, at this juncture, is to me a matter of complete indifference. I don't see why a German who eats a piece of bread should torment himself with the idea that the soil that produces this bread has been won by the sword. When we eat wheat from Canada, we don't think about the despoiled Indians.

The precept that it's men's duty to love one another is theory—and the Christians are the last to practise it! A negro baby who has the misfortune to die before a missionary gets his clutches on him, goes to Hell! If that were true, one might well lament that sorrowful destiny: to have lived only three years, and to burn for all eternity with Lucifer! For Ley,[61] it will be the job of his life to drag that country out of its lethargy. Fields, gardens, orchards. Let it be a country where the work is hard, but the joy pays for the trouble.

We've given the German people what it needed to assert its position in the world. I'm glad that this call to the East has taken our attention off the Mediterranean. The South, for us, is the Crimea. To go further would be nonsense. Let us stay Nordic. In any case, in our country the sunny season sometimes goes on until November. In Berlin, February brings the first promises of spring. On the Rhine, everything flowers in March. In the Ukraine, more than anywhere else, it would be a mistake to install flour-mills that would drain off the wheat from immense territories—over a radius of four hundred kilometres, for example. We should rather build windmills all over the place, to supply regional needs—and export only the wheat demanded by the large centres.

How I regret not being ten years younger! Todt, you will have to extend your programme. As for the necessary labour, you shall have it. Let's finish the road network, and the rail network. We shall have to settle down to the task of rebuilding the Russian track, to restore it to the normal gauge.

There's only one road that, throughout all these last months of campaigning, was of any use to the armies on the central front—and for that I'll set up a monument to Stalin. Apart from that, he preferred to manufacture chains of mud rather than to build roads! What a task awaits us! We have a hundred years of joyful satisfaction before us.

Night of 17th–18th October 1941
May 10th, 1940—Tears of joy—The Schlieffen plan—G.H.Q,. at Felsennest—Paris, a town with a glorious past—22nd June 1941—Kiev, Moscow, St. Petersburg must be destroyed

---

[61] Robert Ley (1890–1945), leader of the German Labour Front from 1933 to 1945.

I never closed an eye during the night of the 9th to 10th of May 1940, or that of the 21st to 22nd of June 1941.

In May 1940, it was especially worry about the weather that kept me awake. I was filled with rage when dawn broke and I realised that it was fifteen minutes earlier than I would been told. And yet I knew that it had to be like that!

At seven o'clock came the news: "Eben Emael has been silenced." Next: "We hold one of the bridges over the Meuse." With a fellow like Witzig,[62] we would have been able to take the bridges of Maastricht before they were blown up. But what difference did it make whether they were blown up, as soon as we held the very high bridge commanding Liège—sixty metres above river-level. If that *had* been blown, our engineers would have found time to put it back into shape. It was wonderful how everything went off as arranged.

When the news came that the enemy was advancing along the whole front, I could have wept for joy: they'd fallen into the trap! It had been a clever piece of work to attack Liège. We had to make them believe we were remaining faithful to the old Schlieffen plan. I had my fears concerning the advance of von Kluge's army, but everything was well prepared. Two days after our arrival at Abbeville, we could already start our offensive to the South.

If I had disposed then of as many motorised troops as I have now, we would have finished the campaign in a fortnight. How exciting it will be, later, to go over those operations once more. Several times during the night I went to the operations-room to pore over those relief-maps.

What a lovely place *Felsennest*[63] was! The birds in the morning, the view over the road by which the columns were going up the line. Over our head, the squadrons of aircraft. There, I knew what I was doing.

In the air attack on Paris, we confined ourselves to the airfields—to spare a city with a glorious past. It's a fact that, from a global point of view, the French are behaving very badly, but all the same they're closely related to us, and it would have hurt me to be obliged to attack a city like Leon, with its cathedral.

On the 22nd of June, a door opened before us, and we didn't know what was behind it. We could look out for gas warfare, bacteriological

---

[62] Rudolf Witzig (1916–2001), the paratrooper in command of the unit which captured the Belgian fortress of Fort Eben-Emael on 10 May, 1940.

[63] The *Felsennest* ("Rocky Eyrie") was Hitler's headquarters in western Germany, used during the invasion of France in 1940..

warfare. The heavy uncertainty took me by the throat. Here we were faced by beings who are complete strangers to us.

Everything that resembles civilisation, the Bolsheviks have suppressed it, and I have no feelings about the idea of wiping out Kiev, Moscow or St. Petersburg.

What our troops are doing is positively unimaginable. Not knowing the great news, how will our soldiers—who are at present on the way home—feel when they're once more on German soil?

In comparison with Russia, even Poland looked like a civilised country. If time were to blot out our soldiers' deeds, the monuments I shall have set up in Berlin will continue to proclaim their glory a thousand years from today.

The Arc de Triomphe, the Pantheon of the Army, the Pantheon of the German people....

18th October 1941, evening
SPECIAL GUESTS: PROFESSOR SPEER[64] AND PROFESSOR BREKER[65]

Churchill conducts the orchestra—Jewry pulls strings—Rapacity of business rogues—State economy must be strengthened

It's a queer business, how England slipped into the war. The man who managed it was Churchill, that puppet of the Jewry that pulls the strings. Next to him, the bumptious Eden,[66] a money-grubbing clown; the Jew who was Minister for War, Hore-Belisha;[67] then the *Eminence grise* of the Foreign Office—and after that some other Jews and business men. With these last, it often happens that the size of their fortune is in inverse ratio to the size of their brains. Before the war even began, somebody managed to persuade them it would last at least three years, and would therefore be a good investment for them.

The people, which has the privilege of possessing such a government, was not asked for its opinion. The business world is made up everywhere of the same rogues. Cold-hearted money-grubbers. The business world gets idealistic only when the workers ask for higher wages. I fully realise that with us, too, the possibilities for people of that kind were greater before 1933. But let the business men weep—it's part

---

[64] Albert Speer (1905–1981), Minister of Armaments and War Production.
[65] Arno Breker (1900–1991), a sculptor famous for his classical artistic style.
[66] Robert Anthony Eden (1897–1977), British Foreign Minister from 1935 to 1938, and again from 1940 to 1945. Later he became Prime Minister of Britain.
[67] Leslie Hore-Belisha (1893–1957), British Secretary for War from 1937 to 1940.

of their trade. I've never met an industrialist without observing how he puts on a careworn expression. Yet it's not difficult to convince each one of them that he has regularly improved his position. One always sees them panting as if they were on the point of giving up their last gasp!

Despite all the taxes, there's a lot of money left. Even the average man doesn't succeed in spending what he earns. He spends more money on cinemas, theatres and concerts than he used to, and he saves money into the bargain.

One can't deprive people of distractions; they need them, and that's why I cannot reduce the activity of the theatres and studios. The best relaxation is that provided by the theatre and the cinema. We have working days that far exceed eight hours, and we shan't be able to change that immediately after the war.

A fault we must never again commit is to forget, once the war is over, the advantages of the autarkic economy. We practised it during the Great War, but with insufficient means, for lack of human potential. The working-capacity lost in the manufacture of unproductive goods must be made good. Instead of thinking of the home market, we hurled ourselves into the foreign markets: before the Great War, out of greed for profits, and, after it, to pay our debts. The fact that we were granted loans, to encourage us along the same path, only plunged us deeper in the mire. We had already succeeded in the manufacture of synthetic rubber: as soon as the war was over, we went back to natural rubber.

We imported petrol; yet the Bergius process[68] had already proved itself! That's our most urgent task for the post-war period: to build up the autarkic economy.

I shall retain rationing of meat and fats as long as I'm not certain that people's needs are largely covered. One realises that this stage has been reached when the rationing coupons are not all used.

What the English were most afraid of, with the Four Year Plan, was an autarkic Germany that they could no longer have at their mercy. Such a policy on our part necessarily entailed for them a great reduction in the profits' of their colonies.

Coffee and tea are all we shall have to import. Tobacco we shall get in Europe. It will also be necessary to produce the soya bean: that will

---

[68] The Bergius process is a method of production of liquid hydrocarbons for use as synthetic fuel, developed in 1913 by the German chemist Friedrich Bergius (1884–1949).

provide oil and fodder for Denmark and Holland. Everybody will be able to participate, under one form or another, in this European economy. If it were only a question of conquering a colony, I would not continue the war a day longer.

For a colonial policy to have any sense, one must first dominate Europe. In any case, the only colony I would like to have back would be our Cameroons—nothing else.

19th October 1941
Above all, large families

The essential thing for the future is to have lots of children. Everybody should be persuaded that a family's life is assured only when it has upwards of four children—I should even say, four sons. That's a principle that should never be forgotten.

When I learn that a family has lost two sons at the front, I intervene immediately. If we had practised the system of two-children families in the old days, Germany would have been deprived of her greatest geniuses. How does it come about that the exceptional being in a family is often the fifth, seventh, tenth or twelfth in the row?

19th October 1941, evening
The art of building—New constructions—The need for standardisation and uniformity—Let the masses enjoy life's amenities—Catechism and typewriting

The art of building is one of the most ancient of human trades. That explains why, in this trade more than any other, people have remained faithful to traditional methods. It's a sphere in which we are terribly behind.

To build a house should not necessarily consist in anything more than assembling the materials—which would not necessarily entail a uniformity of dwellings. The disposition and number of elements can be varied—but the elements should be standardised. Whoever wants to do more than is necessary will know what it costs him. A Croesus[69] is not looking for the "three-room dwelling" at the lowest price.

What's the point of having a hundred different models for wash-basins? Why these differences in the dimensions of windows and doors? You change your apartment, and your curtains are no longer any use to you! For my car, I can find spare parts everywhere, but not for my

---

[69] Croesus was the last king of the Anatolian state of Lydia (reigned c. 560–546) who was renowned for his great wealth.

apartment. These practices exist only because they give shopkeepers a chance of making more money. That's the only explanation of this infinite variety. In a year or two from now, this scandal must have been put a stop to. It's the same with the differences of voltage in the supply of electricity. For example, Moabit and Charlottenburg have different currents. When we rebuild the Reich, we'll make all that uniform.

Likewise, in the field of construction we shall have to modernise the tools. The excavator that's still in use is a prehistoric monster compared to the new spiral excavator.

What economies one could achieve by standardisation in this field! The wish we have to give millions of Germans better living conditions forces us to standardisation, and thus to make use of elements built to a norm, wherever there is no necessity for individual forms. If we make things uniform, the masses will be able to enjoy the material amenities of life. With a market of fifteen million purchasers, it's quite conceivable that it would be possible to build a cheap radio set and a popular typewriter.

I find it a real absurdity that even today a typewriter costs several hundred marks. One can't imagine the time wasted daily in deciphering everybody's scribbles. Why not give lessons in typewriting at primary school? Instead of religious instruction, for example. I shouldn't mind that.

19th October 1941, night
Two scourges of the modern world—Christianity the shadow of coming Bolshevism

The reason why the ancient world was so pure, light and serene was that it knew nothing of the two great scourges: the pox and Christianity. Christianity is a prototype of Bolshevism: the mobilisation by the Jew of the masses of slaves with the object of undermining society. Thus one understands that the healthy elements of the Roman world were proof against this doctrine. Yet Rome today allows itself to reproach Bolshevism with having destroyed the Christian churches! As if Christianity hadn't behaved in the same way towards the pagan temples.

21st October 1941, midday
Prophetic sense of Julian the Apostate—The Aryan origin of Jesus— Distortion of Christ's ideas—The Road to Damascus—Roman tolerance—Materialism and the Jewish religion—Religion as a subversive method—The mobilisation of the slaves—St. Paul and Karl Marx

65

When one thinks of the opinions held concerning Christianity by our best minds a hundred, two hundred years ago, one is ashamed to realise how little we have since evolved. I didn't know that Julian the Apostate had passed judgment with such clear-sightedness on Christianity and Christians. You should read what he says on the subject.

Originally, Christianity was merely an incarnation of Bolshevism the destroyer. Nevertheless, the Galilean, who later was called the Christ, intended something quite different. He must be regarded as a popular leader who took up His position against Jewry. Galilee was a colony where the Romans had probably installed Gallic legionaries, and it's certain that Jesus was not a Jew. The Jews, by the way, regarded him as the son of a whore—of a whore and a Roman soldier.

The decisive falsification of Jesus' doctrine was the work of St. Paul. He gave himself to this work with subtlety and for purposes of personal exploitation. For the Galilean's object was to liberate his country from Jewish oppression. He set himself against Jewish capitalism, and that's why the Jews liquidated him.

Paul of Tarsus (his name was Saul, before the road to Damascus) was one of those who persecuted Jesus most savagely. When he learnt that Jesus' supporters let their throats be cut for His ideas, he realised that, by making intelligent use of the Galilean's teaching, it would be possible to overthrow this Roman State which the Jews hated. It's in this context that we must understand the famous "illumination". Think of it, the Romans were daring to confiscate the most sacred thing the Jews possessed, the gold piled up in their temples! At that time, as now, money was their god.

On the road to Damascus, St. Paul discovered that he could succeed in ruining the Roman State by causing the principle of the equality of all men before a single God to triumph—and by putting beyond the reach of the laws his private notions, which he alleged to be divinely inspired. If, into the bargain, one succeeded in imposing one man as the representative on earth of the only God, that man would possess boundless power.

The ancient world had its gods and served them. But the priests interposed between the gods and men were servants of the State, for the gods protected the City. In short, they were the emanation of a power that the people had created. For that society, the idea of an only god was unthinkable. In this sphere, the Romans were tolerance itself. The idea of a universal god could seem to them only a mild form of madness—for, if three peoples fight one another, each invoking the same god, this means that, at any rate, two of them are praying in vain.

Nobody was more tolerant than the Romans. Every man could pray to the god of his choice, and a place was even reserved in the temples for the unknown god. Moreover, every man prayed as he chose, and had the right to proclaim his preferences.

St. Paul knew how to exploit this state of affairs in order to conduct his struggle against the Roman State. Nothing has changed; the method has remained sound. Under cover of a pretended religious instruction, the priests continue to incite the faithful against the State.

The religious ideas of the Romans are common to all Aryan peoples. The Jew, on the other hand, worshipped and continues to worship, then and now, nothing but the golden calf.

The Jewish religion is devoid of all metaphysics and has no foundation but the most repulsive materialism. That's proved even in the concrete representation they have of the Beyond—which for them is identified with Abraham's bosom.

It's since St. Paul's time that the Jews have manifested themselves as a religious community, for until then they were only a racial community.

St. Paul was the first man to take account of the possible advantages of using a religion as a means of propaganda. If the Jew has succeeded in destroying the Roman Empire, that's because St. Paul transformed a local movement of Aryan opposition to Jewry into a supra-temporal religion, which postulates the equality of all men amongst themselves, and their obedience to an only god. This is what caused the death of the Roman Empire.

It's striking to observe that Christian ideas, despite all St. Paul's efforts, had no success in Athens. The philosophy of the Greeks was so much superior to this poverty-stricken rubbish that the Athenians burst out laughing when they listened to the apostle's teaching. But in Rome, St. Paul found the ground prepared for him. His egalitarian theories had what was needed to win over a mass composed of innumerable uprooted people.

Nevertheless, the Roman slave was not at all what the expression encourages us to imagine today. In actual fact, the people concerned were prisoners of war (as we understand the term nowadays), of whom many had been freed and had the possibility of becoming citizens—and it was St. Paul who introduced this degrading overtone into the modern idea of Roman slaves. Think of the numerous Germanic people whom Rome welcomed. Arminius[70] himself, the first architect of our liberty, wasn't he a Roman knight, and his brother a dignitary of the State? By reason of these contacts, renewed throughout the centuries, the population of Rome had ended by acquiring a great esteem for the Germanic peoples.

It's clear that there was a preference in Rome for fair-haired women, to such a point that many Roman women dyed their hair. Thus Germanic blood constantly regenerated Roman society. The Jew, on the other hand, was despised in Rome. Whilst Roman society proved hostile to the new doctrine, Christianity in its pure state stirred the population to revolt.

Rome was Bolshevised, and Bolshevism produced exactly the same results in Rome as later in Russia. It was only later, under the influence of the Germanic spirit, that Christianity gradually lost its openly Bolshevistic character. It became, to a certain degree, tolerable.

Today, when Christianity is tottering, the Jew restores to pride of place Christianity in its Bolshevistic form. The Jew believed he could renew the experiment. Today as once before, the object is to destroy nations by vitiating their racial integrity. It's not by chance that the Jews, in Russia, have systematically deported hundreds of thousands of men, delivering the women, whom the men were compelled to leave behind, to males imported from other regions. They practised on a vast scale the mixture of races. In the old days, as now, destruction of art and civilisation. The Bolsheviks of their day, what didn't they destroy in Rome, in Greece and elsewhere? They've behaved in the same way amongst us and in Russia.

One must compare the art and civilisation of the Romans—their temples, their houses—with the art and civilisation represented at the same period by the abject rabble of the catacombs. In the old days, the destruction of the libraries. Isn't that what happened in Russia?

The result: a frightful levelling-down. Didn't the world see, carried on right into the Middle Ages, the same old system of martyrs, tortures, faggots? Of old, it was in the name of Christianity. Today, it's in the name of Bolshevism. Yesterday, the instigator was Saul: the instigator today, Mordechai. Saul has changed into St. Paul, and Mordechai into

---

[70] Arminius (c. 18 BC–21 AD), more commonly called Hermann, was the Cherusci tribal chief who led the famous uprising against the attempted Roman occupation of Germania, resulting the cataclysmic Battle of the Teutoburg Forest in 9 AD, in which three Roman legions were destroyed.

Karl Marx. By exterminating this pest, we shall do humanity a service of which our soldiers can have no idea.

21st–22nd October 1941, night
SPECIAL GUEST: REICHSFÜHRER SS HIMMLER

The need for decorum—One Prussian in Rome, another in Munich—The modesty of the Weimar Republic—Role of the new Chancellery—The Ugliness of Berlin—The face of new Berlin—Monuments that will last a thousand years—State and Reich above all—How to be a builder—War memories will fade in the works of peace

As far as my own private existence is concerned, I shall always live simply—but in my capacity of Führer and Head of the State, I am obliged to stand out clearly from amongst all the people around me. If my close associates glitter with decorations, I can distinguish myself from them only by wearing none at all.

We need an impressive décor, and we ought to create one. More and more we should give our festive occasions a style that will remain in the memory. In England, the traditional forms, which from a distance seem baroque, have retained their full youth. They remain vital because they represent customs that have been observed for a long time and without the slightest interruption.

I regard it as a necessity that our ceremonial should be developed during my lifetime. Otherwise one of my successors, if he has simple tastes, could quote me as his authority.

Don't speak to me of Prussian simplicity! We must remember how Frederick the Great took care of his State's finances. Besides, the Prussian spirit is a matter of character and comportment. There was a time when one could say that there was only one Prussian in Europe, and that he lived in Rome. Nowadays one can say that there's only one Roman living amongst the Italians. There was a second Prussian. He lived in Munich, and was myself.

It was one of the characteristic features of the Weimar Republic that, when the Head of the State was receiving diplomats, he had to ask every Ministry to lend him its domestic staff. What can have happened on an occasion when some Ministry was holding a reception itself and couldn't spare its servants? You can see me having recourse to car-hire firms to fetch my guests from their homes and take them back again! The new Chancellery will have to have permanently at its disposal two hundred of the finest motor-cars. The chauffeurs can perform a secondary function as footmen. Whether as chauffeurs or as footmen, these men must be absolutely reliable from the political point of view—quite apart from the fact that they must not be clumsy fools.

It's lucky we have the new Reich Chancellery. There are many things we could not have done in the old one. I've always been fond of Berlin. If I'm vexed by the fact that some of the things in it are not beautiful, it's precisely because I'm so much attached to the city.

During the Great War, I twice had ten days' leave. I never dreamt of spending these leaves in Munich. My pleasure would have been spoilt by the sight of all those priests.

On both occasions, I came to Berlin, and that's how I began to be familiar with the museums of the capital. (Besides, Berlin played a part in our rise to power, although in a different way from Munich. It's at Berlin and Württemberg that I got our financial backing, and not in Munich, where the little bourgeois hold the crown of the road.) What's more, Berlin has the monuments of the days of Frederick the Great. Once upon a time it was the sand-pit of the Empire. Nowadays, Berlin is the capital of the Reich. Berlin's misfortune is that it's a city of very mixed population; which doesn't make it ideal for the development of culture. In that respect, our last great monarch was Frederick-William IV. William I had no taste. Bismarck was blind in matters of art. William II had taste, but of the worst description.

What is ugly in Berlin, we shall suppress. Nothing will be too good for the beautification of Berlin. When one enters the Reich Chancellery, one should have the feeling that one is visiting the master of the world. One will arrive there along wide avenues containing the Triumphal Arch, the Pantheon of the Army, the Square of the People—things to take your breath away!

It's only thus that we shall succeed in eclipsing our only rival in the world, Rome. Let it be built on such a scale that St. Peter's and its Square will seem like toys in comparison! For material, we'll use granite. The vestiges of the German past, which are found on the plains to the North, are scarcely time-worn. Granite will ensure that our monuments last forever. In ten thousand years they'll be still standing, just as they are, unless meanwhile the sea has again covered our plains.

The ornamental theme which we call Germano-Nordic is found all over the earth's surface, both in South America and in the Northern countries. According to a Greek legend, there is a civilisation known as "pre-lunar", and we can see in the legend an allusion to the empire of the lands of Atlantis that sank into the ocean.

If I try to gauge my work, I must consider, first of all, that I've contributed, in a world that had forgotten the notion, to the triumph of the idea of the primacy of race. Secondly, I've given German supremacy a solid cultural foundation. In fact, the power we today enjoy cannot be justified, in my eyes, except by the establishment and expansion of a mighty culture.

To achieve this must be the law of our existence. The means I shall set in operation to this end will far surpass those that were necessary for the conduct of this war. I wish to be a builder.

A war-leader is what I am against my own will. If I apply my mind to military problems, that's because for the moment I know that nobody would succeed better at this than I can. In the same way, I don't interfere in the activity of my colleagues when I have the feeling that they are performing their task as well as I could perform it myself.

My reaction is that of a peasant whose property is attacked and who leaps to arms to defend his patrimony. This is the spirit in which I make war. For me, it's a means to other ends.

The heroic deeds of our troops will turn pale, one day. After the War of the Spanish Succession,[71] nobody thought any longer of the Thirty Years' War.[72] The battles of Frederick the Great made people forget those of the years after 1700. Sedan took the place of the Battle of the Nations[73] fought at Leipzig. Today the Battle of Tannenberg, and even the campaigns of Poland and the Western Front, are blotted out before the battles of the East. A day will come when these battles, too, will be forgotten. But the monuments we shall have built will defy the challenge of time. The Coliseum at Rome has survived all passing events.

Here, in Germany, the cathedrals have done the same. The re-establishment of German unity was Prussia's task, in the last century. The present task, of building Great Germany and leading her to world power, could have been successfully performed only under the guidance of a South German.

[71] The War of the Spanish Succession (1701–1715) was a period of conflict between the claimed heirs of the childless King Charles II of Spain.

[72] The Thirty Years' War (1618–1648), fought primarily between Protestants and Catholics, saw up to 8 million people killed.

[73] The Battle of Leipzig, or the Battle of the Nations, was fought from 16 to 19 October 1813 at Leipzig, Saxony, and saw a coalition of forces from Austria, Prussia, Sweden, and Russia, defeat French Emperor Napoleon Bonaparte's Grande Armée, which consisted of French, Polish, Italians, and Germans from the Confederation of the Rhine.

71

To accomplish my work as a builder, I have recourse especially to men of the South—I install in Berlin my greatest architect.[74] That's because these men belong to a region that from time immemorial has sucked the milk of civilisation.

My acts are always based upon a political mode of thinking. If Vienna expressed the desire to build a monument two hundred metres tall, it would find no support from me. Vienna is beautiful, but I have no reason to go on adding to its beauties.

In any case, it's certain that my successors won't give any city the grants necessary for such works. Berlin will one day be the capital of the world.

24th October 1941, evening
SPECIAL GUEST: LIEUTENANT-GENERAL VON RINTELEN,[75]
COMING FROM ROME

The works of man must perish—Religion versus science—The Church's explanation of natural phenomena—French writers of the classical centuries—Voltaire and Frederick II—Science hits back—The Church and religious beliefs—One hundred and sixty-nine religions are wrong—Stupidity of Russian iconoclasts

On the whole earth there's no being, no substance, and probably no human institution that doesn't end by growing old. But it's in the logic of things that every human institution should be convinced of its everlastingness—unless it already carries the seed of its downfall. The hardest steel grows weary. Just as it is certain that one day the earth will disappear, so it is certain that the works of men will be overthrown.

All these manifestations are cyclical. Religion is in perpetual conflict with the spirit of free research. The Church's opposition to science was sometimes so violent that it struck off sparks. The Church, with a clear awareness of her interests, has made a strategic retreat, with the result that science has lost some of its aggressiveness.

The present system of teaching in schools permits the following absurdity: at 10 a.m. the pupils attend a lesson in the catechism, at which the creation of the world is presented to them in accordance with the teachings of the Bible; and at 11 a.m. they attend a lesson in natural science, at which they are taught the theory of evolution. Yet the two doctrines are in complete contradiction. As a child, I suffered from this contradiction, and ran my head against a wall. Often I complained to

---

[74] Albert Speer.
[75] Enno von Rintelen (1891–1971), the German military attaché in Italy.

one or another of my teachers against what I had been taught an hour before—and I remember that I drove them to despair.

The Christian religion tries to get out of it by explaining that one must attach a symbolic value to the images of Holy Writ. Any man who made the same claim four hundred years ago would have ended his career at the stake, with an accompaniment of *Hosannas*. By joining in the game of tolerance, religion has won back ground by comparison with bygone centuries. Religion draws all the profit that can be drawn from the fact that science postulates the search for, and not the certain knowledge of, the truth.

Let's compare science to a ladder. On every rung, one beholds a wider landscape. But science does not claim to know the essence of things. When science finds that it has to revise one or another notion that it had believed to be definitive, at once religion gloats and declares: "We told you so!" To say that is to forget that it's in the nature of science to behave itself thus. For if it decided to assume a dogmatic air, it would itself become a church.

When one says that God provokes the lightning, that's true in a sense; but what is certain is that God does not direct the thunderbolt, as the Church claims. The Church's explanation of natural phenomena is an abuse, for the Church has ulterior interests. True piety is the characteristic of the being who is aware of his weakness and ignorance.

Whoever sees God only in an oak or in a tabernacle, instead of seeing him everywhere, is not truly pious. He remains attached to appearances—and when the sky thunders and the lightning strikes, he trembles simply from fear of being struck as a punishment for the sin he's just committed.

A reading of the polemical writings of the seventeenth and eighteenth centuries, or of the conversations between Frederick II and Voltaire, inspires one with shame at our low intellectual level, especially amongst the military.

From now on, one may consider that there is no gap between the organic and inorganic worlds. Recent experiments make it possible for one to wonder what distinguishes live bodies from inanimate matter. In the face of this discovery, the Church will begin by rising in revolt, then it will continue to teach its "truths". One day finally, under the battering-ram of science, dogma will collapse. It is logical that it should be so, for the human spirit cannot remorselessly apply itself to raising the veil of mystery without peoples' one day drawing the conclusions.

The Ten Commandments are a code of living to which there's no refutation. These precepts correspond to irrefragable[76] needs of the human soul; they're inspired by the best religious spirit, and the Churches here support themselves on a solid foundation. The Churches are born of the need to give a structure to the religious spirit. Only the forms in which the religious instinct expresses itself can vary. So-and-so doesn't become aware of human littleness unless he is seized by the scruff of the neck, but so-and-so does not need even an unchaining of the elements to teach him the same thing. In the depths of his heart, each man is aware of his puniness. The microscope has taught us that we are hemmed in not only by the infinitely great, but also by the infinitely small—macrocosm and microcosm. To such large considerations are added particular things that are brought to our attention by natural observation: that certain hygienic practices are good for a man—fasting, for example. It's by no means a result of chance that amongst the ancient Egyptians no distinction was drawn between medicine and religion.

If modern science were to ignore such data, it would be doing harm. On the other hand, superstitions must not be allowed to hamper human progress. That would be so intolerable as to justify the disappearance of religions.

When a man grows old, his tissues lose their elasticity. The normal man feels a revulsion at the sight of death—this to such a point that it is usually regarded as a sign of bad taste to speak of it lightly. A man who asks you if you have made your will is lacking intact. The younger one is, the less one cares about such matters.

But old people cling madly to life. So it's amongst them that the Church recruits her best customers. She entices them with the prospect that death interrupts nothing, that beyond our human term everything continues, in much more agreeable conditions. And you'd refuse to leave your little pile of savings to the Church? *Grosso modo,*[77] that's more or less how it goes.

Is there a single religion that can exist without a dogma? No, for in that case it would belong to the order of science.

Science cannot explain why natural objects are what they are. And that's where religion comes in, with its comforting certainties. When incarnated in the Churches, religion always finds itself in opposition to

[76] Not able to be refuted or disproved; indisputable.
[77] In a coarse way.

life. So the Churches would be heading for disaster, and they know it, if they didn't cling to a rigid truth. What is contrary to the visible truth must change or disappear—that's the law of life.

We have this advantage over our ancestors of a thousand years ago, that we can see the past in depth, which they couldn't. We have this other advantage, that we can see it in breadth—an ability that likewise escaped them.

For a world population of two thousand two hundred and fifty millions, one can count on the earth a hundred and seventy religions of a certain importance—each of them claiming, of course, to be the repository of the truth. At least a hundred and sixty-nine of them, therefore, are mistaken! Amongst the religions practised today, there is none that goes back further than two thousand five hundred years. But there have been human beings, in the baboon category, for at least three hundred thousand years. There is less distance between the man-ape and the ordinary modern man than there is between the ordinary modern man and a man like Schopenhauer.[78]

In comparison with this millenary past, what does a period of two thousand years signify? The universe, in its material elements, has the same composition whether we're speaking of the earth, the sun or any other planet. It is impossible to suppose nowadays that organic life exists only on our planet.

Does the knowledge brought by science make men happy? That I don't know. But I observe that man *can* be happy by deluding himself with false knowledge. I grant one must cultivate tolerance. It's senseless to encourage man in the idea that he's a king of creation, as the scientist of the past century tried to make him believe. That same man who, in order to get about quicker, has to straddle a horse—that mammiferous, brainless being! I don't know a more ridiculous claim.

The Russians were entitled to attack their priests, but they had no right to assail the idea of a supreme force. It's a fact that we're feeble creatures, and that a creative force exists. To seek to deny it is folly. In that case, it's better to believe something false than not to believe anything at all.

Who's that little Bolshevik professor who claims to triumph over creation? People like that, we'll break them. Whether we rely on the catechism or on philosophy, we have possibilities in reserve, whilst

---

[78] Arthur Schopenhauer (1788–1860), the German philosopher best known for his 1818 work *The World as Will and Representation*.

they, with their purely materialistic conceptions, can only devour one
another.

25th October 1941, evening
SPECIAL GUESTS: REICHSFÜHRER SS HIMMLER AND SS
GENERAL (OBERGRUPPENFÜHRER) HEYDRICH[79]

*Jews responsible for two world wars—How past civilisations are
effaced—The rewriting of history—The Libraries of antiquity—
Christianity and Bolshevism, aim at destruction—Nero did not burn
Rome—Protestant hypocrisy—The Catholic Church thrives on sin—
Accounts to be settled—The modernist movement—The problem of the
Convents*

From the rostrum of the Reichstag I prophesied to Jewry that, in
the event of war's proving inevitable, the Jew would disappear from
Europe. That race of criminals has on its conscience the two million
dead of the Great War, and now already hundreds of thousands more.
Let nobody tell me that all the same we can't park them in the marshy
parts of Russia! Who's worrying about our troops? It's not a bad idea, by
the way, that public rumour attributes to us a plan to exterminate the
Jews. Terror is a salutary thing.

The attempt to create a Jewish State will be a failure.

The book that contains the reflections of the Emperor Julian[80] should
be circulated in millions. What wonderful intelligence, what discernment, all the wisdom of antiquity! It's extraordinary.

With what clairvoyance the authors of the eighteenth, and especially those of the past, century criticised Christianity and passed judgment on the evolution of the Churches! People only retain from the
past what they want to find there. As seen by the Bolshevik, the history
of the Tsars seems like a blood-bath. But what is *that,* compared with
the crimes of Bolshevism?

There exists a history of the world, compiled by Rotteck,[81] a liberal
of the 'forties, in which facts are considered from the point of view of
the period; antiquity is resolutely neglected. We, too, shall re-write history, from the racial point of view. Starting with isolated examples, we

---

[79] Reinhard Heydrich (1904–1942), head of Reich Security Main Office and Acting Reich-Protector of Bohemia and Moravia.
[80] "Against the Galileans," the book by the Roman Emperor Julian who tried to
reverse the imposition of Christianity throughout the Roman Empire.
[81] Karl von Rotteck (1775–1840), the academic most famous for his nine-volume
work *Allgemeine Geschichte* ("General History")

shall proceed to a complete revision. It will be a question, not only of studying the sources, but of giving facts a logical link. There are certain facts that can't be satisfactorily explained by the usual methods.

So we must take another attitude as our point of departure. As long as students of biology believed in spontaneous generation, it was impossible to explain the presence of microbes.

What a certificate of mental poverty it was for Christianity that it destroyed the libraries of the ancient world! Graeco-Roman thought was made to seem like the teachings of the Devil. "If thou desirest to live, thou shalt not expose thyself unto temptation."

Bolshevism sets about its task in the same way as Christianity, so that the faithful may not know what is happening in the rest of the world.

The object is to persuade them that the system they enjoy is unique in the world in point of technical and social organisation. Somebody told me of a liftman in Moscow who sincerely believed that there were no lifts anywhere else.

I never saw anybody so amazed as that Russian ambassador, the engineer, who came to me one evening to thank me for not having put any obstacles in the way of a visit he paid to some German factories. At first I asked myself if the man was mad! I supposed it was the first time he saw things as they are, and I imagine he sent his Government an indiscreet note on the subject. He was recalled to Moscow a few days later, and we learnt he'd been shot.

Christianity set itself systematically to destroy ancient culture. What came to us was passed down by chance, or else it was a product of Roman liberal writers. Perhaps we are entirely ignorant of humanity's most precious spiritual treasures. Who can know what was there? The Papacy was faithful to these tactics even during recorded history. How did people behave, during the age of the great explorations, towards the spiritual riches of Central America? In our parts of the world, the Jews would have immediately eliminated Schopenhauer, Nietzsche[82] and Kant.

If the Bolsheviks had dominion over us for two hundred years, what works of our past would be handed on to posterity? Our great men would fall into oblivion, or else they'd be presented to future generations as criminals and bandits. I don't believe at all in the truth of

---

[82] Friedrich Wilhelm Nietzsche (1844–1900), perhaps one of the world's most recognizable names in philosophy.

77

certain mental pictures that many people have of the Roman emperors. I'm sure that Nero didn't set fire to Rome. It was the Christian-Bolsheviks who did that, just as the Commune set fire to Paris in 1871 and the Communists set fire to the Reichstag in 1932.

There is a form of hypocrisy, typically Protestant, that is impudence itself. Catholicism has this much good about it, that it ignores the moral strictness of the Evangelicals. In Catholic regions, life is more endurable, for the priest himself succumbs more easily to human weaknesses. So he permits his flock not to dramatise sin. How would the Church earn her living, if not by the sins of the faithful? She declares herself satisfied if one goes to confession. Indulgence, at a tariff, supplies the Church with her daily bread. As for the fruits of sin, the soul that fears limbo is a candidate for baptism, that is to say, another customer, and so business goes on! It is a fact that in Catholic parts of the world there are many more illegitimate births than in Protestant parts.

In Austria, Protestantism was free of all bigotry. It was truly a movement of protest against Catholicism. Moreover, these Protestants were entirely devoted to the German cause.

A scandal is that, when a believer leaves a particular faith, he is compelled to pay the ecclesiastical tax for another year. A simple statement should be enough to free him at once from owing anything further. We'll put all that right as soon as we have peace again.

Take Goebbels,[83] for example. He married a Protestant. At once he was put under the Church's ban. Very naturally, he declared that he would stop paying the ecclesiastical tax. But the Church doesn't see things that way. Exclusion is a punishment, which does not remove the obligation to pay the tax! For my part, the Church held it against me that I was a witness to this marriage. They would certainly have put me under the ban, too, if they had not calculated that it might have won me new sympathies.

Every marriage concluded as the result of a divorce is regarded by the Church as living-in-sin. The result is that, in Austria, for example, nobody cares about the commandments of the Church. From this point of view, Austria was in advance of Germany. The most extraordinary divorce story I know is that of Starhemberg. The Church allowed him to obtain a divorce for a payment of two hundred and fifty thousand schillings. The reason advanced, by agreement between the parties, was

[83] Paul Joseph Goebbels (1897–1945), former *Gauleiter* of Berlin and Reich Minister of Propaganda from 1933 to 1945.

that the marriage was null and void since the contracting parties had come together with the firm intention of not performing their marital duties. Since Starhemberg had no money, the sum was paid by the *Heimwehr*.[84] What *hasn't* the Church discovered as a source of revenue, in the course of these fifteen hundred years? It's an unending circle.

I have numerous accounts to settle, about which I cannot think today. But that doesn't mean I forget them. I write them down. The time will come to bring out the big book! Even with regard to the Jews, I've found myself remaining inactive. There's no sense in adding uselessly to the difficulties of the moment. One acts more shrewdly when one bides one's time . . .

When I read of the speeches of a man like Galen,[85] I tell myself that there's no point in administering pin-pricks, and that for the moment it's preferable to be silent. Why should anyone have room to doubt the durability of our movement? And if I reflect that it will last several centuries, then I can offer myself the luxury of waiting. I would not have reached my final reckoning with Marxism if I hadn't had the strength on my side.

Methods of persuasion of a moral order are not an effective weapon against those who despise the truth—when we have to do with priests, for example, of a Church who know that everything about it is based on lies, and who live by it. They think me a spoil-sport when I rise up in their midst; indeed, I *am* going to spoil their little games.

In 1905 to 1906, when the modernist movement broke out, there were such excesses that some priests, in reaction, over-ran the reformers' objectives and became real revolutionaries. They were at once expelled, of course. The power of the Church was so great that they were ruined. Men like the Abbot Schachleiter[86] suffered a lot. Nowadays, a priest who has been defrocked can build a new career for himself. What gave the power of the Church such a handle was the fact that the civil power didn't want to interfere in these matters at any price. Things have

---

[84] The *Heimwehr* ("Home Guard") was the Austrian equivalent of the German *Freikorps*, or association of former World War One fighters.

[85] Clemens von Galen (1878–1946), the Catholic Bishop of Münster who led Catholic protests against the Nazis. In 1941, he gave three sermons denouncing the government. Despite his open opposition to the Hitler government, he was never arrested and survived the war.

[86] Albanus Schachleiter (1861–1937), Abbot of the Benedictine abbey in Prague, who was one of the few Catholic clerics to publicly welcome the rise of Hitler. He was, as a result, was defrocked in 1933 by the Church.

changed a great deal since then. Nowadays great numbers of priests are forsaking the Church. Obviously, there's a hard core, and I shall never get them all. You don't imagine I can convert the Holy Father. One does not persuade a man who's at the head of such a gigantic concern to give it up. It's his livelihood! I grant, moreover, that, having grown up in it, he can't conceive of the possibility of anything else.

As for the nuns, I'm opposed to the use of force. They'd be incapable of leading any other life. They'd be without support, literally ruined. In this respect, the Catholic Church has taken over the institution of the Vestal Virgins. As soon as a girl becomes a woman, she's faced with the problem of getting a man. If she doesn't find a fiancé, or if she loses him, it's possible that she may refuse to have anything more to do with life, and may prefer to retire to a convent. It can also happen that parents may promise their children to the Church.

When a human being has spent ten years in a monastery or convent, he or she loses the exact idea of reality. For a woman, a part is played by the sense of belonging to a community that takes care of her. When she lacks the support of a man, she quite naturally looks for this support elsewhere. In Germany we have, unfortunately, two million more women than men. A girl's object is, and should be, to get married. Rather than die as an old maid, it's better for her to have a child without more ado! Nature doesn't care the least bit whether, as a preliminary, the people concerned have paid a visit to the registrar. Nature wants a woman to be fertile.

Many women go slightly off their heads when they don't bear children. Everybody says, of a childless woman: "What a hysterical creature!" It's a thousand times preferable that she should have a natural child, and thus a reason for existence, rather than slowly wither.

26th–27th October 1941, evening
SPECIAL GUEST: ADMIRAL FRICKE[87]

Autocracy and military power—Exploitation of the Eastern Territories—A British volte-face—Roosevelt's imposture—Advantage to be gained from European hegemony—A Europe with four hundred million inhabitants—Liquidation of the British Empire

National independence, and independence on the political level, depend as much on autarky as on military power. The essential thing

---

[87] Kurt Fricke (1889–1945), Chief of Staff of the Naval War Command. In December 1944 became head of the Reserve officers corps, and was killed in action during the Battle of Berlin.

for us is not to repeat the mistake of hurling ourselves into foreign markets. The importations of our merchant marine can be limited to three or four million tons. It is enough for us to receive coffee and tea from the African continent. We have everything else here in Europe.

Germany was once one of the great exporters of wool. When Australian wool conquered the markets, our "national" economy suddenly switched over and began importing. I wish today we had thirty million sheep.

Nobody will ever snatch the East from us! We have a quasi-monopoly of potash. We shall soon supply the wheat for all Europe, the coal, the steel, the wood.

To exploit the Ukraine properly—that new Indian Empire—I need only peace in the West. The frontier police will be enough to ensure us the quiet conditions necessary for the exploitation of the conquered territories.

I attach no importance to a formal, juridical end to the war on the Eastern Front. If the English are clever, they will seize the psychological moment to make an about-turn—and they will march on our side. By getting out of the war now, the English would succeed in putting their principal competitor—the United States—out of the game for thirty years. Roosevelt would be shown up as an impostor, the country would be enormously in debt—by reason of its manufacture of war-materials, which would become pointless—and unemployment would rise to gigantic proportions.

For me, the object is to exploit the advantages of continental hegemony. It is ridiculous to think of a world policy as long as one does not control the Continent. The Spaniards, the Dutch, the French and ourselves have learnt that by experience. When we are masters of Europe, we have a dominant position in the world. A hundred and thirty million people in the Reich, ninety in the Ukraine. Add to these the other States of the New Europe, and we'll be four hundred millions, compared with the hundred and thirty million Americans.

If the British Empire collapsed today, it would be thanks to our arms, but we would get no benefit, for we wouldn't be the heirs. Russia would take India, Japan would take Eastern Asia, the United States would take Canada. I couldn't even prevent the Americans from gaining a firm hold in Africa.

In the case of England's being sunk, I would have no profit—but the obligation to fight her successors. A day might come when I could take a share of this bankruptcy, but on condition of its being postponed. At present, England no longer interests me. I am interested only in what's behind her. We need have no fears for our own future. I shall leave behind me not only the most powerful army, but also a Party that will be the most voracious animal in world history.

28th October 1941, evening
The reputed pleasures of hunting

I see no harm in shooting at game. I merely say that it's a dreary sport. The part of shooting I like best is the target—next to that, the poacher. He at least risks his life at the sport. The feeblest abortion can declare war on a deer. The battle between a repeating rifle and a rabbit—which has made no progress for three thousand years—is too unequal. If Mr. So-and-so were to outrun the rabbit, I would take off my hat to him.

Unless I'm mistaken, shooting is not a popular sport. If I were a shot, it would do me more harm in the minds of my supporters than a lost battle.

29th October 1941, evening
SPECIAL GUESTS: FIELD-MARSHAL VON KLUGE,[88] REICH MINISTER DR. TODT, REICHSFÜHRER SS HIMMLER, AND GAULEITER FORSTER[89]

Infantry the queen of battles—Ultra-light tanks are a mistake—A peace in the East free of juridical clauses—Fidelity of the Groats—Memories of Landsberg—The workers of Bitterfeld—The teacher's role—The use of old soldiers—The monuments of Paris—Paris in June 1940

In a campaign, it's the infantryman who, when all is said, sets the tempo of operations with his legs. That consideration should bid us keep motorisation within reasonable limits.

Instead of the six horses that used to pull an instrument of war, they've taken to using an infinitely more powerful motor engine, with the sole object of making possible a speed which is, in practice, unusable—that's been proved. In the choice between mobility and power, the decision in peace-time is given too easily in favour of mobility.

At the end of the Great War, experience had shown that only the heaviest and most thickly armoured tank had any value. This didn't prevent people, as soon as peace had returned, from setting about con-

---

[88] Günther von Kluge (1882–1944), a Field Marshall who held important command posts during the war on both eastern and western fronts.
[89] Albert Forster (1902–1952), *Gauleiter* of Danzig-West Prussia.

structing ultra-light tanks. Within our own frontiers we have a network of perfect roads, and this encourages us to believe that speed is a decisive factor. I desire one thing: that those of our commanders who have front-line experience should give their opinion on this subject, and that it should be respected. To allow us, even in peacetime, to continue our experiments and keep our army at its highest level of efficiency, it's essential that we should have a gigantic plain for manoeuvres, combining all possible war-time conditions. That's why I've set my heart on the Pripet marshes, a region with an area of five hundred kilometres by three hundred. The German Army will retain all its value if the peace we conclude on the Eastern front is not of a formal, juridical character.

If the Croats were part of the Reich, we would have them serving as faithful auxiliaries of the German Führer, to police our marshes. Whatever happens, one shouldn't treat them as Italy is doing at present. The Croats are a proud people. They should be bound directly to the Führer by an oath of loyalty. Like that, one could rely upon them absolutely. When I have Kvaternik[90] standing in front of me, I behold the very type of the Croat as I've always known him, unshakeable in his friendships, a man whose oath is eternally binding.

The Croats are very keen on not being regarded as Slavs. According to them, they're descended from the Goths. The fact that they speak a Slav language is only an accident, they say.

Here's a thing that's possible only in Germany. My present Minister of Justice is the very man who, in his capacity of Bavarian Minister, had me imprisoned in Landsberg.[91] The former director of that prison has become the head of Bavaria's penitentiary services. At the time, I would given my men orders not to leave a prison without first having converted the whole prison staff to National Socialism. The wife of the director of Landsberg became a fervent devotee of the movement. Almost all her sons belonged to the "Oberland" Free Corps.

As for the father—who was not entitled to have an opinion!—it seemed to him reasonable, at the time when he was obliged to rage against me, to spend his nights in the prison, to shelter from household quarrels. None of the guards was offensive in his attitude towards us.

---

[90] Slavko Kvaternik (1878–1947), a founder of the pro-Nazi Croatian Ustaše movement, military commander and Minister of the Armed Forces of the independent State of Croatia, which he declared in April 1941.

[91] Franz Gürtner (1881–1941), who also served as Bavarian Minister of Justice from 1922 to 1933.

The first time I was condemned, for being a threat to public safety, there were four of us, and we had decided to transform the prison into a National Socialist citadel. We arranged things in such a way that, every time one of us was set free, someone else came to take his place. In 1923, when Bruckner[92] was imprisoned, the whole prison was National Socialist—including the director's daughters.

It's not easy to be successful in life, and for some people the difficulties are piled on unjustly. When there's a disparity between the work demanded and the capacities of the man from whom the work is demanded, how can he be expected to work with enthusiasm? Every time we went to Bitterfeld, we were eager to do only one thing—to take the road back. How is one to demand of a worker, in a spot like that, that he should devote himself to his work with joy and gusto? For these men, life didn't begin until they put on their brown shirts. That's why we found them such fanatical supporters. Besides, when one discovers talents in people forced to work in such conditions, the best one can do is to get them away from the place.

Our duty is to smooth the way before them, despite the formalists who are always obsessed by the idea of parchments. Some trades have less need for theoretical knowledge than for a skilled, sure hand. And if these men are awkward in their manners, what does it matter? It's a fault that's quickly cured.

In the Party I've had extraordinary experiences of that sort of thing, even with men who've held the highest jobs. Former farm-workers can pass the tests—and yet what a change from their previous life! On the other hand, we find minor jobs for officials who've been through the usual mill, and whom one can't get anything out of.

The least adaptable are the men who, by temperament, have chosen a trade that calls for no imagination, a trade at which one constantly repeats the same movements. For a teacher, for example, it's necessary to repeat the teaching of the alphabet once a year. If a person like that is called on to do a completely different job, it may lead to the worst mistakes. There's no reason to educate teachers in upper schools. Advanced studies, and then to teach peasants' children for thirty-five years that B—A spells "ba", what a waste!

A man who has been shaped by advanced studies couldn't be satisfied with such a modest post. I've therefore decreed that, in the normal schools for teachers, instruction is not to be carried too far. Neverthe-

[92] Wilhelm Bruckner (1884–1954), Hitler's chief adjutant until October 1940.

less, the most gifted pupils will have the possibility of pursuing their studies somewhere else, at the State's expense.

I'll go a step further. It will be a great problem to find jobs for the re-enlisted sergeants. A great part of them could be made teachers at village schools. It's easier to make a teacher of an old soldier than to make an officer of a teacher!

Those old soldiers will also be excellent gymnastics instructors. But it goes without saying that we shall not give up putting teachers through courses.

Re-enlisted men give the Army the solid structure it needs. It's the weakness of the Italian and Romanian Armies that they haven't anything like that. But since one can't oblige these men to spend all their lives in the Army, it's important to create privileged positions for them. For example, we'll put them in charge of service stations, just as in the old Austria they used to be given tobacconists' shops.

The secret, in any case, is to give each man a chance to get on in life, even outside his own trade. Ancient China used to be a model for that, as long as the teachings of Confucius still throve there. The poorest young village lad would aspire to become a mandarin.

It's all wrong that a man's whole life should depend on a diploma that he either receives or doesn't at the age of seventeen. I was a victim of that system myself. I wanted to go to the School of Fine Arts. The first question of the examiner to whom I would submitted my work, was: "Which school of arts and crafts do you come from?" He found it difficult to believe me when I replied that I hadn't been to any, for he saw I had an indisputable talent for architecture. My disappointment was all the greater since my original idea had been to paint. It was confirmed that I had a gift for architecture, and I learnt at the same time that it was impossible for me to enter a specialised school, because I hadn't a matriculation certificate. I therefore resigned myself to continuing my efforts as a self-taught man, and I decided to go and settle in Germany. So I arrived, full of enthusiasm, in Munich. I intended to study for another three years. My hope was to join Heilmann and Littmann[93] as a designer. I would enter for the first competition, and I told myself that then I would show what I could do! That was why, when the short-listed plans for the new opera-house at Berlin were published,

---

[93] Jakob-Adolf Heilmann (1888–1949) and Max Littmann (1862–1931) were two prominent architects, famous for, respectively, the design of bridges and opera houses.

and I saw that my own project was less bad than those which had been printed, my heart beat high. I had specialised in that sort of architecture. What I still know about it now is only a pale reflection of what I used to know about it at that time.

Von Kluge asked a question: "My Führer, what were your impressions when you visited Paris last year?"

I was very happy to think that there was at least one city in the Reich that was superior to Paris from the point of view of taste—I mean, Vienna. The old part of Paris gives a feeling of complete distinction. The great vistas are imposing. Over a period of years, I sent my colleagues to Paris so as to accustom them to grandeur—against the time when we would undertake, on new bases, the re-making and development of Berlin.

At present Berlin doesn't exist, but one day she'll be more beautiful than Paris. With the exception of the Eiffel Tower, Paris has nothing of the sort that gives a city its private character, as the Coliseum does to Rome. It was a relief to me that we weren't obliged to destroy Paris. The greater the calm with which I contemplate the destruction of St. Petersburg and Moscow, the more I would have suffered at the destruction of Paris. Every finished work is of value as an example. One takes the opportunity of learning, one sees the mistakes and seeks to do better. The Ring in Vienna would not exist without the Paris boulevards. It's a copy of them. The dome of the Invalides makes a deep impression. The Pantheon I found a horrible disappointment. The busts alone can be defended, but those sculptures—what a riot of cancerous tumours! The Madeleine, on the other hand, has a sober grandeur.

Keitel intervened: "Remember how embarrassed we were at the Opera, when you wanted to visit certain rooms!"

Yes, it's queer. The rooms once reserved for the Emperor have been transformed into libraries. The Republic fights to protect its presidents from temptations to the spirit of grandeur. I've known the plans for the Opera since my youth. Being confronted with the reality made me reflect that the opera-houses of Vienna and Dresden were built with more taste. The Paris Opera has an interior decorated in an overloaded style. I paid my visit very early in the morning, between six and nine. I wanted to refrain from exciting the population by my presence. The first newspaper-seller who recognised me stood there and gaped. I still have before me the mental picture of that woman in Lille who saw me from her window and exclaimed: "The Devil!" Finally we went up to the *Sacré Coeur*. Appalling! But, on the whole, Paris remains one of the jewels of Europe.

30th October 1941, midday
Blood sports

The feeling of aversion human beings have for the snake, the bat and the earthworm perhaps originates in some ancestral memory. It might go back to a time when animals of this nature, of monstrous dimensions, terrified prehistoric man.

I learnt to hate rats when I was at the front. A wounded man forsaken between the lines knew he'd be eaten alive by these disgusting beasts.

The Führer turned to Gruppenführer Wolff,[94] who had returned from a shooting-party in the Sudetenland, held for Count Ciano[95] by the Minister for Foreign Affairs, with the participation of the Reichsführer SS and the Finance Minister.

THE FÜHRER: What did you shoot? Eagles, lions...?

WOLFF: No, common rabbits.

THE FÜHRER: Joy must now prevail amongst the rabbits. The air has been cleared.

GENERAL JODL:[96] And you list all that game under the heading of "wild animals"?

WOLFF: Yes.

JODL: Wouldn't it be more appropriate to call them "domestic animals"?

THE FÜHRER: I expect you used explosive bullets... .

WOLFF: Merely lead.

THE FÜHRER: Did you kill or wound any beaters?[97]

WOLFF: No, not to my knowledge.

THE FÜHRER: A pity we can't use you crack shots against the Russian partisans!

WOLFF: The Minister for Foreign Affairs would certainly accept that invitation to take part in a commando.

THE FÜHRER: What was Ciano's bag?

WOLFF: Four hundred.

THE FÜHRER: Only four hundred! If only, in the course of his life as

---

[94] Karl Otto Wolff (1900–1984), Chief of Personal Staff for Himmler.

[95] Gian Ciano (1903–1944), Italian foreign minister under Mussolini.

[96] Alfred Jodl (1890–1946), chief of the Operations Staff of the German Armed Forces High Command.

[97] "Beaters": those humans used to drive animals in a certain direction for hunters.

an airman, he'd shot down even a tiny percentage of that total in enemy aircraft! Your shooting-party came to an end without more slaughter than that?

WOLFF: Shooting is a wonderful relaxation: it makes you forget all your troubles.

THE FÜHRER: Is it indispensable, for relaxation, to kill hares and pheasants? The joy of killing brings men together. It's lucky we don't understand the language of hares. They might talk about you something like this: "He couldn't run at all, the fat hog!" What can an old hare, with a whole lifetime's experience, think about it all? The greatest joy must prevail amongst the hares when they see that a beater has been shot.

JODL: A man needs diversion. He can't be deprived of it, and it's difficult, in that field, to set bounds to his fancy. The important thing is that he should enjoy himself without doing harm to the community.

THE FÜHRER: For two or three years they've been preserving foxes. What damage they've caused! On the one hand, they're preserved for the sake of the hunter, which means a loss of I don't know how many hundred million eggs; and, on the other hand, they make a Four Year Plan. What madness!

30th October 1941, evening
A sharp criticism of the Wilhelmstrasse—Definition of a diplomat—A certain American Ambassador

(The Ministry of Foreign Affairs had just submitted to the Führer a report sent in by a representative of the Wilhelmstrasse[98] in a foreign country. The report consisted of a strongly worded account of the situation in England, but without disclosing whether it represented merely views held by the English opposition and reported by the German diplomat, or gave his own comments on the subject. The Führer was speaking to Minister Hewel,[99] Ribbentrop's representative with the Führer.)

Under the name of "Ministry of Foreign Affairs", we are supporting an organisation one of whose functions is to keep us informed of what is happening abroad—and we know nothing.

We are separated from England by a ditch thirty-seven kilometres wide, and we cannot find out what is happening there! If one studies the matter closely, one realises that the enormous sums swallowed up

[98] The *"Wilhelmstrasse"* is a major road in Berlin. When used in the context above, it meant the German Foreign Office.

[99] Walther Hewel (1904–1945), diplomat and Hitler confidant.

in the Ministry are sheer loss. The only organisation to which we grant foreign currency—the others are paid only in paper—should at least get some information for us. By definition, the diplomat is such a distinguished being that he does not mingle with normal beings. As for you, you're an exception, because you're seen in our company! I wonder in whose company you'd be seen if . . . This attitude is typical of the *carrière*. Diplomats move in a closed circle. Therefore they only know what is said in the society they frequent. When someone talks big to me about a "generally held" opinion, I don't know what he means. One must separate and analyse the current rumours. In addition, one must know the opinions held by one group or another, in order to appreciate the relative value of these elements of information.

Few people can foretell the development of events—but what *is* possible is to give information concerning the opinion of such-and-such a group, or such-and-such, or that other. In your trade, you measure people by the height of their heels. If one of our diplomats were to put up at a third-class hotel, or travel in a taxi, what a disgrace! And yet it could be interesting, sometimes, to sit at the bottom of the table. Young people talk more freely than the mandarins.

Hewel replied: "But, my Führer, all that's out of date, now!"

You defend your shop with a devotion worthy of admiration. Why support such a numerous staff at the legations? I know what diplomats do. They cut out newspaper articles, and paste them together. When I first came to the Reich Chancellery, I received every week a file stuffed with old clippings. Some of them were a fortnight old. Via Dr. Dietrich[100] I knew already by the 2nd of July what the Ministry of Foreign Affairs were going to tell me on the 5th!

An up-to-date legation should include, above all, half a dozen young attachés who would busy themselves with influential women. It's the only way of keeping informed. But if these young people are sentimentals in search of a sister-soul, then let them stay at home. We had a fellow, a man named Lüdecke,[101] who would have made a first-rate agent for critical spots: Iran, Iraq! He spoke French, English, Spanish, Italian, like a native. He'd have been the man for the present situation. Nothing

---

[100] Otto Dietrich (1897–1952), Reich Press Chief and State Secretary in the Ministry of Public Enlightenment and Propaganda.

[101] Kurt Lüdecke (1890–1960), early party member and well-connected international traveller who raised significant amounts of money for the NSDAP. He fell out with Hitler and left Germany in 1936.

escaped him. When I think of our representatives abroad, what a disaster they are! Our ambassador to the King of the Belgians was a timid soul! To think that there was nobody in all this Ministry who could get his clutches on the daughter of the former American ambassador, Dodd—and yet she wasn't difficult to approach. That was their job, and it should have been done. In a short while, the girl should have been subjugated. She was, but unfortunately by others.

Nothing to be surprised at, by the way: how would these senile old men of the *Wilhelmstrasse* have behaved in the ranks? It's the only way. In the old days, when we wanted to lay siege to an industrialist, we attacked him through his children. Old Dodd, who was an imbecile, we would have got him through his daughter. But, once again, what can one expect from people like that?

Keitel[102] enquired: "Was she pretty, at least?"

Von Puttkamer[103] answered: "Hideous!"

Hitler continued: But one must rise above that, my dear fellow. It's one of the qualifications. Otherwise, I ask you, why should our diplomats be paid? In that case, diplomacy would no longer be a service, but a pleasure. And it might end in marriage!

1st November 1941, evening
The interest of the State and private interests—Do nots for Civil Servants

It's urgent, for economic purposes, to work out a statute characterised by the two following principles:

1. The interests of the State have precedence over private interests.

2. In the event of a divergence between the interests of the State and private interests, an independent organisation shall settle the dispute in accordance with the interests of the German people.

The State could not be independent and possess indisputable authority unless those of us who had interests in private undertakings were excluded from the control of public affairs—and the simple fact of owning shares in a private company would be enough.

Every person shall have the alternative of giving them up or of leaving the service of the State.

Servants of the State must not be in any way involved in financial speculations. If they have money, let them buy real property or invest this money in State securities. Thus their wealth would be bound up with the future of the State.

[102] Wilhelm Keitel (1882–1946), chief of the Army High Command.
[103] Robert von Puttkamer (1900–1981), Admiral and Hitler's naval adjutant.

After all, the safety offered by these investments makes them more lucrative in the long run than investments in private industry, which is necessarily liable to booms and slumps.

These regulations apply to members of the Reichstag, members of the Civil Service, regular officers and the chiefs of the Party. These men must be totally unconnected with interests foreign to those of the State.

We see what it leads to when laxity is permitted in this field. England would not have slipped into this war if Baldwin[104] and Chamberlain[105] hadn't had interests in the armaments industry. The decadence of the princely houses began in the same fashion.

Night of 1st–2nd November 1941
The blind machine of administration—The hesitant mind of the jurists— The administration of the Party—In praise of individual qualities—The SS and racial selection—Reform of the magistrature

Our Civil Service often commits crude errors. One day the mayor of Leipzig, Goerdeler, came to offer his resignation. The reason was, he'd wanted to install electric lighting in a street, and Berlin had been against it: it was obligatory to stick to lighting by gas. I enquired into the matter, and found that this asinine decision had been taken by a squirt of a lawyer in the Ministry of the Interior!

Not long ago a staff member of the Ministry of Propaganda contested the right of the man who built Munich opera-house to bear the title of architect, on the grounds that he did not belong to one or another professional organisation. I immediately put an end to *that* scandal.

I'm not surprised that the country is full of hatred towards Berlin. Ministries ought to direct from above, not interfere with details of execution. The Civil Service has reached the point of being only a blind machine. We shan't get out of that state of affairs unless we decide on a massive decentralisation. Even the mere extensiveness of Reich territory forces us to do this. One must not suppose that a regulation applicable to the old Reich or a part of it is automatically applicable to Kirkenaes, say, or the Crimea. There's no possibility of ruling this huge empire from Berlin, and by the methods that have been used hitherto.

---

[104] Stanley Baldwin (1867–1947), British Prime Minister on three occasions, worked in his family business, EP&W Baldwin—one of Britain's largest iron and steel firms—before entering politics.

[105] Neville Chamberlain (1869–1940), British Prime Minister from May 1937 to May 1940, was a director of the Elliott's Metal Company Ltd of Birmingham, and of the Birmingham Small Arms Company (BSA).

The chief condition for decentralisation is that the system of promotion by seniority shall be abandoned in favour of appointment to posts. The former system means simply that, as soon as an official has entered into it, he can be moved regularly into higher grades, no matter what his abilities may be. It also means the impossibility of particularly qualified men's being able to skip whole grades, as it would be desirable that they could.

As regards salaries, I'm likewise of the opinion that new methods should be adopted. The allowance allocated in addition to the basic salary should be in inverse ratio to the number of colleagues employed by the head of a department. This allowance will be all the higher, the fewer the aforesaid departmental head's colleagues. He will thus escape the temptation to see salvation only in the multiplication of his subordinates.

When we get as far as rebuilding Berlin, I'll install the Ministries in relatively confined quarters, and I'll file down their budgets as regards their internal needs. When I think of the organisation of the Party, which has always been exemplary from every point of view, or of the organisation of the State railways, which are better run—much to the irritation of Herr Frick[106]—I can see all the more clearly the weaknesses of our Ministries.

The fundamental difference between the former and the latter is that the former have properly qualified junior staffs. Posts are awarded only with regard to talent, not in virtue of titles that are often no more than valueless pieces of paper.

At the bottom of every success in this war one finds the individual merit of the soldier. That proves the justice of the system that takes account, for purposes of promotion, only of real aptitudes. What indicates an aptitude, to the High Command, is the gift for using each man according to his personal possibilities, and for awakening in each man the will to devote himself to the communal effort.

That's exactly the opposite of what the Civil Service practises towards the citizens, with regard both to legislation and to the application of the laws. In imitation of what used to be done in the old days, in our old police State, the Civil Service, even today, sees in the citizen only a politically minor subject, who has to be kept on the leash. Especially in the sphere of Justice, it is important to be able to rely on a magistra-

---

[106] Wilhelm Frick (1877–1946), Minister of the Interior until 1943, and later governor of the Protectorate of Bohemia and Moravia.

ture that is as homogeneous as possible. Let the magistrates present a certain uniformity, from the racial point of view—and we can expect the magistracy to apply the conceptions of the State intelligently. Take as an example acts of violence committed under cover of the blackout.

The Nordic judge, of National Socialist tendency, at once recognises the seriousness of this type of crime, and the threat it offers society. A judge who is a native of our regions further to the East will have a tendency to see the facts in themselves: a handbag snatched, a few marks stolen. One won't remedy the state of affairs by multiplying and complicating the laws.

It's impossible to codify everything, on the one hand, and, on the other hand, to have a written guarantee that the law will in every case be applied in a sensible manner. If we succeed in grouping together our elite of magistrates, taking race into account, we shall be able to restrict ourselves to issuing directives, instead of putting ourselves in the strait-jacket of a rigid codification. Thus each judge will have the faculty of acting in accordance with his own sound sense.

The English, one may say, have no constitution. What serves them instead of a constitution is an unwritten law, which lives in each one of them and is established by long usage.

The fact of being solidly behind this unwritten law gives every Englishman that attitude of pride, on the national level, which does not exist to such a degree in any other people. We Germans, too, must arrive at the result that every judge resembles every other judge, even in his physical appearance.

I do not doubt for a moment, despite certain people's scepticism, that within a hundred or so years from now all the German elite will be a product of the SS—for only the SS practises racial selection. Once the conditions of the race's purity are established, it's of no importance whether a man is a native of one region rather than another—whether he comes from Norway or from Austria.

Instead of benches of municipal magistrates and juries, we shall set up the single judge, whom we'll pay well, and who will be a model and master for young people who aspire to the same rank. What a judge needs is character.

A plague of which we could, in any case, free the courts at once is the number of suits for insult. It could be decreed that such suits cannot be brought until after a delay of from four to six weeks. The parties would become reconciled in the meantime, and that kind of business would disappear from the rolls. With time, we shall achieve all these things, and others besides.

2nd November 1941, midnight
SPECIAL GUEST: REICHSFÜHRER SS HIMMLER

Poachers in State service—The recruitment of shock troops—Social justice before everything—Away with caste privilege—The masses are the source of the elite—Take leaders where you find them

In the old Austria there were two professions for which they used deliberately to select people formerly convicted: Customs officers and gamekeepers. As regards smugglers, when sentence was passed they were given the choice of serving the sentence or becoming Customs-officers. And poachers were made gamekeepers. The smuggler and the gamekeeper have that sort of thing in their blood. It's wise to offer adventurous natures ways of letting off steam. One man will go into journalism, another will emigrate. The man who remains in the country runs a risk of coming into conflict with the law.

The criminal police in Austria was above all suspicion. Just why that was, it's rather difficult to understand, for the country was quite badly contaminated by the Balkan mentality. Someone must one day have left his personal stamp on the Austrian police, and it was never effaced.

My shock troops in 1923 contained some extraordinary elements—men who had come to us with the idea of joining a movement that was going ahead rapidly. Such elements are unusable in time of peace, but in turbulent periods it's quite different. At that stage these jolly rogues were invaluable to me as auxiliaries. Fifty bourgeois wouldn't have been worth a single one of them. With what blind confidence they followed me! Fundamentally they were just overgrown children. As for their assumed brutality, they were simply somewhat close to nature.

During the war, they'd fought with the bayonet and thrown hand-grenades. They were simple creatures, all of a piece. They couldn't let the country be sold out to the scum who were the product of defeat. From the beginning I knew that one could make a party only with elements like that.

What a contempt I acquired for the bourgeoisie! If a bourgeois gave me a contribution of a hundred or two hundred marks, he thought he'd given me the whole of Golconda.[107] But these fine chaps, what sacrifices they were willing to make! All day at their jobs, and at night off on a

---

[107] Golconda was a fortified centre in Hyderabad, India, famous for its large diamond mines and thus reputed wealth.

mission for the Party—and always with their hearts in the right place. I specially looked for people of dishevelled appearance. A bourgeois in a stiff collar would have bitched up everything.

Of course, we also had fanatics amongst the well-dressed people. Moreover, the Communists and ourselves were the only parties that had women in their ranks who shrank from nothing. It's with fine people like those that one can hold a State.

I always knew the first problem was to settle the social question. To pretend to evade the problem was to put oneself in the situation of a man in the seventeenth or eighteenth century who pretended it was unnecessary to abolish slavery. Men like Scharnhorst[108] and Gneisenau[109] had to fight hard to introduce conscription in Prussia. On the political level, we had to wage a struggle of the same sort. As long as social classes existed, it was impossible to set free the forces of the nation.

I never stopped telling my supporters that our victory was a mathematical certainty, for, unlike Social Democracy, we rejected nobody from the national community. Our present struggle is merely a continuation, on the international level, of the struggle we waged on the national level.

Let everyone, in his own field, take care to do his best, with the knowledge that on every occasion we were pushing the best of us forward; that's how a people surpasses itself and surpasses others. Nothing can happen to us if we remain faithful to these principles, but one must know how to advance step by step, how to reconnoitre the ground and remove, one after another, the obstacles one finds there.

If one neglected to appeal to the masses, one's choice would be rather too much confined to intellectuals. We would lack brute strength. Brute strength consists of the peasant and worker, for the insecurity of their daily life keeps them close to the state of nature. Give them brains into the bargain, and you turn them into incomparable men of action. Above all, we must not allow our elite to become an exclusive society. The son of an official, at the fifth or sixth generation, is doomed to become a lawyer. There, at least, no more responsibility!

So what kind of role can a nation play when it's governed by people of that sort—people who weigh and analyse everything? One couldn't

---

[108] Gerhard von Scharnhorst (1755–1813), Chief of the Prussian General Staff noted for his military theories and reforms implemented in the Prussian army.
[109] August Wilhelm von Gneisenau (1760–1831), Prussian Field Marshal who reformed the Prussian Military and who helped defeat Napoleon Bonaparte.

make history with people like that. I need rough, courageous people, who are ready to carry their ideas through to the end, whatever happens. Tenacity is purely a question of character. When this quality is accompanied by intellectual superiority, the result is wonderful. The bourgeois with whom we flirted at the time of our struggle were simply aesthetes. But what I needed was partisans who would give themselves body and soul, men as ready to break up a Communist meeting as to manage a *Gau*.

In war, it's just the same thing. The commander who interests me is the man who pays with his own hide. A strategist is nothing without the brute force. Better the brute force without the strategist! Intelligence has taken refuge in technique; it flees from situations of utter calm, where one grows fat as one grows stupid.

Since private enterprise adapts itself to the same evolution—nowadays the heads of firms are nearly all former factory hands—one might arrive at the following paradoxical situation: an administration composed of cretins, and private firms capable of forming a brains-trust. Thus, to maintain their role, the officials, for lack of intelligence, would possess only the power they obtain from their functions.

A military unit needs a commander, and the men never hesitate to recognise the qualities that make a commander. A man who is not capable of commanding usually feels no wish to do so. When an idiot is given command, his subordinates are not slow to make his life a burden. If Germany has never had the equivalent of the French Revolution, it's because Frederick the Great and Joseph II once existed.

The Catholic Church makes it a principle to recruit its clergy from all classes of society, without any discrimination. A simple cowherd can become a cardinal. That's why the Church remains militant.

In my little homeland, the bishop a hundred years ago was the son of a peasant. In 1845 he decided to build a cathedral. The town had twenty-two thousand inhabitants. The cathedral was planned to hold twenty-three thousand. It cost twenty-eight million gold crowns. Fifty years later, the Protestants built their largest church, in the State capital. They spent only ten millions.

4 November 1941, evening, and night
November German is the language of Europe—Suppression of Gothic script—Europe's eastern frontier—The permanence of the German race—Deforestation in Italy and fertility in the North—Nordic territories in Roman times

In a hundred years, our language will be the language of Europe. The countries east, north and west will learn German to communicate with us. A condition for that is that the so-called Gothic characters should definitely give place to what we used to call Latin characters, and now call the normal ones. We can see how right we were to make that decision last autumn. For a man who wanted to learn Russian (and *we* shan't make the mistake of doing that), it was already a terrible complication to adapt himself to an alphabet different from ours. I don't believe, by the way, that we're sacrificing any treasure of our patrimony in abandoning Gothic characters. The Nordic runes were written in what were more like Greek characters.

Why should these baroque embellishments be a necessary part of the German genius? In old times Europe was confined to the southern part of the Greek peninsula. Then Europe became confused with the borders of the Roman Empire. If Russia goes under in this war, Europe will stretch eastwards to the limits of Germanic colonisation.

In the Eastern territories I shall replace the Slav geographical titles by German names. The Crimea, for example, might be called Gothenland.

Here and there one meets amongst the Arabs men with fair hair and blue eyes. They're the descendants of the Vandals who occupied North Africa. The same phenomenon in Castille and Croatia. The blood doesn't disappear. We need titles that will establish our rights back over two thousand years.

I would like to remind those of us who speak of the "desolate Eastern territories" that, in the eyes of the ancient Romans, all Northern Europe offered a spectacle of desolation. Yet Germany has become a smiling country. In the same way, the Ukraine will become beautiful when we've been at work there.

We owe the present fertility of our soil to the deforestation of Italy. If it weren't for that, the warm winds of the South would not reach as far as here. Two thousand years ago, Italy was still wooded, and one can imagine how our untilled countries must have looked. The Roman Empire and the Empire of the Incas, like all great empires, started by being networks of roads. Today the road is taking the place of the railway. The road's winning. The speed with which the Roman legions moved is truly surprising. The roads drive straight forward across mountains and hills. The troops certainly found perfectly prepared camps at their staging areas. The camp at Saalburg gives one an idea. I've seen the exhibition of Augustan Rome. It's a very interesting thing. The Roman Empire never had its like. To have succeeded in completely ruling the world! And no empire has spread its civilisation as Rome did.

The world has ceased to be interesting since men began to fly. Until then, there were white patches on the map. The mystery has vanished, it's all over. Tomorrow the North Pole will be a crossroads, and Tibet has already been flown over.

5th November 1941, midday

SPECIAL GUESTS: REICHSFÜHRER SS HIMMLER, SS-STAF. BLASCHKE[110] AND DR. RICHTER[111]

Characteristics of the criminal—The habitual criminal a danger in war-time—A faulty penal system—Juvenile criminals and the old lags—The procedure of appeal

Our penal system has the result only of preserving criminals. In normal times, there's no danger in that. But when the social edifice is in peril, by reason of a war or a famine, it may lead to unimaginable catastrophes. The great mass of the people is, on the whole, a passive element. On the one hand, the idealists represent the positive force. The criminals, on the other hand, represent the negative element.

If I tolerated the preservation of criminals, at a time when the best of us are being killed at the front, I should destroy the balance of forces to the detriment of the nation's healthy element. That would be the triumph of the rabble.

If a country suffers reverses, it runs the risk that a handful of criminals, thus kept under shelter, may cheat the combatants of the fruits of their sacrifice. It's what we experienced in 1918. The only remedy for that situation is to impose the death penalty, without hesitation, upon criminals of this type.

In Vienna before the war, more than eight thousand men used to camp on the edge of the canals. A kind of rats that come rampaging out of their holes as soon as there are rumbles of a revolution. Vienna still possesses gutter-rats such as aren't found anywhere else. The danger is to give these dregs an opportunity to get together.

---

[110] Hugo Blaschke (1881–1959), SS chief dentist and Hitler's personal dentist.

[111] Ronald Richter (1909–1991) an Austrian-born scientist who is most famous for his discovery that the injection of heavy hydrogen (deuterium) caused a nuclear reaction which he could measure with Geiger counters. During the war, he worked on a particle accelerator, and then later moved to Argentina where he worked for the Peron government.

No magistrate, priest or politician can change an inveterate criminal into a useful citizen. Sometimes one can redeem a criminal, but only in exceptional cases. The criminal is very willing, of course, to play the game of the worthy types who work to save delinquents—for he sees in it a possibility of saving his own neck. Afterwards he splits his sides at their expense with his confederates.

Our whole penal system is a mess. Young delinquents belonging to respectable families shouldn't be exposed to living communally with creatures who are utterly rotten. It's already an improvement that, in the prisons, young people are divided into groups. In any case, I'm a believer in the restoration of corporal punishment to replace imprisonment in certain cases. Like that, young delinquents would not risk being corrupted by contact with hardened criminals. A good hiding does no harm to a young man of seventeen, and often it would be enough.

I've had the luck, in the course of my life, to have had a great variety of experiences and to study all the problems in real life. For example, it was in Landsberg gaol that I was able to check the correctness of these ideas.

A young man from Lower Bavaria, who would rather have cut his hand off than stolen, had had fruitful relations with a girl, and had advised her to go to an abortionist. For that he was given a sentence of eight months. Of course, some punishment was necessary. But if he'd been given a sound licking, and then let go, he'd have had his lesson. He was a nice boy. He used to tell us that, for his family, it was a disgrace they could never outlive, to have a son in prison. We often used to comfort him.

As a result, he wrote to us to thank us for what we had done for him, to tell us that he'd never forget it and to promise us that he'd never again commit the slightest evil deed. He used to end by saying that he'd only one wish: to enter the Party. Signed: *Heil Hitler!* The letter was intercepted by the prison censorship, and gave rise to a minute and niggling enquiry.

But there were also real bad lots there. Each of them took up at least half an advocate's time. There were the hibernators, the annual visitors, whom the guards used to see return with a certain pleasure, just as they themselves showed a certain satisfaction at seeing their old cells again. I also remember certain letters from prisoners to respectable people— letters that would wring your heart: "Now I realise what happens when you stop doing what religion teaches."

99

Followed by a reference to such-and-such a wonderful sermon by the prison chaplain.

My men once attended at a sermon. The man of God spoke of fulfilling one's conjugal duties, with tremolos in his voice! Whenever there's a question of granting certain prisoners a remission of their penalty, all sorts of things are taken into account, but these displays of contrition are not the least important factor. Thanks to this play-acting, many customers are let go before their term of sentence has expired.

I completely disagree with the procedure followed in Germany concerning matters taken to appeal. The higher court forms its judgment on the basis of the evidence given before the lower court, and this practice has many drawbacks. In the several dozen cases in which I've been involved, not once was the lower court's verdict altered. The mind of the judge of the higher court is automatically inhibited against this. In my opinion, the latter should know only the form of the accusation or complaint, and should go again from the beginning through the necessary enquiries. Above all, he should be really a higher type of man. The judge's purpose is to discover the truth. As he is only a man, he can achieve this only by means of his intuition—if at all.

5th November 1941, evening
SPECIAL GUESTS: SS COLONEL (STANDARTENFÜHRER)
BLASCHKE AND DR. RICHTER

*Caesar's soldiers were vegetarians—Diet and long life—Living foodstuffs
and sterile diet—Cancer a disease of the degenerate—Disinherited
regions and their inhabitants—An honoured caste called the deer-
stalkers—The helots of Sparta—Progress of the Germanic race—The
impoverished proletariat of Europe—A recrudescence of anti-Semitism
in Britain—Racial doctrine camouflaged as religion—Peculiarities of the
Jewish mind*

There is an interesting document, dating from the time of Caesar, which indicates that the soldiers of that time lived on a vegetarian diet. According to the same source, it was only in times of shortage that soldiers had recourse to meat. It's known that the ancient philosophers already regarded the change from black gruel to bread as a sign of decadence. The Vikings would not have undertaken their now legendary expeditions it they'd depended on a meat diet, for they had no method of preserving meat. The fact that the smallest military unit was the section is explained by the fact that each man had a mill for grain. The purveyor of vitamins was the onion.

It's probable that, in the old days, human beings lived longer than they do now. The turning-point came when man replaced the raw elements in his diet by foods that he sterilises when he eats them. The hypothesis that man ought to live longer seems to be confirmed by the disparity between his short existence as an adult, on the one hand, and his period of growth, on the other.

A dog lives, on the average, eight to ten times as long as it takes him to grow up. On that ratio, man ought normally to live from one hundred and forty to one hundred and eighty years. What is certain is that, in countries like Bulgaria, where people live on polenta, yoghurt and other such foods, men live to a greater age than in our parts of the world.

And yet, from other points of view, the peasant does not live hygienically. Have you ever seen a peasant open a window? Everything that lives on earth feeds on living materials. The fact that man subjects his foodstuffs to a physico-chemical process explains the so-called "maladies of civilisation". If the average term of life is at present increasing, that's because people are again finding room for a naturistic diet. It's a revolution.

That a fatty substance extracted from coal has the same value as olive-oil, that I don't believe at all! It's surely better to use the synthetic fatty substances for the manufacture of soap, for example.

It's not impossible that one of the causes of cancer lies in the harmfulness of cooked foods. We give our body a form of nourishment that in one way or another is debased. At present the origin of cancer is unknown, but it's possible that the causes that provoke it find a terrain that suits them in incorrectly nourished organisms.

We all breathe in the microbes that give rise to colds or tuberculosis, but we're not all phlegmed up or tuberculous. Nature, in creating a being, gives it all it needs to live.

If it cannot live, that's either because it's attacked from without or because its inner resistance has weakened. In the case of man, it's usually the second eventuality that has made him vulnerable.

A toad is a degenerate frog. Who knows what he feeds on? Certainly on things that don't agree with him. It's amazing how lacking in logic men are. The people most devoid of logic are the professors. In two thousand years' time, when they study the origins of the inhabitants of the Ukraine, they'll claim that we emerged from the marshlands. They're incapable of seeing that originally there was nobody in the marshlands, and that it was we who drove the aboriginals into the Pripet marshes in order to install ourselves instead of them in the richer lands.

In Bavaria, the race is handsome in the fertile regions. On the other hand, one finds stunted beings in certain remote valleys. Nevertheless, the men are better than the women; but they content themselves with the women they have. For lack of thrushes, one eats blackbirds!

The fact that the hordes of Huns passed that way can't have helped. Von Kahr[112] must have been a descendant of those people. He was a pure Hun.

The peasant has no talent for romanticism. He sticks to the realism of the soil. He behaves like the townsman who's not interested in the architecture of the shops in which he makes his purchases.

Our ancestors were all peasants. There were no hunters amongst them—hunters are only degenerate peasants. In old times, a man who took to hunting was looked on as a worthless creature, unless he attacked bears and wolves. In Africa, amongst the Masai, lion-hunters belong to a privileged caste, and are honoured as such.

In the times when the population was too numerous, people emigrated. It wasn't necessarily whole tribes that took their departure. In Sparta six thousand Greeks ruled three hundred and forty-five thousand helots. They came as conquerors, and they took everything.

I changed my ideas on how to interpret our mythology the day I went for a walk in the forests where tradition invites us to lay the scene for it. In these forests one meets only idiots, whilst all around, on the plain of the Rhine, one meets the finest specimens of humanity. I realised that the Germanic conquerors had driven the aboriginals into the mountainous bush in order to settle in their place on the fertile lands.

What are two thousand years in the life of peoples? Egypt, the Greek world, Rome were dominant in turn. Today we're renewing that tradition. The Germanic race is gaining more and more. The number of Germanics has considerably increased in the last two thousand years, and it's undeniable that the race is getting better-looking. It's enough to see the children. We ought not to expose ourselves to the mirage of the southern countries. It's the speciality of the Italians. Their climate has

---

[112] Gustav von Kahr (1862–1934), a lawyer who was district president of Upper Bavaria, Bavarian minister president and, from September 1923 to February 1924, Bavarian state commissioner general. One of those who helped sabotage Hitler's 1923 Putsch, he was murdered by a vengeful Nazi in 1934.

a softening effect on us. In the same way, southern man cannot resist our climate.

Fifty years ago, in the Crimea, nearly half the soil was still in German hands. Basically, the population consisted firstly of the Germanic element, of Gothic origin; then of Tartars, Armenians, Jews; and Russians absolutely last. We must dig our roots into this soil.

From a social point of view, the sickest communities of the New Europe are: first, Hungary, then Italy. In England, the masses are unaware of the state of servitude in which they live. But it's a class that ought to be ruled, for it's racially inferior. And England couldn't live if its ruling class were to disappear. Things would go utterly wrong for the common people. They can't even feed themselves. Where would one try to find a peasantry? In the working class? The English are engaged in the most idiotic war they could wage! If it turns out badly, anti-Semitism will break out amongst them—at present it's dormant. It'll break out with unimaginable violence.

The end of the war will see the final ruin of the Jew. The Jew is the incarnation of egoism. And their egoism goes so far that they're not even capable of risking their lives for the defence of their most vital interests. The Jew totally lacks any interest in things of the spirit. If he has pretended in Germany to have a bent for literature and the arts, that's only out of snobbery, or from a liking for speculation. He has no feeling for art, and no sensibility.

Except in the regions where they live in groups, the Jews are said to have reached a very high cultural level! Take Nuremberg, for example: for four hundred years—that is to say, until 1838—it hadn't a single Jew in its population. Result: a situation in the first rank of German cultural life.

Put the Jews all together: by the end of three hundred years, they'll have devoured one another. Where we have a philosopher, they have a Talmudistic pettifogger.

What for us is an attempt to get to the bottom of things and express the inexpressible, becomes for the Jew a pretext for verbal juggleries. His only talent is for masticating ideas so as to disguise his thought. He has observed that the Aryan is stupid to the point of accepting anything in matters of religion, as soon as the idea of God is recognised. With the Aryan, the belief in the Beyond often takes a quite childish form; but this belief does represent an effort towards a deepening of things. The man who doesn't believe in the Beyond has no understanding of religion. The great trick of Jewry was to insinuate itself fraudulently amongst the religions with a religion like Judaism, which in reality is not a religion.

Simply, the Jew has put a religious camouflage over his racial doctrine. Everything he undertakes is built on this lie.

The Jew can take the credit for having corrupted the Graeco-Roman world. Previously words were used to express thoughts; he used words to invent the art of disguising thoughts. Lies are his strength, his weapon in the struggle. The Jew is said to be gifted. His only gift is that of juggling with other people's property and swindling each and everyone.

Suppose I find by chance a picture that I believe to be a Titian. I tell the owner what I think of it, and I offer him a price. In a similar case, the Jew begins by declaring that the picture is valueless, he buys it for a song and sells it at a profit of 5000 per cent.

To persuade people that a thing which has value, has none, and vice versa—that's not a sign of intelligence. They can't even overcome the smallest economic crisis!

The Jew has a talent for bringing confusion into the simplest matters, for getting everything muddled up. Thus comes the moment when nobody understands anything more about the question at issue. To tell you something utterly insignificant, the Jew drowns you in a flood of words. You try to analyse what he said, and you realise it's all wind. The Jew makes use of words to stultify his neighbours. And that's why people make them professors.

The law of life is: "God helps him who helps himself!" It's so simple that everybody is convinced of it, and nobody would pay to learn it. But the Jew succeeds in getting himself rewarded for his meaningless glibness. Stop following what he says, for a moment, and at once his whole scaffolding collapses.

I've always said, the Jews are the most diabolic creatures in existence, and at the same time the stupidest. They can't produce a musician, or a thinker. No art, nothing, less than nothing. They're liars, forgers, crooks. They owe their success only to the stupidity of their victims. If the Jew weren't kept presentable by the Aryan, he'd be so dirty he couldn't open his eyes.

We can live without the Jews, but they couldn't live without us. When the Europeans realise that, they'll all become simultaneously aware of the solidarity that binds them together. The Jew prevents this solidarity. He owes his livelihood to the fact that this solidarity does not exist.

Night of 10th–11th November 1941
Mediocrity of officials in the Eastern Territories—Decorations and the award thereof—The Order of the Party

The Civil Service is the refuge of mediocre talents, for the State does not apply the criterion of superiority in the recruitment and use of its personnel.

The Party must take care not to imitate the State. Indeed, it should follow the opposite path. We don't want any kind of status in the Party similar to the status of officials. Nobody in the Party may have an automatic right to promotion. Nobody may be able to say: "Now it's my turn." Priority for talent, that's the only rule I know! By sticking to these principles, the Party will always have supremacy over the State, for it will have the most active and resolute men at its head.

Amongst our decorations there are three that really have value: the *Mutterkreuz* (Mother's Cross), the *Dienstauszeichnung* (Service Decoration) and the *Verwundetenabzeichen* (Wounds Badge). At the top of them, the *Mutterkreuz* in gold; it's the finest of the lot. It's given without regard for social position, to peasant's wife or Minister's wife. With all the other decorations, even if as a rule they're awarded on good evidence, there are cases of favouritism. During the Great War, I didn't wear my Iron Cross, First Class, because I saw how it was awarded. We had in my regiment a Jew named Guttmann, who was the most terrible coward. He had the Iron Cross, First Class. It was revolting. I didn't decide to wear my decoration until after I returned from the front, when I saw how the Reds were behaving to soldiers. Then I wore it in defiance.

In the Army this question used to be asked: "Can one bestow on a subordinate a decoration that his military superior does not possess?" We do that more easily nowadays than it was done during the Great War; but it's difficult to behave fairly in this matter. One can be a courageous soldier and have no gift for command. One can reward courage by a Knight's Cross, without implying a subsequent promotion to a higher rank. Moreover, the man must have favourable circumstances, if his courage is to reveal itself. Command, on the other hand, is a matter of predisposition and competence.

A good commander can earn only the oak leaves. What is decisive, for him, is to rise in rank. A fighter-pilot receives the swords and diamonds. The commander of the air-fleet neither has them nor can earn them. The Knight's Cross ought to carry a pension with it—against the event of the holder's no longer being able to earn his living. It's the nation's duty similarly to ensure that the wife and children of a soldier who has distinguished himself do not find themselves in need. One could solve this problem by awarding the Knight's Cross posthumously.

To escape any resulting depreciation, I shall create an Order of the Party which will not be awarded except in altogether exceptional cases. Thus all other decorations will be eclipsed.

The State can grant whatever it likes: our decoration will be the finest in the world, not only in its form but also because of the prestige that will be attached to it. The organisation of the Order of the Party will comprise a council and a court, which will be entirely independent of one another and both placed under the immediate authority of the Führer. Thus this distinction will never be awarded to persons undeserving of it.

There are cases in which one no longer knows how to reward a leader who has rendered outstanding services. The exploits of two hundred holders of the *Ritterkreuz* (Knight's Cross) are nothing compared to the services of a man like Todt.

In the Party, the tradition should therefore be established of awarding distinctions only with the utmost parsimony. The best way of achieving that object is to associate such an award with the granting of a pension. The Party's insignia in gold ought to be superior to any distinction granted by the State. The Party distinctions cannot be awarded to a stranger. When I see a man wearing the *Blutorden* (Blood Order) I know that here is somebody who has paid with his own person (wounds or years of imprisonment).

11th November 1941, midday
Antonescu and King Michael—The era of Princes is past—Claims of the Princely Houses of Thuringia—Wars of bygone ages

By the law of nature, the most important person of a nation should be the best man. If I take the example of Romania, the best man is Antonescu.

What are we to say of a State where a man like him is only the second, whilst at the head is a young man of eighteen? Even an exceptionally gifted man could not play such a role before the age of thirty. And who would be capable, at thirty, of leading an army? If he were forty, he would still have things to learn.

I should be surprised to learn that the King of Romania was devoting as much as two hours a day to his studies. He ought to be working ten hours a day, on a very severe schedule.

Monarchy is an out-of-date form. It has a *raison d'être* only where the monarch is the personification of the constitution, a symbol, and where the effective power is exercised by a Prime Minister or some other responsible chief.

The last support of an inadequate monarch is the Army. With a monarchy, therefore, there is always a danger that the Army may be able to imperil the country's interests.

One may draw from the study of history the lesson that the age of princes is over. The history of the Middle Ages becomes confused, when all is said, with the history of a family. For two hundred years we have been watching the decomposition of this system. The princely houses have retained nothing but their pretensions. With these they traffic, and by these they live.

The worst thing of that sort that happened in Germany, happened in Mecklenburg and in Thuringia. The State of Thuringia was formed by the joining together of seven principalities. The seven princely families never stopped making claims upon the poor State of Thuringia, with lawsuits and demands for allowances and indemnities. When we took power in Thuringia, we found ourselves confronted with an enormous deficit. I at once advised these princes to give up their claims.

They were in the habit of clinging to the shirt-tails of "the old gentleman", who had a weakness for them, as if for a child. At the time, I didn't have an easy task with them. It wasn't until from 1934 onwards that my hands were free and I could use the weapons that the law gave me.

I had to threaten them with the enactment of a law compelling them to release their hold. Gürtner was very correct in affairs of that sort. He told me that, from the point of view of simple morality, he considered the princes' claims impudent, but that he was bound by the law of 1918.

Later on, I poked my nose into these families' origins, and realised that they weren't even Germans.

All one had to do was to examine their genealogical trees! If one day we had time to waste, it would be a curious study, that of these princely families, to see how they maintained themselves in power, despite their internal struggles.

Their wars always had the most exalted motives. In reality, it was always a question of odd patches of land, whose possession was bitterly disputed. How much Europe has had to suffer, for eight hundred years, from these practices—and, especially and above all, Germany!

11th November 1941, evening
Friendship of the Church costs too much—The Church is the enemy of the State—The monuments of Christian civilisation—Roosevelt's hypocrisy—The decadence of religion

I've always defended the point of view that the Party should hold itself aloof from religion. We never organised religious services for our supporters. I preferred to run the risk of being put under the ban of the Church or excommunicated. The Church's friendship costs too dear. In case of success, I can hear myself being told that it's thanks to her. I would rather she had nothing to do with it, and that I shouldn't be presented with the bill!

Russia used to be the most bigoted State of all. Nothing happened there without the participation of the Orthodox priests. That didn't prevent the Russians from getting beaten. It seems that the prayers of a hundred and forty million Russians were less convincing, before God, than those of a smaller number of Japanese. It was the same thing in the Great War. Russian prayers had less weight than ours. Even on the home front, the cowls[113] proved incapable of ensuring the maintenance of the established order. They permitted the triumph of Bolshevism.

One can even say that the reactionary and clerical circles helped on this triumph, by eliminating Rasputin. They thus eliminated a force that was capable of stimulating the healthy elements in the Slav soul.

But for the Nationalist volunteers of 1919–20, the clergy would have fallen victim to Bolshevism just as much in Germany as they did in Russia. The skull-cap is a danger to the State when things go badly.

The clergy takes a sly pleasure in rallying the enemies of the established order, and thus shares the responsibility for the disorders that arise. Think of the difficulties the Popes continually caused the German emperors! I would gladly have recourse to the shavelings,[114] if they could help us to intercept English or Russian aircraft. But, for the present, the men who serve our anti-aircraft guns are more useful than the fellows who handle the sprinkler.

In the Latin countries, we've often been within a hair's breadth of seeing Bolshevism triumph, and thus administer the death-blow to a society that was always on the point of collapse.

---

[113] *Cowl:* used in this sense, a hood or long hooded cloak of a monk.

[114] "Shaveling": A deliberately derogatory term for a priest with the crown of their hair cut off, leaving only a "ring" around the back of the head and above the ears, a practice known as tonsuring.

When, in ancient Rome, the *plebs* were mobilised by Christianity, the *intelligentsia* had lost contact with the ancient forms of worship. The man of today, who is formed by the disciplines of science, has likewise ceased taking the teaching of religion very seriously. What is in opposition to the laws of nature cannot come from God. Moreover, thunderbolts do not spare churches. A system of metaphysics that is drawn from Christianity and founded on outmoded notions does not correspond to the level of modern knowledge. In Italy and in Spain, that will all end badly. They'll cut each other's throats. I don't want anything of that sort amongst us.

We can be glad that the Parthenon is still standing upright, the Roman Pantheon and the other temples. It matters little that the forms of worship that were practised there no longer mean anything to us. It is truly regrettable that so little is left of these temples. The result is, we are in no risk of worshipping Zeus.

Amongst us, the only witnesses of our greatness in the Middle Ages are the cathedrals. It would be enough to permit a movement of religious persecution to cause the disappearance of all the monuments that our country built from the fifth to the seventeenth century. What a void, and how greatly the world would be impoverished! I know nothing of the Other World, and I have the honesty to admit it. Other people know more about it than I do, and I'm incapable of proving that they're mistaken. I don't dream of imposing my philosophy on a village girl. Although religion does not aim at seeking for the truth, it is a kind of philosophy which can satisfy simple minds, and that does no harm to anyone. Everything is finally a matter of the feeling man has of his own impotence. In itself, this philosophy has nothing pernicious about it. The essential thing, really, is that man should know that salvation consists in the effort that each person makes to understand Providence and accept the laws of nature.

Since all violent upheavals are a calamity, I would prefer the adaptation to be made without shocks. What could be longest left undisturbed are women's convents. The sense of the inner life brings people great enrichment. What we must do, then, is to extract from religions the poison they contain. In this respect, great progress has been made during recent centuries.

The Church must be made to understand that her kingdom is not of this world. What an example Frederick the Great set when he reacted against the Church's claim to be allowed to interfere in matters of State! The marginal notes, in his handwriting, which one finds on the pleas addressed to him by the pastors, have the value of judgments of Solomon. They're definitive. Our generals should make a practice of reading them daily. One is humiliated to see how slowly humanity progresses.

The house of Habsburg produced, in Joseph II, a pale imitator of Frederick the Great. A dynasty that can produce even one intellect in the class of Frederick the Great's has justified itself in the eyes of history. We had experience of it during the Great War: the only one of the belligerents that was truly religious was Germany. That didn't prevent her from losing the war.

What repulsive hypocrisy that arrant Freemason, Roosevelt, displays when he speaks of Christianity! All the Churches should rise up against him—for he acts on principles diametrically opposed to those of the religion of which he boasts.

The religions have passed the climacteric; they're now decadent. They can remain like that for a few centuries yet. What revolutions won't do, will be done by evolution. One may regret living at a period when it's impossible to form an idea of the shape the world of the future will assume. But there's one thing I can predict to eaters of meat, that the world of the future will be vegetarian!

12th November 1941, midday
The Bolshevik workers' paradise—Recurrent Asiatic assaults—
Preparations for German dominion—Sops for the local inhabitants

It's a huge relief for our Party to know that the myth of the Workers' Paradise to the East is now destroyed. It was the destiny of all the civilised States to be exposed to the assault of Asia at the moment when their vital strength was weakening.

First of all it was the Greeks attacked by the Persians, then the Carthaginians' expedition against Rome, the Huns in the battle of the Catalaunian Fields, the wars against Islam beginning with the battle of Poitiers, and finally the onslaught of the Mongols, from which Europe was saved by a miracle—one asks what internal difficulty held them back. And now we're facing the worst attack of all, the attack of Asia mobilised by Bolshevism. A people can prove to be well fitted for battle even although it is ill fitted for civilisation. From the point of view of their value as combatants, the armies of Genghiz Khan were not inferior to those of Stalin (provided we take away from Bolshevism what it owes to the material civilisation of the West).

110

Europe comes to an end, in the East, at the extreme point reached by the rays of the Germanic spirit. The Bolshevik domination in European Russia was, when all is said, merely a preparation (which lasted twenty years) for the German domination. Prussia of the time of Frederick the Great resembled the Eastern territories that we are now in process of conquering.

Frederick II did not allow the Jews to penetrate into West Prussia. His Jewish policy was exemplary.

We shall give the natives all they need: plenty to eat, and rot-gut spirits. If they don't work, they'll go to a camp, and they'll be deprived of alcohol.

From the orange to cotton, we can grow anything in that country. It's all the more difficult to conquer because it hasn't any roads. What luck that *they* didn't arrive, with their vehicles, on *our* roads!

12th November 1941, evening

SPECIAL GUESTS: SS-STAF. BLASCHKE AND DR. RICHTER

*We must remain faithful to autocracy—An end to unemployment—
Difficulties with the Minister of Economic Affairs—Gold is not
necessary—Financial juggling by the Swiss—The Ukraine's agricultural
potential—Himmler's work—War on the economists*

We committed the capital fault, immediately after the last war, of re-entering the orbit of world economy, instead of sticking to autarky. If at that time we had used, within the framework of autarky ,the sixteen million men in Germany who were devoted to an unproductive activity, we would have not had any unemployment.

The success of my Four Year Plan is explained precisely by the fact that I set everybody to work, in an economy within a closed circle. It wasn't by means of rearmament that I solved the problem of unemployment, for I did practically nothing in that field during the first years.

Vögler[115] submitted to me right away a project for the production of synthetic petrol, but it was impossible to get the project accepted by the Ministry of Economics. It was objected that, since the foreign market was offering petrol at nine *pfennige*, it was ridiculous to produce it at home for double that price. It was no use my replying that our unemployed were costing us thousands of millions, and that we would save on these thousands of millions by setting these unemployed to work; I was met with faulty arguments.

---

[115] Albert Vögler (1877–1945), founder and chairman of the Vereinigte Stahlwerke AG company, and a major financial backer of the NSDAP

It was discovered, or so I was told, that the processes of manufacture had not been worked out. As if our industrialists, with their well-known caution, would have rashly undertaken a method of manufacture without knowing its secrets! Later on, I could have kicked myself for not having thrown all that crew overboard. I broke with Feder,[116] by the way, because he wasn't keen on this project.

Then came Keppler's turn.[117] He was duped by the charlatan of Düsseldorf. In this way we wasted nine months. All the scientists had asserted that something would come of it. This was the period when every charlatan had some project to put before me. I told the alchemists that I had no interest in gold—either natural or synthetic.

At last, we began to build factories. How glad I would have been in 1933 to find the possibility, in one way or another, of giving the workers jobs! Night and day I racked my brains to know how to set about it in order to bring the ponderous machine of the economy back into motion.

Whoever opened a new firm, I freed him from taxes. When business is going well, the money flows back into the State's coffers! Our opponents have not yet understood our system. We can be easy in our minds on that subject; they'll have terrible crises once the war is over.

During that time, we'll be building a solid State, proof against crises, and without an ounce of gold behind it. Anyone who sells above the set prices, let him be marched off into a concentration camp!

That's the bastion of money. There's no other way. The egoist doesn't care about the public interest. He fills his pockets, and sneaks off abroad with his foreign currency. One cannot establish a money's solidity on the good sense of the citizens. The Dutch live on their colonies. The Swiss have no other resources than their fraudulent manipulations. They're completely mad to transfer all their money to America. They won't see it again!

The conversations we've just had with the Danes have had a considerable effect. A company has just been formed in Denmark to share in the exploitation of the Eastern territories. We're thus creating bases for Europe.

---

[116] Gottfried Feder (1883–1941), a civil engineer, economic theorist, and key early NSDAP activist.

[117] Wilhelm Keppler (1882–1960), a NSDAP and one of Hitler's early economic advisors. He was famously taken in by Heinrich Kurschildgen, a professional con man who claimed he could make gasoline from water.

One day I received a visit from a big Belgian industrialist who saw no way out of the problems confronting him. If he was simply reasonable, he said, he would close his factory. He was caught in the dilemma: a desire to continue an enterprise created by his father, and a fear of the reproaches he would have to heap upon himself if he persevered.

Belgium, Holland, Norway will have no more unemployed. England is beginning to take heed of the situation.

If we increase agricultural production in the Ukraine by only 50 per cent, we provide bread for twenty-five to thirty million more people. To increase the production of the Ukraine by 50 per cent is a trifle, for it would still be 30 per cent lower than the average production of the soil in Germany. The same point of view is equally applicable to the Baltic countries and White Russia, which also have a surplus production. It would be ridiculous not to put some sort of order into this continent.

Our economy must be organised with care. But it will be prudent not to become too far involved in motorisation. The solution of the problem of meat and fat is at the same time that of the problem of leather and manures. On one side, we have in Europe highly civilised peoples who are reduced to breaking their stones for themselves. On the other side, we have at our disposal those stupid masses in the East. It's for these masses to perform our humbler tasks.

Thus the native population of the East will be better fed than it has ever been hitherto—and it will also receive the household utensils it needs. The alluvial deposits on the shores of the North Sea are the best manure in the world.

The nuisance is, transport is expensive, and besides, who are the men who will go and collect these deposits? I have a hundred and fifty thousand convicts who are making list slippers![118] One day Himmler will be our biggest industrialist. With our new economic organisation, the political centre of Europe is shifting. England will be nothing but a vast Holland. The Continent is coming back to life.

For the next ten years, the essential thing is to suppress all the chairs of political economy in the universities.

16th November 1941, noon
SPECIAL GUESTS: REICHSFÜHRER SS HIMMLER, SS-STAF.
BLASCHKE AND DR. RICHTER
Misdeeds of the Central Administration—Twice too many officials—The lure of paper-work—Juridical scruples

---

[118] "List slippers" were soft-soled shoes worn in the navy.

Amongst us, the conception of the monolithic State implies that everything should be directed from a centre. The logical extreme of this attitude is that the most modest of officials should finally have more importance than the mayor of Essen. The English in India do exactly the opposite. A hundred and forty-five thousand men govern a hundred and fifty millions. In their place, we would need millions of officials! The French have no administrative autonomy. For us they're the worst possible example, but it's the ideal State from the point of view of our lawyers and advocates! We must reorganise our administration so that it will make the best use on the spot of the most effective men. It's the only way of overcoming the difficulties on which the lawyers' State must stumble. In this reorganisation, the first thing to do will be to chase the lawyers out of the Ministries. We'll find subordinate jobs for them.

It's likewise nonsense to try to control all a province's expenditure from Berlin. What *is* good is to keep a check on the expenditure authorised by the central authority. Whether a second-grade official should be promoted to the first grade, that should be decided on the spot—and not in Berlin, by the Ministry of the Interior in agreement with that of Finance. Again, if the theatre at Weimar wants to renew its equipment, it should not have to make a request to Berlin. It's a local problem.

To act otherwise is to encourage people to forget their sense of responsibilities, and to encourage the development of the satrap's mentality. Our officials are trained not to take any initiative, to render an account for everything, and to have themselves covered in all they do by a hierarchical superior.

For Berlin, that's the ideal type of official! We must use the axe ruthlessly on that sort of thing. We can easily get rid of two-thirds of them. Let's regard the jurist as an adviser, and not give him any authority to give orders. How can a man who has spent his whole life with his nose buried in files understand anything at all about live problems? He knows nothing.

I never miss an opportunity of being rude about jurists. That's because I hope to discourage young people who would like to rush into such a career. One must decry the profession to such a point that in future only those who have no other ideal but red tape will have the wish to devote themselves to it.

What weight have juridical scruples when something is necessary in the interests of the nation? It's not thanks to the jurists, but despite

114

them, that the German people is alive. I'm not the first to regard these people as a cultural medium for bacilli. Frederick the Great had the same sort of ideas.

16th November 1941, evening
SPECIAL GUESTS: REICHSLEITER ROSENBERG[119] AND SS REICHSFÜHRER HIMMLER

Cast out the outcasts—Customary rights of ancient days—The abuse of formalism—Clean up the legal profession—A public Counsel for the Defence—On Treason—The right of amnesty—Serrano Suñer[120]

It always fills me with nervous irritation to see in what spirit the magistrates deliver their verdicts. The authors of crimes against morality are as a rule recidivists—and they usually crown their career with some filthy misdeed. Why not wipe out these individuals at once? When I consider the question of responsibility, I don't regard the fact that a being is abnormal as an extenuating circumstance—it's an aggravating circumstance.

What harm do you see in it if an abnormal being is punished as much as a normal being? Society should preserve itself from such elements. Animals who live in the social state have their outlaws. They reject them.

The popular judge of former times, who applied a law established by custom, has been gradually transformed into a professional judge. Originally, royalty identified itself with the law. Theoretically, it still does so—since a country's highest magistrate is the Head of the State.

The law should take account, on the one hand, of the circumstances of the period, and, on the other hand, of special cases. Our ancestors were particularly tolerant towards thefts of food. When the delinquent could prove that his only motive had been hunger, and that he had stolen only what he needed to appease his hunger, he was not punished. A distinction was made between acts, according as to whether or not they threatened the life of the group. According to present law, it can happen that a man who has killed a hare is more severely punished than a man who has killed a child.

---

[119] Alfred Rosenberg (1893–1946), a key NSDAP ideologue and head of the Reich Ministry for the Occupied Eastern Territories.

[120] Ramón Serrano Suñer (1901–2003), a Spanish Falangist, Interior and Foreign Affairs Minister who was forced to resign in August 1942 after attempting to downplay an assassination attempt by a fellow Falangist upon the life of the Royalist supporting Minister of the Army, General José Enrique Varela.

I put my signature beneath every new law, but only a short time ago I hadn't the power to refuse, by a simple written declaration, a legacy that was offered me. No, it was necessary for a notary to put himself out so that I could declare in valid style that such was my will. My signature alone had no validity. At that point, I came to a compromise. Since then it has been Lammers[121] who attests, in place of the notary, that such is my will.

That reminds me of a fantastic story that took place at the beginning of the war. I had myself just been making a holograph will[122] (which I passed on to Lammers), when the following case was laid before me. A Hamburg businessman leaves his fortune to a woman. He then dies, and his sister disputes the validity of the will. Her plea is rejected at the first hearing.

On appeal, the Court decides that, although there is no doubt of the testator's intention, the will must be annulled for a vice of form: the will is properly drawn up, in the man's own handwriting, but the name of the place is printed on the paper, whereas it ought to be written by hand. I said to Gürtner: "I'll have the whole Court of Appeal arrested!" By the terms of this judgment, my own will would not have been valid . . .

When a thing like that happens to one of us, we have the possibility of defending ourselves. But what about the man in the street? He finds himself up against a wall, and he must think there is no justice. Such a conception of the law can have been born only in atrophied brains.

In my own law-suits I've experienced incidents that would make one's hair stand on end. The advocate's profession is essentially unclean, for the advocate is entitled to lie to the Court. The degree of disrepute this profession has achieved is shown by the fact that they've re-baptised it. There are only two professions that have changed their names: teachers and advocates.

The former wish to be known in future under the name of *Volksbildner* (people's educators), and the latter under the name *of Rechtswahrer* (guardians of the law). Let advocates remain advocates, but let the profession be purified! Let it be employed in the service of the public interest. Just as there is a public prosecutor, let there be a public defender, and may he be bound by the oath to act in accordance with the

---

[121] Hans Lammers (1879–1962), a jurist and Chief of the Reich Chancellery.
[122] A holographic will is a will completely written and signed in the person's own handwriting.

interests of truth. We need a renovated magistrature: few judges, but let them have great responsibilities and a high sense of their responsibilities. Today there's no middle course. Either exaggeratedly severe sentences (when *they* feel they are supported by public opinion), or else a misplaced leniency. When somebody speaks to me about a traitor, it doesn't interest me to know just how he betrayed, or whether his treachery was successful, or what it concerned. For me, the only question is: "Did he act for or against Germany?"

As regards certain offences committed with the aggravating circumstance of perversity, that's just the same. To catch an offender, shut him up, let him go again, watch over him, catch him again, what's the sense in all that?

Really, the jurists look after the underworld with as much love as owners of shoots taking care of their game during the close season. When I think of the sentences passed on persons guilty of assault during the black-out! There will always be one of those jurists who will juggle with the facts until the moment comes when he finds an extenuating circumstance. A swine will always be a swine. I reserve my pity for the brave man amongst my compatriots. It's my duty to protect them against the underworld.

This imaginary world of juridical notions is a world into which we may not enter. A court is asking me to show clemency to a man who, having made a girl pregnant, drowned her in the Wannsee. The motive: he acted in fear of the illegitimate child. I noticed on this occasion that all those who had committed an analogous crime had been pardoned. Hundreds of cases. And yet isn't it the filthiest of crimes?

I said to Gürtner: "Criminals of that sort, I shall never pardon a single one of them. There's no use in suggesting it to me." One day Meissner[123] proposed to me that I should pardon a young girl who had made herself guilty of treason. Why should she be pardoned? Because she had studied philosophy! I said to Meissner: "Are you mad?" When a young man makes a mistake, and I can persuade myself that he's simply an imbecile—then, all right! But not in a case like this.

With such a system of law, our Reich would be in full decadence, if I hadn't decided that today society is in a state of legitimate defence, and hadn't therefore provided the laws, as they are applied, with the necessary correctives.

---

[123] Otto Meissner (1880–1953), head of the Office of the President of Germany from 1920 to 1945, serving all 13 Weimar Presidents, and finally Hitler.

The officer and the judge should be the defenders of our conception of society. But the condition of this discretionary power which is granted to the judge is that the magistrature should be racially so homogeneous that the smallest sign should be sufficient to make it understand us.

Franco's[124] brother-in-law is becoming Minister for Foreign Affairs. It's not usual for one family to monopolise all the talent. Nepotism has never been a happy formula; and this is how a work cemented by the blood of a people can be systematically destroyed.

19th November 1941

Stupidity of the bourgeois parties—The struggle for power and the international struggle—Misplaced pity for the bourgeoisie—Providence and the selection of the ablest—No room for the lukewarm in the Party

Above all, it was essential that the Party should not allow itself to be overrun by the bourgeois. I took care, by applying appropriate methods, to welcome nobody into it but truly fanatical Germans, ready to sacrifice their private interests to the interests of the public.

The bourgeois parties carried their stupidity so far as to claim that it's always tie more intelligent who should yield. I, on the other hand, have always had a single aim: to assert my demands at all costs, come wind, come weather.

The basic notions that served us in the struggle for power have proved that they are correct, and are the same notions as we apply to-day in the struggle we are waging on a world scale. We shall triumph in this undertaking, likewise: because we fight fanatically for our victory, and because we believe in our victory.

This snivelling in which some of the bourgeois are indulging nowadays, on the pretext that the Jews have to clear out of Germany, is just typical of these holier-than-thou's. Did they weep when every year hundreds of thousands of Germans had to emigrate, from inability to find a livelihood on our own soil?

These Germans had no kinsfolk in various parts of the world; they were left to their own mercies, they went off into the unknown. Nothing of that sort for the Jews, who have uncles, nephews, cousins everywhere. In the circumstances, the pity shown by our bourgeois is particularly out of place. In any case, is it we who created nature, established its laws? Things are as they are, and we can do nothing to change them.

---

[124] Francisco Franco (1892–1975), ruler of Spain from 1939 to 1975.

Providence has endowed living creatures with a limitless fecundity; but she has not put in their reach, without the need for effort on their part, all the food they need.

All that is very right and proper, for it is the struggle for existence that produces the selection of the fittest. The Party must continue to be as tough as it was during the conquest of power. It's necessary that the Führer should at all times have the certainty that he can count on the unshakable support of the members of the Party, and that he can count on it all the more inasmuch as certain compatriots, beneath the weight of circumstances, should prove to be waverers.

The Party cannot drag dead weights with it, it can do nothing with the lukewarm. If there are any such amongst us, let them be expelled! To those who hold in their hands the destinies of the country, it can be a matter of indifference that not all the bourgeois are behind them; but they must have this certainty—that the Party forms a buttress as solid as granite to support their power.

20th November 1941
Germany's sense of duty.

If the mental picture that Christians form of God were correct, the god of the ants would be an ant, and similarly for the other animals.

Even for the Bolsheviks, the notion of collective ownership has its limits. Trousers, shirt, handkerchief—for those who have such a thing—are regarded as private property.

We Germans have that marvellous source of strength—the sense of duty—which other peoples do not possess. The conviction that, by obeying the voice of duty, one is working for the preservation of the species, helps one to take the gravest decisions.

What would have happened if Italy, instead of becoming Fascist, had become Communist? We ought to be grateful to the Duce for having dispelled this danger from Europe. That's a service he has rendered that must never be forgotten. Mussolini is a man made to the measure of the centuries. His place in history is reserved for him.

What doesn't Italy owe to Mussolini? What he has achieved in every sphere! Even Rhodes, that island asleep in the *far niente*,[125] he created out of the void.

Compare that fertile island with the Greek isles, and you understand what Mussolini has done for his country.

---

[125] Italian for "doing nothing."

30th November 1941, evening
SPECIAL GUESTS: THE REICHSFÜHRER SS HIMMLER AND
GENERAL DIETL

National Socialist demonstration at Coburg—Successful rioting—
Dispersion of the Reds—The devil loses his sword—A throw-back from
Bismarck—Capitulation of the Trades Unions—A new era—The Party's
printer—The Völkischer Beobachter—Dietl's part—National Socialism
would not work in France

Coburg.[126] It was the first time we received a positive invitation. I
accepted immediately. We must not let such an opportunity escape us.
I took eight hundred men. Others were to join us, from Saxony and
Thuringia. At Nuremberg we had our first encounter. Our train, which
was beflagged, was not to the taste of some Jews installed in a train
halted beside ours. Schreck[127] leapt into the midst of them and started
laying about him.

In Coburg station, the reception-committee was waiting for us. Dietrich[128] came hobbling over to me to tell me that he'd made an agreement with the Trades Unions, by the terms of which we undertook not
to march in ranks, with flags and music in front of us. I pointed out
that he had no authority to give undertakings in my name, and that I
would pay no attention to them. I ordered the flags and music to go in
front, and the procession was formed. When I appeared, I was greeted
by the unanimous shout of a thousand voices: "Rogues, bandits!" A real
populace! Things were going to warm up.

At once I put myself at the head. We were led, not to the rifle-range,
but to the Hofbräuhaus. Around us was an innumerable crowd, shouting, howling, threatening.

When we were inside, Dietrich told me that for the present it was
impossible for us to go to our billets. At this moment the gate of the
beer-hall was barricaded by the police. "Good God!" I exclaimed. A
policeman came and told me we were forbidden to leave the building,

---

[126] On October 14, 1922, Hitler led 800 Brownshirts to take part in a joint nationalist ceremony in the town of Coburg. There, the nationalists were attacked
by Communists, and a street fight took place which ended in a Nazi victory. The
town's population—previously staunch communists—changed allegiance and the
town was the first in all Germany to elect a NSDAP council.

[127] Julius Schreck (1898–1936), a founding member of the Brownshirts, and first
leader of the SS. He was also Hitler's chauffeur until his death from meningitis.

[128] Hans Dietrich (1898–1945), and early NSDAP Reichstag member for Coburg.

since the police declared themselves unable to guarantee our protection. I replied that this protection of theirs was no concern of mine, that we were capable of protecting ourselves, and that I ordered him to open the gate. This he did, but explaining that I was compelling him to bow to force.

I said to myself: "If I see a single one of our fellows flinch, I'll tear off his brassard!" Once we were outside, we gave them such a thrashing that in ten minutes' time the street was cleared. All our weapons came in useful: our musicians' trumpets came out of the affray twisted and dented. The Reds were scattered, and fled in all directions. We slept on straw. During the night I learnt that a group of my supporters had been attacked. I sent a few men to the rescue, and soon afterwards three Reds were brought back to me—three Reds whose faces were no longer human. It was at this moment that a policeman confided to me: "You can't imagine how we suffer under the domination of these dogs. If only we had known that you'd settle their hash like that!" I told him that this was the special treatment we reserved for the rabble.

Next day, all the talk was of "Bavarian gangsters" who had broken into the town. Leaflets were distributed in the street, inviting the population to a counter-manifestation. At the hour stated, we were on the scene. We saw about a hundred and fifty Reds assembling, but at sight of us they took flight. We then went, in procession, to the Citadel, and came down again from it. I would ordered my men to strike down the first man who hesitated. After our return, we were greeted with cheers from all the windows. The bourgeoisie had regained courage. That evening at the Hofbräuhaus, the citizens were rejoicing at the thought that the devil's fangs had been drawn. Jürgen von Ramin[129] was there. I said to him: "That's typical of your bourgeois world. Cowards at the moment of danger, boasters afterwards."

"We fight with the weapons of the spirit," he replied.

"They'll do you a lot of good, your spiritual weapons," Dietrich said with a shout of laughter.

"Excuse me," Ramin replied, "you forget that I'm a descendant of Bismarck." On which I observed that one couldn't blame Bismarck for having such a scion.

For our return to Munich, the Railwaymen's Trade Union told us that it refused to give us transport. "Very well," I said to their delegates,

---

[129] Jürgen von Ramin (1884–1962), an early NSDAP Reichstag member for East Prussia and member of the landed nobility Prussia Junker class.

"I'll start by taking *you* as hostages, and I'll have a round-up of all your people who fall into our hands. I have locomotive-drivers amongst my men; they'll drive us. And I'll take you all on board with us. If anything at all happens, you'll accompany us into the Other World!" Thereupon I had them all rounded up, and half an hour later the "proletariat" decided to let us go.

At that date, it was indispensable to act without hesitations. It was the beginning of a new era.

At Munich an action was brought against us on the pretext that at Coburg we had severely wounded a number of manifesters. It was even said that we had used machine-guns. In reality, somebody had confused a music-stand with a machine-gun. The affair was pigeon-holed. Later on, the Reds we had beaten up became our best supporters.

When the Falange[130] imprisons its opponents, it's committing the gravest of faults. Wasn't my party, at the time of which I'm speaking, composed of 90 per cent of left-wing elements? I needed men who could fight. I had no use for the sort of timid doctrinaires who whisper subversive plans into your ear. I preferred men who didn't mind getting their hands dirty.

Bearing in mind our origins, one can only be stupefied by the results obtained in four years. I had Munich, and I controlled a newspaper. The press hostile to us had a total circulation ten times greater than ours. Our printer, Adolf Müller,[131] a man of an infinite flexibility of views, had printed them all. He had a number of Communists on his staff, and was in the habit of saying to them that, if anything displeased them in the activities of the firm, he would offer to pay them their week's wages in orthodox opinions instead of in money.

This Müller was a *self-made man*. There was a period when he was constantly coming to demand money from us. We were convinced that he was exploiting us. For this reason, Amann[132] used every week to wage a war to the knife against him with the object of making him lower his rates.

---

[130] The *Falange Española Tradicionalista y de las Juntas de Ofensiva Nacional Sindicalista* (FET y de las JONS), was the ruling party of Spain under Francisco Franco.
[131] Adolf Müller (1884–1945), owner of the *Münchner Buchgewerbhaus M. Müller & Sohn* printing works. An intimate friend of Hitler, Müller fetched Hitler from Landsberg after his release from prison.
[132] Max Amann (1891–1957), first NSDAP business manager and head of the party's publishing house. He was also Hitler's First World War company sergeant.

The best trick I played on him was the adoption of the large format for the *Völkischer Beobachter*. Müller had thought himself the cunning one, for he supposed that, by being the only man who possessed a machine corresponding to our new format, he was binding us to him. In reality, it was he who was binding himself to our newspaper, and he was very glad to continue to print us, for no other newspaper used our format.

Müller had become the slave of his machine. Moreover, we were the only newspaper that never had a fall in circulation. It was a piece of luck that we didn't have our own printing-shop, for the Party comrades who would have been our customers would have needed a lot of coaxing to make them pay their bills: "What about Party solidarity?" they'd have said.

In his own way, Adolf Müller was a good sort. He looked carefully after the well-being of his employees, and he always defended his workers' interests, even before the Labour Front existed. Himself an offspring of the people, he knew how to practise the art of "live and let live".

It's at this period that we laid the first foundations of our present Reich. When I think of the persecutions we met with! Newspapers suspended, meetings forbidden or sabotaged. Seen in retrospect, this was the golden age of our struggle. My entry into the Chancellery marks the end of that inspiring life. Until then, nine out of ten of the men with whom I was in contact belonged to the people. From that moment onwards, nine out of ten belonged to distinguished society. It was a turning upside down of my entire existence. Today I once more find the old contact with the people in popular gatherings.

Addressing Dietl, the Führer continued: All that—I owe it to you, for, at the origin of the movement, it was with your men that you permitted me to act. To tell the truth, you contributed to the birth of the Third Reich.

I understand why the bourgeois bristle at the prospect of being governed by people like us. Compared with us, the Social Democrats numbered in their ranks men with much better outward qualifications— from the point of view of the bourgeois, I mean. The bourgeois could only be terrified as they witnessed the coming of this new society. But I knew that the only man who could be really useful to us was the man capable of mounting on the barricades.

Turning towards Hewel, the Führer went on: 1923. At that period you already had magnificent uniforms. But 1920, 1922! The uniform was indispensable.

With some people well dressed and others miserably, one cannot build a coherent formation. It's difficult to imagine that sort of thing nowadays.

It's because I'm aware of all that, that I know, too, that our movement is inimitable. What has happened in our midst is something unique—inconceivable in France, for example. And the French will never have a chief like the Duce.

Night of 1st December 1941

German women married to Jews—"Decent" Jews—The Jews and the Fourth Commandment—Society's debt to the Jews—Peculiarities of the Jewish-Aryan half-caste—Microcosm and macrocosm—The laws of nature—The preservation of the race—The importance of the beautiful

Walter Hewel questioned whether it was right to reproach a woman for not having taken the decision, after 1933, to obtain a divorce from a Jewish husband. He questioned, incidentally, whether the desire to obtain a divorce in such circumstances did not rather betoken a conformism that, from a humane point of view, was not very creditable.

E.D.[133] interposed that the fact that a German woman had been capable of marrying a Jew was the proof of a lack of racial instinct on her part, and that one could infer from this fact that she had ceased to form a part of the community.

The Führer interrupted: Don't say that. Ten years ago, our intellectual class hadn't the least idea of what a Jew is.

Obviously, our racial laws demand great strictness on the part of the individual. But to judge of their value, one must not let oneself be guided by particular cases. It is necessary to bear in mind that in acting as I do I am avoiding innumerable conflicts for the future.

I'm convinced that there are Jews in Germany who've behaved correctly—in the sense that they've invariably refrained from doing injury to the German idea.

It's difficult to estimate how many of them there are, but what I also know is that none of them has entered into conflict with his co-racialists in order to defend the German idea against them. I remember a Jewess who wrote against Eisner[134] in the *Bayrischer Kurier*.

---

[133] Eduard Dietl.

[134] Kurt Eisner (1867–1919), the Jewish revolutionary who organized the com-

But it wasn't in the interests of Germany that she became Eisner's adversary, but for reasons of opportunism. She drew attention to the fact that, if people persevered in Eisner's path, it might call down reprisals on the Jews. It's the same tune as in the Fourth Commandment. As soon as the Jews lay down an ethical principle, it's with the object of some personal gain! Probably many Jews are not aware of the destructive power they represent.

Now, he who destroys life is himself risking death. That's the secret of what is happening to the Jews. Whose fault is it when a cat devours a mouse? The fault of the mouse, who has never done any harm to a cat?

This destructive role of the Jew has in a way a providential explanation. If nature wanted the Jew to be the ferment that causes peoples to decay, thus providing these peoples with an opportunity for a healthy reaction, in that case people like St. Paul and Trotsky are, from our point of view, the most valuable.

By the fact of their presence, they provoke the defensive reaction of the attacked organism. Dietrich Eckart[135] once told me that in all his life he had known just one good Jew: Otto Weininger,[136] who killed himself on the day when he realised that the Jew lives upon the decay of peoples.

It is remarkable that the half-caste Jew, to the second or third generation, has a tendency to start flirting again with pure Jews. But from the seventh generation onwards, it seems the purity of the Aryan blood is restored. In the long run nature eliminates the noxious elements.

One may be repelled by this law of nature which demands that all living things should mutually devour one another. The fly is snapped up by a dragon-fly, which itself is swallowed by a bird, which itself falls victim to a larger bird.

This last, as it grows old, becomes a prey to microbes, which end by getting the better of it. These microbes, in their turn, find their predestined ends.

---

munist revolution in Munich in 1918, a venture which created the short lived "Peoples' State of Bavaria."

[135] Dietrich Eckart (1868–1923), one of the founders of the precursor to the NS-DAP, the German Workers' Party, and first publisher of the party newspaper.

[136] Otto Weininger (1880–1903), an Austrian-Jewish philosopher convert to Christianity. His book, *Geschlecht und Charakter* ("Sex and Character"), contained a strongly anti-Semitic chapter. He committed suicide in the house where Ludwig van Beethoven, one of his heroes, had died.

If we had more powerful microscopes, we would discover new worlds. In the absolute, moreover, nothing is either great or small. Things are big or little by the standard one selects. What is certain, in any case, is that one cannot change anything in all that. Even a man who takes his own life returns finally to nature—body, soul and mind.

The toad knows nothing of his previous existence as a tadpole, and our own memory serves us no better as regards our own previous state. That's why I have the feeling that it's useful to know the laws of nature— for that enables us to obey them.

To act otherwise would be to rise in revolt against Heaven. If I can accept a divine Commandment, it's this one: "Thou, shalt preserve the species." The life of the individual must not be set at too high a price.

If the individual were important in the eyes of nature, nature would take care to preserve him.

Amongst the millions of eggs a fly lays, very few are hatched out— and yet the race of flies thrives. What is important for us, who are men, is less the sum of knowledge acquired than the maintenance of conditions that enable science constantly to renew itself.

Nobody is compelled to consider life from a point of view that makes it unworthy to be lived. Man has a gift for seizing hold of what is beautiful. And what inexhaustible riches the world contains for the man who knows how to enjoy his senses!

Moreover, nature has given man the desire to make others share in the joys he feels. The beautiful always claims its right to primacy. Otherwise, how is one to explain the fact that in periods of misfortune so many beings are ready to sacrifice their lives simply to ensure the continuity of their race?

The catastrophe, for us, is that of being tied to a religion that rebels against all the joys of the senses. Apropos of that, the hypocrisy of the Protestants is worse than that of the Catholics. Protestantism has the warmth of the iceberg.

The Catholic Church, that still has its thousand years of experience and has not lost contact with its Jewish origins, is obviously more adroit. She permits the orgies of Carnival, firstly because she is powerless to prevent them, and secondly because she recaptures the sinner on Ash Wednesday.

By picturing to him the sufferings of Hell, she succeeds in inciting him to be properly generous. After periods of repentance, there's room for relaxation!

126

13th December 1941, midday
SPECIAL GUESTS: RIBBENTROP,[137] ROSENBERG, GOEBBELS,
TERBOVEN[138] AND REICHSLEITER BOUHLER[139]

Time to solve the religious problem—Condemnation of the organised
falsehood—The SS and religion—St. Paul and pre-Bolshevism—
Paradise: according to Christians and according to Mahommedans—
Negro taboos and the Eucharist—The Japanese and religion—Mussolini
makes a mistake

The war will be over one day. I shall then consider that my life's final task will be to solve the religious problem. Only then will the life of the German native be guaranteed once and for all.

I don't interfere in matters of belief. Therefore I can't allow churchmen to interfere with temporal affairs. The organised lie must be smashed. The State must remain the absolute master.

When I was younger, I thought it was necessary to set about matters with dynamite. I've since realised that there's room for a little subtlety. The rotten branch falls of itself.

The final state must be: in St. Peter's Chair, a senile officiant; facing him, a few sinister old women, as gaga and as poor in spirit as anyone could wish. The young and healthy are on our side.

Against a Church that identifies itself with the State, as in England, I have nothing to say. But, even so, it's impossible eternally to hold humanity in bondage with lies. After all, it was only between the sixth and eighth centuries that Christianity was imposed on our peoples by princes who had an alliance of interests with the shavelings. Our peoples had previously succeeded in living all right without this religion. I have six divisions of SS composed of men absolutely indifferent in matters of religion. It doesn't prevent them from going to their deaths with serenity in their souls.

Christ was an Aryan, and St. Paul used his doctrine to mobilise the criminal underworld and thus organise a proto-Bolshevism. This intrusion upon the world marks the end of a long reign, that of the clear Graeco-Latin genius.

What is this God who takes pleasure only in seeing men grovel before Him? Try to picture to yourselves the meaning of the following, quite simple story. God creates the conditions for sin. Later on He

---

[137] Joachim von Ribbentrop (1893–1946), Minister of Foreign Affairs.
[138] Josef Terboven (1898–1945), *Reichskommissar* for Norway.
[139] Philipp Bouhler (1899–1945), Chief of the Chancellery of the Führer.

succeeds, with the help of the Devil, in causing man to sin. Then He employs a virgin to bring into the world a son who, by His death, will redeem humanity! I can imagine people being enthusiastic about the paradise of Mahomet, but as for the insipid paradise of the Christians!

In your lifetime, you used to hear the music of Richard Wagner. After your death, it will be nothing but hallelujahs, the waving of palms, children of an age for the feeding-bottle, and hoary old men. The man of the isles pays homage to the forces of nature. But Christianity is an invention of sick brains: one could imagine nothing more senseless, nor any more indecent way of turning the idea of the Godhead into a mockery. A negro with his taboos is crushingly superior to the human being who seriously believes in transubstantiation.

I begin to lose all respect for humanity when I think that some people on our side, Ministers or generals, are capable of believing that we cannot triumph without the blessing of the Church. Such a notion is excusable in little children who have learnt nothing else.

For thirty years the Germans tore each other to pieces simply in order to know whether or not they should take Communion in both kinds. There's nothing lower than religious notions like that. From that point of view, one can envy the Japanese. They have a religion which is very simple and brings them into contact with nature. They've succeeded even in taking Christianity and turning it into a religion that's less shocking to the intellect.

By what would you have me replace the Christians' picture of the Beyond? What comes naturally to mankind is the sense of eternity and that sense is at the bottom of every man. The soul and the mind migrate, just as the body returns to nature. Thus life is eternally reborn from life. As for the "why?" of all that, I feel no need to rack my brains on the subject. The soul is unfathomable.

If there is a God, at the same time as He gives man life, He gives him intelligence. By regulating my life according to the understanding that is granted me, I may be mistaken, but I act in good faith. The concrete image of the Beyond that religion forces on me does not stand up to examination.

Think of those who look down from on high upon what happens on earth: what a martyrdom for them, to see human beings indefatigably repeating the same gestures, and inevitably the same errors! In my view, H. S. Chamberlain was mistaken in regarding Christianity as a reality upon the spiritual level.

Man judges everything in relation to himself. What is bigger than himself is big, what is smaller is small. Only one thing is certain, that one is part of the spectacle. Everyone finds his own role. Joy exists for everybody. I dream of a state of affairs in which every man would know that he lives and dies for the preservation of the species. It's our duty to encourage that idea: let the man who distinguishes himself in the service of the species be thought worthy of the highest honours.

What a happy inspiration, to have kept the clergy out of the Party! On the 21st March 1933, at Potsdam,[140] the question was raised: with the Church, or without the Church? I conquered the State despite the malediction pronounced on us by both creeds. On that day, we went directly to the tomb of the kings whilst the others were visiting religious services. Supposing that at that period I would made a pact with the Churches, I would today be sharing the lot of the Duce. By nature the Duce is a freethinker, but he decided to choose the path of concessions. For my part, in his place I would have taken the path of revolution.

I would have entered the Vatican and thrown everybody out—reserving the right to apologise later: "Excuse me, it was a mistake." But the result would have been, they'd have been outside! When all is said, we have no reason to wish that the Italians and Spaniards should free themselves from the drug of Christianity. Let's be the only people who are immunised against the disease.

14th December 1941, midday
SPECIAL GUESTS: ROSENBERG, BOUHLER, HIMMLER
Incompatibility of National Socialism and Christianity—The Popes of the Renaissance—A poisoned source

Kerrl,[141] with the noblest of intentions, wanted to attempt a synthesis between National Socialism and Christianity. I don't believe the thing's possible, and I see the obstacle in Christianity itself.

I think I could have come to an understanding with the Popes of the Renaissance. Obviously, their Christianity was a danger on the practical level—and, on the propaganda level, it continued to be a lie. But a Pope, even a criminal one, who protects great artists and spreads beauty around him, is nevertheless more sympathetic to me than the Protestant minister who drinks from the poisoned spring.

---

[140] March 21, 1933 was the inaugural celebrations of the first Reichstag convened after the Reichstag building was burned down by a Dutch communist.

[141] Hanns Kerrl (1887–1941), a NSDAP activist who was Reichsminister of Church Affairs.

Pure Christianity—the Christianity of the catacombs—is concerned with translating the Christian doctrine into facts.

It leads quite simply to the annihilation of mankind. It is merely whole-hearted Bolshevism, under a tinsel of metaphysics.

14th December 1941, evening

SPECIAL GUESTS: DR. GOEBBELS AND HIMMLER

Pan-Germanic supporters and the Austrian Christian Socialists— Schönerer and Lueger—A great mayor—Anti-Semitism in Vienna— Opposition to the Habsburg—Richard Wagner and the mayor of Leipzig—Other mayors

There was a man in Vienna, before the Great War, who was always in favour of an understanding with anti-Semitic Romania—and he saw in it the best way of preventing Hungary from acquiring too much importance. That was Lueger.[142] Lueger was also of the opinion that it was possible to maintain the Austrian State, but on condition that Vienna regained all its supremacy. Schönerer, on the other hand, took as his point of departure the idea that the Austrian State ought to disappear. His attitude towards the house of Hapsburg was brutally radical. From that time dates the first attempt to oppose the Germanic racial community to the monarchy. On that point, Lueger and Schönerer[143] parted company.

Lueger, who had belonged to the Pan-Germanist movement, went over to the Christian-Social party, for he thought that anti-Semitism was the only means of saving the State.

Now, in Vienna, anti-Semitism could never have any foundation but a religious one. From the point of view of race, about 50 per cent of the population of Vienna was not German. The number of Jews, amongst a million eight hundred thousand inhabitants, was close on three hundred thousand. But the Czechs of Vienna were anti-Semitic. Lueger succeeded in filling thirty-six of the hundred and forty-eight seats of the Vienna Municipal Council with anti-Semites.

When I arrived in Vienna, I was a fanatical opponent of Lueger. As a Pan-German, and as a supporter of Schönerer, I was accordingly an enemy of the Christian-Socials. Yet in the course of my stay in Vienna I couldn't help acquiring a feeling of great respect for Lueger personally.

---

[142] Karl Lueger (1844–1910), leader of Austrian Christian Social Party, served as mayor of Vienna from 1897 onward.

[143] Georg Ritter von Schönerer (1842–1921), Austrian politician best known for his pan-Germanism.

It was at the City Hall that I first heard him speak. I had to wage a battle with myself on that occasion, for I was filled with the resolve to detest Lueger, and I couldn't refrain from admiring him.

He was an extraordinary orator. It's certain that German policy would have followed another direction if Lueger hadn't died before the Great War, as a result of blood-poisoning, after having been blind for the last years of his life.

The Christian-Socials were in power in Vienna until the collapse in 1918. Lueger had royal habits.

When he held a festivity in the City Hall, it was magnificent. I never saw him in the streets of Vienna without everybody stopping to greet him. His popularity was immense.

At his funeral, two hundred thousand Viennese followed him to the cemetery. The procession lasted a whole day. Lueger was the greatest mayor we ever had. If our Commons acquired a certain autonomy, that was thanks to him.

What in other cities was the responsibility of private firms, he converted in Vienna into public services. Thus he was able to expand and beautify the city without imposing new taxes.

The Jewish bankers one day hit on the idea of cutting off his sources of credit. He founded the municipal savings-bank, and the Jews at once knuckled under, overwhelming him with offers of money.

Schönerer and Lueger remained opponents until the end, but they were both great Germans. In their dealings with the house of Habsburg, they both had the habit of behaving as one great power treating with another.

Schönerer was the more logical of the two, for he was determined to blow up the Austrian State. Lueger, on the other hand, believed that it was possible to preserve this State within the German community.

A city like Hamburg is supremely well governed. The lowest point was reached in Leipzig, at the time when Kreisleiter Dönicke[144] was mayor there. He was an excellent Kreisleiter, but a mere cypher as a mayor.

I have several original scores of Richard Wagner, which was something that not even Dönicke could overlook. The result was that one day, in the course of a ceremony, to the accompaniment of speeches in Saxon dialect, I received from Dönicke's innocent hands a lithographed

---

[144] Kurt Dönicke (1899 1945), held the post of mayor of Leipzig from October 1937 to October 1938.

score of Wagner, which he quite simply confused with a manuscript. Dönicke was beaming with satisfaction. The following is approximately the opening of the speech he made before the whole assembled university: "In Leipzig was born the celebrated composer Richard Wagner, author, amongst others, of the opera *Tannhäuser*." The professors looked at one another in embarrassment. I myself was looking for a trap-door through which I might disappear. As I left, I said to Mutschmann:[145] "Let me know within a week the name of your new mayor!"

Our best municipal administrator is, beyond all doubt, Fiehler,[146] but . . .[147]

Liebel[148] is a personality. He doesn't yet know that I've found the *Goblet* by Jamnitzer[149] for him. He supposes it's still at the Hermitage. The Jews had sold it, and I bought it back in Holland at the same time as the objects of the Mannheimer collection.[150]

The *Festival of the Rosary* by Albrecht Dürer is still in Prague. So Liebel never misses an opportunity of reminding me that he possesses the frame of this picture. "Very well," I said to him on the last occasion, "we'll have a copy made!"

Every time something turns up in the Prague neighbourhood, I receive more or less veiled allusions from Nuremberg to the fact that it would perhaps be appropriate to remove such-and-such or such-and-such a work to a place of safety. Cracow had scarcely fallen when Liebel had already succeeded by some wangle, without anybody's noticing, in having the sculptures of Veit Stoss[151] taken down from their pedestals and repatriated to Nuremberg.

Liebel regards the inhabitants of Fuerth as parasites. He has discovered numerous arguments proving that they've cheated the city of

---

[145] Martin Mutschmann (1879–1947), *Gauleiter* of the state of Saxony.

[146] Karl Fiehler (1895–1969), Mayor of Munich from 1933 until 1945.

[147] It is not known what was meant to be inserted here.

[148] Friedrich Liebel (1897–1945), Mayor of Nuremberg from 1933 to 1945.

[149] The "goblet" is a work dating from around 1600 by the famous Dresden goldsmith Christoph Jamnitzer (1563–1613). It is a silver ceremonial drinking vessel in the shape of an African's head, and is adorned with precious stones.

[150] Fritz Mannheimer (1890–1939) was a German Jewish banker and art collector who was the director of the Amsterdam branch of the Berlin-based investment bank Mendelssohn & Co. His art collection was purchased by Hitler in 1941. It was seized by the Allies in 1945 and is now in the Rijksmuseum in Amsterdam.

[151] Veit Stoss (1450–1533), a foremost German wood sculptor of the late Gothic and the Northern Renaissance phase.

Nuremberg. If it depended on him, the city of Fuerth would be exterminated. For lack of that, he would be contented with annexing it!

An excellent mayor was Siebert,[152] at Rothenburg and Lindau. Siebert is a personality of the first order. He's a counterweight to Wagner,[153] who, for his part, has more gifts for propaganda. Siebert, what's more, has a feeling for the arts. It's to him, especially, that we owe the restoration of the keep at Nuremberg.[154]

Liebel let him do it without saying a word, and then, when the work was finished, he suggested to Siebert that the keep should be offered to the Führer (but Liebel knew very well that I would never accept such a gift). So Siebert came and solemnly offered me the keep.

Next day it was Liebel who came to tell me how glad he was to learn that I would accepted. "You're mistaken," I said, "I do not accept this gift." Liebel thereupon asked me whether he could beg of me the favour of returning the keep to him on behalf of the ancient and noble city of Nuremberg.

Siebert came to see me again, but this time to weep on my bosom. He complained, with some justice, of Liebel's not very regular proceedings. After all, it was he (Siebert) who had provided all the money. If I'm not mistaken, the matter was settled in such a way that Nuremberg finally got the keep!

The mayor of Regensburg is also excellent. He's our greatest builder of cities for workers. I'm always disappointed when I observe that certain cities that have great pasts are not governed by first-rate administrators. The authority is vested in the Reich, but the administration should be decentralised. Otherwise what we would have had would be the reign of State officials, and the talents budding on the spot would be systematically ignored.

Night of 17—18th December 1941
SPECIAL GUEST: DR. GOEBBELS

A new calendar?—Military traditions—The flags and standards of the Reich

I was faced with that question when we first took power. Should we preserve the Christian chronology, or should we inaugurate a new era?

---

[152] Ludwig Siebert (1874–1942), who in 1930 became the first Nazi Lord Mayor in Bavaria. He later became Minister President of Bavaria from 1933 to 1942.

[153] Adolf Wagner (1890–1944), *Gauleiter* in Munich and Interior Minister of Bavaria until his death.

[154] Sinwell Tower, the inner part of Nuremberg Castle.

I reasoned that the year 1933 merely renewed our link with a military tradition.

At that time the notion of the Reich had been, so to speak, lost, but it has again imposed itself on us and on the world. When one speaks of Germany, wherever one may be, one no longer says anything but "the Reich". The army of the Reich must gradually be steeped in the old traditions—especially those of Prussia, Bavaria and Austria.

It's regrettable that we have not yet arrived at a uniform style for the eagles and standards of our various arms. What a fine thing it is, the war-flag of the Reich! But it's used only by the Navy. Raeder[155] knew that, when a ship hoists its colours, it's hoisting the colours of the nation. Fritsch,[156] on the other hand, wanted to give the Army an independent personality, and that's why our regimental flags are, in a sense, the flags of an association.

They emphasise whatever personifies each particular arm, whereas what should be accented is whatever recalls that they belong to the Reich. The Crusaders, in their struggle against the Saracens, all fought under the emblem of Christendom. The Romans, also, all had the same standard.

18th December 1941, noon
SPECIAL GUEST: HIMMLER
Had the British but understood—Dutch regrets—Japan and the white races—Kiaochow

What is happening in the Far East is happening by no will of mine. For years I never stopped telling all the English I met that they'd lose the Far East if they entered into a war in Europe. They didn't answer, but they assumed a superior air. They're masters in the art of being arrogant! I was moved when Mussert[157] said to me: "You will surely understand me at this hour. Three centuries of effort are going up in smoke."

Himmler intervened: "We must consider this much compensation, that in this way the Dutch people will maintain its integrity, whereas, before, it was running the risk of corrupting itself with Malayan blood."

---

[155] Erich Raeder (1876–1960), Grand Admiral of the navy who resigned in January 1943 and was replaced by Karl Dönitz.

[156] Werner von Fritsch (1880–1939), Commander-in-Chief of the German Army from 1934 until 1938. He was killed in action in Poland.

[157] Anton Mussert (1894–1946), leader of the *Nationaal-Socialistische Beweging in Nederland* (Dutch National Socialist Movement, or NSB).

Hitler continued: The Japanese are occupying all the islands, one after the other. They will get hold of Australia, too. The white race will disappear from those regions. This development began in 1914, at the moment when the European powers authorised Japan to lay her hands on Kiaochow.[158]

Night of 23rd-24th December 1941
The Museum at Linz—Belittling of great paintings by Jewish critics—
Incompetence of the bourgeois leaders—The Venus of Bordone

It occurs to me that already Linz Museum can bear comparison with no-matter-which museum in New York. In the years 1890 to 1900, one could still form great collections. After that, it became practically impossible to lay one's hand on the truly great works. The Jews mounted guard and monopolised the lot. If I would had money sooner, I would have been able to keep in Germany a number of works that have emigrated.

It's lucky I got there finally. Otherwise we would have had nothing left but rubbish, for the Jews do their business in works of real value.

They made use of literature to achieve this. What we should blame is, firstly, the cowardice of our bourgeoisie, and, next, the state of society (for which the bourgeoisie is equally responsible) whereby only a tiny fraction of the population is interested in art. The Jew was able to say to himself: "These Germans, who accept perverse pictures of the crucified Christ, are capable of swallowing other horrors, too, if one can persuade them that these horrors are beautiful!" The people were not concerned in such matters. It was all the affair of the so-called elite, who believed in their own competence, whereas in reality they were not capable of telling the difference between what was beautiful and what was ugly. This set-up was useful to me at the period when, although I still hadn't much money, I began to buy.

Another thing that was useful to me, in England, was the fact that certain works, by reason of their subjects, did not fit in with the conformist morals of society. So it was that I was able to take possession of the admirable *Venus* by Bordone,[159] which formerly belonged to the

---

[158] Kiaochow (now Jiaozhou Bay in Tsingtau, China). China leased it for 99 years to the German Empire in 1898, but the colony was seized by British and Japanese forces in 1914.

[159] "Venus and Cupid," by Paris Bordone (1500–1571). Hitler purchased the painting in 1936 from the Berlin art dealer Karl Haberstock (1878–1956). The painting was seized by the American Army, and given to the Warsaw National Museum.

Duke of Kent. I'm delighted that I succeeded in obtaining in England some works of the highest level in exchange for some horrors boosted by the Jewish critics. Those are real forgers' tactics on the Jews' part, for they're perfectly well aware of the worthlessness of the works they're boosting.

They've used this transvaluation of values to buy, surreptitiously and at a favourable price, the masterpieces they had depreciated.

Night of 28th–29th December 1941

*A diet deprived of biological quality—The observatory at Linz—
Everything dependent on man—The case of Julius Streicher[160]—Streicher
idealised the Jew—True to one's old comrades—Dietrich Eckart and his
hams—Severing's love letters—Succour for honourable foes*

When I was a young man, the doctors used to say that a meat diet was indispensable for the formation of bones. This was not true. Unlike peoples who eat polenta, we have bad teeth. It occurs to me that this has something to do with a diet that's more or less rich in yeast. Nine-tenths of our diet are made up of foods deprived of their biological qualities.

When I'm told that 50 per cent of dogs die of cancer, there must be an explanation for that. Nature has predisposed the dog to feed on raw meat, by tearing up other animals. Today the dog feeds almost exclusively on mixed bread and cooked meat. If I offer a child the choice between a pear and a piece of meat, he'll quickly choose the pear. That's his atavistic instinct speaking.

Country folk spend fourteen hours a day in the fresh air. Yet by the age of forty-five they're old, and the mortality amongst them is enormous. That's the result of an error in their diet. They eat only cooked foods.

It's a mistake to think that man should be guided by his greed. Nature spontaneously eliminates all that has no gift for life. Man, alone amongst the living creatures, tries to deny the laws of nature.

The great tragedy for man is that he understands the mechanism of things, but the things themselves remain an enigma to him. We are capable of distinguishing the component parts of a molecule. But when it's a question of explaining the why of a thing, words fail us. And that's what leads men to conceive of the existence of a superior power.

---

[160] Julius Streicher (1885–1946), *Gauleiter* of Franconia, most infamous for the virulently anti-Semitic newspaper *Der Stürmer*. His extremism alienated many top Nazis, and he was stripped of his party offices in February 1940.

If I have an observatory built at Linz, I'll have the following words carved on its front: "The heavens proclaim the glory of the eternal."

It's marvellous that this is how mankind formed the idea of God. The almighty being that made the worlds has certainly granted to each being that he should be motivated by awareness of his function. Everything in nature happens in conformity with what ought to happen.

Man would certainly have gone mad if he had suddenly learnt, a hundred thousand years ago, all that we know today. The human being does not develop solely through the obligations life imposes on him, but also through the habits that make up the climate of his period. Thus the youth of today regards as quite natural various notions that seemed revolutionary to the generation before.

I've totally lost sight of the organisations of the Party. When I find myself confronted by one or other of these achievements, I say to myself: "By God, how that has developed!" So it's not correct when I'm told, for example: "It's only because of you, my Führer, that *Gauleiter* So-and-so has succeeded in doing that." No, it depends essentially on the men who do the job. I realise that nowadays in military matters. Everything depends on the men. Without them, I could do nothing.

Nowadays certain small peoples have a greater number of capable men than the whole British Empire.

How many times I've heard it said in the Party that a new man should be found for such-and-such a post. Unfortunately I could only reply: "But by whom will you replace the present holder?"

I'm always ready to replace an inadequate man by another with better qualifications. In fact, whatever may be said about the bonds of loyalty, it's the quality of the man who assumes responsibilities that's finally decisive.

Of one thing there is no doubt, that Streicher has never been replaced. Despite all his weaknesses, he's a man who has spirit. If we wish to tell the truth, we must recognise that, without Julius Streicher, Nuremberg would never have been won over to National Socialism. He put himself under my orders at a time when others were hesitating to do so, and he completely conquered the city of our Rallies. That's an unforgettable service. More than once Dietrich Eckart told me that Streicher was a school-teacher, and a lunatic, to boot, from many points of view. He always added that one could not hope for the triumph of National Socialism without giving one's support to men like

Streicher. Despite everything, Eckart was very fond of him. Streicher is reproached for his *Stürmer*. The truth is the opposite of what people say: he *idealised* the Jew. The Jew is baser, fiercer, more diabolical than Streicher depicted him.

It's not a crime to speak publicly of affairs of State, for the State needs the people's approval. Of course, there are cases in which it's inopportune to speak of certain matters. Whoever is guilty of doing so is committing, as a rule, nothing worse than an offence against discipline. Frick told me once that Streicher's stock had completely slumped at Nuremberg. I went to Nuremberg to try to form an opinion. Streicher came into the room, and there was a hurricane of enthusiasm!

I went once to a women's gathering. It took place at Nuremberg, and I would been warned that Elsbeth Zander[161] was a very serious competitor to Streicher. The meeting was held in the Hercules hall for bicycle-races. Streicher was welcomed with an indescribable enthusiasm. The oldest adherents of the Party all spoke in favour of Streicher and against Elsbeth Zander. There was nothing for me to do but take my departure.

It goes without saying that the organisation of the *Gau* was very imperfect. If I take a functionary of the Civil Service as my criterion, the comparison is obviously not to Streicher's advantage. But I must recall that it wasn't a functionary who took Nuremberg for me in 1919.

When all is said, it was the *Gauleiters* themselves who asked me to be indulgent with Streicher. In all the circumstances, there was no comparison between the faults he committed and his recognised merits, which were brilliant.

As usual, one must look for the feminine angle! Who escapes from criticism? I myself, if I disappear today, realise that a time will come, in a hundred years, perhaps, when I shall be violently attacked. History will make no exception in my favour. But what importance has that? It takes only another hundred years for these shadows to be effaced. I don't concern myself with such things, I go my way.

This Streicher affair is a tragedy. At the origin of the conflict lies the hatred sworn between two women. In any case, there's just one statement I have to make, that Streicher is irreplaceable. His name is engraved in the memory of the people of Nuremberg. There's no question of his coming back, but I must do him justice. If one day I write my

[161] Elsbeth Zander (1888–1963), founder of the German Women's Order and head of the NS Women's Association.

memoirs, I shall have to recognise that this man fought like a buffalo in our cause. The conquest of Franconia was his work.

I have a bad conscience when I get the feeling that I've not been quite fair to somebody. When I go to Nuremberg, it's always with a feeling of bitterness. I can't help thinking that, in comparison with so many services, the reasons for Streicher's dismissal are really very slender.

All that's said about his alleged disease is false. Streicher had only one disease, and that was nympholepsy.[162]

In one way or another, we shall have to find a solution. I cannot dream of holding a rally at Nuremberg[163] from which the man who gave Nuremberg to the Party is banished. I can install some mediocrity in Streicher's place. He'll administer the *Gau* perfectly, as long as circumstances are normal. If a catastrophe occurs, the mediocrity will disappear.

The best advice I can give my successors is in such a case to be loyal. Frau Streicher is outside this business. Frau Liebel is an ambitious woman.

Probably none of us is entirely "normal". Otherwise we should spend all our days in the café on the corner. The Catholics, the bourgeois, everybody has accused me of being crazy because, in their eyes, a normal man is one who drinks three glasses of beer every evening. "Why all this fuss? It's obviously the proof that he's mad." How many men of our Party were regarded in their families as black sheep! When I examine the faults for which Streicher is blamed, I realise that no great man would pass through this sieve.

Richard Wagner was attacked because he wore silk pyjamas: "Prodigality, insensate luxury, no knowledge of the value of money. The man's mad!" As regards myself, it's enough that I could be blamed for entrusting money to all and sundry, and without having any guarantee that the money was wisely invested. The man who wants to kill my dog begins by saying that it has rabies! It does not affect me at all that I myself should be judged in this fashion. But I should be ashamed if I used such criteria in passing judgment on others.

---

[162] Nympholepsy, from the ancient Greek belief that individuals could be possessed by nymphs. In the sense used above, it indicates an overly interest in beautiful women.

[163] The last Nazi rally at Nuremberg was held in 1938. The outbreak of the war the next year put an permanent end to these events. From the above, it is clear that Hitler sought to resume them after the war.

All sanctions are justified when it's a question of a real offence: treason to the Movement, for example. But when a man has made a mistake in good faith? Nobody has the right to photograph a man surprised in intimacy. It's too easy to make a man seem ridiculous. Let every man ask himself the question, what would he do if he had the bad luck to be photographed unawares in a delicate situation? The photos in question were taken from a house opposite. It was a disgusting way of behaving, and I've forbidden any use to be made of the photos.[164]

It's not fair to demand more of a man than he can give. Streicher has not the gifts of a great administrator. Would I have entrusted the editorship of a great newspaper to Dietrich Eckart? From the financial point of view, there'd have been a terrifying mess. One day the newspaper would have come out, the next day not. If there'd been a pig to share out, Eckart would have promised it left and right, and distributed at least twenty-four hams. Those men are made like that, but without them it's impossible to get anything started.

I haven't myself the talents of a great administrator, but I've known how to surround myself with the men I needed. Dietrich Eckart could not, for example, have been the Director of the National Institute of Arts and Letters. It would be like asking me to devote myself to agriculture. I'm quite incapable of it.

One day I had in my hands a pile of letters from Severing.[165] If they'd been published, he'd have been annihilated. They were the outpourings of a draper's assistant. I said to Goebbels: "We haven't the right to make use of these." Reading these letters had made Severing seem to me more sympathetic than otherwise, and perhaps that's one of the reasons why later on I didn't persecute him. In the same way, I have in the State archives photographs of Mathilde von Kemnitz.[166] I forbid them to be published. I don't think a man should die of hunger because he has been my opponent. If he was a base opponent, then off to the concentration camp with him!

---

[164] The details of this incident are unknown, but, given Hitler's earlier comments, must have involved an extra-marital affair involving Streicher.

[165] Carl Severing (1875–1952), a Social Democrat Minister of the Interior from 1928 to 1930.

[166] Mathilde von Kemnitz (1877–1966) was a psychiatrist and proponent of an esoteric anti-Christian and anti-Semitic nationalism. The wife of General Erich Ludendorff, an early prominent NSDAP activist, she and her husband took on such extreme public positions that they fell out with the NSDAP. The images to which Hitler here refers have never emerged in public and their details are unknown.

But if he's not a swindler, I let him go free, and I see that he has enough to live on. That's how I helped Noske[167] and many others. On my return from Italy, I even increased their pensions, saying to myself: "God be praised, thanks to these people we've been rid of the aristocratic riff-raff that's still ruining Italy." Barring errors on my part, their pension is at present eight hundred marks a month.

What I couldn't allow, though, was that they should make some financial arrangement in my favour—as Severing, for example, offered to do more than once. I would seem to have bought them. In the case of one of them, I know what he has said about us: "On the path towards Socialism, the results surpass all we had dreamed of."

Thälmann himself is very well treated in his concentration camp. He has a little house to himself. Torgler has been set free. He's peacefully busy with a work on Socialism in the nineteenth century. I'm convinced he was responsible for the burning of the Reichstag, but I can't prove it.

Personally, I have nothing against him. Besides, he has completely calmed down. A pity I didn't meet the man ten years earlier! By nature, he's an intelligent fellow. That's why it's crazy of Spain to persecute genuine Falangists.[168] Thank God, I've always avoided persecuting my enemies.

29th December 1941
SPECIAL GUESTS: DR. TODT AND DIRECTOR-GENERAL PLEIGER[169]

Industrialisation of the Reich—Coal and iron—Work done by Russian prisoners—Take the long view

The industrialisation of the Reich began with the exploitation of the coal in the Ruhr district. Then followed the development of the steel industry, with, as a consequence, heavy industry generally—which itself was the origin of the chemical industry and all the others. The main problem today is a problem of labour. Then comes the problem of the

---

[167] Gustav Noske (1868–1946), Social Democratic Party Minister of Defence of the Weimar Republic who suppressed the Communist Revolutions in Germany in 1919

[168] Some members of Spain's Falangist movement refused to support Franco's rule on the grounds that it was still too deeply embedded with the Catholic Church. The clash with the "genuine" Falangists continued for years.

[169] Paul Pleiger (1899–1985), a German industrialist who served the Nazi state in various economic and industrial advisory capacities, including Reich commissioner for coal and the eastern economy.

basic raw materials: coal and iron. With men, coal and iron one can solve the transport problem. At this stage, all the conditions are fulfilled for the functioning of a gigantic economy. How can we manage to increase the production of coal and ores?

If we employ Russian labour, that will allow us to use our nationals for other tasks. It's better worthwhile to take the trouble of knocking the Russians into shape than to fetch Italians from the South, who will say good-bye after six weeks! A Russian is not so stupid, after all, that he can't work in a mine. In any case, we're completely geared for standardisation. What's more, we'll do less and less turning. Presses will henceforward take the place of lathes. With the help of this colossal human material—I estimate the employable Russian labour at two and a half millions—we'll succeed in producing the machine-tools we need. We can give up the notion of building new factories if we progressively introduce the double-shift system.

The fact that the night-shift doesn't turn out as much as the day-shift is not an insuperable inconvenience. The compensation is that we economise on the materials needed for the construction of new factories. One must take long views.

30th December 1941, midday
SPECIAL GUEST: HIMMLER

Damaged ships—A British example—Sabotage

The English are very quick about restoring to seaworthiness those of their ships that have been damaged in the course of operations. This makes one think that they know how to restrict themselves to the indispensable repairs, whilst we insist on finicking about—which loses us precious time. In many fields we remain faithful to the old habit of always and everywhere achieving the best. I ask you, what good does it do us if a ship we need at one particular moment is made of a steel that outlasts the centuries?

Besides, what finally matters, in war or peace, is that a thing should do the job asked of it, at the moment when one needs it. Very often people cling to the old rules because they're afraid to take a responsibility.

And everybody thanks God: there's a regulation that removes the opportunity to take the initiative! That's a sort of passive resistance induced by indolence and laziness of the mind. I think there are cases in which faithfulness to the letter of a regulation is a sort of sabotage.

Night of 31st December 1941–1st January 1942
The white races and the Far East—Japan has no social problem—
Holland and Japan—The imminent fall of Singapore

It would have been possible to hold the Far East if the great countries of the white race had joined in a coalition for the purpose. If things had been thus arranged, Japan would never have been able to make her claims prevail. The Japanese have no need of a National-Socialist revolution. If they rid themselves of certain superfluous contributions from the West, they'll avoid the necessity of the social question arising amongst them. Whether a Japanese factory belongs to the State or to an individual is purely a formal question. Japan has no great landed class, only small proprietors. The middle class is the backbone of the population.

The social question could arise in Japan only if the country acquired enormous wealth. Oshima[170] reckons that we are lucky because the Russian spaces we are conquering have a wild, rough climate. He observes that, on the other hand, the archipelagos on which his compatriots are establishing themselves have a softening climate.

If the Dutch were linked with Japan by a commercial agreement, that would have been a clever calculation on their part. Under English pressure, they've done exactly the opposite during the last few years. It's possible the Dutch may decide on such an agreement as soon as Singapore has fallen. Thanks to the Germans whom the Japanese will employ in the archipelago, we'll have excellent outlets in those regions.

PART TWO
January to September 1942
1st January 1942, midday
SPECIAL GUESTS: HIMMLER, REICH MINISTER DORPMÜLLER[171]
AND UNDER-SECRETARY OF STATE KLEINMANN[172]
Do not waste German man-power

I'm in favour of great public works (building of tunnels, etc.) being carried out for the duration of hostilities by prisoners-of-war. Any fool

---

[170] Baron Hiroshi Ōshima (1886–1975), a Japanese general who served as ambassador to Germany from 1938 to 1945.
[171] Julius Dorpmüler (1869–1945), Manager of the German Railways (from 1926) and Minister for Transport from 1937 to 1945.
[172] Wilhelm Kleinman (1876-1945) State Secretary to the Ministry of Transport.

can be put in charge of them. It would be wasting German labour to impose such tasks on it.

1st January 1942, evening
SPECIAL GUEST: HIMMLER
The permission to gamble in Baden-Baden

I never bother about the price of things except when we are concerned with purchasers of modest means. As for the rich, opportunities should be invented of making them spend their money! One day the *Gauleiter* of Baden came to confide in me his fears concerning Baden-Baden, which he told me was losing its source of revenue. The Jews, who formerly had been the mainstay of its clientele, had been deserting the resort since 1933. There was no question of granting Baden-Baden a subsidy. The resort was viable, on condition it was endowed with a casino. I didn't hesitate for a second, and I authorised gambling there.

Night of 1st – 2nd January 1942
You cannot avoid God—The marriage ceremony—The official who doesn't think—Monserrat. . .

Discussing a letter from Frau von Oeynhausen, Chr. Schr.[173] examined the possibility of replacing religious instruction in schools by a course of general philosophy, so that children should not lose the sense of respect in the presence of things that transcend our understanding. Someone proposed that this new type of instruction should not be described as "philosophy". It would be more like an exegesis of National Socialism.

The Führer gave his opinion: It's impossible to escape the problem of God. When I have the time, I'll work out the formulae to be used on great occasions. We must have something perfect both in thought and in form.

It's my opinion that we should organise marriage in such a way that couples do not present themselves one by one before the officer of the civil authority. If each couple assembles a following of ten relatives or friends, with fifty couples we shall have five hundred participants—all the elements of a majestic ceremony! At present the officer of the civil authority is faced with an impossible task. How do you expect the man to make an inspired-speech ten times a day? But what insipid twaddle they do sometimes pour forth! The expression "officer of the civil authority" is itself not very poetic. When I hear it, it reminds me of my father. I used occasionally to say to him: "Father, just think . . ." He used

---

[173] Christa Schroeder, one of Hitler's secretaries.

immediately to interrupt me: "My son, I have no need to think, I'm an official."

Hitler is engaged in skimming through an illustrated book on Spain: Monserrat! The word makes the legend come alive. It has its origin in the hostile encounter between the Moors and the Romano-Germanic elements. A lovely country. One can imagine the castle of the holy grail there.

Night of 2nd–3rd January 1942
Memories of Obersalzberg—Professor Hoffmann—The paintings of Rottmann—Animals

When I go to Obersalzberg, I'm not drawn there merely by the beauty of the landscape. I feel myself far from petty things, and my imagination is stimulated. When I study a problem elsewhere, I see it less clearly, I'm submerged by the details. By night, at the *Berghof,*[174] I often remain for hours with my eyes open, contemplating from my bed the mountains lit up by the moon. It's at such moments that brightness enters my mind.

During my first electoral campaign, the question was how to win seats. Only the parties that had a certain importance had any hopes of doing so. I had no original formula for the campaign. I went up to Obersalzberg. At four o'clock in the morning I was already awake, and I realised at once what I had to do. That same day I composed a whole series of posters. I decided to overwhelm the adversary under the weight of his own arguments. And what weapons he supplied us with! All my great decisions were taken at Obersalzberg. That's where I conceived the offensive of May 1940 and the attack on Russia.

When Hoffmann[175] is away for a few days, I miss him.

Chr. Schr. exclaims: "My Führer, if Professor Hoffmann knew that, he'd be delighted." But he knows it very well. Not long ago he wanted to give me a Menzel.[176] It was really very nice of him. I refused it. Even though I liked it, I wasn't going to deprive him of the picture. Besides, what would I have done with it? There'd have been no place for it at Linz. But, for Hoffmann's house, it's a treasure. The way in which Hoffmann can do me a service is by finding a Rottmann,[177] for example, for my collection. Rottmann's Greek and Roman landscapes at the Pinakothek

[174] The name of Hitler's house in Berchtesgaden.
[175] Heinrich Hoffmann (1885–1957), Hitler's official photographer.
[176] Adolph von Menzel (1815–1905), a leading Realist artist.
[177] Carl Rottmann (1797–1850), a prominent German landscape painter.

have some extraordinary lighting effects. We have only one picture by him, for Linz. But, after all, we can't have everything. If anyone wants to study Rottmann, he has only to go to Munich.

Why is it that the screech of an owl is so disagreeable to a man? There must be some reason for that. I imagine it to be the confused hubbub of the virgin forest. Animals cry aloud when they're hungry, when they're in pain, when they're in love.

The language of the birds is certainly more developed than we think. We say that cats are playful creatures. Perhaps they think the same of us. They endure us as long as they can, and when they've had enough of our childishness, they give us a scratch with their claws!

3rd January 1942, midday
Great Britain should have avoided war—Nomura and Kurusu, two Japanese diplomats[178]—How to deceive

If there was a country that had particular reasons to avoid war, it was certainly Great Britain. The only way for her to keep her Empire was to have a strong air force and a strong navy.

That was all she needed. Oshima told me that, to deceive the Americans, they were sent N. and K.—for it was notorious that both of them had always been in favour of an understanding with the United States.

When one wants to deceive an adversary by simulating weakness, what a mistake to use a brave man and ask him to simulate the weakness for you! It's better to choose somebody who is out-and-out weak.

Night of 3rd—4th January 1942
Recruitment of the SS—Himmler's value—Origins of the SS and the SA—Sepp Dietrich[179]—Seven hundred seats in the Reichstag— Schoolmasters—Göring[180] and German honour—In praise of optimism— Women love males—Forty degrees below zero—Rommel's tanks—The Diet of Worms—Origin of the German salute—The term "Führer" explained.

---

[178] Kichisaburō Nomura (1877–1964), ambassador to the United States in 1941. Saburō Kurusu (1886–1954) was a career diplomat sent to Washington DC in April 1941 in order to try and negotiate with the US Government. Both men were unaware of the planned Japanese attack on Pearl Harbour.

[179] Josef "Sepp" Dietrich (1892–1966), a senior SS figure who held commands in a number of units before and during the war, including Hitler's bodyguard unit, the *Leibstandarte SS Adolf Hitler*, and several panzer armies.

[180] Hermann Göring (1893–1946), early and famous NSDAP member who became President of the Reichstag, commander of the German air force, and, from 1941 to 1945, Hitler's deputy.

The SS shouldn't extend its recruiting too much. What matters is to keep a very high level. This body must create upon men of the elite the effect of a lover. People must know that troops like the SS have to pay the butcher's bill more heavily than anyone else—so as to keep away the young fellows who only want to show off. Troops inspired by a fierce will, troops with an unbeatable turn-out—the sense of superiority personified! As soon as peace has returned, the SS will have to be given its independence again—a complete independence. There has always been a rivalry between troops of the line and guardsmen.

That's why it's a good thing that the SS should constitute, in relation to the others, an absolutely distinct world. In peace-time it's an elite police, capable of crushing any adversary.

It was necessary that the SS should make war, otherwise its prestige would have been lowered. I am proud when an army commander can tell me that "his force is based essentially on an armoured division and the SS Reich Division". Himmler has an extraordinary quality. I don't believe that anyone else has had like him the obligation to deploy his troops in such constantly difficult conditions. In 1934, "the old gentleman" was still there. Even afterwards, a thousand difficulties arose.

Being convinced that there are always circumstances in which elite troops are called for, in 1922–23 I created the "Adolf Hitler Shock Troops". They were made up of men who were ready for revolution and knew that one day or another, things would come to hard knocks.

When I came out of Landsberg, everything was broken up and scattered in sometimes rival bands. I told myself then that I needed a bodyguard, even a very restricted one, but made up of men who would be enlisted without restriction, even to march against their own brothers. Only twenty men to a city (on condition that one could count on them absolutely) rather than a suspect mass.

It was Maurice,[181] Schreck and Heiden[182] who formed in Munich the first group of "tough 'uns", and were thus the origin of the SS. But it was with Himmler that the SS became that extraordinary body of men, devoted to an idea, loyal unto death. I see in Himmler our Ignatius de

---

[181] Emil Maurice (1897–1972), an early NSDAP member, co-founder of the SS, and Hitler's first personal chauffeur. His great-grandfather was Jewish, a fact which was well-known to Hitler and the top Nazi leadership.

[182] Erhard Heiden (1901–1933), early NSDAP member and the third SS commander. He was murdered by unknown persons in 1933.

Loyola.[183] With intelligence and obstinacy, against wind and tide, he forged this instrument.

The heads of the SA, for their part, didn't succeed in giving their troops a soul. At the present time we have had it confirmed that every division of the SS is aware of its responsibility.

The SS knows that its job is to set an example, to be and not to seem, and that all eyes are upon it. The role of Sepp Dietrich is unique. I've always given him opportunity to intervene at sore spots. He's a man who's simultaneously cunning, energetic and brutal. Under his swashbuckling appearance, Dietrich is a serious, conscientious, scrupulous character. And what care he takes of his troops! He's a phenomenon, in the class of people like Frundsberg, Ziethen and Seydlitz.[184] He's a Bavarian Wrangel,[185] someone irreplaceable. For the German people, Sepp Dietrich is a national institution. For me personally, there's also the fact that he is one of my oldest companions in the struggle.

One of the tragic situations we've been through was in Berlin in 1930. How Sepp Dietrich could impose his personality! It was just before the elections on which everything depended. I was waiting at Munich for the results of the counting. Adolf Müller came in, very excited, and declared: "I think we've won. We may get sixty-six seats."

I replied that if the German people could think correctly, it would give us more than that. Within myself I was saying: "If it could be a hundred!" Suddenly, we found ourselves with the certainty of a hundred seats. Müller offered to stand a round of drinks. It went up to a hundred and seven! How to express what I felt at that moment? We had gone up from twelve seats to a hundred and seven.

I cannot endure schoolmasters. As always, the exceptions confirm the rule, and that's why young people become all the more attached to the exceptional ones. After the Great War, the situation at the universities was difficult. The young officers who had a short time ago been at the front were somewhat awkward pupils.

---

[183] Ignatius of Loyola (1491–1556), a Spanish Catholic priest and co-founder and driving force of the Society of Jesus, better known as the Jesuits.

[184] All prominent historical German military figures. Georg von Frundsberg (1473–1528) was one of the leading soldiers of the 1494 to 1559 between the Imperial House of Habsburg and various Italian and French opponents. Hans Joachim von Ziethen (1699–1786) was cavalry general in Frederick the Great's Prussian Army. Friedrich von Seydlitz (1721–1773) is known as one of the greatest Prussian cavalry generals.

[185] Friedrich von Wrangel (1784–1877), Field Marshall in the Prussian Army.

One day I had an opportunity to hear a speech by Göring, in which he declared himself resolutely on the side of German honour. My attention had been called to him. I liked him. I made him the head of my SA. He's the only one of its heads who ran the SA properly. I gave him a dishevelled rabble. In a very short time he had organised a division of eleven thousand men.

Young Lutze[186] has gone off to the front as a volunteer. Let's hope nothing happens to him. He's truly a pattern of what a young man should be—perfect in every way. When he has had a long enough period of training at the front, I'll take him onto my staff. He has plenty of breeding. On one occasion, Inge[187] and he had come to Obersalzberg. They must have been thirteen and fourteen years old. Inge had done something that was not too well-behaved, no doubt. He turned to us and made the observation: "What young people are coming to, nowadays!"

I was present one day at the burial of some National Socialist comrades who'd been murdered. I was struck by the dignified attitude of their families. Sometime later, at Nuremberg, they were burying the Austrian soldier, Schumacher,[188] who had likewise been murdered. Everything was cries and lamentations, an appalling spectacle.

Have pity on the pessimist. He spoils his own existence. In fact, life is endurable only on condition that one's an optimist. The pessimist complicates things to no purpose. In my section[189] there was a spirit of open larking. Apart from the runners, we had no link with the outside world. We had no radio set. What would have happened to us, by Heaven, if we had been a group of pessimists!

The worst thing of all is a pessimistic commanding officer. A man like that can paralyse everything. At that stage, a man is no longer a pessimist, he's a defeatist. How could I have been successful without that dose of optimism which has never left me, and without that faith that moves mountains? A sense of humour and a propensity for laugh-

---

[186] Viktor Lutze junior (1924–1944) was the son of the SA ("Brownshirts") leader, Viktor Lutze senior (1890–1943). Viktor senior died in a motor vehicle accident, and Viktor junior was killed in action in Normandy.

[187] Inge Lutze (1925–1943) was Viktor senior's daughter, who died in the motor vehicle accident which killed her father.

[188] Herbert Schumacher (1913–1932), was shot and then beaten to death by members of the Communist Party in Greifswald in July 1932.

[189] During the First World War.

ter are qualities that are indispensable to a unit. On the eve of our setting out for the battle of the Somme, we laughed and made jokes all night. Young people are optimists by nature. That's an inclination that should be encouraged. One must have faith in life.

It's always useful to be able to make comparisons between events. Thus, when faced with a difficult situation, I always remember what our situation was like in 1933. It's not enough to be inclined to optimism, one must have a certain youthfulness into the bargain. It's lucky that I went into politics at thirty, became Chancellor of the Reich at forty-three, and am only fifty-two today.

One is born an optimist, just as one is born a pessimist. With age, optimism gets weaker. The spring relaxes. When I suffered my setback in 1923,[190] I had only one idea, to get back into the saddle. Today I would no longer be capable of the effort which that implies. The awareness that one is no longer capable of that has something demoralising about it. I believe blindly in my nation. If I lost that belief, we would have nothing left to do but to shut up shop. A poor man like Wiedemann,[191] what's left for him to do now? Every crisis has an end. The only question is whether one will survive the crisis. A winter in which the thermometer remains frozen at 50° below freezing-point simply doesn't exist! What matters is, not to give way in any circumstances. It's wonderful to see a man come through a desperate situation. But it's not given to many beings to master a hostile fate.

Throughout my life, that was my daily bread. First of all, the poverty I experienced in my youth. After that, the sometimes inextricable difficulties of the Party. Next, the government of the country. But luckily

---

[190] Hitler's imprisonment following the failed *putsch*.

[191] Fritz Wiedemann (1891–1970), one of Hitler's superior officers on the Western Front during the First World War. Hitler offered him the leadership of the SA ("Brownshirts") in 1921, an offer he declined. When however, his dairy business went bankrupt in 1933, he asked Hitler for a job. By 1934 he had been given a position as adjutant to Hitler's deputy, Rudolf Hess, and became a member of the NSDAP, despite being on the party's "untrustworthy" proscribed list. By 1935, he became Hitler's adjutant, and was elected to the Reichstag in 1938. After falling out with Hitler in 1939, he was dismissed him from all his positions, and given the job of consul general in San Francisco, USA. There, Wiedemann openly moved against Hitler, offering his services to the Allied Secret Services. When the German consulate was closed, Wiedemann returned to Germany, only to be appointed Consul General in Tianjin, China. He was arrested in 1945, brought back to Germany and testified about his superiors at the Nuremberg Trials.

nothing lasts forever—and that's a consoling thought. Even in raging winter, one knows that spring will follow.

And if, at this moment, men are being turned to blocks of ice, that won't prevent the April sun from shining and restoring life to these desolate spaces. In the South, the thaw starts in May. In the Crimea, it's warm in February. At the end of April, it's as if someone had waved a magic wand: in a few days the snow melts, and everything becomes green again. This passage from one season to the next is made, so to speak, without transition. It's a powerful thrusting up of sap. Nothing that can be compared to what happens in our part of the world.

Man loses in a moment the memory of the things that have made him suffer. Otherwise man would live in constant anguish. At the end of nine months, a woman forgets the terrible pains of childbirth. A wound is forgotten at once.

What is strange, indeed, is that at the moment of being wounded one has merely the sense of a shock, without immediate pain. One thinks that nothing important has occurred. The pain begins only when one is being carried away. All that gave rise to incredible scenes, especially in 1914, at the period when formalism had not yet lost its rights. The wounded, who could hardly remain on their feet, used to stand at attention to ask their captain for leave to be evacuated! At bottom, all that's excellent for our race. It's excellent also for the German woman; for the women adore the males. The men of the Nordic countries have been softened to this point, that their most beautiful women buckle their baggage when they have an opportunity of getting their hooks on a man in our part of the world. That's what happened to Göring with his Karin.[192] There's no rebelling against this observation.

It's a fact that women love real men. It's their instinct that tells them. In prehistoric times, the women looked for the protection of heroes. When two men fight for the possession of a woman, the latter waits to let her heart speak until she knows which of the two will be victorious. Tarts adore poachers.

At this moment, on the Eastern front, I would prefer to lead a section of poachers in an attack rather than a section of those lawyers who condemn poachers.

I'm impressed by the opinion of the Japanese, who consider that the Englishman is a much better soldier than the American. The fact that

---

[192] Karin Göring (née Fock), (1888–1931) was the Swedish first wife of Hermann.

the Englishman was beaten by us will not prevent him from believing in his superiority. It's a matter of upbringing. At the beginning of the Great War, the English were not accustomed to artillery fire. After a bombardment of four hours, they were broken, whereas our fellows could hold out for weeks.

The English are particularly sensitive to threats on their flanks. All in all, the English soldier has not improved since the Great War. The same thing is true, by the way, of all our opponents, including the Russians. One can even say that the Russians fought better during the Great War.

I intended to attack in the West right away in the autumn of 1939. But the season was too far on. The battle in Africa is at present a battle of materials. Rommel[193] has been lacking tanks—the others still had some. That explains everything. And if Rommel lacked tanks, that's because we couldn't transport them.

The expression "Blitzkrieg" is an Italian invention. We picked it up from the newspapers. I've just learnt that I owe all my successes to an attentive study of Italian military theories.

In former days, when I arrived by motor-car in a town where I was expected, I always stood, bare-headed—and I stayed like that sometimes for hours, even in the worst weather. I sincerely regret that age and my health no longer allow me to do that. At bottom, I could endure much more than the others, including those who were waiting for me in the open air, whatever the weather.

The military salute is not a fortunate gesture. I imposed the German salute for the following reason. I would given orders, at the beginning, that in the Army I should not be greeted with the German salute. But many people forgot. Fritsch drew his conclusions, and punished all who forgot to give me the military salute, with fourteen days' confinement to barracks. I, in turn, drew *my* conclusions and introduced the German salute likewise into the Army.

On parades, when mounted officers give the military salute, what a wretched figure they cut! The raised arm of the German salute, that has quite a different style! I made it the salute of the Party long after the Duce had adopted it.

I would read the description of the sitting of the Diet of Worms, in the course of which Luther was greeted with the German salute. It

---

[193] Erwin Rommel (1891–1944), the Field Marshal whose exploits in North Africa became legendary. He committed suicide after being implicated in the July 20, 1944, plot to kill Hitler.

was to show him that he was not being confronted with arms, but with peaceful intentions.

In the days of Frederick the Great, people still saluted with their hats, with pompous gestures. In the Middle Ages the serfs humbly doffed their bonnets, whilst the noblemen gave the German salute. It was in the *Ratskeller* at Bremen, about the year 1921, that I first saw this style of salute. It must be regarded as a survival of an ancient custom, which originally signified: "See, I have no weapon in my hand!"

I introduced the salute into the Party at our first meeting in Weimar. The SS at once gave it a soldierly style. It's from that moment that our opponents honoured us with the epithet "dogs of Fascists".

Thinking of that time reminds me of Scheubner-Richter's[194] sacrifice. What dignity his wife displayed! It's a heartbreaking grief to me that Dietrich Eckart did not live to see the Party's rise.

What a revenge and what an achievement that was, for all those who were with us as long ago as 1923! Our old Nazis, they were grand fellows. They'd everything to lose, at that time, and nothing to win by coming with us.

In ten years, the expression "the Führer" will have acquired an impersonal character. It will be enough for me to give this title an official consecration for that of Reich Chancellor to be blotted out. Even in the Army they now say "the Führer". This title will later be extended to cover persons who will not have all the virtues of a leader, but it will help to establish their authority.

Anyone at all can be made a president, but it's not possible to give the title of "Führer" to a nobody. Another good thing is that every German can say "my Führer"—the others can only say "Führer". It's extraordinary how quickly this formula has become popular. Nobody addresses me in the third person.

Anyone can write to me: "My Führer, I greet you." I've killed the third person and dealt a death-blow to the last vestiges of servility, those survivals of the feudal age.

I don't know how the expression was born, I've nothing to do with it. It suddenly implanted itself in the people, and gradually acquired the strength of usage. What a happy inspiration I had, to refuse the title of President of the Reich. You can imagine it: President Adolf Hitler! There is no finer title than that of Führer, for it was born spontaneously

---

[194] Ludwig Erwin von Scheubner-Richter (1884–1923) an early NSDAP member who was killed in the 1923 Putsch.

in the people. As for the expression "my Führer", I imagine it was born in the mouth of women. When I wished to influence "the old gentleman", I used to address him as "Herr Generalfeldmarschall". It was only on official occasions that I used to say to him: "Herr Präsident".

It was Hindenburg,[195] by the way, who gave prestige to the presidential title. These fine shades may seem to be trifles, but they have their importance. They're what give the framework its rigidity.

The destiny of a word can be extraordinary. For two thousand years the expression "Caesar" personified the supreme authority. The Japanese also have their own expression to indicate the highest authority: they say "Tenno", which means "Son of Heaven". The Japanese are still at the point where we were sixteen hundred years ago, before the Church crept into the affair.

One must never admit that the authority of the State and the authority of the Party are two different things. The control of a people and the control of a State have to be combined in one person.

4th January 1942, midday
SPECIAL GUESTS: SEPP DIETRICH AND COLONEL ZEITZLER[196]
The Italian High Command made three mistakes—On publicity—The beer demagogues—The first loud-speakers—Air travel and weather forecast

The Italian High Command has committed three great mistakes in strategy. The resulting disasters have deprived the Italian Army of its former confidence. That's the explanation of its present mediocrity. It was first of all a mistake to hurl the best regiments of *Bersaglieri*[197] against solidly fortified French positions, the plans of which were utterly unknown to the Italian Command, and to do so in the snow at a height of three thousand metres, and that precisely at a time when aircraft could play no part.

It's not surprising that these regiments were so sorely tested. We ourselves could not have achieved any result in such conditions. If they'd listened to me, they'd have taken the French in the rear by the Rhine valley. The second mistake was Africa. The Italians had no pro-

---

[195] Paul von Hindenburg (1847–1934), former leader of the Imperial German Army during World War I and later President of Germany.
[196] Kurt Zeitzler (1895–1963), a senior officer who in 1942 became Chief of the Army General Staff with the rank of General. He resigned his post in July 1944.
[197] The *Bersaglieri* (Italian for "sharpshooter") were the elite of the Italian Army's infantry corps.

tection against the British tanks, and they were shot like rabbits. Many senior officers fell beside their guns. That's what gave them their panic terror of tanks.

The third mistake was their fatal enterprise against Albania. For this attack they used troops from Southern Italy—exactly what was needed for a winter campaign in mountainous country, without proper equipment, over an impracticable terrain, and without any organisation in depth!

Speaking of that, Keitel, we must see to it that the regiment of *bersaglieri* we're expecting is sent immediately onto the job. They couldn't endure a long march in this season and in such conditions. Let's prevent these *bersaglieri* from becoming demoralised before they've even arrived at the front!

Hitler turns to Sepp Dietrich: Hoffmann often speaks of his desire to have me visit his model farm. I can see from here what would happen. He'd photograph me entering a barn. What publicity for the sales of his milk! I would be posted up in all the dairies.

If I agreed to be photographed with a cigar between my teeth, I believe Reemtsma[198] would immediately offer me half a million marks! And why not just as well some publicity for a master furrier? A pelisse[199] on my back, a muff in my hand, on the look-out to shoot rabbits! I once did myself incalculable harm by writing an open letter to an inn-keeper. I reproached him with the commercial demagogy of the brewers, who made themselves out to be benefactors of the small man, struggling to ensure him his daily glass of beer. Very soon I saw Amann appear, completely overwhelmed, to tell me that the big beer-halls were cancelling their advertising contracts with the newspaper. That meant an immediate loss of seven thousand marks, and of twenty-seven thousand over a longer period. I promised myself solemnly that I would never again write an article under the domination of rage.

At the beginning of our activity, there were still no loudspeakers. The first ones that existed were the worst imaginable. Once, at the Sports Palace in Berlin, there was such a cacophony that I had to cut the connection and go on speaking for nearly an hour, forcing my voice. I stopped when I realised that I was about to fall down from exhaustion. Kube[200] was the man who had the most powerful voice of us all, the

---

[198] One of the largest tobacco companies in Germany.

[199] A fur-lined cloak.

[200] Wilhelm Kube (1887–1943), an early NSDAP activist in East Prussia, and later

voice of a rhinoceros. He held out for only twenty minutes. Another time, at Essen, it was an utter flop. The whole population had come to our meeting. Nobody understood a word. I was admired simply for my endurance. I had witnesses. Your wife, Brandt,[201] herself confessed to me that it was completely incomprehensible.

It was only gradually that we learnt the necessity of distributing the loud-speakers through the hall. One needs about a hundred—and not just one, placed behind the platform, which was what we had at the Sports Palace. Every word was heard twice: once from my mouth, and then echoed by the loud-speaker.

I also remember the German Day of 1923, in Nuremberg. It was the first time I spoke in a hall that could hold two thousand people. I had no experience as an orator. At the end of twenty minutes, I was speechless.

Hitler again turns to Sepp Dietrich: Burdened with responsibilities as I am at this moment, I don't take unnecessary risks in moving about by aircraft. But you know that in the heroic days I shrank from nothing. I only once had to abandon a flight, and that was against my will. It was at the end of an electoral campaign. I would spoken at Flensburg, and I wanted to get back to Berlin, breaking my journey at Kiel.

Captain Baur[202] interposes: "Yes, my Führer, it was I who insisted on your giving up that flight. First of all, it was a night flight, and our course was thick with heavy storms. Moreover, I had no confidence in the Met. I was sure of one thing, that some people would have been delighted to learn that we had broken our necks."

<h3 style="text-align:center">4th January 1942, evening</h3>

SPECIAL GUESTS: SEPP DIETRICH AND COLONEL ZEITZLER

The desert is ideal for tanks—Supplying Rommel—The never-ceasing demand for new weapons

It has always been supposed that the employment of tanks depended on the existence of roads. Well, it has just been realised that the desert is the ideal terrain for them. It would have been enough for Rommel to have two hundred more tanks. If we succeed in neutralising Malta and getting new tanks to Africa, Rommel will be able to recapture the op-

---

Gauleiter. His last office was that of Commissioner-General for West Ruthenia in occupied Byelorussia, where he was assassinated by a Soviet partisan.

[201] Karl Brandt (1904–1948), Hitler's SS escort doctor.

[202] Johannes "Hans" Baur (1897–1993), Hitler's personal pilot and commander of the small squadron of aircraft at Hitler's disposal.

erational initiative. It's proper not to exaggerate, we haven't lost much. In any case, there's no question—quite the opposite—of giving up the game. In my opinion, their victory will make the English withdraw a part of their forces from Africa.

It's likely, for nobody in this war has sufficient reserves of aircraft to permit himself to immobilise them in sectors where they're not indispensable. On their side, especially, all their forces are constantly in the line—in fact, we are the only ones who still have a few reserves. The only problem for us is that of forcing the passage between Sicily and Tripolitania. On their side, they have to go all round Africa. They're aware of our strength in the Mediterranean, and dare not use the classic route to India. As soon as they've stripped that sector, I'll send Rommel what he needs.

The hollow charge[203] means the death of the tank. Tanks will have finished their career before the end of this war. We haven't used the hollow charge so far, but there's no more reason to wait, since Italy has suggested to us a similar weapon. Secrets are badly kept amongst the Italians, and what Italy has today, the rest of the world will have soon! If the others have it, there'll be nothing left for us to do, either, but to pack up our tanks. With the help of this weapon, anyone at all can blow up a tank. When the Russians start up again in the spring, their tanks will be put out of action. Two years ago I had a new heavy anti-tank gun. In the meantime the new enemy tanks have come into the line. Necessity teaches men not merely to pray, but ceaselessly to invent, and above all to accept the inventions that are suggested to them. Every new invention so much reduces the value of the previous material that it's a ceaselessly renewed struggle to introduce a novelty.

Night of 4th–5th January 1942
SPECIAL GUEST: SEPP DIETRICH

The Jews and the new Europe—The Jews and Japan—The two impostors, Churchill and Roosevelt—The courage of the Spanish soldiers

The Jews didn't believe the New Europe would be born. They could never settle themselves in Japan. They've always mistrusted this world

---

[203] A hollow charge, also called a "shaped charge," is an shell which has explosive charge formed in such a way as to focus its detonation's energy. Although first developed in Germany in 1883, the most famous use of a hollow charge was the German *Panzerfaust,* a weapon which became the model for all hand-held anti-tank devices such as the more famous Russian "Hand-held Anti-tank Grenade Launcher" or "RPG."

wrapped up in itself, they've always seen in it a powerful danger to themselves—and that's why they've constantly striven to keep England and America away from Japan.

Just as there have always been two Germanys, so there have always been two Japans: the one, capitalist and therefore Anglophile—the other, the Japan of the Rising Sun, the land of the *samurai*. The Japanese Navy is the expression of this second world. It's amongst the sailors that we've found the men nearest to ourselves.

Oshima, for example, what a magnificent head he has! On the other hand, certain men belonging to the Mikado's[204] entourage have given me an impression of decadence.

Throughout a period of two thousand six hundred years, Japan never had war on her own soil. One thing for which one must be grateful to Ribbentrop is having understood the full significance of our pact with Japan, and drawn the conclusions from it with great lucidity. Our Navy was inspired by the same state of mind, but the Army would have preferred an alliance with China.

I'm very glad I recently said all I think about Roosevelt. There's no doubt about it, he's a sick brain. The noise he mace at his press conference was typically Hebraic. There's nobody stupider than the Americans. What a humiliation for them! The further they fall, the greater their disillusionment.

In any case, neither of the two Anglo-Saxons is any better than the other. One can scarcely see how they could find fault with one another! Churchill and Roosevelt, what impostors! One can expect utterly extravagant repercussions.

In the secrecy of their hearts, the South Americans loathe the Yankees. I don't believe the Americans are attacking the Azores. They've let the moment go by.

From this moment the Dutch, whether they like it or not, are bound up with our fortunes.

Zeitzler told me today that the Italian regiment of tanks has made a very incisive counter-attack.

To troops, the Spaniards are a crew of ragamuffins. They regard a rifle as an instrument that should not be cleaned under any pretext. Their sentries exist only in principle. They don't take up their posts, or, if they do take them up, they do so in their sleep. When the Russians arrive, the natives have to wake them up. But the Spaniards have never

---

[204] The Emperor of Japan.

yielded an inch of ground. One can't imagine more fearless fellows. They scarcely take cover. They flout death. I know, in any case, that our men are always glad to have Spaniards as neighbours in their sector. If one reads the writings of Goeben[205] on the Spaniards, one realises that nothing has changed in a hundred years. Extraordinarily brave, tough against privations, but wildly undisciplined.

What is lamentable with them is the difference in treatment between officers and men. The Spanish officers live in clover, and the men are reduced to the most meagre pittance.

The Hungarians are good auxiliaries for us. With proper stiffening, we find them very useful. As for Romania, she has only one man, Antonescu!

5th January 1941, midday
SPECIAL GUESTS: DR. TODT, SEPP DIETRICH, GENERAL GAUSE[206] AND COLONEL ZEITZLER
The British lose the Far East—India or Tripoli—British thunder—The American soldier

The situation of the English, on the military level, is compromised in two sectors of vital importance. One of their great bases is Iran, Iraq and Syria. That's where their fleet takes on supplies. The other is the Malay archipelago, where they're losing all their refuelling-points for oil. They can trumpet abroad their intentions concerning Europe, but they know very well that it's the possession of India on which the existence of their Empire depends. If I were in their place, I would say: "It will be impossible to reconquer India once it's lost." My chief care would be to put everything I had on the road there, even if it were only one division. I have a clear impression that they're ransacking their cupboards to try to save their positions in the Far East.

Projects are one thing, but it's the event that calls the tune. It would be conceivable that the English should have Indian units moved to Europe—but these are mere movements for movement's sake, such as reduce an Army's effectiveness.

They'd lose in the one quarter without gaining in the other. If things go on following this rhythm, in four weeks the Japanese will be in Singapore. It would be a terribly hard blow. And the space there is so vast

---

[205] August Karl von Goeben (1816–1880), a Prussian general who served with Spanish troops in Morocco and wrote two books on his experiences.
[206] Alfred Gause (1896–1967), Rommel's chief of staff in North Africa and later Chief of Staff of the 6th Panzer Army.

that there could be no question of holding it with a division. The situation would be entirely different if the English had a few thousand tons of fuel in reserve.

Some time ago, when we were transporting material from Sicily to Tripolitania, the English evaded battle in an incomprehensible fashion. Yet for them it's a matter of life or death to prevent us from supplying our troops in Africa. If our today's convoy succeeds in getting through, that will be a poor look-out for them. If I were faced with the alternatives of losing either Tripoli or India, I would not hesitate to give up Tripoli and concentrate my efforts on India.

General Gause declared: "It was a relief for us to learn of Japan's entry into the war"

Yes, a relief, an immense relief. But it was also a turning point in history. It means the loss of a whole continent, and one must regret it, for it's the white race which is the loser.

In 1940 the English told us that the Flying Fortresses would "pulverise" Germany. They told the Japanese that Tokyo would be razed to the ground within nine hours. On the basis of these boastings, we were entitled to suppose that during 1941 they would multiply their efforts in the field of air-warfare. To cope with this possibility, I had our flak reinforced, and, above all, I had enormous reserves of ammunition built up. In actual fact, during 1941 we used only one quarter of the ammunition used the previous year.

I believe that if we can get through to Rommel enough gasoline, tanks and anti-tank guns, the English will have to dig in on the defensive, and we shall again have the chance of getting them on the run. Just about now, Rommel should be receiving two hundred tanks.

I'll never believe that an American soldier can fight like a hero.

Night of 5th–6th January 1942
SPECIAL GUEST: SEPP DIETRICH

Stalin, successor to the Tsars—The Germans saved Europe in 1933— Reasons for our attack on Russia—The matériel of the Russians—Asian inferiority

Stalin pretends to have been the herald of the Bolshevik revolution. In actual fact, he identifies himself with the Russia of the Tsars, and he has merely resurrected the tradition of Pan-Slavism. For him Bolshevism is only a means, a disguise designed to trick the Germanic and Latin peoples. If we hadn't seized power in 1933, the wave of the Huns would have broken over our heads. All Europe would have been affected, for Germany would have been powerless to stop it. Nobody suspected it, but we were on the verge of catastrophe.

To what an extent people failed to suspect it, I have some evidence. A few days before our entry into Russia, I told Göring that we were facing the severest test in our existence. Göring fell off his perch, for he'd been regarding the campaign in Russia as another mere formality.

What confirmed me in my decision to attack without delay was the information brought by a German mission lately returned from Russia, that a single Russian factory was producing by itself more tanks than all our factories together. I felt that this was the ultimate limit.

Even so, if someone had told me that the Russians had ten thousand tanks, I would have answered: "You're completely mad!"

The Russians never invent anything. All they have, they've got from others. Everything comes to them from abroad—the engineers, the machine-tools. Give them the most highly perfected bombing-sights. They're capable of copying them, but not of inventing them. With them, working-technique is simplified to the uttermost. Their rudimentary labour-force compels them to split up the work into a series of gestures that are easy to perform and, of course, require no effort of thought.

They eat up an incredible number of tractors, for they're incapable of performing the slightest repair. Even the Czechs, who are the most efficient of the Slavs, have no gift for invention—and yet they're hard-working and careful. When Skoda was started, it was by Austrians and Germans.

Destroy their factories, and the Russians can't rebuild them and set them working again. They can barely manage to set a factory working that works all by itself. Although they've always bought licences for the most modern aircraft, their *Rata*[207] is a flop. Their most recent models are still far from catching up with our 109.[208]

The Japanese are capable of improving something that exists already, by borrowing from left and right whatever makes it go better. At the time of the Pact, the Russians displayed a wish to possess a specification of each of our ships. We couldn't do otherwise than hand over to them inventions some of which represented for us twenty years of

---

[207] The Polikarpov I-16 Soviet fighter was nicknamed the *Rata* (the "rat" in Spanish) during the Spanish Civil War on account of its shape.

[208] The Messerschmitt Bf 109 was the standard single seater aircraft fighter of the war. It was constantly improved, and in this way remained on a more than equal basis with all the latest Allied fighter aircraft until the end of the war.

research. These peoples were always inferior to us on the cultural level. Compare the civilisation of the Greeks with what Japan or China was at the same period: it's like comparing the music of Beethoven with the screeching of a cat. In the sphere of chemistry, for example, it's been proved that everything comes to them from us. But the Japanese are at least discreet. They keep to themselves the secrets that are entrusted to them. Our two Navies have always worked in a pleasant spirit of collaboration. We owe precious information to the Japanese.

What was painful to me, was to endure the visit of the Russian commercial delegation. The Russians probably learnt the secret of the rockets by some piece of treachery committed before we took power. In fact, they've remained at the stage of technique of the period, and haven't profited by the progress we've made since. Nevertheless, they've adopted a guiding rail, which perhaps they've got from the French.

On our side, nobody in the Army knew we had the rocket. The Russians attached importance to the fact that the rocket goes off without making a noise. Our heavy rockets make such a hellish din that nobody can endure it. It has a psychological effect in addition to the material effect. There's no point in hiding the discharge of the shot from the enemy, for in any case there's no means of protecting oneself against it.

I didn't realise that ricochet firing had such a destructive effect. Keitel has always favoured that technique. A shell from one of our field-guns, which weighs only sixteen kilos, produces on the enemy the effect of a heavy shell. In the technique of armament, we shall always be superior to the others. But we ought to preserve the lesson of history and take care, after the war, not to allow the others to penetrate our secrets. No new invention will be permitted to be published without a special authorisation issued by an office set up for this purpose—even as regards countries with which we're linked by agreements.

6th January 1942, midday
The corruptive practices of Freemasonry—Daladier, Chamberlain and the warmongers—The fictitious value of gold—The catastrophe of 1940— The scapegoat

I've realised one thing. The worst of Freemasonry is not so much the philosophic side as the fact that it's an immense enterprise of corruption. It's a handful of men who are responsible for the war. Churchill's predestined opponent was Lloyd George.[209] Unfortunately, he's twenty

---

[209] David Lloyd George (1863–1945), Prime Minister of the United Kingdom from 1916 to 1922.

years too old. The critical moment was when Chamberlain and Daladier[210] returned from Munich. Both of them should have seen very clearly that the first thing to do was to dissolve their parliaments. If Daladier had organised an election, the fire-eaters would have been routed. The whole people would have approved of the peace-policy. But it was only a respite, and the agitators were not slow to raise their heads again.

England and France are engaged in losing what in our eyes is only a fictitious wealth—that is to say, gold and foreign holdings. Their true wealth, which nobody can take away from them, is their human potential (but on condition that it's used in such a way as to exploit the country's natural resources).

This war will have helped to originate one of the world's great upheavals. It will have consequences that we did not seek—for example, the dismemberment of the British Empire. Who are the guilty parties? The Jews. What happens to England is totally indifferent to them. A Hore-Belisha, who grew up in the ghetto, couldn't have the same reflexes as an Englishman.

Experience teaches us that after every catastrophe a scapegoat is found. In England, it will probably be the Jew. But let them settle that between themselves. It's not our mission to settle the Jewish question in other people's countries!

6th January 1942, evening
GUEST: GENERAL DIETL

Order and cleanliness—Pedantry of the administrative services.

In peace-time, it's necessary to govern in a spirit of economy. For that there's one condition, which is that order should prevail. Another condition, for that matter, is that cleanliness should prevail.

In every organisation, the art consists in finding a formula in which the necessary strictness of the rule is tempered by the generosity called for by the facts. We shall never completely eliminate from the administrative services the spirit of pedantry that paralyses all initiative. In important cases, we must arrange for a third authority to intervene, equipped with the necessary power of decision.

It's really moving to observe what is happening just now about the collection of wool for the Russian front. Civilians deprive themselves of their most precious possessions. But they must have the conviction

---

[210] Édouard Daladier (1884–1970), the French Radical-Socialist Prime Minister of France.

that everything is being put through without the slightest fraud, and that every object will reach its proper destination. Let anyone beware, therefore, who might try to interfere with the proper channels and intercept, for example, such-and-such a sumptuous fur, which will be worn perhaps by the simplest of our soldiers!

Night of 6th–7th January 1942
The changing of the guard at Rome—The Duce's difficulties—Check to Brauchitsch[211]

The changing of the guard at Rome is not good news, I think. In my view, too frequent changes of leading figures are a mistake. A responsible chief who knows that he probably won't have time to complete a job that he'd like to embark on, generally sticks to routine. I don't understand why one should create such situations. In that way one merely aggravates one's own troubles. The reason why I can carry the new responsibilities I am undertaking is that gradually I've been freed from certain responsibilities, by colleagues to whom I've given the chance to reveal themselves, and who've succeeded in deserving my trust. It's possible that the Duce can't find amongst his advisers the sort of collaboration he needs. For my part, I've had the luck to do so.

If Brauchitsch had remained at his post, even if only for another few weeks, the matter would have ended in catastrophe. He's no soldier, he's but a poor thing and a man of straw. Later on, people's eyes will be opened to what these four weeks were for me.[212]

7th January 1942, evening
Churchill in American pay—Separate peace with Britain—Consequences of the loss of Singapore—Frontiers between East and West—Opposition to Churchill—Japanese predominance in the Pacific—The evils of Americanism

I never met an Englishman who didn't speak of Churchill with disapproval. Never one who didn't say he was off his head.

Supposing we had lost the war right at the beginning, there would nevertheless be a hegemony on the Continent. The hegemony of Bolshevism. And that's what the English would have been fighting for! The fact that America is insisting on England's abandoning the Far East will

---

[211] Walther von Brauchitsch (1881–1948), Field Marshal and the Commander-in-Chief of the German Army from 1938 to 1941. He suffered a heart attack in November 1941 which caused his retirement.

[212] The German army had been repulsed before the gates of Moscow, the first major military reverse which Hitler had suffered.

obviously never bring about any change in Churchill's attitude towards America: the man is bought.

One thing may seem improbable, but in my view it's not impossible—that England may quit the war. As a matter of fact, if today every nation were to reckon up its own private balance, England would today still be the best off. Now, if there's one nation that has nothing to gain from this war, and may even lose everything by it, that's England.

When the English have abandoned Singapore, I don't quite see how they can face Japan with any chance of success.

Thanks to her bases, Japan dominates the sea as well as the air. The only possible hope for the English is that the Russians should help them, from Vladivostok. If the English knew they could get out of it all simply with a black eye, I believe they wouldn't hesitate for a moment. India being only a land power, she ceases to have any interest for them, on the strategic level, as soon as Singapore has fallen.

Men like Eden are no longer fighting for their pockets, but solely in the hope of saving their skins. Besides, all the guilty men are still there, except Hore-Belisha. If it turns out badly, their compatriots will have bones to pick with them.

The English were generous as long as it was only a question of distributing other people's property. Today they're not just fighting for new profits, but to try to save their Empire. Hitherto they've been able to accept things philosophically, to say that Europe was not their direct concern, that the conquered countries were not theirs. But after the fall of Singapore, everything will be different. Where, in fact, is the frontier between East and West to be laid down? Will England be in a position to hold India? That will depend on the maintenance of sea-communications, since there are no communications by land.

Churchill is a bounder of a journalist. The opposition to Churchill is in the process of gaining strength in England. His long absence has brought it on him. If a nation were to quit the war before the end of the war, I seriously think it might be England. I don't definitely say so, but it seems to me possible.

England and America have now decided to produce synthetic rubber. It's not just a matter of building factories—they also need coal! The problem will become really acute for them in the next six months. At this moment all States have similar difficulties to overcome, and are living from one day to the next. But it's certain that, for England, her present difficulties have incalculable implications. One safeguard for the future is that the Japanese should never give up the preponderance they are obtaining in the Pacific. The important question for England will be whether she can hold India. It might be possible to negotiate a separate peace which would leave India to England.

In that case, what would happen to the United States? They would be territorially intact. But one day England will be obliged to make approaches to the Continent. And it will be a German-British army that will chase the Americans from Iceland.

I don't see much future for the Americans. In my view, it's a decayed country. And they have their racial problem, and the problem of social inequalities. Those were what caused the downfall of Rome, and yet Rome was a solid edifice that stood for something. Moreover, the Romans were inspired by great ideas.

Nothing of the sort in England today. As for the Americans, that kind of thing is non-existent. That's why, in spite of everything, I like an Englishman a thousand times better than an American. It goes without saying that we have no affinities with the Japanese. They're too foreign to us, by their way of living, by their culture. But my feelings against Americanism are feelings of hatred and deep repugnance. I feel myself more akin to any European country, no matter which.

Everything about the behaviour of American society reveals that it's half Judaised, and the other half negrified. How can one expect a State like that to hold together—a State where 80 per cent of the revenue is drained away for the public purse—a country where everything is built on the dollar? From this point of view, I consider the British State very much superior.

Night of 8th–9th January 1942

Childhood memories—Religious instruction—The Abbé Schwarz—"Sit down, Hitler!"—Preparation for confession—The story of Petronella

In Austria, religious instruction was given by priests. I was the eternal asker of questions. Since I was completely master of the material, I was unassailable. I always had the best marks.

On the other hand, I was less impeccable under the heading of Behaviour. I had a particular liking for the delicate subjects in the Bible, and I took a naughty pleasure in asking embarrassing questions.

Father Schwarz, our teacher, was clever at giving me evasive answers. So I kept on insisting until he lost his patience. One day—I've forgotten with reference to what—he asked me if I said my prayers in the morning, at midday and at night.

"No, sir, I don't say prayers. Besides, I don't see how God could be interested in the prayers of a secondary schoolboy."

"Sit down, then!"

When Father Schwarz entered the classroom, the atmosphere was at once transformed. He brought revolution in with him. Every pupil took to some new occupation. For my part, I used to excite him by waving pencils in the colours of Greater Germany. "Put away those abominable colours at once!" he would say. The whole class would answer with a long howl of disapproval. Then I would get up and explain to him that it was the symbol of our national ideal.

"You should have no other ideal in your heart but that of our beloved country and our beloved house of Hapsburg. Whoever does not love the Imperial family, does not love the Church, and whoever does not love the Church, does not love God. Sit down, Hitler!"

Father Schwarz had a huge, blue handkerchief that he used to fish up from the lining of his cassock. You could hear it crackle when he spread it out. One day he had dropped it in class. During break, when he was talking with some other teachers, I went up to him holding the handkerchief at arm's length, and disguising my disgust: "Here's your handkerchief, sir." He grabbed hold of it, glaring at me. At that moment the other boys, who had gathered round me, burst out into a noisy, artificially prolonged laughter.

In the Steinstrasse, Father Schwarz had a female relative, of the same name as himself, who kept a little shop. We used to visit her in a group and ask for the silliest objects: women's bloomers, corsets, etc. Of course, she didn't stock that kind of article. We left the shop indignantly, complaining in loud voices.

Opposite the school, in the Herrengasse, there was a convent. An excellent recruit came to us from Vienna, a real scamp. He used to blow kisses to the nuns when they passed a window. One day one of them smiled back at him. At once an old prude got up and drew the curtain violently. We even heard a cry. Half an hour later, our Rector gave us a scolding, expressing his amazement at our lack of respect.

If there hadn't been a few teachers who would intercede for me on occasion, the affair would have ended badly for me. Before Easter we had lessons to prepare us for confession. It was a tremendous rag. As we had to give examples of sins to confess, we chose them in such a way as to tease Father Schwarz. One boy confessed that he had had bad thoughts about his teacher, another said he had deliberately vexed him, and so on. The priest told us we were guilty of a grave sin in not going more deeply into ourselves, and in confining ourselves to these superficial confessions. So we agreed, we would confess to a series of appalling sins.

During break I wrote out on the blackboard a terrifying confession, headed by the words: "Copy out." I was busy at work when there was a whistle. It was the signal from the boy whom we had posted to keep watch. I knocked the blackboard over and rushed to my form. The holidays went by, and everybody, including myself, forgot the matter.

At the beginning of next term, a boy was answering questions. He filled the empty side of the blackboard, which was facing him, and when he got to the bottom of the blackboard, he turned it round. The words I would written came into sight: "I have committed fleshly sin, outside of marriage. . ."

The teacher studied the handwriting, thought he recognised it as mine, and asked me if I was the author. I explained to him that this was an example of deep introspection—Father Schwarz having told us to be very precise on this subject. "You, Hitler, keep your examples to yourself. Otherwise I'll make an example of somebody . . ."

Often I promised myself to moderate my ways, but I couldn't help it, I couldn't endure all those hypocrisies. I can still see that Schwarz, with his long nose. I saw red when I looked at him. And I retorted as best I could!

One day my mother came to the school, and he took the opportunity to pounce on her and explain that I was a lost soul.

"You, unhappy boy. . ." he apostrophised me.

"But I'm not unhappy, sir."

"You'll realise you *are*, in the Next World."

"I've heard about a scientist who doubts whether there *is* a Next World."

"What do *you*[213] mean?"

"I must inform you, sir, that you are addressing me as 'thou.'"

"You won't go to Heaven."

"Not even if I buy an indulgence?"

I was very fond of visiting the cathedral. Without my realising it, this was because I liked architecture. Somebody must have informed Father Schwarz of these visits, and he supposed I went there for some secret reason. The fact was, I was full of respect for the majesty of the

[213] In German, the word "Du" means "you" and "thou."

place. One day, on leaving, I found myself face to face with the priest. "And there was I thinking you were a lost soul, my son! Now I see you're nothing of the sort."

This happened at a moment when Schwarz's opinion was not a matter of indifference to me, for it was the day before the examinations. So I carefully refrained from enlightening him. But he never knew what to think of me, and that vexed him. I had read a lot of works by free thinkers, and he knew it. When I bearded him with my ill-digested scientific knowledge, I drove him nearly out of his wits.

At Linz there was an association of "persons physically separated", for at that time not even civil divorce existed in Austria. The aforesaid organisation used to organise demonstrations against this barbarism. Public demonstrations were forbidden, but private meetings were allowed, on condition that only members of the association were present. I went to one of these meetings, signed a form of membership at the door, and was seized with virtuous indignation when I heard the speaker's account of the situation.

He described men who were models of ignominy, and whose wives, by law, could never separate from them. I at once convinced myself that it was my duty to spread the truth amongst the public, and I wrote a play on the subject. Since my writing was illegible, I dictated the play to my sister, pacing up and down in my room.

The play was divided into a number of scenes. I displayed a lofty, burning imagination. At that time I was fifteen years old. My sister said to me: "You know, Adolf, your play can't be acted." I couldn't persuade her that she was mistaken. She even persisted in her obstinacy to such a point that one day she went on strike, and that was the end of my masterpiece. But the thoughts I would had on the subject were useful as providing fuel for my conversations with Schwarz. At the first opportunity, still burning with indignation, I tackled him on the matter.

"I really don't know, Hitler, how you manage to discover such subjects."

"Because it interests me."

"It *oughtn't* to interest you. Your blessed father is dead . . ."

"But my father has nothing to do with it. It's I who am a member of the Association of Persons Physically Separated."

"You're *what*? Sit down!"

I would had Schwarz for three years. Before him (his name comes back to me now) it was Father Silizko—a great enemy of ours.

One of our teachers, a certain Koenig, had been a superintendent in charge of steam boilers. One day an explosion gave him a physical shock that expressed itself in a defective pronunciation. He could no longer pronounce the letter "h". When he read out the names of the class, at his first lesson, I pretended not to hear, although I was sitting right in front of him. He repeated it several times, but without result. When he had identified me, he asked me why I didn't answer. "My name's not Itler, sir. My name is Hitler." I've always wondered why our teachers were so careless of their persons.

At Steyr we had a Jew as teacher. One day we shut him up in his laboratory. In his class things were like in a Jewish school—everything was anarchy. This teacher had no authority at all. The boys were afraid of him at first, so it seems—because he used to howl like a madman. Unfortunately for him, one day he was caught laughing immediately after being angry. The boys realised that his bouts of anger were mere play-acting, and that was the end of his authority.

I had discovered in my landlady's house a huge scarf, which I borrowed from her. I tied it round my neck, and went to school in this rig. The teacher asked what was the matter with me, and I answered in an indistinct murmur, making him think that I couldn't speak. He was scared of a possible infection, supposing I was in very bad shape, and at once exclaimed: "Be off, be off! Go home, take care of yourself!"

I always had the habit of reading during lessons—reading books, of course, that had nothing to do with the aforesaid lessons. One day I was reading a book on diseases caused by microbes, when the teacher pounced on me, tore the book from my hands, and threw it into a corner. "You should take an example from me, and read serious works, if read you must."

Steyr was an unpleasant town—the opposite of Linz. Linz, full of national spirit. Steyr, black and red—the clergy and Marxism. I lodged with a school-companion in Grünmarkt, No. 9, in a little room overlooking the courtyard.

The boy's first name was Gustav, I've forgotten his surname. The room was rather agreeable, but the view over the courtyard was sinister. I often used to practise shooting rats from the window. Our landlady was very fond of us. She regularly took sides with us against her husband, who was a cipher[214] in his own house, so to speak. She used

---

[214] When a person is a *cipher,* it means that they are a person without power and only used by others.

to attack him like a viper. I remember the sort of quarrel they often used to have. A few days before, I had asked my landlady—very politely—to give me my breakfast coffee a little less hot, so that I should have time to swallow it before we set off. On the morning of this quarrel, I pointed out to her that it was already half-past the hour, and I was still waiting for my coffee. She argued about whether it was so late. Then the husband intervened. "Petronella," he said, "it's twenty-five to." At this remark, made by someone who had no right to speak, she blew up. Evening came, and Petronella had not yet calmed down. On the contrary, the quarrel had reached its climax.

The husband decided to leave the house, and, as usual, asked one of us to come with him—for he was afraid of the rats, and had to be shown a light. When he'd gone, Petronella bolted the door. Gustav and I said to one another: "Look out for squalls!" The husband at once injured his nose on the shut door, and politely asked his wife to open. As she didn't react, except by humming, he ordered her to do as she was told, but without any better success.

From threats he passed to the most humble supplication, and ended by addressing himself to me (who could only answer that his charming spouse had forbidden me to obey him). The result was that he spent the night out of doors, and could not return until next morning with the milk, pitiful and cowed. How Gustav and I despised the wet rag! Petronella was thirty three years old. Her husband was bearded and ageless. He was a member of the minor nobility, and worked as an employee in the service of the municipality.

At that time Austria contained a great number of noble families in straitened circumstances. I wonder whether Petronella is still alive? We were very fond of her. She looked after us in all sorts of small ways, she never missed an opportunity of stuffing our pockets with dainties. In Austria the good women who provided lodgings for students were usually called by the Latin word, *crux.*[215]

After the examinations, we organised a great party. It's the only time in my life I've been drunk. I had obtained my certificate, next day I was to leave Steyr and return to my mother. My comrades and I secretly gathered over a quart of local wine. I've completely forgotten what happened during that night. I simply remember that I was awoken at dawn, by a milk woman, on the road from Steyr to Karsten. I was in a

---

[215] In Latin, *crux* means literally an instrument of torture, often a cross, and figuratively, the torture inflicted by such an instrument.

lamentable state when I got back to the house of my *crux*. I had a bath and drank a cup of coffee. Then Petronella asked me whether I had obtained my certificate. I wanted to show it to her, I rummaged in my pockets, I turned them inside out. Not a trace of my certificate! What could I have done with it, and what was I to show my mother? I was already thinking up an explanation: I had unfolded it in the train, in front of an open window, and a gust of wind had carried it off! Petronella did not agree with me, and suggested that it would be better to ask at the school for a duplicate of the document. And, since I had drunk away all my money, she carried her kindness so far as to lend me five gulden. The director began by keeping me waiting for quite a long time. My certificate had been brought back to the school, but torn into four pieces, and in a somewhat inglorious condition. It appeared that, in the absent-mindedness of intoxication, I had confused the precious parchment with toilet paper. I was overwhelmed. I cannot tell you what the director said to me, I am still humiliated, even from here. I made a promise to myself that I would never get drunk again, and I've kept my promise. I was fifteen to sixteen years old, the age when all young people write poetry.

I liked visiting the waxworks, and I passed for choice through the door surmounted by the label *For Adults Only*. This is the age when one wants to know all, and be ignorant of nothing. I remember visiting a cinema near the Southern Station at Linz. What a horror of a film!

Speaking of the cinema, I was present once at a showing given in aid of some charity. What was curious was the choice of films, which was more than doubtful from the point of view of morals. The Austrian State was tolerant in that sphere! I found myself cheek by jowl with a teacher named Sixtel. He said to me, laughing: "So you, too, are a keen supporter of the Red Cross!" This remark seemed to me shocking.

(E. D.[216] asked whether any of Hitler's teachers had witnessed his rise to power.) Yes, some of them. I was not a model pupil, but none of them has forgotten me. What a proof of my character!

Night of 9th–10th January 1942

Health and sickness—Air travel and electoral campaigns—The Führer's plot—Travel facilities in the Eastern Territories

I haven't been sick since I was sixteen. The last time I was in bed was in 1918, in a military hospital. The fact that I've never been sick makes

---

[216] Eduard Dietl.

me think that, when an illness attacks me, it will have a more violent effect on me. I have the impression that it won't drag on and on! Only ten years ago, I could fly in an aircraft at a height of 6,000 metres without the help of oxygen. The two Dietrichs fainted. It would have been different if I would had to move, no doubt. Anyway, it was lucky that it was so, for there were never enough masks for everybody.

Another time we were flying at only 4,000 metres, but Baur had to come down with all speed to escape a storm that was beneath us. It gave me terrible headaches, which lasted all day long. That's why I greatly admire Stuka pilots.

Recently Göring expressed his dissatisfaction to me that Baur had been flying a Heinkel. He insists that Baur should always use the same type of aircraft. If he always flew a Heinkel, that would be different. As regards Baur himself, he's delighted to have the new Condor.

There is always an element of danger in flying. One is dependent, in short, on a single man. It's enough for this man to have a moment of weakness, and everything's finished. Moreover, there are the atmospheric conditions. If one's caught by ice on the wings, there's nothing to do but try a chance landing, which isn't always easy.

Formerly I used to fly all the time. Today I take care that nothing should happen to me. When the situation is easier, I'll pay less attention to the matter. I've made two landings in a fog. One comes down, and doesn't know what one might run into. Once, it was at Munich. We saw very dimly the red flares of the ground-lighting.

Baur, who has an extraordinary speed of decision, at once dived without bothering about the direction of the wind. We were in an old Rohrbach. I had the feeling that we were descending at mad speed. Suddenly the ground rose to meet us. Baur levelled out the aircraft at the very last moment. Already our wheels were down. But there was still the risk of running into an obstacle. Baur succeeded in turning within a few yards of the hangars.

Another time, we tried to put ourselves in the same situation at Bremen. At that period the Lufthansa was infested by Jews. They let me fly when it was forbidden to fly all over Reich territory. They obviously had only one wish—that I should end my career in an aircraft accident! We were coming down blindly when the ground rose up. Baur had just time to level out and thus avoid a herd of cattle.

Yet another time, we had to go through three storms in succession. It was in the direction of Brunswick. How many times we made forced landings in the fields! On the 28th of July 1932, for example, at Ulm. On another occasion, I said to Baur: "We must go, we're expected at Munich." We had no equipment for night flying. So Baur had had an improvised lighting system installed. On arriving at Munich, we wheeled around above the stadium.

It was at the time of the Papen elections, when we got our two hundred and ninety-seven seats. That same day I would had meetings at Constance, Friedrichshafen and Kempten. At the meeting in Munich, I could hardly speak. I was dizzy. As I went back home, I thought I was going to faint. I got nothing easily in those days! I remember I once spoke at Stralsund at three o'clock in the morning.

These rapid, incessant moves were due to the necessity of my speaking sometimes in great halls and sometimes in the open air, and we didn't always have a choice of dates. For example, on my birthday in 1932. The day before, I would held six meetings at Königsberg, the last ending at half-past two in the morning. I was in bed by five, and by half-past eight I was back on the airfield. A young girl of ravishing beauty offered me a nosegay, and I regarded that as a happy omen. Meetings at Schneidemühl, at Kassel, then at Göttingen, where from forty to fifty thousand people were waiting for us in the night, under torrential rain.

Next day, at three o'clock in the morning, we set out by car for Wiesbaden, Trier and Koblenz. The organisation of these round-trips was very difficult, for we had to take mainly into account the possibility of getting halls. Often I had to use a little Junker single-motor that had belonged to Sepp Dietrich. It was a rather unstable aircraft, and we were violently shaken by the bad weather. Baur once set it down on a race-course. He did better than that, for he succeeded in starting off again in black darkness.

As a matter of fact, we had no meteorological protection. My very first flight, Munich to Berlin, was so unfavourable that I spent years without entering an aircraft again.

My weakness is for motor-cars. I owe it some of the finest hours of my life. The Rhine seen from the air is no great shakes. In a car it's better. But the ideal thing is in a boat.

As regards the East, the only means of locomotion is the aircraft. Here, there's nothing to lose. When we have built our first *autobahnen*, dotted every hundred kilometres by a little town that will remind us of Germany, that will already be better. These *autobahnen* will have to be different from ours, or else the travellers will be seized by the boredom of the journey and will have crises of agoraphobia.[217] The way from Cologne to Bonn is already difficult to endure. When I go from Berlin to Munich, my fancy is continually being taken by lovely things. But a thousand kilometres over a plain, that's terrifying!

We shall have to populate that desert. The *autobahnen* of the East will have to be built on ridges, so that they'll remain clear during the winter. The wind must be able to sweep them continually.

9th January 1942, evening
Whale oil and vegetable oils

Nowadays humanity depends basically on the whale for its nourishment with fats. I gather that the number of whales in the seas of the world tends rather to fall than to increase. The East will supply us with the vegetable fats that will replace whale-oil.

10th January 1942, evening
Japan's sudden rise to wealth—Capitalist exploitation of India—The blood-sucker of widows—India or the control of Europe

Japan is in process of making itself independent in all fields. It's guaranteeing its supplies of rubber, oil, zinc, wolfram and a number of other products. Japan will be one of the richest countries in the world. What a transformation! This country that as recently as a few weeks ago was regarded as one of the poorest! There are few examples in world history of a more rapid and complete reversal of the situation.

The wealth of Great Britain is the result less of a perfect commercial organisation than of the capitalist exploitation of the three hundred and fifty million Indian slaves. The British are commended for their worldly wisdom in respecting the customs of the countries subject to them. In reality, this attitude has no other explanation than the determination not to raise the natives' standard of living. If we took India, the Indians would certainly not be enthusiastic, and they'd not be slow to regret the good old days of English rule! The climax of this cynical behaviour of the English is that it gives them the prestige of liberalism and tolerance.

The prohibition of *suttee*[218] for widows, and the suppression of starvation-dungeons, were dictated to the English by the desire not to reduce the labour-force, and perhaps also by the desire to economise wood! They set so cleverly about presenting these measures to the

---

[217] The fear of entering open or crowded places.

[218] The Indian custom of a wife immolating herself either on the funeral pyre of her dead husband or in some other fashion soon after his death.

world that they provoked a wave of admiration. That's the strength of the English: to allow the natives to live whilst they exploit them to the uttermost.

There's not a single Englishman, at this moment, who isn't thinking constantly of India. If one were to offer the English this alternative, to keep India whilst abandoning Europe to Germany, or to lose India whilst retaining the control of Europe, I'm sure that 99 per cent of them would choose to keep India. For them, India has likewise become a symbol, for it's on India that she built the Empire. Out of four hundred and fifty million subjects, the King of England has three hundred and fifty million Indians.

Confronted with America, the best we can do is to hold out against her to the end.

13th January 1942, midday
SPECIAL GUESTS: DR. PORSCHE[219] AND JACOB WERLIN[220]
The air-cooled motor

The water-cooled engine will have to disappear completely. Instead of obtaining petrol from coal by a complicated process, it's preferable to compel certain categories of users to employ vehicles equipped with gas-generators.

Night of 12th–13th January 1942
Confirmation of orders—Supply problems on the Eastern front—Making the best use of things—The suddenness of the Russian winter—An outworn political conception—European balance of power—The liar Halifax[221]—Duff-Cooper[222] and Hore-Belisha—The Indian boomerang— Mosley's[223] solution

---

[219] Ferdinand Porsche (1875–1951), the Austrian-born engineer and founder of the Porsche motor company, best known for creating the first gasoline–electric hybrid vehicle, and the Volkswagen Beetle.

[220] Jakob Werlin (1886–1965), an Austrian-born auto salesman used by the NS-DAP to purchase vehicles. An early close friend of Hitler's, he became an informal advisor to the German leader on all matters automotive.

[221] Edward Wood, 1st Earl of Halifax (1881–1959), British Foreign Secretary between 1938 and 1940, and thereafter, ambassador to the United States until 1945.

[222] Alfred Duff Cooper, 1st Viscount Norwich (1890–1954), was the British First Lord of the Admiralty from 1937 to 1938, and previously Secretary of State for War from 1935 to 1937.

[223] Oswald Mosley, (1896–1980), served in Parliament for the British Conservative, Labour and Liberal parties before founding the British Union of Fascists (BUF) in 1932.

In the *Wehrmacht* there used until now to be no obligation to confirm the carrying out of an order, except at lower levels. I've just changed that. Without this obligation, there's a risk that people may consider an order as having been carried out simply because it has been given. One must have a confirmation, so as to be quite sure.

The supplying of the front creates enormous problems. In this matter, we've given proof of the most magnificent gifts of improvisation. Amongst the unforeseen matters in which we've had to improvise was that catastrophe of the temperatures falling, in two days, from 2° below zero to 38° below. That paralysed everything, for nobody expected it. The natives themselves were surprised; they confirm that winter came on in a quite unusual fashion.

Given the present war-time conditions, one may ask whether the most competent officers should be at the front or the rear. I say they should be at the front. During the Great War, we had a total of forty thousand motorised vehicles. Today a single one of our units has as many. What was the situation eight years ago? We had seven divisions of infantry and three of cavalry. Nowadays we have nothing but armoured divisions and motorised divisions. That's why I need officers, always more officers.

In the spring of 1938, we entered Austria. On the stretch from Linz to Vienna we saw over eighty tanks immobilised by the side of the road—and yet what an easy road it was! Our men hadn't enough experience. A year later, we went into Czechoslovakia, and nothing of the sort happened.

We need a suitable organisation for the interior. We're forced to entrust some officer with responsibility for a dump of materials. Now, he may be a lieutenant of the reserve, a dentist or teacher in civil life. Naturally, these good fellows have no idea of the maintenance of material, and they have to begin by gaining their own experience. Let's not forget that the German Army has gone ahead with crazy speed. Our present difficulties are the same, in a worse form, as those we met with in 1938, during our advance on Vienna. Next winter none of that will be reproduced. We'll not see a single truck or locomotive immobilised—because of the weather, I mean.

As soon as these regions are incorporated in our rail network, we'll build locomotives adapted to local conditions. In this field I make no reproaches to anybody. Material of that sort can't be conjured up, it has to be built, but until now we had no reason to make machines designed for any other climate than our own. Even this year the winter wouldn't have caused us any difficulties if it hadn't surprised us by its suddenness. Yet it's lucky it came so suddenly, for otherwise we would have advanced another two or three hundred kilometres. In that case, the adaptation of the railway to our gauge wouldn't have been possible. In such temperatures, we're obliged to have recourse to traction by animals.

On the front at Leningrad, with a temperature of 42° below zero, not a rifle, a machine-gun or a field-gun was working, on our side. But we've just received the oil we unfortunately lacked two months ago.

We lack two things: a fur helmet and a celluloid mask. Göring tells me that he knew, because he'd used them when shooting, the warming bags one finds on Russian soldiers.

How long have I been clamouring for an air-cooled motor? But it's like talking to a wall. The thickest wall of all is human stupidity. The military were against it, in the same way as they were against the Volkswagen, at first. What a price the special petrol for starting up our engines is now costing us. It goes without saying that it would be different if we had under every bonnet a heater working by catalysis. I gave an order for them, it will be forbidden in future to build engines except with air-cooling.

Almost everything we lack today, we already had in the Great War. It's strange to see how quickly a human being forgets. Everything has to be constantly re-invented.

Churchill is a man with an out-of-date political idea—that of the European balance of power. It no longer belongs to the sphere of realities. And yet it's because of this superstition that Churchill stirred England up to war. When Singapore falls, Churchill will fall, too; I'm convinced of it.

The policy represented by Churchill is to nobody's interest, in short, but that of the Jews. But *that* people was chosen by Jehovah because of its stupidity. The last thing that their interest should have told the Jews to do was to enter into this war.

All that they'll have gained by it is to be chased out of Europe, for the longer the war lasts, the more violently the peoples will react against them.

At the bottom of all this upheaval are a few imbeciles. In fact, one must see things as they are. What *is* that Moroccan Jew whom Great Britain made a Minister of War? The generals finally broke him—as

Wavell[224] has just done to Duff-Cooper. I regard Halifax as a hypocrite of the worst type, as a liar. On the whole, it's visible that sympathy between the English and Americans is not booming. On the side of the English, it's antipathy that's booming, in fact. But for Japan's intervention in the war, their accounts would have balanced, but now it's definitely England who's paying for the broken crockery.

Will fine speeches from Roosevelt be enough to make up for the loss of India? I don't think the Japanese will embark on the conquest of India. They'll surely confine themselves to blockading it. And if their communications with India are broken, what will be the gain for the English in being still masters there? Besides, their position is very peculiar. There are three hundred and fifty thousand of them, to govern three hundred and fifty million people. If suddenly the three hundred and fifty millions declare they won't fight any more, what are the English to do? I suppose that in Germany, at the time of the Weimar Republic, the General Strike would have been rigorously applied—what could an army of a hundred thousand men have done against that?

There are no bloody insurrections in India today, but the difficulty for the Indians is to reconcile the divergent interests of such a diverse population. How are the princes and the Brahmins, the Hindus and the Mussulmans, all these hierarchised and partitioned castes to be combined in a common front? If a British newspaper in India writes an article today attacking Churchill, that's because it can't do anything else—or it would lose its whole public. The Press doesn't give an exact picture of the reality. In India, revolt is an endemic condition.

Gandhi tried to succeed by pacific methods, but whatever be the methods chosen, the Indians are unanimous in their desire to shake off the British yoke. Some of them would like to try Bolshevism for that purpose, others would like to try us.

Others would prefer to owe nothing to the foreigner. For all, the object is the same, it's liberty—and nobody cares about the state of anarchy that will follow in India upon the departure of the English.

When one treats a people as the English have continually treated the Indians, the unpardonable folly is to send the youth of the country

---

[224] Archibald Percival Wavell, 1st Earl Wavell, (1883–1950), British Field Marshal and Commander-in-Chief Middle East, until 1941, and thereafter Commander-in-Chief, India until June 1943. Duff Cooper, then Minister Resident in Singapore, was recalled to London after Wavell was appointed head of Allied forces in South East Asia.

to the universities, where it learns things that it would be better for it not to know. After all, Singapore is not Crete. I try to imagine what *we* would do if such a blow fell on us. But there's no means of comparison, for we don't possess a world-wide empire.

How are they going to react to that? Of course, they have in reserve men like Mosley. When I think that Mosley and more than nine thousand of his supporters—including some belonging to the best families—are in prison because they didn't want this war! Mark my words, Bormann, I'm going to become very religious.

Bormann: "You've always been very religious."

I'm going to become a religious figure. Soon I'll be the great chief of the Tartars. Already Arabs and Moroccans are mingling my name with their prayers. Amongst the Tartars I shall become Khan. The only thing of which I shall be incapable is to share the sheiks' mutton with them. I'm a vegetarian, and they must spare me from their meat. If they don't wait too long, I'll fall back on their harems!

13th January 1942, evening
SPECIAL GUESTS: FIELD-MARSHAL LEEB[225] AND TERBOVEN

Pro-German Czechs and the adherents of Benea—Czechs in the Austro-Hungarian Empire—Hácha[226] and Morell's[227] inoculation

I know the Czechs. At present they're very undecided. Some of them would like an understanding with Germany. The others are supporters of Beneš.[228] A weak policy in Czechoslovakia would be the equivalent on our part to a deliberate hunt for disaster. If the Austrian State had acted energetically towards them, it would have avoided dismemberment. My first intervention dates two and a half years back. We had to shoot nine agitators and send two thousand five hundred people into concentration camps. Order was restored instantly.

The Czechs' behaviour towards the old Austria was a complete expression of the meaning of the phrase: "passive resistance". The most impertinent are always those who are treated with the greatest respect.

---

[225] Wilhelm von Leeb (1876–1956), a Field Marshall who commanded armies in France and the Soviet Union.

[226] Emil Hácha (1872–1945), president of Czechoslovakia from 1938 to 1939, and then president of the German Protectorate of Bohemia and Moravia. He was murdered by Soviet agents in 1945.

[227] Theodor Morell (1886–1948), Hitler's personal physician.

[228] Edvard Beneš (1884–1948), president of Czechoslovakia from 1935 to 1938, and again from 1945 to 1948.

In their eyes, consideration is a sign of weakness or stupidity. I would rather be regarded as a brute than as an idiot.

I'm convinced that the Czechs will end by regarding Hácha as one of the greatest political figures in their history! In 1939 I gave them an ultimatum by the terms of which they had until six o'clock to accept my proposals—otherwise German aircraft would be over Prague. I would have irremediably lost face if I would had to put this threat into execution, for at the hour mentioned fog was so thick over our airfields that none of our aircraft could have made its sortie. At three o'clock the meeting with Hácha was over. He informed his Government, and three-quarters of an hour later we were notified that the order had been carried out. German troops would enter Czechoslovakia without striking a blow.

The Czechs had their army well under control. The order sent by Hácha had been framed by my advisers. Hácha's visit caused me concern, for he was a very fragile old gentleman.

Imagine the uproar in the foreign press if anything had happened to him! In the morning he was animated by a spirit of resistance that contrasted with his usual behaviour. He especially opposed the idea that his Minister of Foreign Affairs should countersign our agreement.

I said to myself: "Look out! Here's a lawyer I have facing me." Perhaps there was an arrangement in Czechoslovakia giving the force of a law only to an agreement of this sort if it was countersigned by the Minister in question? On the following day, in Prague, Hácha asked me what we had done to make such a different man of him. He was himself astonished to have suddenly shown such obstinacy. It was probably the result of the injection Morell had given him to build him up again. His renewed energy turned against us! At present I receive from Hácha the warmest messages of sympathy. I don't publish them, so as not to create the impression that we need the support of an underdog.

Night of 13th–14th January 1942
The composer Bruckner[229]—Brahms at his height—Wagner and Göring—
Great architects—Talent must be encouraged

After a hearing of Bruckner's Seventh Symphony: This work is based on popular airs of upper Austria. They're not textually reproduced, but repeatedly I recognise in passing Tyrolean dances of my youth. It's wonderful what he managed to get out of that folklore. As it happened,

---

[229] Josef Anton Bruckner (1824–1896), an Austrian composer whose music was particularly popular in Nazi Germany.

it's a priest to whom we must give the credit for having protected this great master.

The Bishop of Linz used to sit in his cathedral for hours at a time, listening to Bruckner play the organ. He was the greatest organist of his day. One can imagine this obscure peasant's arrival in Vienna, amidst an effete society. One of Bruckner's opinions of Brahms was published in a newspaper recently, and further increased the sympathy I felt for him: "Brahms's music is very beautiful, but I prefer my own." There you have the self-awareness, full both of humility and of pride, such as a peasant can feel, in all simplicity, when he is inspired by a true conviction.

The critic Hanslick[230] depicted Bruckner's life in Vienna as a real hell for him. When the moment came when it was no longer possible to ignore his work, he was covered with decorations and overwhelmed with honours. What did all that mean to him? Wouldn't it have been better not to have misunderstood him so long? Jewry had raised Brahms to the pinnacle. He was lionised in the *salons* and was a pianist of theatrical gestures. He exploited effects of the hands, effects of the beard and hair. Compared with him, Bruckner was a man put out of countenance, an abashed man.

Wagner also had the feeling for gesture, but with him it was innate. Wagner was a man of the Renaissance—like Göring in a certain aspect (and it would be silly to blame him).

There is nothing crueller than to live in a milieu that has no understanding for a work already achieved or in process of gestation. When I think of a man like Schiller[231] or Mozart![232] Mozart who was flung, nobody knows where, into a communal grave . . . What ignominy! If I hadn't been there to prevent it, I believe the same thing would have happened to Troost.[233] That man revolutionised the art of building. Perhaps it would have taken a few years—and he'd have died without anyone having the slightest idea of his genius. When I got to know him, he was depressed, embittered, disgusted with life. It often happens that ar-

---

[230] Eduard Hanslick (1825–1904), chief music critic of the *Neue Freie Presse*.
[231] Friedrich von Schiller (1759–1805), playwright, poet, and philosopher.
[232] Wolfgang Amadeus Mozart (1756–1791), one of the Classical music period's most famous and prolific composers. He was buried in an unmarked commoner's grave at the St. Marx Cemetery in Vienna.
[233] Paul Ludwig Troost (1878–1934), Hitler's favourite neoclassical architect who designed many of the most striking early buildings in Nazi Germany.

chitects are hypersensitive people. Think merely of Hansen,[234] who was the most richly gifted of the architects of Vienna. And Hasenauer?[235] The critics had attacked him so savagely that he committed suicide before his great work was finished—and yet the Vienna opera-house, so marvellously beautiful, puts the Paris *Opéra* into the shade. To know that one is capable of doing things that nobody else can do—and to have no possibility of giving proof of it! It seems that people should make sacrifices for their great men as a matter of course. A nation's only true fortune is its great men.

A great man is worth a lot more than a thousand million in the State's coffers. A man who's privileged to be the Head of a country couldn't make a better use of his power than to put it at the service of talent. If only the Party will regard it as its main duty to discover and encourage the talents! It's the great men who express a nation's soul. I had extraordinary luck, but the German people had even more. The seven infantry divisions and three cavalry divisions of 1933 would not have stopped the tidal wave from the East!

15th January 1942, evening
Churchill's return from U.S.A.—Miracles don't happen—Over-population and vaccination

On his return to England, Churchill will have no difficulty in getting round the House of Commons—but the people whose fortunes are in India won't let the wool be pulled over their eyes. Already an English newspaper is so bold as to write: "Send everything to India, without bothering about Russia or North Africa."

Nowadays the possessing class has only one idea: "How are we to save the Empire?" It's not impossible that a miracle may take place and England may withdraw from the war. A year ago she could have made

---

[234] Theophil Edvard von Hansen (1813–1891), a Danish-born architect who became an Austrian citizen. He designed many now famous buildings in Vienna and Athens, including the Austrian Parliament Building and the Academy of Athens.
[235] Baron Karl von Hasenauer (1833–1894), a neo-Baroque architect responsible for many famous designs in Vienna including the Maria-Theresia Memorial, the "Kunsthistorisches Museum" (Museum of Art History), the Burgtheater, and the "Neue Hofburg." He did not commit suicide, and also was not the architect of the Vienna Opera House. That building was designed by Eduard van der Null (1812–1868) and August Sicard von Sicardsburg (1813–1868). It was Van der Null hanged himself after the building was criticized by Emperor Franz Josef I and in the press. It is unclear if this was indeed an uncharacteristic error by Hitler on his favourite topic, or merely a transcription error.

peace and retained all her prestige. In this war, in the event of victory, only America will gain an advantage. In the event of defeat, it's England who will be the only loser.

I read today that India at present numbers three hundred and eighty-eight million inhabitants, which means an increase of fifty-five millions during the last ten years. It's alarming. We are witnessing the same phenomenon in Russia. The women there have a child every year. The chief reason for this increase is the reduction in mortality due to the progress made by the health services. What are our doctors thinking of? Isn't it enough to vaccinate the whites? So much the worse for the whites who won't let themselves be vaccinated! Let 'em croak! All the same, because of these people's fixed ideas, we can't sterilise all the natives.

Bormann put in that of the fifty families in Obersalzberg, twenty-four had children in 1941.

That brings us close to the Russian birth-rate! I've always said that the only problem for us is the housing problem. The children will come of themselves. A great convenience for the parents is blocks of buildings with communal gardens inside, where the children can play freely and still be under supervision.

It's no longer possible to leave them on the road. When they're all together, it's easier to make social beings of them. At Regensburg I saw a settlement teeming with children. In Germany, likewise, the birth-rate is rising.

Night of 15th–16th January 1942
Nowhere without influence in old Austria—Corruption in the old days—A woman of genius—The Arts must be protected

In the old Austria, nothing could be done without patronage. That's partly explained by the fact that nine million Germans were in fact rulers, in virtue of an unwritten law, of fifty million non-Germans. This German ruling class took strict care that places should always be found for Germans. For them this was the only method of maintaining themselves in this privileged situation. The Balts of German origin behaved in the same way towards the Slav population.

One got absolutely nothing in Austria without letters of introduction. When I arrived in Vienna, I had one to Roller,[236] but I didn't use

---

[236] Alfred Roller (1864–1935), an Austrian painter, graphic designer, and chief stage designer to the Vienna State Opera.

it. If I would presented myself to him with this introduction, he'd have engaged me at once. No doubt it's better that things went otherwise. It's not a bad thing for me that I had to have a rough time of it.

In the old days there was ten times as much corruption as today. The difference is that one didn't talk about it. When we condemn a swindler, it's not necessary to take that as an occasion for loud shouts. We haven't any endemic disease, only particular cases.

I'm convinced of the necessity of the Führer's not having protégés and not admitting any system of favouritism around him. I myself have never had recourse to it. I owe it to my job to be absolutely deaf in that respect. Otherwise where would we go? I'll take a case, for example, in which I might spontaneously have the intention of doing something for someone. It would be sufficient for one of the people near to me to propose something similar, and I would be obliged to give up my idea, for people might suppose I wasn't acting freely, and I don't want to create the impression that it's possible to have influence with me.

In the *Wehrmacht* it takes five days for an order from me to be translated into action. In the Party, everything is done quickly and simply. It's in the Party that we find our power of action.

If the Italians had succeeded in former times in getting their hands on the Erzberg,[237] their requirements of iron-ore would have been covered for two hundred years to come. Those are the strategic reserves that drove them in that direction. I think the world's stocks of iron-ore will run out. But we already possess light metals that are harder than steel. Coal will run out, too. We'll replace it by other natural forces: air and water.

Two dangerous trades: the miner's and the sailor's.

It's claimed that women have no creative genius. But there's one extraordinary woman, and it irritates me that men don't do her justice. Angelica Kauffmann[238] was a very great painter. The most illustrious of her own contemporaries admired her.

For Linz Museum I can think of only one motto: "To the German people, that which belongs to it."

---

[237] Erzberg is still Austria's largest iron ore mine, located in Styria. Hitler is referring to the First World War, when the Italian army unsuccessfully attempted to invade Austria.

[238] Maria Anna Angelika Kauffmann (1741–1807), a Swiss-Austrian neoclassical painter who worked in London and Rome. Her themes were mainly classical history or mythology.

The Munich Pinakothek is one of the most magnificent achievements in the world. It's the work of one man. What Munich owes to Ludwig I[239] is beyond computing. And what the whole German people owes to him! The palace of the Uffizi at Florence does honour not to Florence alone, but to all Italy.

I must do something for Königsberg. With the money Funk has given me, I shall build a museum in which we shall assemble all we've found in Russia. I'll also build a magnificent opera house and a library.

I propose to unify the museums of Nuremberg. That will result in a wonderful collection. And I'll have a new Germanic Museum built in that city. On the present sites, I'm always afraid a fire may break out.

During the past century, the German people has had pleasure from the museums of Berlin, Munich, Dresden, Vienna and Kassel. There's nothing finer than to offer the nation monuments dedicated to culture.

I also want to see to the new Trondheim.

In time, wars are forgotten. Only the works of human genius are left.

Night of 16th–17th January 1942

A wild region—The discovery of Obersalzberg—The adventures of Dietrich Eckart—Hitler incognito—Reunions at Passau and Berchtesgaden—Local stories—The construction of the Berghof—First Christmas at Obersalzberg—Journey to Buxtehude—A providential fire—Dietrich Eckart, mentor—Picturesque quarrels—The first of the Faithful

The Hochlenzer[240] was built in 1672. It's a region where there are traces of very ancient habitation. There's a reason for that, for through here passed the old salt route that led from Hallein to Augsburg, passing through Salzburg and Berchtesgaden.

Hallthurm was a landmark on this route. I don't suppose our ancestors considered this region very inviting. Every year, about Christmas, the children rig themselves out in terrifying masks—a survival of a period when people thought that in this way they could chase away evil spirits.

Bad spirits gather in wild and desolate regions! Imagine this narrow road, where the traders obliged to pass that way lived in constant fear of attack, either by wild beasts or by brigands. They needed a whole day to cover a distance that today takes us twenty minutes.

---

[239] Ludwig I (1786–1868), King of Bavaria from 1825 until 1848.
[240] The Gasthof (Guesthouse) Hochlenzer at Berchtesgaden was often visited by Hitler before he settled in the area.

In the spot where I have my house, there was nothing before 1917. Nothing but fields. I think it was in 1917 that the Winter family, of Buxtehude, built the little house on whose site I built mine.

The visit to Obersalzberg that made the keenest impression on me was the visit I made at the time when my house was being built. It was my first for several months, and I was full of the excitement of discovery. The main work had only just been finished.

The dimensions of the house made me somewhat afraid it would clash with the landscape. I was very glad to notice that, on the contrary, it fitted in very well. I had already restricted myself for that reason—for, to my taste, it should have been still bigger.

The house that belonged to Cornelius, *Sonnenköpfl,*[241] was celebrated. The Bechsteins[242] wanted me to acquire it. But I set too much store by the view in the direction of Salzburg, perhaps out of nostalgia for my little fatherland. Moreover, it's too warm in summer at *Sonnenköpfl.* The *Berghof*[243] has a truly ideal situation. How I would like to be up there! It will be a glorious moment when we can climb up there again. But how far away it is, terribly far!

To put it briefly, it was Dietrich Eckart who introduced me to Obersalzberg. There was a warrant out for his arrest, and we were seeking to hide him.

First of all he'd taken refuge at Munich, with the Lauböcks.[244] But he couldn't resist the temptation to telephone right and left. Already by the second day, he was clamouring that his girl-friend Anna should go and visit him. "I'm incapable of hiding," he used to say.

We decided to fetch him back to his home. As a precautionary measure, patrols of ours used to watch the house. Here and there one could see the silhouette of a policeman sticking up, but they were too cowardly to embroil themselves with us. Christian Weber[245] came to see me

---

[241] Carl Maria Cornelius (1868–1945), a renowned art historian. His summer residence on the *Sonnenköpfl* was sold in 1935 for financial reasons.

[242] The Bechstein family—most famous for their pianos which are still manufactured to the present day—were ardent supporters of Hitler. Helene Bechstein (1876–1951) was a close friend of Hitler, and the family's residence at the Obersalzberg was frequently used by Hitler and other leading NSDAP members.

[243] Hitler's own house at the Obersalzberg, destroyed completely after the war.

[244] Theodor Lauböck (1874- ?) a Reich railways employee and founder of the first NSDAP organisation in Rosenheim, Bavaria.

[245] Christian Weber (1883–1945), SS-Brigadeführer and important party man in Munich.

and tell me about the Büchners[246] of Obersalzberg, whom I didn't yet know. Weber had been their paying guest, and he thought it would be just the place for hiding Dietrich Eckart. The Büchners ran the pension Moritz.

One day Röhm[247] telephoned to me, asking me to go and see him immediately at the office of our military administration. There was a "wanted persons" service there that functioned in parallel with that of the civil police. Röhm told me that an attempt would be made to arrest Eckart during the night, and he advised me to take him elsewhere. I would myself observed that the house was beginning to be hemmed in by policemen. A little later in the day I learnt from Röhm that all the roads round Munich had been barred. "Take him to the English Garden,"[248] he told me. "There you'll find a *Reichswehr* vehicle that I'm putting at his disposal."

I commented to Röhm that Eckart would certainly not consent to depart by himself. "So much the better," said Röhm. "It will be excellent if the vehicle is full." I went to see Drexler,[249] and asked him if he would like to go off for a few weeks with Dietrich Eckart.

He was enthusiastic at the proposal. Eckart began by jibbing at the idea, but in the evening he let himself be led off. All this happened during the winter 1922–1923. So they went up to Obersalzberg, where there was still a lot of snow. I've had no details of that journey.

Next day the police came to my house. They knew nothing, of course. That reminds me that we used to treat these police fellows very rudely.

When we were telephoning, and suspected that the line was tapped, we used to exclaim at once: "Good God, another of these chimpanzees taking an interest in us!"

---

[246] Bruno Büchner (1871–1943), owner and manager of the Platterhof Hotel on the Obersalzberg, and used occasionally by Hitler.

[247] Ernst Röhm (1887–1934), early NSDAP member and co-founder of the SA ("Brownshirts"). Although initially a close ally of Hitler, Röhm was an integral part of the 1934 plot to overthrow the German leader and replace him with a more "socialist" program. He was arrested and executed in 1934 in the so-called "Night of the Long Knives."

[248] The *Englischer Garten* is a large public park in the centre of Munich.

[249] Anton Drexler (1884–1942), the founder and first leader of the German Workers' Party (DAP), the party which became the Party (NSDAP). Hitler replaced him as leader, and Drexler appointed to the symbolic position of honorary president. He left the party in 1923 and only rejoined in 1933.

Christian Weber gave us news regularly. All that I knew was that they were in a boarding-house somewhere near Berchtesgaden.

One day in April I went to Berchtesgaden, accompanied by my young sister. I told her that I had to have an interview on the mountain, and I asked her to wait for me. I set off on foot with Weber. The path rose sharply, and went on and on: a narrow path, through the snow. I asked Weber whether he took me for a chamois, and threatened to turn back and return by day. Then we found a house before us, the Pension Moritz.[250]

Weber said to me: "No knocks at the door; we can go in." As a precaution, we had not announced ourselves. Eckart, brought from his bed, came to meet us in his nightshirt, displaying heels bristling with hair like barbed-wire. He was very much moved.

I asked Eckart at what hour I should get up next day in order to admire the landscape. He told me that it was marvellous at 7.30. He was right—what a lovely view over the valley! A countryside of indescribable beauty.

Eckart was already downstairs. He introduced me to the Büchners: "This is my young friend, Herr Wolf." Nobody could think of forming any connection between this person and that crazy monster Adolf Hitler. Eckart was known at the boarding-house under the name of Dr. Hoffmann. At midday he took me to the *Türken* inn,[251] promising me a genuine goulash. He was addressed there as "Herr Doktor", but I saw at once that everybody knew his real identity. When I mentioned this to him, he answered that there were no traitors in Obersalzberg.

After a meeting at Freilassing, he had spoken under the name of Hoffmann, but during the speech he had become carried away by passion and had so far forgotten himself as to say: "What's that nonsense you're telling me? Why, I'm better informed than you are. I'm Dietrich Eckart!"

I didn't stay there long, and went back to Munich. But every time I had a few free days, I used to return up there. We often went on excursions. Once we were caught in the Purtscheller hut by a terrible storm, so fierce we thought the hut was about to fly away. Dietrich Eckart cursed: "What folly to have shut myself up in such a wretched shanty!"

Another time, Büchner took Eckart on his motor-cycle. I can still see them climbing at full speed the stiff, winding path to Obersalz-

---

[250] To be renamed as the Platterhof.
[251] The Hotel zum Türken on the Obersalzberg.

berg. What a team! A day came when it was impossible to keep Eckart at the boarding-house any longer. People were saying everywhere that a horde of policemen was coming to pick him up. One afternoon we moved him into Göll's little house. As he always did when he moved, he took with him his bed and his coffee-grinder.

I had become immediately attached to Obersalzberg. I would fallen in love with the landscape. The only people who knew who I was were the Büchners, and they'd kept the secret. All the others thought of me as Herr Wolf. So it was very amusing to hear what people said at table about Hitler.

I would decided to go to Passau for a meeting. Our boarding house had a customer accompanied by a very pretty wife. We were chatting together, and suddenly he said to me: "I've come from Holstein as far as Berchtesgaden. I refuse to miss the opportunity of seeing this man Hitler. So I'm going to Passau."

It seemed to me that this was a bad omen for me, and that I would lose my incognito. I told him I was going there, too, and offered to take him in my car. When we reached Passau, a car was waiting for me. I went ahead and warned my friends that I was Herr Wolf, asking them to avoid any gaffes with the braggart whom I was leaving in their care. I invited the braggart to come into the meeting with my friends, telling him I would join him in the hall. The fact was that I had to take off the overalls hiding my uniform.

I immediately recognised my man by his stupidly scarred face, lost in the confused uproar of the hall. When he saw me mount the platform and begin to speak, he fixed his eyes upon me as if I were a ghost. The meeting ended in a terrible brawl, in the course of which Schreck was arrested. I took my companion back to Obersalzberg. He was dumbfounded. I begged him to keep my secret, telling him that if I were recognised I should be obliged to change my place of refuge, and that this would be a great vexation. He gave me his word.

On the way back, it was Göring who was at the wheel. He drove like a madman. On a bend, before we arrived at Tittmoning, we suddenly found ourselves on a dung-heap. Maurice took over the wheel again, and drove us back to Berchtesgaden without further obstacle.

Next day I could see, from the way the braggart's wife had of staring at me, that he had spoken to her. But towards the others he had been entirely discreet. For a long time a meeting had been arranged at Berchtesgaden. The moment came when it was no longer possible to avoid it. "German Day at Berchtesgaden. Present: Comrade Adolf Hitler." Great sensation at Obersalzberg. The whole boarding-house, forty to fifty people in all, came down into the valley to see the phenomenon. Dinner-time had been advanced so that they could arrive punctually.

I came down by motor-cycle. At the Crown inn, I was welcomed by a formidable ovation. All my boarding-house was gathered in front of the door—but the good people were in no way surprised, being convinced that every new arrival was greeted in this vociferous fashion. When I climbed on the platform, they stared at me as if I would gone mad. When they became aware of the reality, I saw that it was driving them out of their minds.

When Wolf returned to the boarding-house, the atmosphere there was poisoned. Those who had spoken ill of Adolf Hitler in my hearing were horribly embarrassed. What a pity! The pleasant period was when my features weren't known, and I could travel in peace all over the Reich. What a pleasure it was for me to be mistaken for no matter whom!

One of my first escapades after my emergence from prison, in 1925, consisted in a visit to Berchtesgaden. I told the Büchners that I had work to do and needed absolute quiet. I accordingly installed myself in the small annexe.

Then the Büchners went away. I shall always follow their fortunes with interest. I judge people according to how they treated us at the period of our struggle. The Büchners were admirable to us at a time when we were weak. Büchner was a very nice fellow, and his wife was a person full of energy. They gave way, in 1926 or 1927, to Dressel, a Saxon. What a change! Dressel was horribly lazy, his house was ill-kept, his food uneatable. A drunken brother-in-law into the bargain.

The café was kept by a charming girl, who today works with Amann, and whom Dressel mistreated. She was the daughter of a porcelain-manufacturer, Hutschenreuther, whose business had turned out badly. What a relief for her when Amann got her out of there! Dressel even withheld from his staff the 10 per cent for service to which they were entitled. All this was so disgusting that we decided not to stay there any longer. After that I stayed at the *Marineheim*. The Bechsteins were there, and had begged me to keep them company. But the atmosphere was intolerable. The Bechsteins, who were people of the world, themselves admitted it. A society entirely lacking in naturalness, characters swollen with pretentiousness, the quintessence of everything that revolts us! After the incident of Herr Modersohn's luggage, I went away. I couldn't remain any longer in a house inhabited by such puppets. Then I selected the *Deutsche Haus* in Berchtesgaden. I lived there for nearly two years, with breaks. I lived there like a fighting-cock. Every day I went up to Obersalzberg, which took me two and a half hours' walking there and back. That's where I wrote the second volume of my book. I was very fond of visiting the *Dreimäderlhaus,* where there were always pretty girls. This was a great treat for me. There was one of them, especially, who was a real beauty.

In 1928 I learnt that the *Wachenfeld* house would be coming up to let. I thought this would be an excellent solution, and I decided to go and look at it. Nobody was there. Old Rasp, whom I met there, told me that the two ladies had just gone out. Winter, who had had the house built, was at that time a big industrialist in Buxtehude. He'd given it his wife's maiden name, *Wachenfeld.*

The two ladies came back. "Excuse me, ladies. You are the proprietors of this house. I've been told that you wanted to let it."

"You are Herr Hitler? We are members of the Party."

"Then we are wonderfully suited."

"Come in, come and have a cup of coffee." Then I visited the house, and was completely captivated. We at once came to an agreement. The proprietors were delighted to let the entire house by the year, for a hundred marks a month. They considered that I was doing them a service in not leaving the house empty. They were so kind as to add that, in the event of sale, which was improbable, they would give me the first option.

I immediately rang up my sister in Vienna with the news, and begged her to be so good as to take over the part of mistress of the house. Since my sister was often alone, with a little servant-girl, I procured two watch-dogs for her. Nothing ever happened to her.

I went once to Buxtehude. Since I would invested a lot of money in the house, I wanted a price, against the event of sale, to be fixed before a lawyer. The most agreeable thing for me would have been to buy at once, but Frau Winter couldn't make up her mind to sell the house, which she had from her late husband.

We had arrived by car from Hamburg. When I asked where was the Winter factory, I was told that it had burned down precisely the night before. I told myself that I would come at the proper moment. I visited Frau Winter in her house. I was received at first by her daughter. The mother came, beaming: "What a coincidence!" she said. "*You* arrive, and the factory was burnt down last night. Two pieces of luck!" The fact was that during the inflation, two Jews had bought the factory for nothing, profiting by a widow's weakness.

She added: "This is such a good day for me that I agree to sell you the house." She led me in front of a photograph: "Look at this scamp!" she said. "For three weeks he's been with the Army, and I've had no letter from him."

I tried to explain to her that perhaps the young man was on manoeuvres and unable to write. She was delighted that I would supplied her with a pretext for regarding herself as having been unjust to the boy. I was entirely subjugated by this adorable old lady of eighty. She reminded me of Frau Hoffmann—only taller, thinner and more alert.

I went for a short walk with the old lady, and learnt that she had the right to dwell only in the house belonging to the factory. By good luck, although the lightning had struck the factory, the living-house had been spared! That's how I became a property owner at Obersalzberg.

Yes, there are so many links between Obersalzberg and me. So many things were born there, and brought to fruition there. I've spent up there the finest hours of my life. My thoughts remain faithful to my first house. It's there that all my great projects were conceived and ripened. I had hours of leisure, in those days, and how many charming friends! Now it's stultifying hard work and chains. All that's left to me now is these few hours that I spend with you every night.

For the baroness, I was somebody interesting. Eckart had introduced me as follows: "Here's a young friend who one day will be a very important man." How she wanted to know what I did! I told her I was a writer.

How I loved going to see Dietrich Eckart in his apartment in the Franz Josephsstrasse. What a wonderful atmosphere in his home! How he took care of his little Anna! When he died, she told me with all the tears of bitterness that she would never again meet a man as disinterested as he was.

We've all taken a step forward on the road of existence, and we could no longer picture to ourselves exactly what Dietrich Eckart was for us. He shone in our eyes like the polar star. What others wrote was so flat. When he admonished someone, it was with so much wit. At the time, I was intellectually a child still on the bottle. But what comforted me was that, even with him, it hadn't all sprouted of itself—that everything in his work was the result of a patient and intelligent effort. There are things I wrote ten years ago that I can no longer read. Our society, at the boarding-house, was composed of Dietrich Eckart, with his girl-friend, Anna, of Gansser, the Baroness Abegg,[252] Esser, Heinrich Hoff-mann and Drexler.

I remember bringing up from Berchtesgaden, in a basket, a bust acquired by the Baroness that everybody attributed to Donatello. I re-gretted the sweat it cost me all the more since, when I dragged it from the basket, it proved to be a bad copy in clay.

We often spent agreeable evenings in the *Deutsche Haus,* sometimes in the café, sometimes in one or other of our rooms. Gansser used to fill the house with the booming of his voice and his Bavarian accent. He scented traces of plots everywhere.

Miezel was a delightful girl. At this period I knew a lot of women. Several of them became attached to me. Why, then, didn't I marry? To leave a wife behind me? At the slightest imprudence, I ran the risk of going back to prison for six years. So there could be no question of marriage for me. I therefore had to renounce certain opportunities that offered themselves.

Dr. Gansser[253] deserves eternal gratitude from the Party. I owe him a whole series of very important relationships. If I hadn't, thanks to him, made the acquaintance of Richard Frank—the wheat man—I wouldn't have been able to keep the *Beobachter* going in 1923.

The same is true of Bechstein. For months I travelled in his car when it was loaded with dynamite. He used to say, to calm me: "I can't use any other chauffeur, for this one is so completely stupid that I can say anything at all in front of him. If he runs into another car, it can't be helped; up in the air we'll go!"

When it was a question of setting off on a journey, Eckart was the most precise man on earth, Gansser the most imprecise. Eckart would arrive at the station an hour and a half before the train's departure. Gansser was never there.

Eckart used to say to me: "Have you any news of Gansser? I'm afraid he's late again. You—don't go away, or I'll be left alone!" The train would be leaving the platform when we would see Gansser, overflowing with his luggage, having traversed the whole train after having succeeded

---

[252] Claire von Abegg, born Frerichs, (1874–1935), an early supporter of Hitler, left her property to the NSDAP when she died.

[253] Emil Gansser (1874 1941), an explosives expert who worked for Siemens, and an early Reichstag party member.

in bringing off a flying leap into the last carriage. Eckart would apostrophise him: "You, you're a man born after his time. That explains everything!"

Eckart was born a Protestant. When he was with Gansser, he used to defend Catholicism. "But for Luther, who gave Catholicism new vigour, we would have finished with Christianity much sooner." Gansser, as a pastor's son, used to defend Luther.

One day Eckart brought their traditional dispute to the following conclusion: "I must tell it to you now. You're merely a sub-product of Protestant sexuality—that is to say, of a sexuality that's not at ease in good society."

I had a great number of loyal supporters in Munich. They had everything to lose, by adopting this position, and nothing to win. To-day, when I happen to meet one of them, it moves me extraordinarily. They showed a truly touching attachment towards me. Small stall keepers of the markets used to come running to see me "to bring a couple of eggs to Herr Hitler".

There were important ones like Pöschl, Fuess and Gahr, but also quite small men, whom today I find much aged. I'm so fond of these unpretentious fellows. The others, the ten thousand of the elite, whatever they do is the result of calculation.

Some of them see me as an attraction to their drawing rooms, others seek various advantages. Our newspaper-sellers were often boycotted and beaten up. One of our most faithful supporters, since 1920, was old Jegg. My happiest memories are of this time. The attachment I then felt to the people has never left me.

There are such bonds joining me to them that I can share in their troubles and joys. I put myself spontaneously in their place. For years I lived on Tyrolean apples, and so did Hess. It's crazy what economies we had to make. Every mark saved was for the Party. Another loyal supporter was little Neuner, Ludendorff's valet.

There were also noblemen: Stransky, Scheubner-Richter, von der Pfordten. I realised the similarity of opposites. My comrades at the beginning already came from all parts of Germany. Nothing in the groundwork of the Party has changed. I still rely on the same forces.

It's a great time, when an entirely unknown man can set out to conquer a nation, and when after fifteen years of struggle he can become, in effect, the head of his people. I had the luck to number some strong personalities among my supporters.

Night of 17th–18th January 1942
Sledge-hammer blows of the Russian campaign—German and American aircraft—The torment of Malta—Grave Italian errors

"First of all snow, later frost!" That's all one could read in the books about Russia. And Hilger[254] himself has no more to tell. It's a proof that one can't trust all these observations. It's obviously easy to calculate the average temperatures, based on the results over several years, but it would be indispensable to add that in some years the variations in temperature can be greater, and far greater, than the calculated averages allow one to suppose.

The staggering blow for us was that the situation was entirely unexpected, and the fact that our men were not equipped for the temperatures they had to face. Moreover, our Command could not at once adapt its tactics to the new conditions. Nowadays we allow the Russians to infiltrate, whilst we remain where we are without budging. They get themselves wiped out behind our lines, or else they gradually wither away in the villages for lack of supplies. It takes solid nerves to practise such tactics. I can even say openly that my respected predecessor had not the nerves required for that. Generals must be tough, pitiless men, as crabbed as mastiffs—cross-grained men, such as I have in the Party. Those are the sort of soldiers who impose their will on such a situation.

If the frost hadn't come, we would have gone on careering forward—six hundred kilometres, in some places. We were within a hair's breadth of it. Providence intervened and spared us a catastrophe. The oil we needed at that moment, we already had—and all we needed was this intervention. The idiot who bestowed that "all temperatures" oil upon us! I hate those specialists' jobs.

I regard everything that comes from a theoretician as null and void. Aesthetical forms, mechanical finish—let's keep these preoccupations for peace-time. What I need at this moment are locomotives that will stand the grind for five or six years. All these details, which result in a machine remaining on record for another ten years, are a matter of complete indifference to me.

Recently one of our new Messerschmitts fell into enemy hands. They were dumbfounded. An American magazine wrote that the opinion was widespread that the Germans had only mediocre material, but that it was necessary to yield to the evidence that within three years, at

[254] Gustav Hilger (1886–1965), a professional diplomat, Weimar period German ambassador in Moscow and expert on the Soviet Union.

least, the United States would not be able to produce an aircraft of that quality.

"To oppose it with the aircraft at present in service," it added, "would be to send our pilots to suicide." It must be observed, while we're on the subject, that a German aircraft requires at least six times as much work as an American aircraft. The Italian fighters, too, are superior to the Hurricanes.

At Malta, our tactics consist in attacking without respite, so that the English are compelled to keep on firing without interruption.

The Italians have just launched another torpedo-attack on the harbour of Alexandria. In the opinion of the English, these attacks are the work of very brave men.

What we've just experienced in Russia, because of the weather—the sort of upset that leaves you groggy for a moment—*is* something the Italians experienced before us: as a result of the serious mistakes they made in the employment of their forces. We recovered from it quickly—but will *they* recover?

18th January 1942, evening
Persuading other people—Hindenburg, the "Old Gentleman"—First contacts with the Marshal—Germany, Awake!—Von Papen's milliards—Versailles blackmail—If the French had occupied Mainz

My whole life can be summed up as this ceaseless effort of mine to persuade other people. In 1932 I had a conversation at the *Kaiserhof* with Meissner. He told me that, if he was a democrat, it was in a perhaps slightly different way than we imagined—and that, in fact, we weren't so far removed from one another.

He promised me that, in any case, he would do what he could for me with Field-Marshal Hindenburg. "It won't be easy," he added, "for the 'old gentleman's' habits of thinking and feeling are in revolt against all you represent."

I must recognise that Meissner was the first man who made me understand Hindenburg's exact situation. In whom could the Field-Marshal find support? In any case, not among the German Nationalists, who were a lot of incompetents. He was not disposed to violate the constitution.

So what could we do? It required a great effort from him to collaborate with certain Social-Democrats and certain representatives of the Centre. He also had an aversion for Hugenberg (who had one day described him as a "traitor" for having maintained Meissner in his job).

Hindenburg invited me: "Herr Hitler, I wish to hear from your own mouth a summary of your ideas." It is almost impossible, across such a gap, to communicate to others one's own conception of the world. I tried to establish contact with the Field-Marshal by having recourse to comparisons of a military nature. Connection was fairly rapidly made with the soldier, but the difficulty began the instant there was a question of extending our dawning comprehension to politics.

When I would finished my summary, I felt that I would moved Hindenburg and that he was yielding. At once he made this a pretext for reproaching me with an incident that had occurred in East Prussia:

"But your young people have no right to behave as they do. Not long ago, at Tannenberg, they shouted out, so that I could hear: 'Wake up, wake up!' And yet I'm not asleep!" Certain charitable souls had given "the old gentleman" to suppose that the shout was meant for him personally, whereas in reality our supporters were shouting: "Wake up, Germany!" *(Deutschland, erwache)*.

Shortly after this interview, Hindenburg informed me that he would consult me whenever there was a decision to take. But the influence of the enemies I numbered amongst those about me remained so strong that even in 1933 I couldn't see him except in the presence of Papen.

One day, Papen being absent, I appeared in the Field-Marshal's presence by myself. "Why is Herr von Papen always with you?" he asked. "But it's you I want to talk to!" When Papen came back, he must have regretted the trip that had called him away.

"The old gentleman" regarded Papen as a sort of greyhound, but I think he was fond of him. Papen knew admirably how to handle him. We owe a debt of gratitude to Papen, by the way, for it was he who opened the first breach in the sacred constitution. It's obvious one couldn't expect more from him than that.

Unless Antonescu gains the ear of the people, he's undone. The commander who has no troops behind him cannot maintain himself for long. It's thanks to the People's Party that Atatürk[255] assured his rule. It's the same thing in Italy. If Antonescu were to disappear today, there would be a terrible struggle in the Army between the claimants to his succession. That wouldn't happen if there were an organisation that could impose his successor. In his place, I would have made the Legion the basis of power, after first shooting Horia Sima. Without a solid po-

---

[255] Mustafa Kemal Atatürk (1881–1938), a Turkish field marshal, revolutionary, and the founder of the Republic of Turkey which overthrew the Ottoman rulers.

litical basis, it's not possible either to settle a question of succession or to guarantee the normal administration of the State. From this point of view, the Romanians are in a state of inferiority in relation to the Hungarians. The Hungarian State has the advantages of a parliament. For us, such a thing would be intolerable; but theirs is one whose executive power is, in practice, independent.

Papen's misfortune was that he had no support. We were not strong enough to shore him up. Anyway, I wouldn't have done it, for Papen was not our man. The sum total of the deficits of the Reich and the German States was reaching the yearly figure of five and a half thousand millions. On top of that, we had to pay five thousand millions to our enemies. "Marvellous result!" Papen said to me, after his return from Geneva, speaking of the hundred and fifty thousand millions that appeared on paper. "With that, on the 30th of January, we'll have eighty-three millions in the Reich's vaults!"

Then we had the following dialogue: "With what do you propose to pay?"

"But we'll *have* to pay, otherwise they'll make us go bankrupt."

"How will they do that? They have nothing to distrain on!" When I demanded three thousand millions for rearmament, I again met this objection of what we owed abroad. I replied: "You want to give this money to foreigners? Let's rather use it in our own country!" I made my point of view clear to the British Ambassador when he presented his credentials. His reply was: "You mean to say that the new Germany does not recognise the obligations of preceding governments?"

I replied: "Freely negotiated agreements, yes! But blackmail, no! Everything that comes under the heading of *Treaty of Versailles* I regard as extortion."

"Well, I never!" he said. "I shall immediately inform my Government of that." Never again, from that day on, did England or France think themselves entitled to claim the smallest payment from us.

As regards the English, I had no worries. But I feared that the French might take this pretext for occupying Mainz, for example.

Night of 18th–19th January 1942
The Party programme—The unthinking public—The Russian winter—
Rhetoric and common sense—On the Neanderthal man—Our ancestors
the Greeks

I'm sometimes asked why I don't modify the Party programme. To which I reply: "And why *should* I modify it?"

This programme belongs to history. It was already ours on the day of the foundation of the Party, on the 24th February 1919. If anything should be changed, it's for life to take the initiative. I haven't got to identify myself with a medical review or a military publication—things which have to present matters under discussion in their latest state.

What luck for governments that the peoples they administer don't think! The thinking is done by the man who gives the orders, and then by the man who carries them out. If it were otherwise, the state of society would be impossible. The difficulty of the situation is not so much the winter in itself, but the fact of having men, and not knowing how to transport them; of disposing abundantly of ammunition, and not knowing how to get it on the move; of possessing all the necessary weapons, and not knowing how to put them in the hands of the combatants.

As for the railways, I'm keeping them behind. If they don't do better next time, I'll have a word to say to them! All the same, it's better that it should be I who speaks on the 30th, and not Goebbels.

When it's a question of raising morale, I know how to preserve the golden mean between reason and rhetoric. In his last appeal, Goebbels exhorted the soldiers at the front to remain tough and calm. I would not have expressed myself like that. In such a situation, the soldier is not calm, but resolved. One must have been through it to understand these matters.

A skull is dug up by chance, and everybody exclaims: "That's what our ancestors were like." Who knows if the so-called Neanderthal man wasn't really an ape?

What I can say, in any case, is that it wasn't *our* ancestors who lived there in prehistoric times. The soil we live on must have been so desolate that our ancestors, if they passed that way, certainly continued their journey. When we are asked about our ancestors, we should always point to the Greeks.

19th January 1942, evening
Stupidity of duelling—Some duels—Village scuffles—Honour is not a caste privilege

I've always had a lot of trouble in stopping my men from fighting duels. In the end I was forced to forbid duelling. We lost some of our best people in that stupid fashion. Just try to imagine the reasons for some of these duels! One day we were at the Reichsadler. Hess was there, with his wife and sister-in-law. In comes a half-drunk student, who permits himself to make some impertinent remarks about them.

Hess asks him to come out of the inn with him and clarify his views. Next day two hobbledehoys[256] come to see Hess and ask him to explain the insult to their comrade!

I forbade Hess to become involved in this ridiculous affair, and asked him to send me the two seconds. I said to them: "You're trying to pick a quarrel with a man who fought against the enemy for four years. Aren't you ashamed?"

Our friend Holzschuher[257] was involved in an affair that might have ended in a duel. The pretext was grotesque. I said to the people concerned: "I know some Communist hide-outs where, for any of our chaps, the mere fact of showing oneself is to risk one's life. If any of us is tired of living, let him go and make a trip round those places!" I've never known a single case of a duel that deserved to be taken seriously.

We had an irreparable loss in Strunk[258]—our only journalist in the international class. His wife was insulted—*he* was killed.

Where's the logic? In 1923, Dietrich Eckart was simultaneously challenged to a duel by sixteen or seventeen flabby adolescents. I intervened, and put the whole affair in good order. In my presence, nobody turned a hair.

Obviously there are cases in which two individuals have a conflict that no tribunal could settle. Let's assume they quarrel over a woman. A solution must be found. One of the two has got to disappear. But in time of war there's no question of condoning affairs of that kind. The country can't afford such superfluous deaths.

For peasants' brawls, I'm inclined to be extremely indulgent. The young man whose honour is in question can no longer show himself in the village unless he has fought for his sweetheart. There's nothing tragic in affairs of that sort.

It sometimes happens that a court finds a man guilty of murder when he's really only guilty of culpable homicide. It's sufficient if the accused has once, in bravado, threatened to kill the other man. Then at once people wish to interpret the act as the execution of a well-con-

---

[256] A clumsy or awkward youth.

[257] Wilhelm von Holzschuher (1893–1965), SS-*Gruppenführer* and NSDAP District President of Lower Bavaria and Upper Palatinate.

[258] A pistol duel between NSDAP newspaper journalist Roland Strunk (1900–1937) and a senior Hitler Youth Officer, Horst Krutschinna (1909–1945) over an affair between Strunk's wife and Krutschinna ended with Strunk's death.

sidered plan. What would happen if all those who have offered threats of this sort, in the country areas, were regarded as murderers? In such cases, and when I see that the accused is a decent lad, I wink an eye. The penalty is first of all commuted into imprisonment. After some time, it becomes conditional liberation.

Who, in Germany, is allowed to see justice done for himself, even on a point of honour? I don't see that honour is the privilege of a caste. If the Labour Front demanded that its members should have the right to duel, there'd soon be nobody left in Germany except abortions with no sense of honour.

In principle, I would be inclined to permit duelling between priests and between lawyers. For decent people, there are more noble and more effective ways of serving one's country. In this sphere, it's time to impose a scale of values that has some relation to reality. In comparison with the important things of life, these incidents seem mere trifles.

How many families are wearing black because of this ridiculous practice? Besides, it proves nothing. In duelling, what matters is not to have right on your side, but to aim better than your opponent.

20th January 1942, midday
SPECIAL GUEST: REICHSFÜHRER SS HIMMLER
The worker and the German community—Men worthy of command—The age of officers

In the old Imperial Army, the best rubbed shoulders with the worst. Both in the Navy and in the Army, everything was done to exclude the worker from the German community, and that's what gave rise to Social-Democracy. This attitude did a lot of harm.

The institution of the warrant-officer doing an officer's job was a serious mistake. In every regiment there are officers who are particularly gifted and therefore destined for rapid promotion. Numerous warrant-officers would have deserved to have the same chances of promotion, but their way was barred, the question of an N.C.O. in the officers' caste being practically impossible. On the other hand, the most junior teacher could automatically become an officer. And what's a teacher?

One must not generalise, either to one effect or to the other, and it's only when a man has proved himself that one knows whether he is worthy of command. If he is, then he must be given the prerogatives corresponding to his functions. The man who commands a company must necessarily have the rank of captain. It's due to him, if only to give him the authority he needs. Cases are not rare of warrant-officers who had to command a company for more than two years—and of lieutenants who had to command a battalion. It's a duty towards the soldiers to give those who command them the rank that corresponds to their functions—assuming, of course, that they deserve it. But it's impermissible, when a major has been put in command of a regiment, to refuse him, on grounds of sheer red tape, the rank of colonel to which he's entitled. In peacetime, obviously, everything finds its proper level again.

I distrust officers who have exaggeratedly theoretical minds. I would like to know what becomes of their theories at the moment of action. In modern war, a company-commander aged more than forty is an absurdity. At the head of a company one needs a man of about twenty-six, at the head of a brigade a man of about thirty-five, at the head of a division a man of forty. All these men are exaggeratedly old. From now on, I shall pay no attention to the table of seniority when it's a matter of assigning a post.

22nd January 1942, midday
SPECIAL GUESTS: REICHSFÜHRER SS HIMMLER AND
GAULEITER RAINER[259]
The problem of nationalities—Czechs, Hungarians and Romanians—The Czech complex—The SS as a nursery for leaders

It's not impossible that we may succeed, by the end of two hundred years of rule, in solving the problem of nationalities. The problem was solved at the time of the outbreak of the Thirty Years' War.

About 1840, a Czech was ashamed of his language. His pride was to speak German. The summit of his pride was to be taken for a Viennese. The institution of universal suffrage in Austria was necessarily to lead to the collapse of German supremacy.

As a matter of principle, the Social-Democrats made common cause with the Czechs. The high aristocracy behaved in the same way. The German people are too intelligent for such fellows. They always had a preference for the backward peoples on the periphery.

The Czechs were better than the Hungarians, Romanians and Poles. There had grown up amongst them a hard-working and conscientious small bourgeoisie, quite aware of its limitations.

Today they'll bow before us again, with the same sense of mingled rage and admiration as before: "People like us, people from Bohemia, are not predestined to rule," they used to say. With the habit of rule, one learns to command. The Czechs would probably have lost their in-

---

[259] Friedrich Rainer (1903–1950), Gauleiter of Salzburg and Carinthia.

feriority complex by gradually observing their superiority to the other peoples who, like them, belonged to the periphery of the empire of the Habsburgs. The situation before March 1939 is no longer conceivable. How was all that possible?

After so many centuries of withdrawal, it's important that we should once again become aware of ourselves. We've already proved that we are capable of ruling peoples. Austria is the best example of it. If the Habsburgs hadn't linked themselves so closely to the outer elements of their empire, the nine million Germans would have easily continued to rule the other fifty millions.

It's said that the Indians fight for the English. That's true, but it was just the same with us. In Austria everybody fought for the Germans.

The gift of command comes naturally to everyone in Lower Saxony. Wasn't it from there that Great Britain got its ruling class?

Thanks to its method of recruiting, the SS will be a nursery of rulers. In a hundred years' time from now, we'll control this whole empire without having to rack our brains to know where to find the proper men. The essential thing is to leave behind the pettinesses of the parochial spirit. That's why I'm so glad we're installed in Norway and all over the place.

The Swiss are only suckers of the Germanic tree.

We've lost some of our Germanics! The Berbers of North Africa, the Kurds of Asia Minor. One of them was Kemal Atatürk, who had nothing to do with his compatriots, from the racial point of view.

22nd January 1942, evening
SPECIAL GUEST: ADMIRAL FRICKE
The Bavarians and the Navy—Fish as food—Meat-eaters and vegetarians—Vegetarian atavism—Alcohol and smoking

Of all the areas of the Reich, it's Bavaria that used proportionally to have the greatest number of seamen. The smallest bookshop in Munich used to display books about the Navy. The chief publisher of works on the Navy had his headquarters in Munich—I mean J. F. Lehmann.

Germany consumes, yearly, an average of twelve kilogrammes of fish per head. In Japan the average is from fifty to sixty kilos. We still have leeway to make up!

To encourage the consumption of fish is above all a matter of organisation and presentation, for it's essentially a perishable commodity. Before the Great War, it was incomparably easier to find fish in Munich than in Vienna, for example. It seems that since then conditions in

Austria have much improved. It's very difficult to persuade a cannibal not to eat human flesh. According to his ideas, it's a law of nature.

Hitler turns towards Admiral Fricke: Above all, don't go believing that I'll issue a decree forbidding the Navy to eat meat! Supposing the prohibition of meat had been an article of faith for National Socialism, it's certain our movement wouldn't have succeeded. We would at once have been asked the question: "Then why was the leg of the calf created?" At present, the base of our diet is the potato—and yet only 1 per cent of the soil in Germany is devoted to growing the potato. If it was 3 per cent, we would have more to eat than is needed. Pasturages cover 37 per cent of the surface of our country.

So it's not man who eats grass, it's his cattle. Amongst the animals, those who are carnivores put up performances much inferior to those of the herbivores. A lion's in no shape to run for a quarter of an hour—the elephant can run for eight hours! The monkeys, our ancestors of prehistoric times, are strictly vegetarian. Japanese wrestlers, who are amongst the strongest men in the world, feed exclusively on vegetables. The same's true of the Turkish porter, who can move a piano by himself.

At the time when I ate meat, I used to sweat a lot. I used to drink four pots of beer and six bottles of water during a meeting, and I would succeed in losing nine pounds! When I became a vegetarian, a mouthful of water from time to time was enough.

When you offer a child the choice of a piece of meat, an apple or a cake, it's never the meat that he chooses. There's an ancestral instinct there. In the same way, the child would never begin to drink or smoke if it weren't to imitate others.

The consumption of meat is reduced the moment the market presents a greater choice of vegetables, and in proportion as each man can afford the luxury of the first fruits.

I suppose man became carnivorous because, during the Ice Age, circumstances compelled him. They also prompted him to have his food cooked, a habit which, as one knows today, has harmful consequences. Our peasants never eat any food that hasn't been cooked and recooked, and thus deprived of all its virtues. The southern peoples are not acquainted either with a meat diet or with cooking. I lived marvellously in Italy. I don't know any country that enlivens one more. Roman food, how delicious it is!

Not long ago, I drank for the first time in my life a really good wine, with an extraordinary bouquet. The drinkers with me said it was too sweet. I know people who seem normal and yet suddenly hurl themselves on drinks that on me have the effect of vitriol. If Hoffmann were bitten by a serpent, I suppose the serpent would fall down stiff in a moment, dead-drunk.

When I go into an inn where people are smoking, within an hour I feel I've caught a cold. The microbes hurl themselves upon me! They find a favourable climate in the smoke and heat.

Night of 22nd–23rd January 1942
The story of the dog Foxl[260]

How many times, at Fromelles, during the Great War, I've studied my dog Foxl. When he came back from a walk with the huge bitch who was his companion, we found him covered with bites. We had no sooner bandaged him, and had ceased to bother about him, than he would shake off this unwanted load.

A fly began buzzing. Foxl was stretched out at my side, with his muzzle between his paws. The fly came close to him. He quivered, with his eyes as if hypnotised. His face wrinkled up and acquired an old man's expression. Suddenly he leapt forward, barked and became agitated. I used to watch him as if he'd been a man—the progressive stages of his anger, of the bile that took possession of him. He was a fine creature.

When I ate, he used to sit beside me and follow my gestures with his gaze. If by the fifth or sixth mouthful I hadn't given him anything, he used to sit up on his rump and look at me with an air of saying: "And what about me, am I not here at all?"

It was crazy how fond I was of the beast. Nobody could touch me without Foxl's instantly becoming furious. He would follow nobody but me. When gas-warfare started, I couldn't go on taking him into the front line. It was my comrades who fed him. When I returned after two days' absence, he would refuse to leave me again. Everybody in the trenches loved him.

During marches he would run all round us, observing everything, not missing a detail. I used to share everything with him. In the evening he used to lie beside me. To think that they stole him from me! I would made a plan, if I got out of the war alive, to procure a female companion for him. I couldn't have parted from him. I've never in my life sold a dog. Foxl was a real circus dog. He knew all the tricks. I remember, it was before we arrived at Colmar. The railway employee who coveted

[260] Foxl was originally a British soldier's dog who had wandered across the front line into the German side in 1915.

Foxl came again to our carriage and offered me two hundred marks. "You could give me two hundred thousand, and you wouldn't get him!" When I left the train at Harpsheim, I suddenly noticed that the dog had disappeared. The column marched off, and it was impossible for me to stay behind! I was desperate. The swine who stole my dog doesn't realise what he did to me.[261]

It was in January 1915 that I got hold of Foxl. He was engaged in pursuing a rat that had jumped into our trench. He fought against me, and tried to bite me, but I didn't let go.

I led him back with me to the rear. He constantly tried to escape. With exemplary patience (he didn't understand a word of German), I gradually got him used to me. At first I gave him only biscuits and chocolate (he'd acquired his habits with the English, who were better fed than we were). Then I began to train him. He never went an inch from my side. At that time, my comrades had no use at all for him. Not only was I fond of the beast, but it interested me to study his reactions. I finally taught him everything: how to jump over obstacles, how to climb up a ladder and down again.

The essential thing is that a dog should always sleep beside its master. When I had to go up into the line, and there was a lot of shelling, I used to tie him up in the trench. My comrades told me that he took no interest in anyone during my absence. He would recognise me even from a distance. What an outburst of enthusiasm he would let loose in my honour! We called him Foxl. He went through all the Somme, the battle of Arras. He was not at all impressionable. When I was wounded, it was Karl Lanzhammer who took care of him. On my return, he hurled himself on me in frenzy. When a dog looks in front of him in a vague fashion and with clouded eyes, one knows that images of the past are chasing each other through his memory.

23rd January 1942, midday
SPECIAL GUESTS: LAMMERS, HIMMLER AND COLONEL ZEITZLER

Appreciation of the Czechs—The internal policy of the Habsburgs—When the Popes harried the Jews—The "decent" Jews

The man who shaped the old Reich hadn't the slightest notion of what people are like. They grew up in a climate of stupidity. They understand nothing about Austria. The fact that Austria was not a State,

---

[261] Hitler's portfolio of sketches and drawings was also stolen along with the dog.

in the meaning we give the term, but a fruit-salad of peoples, is one that escapes them. *Sancta simplicitas.*[262] There was no such thing, properly speaking, as an Austrian Army, but an Army composed of Czech, Croat, Serb units, etc.

Every Czech is a born nationalist who naturally relates everything to his own point of view. One must make no mistake about him: the more he curbs himself, the more dangerous he is. The German of the Old Reich lets himself be duped by the apparent obligingness of the Czech, and by his obsequiousness. Neurath[263] let himself be completely diddled by the Czech nobility. Another six months of that regime and production would have fallen by 25 per cent.

Of all the Slavs, the Czech is the most dangerous, because he's a worker. He has a sense of discipline, he's orderly, he's more a Mongol than a Slav. Beneath the top layer of a certain loyalty, he knows how to hide his plans. Now they'll work, for they know we're pitiless and brutal. I don't despise them, I have no resentment against them. It's destiny that wishes us to be adversaries. To put it briefly, the Czechs are a foreign body in the midst of the German community. There's no room both for them and for us. One of us must give way.

As regards the Pole, it's lucky for us that he's idle, stupid and vain. The Czech State—and that's due to the training the Czechs have had— was a model of honesty. Corruption practically didn't exist amongst them. Czech officials are generally inspired by a sense of honour. That's why a man like Hácha is more dangerous than a rogue of a journalist. He's an honest man, who won't enrich himself by a crown in the exercise of his functions. Men liable to corruption are less dangerous.

Those are things that the Second Reich never understood. Its way of behaving towards the Poles was a deplorable set-back. It only succeeded in strengthening their sense of patriotism. Our compatriots of the frontier regions, who would know how to set about things with the neighbouring peoples, were repressed by the kindly Germans of the interior—who suppose, for their part, that kindliness is the way to win these foreign hearts for Germany.

At the time of Maria Theresa everything was going well, and one can say that in the 'forties there was no question of a Polish patriotism. With the rise to power of the bourgeoisie, the conquered territory was

---

[262] "Holy Innocence," a phrase used to refer to a person's naïveté.
[263] Konstantin von Neurath (1873–1956), a career diplomat who served as Foreign Minister between 1932 and 1938.

lost again. The Tsar Ferdinand of Bulgaria said to me one day: "Do you know who's the most dangerous man? Beneš. Titulescu[264] is venal, but Beneš, I don't believe he is." Ferdinand was really very clever.

It's the duty of the Party to settle these questions once and for all in the course of the next five hundred years. The Habsburgs broke their teeth on them. They believed they could smoothe everything down by kindness. The Czechs didn't have the feeling that they were being treacherous in acting as they did. In any case, it's one of the incomprehensible circumstances of history that the ancient Bavarians left those territories and the Czechs settled there. Such a situation is unbearable from the geopolitical point of view. The result has been, we have the Poles close at hand, and, between them and the Czechs, nothing but the narrow Silesian strip.

If I withdraw fifty thousand Germans from Volhynia, that's a hard decision to take, because of the sufferings it entails. The same is true of the evacuation of Southern Tyrol.

If I think of shifting the Jew, our bourgeoisie becomes quite unhappy: "What will happen to them?" Tell me whether this same bourgeoisie bothered about what happened to our own compatriots who were obliged to emigrate? One must act radically. When one pulls out a tooth, one does it with a single tug, and the pain quickly goes away. The Jew must clear out of Europe. Otherwise no understanding will be possible between Europeans. It's the Jew who prevents everything. When I think about it, I realise that I'm extraordinarily humane. At the time of the rule of the Popes, the Jews were mistreated in Rome.

Until 1830, eight Jews mounted on donkeys were led once a year through the streets of Rome. For my part, I restrict myself to telling them they must go away. If they break their pipes on the journey, I can't do anything about it. But if they refuse to go voluntarily, I see no other solution but their rooting out. Why should I look at a Jew through other eyes than if he were a Russian prisoner-of-war?

In the P.O.W. camps, many are dying. It's not my fault. I didn't want either the war or the P.O.W. camps. Why did the Jew provoke this war? A good three hundred or four hundred years will go by before the Jews set foot again in Europe. They'll return first of all as commercial travellers, then gradually they'll become emboldened to settle here—the better to exploit us. In the next stage, they become philanthropists, they

---

[264] Nicolae Titulescu (1882–1941), Minister of Foreign Affairs of Romania from 1927 to 1928, and President of the League of Nations from 1930 to 1932.

endow foundations. When a Jew does that, the thing is particularly noticed—for it's known that they're dirty dogs. As a rule, it's the most rascally of them who do that sort of thing. And then you'll hear these poor Aryan boobies telling you: "You see, there *are* good Jews!"

Let's suppose that one day National Socialism will undergo a change, and become used by a caste of privileged persons who exploit the people and cultivate money. One must hope that in that case a new reformer will arise and clean up the stables.

24th January 1942, evening
Raw materials, synthetic materials and the Four Year Plan—Two possibilities for the British—Out with Churchill and Roosevelt! Even in peace-time it is important, when arming oneself, to concentrate solely on those raw materials which one knows one will have in time of war

When the Four Year Plan was hatched, in 1936, circumstances forced us to have recourse to substitute products. One can have no idea what it takes, even only in optical instruments, to equip an army of several million men.

One day the English will realise that they've nothing to gain in Europe. Sixteen thousand millions of debts from the Great War, to which have since been added nearly two hundred thousand millions! The Conservatives must reckon that, in order to gain a rapid success in Northern Norway, for example, they would have to pay for this by abandoning India.

But they're not so mad as to envisage such a solution! If they want to save New Zealand and Australia, they can't let India go.

The English have two possibilities: either to give up Europe and hold on to the East, or *vice versa*. They can't bet on both tables. When it's a matter of the richest country in the world (from the capitalist point of view), one understands the importance of such a dilemma. It would be enough for them to be aware of it for everything to be changed. We know that the bourgeoisie becomes heroic when its pocket-book is threatened.

A change of government would be associated, in England, with the decision to abandon Europe. They'll keep Churchill in power only as long as they still have the will to pursue the struggle here. If they were really cunning, they'd put an end to this war, thus dealing a mortal blow to Roosevelt. They would have the following excuse: "We're no longer strong enough to continue the war, and you cannot help us. This leads us to reconsider our attitude towards Europe." This would result in the collapse of the American economy, and also the personal collapse of Roosevelt. Simultaneously, America would have ceased to be a danger to England.

24th January 1942, evening
SPECIAL GUEST: HIMMLER
Reorganisation of the administrative services—Taxes—The importance of bureaucracy must be lessened—The Ministry of Propaganda—A dialogue with von Papen—Tribute payable to nature

Göring wanted to get from me a decree conferring powers on Stuckart[265] and Reinhardt[266] so that they could undertake the reorganisation of our administrative services with a view to simplifying them. I refused. Why entrust these men with such a mission when it's precisely the Ministry of Finance and Interior, which are their field, whose administrations are plethorically swollen? There are two ways of revising the administration: a reduction of the Budget, or a reduction of personnel. The fiscal system is uselessly complicated. Since the days when people paid the Crown its tenth, there's been no end to the process of adding supplementary taxes to this tenth! The simplest method consists in restricting oneself to the four following taxes:

1. A tax on luxury goods.
2. A stamp duty. (Everybody obtains the stamps he needs.

It does not require any costly administrative apparatus. And it's a tax that's not oppressive. Old Austria had this tax. No tradesman could sell anything at all without stamps. He bought them at the post office, which confined itself to keeping an account of the sums realised.)

3. A tax on private means.
4. A tax on commercial profits.

As regards direct taxes, the simplest is to take as a basis the amount paid the previous year. The tax-payer is told: "You'll pay the same sum as last year. If this year your earnings are lower, you'll report that fact. If they're higher, you'll immediately pay a proportionate supplement. If you forget to announce the increase in your income, you'll be severely punished."

If I explain this system to the Ministry of Finance or to Reinhardt, the reply will be, after an instant's reflection: "My Führer, you're right." But within six months they'll certainly have forgotten everything! Thanks to this method, one might reduce the bureaucracy to a third

---

[265] Wilhelm Stuckart (1902–1953), State Secretary to the Ministry of the Interior.
[266] Friedrich Reinhardt (1895–1969), State Secretary to the Ministry of Finance.

of its present importance. The snag is that a tax which is easy to collect doesn't suit these gentlemen of the administration. What would be the use of having been to a University? Where would one find jobs for the jurists? There'd be no more work for them, for everything could be done by means of an extremely simple piece of apparatus, and the Chinese puzzle of declaring one's taxes would be done away with.

Lammers told me: "My Führer, I've been using the simplified method since the beginning, and it works. All the other systems are too cumbrous." If I now give a jurist the job of simplifying the mechanism of the administration, his first care will be to create an office of which he will be at the head, with the idea that finally it will entitle him to a Minister's portfolio.

I've had the same experience in the Party. One decides to create a group of the Hitler Youth at Salzburg. Suddenly they need a building of five hundred rooms—now, I've run a party of eight hundred thousand members, and I housed all my administration in a few attics—(*Schwarz listens impassively to the demand formulated, then he cuts in: "We'll start with twelve rooms"*[267]).

I'm all in favour of installing Ministries in monumental and majestic buildings, but on condition that everything is reckoned out in advance in such a way that no enlargement can prove to be possible, not even in height. In this way a Ministry learns to make use of its organs of execution. It confines itself to controlling, it avoids direct administration.

The Republic of Venice, which used to reign over the Adriatic Sea, was installed in the palace of the Doges, which today still houses the entire administration of the city.

I created the Ministry of Propaganda with the idea that it should be at everybody's service. Thus I myself can do without a propaganda service. It's enough for me to have the possibility of taking my telephone off the hook and asking the question: "Herr Doktor, how am I to set about such-and-such a matter?" Yet there practically doesn't exist a Ministry today that hasn't its own press-service. They ought to find the services of the Ministry of Propaganda enough.

Since it's I who give the Reich's Propaganda Ministry its directives, why should I maintain a private press-section? In the days when there was a Vice-Chancellery, that service had a budget of six hundred thousand marks. One day I asked Lammers: "What *is* that shop?" He re-

---

[267] Franz Schwarz (1875–1947), SS Senior Leader and National Treasurer of the NSDAP.

plied: "It's a swindle." Lammers had held an enquiry and had discovered that all the people I would sacked from the Chancellery had found jobs again in the Vice-Chancellery.

When Papen proposed the Vice-Chancellery to me, I explained to him: "A Vice-Chancellor never becomes active except when the Chancellor is ill. If I am the Vice-Chancellor, you will never be ill. So I refuse the Vice-Chancellery." Personally, Papen was an inoffensive man—but, by a sort of fatality, he surrounded himself with people who all had something on their conscience.

Jodl interposed: "For the Wehrmacht, the bureaucracy has become frightful. The Minister for War has made it a point of honour to imitate the other Ministers, as concerns both style and practice. The individual personality has disappeared behind the administrative entities, and I consider that unworthy of a soldier. Nobody speaks any longer in the first person. Everybody expresses himself in the name of an entity. It's the triumph of impersonality."

Himmler interposed in turn: "I've arranged that each of my subordinates shall sign everything that issues from our offices, with his own name and in a legible fashion. Thus one always knows with whom one is dealing, and nobody can take refuge behind abstractions. What is scandalous is the tone of our administrative people in their relations with the public. Every summons to a meeting, every tax demand, is, in its general effect, an offence against the citizen. I've had all our forms of summons cancelled and ordered them to be replaced. Now the first summons is in the following set terms: 'I request you, on behalf of the President of Police, to be so kind . . . If you are unable to attend, I should be grateful if you would inform me in writing concerning the matter mentioned above.' If the recipient makes no move, he receives a second letter as follows: ' You did not answer my summons. I draw your attention to the fact that you are obliged to...'"

The Führer replied: That's why I've never been able to make up my mind to praise publicly the body of officials generally. All that should be reviewed from top to bottom. The best thing you've done, Himmler, is to have transformed the incendiary into a fireman. Thus the fireman lives under the threat of being hanged if there is an outbreak of fire.

I've sometimes wondered whether the tax the peasant pays in money couldn't be replaced by a tax paid in produce. In Russia, it will be absolutely necessary to do things like that. There'll be barracks there where one will be able to collect tithes. It's easier for the peasant to pay in produce than to trot out the ready money. Life used to be very hard for the peasants. To them a good crop used to mean more work, and not more money. A bad crop was simply a disaster. It was the middleman who pocketed the profits!

Night of 24th–25th January 1942
Origin of Tristan and Isolda—Cosima Wagner—Wahnfried—The Makart style—Bayreuth—On the Nuremberg Congress

Whatever one says, *Tristan* is Wagner's masterpiece, and we owe *Tristan* to the love Mathilde Wesendonck[268] inspired in him. She was a gentle, loving woman, but far from having the qualities of Cosima.[269] Nobody like Wagner has had the luck to be entirely understood by a woman. Those are things that life does not owe a man, but it's magnificent when it happens.

Neither Mozart nor Beethoven, neither Schiller nor Goethe,[270] have had a share of such happiness. In addition to all Wagner's gifts, Cosima was femininity personified, and her charm had its effect on all who visited Wahnfried.[271]

After Wagner's death, the atmosphere at Wahnfried remained what it had been during his lifetime. Cosima was inconsolable, and never ceased to wear mourning. She had wanted her own ashes to be scattered over her husband's tomb, but she was refused this satisfaction. Nevertheless, her ashes were collected in an urn, and this urn was placed on the tomb. Thus death has not separated these two beings, whom destiny had wished to live side by side! Wagner's lifetime was also that of a man like Meyerbeer![272] Wagner is responsible for the fact that the art of opera is what it is today. The great singers who've left names behind became celebrated as interpreters of Wagner. Moreover, it's since him that there have been great orchestra-leaders. Wagner was

---

[268] Mathilde Wesendonck (1828–1902), a poet and author whose beauty captivated Richard Wagner to the point where it broke up his marriage and caused him to pause writing his Ring trilogy and start writing Tristan und Isolde.

[269] Cosima Wagner (1837–1930), daughter of Franz Liszt and Richard Wagner's second wife.

[270] Johann Wolfgang von Goethe (1749–1832), perhaps the most influential German writer of all time.

[271] The name given by Richard Wagner to his home in Bayreuth. It is a compound noun made up of two German words: *Wahn* (delusion) and *Fried* (peace).

[272] Giacomo Meyerbeer (1791–1864), a Jewish German opera composer (born Jakob Liebmann Beer) who was the first to combine German orchestra style with the Italian vocal tradition, setting a standard which quickly became the norm.

typically a prince. His house, Wahnfried, for example! It's been said that the interior, in Makart[273] style, was overloaded.

But should a house be mistaken for a gallery of works of art? Isn't it, above all, a dwelling, the framework for a private life, with its extensions and its radiance? If I possess a gallery of ancestors, should I discard it on the pretext that not all the pictures in it are masterpieces?

The houses of that period—and the same remark is equally true of Makart's studio—were filled with private memories. As far as I'm concerned, I keenly regret that Makart's studio hasn't been kept as it was in the artist's lifetime. Respect for the venerable things that come to us from the past will one day benefit those who today are young. Nobody can imagine what Makart's vogue was like. His contemporaries extolled him to the heights.

At the beginning of this century there were people called Wagnerians. Other people had no special name. What joy each of Wagner's works has given me! And I remember my emotion the first time I entered Wahnfried. To say I was moved is an understatement! At my worst moments, they've never ceased to sustain me, even Siegfried Wagner. (Houston Stewart Chamberlain wrote to me so nicely when I was in prison.) I was on Christian-name terms with them. I love them all, and I also love Wahnfried.

So I felt it to be a special happiness to have been able to keep Bayreuth going at the moment of its discomfiture. The war gave me the opportunity to fulfil a desire dear to Wagner's heart: that men chosen amongst the people—workers and soldiers—should be able to attend his Festival free of charge. The ten days of the Bayreuth season were always one of the blessed seasons of my existence.

And I already rejoice at the idea that one day I shall be able to resume the pilgrimage! The tradition of the Olympic Games endured for nearly a thousand years. That results, it seems to me, from a mystery similar to that which lies at the origin of Bayreuth. The human being feels the need to relax, to get out of himself, to take communion in an idea that transcends him.

The Party Congress answers the same need, and that's why for hundreds of years men will come from the whole world over to steep themselves anew, once a year, in the marvellous atmosphere of Nuremberg. They'll come, and they'll see side by side the proofs we shall have left of

---

[273] Hans Makart (1840–1884), an Austrian painter, designer, and decorator who specialized in classical style works.

our greatness, and at the same time the memories of old Nuremberg.

On the day following the end of the Bayreuth Festival, and on the Tuesday that marks the end of the Nuremberg Congress, I'm gripped by a great sadness—as when one strips the Christmas tree of its ornaments. The Congress, for me, is a terrible effort, the worst moment of the year. We shall prolong its duration to ten days, so that I may not be obliged to speak continually. It's because of the superhuman effort which that demands of me that I was already obliged to have the opening proclamation read out. I no longer have the strength to speak as long as I used to. So I'll withdraw when I realise I'm no longer capable of giving these festivities the style that suits them.

The most difficult effort comes at the march-past, when one has to remain motionless for hours. On several occasions it has happened to me to be seized by dizziness. Can anyone imagine what a torture it is to remain so long standing up, motionless, with the knees pressed together? And, on top of that, to salute with outstretched arm? Last time, I was compelled to cheat a little. I also have to make the effort of looking each man in the eyes, for the men marching past are all trying to catch my glance. In future I must be given cover against the sun. The Pope is generally a frail old gentleman. He's therefore carried under a baldaquin.[274] They used to wave palms around the Pharaohs, to give them some air.

After the war, it will perhaps be best to have the columns march past sixteen deep, and not twelve deep as hitherto. The march-past would last four hours instead of five—and that would always be so much gained!

Night of 24th–25th January 1942
The Führer's chauffeurs—Driving a car—Some instructions

My life is in the hands of a few individuals: my driver, my orderlies, perhaps also a cook. Kempka[275] begged me, in spring, to allow him to rejoin an armoured unit.

I wonder which is the more useful to the nation: the man who shoots down some enemy tanks—which others could do in his place—or the man who continues to be the driver who enjoys all my confidence? He's been in my service for nine years, now, and I've nothing but praise for him. His predecessor, Schreck, was a companion of the

---

[274] A ceremonial canopy, usually over an altar.
[275] Erich Kempka (1910–1975), Hitler's chauffeur from 1936 to April 1945.

years of struggle. When things went badly around us, the front-line soldier awoke in him. In such situations, Kempka would perhaps have fainted! But he drives with extraordinary prudence—always excepting when he's suffering from unrequited love, and *that* I notice at once. After all, I can't devote my time, at the present juncture, to training a new driver. If I were certain that Kempka would return safe and sound, I would perhaps give in. How many of my drivers I've had who lost their heads simply because I was sitting beside them! Kempka is calm personified. Besides, I'm accustomed to chatting with him. Eickenberg drives well, but I would have to train him. He drives well mechanically, but he hasn't the initiative.

I've done more than two and a half million kilometres by car, without the slightest accident. When I rode with drivers for whose training I was not responsible, it was a matter of luck that nothing happened. I've always insisted with my drivers, Maurice, Schreck and Kempka, that the speed at which they drive should allow them to pull up in time in any circumstances.

If one of my drivers killed a child, and excused himself by saying that he'd sounded his horn, I would tell him: "A child has no judgment, it's for you to think." I find it unpleasant when a car splashes mud on people lined up on the edge of the road, especially when they're people in their Sunday clothes. If my car passes a cyclist, I don't allow my driver to keep up the same speed, except when the wind immediately scatters the dust we raise.

When the rear tyres shriek, that's a sign that the driver has taken a bend badly. It's a rule that one should accelerate only in the bend, never before. The more our drivers succeed, on the whole, in driving well (although not always exactly in the manner that suits me), the more our ruling class drives miserably.

Of course, I've not invented the theory of driving, but I can learn from other people's experience. Adolf Müller once took me in his car. Thanks to him, I learnt more in a few hours than during the years that had gone before.

In former times I used to read regularly the publications devoted to the motor-car, but I no longer have the time. Nevertheless, I continue to be interested in all new advances made in that field. I talk about them with Kempka. *He's* a man who knows all the motor-cars in the world! It's a pleasure to see—since it's his job to bother about that— how well our motor-car park is kept. Junge, too, asked me for leave to return to the front. If I had the feeling that he didn't want to spend his life with me, I would give him permission to leave me, in his own interests. It would be better for his future. Junge's by far the most gifted of my orderlies.

I hadn't realised that until I went to *Felsennest*. There, during our air-raid alerts, I often had the opportunity to talk with him. You've no notion what a cultivated boy he is.

Linge's[276] a good chap, but less intelligent, and very absent-minded into the bargain. As for Bussmann, he's of a distinctly inferior class. Krause had a morbid tendency to tell idle stories. It was no part of his duties. He used to tell lies absolutely without motive.

I'm a very tolerant employer, and I readily admit that one can occasionally be inattentive. In such a case I confine myself to drawing the silly fellow's attention to his fault, and I ask him to be less absent-minded next time. But I cannot endure lying.

Night of 25th–26th January 1942
On marriage—Some beautiful women

It's lucky I'm not married. For me, marriage would have been a disaster. There's a point at which misunderstanding is bound to arise between man and wife; it's when the husband cannot give his wife all the time she feels entitled to demand. As long as only other couples are involved, one hears women say: "I don't understand Frau So-and-so, I wouldn't behave like that."

But when she herself is involved, every woman is unreasonable to the same degree. One must understand this demandingness. A woman who loves her husband lives only for his sake. That's why, in her turn, she expects her spouse to live likewise for *her* sake. It's only after maternity that the woman discovers that other realities exist in life for her. The man, on the other hand, is a slave to his thoughts.

The idea of his duties rules him. He necessarily has moments when he wants to throw the whole thing overboard, wife and children too. When I think of it, I realise that during the year 1932, if I would been married, I would scarcely have spent a few days in my own home. And even during these few days, I would have not been my own master. The wife does not complain only of her husband's absence. She also resents his being preoccupied, having his mind somewhere else. In a woman, the grief of separation is associated with a certain delight. After the

---

[276] Heinz Linge (1913–1980), Hitler's personal valet.

separation, the joy of meeting again! When a sailor returns home, after a long voyage, he has something like a new marriage. After months of absence, he enjoys some weeks of complete liberty. That would never have been the case with me, and my wife would justly have been bored to death. I would have had nothing of marriage but the sullen face of a neglected wife, or else I would have skimped my duties. That's why it's better not to get married.

The bad side of marriage is that it creates rights. In that case, it's far better to have a mistress. The burden is lightened, and everything is placed on the level of a gift.

The Führer noticed two guests who looked somewhat crestfallen, J.W.[277] and Chr. Schr.[278] He turned towards Schr., and explained: What I've said applies only to men of a higher type, of course! *Relieved, Schr. exclaimed: "That's just what I was thinking, my Führer."*

I don't believe that W. H.[279] will ever get married. He has created an ideal image of a woman, taking her silhouette from one, her hair from the next, her intelligence from a third, from still another her eyes—and it's with this image in his mind that he approaches every woman; but there's nothing like it in nature.

One must declare oneself satisfied when one finds *one* perfect detail in a woman. A girl of eighteen to twenty is as malleable as wax. It should be possible for a man, whoever the chosen woman may be, to stamp his own imprint upon her. That's all the woman asks for, by the way.

Dora's a sweet girl, but I don't think that Kempka and she will be happy. For a girl like her, it seems to me that Kempka is too exclusively interested in mechanics. She's too intelligent for him! What lovely women there are in the world!

We were sitting in the *Ratskeller* at Bremen. A woman came in. One would truly have thought that Olympus had opened its gates. Radiant, dazzling. The diners unanimously put down their knives and forks, and all eyes were fixed on her.

Another time, at Brunswick, a young girl rushed towards my car to offer me a bouquet. She was blonde, dashing, wonderful. Everyone around me was amazed, but not one of these idiots had the idea of ask-

---

[277] Johanna Wolf (1900–1985), Hitler's chief secretary from 1929 to 1945.

[278] Christa Schroeder.

[279] Walther Hewel. See note 97. In fact, Hewel did get married in 1944, to a nurse who had tended to him after he was injured in an aircraft crash.

ing the girl for her address, so that I could send her a word of thanks. I've always reproached myself most bitterly.

On yet another occasion, I was at a reception at the *Bayrischer Hof.* There were splendid women there, elegant and covered with jewels. A woman entered who was so beautiful that all the others were eclipsed. She wore no jewels. It was Frau Hanfstaengl.[280]

I saw her again just once, with Mary Stuck at Erna Hanfstaengl's. Three women together, one more beautiful than the others. What a picture! In my youth, in Vienna, I knew a lot of lovely women.

Night of 25th–26th January 1942

More about dogs—Origins of the human race—Beauty and the ancient Greeks—The significance of mythology—Thoughts on the prehistoric— The cosmic theories of Hörbiger—Human genius and politics

I love animals, and especially dogs. But I'm not so very fond of boxers, for example. If I had to take a new dog, it could only be a sheepdog, preferably a bitch. I would feel like a traitor if I became attached to a dog of any other breed. What extraordinary animals they are—lively, loyal, bold, courageous arid handsome!

The blind man's dog is one of the most touching things in existence. He's more attached to his master than to any other dog. If he allows a bitch to distract his attention for a moment, it's for hardly any time and he has a bad conscience. With bitches it's more difficult. When they're on heat, they can't be restrained.

During the winter of 1921–22, I was offered a sheep-dog. He was so sad at the thought of his old master that he couldn't get accustomed to me. I therefore decided to part with him. His new master had gone a few steps, when he gave him the slip and took refuge with me, putting his paws on my shoulders. So I kept him.

When Graf made me a present of Muckl,[281] the process of getting accustomed was quicker. He came up the stairs rather hesitantly. When he saw Blondi, he rushed towards her, wagging his tail. Next day, it was

---

[280] Helena Hanfstaengl, wife of Ernst Hanfstaengl (1887–1975). Ernst was a dual German-American citizen, who lived in America during the First World War and upon his return to Germany in 1992, became an ardent Hitler supporter and close friend. He participated in the failed November 1923 Putsch, and eventually became Hitler's foreign press secretary. He fell out with Hitler in 1938, and returned to America, where he became famous as a bitter opponent of his former friends.

[281] Hitler owned Muckl from 1928 until January, 1935, when the dog was poisoned, supposedly by an enemy of his owner.

indescribable. A dog gets used to a new master more quickly when there's already a dog in the house. It's enough even if he learns from the scent that his new master has recently had a dog; he feels himself trusted.

The dog is the oldest of the domestic animals. He has been man's companion for more than thirty thousand years. But man, in his pride, is not capable of perceiving that even between dogs of the same breed there are extraordinary differences. There are stupid dogs and others who are so intelligent that it's agonising.

I once possessed a work on the origins of the human race. I used to think a lot about such matters, and I must say that if one examines the old traditions, the tales and legends, from close up, one arrives at unexpected conclusions.

It's striking to realise what a limited view we have of the past. The oldest specimens of handwriting we possess go back three or four thousand years at most. No legend would have reached us if those who made and transmitted them hadn't been people like ourselves. Where do we acquire the right to believe that man has not always been what he is now? The study of nature teaches us that, in the animal kingdom just as much as in the vegetable kingdom, variations have occurred.

They've occurred within the species, but none of these variations has an importance comparable with that which separates man from the monkey—assuming that this transformation really took place.

If we consider the ancient Greeks (who were Germanics), we find in them a beauty much superior to the beauty such as is widespread to-day—and I mean also beauty in the realm of thought as much as in the realm of forms. To realise this, it's enough to compare a head of Zeus or of Pallas Athene with that of a crusader or a saint!

If one plunges further into the past, one comes again with the Egyptians upon human beings of the quality of the Greeks. Since the birth of Christ, we have had scarcely forty successive generations on the globe, and our knowledge goes back only a few thousand years before the Christian era. Legend cannot be extracted from the void, it couldn't be a purely gratuitous figment. Nothing prevents us from supposing—and I believe, even, that it would be to our interest to do so—that mythology is a reflection of things that have existed and of which humanity has retained a vague memory. In all the human traditions, whether oral or written, one finds mention of a huge cosmic disaster. What the Bible tells on the subject is not peculiar to the Jews, but was certainly

221

borrowed by them from the Babylonians and Assyrians. In the Nordic legend we read of a struggle between giants and gods.

In my view, the thing is explicable only by the hypothesis of a disaster that completely destroyed a humanity which already possessed a high degree of civilisation. The fragments of our prehistory are perhaps merely reproductions of objects belonging to a more distant past, and it's by means of these, doubtless, that the road to civilisation was discovered anew.

What is there to prove to us that the stone axe we re-discover in our parts was really an invention of those who used it? It seems to me more likely that this object is a reproduction in stone of an axe that previously existed in some other material.

What proof have we, by the way, that beside objects made of stone there were not similar objects made of metal? The life of bronze is limited, and that would explain that in certain earthy deposits one finds only objects made of stone. Moreover, there's no proof that the civilisation that existed before the disaster flourished precisely in our regions. Three-quarters of the earth are covered by water, and only an eighth of the earth's surface is in practice accessible. Who knows what discoveries would be made if we could explore the ground that is at present covered by the waters?

I'm quite well inclined to accept the cosmic theories of Hörbiger.[282] It's not impossible, in fact, that ten thousand years before our era there was a clash between the earth and the moon that gave the moon its present orbit. It's likewise possible that the earth attracted to it the atmosphere which was that of the moon, and that this radically transformed the conditions of life on our planet. One can imagine that, before this accident, man could live at any altitude—for the simple reason that he was not subject to the constraint of atmospheric pressure.

One may also imagine that, the earth having opened, water rushed into the breach thus formed, and explosions followed, and then diluvian torrents of rain—from which human couples could escape only by taking refuge in very high regions. It seems to me that these questions will be capable of solution on the day when a man will intuitively es-

---

[282] Hans Hörbiger (1860–1931), a German engineer who developed a theory of "cosmic ice" which entailed the suggestion that space is filled with cosmic ice, and stellar systems are generated when a large block of cosmic ice collides with a hot star. The theory, never proven, is based upon the idea of extreme temperature variations being the cause of solar systems.

tablish the connection between these facts, thus teaching exact science the path to follow. Otherwise we shall never raise the veil between our present world and that which preceded us.

If one takes our religions at their beginning, one discovers in them a more human character than they subsequently acquired. I suppose religions find their origin in these faded images of another world of which human memory had retained the distant image. The human mind has kneaded such images together with notions elaborated by the intelligence, and it's thus that the Churches have created the ideological framework that today still ensures their power.

The period stretching between the middle of the third and the middle of the seventeenth century is certainly the worst humanity has ever known: blood-lust, ignominy, lies.

I don't consider that what has been should necessarily exist for the simple reason that it has been. Providence has endowed man with intelligence precisely to enable him to act with discernment. My discernment tells me that an end must be put to the reign of lies. It likewise tells me that the moment is not opportune.

To avoid making myself an accomplice to the lies, I've kept the shavelings out of the Party. I'm not afraid of the struggle. It will take place, if really we must go so far. And I shall make up my mind to it as soon as I think it possible.

It's against my own inclinations that I devoted myself to politics. I don't see anything in politics, anyway, but a means to an end. Some people suppose it would deeply grieve me to give up the activity that occupies me at this moment. They are deeply mistaken, for the finest day of my life will be that on which I leave politics behind me, with its griefs and torments.

When the war's over, and I have the sense of having accomplished my duties, I shall retire. Then I would like to devote five or ten years to clarifying my thought and setting it down on paper. Wars pass by. The only things that exist are the works of human genius.

This is the explanation of my love of art. Music and architecture—is it not in these disciplines that we find recorded the path of humanity's ascent? When I hear Wagner, it seems to me that I hear rhythms of a bygone world. I imagine to myself that one day science will discover, in the waves set in motion by the *Rheingold,* secret mutual relations connected with the order of the world. The observation of the world perceived by the senses precedes the knowledge given by exact science as well as by philosophy. It's in as far as percipient awareness approaches truth that it has value.

The notion that the cosmos is infinite in all senses should be expressed in an accessible fashion. It is infinite in the sense of the infinitely great as well as in the sense of the infinitely small. It would have been a mistake at the beginning of the positivist era to picture space as limited by the bounds perceived by the instruments. We should reason in the same fashion today, despite the progress made in methods of measurement—and that applies both on the microscopic and also on the macroscopic scale. Seen in the microscope, a microbe acquires gigantic proportions. In this direction, too, there is no end.

If somebody else had one day been found to accomplish the work to which I've devoted myself, I would never have entered on the path of politics. I would have chosen the arts or philosophy. The care I feel for the existence of the German people compelled me to this activity. It's only when the conditions for living are assured that culture can blossom.

26th January 1942, evening
Women in politics—American methods of production—Towards another economic crash

I detest women who dabble in politics. And if their dabbling extends to military matters, it becomes utterly unendurable.

In no local section of the Party has a woman ever had the right to hold even the smallest post. It has therefore often been said that we were a party of misogynists, who regarded a woman only as a machine for making children, or else as a plaything. That's far from being the case. I attached a lot of importance to women in the field of the training of youth, and that of good works.

In 1924 we had a sudden upsurge of women who were attracted by politics: Frau von Treuenfels and Matilde von Kemnitz. They wanted to join the Reichstag, in order to raise the moral level of that body, so they said. I told them that 90 per cent of the matters dealt with by parliament were masculine affairs, on which they could not have opinions of any value. They rebelled against this point of view, but I shut their mouths by saying: "You will not claim that you know men as I know women."

A man who shouts is not a handsome sight. But if it's a woman, it's terribly shocking. The more she uses her lungs, the more strident her voice becomes. There she is, ready to pull hair out, with all her claws showing. In short, gallantry forbids one to give women an opportunity of putting themselves in situations that do not suit them.

Everything that entails combat is exclusively men's business. There are so many other fields in which one must rely upon women. Organising a house, for example. Few men have Frau Troost's talent in matters concerning interior decoration. There were four women whom I give star roles: Frau Troost, Frau Wagner, Frau Scholtz-Klink[283] and Leni Riefenstahl.[284]

The Americans are admirable at mass-production, when it's a question of producing a single model repeated without variation in a great number of copies. That's lucky for us, for their tanks are proving unusable. We could wish them to build another sixty thousand this year.

I don't believe in miracles, and I'm convinced that when they come along with their twenty-eight-tonners and sixty-tonners, the smallest of our tanks will outclass them. They have some people there who scent an economic crisis far surpassing that of 1929. When one has no substitute product for materials like copper, for example, one is soon at the end of one's tether.

27th January 1942, midday
SPECIAL GUEST: HIMMLER
The blood of others—The British and the capitalist system—History but for the advent of Christianity—Constantine the Great and Julian the Apostate—Chamberlain's return to Munich—Sir Samuel Hoare— The privileged position of Mosley—Class prejudice in Germany and Britain—The process of selectivity—The faith of the German people

The soldiers whom England used for her wars were for the most part men of German blood. The first great outpouring of blood that could properly be described as English took place in the Great War. And how one understands that that ordeal left its mark on them! So as not to suffer the after-effects of the present war on the economic level, the English should have abandoned their capitalistic system, or else shaken off the burden of a debt that was reaching a billion four hundred thousands.

They made a timid attempt in that direction, by the classic method: by reducing their armaments budget to a minimum, so as to be able thus to pay the interest on their debt. Their situation after the Na-

---

[283] Gertrud Emma Scholtz-Klink (1902–1999), leader of the National Socialist Women's League.

[284] Amalie "Leni" Riefenstahl (1902–2003), one of the Reich's famous film makers.

poleonic wars was somewhat similar to that after 1918. They passed through a long period of exhaustion, didn't become themselves again until under Victoria's reign.

A people cannot lay claim to mastery of the world unless it's ready to pay with its blood. The Roman Empire had recourse to mercenaries only when its own blood was exhausted. In fact, it was only after the Third Punic War that Rome had legions of mercenaries.

But for the coming of Christianity, who knows how the history of Europe would have developed? Rome would have conquered all Europe, and the onrush of the Huns would have been broken on the legions. It was Christianity that brought about the fall of Rome—not the Germans or the Huns.

What Bolshevism is achieving today on the materialist and technical level, Christianity had achieved on the metaphysical level. When the Crown sees the throne totter, it needs the support of the masses.

It would be better to speak of Constantine the traitor and Julian the Loyal than of Constantine the Great and Julian the Apostate. What the Christians wrote against the Emperor Julian is approximately of the same calibre as what the Jews have written against us.

The writings of the Emperor Julian, on the other hand, are products of the highest wisdom. If humanity took the trouble to study and understand history, the resulting consequences would have incalculable implications.

One day ceremonies of thanksgiving will be sung to Fascism and National Socialism for having preserved Europe from a repetition of the triumph of the Underworld.

That's a danger that especially threatens England. The Conservatives would face a terrible ordeal if the proletarian masses were to seize power. If Chamberlain, on his return from Munich, had based elections on the choice between war and peace, he'd have obtained a crushing majority in favour of peace. When I took possession of Memel, Chamberlain informed me through a third party that he understood very well that this step had to be taken, even although he could not approve of it publicly.

At this period, Chamberlain was being fiercely attacked by the Churchill clan. If he'd had the presence of mind to organise an election, he'd have been saved. In similar cases, I've always made arrangements for a plebiscite to be held. It produces an excellent effect, both at home and abroad. It wasn't at this juncture that the Labour Party could return into the lists. The Jews had set the cat among the pigeons. If Samuel Hoare[285] were to come to power today, as is desirable, all he'd have to do would be to set free the Fascists.

The English have to settle certain social problems which are ripe to be settled. At present these problems can still be solved from above, in a reasonable manner. I tremble for them if they don't do it now. For if it's left to the people to take the initiative, the road is open to madness and destruction.

Men like Mosley would have had no difficulty in solving the problem, by finding a compromise between Conservatism and Socialism, by opening the road to the masses but without depriving the elite of their rights.

Class prejudices can't be maintained in a socially advanced State like ours, in which the proletariat produces men of such superiority. Every reasonably conducted organisation is bound to favour the development of beings of worth.

It has been my wish that the educative organisations of the Party should enable the poorest child to lay claim to the highest functions, if he has enough talent. The Party must see to it, on the other hand, that society is not compartmentalised, so that everyone can quickly assert his gifts.

Otherwise discontent raises its head, and the Jew finds himself in just the right situation to exploit it. It's essential that a balance should be struck, in such a way that dyed-in-the-wool Conservatives may be abolished as well as Jewish and Bolshevik anarchists.

The English people are composed of races that are very different from one another and have not been blended together as in many other countries. There lies the danger that amongst them a class war may be transformed into a racial war.

The English could escape this risk by ceasing to judge their fellow citizens in accordance with their outward aspects and paying attention, instead, to their real qualities. One can be the son of a good family and have no talent. If the English behaved as we behave in the Party, they would give advancement only to the most deserving.

---

[285] Samuel Hoare (1880–1959), a senior British Conservative politician who served as Secretary of State for Air, Secretary of State for India, Secretary of State for Foreign Affairs, Home Secretary, and Lord Keeper of the Privy Seal. He was vehemently opposed to going to war with Germany, and was one of those removed from office in 1940 to make way for those in favour of the war.

It's good that the professions should be organised, but on condition that each man finds his place. It's folly to have a man build roads who would at best be capable of sweeping them, just as it is scandalous to make a road-sweeper of a man who has the stuff of an engineer.

National Socialism has introduced into daily life the idea that one should choose an occupation because one is predisposed to it by one's aptitudes, and not because one is predestined for it by birth. Thus National Socialism exercises a calming effect. It reconciles men instead of setting them against one another. It's ridiculous that a child should ever feel obliged to take up his father's profession. Only his aptitudes and gifts should be taken into consideration.

Why shouldn't a child have propensities that his parents didn't have? Isn't everyone in Germany sprung from the peasantry? One must not put a curb on individuals. On the contrary, one must avoid whatever might prevent them from rising. If one systematically encourages the selection of the fittest, the time will come when talents will again be, in a sort of way, the privilege of an elite. I got this impression especially strongly on the occasion of the launching of the *Tirpitz*.[286] The workers gathered for that ceremony gave an extraordinary impression of nobility.

Evolution usually occurs in one direction—that is to say, in the direction of the development of intellectuality. One has a tendency to forget what the potential of energy to be found in the people means for the nation's life.

For the maintenance of social order, it's important that room should be found not only for the intellect but also for strength. Otherwise the day comes when strength, having divorced the intellect, rebels against it and crushes it. The duel between intellect and strength will always be decided to the advantage of strength. A social class made up solely of intellectuals feels a sort of bad conscience.

When a revolution occurs, this class is afraid to assert itself; it sits on its sacks of coin; it plays the coward. My own conscience is clean. If I am told that somewhere there exists a young man who has talent, I myself will do what I can for him. Nothing could be more agreeable to me than to be told, when somebody is introduced to me: "Here's a man of rare talent. Perhaps one day he'll be the Führer of the nation."

Precisely because I favour a maximum of equity in the established social order, for that very reason I feel myself entitled to rage with pit-

[286] The battleship *Tirpitz* was launched in Wilhelmshaven in 1938.

iless severity against whoever might try to undermine that order. The order I'm building must be solid enough to withstand all trials, and that's why we shall drown in blood any attempt to subvert that order. But in this National Socialist society nothing will be left undone to find their proper place for competence and talent. We really want every man to have his chance. Let those who have an aptitude for commanding, command, and let the others be the agents who carry these commands out. It's important to appreciate, without prejudice, everyone's aptitudes and faults—so that everyone can occupy the place that suits him, for the greatest good of the community.

On the day when the English set free their nine thousand Fascists, these men will tear the guts out of the plutocrats, and the problem will be solved. In my view, when there are nine thousand men in a country who are capable of facing prison from loyalty to an idea, this idea remains a living one. And as long as a man is left to carry the flag, nothing is lost. Faith moves mountains.

In that respect, I see things with the coldest objectivity. If the German people lost its faith, if the German people were no longer inclined to give itself body and soul in order to survive—then the German people would have nothing to do but disappear!

27th January 1942, evening
Capitalist economy and prosperity—Sabotage of synthetic petrol in 1933—Deterding[287] backs Schacht—The British have ruined the solidarity of the white races—History will justify Lloyd George—The Jew must be rooted out from Europe

America should be living in abundance. But rationalisation is the beginning of an unspeakable poverty. The counterpart of this poverty is the insolent opulence of the privileged caste. Obviously the Jew thinks as a capitalist, and not as an economist.

I believe the United States have promised Brazil to buy up its crop of coffee after the war. The Brazilians must have been lured in one way or another. States like Brazil should understand that such a policy will more and more drive Europe to autarky.

Vögler made me the proposal, in 1933, to supply us with two million tons of synthetic petrol in the space of three years, on condition that we

---

[287] Henri Deterding (1866–1939), chairman of the combined Royal Dutch/Shell oil company, head of the Royal Dutch Petroleum Company and its general manager for 36 years. Deterding was a staunch anti-communist and known for his support of the NSDAP.

should undertake to buy his entire output, at a price fixed beforehand, for a period of ten years. His offer covered our entire needs for the year 1934. The Ministry of Economics torpedoed the scheme. It was arranged in advance that the IG. Farben would finance the construction of the factories. The scheme furthermore guaranteed employment for hundreds of thousands of workers. As a result of this piece of torpedoing, I sacked some high officials of the Ministry of Economics, and I installed Keppler there. Thereupon they tripped him up with the knave of Düsseldorf. And thus another nine months were wasted.

Behind Schacht was Deterding. I would much like to know who *wasn't* corrupt in that bucket-shop! These circumstances led me to set afoot the Four Year Plan, at the head of which I placed Göring.

As regards buna,[288] there were the same kinds of resistance. Whatever I did, things didn't go forward. Things began to change at the Ministry of Economics when Funk took it in hand.

It was only after the beginning of the winter of 1936 that I began to have something to say about the State Railways. Until then, it was the clauses of the Treaty of Versailles that were operative. I cancelled these clauses by a law that I had passed by the Reichstag, so that no lawyer could come and argue with me about the illegality of the measures on which I decided. Thus the State Railways, the State Bank and the Kaiser Wilhelm Canal came back beneath our sovereignty. What troubles I had, until the moment when I could regain the effective control of German affairs in their entirety! It's an imperative obligation for the white man, in the colonies, to keep the native at a distance.

The Japanese haven't any transport problems to solve. Wherever they install themselves, they can live on the resources of the region. All they need is ammunition. The Americans, on the other hand, need a gigantic transport fleet. All the same, what happened wasn't inevitable. The English had a right to be cowards, but at least they had to be clever. A policy of friendship with us would have entailed their offering us Guinea, for example. Now, because of their stupidity, they're losing a whole world—and they've turned *us* into allies of the Japanese!

What would have happened on the 13th March 1936, if anybody other than myself had been at the head of the Reich! Anyone you care to mention would have lost his nerve. I was obliged to lie, and what saved us was my unshakeable obstinacy and my amazing aplomb. I

---

[288] Buna rubber was a synthetic polybutadiene rubber first produced in Germany.

threatened, unless the situation eased in twenty-four hours, to send six extra divisions into the Rhineland. The fact was, I only had four brigades. Next day, the English newspapers wrote that there had been an easing of the international situation.

I must recognise that Ribbentrop is not a particularly agreeable companion, but he's a sturdy and obstinate man. Neurath displayed the same qualities on that occasion. A retreat on our part would have spelt collapse.

Our negotiators were in a situation similar to that of 1919. They could have obtained much more favourable peace conditions. But was it in the interests of the German people?

That was quite another question. What did it matter, after all, to obtain an Army of two or three hundred thousand men in place of the Army of a hundred thousand? What matters to a nation is to be free. And it was the German nation's despair that gave birth to National Socialism.

We had a fundamental problem to deal with, and it's only after the event that one can say that a certain good could be born of evil. But it goes without saying that the task of a negotiator is to extract the best possible conditions from his adversary. Amongst the Social-Democrats there were men who favoured an energetic policy, and were willing to take the risks. It was two Catholics, Wirth and Erzberger, who gave in.

If we had had an Army of two or three hundred thousand men, the French Army would not have degenerated as it did. That circumstance stood us in good stead. The French having fallen into indolence, we recovered much more quickly than they did.

The man who, without any doubt, will find himself justified by history is Lloyd George. In a memorandum drafted at the time, Lloyd George declared that, if peace were made in the conditions foreseen, it would help to start a new war. "The Germans fought so heroically", he wrote "that this proud nation will never be content with such a peace." If Lloyd George had had the necessary power, he would certainly have been the architect of a German-English understanding. The British Navy was the chief partisan of such an understanding.

It was the jumping-jacks of politics, inspired by world Jewry, who set themselves against it. The sailors thought that the German fleet represented the necessary supplement to the British fleet to guarantee the policing of the seas. In a conflict of no interest to Europe, the German

Navy would have had as its mission to guard the safety of European waters, which would have set free the entirety of the British fleet. Events missed actually taking that direction only by a hair's breadth.

The Jews must pack up, disappear from Europe. Let them go to Russia. Where the Jews are concerned, I'm devoid of all sense of pity. They'll always be the ferment that moves peoples one against the other. They sow discord everywhere, as much between individuals as between peoples. They'll also have to clear out of Switzerland and Sweden. It's where they're to be found in small numbers that they're most dangerous. Put five thousand Jews in Sweden—soon they'll be holding all the posts there. Obviously, that makes them all the easier to spot.

It's entirely natural that we should concern ourselves with the question on the European level. It's clearly not enough to expel them from Germany. We cannot allow them to retain bases of withdrawal at our doors. We want to be out of danger of all kinds of infiltration.

28th January 1942, midday
SPECIAL GUESTS: FIELD-MARSHAL MILCH[289] AND THE AIRMEN JESCHONNEK[290] AND GALLAND[291]

Frederick the Great

When one reflects that Frederick the Great held out against forces twelve times greater than his, one gets the impression: "What a grand fellow he must have been!" This time, it's we who have the supremacy. I'm really quite ashamed of it.

Night of 28th–29th January 1942
Birth control and the victory of Christianity—Families of two or three in France—Propagating German blood—The rights born of conquest

Do you know what caused the downfall of the ancient world? The ruling class had become rich and urbanised. From then on, it had been inspired by the wish to ensure for its heirs a life free from care. It's a state of mind that entails the following corollary: the more heirs there are, the less each one of them receives. Hence the limitation of births.

The power of each family depended to some extent on the number of slaves it possessed. Thus there grew up the *plebs* which was driven to multiplication, faced by a patrician class which was shrinking. The

---

[289] Erhard Milch (1892–1972), State Secretary in the Ministry of Aviation and Inspector General of the Air force in charge of aircraft production and supply. His father was allegedly Jewish.
[290] Hans Jeschonnek (1899–1943), Luftwaffe Chief of the General Staff.
[291] Adolf Galland (1912–1996), Luftwaffe Lieutenant General and fighter ace.

day when Christianity abolished the frontier that had hitherto separated the two classes, the Roman patriciate found itself submerged in the resulting mass. It's the fall in the birth-rate that's at the bottom of everything. France, with its two-children families, is doomed to stagnation and its situation can only get worse. The products of French industry do not lack quality. But the danger, for France, is that the spirit of routine may triumph over the generative impulses of progress.

It's the feeding-bottle that will save us. Even if this war costs us two hundred and fifty thousand dead and a hundred thousand disabled, these losses are already made good by the increase in births in Germany since our seizure of power. They will be paid for several times over by our colonisation in the East.

The population of German blood will multiply itself richly. I would regard it as a crime to have sacrificed the lives of German soldiers simply for the conquest of natural riches to be exploited in capitalist style. According to the laws of nature, the soil belongs to him who conquers it. The fact of having children who want to live, the fact that our people is bursting out of its cramped frontiers—these justify all our claims to the Eastern spaces. The overflow of our birth-rate will give us our chance. Overpopulation compels a people to look out for itself. There is no risk of our remaining fixed at our present level. Necessity will force us to be always at the head of progress. All life is paid for with blood. If a man doesn't like this notion of life, I advise him to renounce life altogether—for it proves he is not suited for the struggle. In any case, on the margin of this continual struggle, there's so much pleasure in living. So why be sad at what is so, and could not be otherwise! The creative forces make their home in the bosom of the optimist. But faith is at the bottom of everything.

30th January 1942, midday
SPECIAL GUESTS: DR. LEY, HEYDRICH, DR. WEBER[292] AND
BENNO VON ARENT [293]

*A French agent—Further misdeeds of the jurists—Memories of prison—
Hácha*

As an orator, my most dangerous opponent was Ballerstedt.[294] What a feat it was to hold my own against him! His father was a Hessian, his

---

[292] Friedrich Weber (1892–1955), a vet and November 1923 Putschist.

[293] Benno von Arent (1898–1956), a film director and SS General Staff member.

[294] Otto Ballerstedt (1887–1934), leader of an early NSDAP competitor party. He was murdered by unknown persons in 1934.

mother was from Lorraine. He was a diabolical dialectician. To give his hearers the impression that he agreed with them, he'd begin with a eulogy of the Prussians. I've been condemned several times for accusing this man of treason—and yet he was in fact sold to the French.

Finally I got three months' imprisonment for breaking up one of his meetings.[295] In the reasons adduced for the verdict, the point of view was put in evidence that the fact of regarding Ballerstedt's policy as treason towards the Reich did not correspond to any objective reality. The Court recorded that this was simply a matter of a policy which I, personally, regarded as treason.

The experience I've had, in the course of my life, of the stupidity of lawyers has resulted in these people's being definitely classified, in my view. They're the people who used to burn witches! Originally I used to think it was an idiosyncrasy of Dietrich Eckart's continually to attack lawyers. He used to say that the mere fact of wanting to be a lawyer came from a mental deficiency. Alternatively, he used to explain, the mental deficiency came of being a lawyer. It was Eckart who asked the advocate Zetzschwitz, on whom some dignity had just been conferred: "Was it to reward you for having lost all your cases?"

My first long term of imprisonment was at Stadelheim. As he led me into my cell, the warder amiably pointed out to me that a number of celebrated men had lived there before: Ludwig Thoma,[296] for example—and likewise Kurt Eisner. Kriebel[297] continually complained at Landsberg. During the first days, it was because of the heating. He spent his time finding fault with the warders. One day he had the idea of sending for the prison regulations, which dated from 1860. He read them attentively and discovered that the prisoners were entitled, notably, to a chest of drawers.

Another day it was revealed to him that the reverend priests were obliged to visit the prisoners, and he complained of not yet having seen the shadow of a cassock. The Mufti[298]—this was the name we gave the

[295] Hitler served one month of this sentence from 24 June to 27 July 1922 in Munich's Stadelheim prison

[296] Ludwig Thoma (1867–1921), a popular author who was imprisoned in 1906 for publishing a poem which insulted "members of a social morality organisation"—members of the clergy in Cologne.

[297] Hermann Kriebel (1876–1941), an early party member, November 1923 Putschist, and later German consul general in Shanghai.

[298] A Muslim legal expert who is empowered to give rulings on religious matters. In this case, the director of the prison.

director of the prison—was at his wits' end and came and consulted me: "Might Colonel Kriebel be a war-wounded?"

"What do you mean by that?"

"He's raving mad."

"I think he once had malaria."

"So he should be treated with care?"

"I think that would be the proper course."

We must present Hácha as one of the greatest men who've ever lived—but on condition that he leaves the Czechs a legacy that will destroy them forever. We must not hesitate to make at least as much of him as King Wenceslas[299]—so that until the end of time all the cowards can complain of him. His successor? It doesn't matter who, as long as he's a lecher. We'll always get along better with cads than with men of character! We'll settle the Czechs' hash if we follow a consistent policy with them, without letting this policy be influenced by accidents of persons.

Since the Battle of the White Mountain,[300] in 1620, and until 1867, the Austrian State pursued this policy towards the Czechs. Thus the Czechs ended in being ashamed of speaking their own tongue. A great part of the Czechs are of Germanic origin, and it's not impossible to re-Germanise them.

31st January 1942, evening

Former German colonies—The British plutocracy—The psychological moment to stop the war—Possibility of collaboration with France—The era of Italian Fascism—The birth of the SA—Two worlds cheek by jowl— The fossils of the Italian Court—Venice, Naples, Rome, Florence—The third Power

The German colonies suffered from a lack of skilled labour. That explains why there was no possibility for big investments. Yet they were territories populated by three or four million natives. In India, the English invested huge sums: railways and other methods of transport, factories and port installations. If each of three hundred and eighty million Indians merely buys a reel of cotton every year, imagine what a volume of business that adds up to! Cotton goods were at first manufactured in England. It's only little by little that factories were built in India herself. It's the capitalist notion of business that led to that result.

---

[299] Also spelled Wenceslaus I (907–935), Duke of Bohemia.
[300] The Battle of White Mountain (8 November 1620) during the Thirty Years' War led to the defeat of the Bohemian Revolt and ensured Habsburg control.

People thought that the saving on transport costs and the employment of less expensive labour would increase the margin of profit.

For a capitalist, it would be a crime to waste a crumb. What was the result? Today England has an army of two million and a half unemployed. There are in Great Britain more than four hundred tax-payers with a yearly income of more than a million pounds. In Germany, only the Kaiser, Henckel von Donnersmarck and Thurn-and-Taxis had incomes of three to four million marks. A man who had a fortune of a million marks was already regarded as a nabob.[301]

But for the Great War, the English would have gone on enjoying the blessings of the Victorian Age. What is Libya to Great Britain? Another desert. Every war comes to an end at the moment when one of the belligerents decides he must cut costs. In this war it's the English who'll throw in the sponge.

Strategic successes can make no difference to the Empire's precarious situation. England can continue to be viable only if she links herself to the Continent. She must be able to defend her imperial interests within the framework of a continental organisation. It's only on this condition that she'll keep her Empire. But nothing is more difficult than to come down from a pedestal. Thus Austria clung until 1866 to the fiction of supremacy—and then it took her another seventy years to learn from the facts.

British military prestige has been re-established by the conquest of Benghazi. It was the psychological moment to put an end to the war. But Churchill had Russia at the back of his mind-and he didn't see that, if Russia were to triumph over Germany, Europe would at once come under the hegemony of a Great Power. Too many Jews had an interest in seeing events take this turn. The Jew is so stupid that he himself saws through the branch on which he's sitting. In 1919, a Jewess wrote in the *Bayrischer Kurier:* "What Eisner's doing now will recoil upon *our* heads." A rare case of foresight.

France remains hostile to us. She contains, in addition to her Nordic blood, a blood that will always be foreign to us. In addition to Paris, which is more spontaneous in its reactions, she has the clerical and Masonic South. In imitation of Talleyrand[302] in 1815, the French try to

---

[301] Originally, a Muslim official or governor under the Mogul empire. In the sense above, a person of conspicuous wealth or high status.

[302] Charles-Maurice de Talleyrand-Périgord (1754–1838), Prime Minister of France following the downfall of Napoleon Bonaparte.

profit by our moments of weakness to get the greatest possible advantage from the situation. But with me they won't succeed in their plans. There's no possibility of our making any pact with the French before we've definitely ensured our power. Our policy, at this moment, must consist in cleverly playing off one lot against the other.

There must be two Frances. Thus, the French who have compromised themselves with us will find it to their own interests that we should remain in Paris as long as possible. But our best protection against France will be for us to maintain a strong friendship, lasting for centuries, with Italy.

Unlike France, Italy is inspired by political notions that are close to ours. I was thinking of the Italian delegation I received yesterday. I met men who have rulers' qualities such as are very much to my taste. What handsome individuals, and what a resolute air! Those are men who could play a part at the top level.

The Fascists paid with their blood much more than we did. The story of the conquest of power in Italy is an heroic epic. It always warms my heart to think of it. I can understand their emotion when they once more live through the time of the March on Rome.

Why should such men suddenly become worthless as soldiers? It's quite simply because they lack a command. The Italian people is idealistic, but the cadres of the Italian Army are reactionary.

It's strange how, throughout the last hundred years, our two peoples have had perceptibly the same destiny. First of all, the wars for unity, then the fact that each was cheated of its rights. Then, more recently, the two sister revolutions that knew nothing of one another.

It was in 1921 that I first heard Fascism mentioned. The SA was born in 1920, without my having the least idea of what was going on in Italy.

Italy developed in a manner at which I was the first to be surprised. I could see fairly clearly the orientation that it would be proper to give the Party, but I had no ideas concerning paramilitary organisations. I began by creating a service to keep order, and it was only after the bloody brawls of 1920 that I gave these troops the name *of Sturm-Abteilung* (SA), as a reward for their behaviour.

I had taught them the technique of concentrating their efforts on limited objectives, and at meetings to attack the opponent table by table. But it was confined to that. When the brassard proved no longer sufficient, I equipped them with a specially designed cap. That was after

Coburg. The skier's cap didn't cost much. It was all done in a very empirical manner. Nothing of that sort was thought out in advance.

The SS started with formations of seven or eight men. In these we gathered the "tough 'uns." Things developed spontaneously, and subsequently acquired a speed comparable to that of developments in Italy. The Duce himself has told me that at the moment when he undertook the struggle against Bolshevism, he didn't know exactly where he was going.

What crowns these parallel destinies is that today we are fighting side by side against the same Powers and against the same personages.

At the same period, the Duce and I were both working in the building-trade. This explains that there is also a bond between us on the purely human level. I have a deep friendship for this extraordinary man. From the cultural point of view, we are more closely linked with the Italians than with any other people. The art of Northern Italy is something we have in common with them: nothing but pure Germans.

The objectionable Italian type is found only in the South, and not everywhere even there. We also have this type in our own country. When I think of them: Vienna-Ottakring, Munich-Giesing, Berlin-Pankow! If I compare the two types, that of these degenerate Italians and our type, I find it very difficult to say which of the two is the more antipathetic.[303]

There is a difference as between day and night, between the genuine Fascists and the others. Those society people with whom we are compelled to associate, that cosmopolitan world, they're more or less the same there and here. But the man of the people has plenty of spirit and, even physically, quite a different bearing. Compare that man with the parade-ground Fascists who people the Embassy—why, it's like in Germany, with our diplomats from the *Wilhelmstrasse*—excuse me, Hewel! All these people are intolerable—deceivers, hypocrites, liars. I've never seen anything worse than those courtiers at Naples.

As for the bodyguard they so kindly gave me—what foul creatures, what gallows-birds! The Fascists and the others, they're really two worlds in water-tight compartments. The Fascists call the courtiers "lobsters", because of their red livery.

I was greeted at the station by the Duke of Pistoia, a real degenerate. Beside him was another duke, no less degenerate. There was an admiral there who looked like a court toad, a bogus coin, a liar. Happily there

[303] "Antipathetic": showing or feeling a strong aversion.

was also a group of Fascists. All of them, even Ciano, spoke with the deepest contempt of this ridiculous masquerade.

During my excursions with the Duce, my breath was taken away by the skill and audacity of the motor-cyclists who escorted us. What a handsome race! When I went out with the Court, I was perched on a badly slung carnival carriage, which hobbled along in a lamentable fashion. The least depressing people there were the *carabinieri* who escorted us. "There's hope", the Duce said to me, "that in fifty years' time the Court will discover the internal-combustion engine."

The officers' corps belongs to this fossilised world. The senior officers have no contact with the people. Zeitzler told me he had a meal of five or six courses, given by front-line officers. Meanwhile the other ranks were supplied with a watery soup.

I consider it scandalous that such a thing can happen in the middle of a war. It must either feed the soldier's hatred for his officers, or make him indifferent to everything. Our own fellows say the Italian simple soldier is a man full of good will, inclined to enthusiasm for any cause, and that one could get all one wanted out of him if he were well led.

Perhaps the Duce came on the scene a year or two too early with his revolution. He probably should have let the Reds have their own way for a bit first—they'd have exterminated the aristocracy. The Duce would have become Head of a Republic. Thus the abscess would have been lanced.

When I was with Mussolini, the crowd shouted: "Duce! Duce!" When I was with the King, it shouted: "Führer! Führer!"

In Florence I was alone with the Duce, and I read in the eyes of the population the respect and burning love they devoted to him. The common people gazed at him as though they'd have liked to eat him.

Rome captivated me. At Naples, I was interested above all by the harbour. At the Court, I was aware only of the hostile atmosphere. But at Florence, everything was quite different—simply because the Court, that foreign body, wasn't there.

I've retained a painful memory of a visit I paid to units of the fleet in the Bay of Naples. The little king didn't know where to look; nobody paid him any attention. At table I was surrounded only by courtiers. I would rather have entertained myself with the Marshals.

During the parade, at Rome, the front row was occupied by old nanny-goats, dried-up and enamelled, and wearing outrageously low-necked dresses, what's more, with a crucifix hanging between their withered breasts. The generals were in the second row. Why display this come-down of the human race?

At the palace in Venice, on the other hand, everything teemed with lovely girls. But they managed to apologise to me for the *faux pas* that had been committed. Some mannequins from a fashion-house in Rome, I was told, had strayed into the audience!

The difficulty for the Duce is that he's made himself a sort of prisoner to this society, and has thus to some extent betrayed his own men. In his place, I would invite some lovely girls from the Campagna to my receptions—the place overflows with them.

It wouldn't occur to me to compete with the King on his own ground, I would be beaten in advance. These misunderstandings arise because the situation is not clear. The poor Duce; I'm often sorry for him. All the affronts he has to swallow. I don't think I would endure them.

There's also the third power—the Vatican. Don't forget that! Why be surprised if our confidential letters are broadcast to the world a few days after being received? I'll never forget the gratitude we owe to Noske, Ebert[304] and Scheidemann[305] for having rid us of such people. Their intentions weren't pure, and that's why they've been punished, but we've reaped all the profit!

1st February 1942, evening
SPECIAL GUEST: HIMMLER
The instigators of the 1918 revolution—Attitude towards former opponents—The Bavarian police—The arms traffic

Amongst the men who became conspicuous during the events of 1918, I draw certain distinctions. Some of them, without having wished it, found themselves dragged into the revolution. Amongst these was first of all Noske, then Ebert, Scheidemann, Severing—and, in Bavaria, Auer.[306] In the struggle that set these men against us, I was merciless. It was only after our victory that I could say to them: "I understand the motives that drove you on." Those who were truly base were men of the Catholic Centre—Spiecker, for example. Tortuous methods and lies. Brüning utterly lacked character, and Treviranus was a bounder.

---

[304] Friedrich Ebert (1871–1925) Social Democratic Party of Germany president of Germany from 1919 until 1925.

[305] Philipp Scheidemann (1865–1939), Social Democratic Party politician and first Minister President of the Weimar Republic.

[306] Erhard Auer (1874–1945), leader of the Social Democratic Party in Bavaria and Minister of the Interior of the Free State of Bavaria.

I'm full of understanding for a worker who was hurled into a hostile world, and, quite naturally, found himself exposed to the seductions of Marxism. But not for those swine of theoreticians like Hilferding and Kautsky. Braun was not the worst of them. In any case, he was quick to put water in his wine. Luppe, at Nuremberg, was not a bad mayor. As for Scharnagel, he was a baker from head to foot.

In Bavaria, men like Stützel, Schweyer, Koch and others were not bribeable, but this did not prevent them from being fundamentally base. Lerchenfeld and Lortz were just poor devils. Matt was more a fool than a knave. Several of them were descended from Mongols and Huns. Some of them succeeded in improving themselves in the following generation.

I've been particularly correct towards my opponents. The Minister who condemned me, I've made him my Minister of Justice. Amongst my prison guards, several have become chiefs of the SA. The director of my prison has risen in rank. The only one whose situation I've not improved is Schweyer. On the contrary, I've suppressed his plurality of offices, for on top of his pension as Minister he used to receive eighteen thousand marks as administrator of Bavarian Electricity. Social-Democracy of the time lacked only a leader. Its worst mistake was to persevere in a path condemned by the facts.

I was pitiless to all who indulged in Separatism—if only by way of warning, and to get it into everyone's head that in that sort of thing we have no time for jokes. But, in a general way, I can say I've been full of moderation.

My conversations with Nortz, the Police President, were amusing. In 1923, two days before the 27th January, he claimed the right to compel me to hold in a hall a meeting that I wanted to hold in the open air. He invoked the security of the State as an argument in support of his decision, and likewise the fact that he had not enough police forces to guarantee our safety. I retorted that we were capable of guaranteeing order by our own methods. Moreover, I claimed the right to hold a dozen meetings in succession, not just one. I added that if he opposed our decision, the blood that would be shed would be upon his head. Our haggling continued, and Nortz finally proposed that we should split the baby in two: six meetings, instead of twelve, held simultaneously in the Circus[307] and on the Marsfeld in front of the Circus (for I

---

[307] The Circus Krone building in Munich was originally designed as a circus venue, but its size allowed it to be hired out as a meeting hall.

would declared that the Circus wasn't big enough to hold all my supporters). Finally, Nortz granted me my twelve meetings, but in the following form: we would hold simultaneously six times two meetings. For him that made six—for us, twelve!

I had another conflict with him concerning an individual whom the police maintained in our midst. The man was, in any case, ill-chosen, for he stank of the police spy at a radius of a hundred metres.

One day I was visited by a policeman who announced himself to me as an old comrade from the front. He said he was racked by remorse, for it was he who took down the spy's reports from dictation. I asked the comrade from the front to go on recording what the spy had to say, but on condition that he sent me a copy every time. In reality, the comrade in question was inspired quite simply by a desire for revenge, as I subsequently learnt. He was the victim of our spy, who was cuckolding him!

When I asked for the Circus for our demonstration on the 1st May, Nortz refused it me on the pretext that his forces were not enough to ensure order, and that my men continually provoked their adversaries. I leapt on the word "provoke". "My men!" I said. "But it's you who send us provocative agitators in plain clothes. It's *your* spies who urge my innocent lambs on to illegal acts."

Nortz supposed I was exaggerating. When I insisted, and offered him proofs, he sent for his colleague Bernreuther. The latter, who was certainly well informed, tried to calm me down. It was only when I threatened them that I would publish in my newspaper a replica of the reports in my possession, that the affair was settled. An hour later, we had the authorisation to hold our meeting.

There had been talk of attempting a *coup*, in agreement with the bourgeois parties. It was to take place here and there all over Germany, especially in Thuringia. I would been well let down by the bourgeois over the business, which I remember as the finest of our mess-ups. But Nortz couldn't prevent our march on Oberwiesenfeld.

At three o'clock in the morning, after taking possession of our weapons, we occupied Oberwiesenfeld according to plan. The hours passed, and still nothing happened. Our bourgeois allies had stayed in their beds. Calm prevailed throughout Germany, whilst we awaited from all quarters the confirmation of the expected risings. At six o'clock, gangs of Reds gathered to meet us. I sent some men to provoke them, but they didn't react.

Ten o'clock, eleven o'clock, and the Reich still did not emerge from its stupor—and we were still there on the look-out, armed to the teeth! We had to make up our minds to go home. During the return march, we met a few inoffensive Reds, fellows who could be dispersed by a flourish of trumpets. We beat them up a little, in the hope of getting a big row started, but it was no use.

Everything was over when a trotting, horse-drawn battery, which I hadn't sent for, arrived from Tölz. It unfolded like a flower, right in the face of the police. I would done well to swear never again to undertake anything in collaboration with the bourgeois.

Three days later I was summoned to appear before the Prosecutor General, a bloody man, to reply to the accusation of having endangered public security. "I in no way infringed public order," I said. "But an attempt was made to do so."

"Who says that?"

"The law declares that the fact of arming gangs . . ."

"Who is speaking of gangs? My men are perfectly disciplined. As for my weapons, they were stored in the State arsenals."

"So you possess weapons?"

"Of course. Are you not aware that the others possess them, too?" This inculpation had no consequences. In the circumstances, Stenglein and Ehardt were sitting pretty.

This was how I would procured weapons. A certain Councillor Schäffer had a store of weapons at Dachau, and he offered to sell them to me. At that time I made it a principle to leave weapons in the hands of the civic guards, reasoning that they would keep them in good condition as long as there was no question of using them, and that in case of need they would ask nothing better than to hand them over to us, so that we could take their place in the first rank. Nevertheless, I thought it opportune not to reject Schäffer's proposal. I therefore went to Dachau with Göring. We had the impression we had fallen into a bandits' lair. Their first concern was to ask us for the password. We were led into the presence of a woman. I remember her, for this was the first time I saw a woman with her hair dressed like a boy's. She was surrounded by a gang of individuals with gallows-birds' faces.

This was Schäffer's wife. We drove the bargain, although not without my warning them that they wouldn't see the colour of my money until the weapons were in my possession. We also found, on the airfield at Schleissheim, thousands of rifles, mess-tins, haversacks, a pile of useless junk. But, after it had been repaired, there would be enough to equip a regiment.

I went to see Lossow[308] and handed him all this material, urging him to take care of it and telling him, moreover, that I would make no use of it except in the event of a show-down with Communism. It was thus solemnly agreed that the material would remain in the hands of the Reichswehr as long as this eventuality did not arise. Amongst the mixed parcels, there were notably seventeen guns of all calibres.

I got my hands on the second parcel in particularly comic circumstances: Somebody had mysteriously rung me up on the telephone to ask me to "take possession of the crates". I didn't waste time in having the whole bill of fare read out to tell me what it was all about. I thought to myself that there were crates going for the asking, and I told myself that it was at least worth the trouble of going to find out. Nevertheless, I asked my interlocutor's name.

"Voll," he said, "the brother-in-law of the proprietor of the warehouse." I arrived at this warehouse, which was in the Landsbergerstrasse, and, sure enough, I found there forty-eight crates that had been deposited there in my name. Voll told me that they contained arms, and that it was impossible for him to keep them any longer, for there were numerous Communists amongst his workers. He begged me to have the crates removed as soon as possible. I went first to see Röhm to ask him if he could put any trucks at my disposal. He replied that he couldn't do that immediately. I then applied to Zeller. He accepted, refusing any payment but laying it down as a condition that he should share the booty with me. Agreed.

When we were loading the trucks, up came Major Stefani. He claimed that the arms were his. "They're in my name," I replied, "and nobody will stop me from taking possession of them."

Three days later, Zeller told me that the aforesaid arms were from his own warehouse in the Franz Joseph Strasse, from which they'd been stolen. "What are you complaining about?" I said. "Haven't you recovered half of them?" There were arms practically everywhere in those days: in monasteries, on farms, amongst groups of civic guards. It was to the citizens' credit that they thus assembled arms that had been

---

[308] Otto von Lossow (1868–1938), an Army officer who, along with Gustav Ritter von Kahr, Minister President of Bavaria and Colonel Hans Ritter von Seisser, head of the Bavarian State Police, formed the ruling triumvirate in Bavaria at the time of the November 1923 Putsch.

thrown away by soldiers returning, demoralised, from the front—and that others had pillaged at the depots.

4th February 1942, midday
Churchill and Robespierre—The citadel of Singapore—In praise of François-Poncet[309]—Inadequacy of the diplomats—Reorganisation of German diplomacy

Churchill is like an animal at bay. He must be seeing snares everywhere. Even if Parliament gives him increased powers, his reasons for being mistrustful still exist. He's in the same situation as Robespierre on the eve of his fall. Nothing but praise was addressed to the virtuous citizen, when suddenly the situation was reversed. Churchill has no more supporters.

Singapore has become a symbol to the entire world. Before 1914, it was only a commercial harbour. It was between the two wars that Singapore began its great rise and acquired the strategic importance that it's recognised to have today. When one builds a citadel like Singapore, it must be made an impregnable position—else it's a waste of money. The English have lived on the idea of an invincibility whose image is invoked for them by the magic names of Shanghai, Hong Kong and Singapore. Suddenly they have to sing smaller, and realise that this magnificent façade was merely a bluff. I agree, it's a terrible blow for the English.

I've been told that an English statesman left a will in which he reminded his compatriots of the following sacred truth: that the only danger to England was Germany!

François-Poncet did not want the war. The reports dating from the end of his mission to Berlin are worthless, in my view. The little vulgarities in which he indulged at my expense had no other object but to prove to his compatriots that he wasn't contaminated by us. If he had said in his reports what he really thought, he'd have been recalled at once. In all his reports, he insisted on the necessity of following the evolution of the situation in Germany with close attention.

Poncet is the most intelligent of the diplomats I've known—including the German ones, of course. I would not have risked discussing German literature with him, for I would have been put out of countenance. When he said good-bye to me at the Obsersalzburg, he was very much moved. He told me he'd done everything humanly possible,

---

[309] André François-Poncet (1887–1978), French Ambassador to Germany from 1931 to 1938.

but that in Paris he was regarded as a man won over to our cause. "The French are a very clever people," he added. "There's not a Frenchman who doesn't believe that in my place he would do much better than I."

François-Poncet speaks absolutely perfect German. He once made a speech at Nuremberg that began: "Now that I've had conferred upon me the dignity of an orator of the National-Socialist Party . . ."

I've forgiven him all his remarks about me. If meet him, I shall confine myself to saying to him: "It's dangerous to give one's opinion in writing on people whom one does not entirely know. It's better to do it *viva voce*." Our difficulties on the subject of Morocco were smoothed out by him in two days.

Henderson[310] and Poncet certainly both had connections in industry. Henderson, for his part, was interested in seeing to it that war should come. Poncet was the proprietor of some factories in Lorraine. But, tell me, do you know a diplomat who poked his nose into everything, as he did, who was connected with everybody and knew everything? Nothing escaped him. What didn't he distribute, like sweets!

A supplementary attraction of his was his wife. What natural behaviour! She hadn't the slightest affectation. Truly, an exceptional woman.

One day there was a dramatic incident! A foreign statesman passing through Berlin paid François-Poncet a visit. It was the hour when children were leaving school. His children rushed into the drawing-room, shouting "Heil Hitler!" When he told me the story, Poncet appealed to me: "It was very embarrassing for me. Put yourself in my place!"

Soon afterwards, François-Poncet went to Paris, and returned to Berlin without his children. I asked him if his children weren't happy in Berlin. "Young people are easily influenced," he said. "Just think, my children don't know who is the President of the Republic. I'm aghast! The other day we were passing by a monument in Paris and suddenly they exclaimed: 'Look, daddy, there's Bismarck!' I decided to send them to a good school in France."

In my opinion, the man most guilty of all is Churchill—then Belisha, Vansittart[311] and a swarm of others. The French let themselves be dragged in. In a general way, they supposed that Germany was about to collapse immediately. The Polish ambassador Lipski[312] had the cheek to

[310] Nevile Henderson (1882–1942), British ambassador in Berlin (1937–1939).
[311] Robert Vansittart (1881–1957), British Permanent Under-Secretary of State for Foreign Affairs and later Chief Diplomatic Adviser to the British Government.
[312] Józef Lipski (1894–1958), Polish ambassador to Germany from 1934 to 1939.

write in a report that he knew from a sure source that Germany could hold out only for a week. People like that bear a great share of responsibility for what has happened. Lipski, particularly, used to frequent the Dirksens' receptions. If a man like Lipski could believe such a thing—a man who was present at all the Party demonstrations—what can the other diplomats have written? I attach absolutely no value to what these people say.

Each time he changes his post, the diplomat begins by paying his formal visits in the city where he's now residing. He exchanges conventional remarks with all and sundry. He has fulfilled the essential part of his mission. After that he moves in a closed world, with no windows open on the outside, and knows nothing of what is happening in the country, except through the tittle-tattle of a barber, a manicurist or a chauffeur.

But these latter, by dint of living in the narrow circle of their clientele, have themselves lost contact with the people. In any case, they're cunning enough to tell tendentious old wives' tales, if they think it appropriate. The less these diplomats know, the more they talk. They've nothing to do, and it would never occur to any of them to profit by his leisure to learn something.

François-Poncet is the only one I knew who used to run about continually, taking an interest in everything—to the point even of sometimes embarrassing me a little.

Besides the big mandarins, one usually has to deal with agents of the needy, sponging type. They're timid, scared—always groping to know whether they should or should not pass on certain information. At the slightest slip or indiscretion, they might lose their jobs, be switched on to a side-track. In many cases, it seems to me it would be better to replace them by more modest representatives, who would confine themselves to receiving and sending despatches. Of what use were our own diplomats to us? What did they teach us before the Great War? Nothing! During the Great War? Nothing! After the Great War? Nothing! I suppose that for the others it must be very much the same.

Diplomacy should be reorganised from top to bottom. Take the case of the Far East. What useful information did I get from our services? A man like Colin Ross,[313] for example, gave me infinitely more precious

---

[313] Colin Ross (1885–1945), a Vienna-born German of Scottish descent—hence his name—was one of the 1920s' most popular travel writers in Germany and Austria. He was also a dedicated Hitler supporter.

information on the subject. And yet Kriebel, whom we had out there, was one of our men. It was he who wrote to me that the Japanese were not nearly strong enough to settle with the Chinese. I recalled him, and he tried to justify himself in my eyes by insisting: "But it's what everyone was saying in Shanghai!" That kind of thing is obviously explained by the company he kept. All of the same kidney, as is usual amongst diplomats. Colin Ross, on the other hand, saw all kinds. His view was that the Japanese would win the war, but that in the long run they'd be absorbed by the Chinese. I am speaking now only of the diplomats of the classic sort.

Amongst these, I admit only two exceptions: François-Poncet and Böttscher[314]—the only ones who ruled the roost. Men like Abetz[315] will always be regarded as amateurs by the careerists. The Dutch representative was a man who knew what he was about. He worked hard, and he gave his Government valuable information.

The Belgian, he was a dwarf! As for the Swiss, he did his daily dozen, sent a report every day. To say what? God preserve me from such bureaucrats! I rack my brains wondering how to improve our diplomacy.

On the one hand, one would like to keep men for a long time at the same post, so that the experience they acquire may be of use to them— knowledge of the language, and of local customs.

On the other hand, one would like to prevent them from sinking into a rut. What is one to do? Probably the English have the best system. Besides their official representatives, they have a great number of spies. It would be very useful to me at this moment, for example, to be informed concerning the importance of the opposition in England, to know who belongs to it. As it is, all I know on this subject is what I've learnt by reading the newspapers! Besides, can't I learn from my diplomats what Washington has in store?

2nd February 1942, evening
Importance of coal and iron—Superiority of American technique— Production and unemployment—Economy of labour—The defeat of stagnation

We must achieve higher yields of coal and steel—the rest will follow automatically. Why are some countries industrialised, and others not? There are permanent reasons for that.

---

[314] Karl Böttcher (1889–1973), commander of the 21st Panzer Division.
[315] Otto Abetz (1903–1958), German ambassador for the Vichy-Government from 1940 to 1944.

France, for example, has always suffered from lack of coal, and that's why she has never been a great industrial Power. The opposite example is that of Great Britain. With us, it's the same. Here everything is based on coal and iron.

Hitherto we haven't reached our ceiling in any field of industry. It's not until we've solved the problem of the raw materials that we'll be able to have our factories giving 100 per cent production, thanks to ceaselessly alternating shifts.

Another factor with which we should reckon is the simplification and improvement of processes of manufacture, with the object of economising on raw material. The mere fact of reducing by two-thirds the wastage in manufacture entails an economy of transport that is far from being negligible. Thus the improvements made in manufacture help to solve the vital transport problem.

The great success of the Americans consists essentially in the fact that they produce quantitatively as much as we do with two-thirds less labour. We've always been hypnotised by the slogan: "the craftsmanship of the German worker".

We tried to persuade ourselves that we could thus achieve an unsurpassable result. That's merely a bluff of which we ourselves are the victims. A gigantic modern press works with a precision that necessarily outclasses manual labour.

American cars, for example, are made with the least possible use of human labour. The first German manufacture of the sort will be the Volkswagen. In this respect, we are far behind the Americans. Moreover, they build far more lightly than we do. A car of ours that weighs eighteen hundred kilos would weigh only a thousand if made by the Americans.

It was reading Ford's books that opened my eyes to these matters. In the 'twenties, the Ford used to cost about two hundred and fifty-five dollars, whilst the least expensive of our cars, the little Opel, cost four thousand six hundred marks. In America everything is machine-made, so that they can employ the most utter cretins in their factories. Their workers have no need of specialised training, and are therefore interchangeable.

We must encourage and develop the manufacture of machine tools. The prejudice has for a long time prevailed that such practices would inexorably lead to an increase in unemployment. That's actually true only if the population's standard of living is not raised.

Originally, all men were cultivators. Each of them produced everything he needed, and nothing else. In the degree to which methods were improved, men were set free from working on the soil and could thereafter devote themselves to other activities. Thus the artisan class was born. Today only 27 per cent of the population of Germany is engaged in tilling the soil. In the artisan class there has been a similar evolution.

The improvement in methods of manufacture has made it possible to economise on labour. One day an idiot had the idea that men had reached a stage that could not be surpassed. Yet progress consists in making life, within the limits of the possible, more and more agreeable for human beings. It does not consist in stagnation. My idea is that we shall never economise enough on labour.

If I found that I needed only half as much labour to build an *autobahn*, well, I would build it twice as wide. All this confusion is the work of professors of political economy. The pontiff of Munich teaches a universal doctrine which is entirely different from the universal doctrine taught by the pontiff of Leipzig. Only one doctrine, however, can correspond to reality, and that's not necessarily the doctrine taught by either of these pontiffs.

It is certainly possible to economise another 30 per cent on our labour. Necessity will make us ingenious.

3rd February 1942, evening
German Freemasonry—Ludendorff's gaffe—A Masonic manoeuvre—
Democratic ritual—Bismarck beaten by a shoemaker

There used to be a large number of Freemasons in Germany who didn't at all know what exactly Freemasonry was. In our lodges, it was above all an occasion for eating, drinking and amusing oneself. It was a very cleverly adjusted organisation. People were kept on the alert, they were entertained with children's rattles the better to divert their gaze from the essential truth. I knew little towns that were entirely under the dominion of masonry, much more so than the big towns—for example, Bayreuth and Gotha. Zentz[316] once invited us—Ludendorff,[317] Pöhner[318]

---

[316] Eugen Zentz (1870–1945), Munich politician most famous for being the chairman at the meeting where the November 1923 Putsch was launched.

[317] Erich Ludendorff (1865–1937), Army General and one of the participants in the failed November 1923 Putsch. He thereafter distanced himself from Hitler, and took no further part in the party.

[318] Ernst Pöhner (1870–1925), Munich Chief of Police from 1919 to 1922, He was

and myself—to be present at a full-dress gathering of the Lodge of St. John. I refused the invitation, and Zentz reproached me with passing judgment without knowing. I said to him: "Save your saliva. For me, Freemasonry's poison."

Ludendorff and Pöhner went there. And Ludendorff was even so ill-advised as to put his signature in their register, under some stupidly compromising phrase. A few days later, I happened to be visiting Pöhner. He was grinning like a monkey. He told me they'd played the same trick on him as on Ludendorff, and that he'd written in their book: "Hitherto I believed that Freemasonry was a danger to the State. I now believe additionally that it should be forbidden for the offence of major imbecility."

Pöhner had been dumbfounded by the ridiculousness of these rites, which transformed men who were quite sane and sober in their ordinary lives into informed apes. The Freemasons tried to use Ludendorff's clumsy declaration for publicity purposes—but it goes without saying that with former's, they were more discreet.

Richard Frank is one of the greatest idealists I've known. Since we needed headquarters, he made efforts to procure the money for us. With this object, he introduced me, in Munich, to a certain Dr. Kuhlo. On Frank's initiative, this Kuhlo had formed a syndicate to buy the Hotel Eden, situated near the station. It was obviously out of the question to make this purchase with the Party's money. This was in 1923, and the sellers demanded payment in Swiss francs.

When all was ready, the syndicate met, with Kuhlo in the chair. The latter rose to his feet and announced that the hotel would be put at the Party's disposal for a modest rental. He suggested, in passing, that perhaps the Party might suppress the article in its programme concerning Freemasonry. I got up and said good-bye to these kindly philanthropists. I would fallen unawares into a nest of Freemasons!

How many times subsequently I've heard comments of this sort: "Why declaim against the Freemasons? Why not leave the Jews in peace?" It's by means of these continual blackmailings that they succeeded in acquiring the subterranean power that acts in all sectors, and each time by appropriate methods. After the prohibition of the Lodges, I often heard it said that, amongst the former masons, there were many

---

earmarked as Bavaria's minister president should the November 1923 Putsch have succeeded, and was convicted with Hitler in 1924 of high treason. Sentenced to five years in prison, he served only three months.

who felt a sense of relief at the idea that we had freed them from this chain.

Not only has there always been an incompatibility between membership of a Lodge and membership of the Party, but the fact of having been a Freemason forbids access to the Party. Of course, there are men who are so stupid that one knows very well that it was only from stupidity that they became masons. The very rare cases in which an exception can be made come exclusively under my authority. And I grant absolution only to men whose entire lives bear witness to their indisputably nationalist feelings.

We were obliged to call a general meeting of the Party each year to elect the Directing Committee. The result of the vote, recorded in a minute, had to appear in the Register of Societies, But for this formality, the Party would have lost its juridical personality and accompanying rights. This annual meeting had something of farce about it. I would offer my resignation. Two accountants, in the space of two hours, would succeed in checking a balance for a total movement of funds of six hundred and fifty millions. The President of the Assembly, elected *ad hoc,* would conduct the debates and proceed to the election of the new Committee.

Voting was by a show of hands. "Who is for, who is against?" he would ask. His silly questions would arouse storms of mirth.

I would then present myself to the Registry of the Court to have our documents registered. The anti-democratic parties, just like the democratic parties, had to go through these grotesque ceremonies.

The other parties had practically no paying members. We, with our two and a half million members, banked two and a half million marks every month.

Many members paid more than the subscription demanded (at first it was fifty pfennig a month, then it was raised to a mark). Fräulein Schleifer, from the post-office, used to pay ten marks a month, for example.

Thus, the Party disposed of considerable sums. Schwarz was very open-handed when it was a question of large matters, but extremely thrifty in small ones. He was the perfect mixture of parsimony and generosity. It was necessary to have a minimum of sixty thousand votes in a district to be entitled to a mandate. Our base was in Bavaria. Here we had six mandates, to start with, which gave us an equal number of delegates to the Reichstag.

There were some extraordinary parties in that Republic. The most incredible was Häusser's.[319] I happened to be passing through Stuttgart. This was in 1922 or 1923. Frau Waldschmidt suggested that I should go and see this phenomenon, without committing myself. I'm fairly sure Häusser was an Alsatian. If my memory is correct, he addressed his audience more or less as follows: "You, you filthy rabble. . ." And it went on in the same tone, consisting solely of insults. In the Munich district, he got a greater number of votes than Stresemann.

As for us, we had all the difficulty in the world to have Epp[320] elected. What scatter-brains we sometimes had opposed to us! Let's not complain about it too much—it must not be forgotten that one day Bismarck was beaten by a cobbler.[321]

Night of 3rd–4th February 1942
Memories of Bayreuth—The automobile craze—Leaving Landsberg—Reconstitution of the Party—The world will recapture its sense of joy

I've been lucky that I never had an accident while travelling. You know the story of the *Hound of the Baskervilles*.[322] On a sinister, stormy night I was going to Bayreuth through the Fichtelgebirge. I would just been saying to Maurice: "Look out on the bend!" I would scarcely spoken when a huge black dog hurled itself on our car. The collision knocked it into the distance. For a long time we could still hear it howling in the night.

I would settled down with the Bechsteins, within a few yards of Wahnfried. On the morning of my arrival, Cosima Wagner paid me a visit, which I returned in the course of the day. Siegfried was there. Bayreuth exerted its full charm upon me.

---

[319] Ludwig Christian Häusser (1881–1927) was a mentally-ill lay preacher who set up a party, the *Christlich-Radikale Partei* ("Christian Radical Party") which literally proclaimed him as the new messiah.

[320] Franz Epp (1868–1947), a First World War general who was elected as one of the first NSDAP members of the Reichstag in 1928.

[321] A reference to the struggle between the co-founder of the Social Democratic Party, the craftsman August Bebel (1840–1913), and Otto von Bismarck. Despite being imprisoned by the state for libelling the Prussian Chancellor, Bebel went on to lead the SPD in the elections of 1890, winning nearly 20 percent of the vote, and becoming Bismarck's greatest opponent. Ultimately, the failure of Bismarck's anti-Socialist law led to his dismissal from office.

[322] The 1902 book, *The Hound of the Baskervilles,* is one of British writer Arthur Conan Doyle's Sherlock Holmes mysteries, and involves a mysterious and allegedly ghostly hound which kills heirs to the Baskerville family.

I was thirty-six years old, and life was delightful. I had all the pleasures of popularity, without any of the inconveniences. Everybody put himself out to be nice to me, and nobody asked anything of me. By day I would go for a walk, in leather shorts. In the evening, I would go to the theatre in a dinner-jacket or tails.

Afterwards, we would prolong the evening in the company of the actors, either at the theatre restaurant or on a visit to Berneck. My supercharged Mercedes was a joy to all. We made many excursions, going once to Luisenberg, another time to Bamberg, and very often to the Hermitage.

There are a lot of photos of me taken at this time which Frau Bechstein has. She used often to say to me: "You deserve to have the finest motor-car in the world. I wish you had a Maybach." The first thing I did on leaving the prison at Landsberg, on the 20th December 1924, was to buy my supercharged Mercedes.

Although I've never driven myself, I've always been passionately keen on cars. I liked this Mercedes particularly. At the window of my cell, in the fortress, I used to follow with my eyes the cars going by on the road to Kaufbeunen, and wonder whether the time would return when I would ride in a car again. I discovered mine by reading a prospectus. At once I realised that it would have to be this or none. Twenty-six thousand marks, it was a lot of money!

I can say that, as to what gives the Mercedes-Benz its beauty nowadays, I can claim the fatherhood. During all these years I've made innumerable sketches with a view to improving the line.

Adolf Müller had taught me to drive all right, but I knew that at the slightest accident my conditional liberty would be withdrawn, and I also knew that nothing would have been more agreeable to the Government. In November 1923, I was already owner of a marvellous Benz. On the 9th, it was in Müller's garage under lock and key. When the police came to seize it, they must have filed through the chain. But they dared not use it in Munich, for the whole population would have risen in revolt, shouting: "Car-thieves!" So they sent it to Nuremberg, where it immediately had an accident. I've bought it back since, and it can be seen among our relics.

It was a queer experience when the Mufti of the prison came to tell me, with all sorts of circumlocution, and panting with emotion: "You're free!" I couldn't believe it was true. I would been sentenced to six years! I owe my liberation to the juryman Hermann, a scowling, supercilious man, who throughout the trial had looked at me with a grim expression. I supposed him to be a member of the Bavarian People's Party, reflecting that the Government had doubtless appointed jurymen to suit it.

Through Hermann I learnt the details of my trial. The jury wanted to acquit me. On the evidence of my defence, they were convinced that Kahr, Lossow and Seisser must have been equally guilty. They were informed of the objection that an acquittal might entail the risk of having the affair referred to the Court at Leipzig. This made the jury reflect. They decided it was prudent to have me found guilty, the more so as they had been promised a remission of the sentence after six months. This had been a little piece of knavery on the Court's part, for they had no reason to suppose that an appeal by the public prosecutor could have resulted in the case being referred to the Supreme Court. In fact it's certain that Kahr, Lossow and Seisser would not have appeared at Leipzig. Since the promise of conditional liberation was not kept, Hermann wrote to the Government informing it that the three jurymen would appeal to public opinion if I were not set free immediately.

When I left Landsberg, everybody wept (the Mufti and the other members of the prison staff)—but not I! We had won them all to our cause. The Mufti came to tell me that Ludendorff, on the one hand, and the Popular Block, on the other, wanted to send a car for me. Since he was afraid of demonstrations, I reassured him by saying: "I'm not keen on demonstrations, I'm keen only on my freedom." I added that I would make no use of the offers of transport, but it would be agreeable to me if my printer, Adolf Müller, might come and fetch me.

"Do you permit me," he asked, "to inform the Government to that effect? These gentlemen would be much reassured." Müller accordingly arrived, accompanied by Hoffmann.

What a joy it was for me to be in a car again! I asked Müller whether he couldn't accelerate. "No," he replied. "It's my firm intention to go on living for another twenty-five years." At Pasing we met the first messengers on motor-cycles. I found them gathered at my door, in the Thierschstrasse, in Munich, men like Fuess, Gahr and the other old faithfuls. My apartment was decorated with flowers and laurel wreaths (I've kept one of them). In his exuberant joy, my dog almost knocked me down the stairs.

The first visit I paid was to Pöhner. He could almost have kissed me—he who had in front of him what I had behind me. He had a con-

255

versation with Cramer Cletl, asking him to inform Held that I maintained my demand that all my men should also be set at liberty.

Held granted me an appointment, and I must acknowledge that his attitude was entirely correct. Thus, later on, I refrained from making any trouble for him, unlike what I did for Schweyer. Held asked me whether, if I started the Party up again, I contemplated associating myself with Ludendorff.

I told him that such was not my intention. Held then told me that, because of the attitude taken up by Ludendorff towards the Church, he found himself obliged to oppose him. I assured him that the Party programme did not entail a struggle with the Church, and that Ludendorff's affairs were no concern of mine. Held undertook to get in touch with the Minister of Justice and to inform me of the decisions that would be taken concerning my men.

The news reached Pöhner that Gürtner, the Minister of Justice, refused to be persuaded that my demand was justified. I again visited Held, who advised me to go and see Gürtner.

There, I fell in with a lawyer! He opposed me with a lawyer's arguments. My men, he claimed, had not been imprisoned so long as I had. In any case, he couldn't set them free before the vacation. Besides, he hadn't the files. I had no difficulty in replying to him that the files were not necessary, that I knew all the names! During my enumeration, he reacted violently at the name of Hess: "Not him, in any case! He exposed Ministers to the risk of being stoned by the crowd!"

"What can *we* do about that? Is it our fault if you are so unpopular? Besides, nothing happened to you!"

My point of view was as follows: it was not possible for my men to remain in prison whilst I, who was responsible for everything, was at liberty. Held confessed to me that he did not understand Gürtner's attitude. The latter, by reason of his belonging to the National-German Party, should have felt closer to me than Held himself. It was finally Pöhner who, with extreme brutality, informed Gürtner of his views. On returning home one evening, I found a message signed by my thirteen companions. They had just been set free. Next morning, Schaub came to fetch my mail. He had lost his job. He has never left me since that moment.

I had already borrowed three hundred marks to pay for the taxis that the newly liberated men had to take when they left Landsberg—but they were already in Munich when I learnt of their liberation.

I didn't know what to do with my first evening of freedom. I had the impression that at any moment a hand would be laid on my shoulder, and I remained obsessed by the idea that I would have to ask leave for anything I wanted to do! During the first weeks, I remained quite quiet, but time seemed to me to drag. I regained contact with reality, and began by reconciling the enemy brothers. On the 27th January 1925, I again founded the Party.

My thirteen months of imprisonment had seemed a long time—the more so because I thought I would be there for six years. I was possessed by a frenzy of liberty. But, without my imprisonment, *Mein Kampf* would not have been written. That period gave me the chance of deepening various notions for which I then had only an instinctive feeling. It was during this incarceration, too, that I acquired that fearless faith, that optimism, that confidence in our destiny, which nothing could shake thereafter.

It's from this time, too, that my conviction dates—a thing that many of my supporters never understood—that we could no longer win power by force. The State had had time to consolidate itself, and it had the weapons. My weakness, in 1923, was to depend on too many people who were not ours.

I would warned Hess that it would take us two years to give the Party a solid foundation—and, after that, the seizure of power would only be a matter of five to ten years. It was in accordance with these predictions that I organised my work.

There are towns in Germany from which all joy is lacking. I'm told that it's the same thing in certain Calvinistic regions of Switzerland. In Trier and Freiburg, women have addressed me in so ignoble a fashion that I cannot make up my mind to repeat their words. It's on such occasions that I become aware of the depth of human baseness. Clearly, one must not forget that these areas are still feeling the weight of several centuries of religious oppression.

Near Würzburg, there are villages where literally all the women were burned. We know of judges of the Court of the Inquisition who gloried in having had twenty to thirty thousand "witches" burned. Long experience of such horrors cannot but leave indelible traces upon a population. In Madrid, the sickening odour of the heretic's pyre remained for more than two centuries mingled with the air one breathed. If a revolution breaks out again in Spain, one must see in it the natural reaction to an interminable series of atrocities.

One cannot succeed in conceiving how much cruelty, ignominy and falsehood the intrusion of Christianity has spelt for this world of ours. If the misdeeds of Christianity were less serious in Italy, that's because the people of Rome, having seen them at work, always knew exactly the worth of the Popes before whom Christendom prostrated itself. For centuries, no Pope died except by the dagger, poison or the pox.

I can very well imagine how this collective madness came to birth. A Jew was discovered to whom it occurred that if one presented abstruse ideas to non-Jews, the more abstruse these ideas were, the more the non-Jews would rack their brains to try to understand them. The fact of having their attention fixed on what does not exist must make them blind to what exists. An excellent calculation of the Jew's part. So the Jew smacks his thighs to see how his diabolic stratagem has succeeded.

He bears in mind that if his victims suddenly became aware of these things, all Jews would be exterminated. But, this time, the Jews will disappear from Europe. The world will breathe freely and recover its sense of joy, when this weight is no longer crushing its shoulders.

4th February 1942, evening
SPECIAL GUEST: HIMMLER

Charlemagne—The call of the South—Struggling through the mud—Henry the Lion—The sweetness of life—Improving living conditions—For the Reich no sacrifice is too great

The fact that Charlemagne was able to federate the quarrelsome and bellicose Germans shows that he was one of the greatest men in world history.

We know today why our ancestors were not attracted to the East, but rather to the South. Because all the regions lying east of the Elbe were like what Russia is for us today. The Romans detested crossing the Alps. The Germanic peoples, on the other hand, were very fond of crossing them—but in the opposite direction. One must bear in mind that at this period Greece was a marvellous garden, in which oak-forests alternated with orchards. It was only later that olive-growing was introduced into Greece.

The reason why the climate has become temperate in Upper Bavaria is that Italy was deforested. The warm winds of the South, which are no longer held in check by the vegetation, pass over the Alps and make their way northwards.

The Germanic needed a sunny climate to enable his qualities to develop. It was in Greece and Italy that the Germanic spirit found the first terrain favourable to its blossoming. It took several centuries to create, in the Nordic climate, the conditions of life necessary for civilised man. Science helped there.

For any Roman, the fact of being sent to *Germania* was regarded as a punishment—rather like what it used to mean to us to be sent to Posen. You can imagine those rainy, grey regions, transformed into quagmires as far as eye could see. The megalithic monuments were certainly not places of worship, but rather places of refuge for people fleeing from the advance of the mud. The countryside was cold, damp, dreary. At a time when other people already had paved roads, we hadn't the slightest evidence of civilisation to show. Only the Germanics on the shores of the rivers and the sea-coasts were, in a feeble way, an exception to this rule. Those who had remained in Holstein have not changed in two thousand years, whilst those who had emigrated to Greece raised themselves to the level of civilisation.

What persists, through the centuries, in a people's customs is what relates to their habits of eating. I'm convinced that the soup of Holstein is the origin of the Spartan gruel.

As regards the archaeological discoveries made in our part of the world, I'm sceptical. The objects in question were doubtless made in entirely different regions. Their presence would indicate that they were articles of exchange, which the Germanics of the coast obtained for their amber. In the whole of Northern Europe, the level of civilisation cannot much have surpassed that of the Maoris.

Nevertheless, the Greek profile, and that of the Caesars, is that of the men of this North of ours, and I would wager that I could find amongst our peasants two thousand heads of that type.

If Henry the Lion had not rebelled against the Imperial power, certainly nobody would ever have had the notion of expanding to the East. Supposing he'd succeeded, the Slav world would have been given a Germanic ruling class, but it wouldn't have gone further than that. All these strivings towards the East were translated into a loss of Germanic blood, to the profit of the Slavs.

I prefer to go to Flanders on foot rather than eastwards in a sleeping-car. It has always been my delight, towards March, to leave Munich and go to meet the spring in the Rhineland.

On the way back, one leaves the sweetness of living behind as one passes the mountains of Swabia. There is still a smiling valley near Ulm, and then one is definitely caught once more by the rude climate of the high Bavarian plain. I'm sorry for those who have to suffer this hardening process permanently.

Yet we've made those inclement regions habitable. In the same way, we'll transform the spaces of the East into a country in which human beings will be able to live. We must not forget that over there are found iron, coal, grain and timber. We'll build welcoming farms and handsome roads there. And those of our people who thrust as far as that will end by loving their country and loving its landscapes—as the Germans on the Volga used to do.

You'll understand, Himmler, that if I want to establish a genuine civilisation to the North and East, I'll have to make use of men from the South. If I were to take official architects of the Prussian Government to beautify Berlin, for example, I would do better to abandon the project!

In our ambition to play a role on the world level, we must constantly consult Imperial history. All the rest is so new, so uncertain, so imperfect. But Imperial history is the greatest epic that's been known since the Roman Empire. What boldness! What grandeur! These giants thought no more of crossing the Alps than crossing a street.

The misfortune is that none of our great writers took his subjects from German Imperial history. Our Schiller found nothing better to do than to glorify a Swiss cross-bowman![323] The English, for their part, had a Shakespeare—but the history of his country has supplied Shakespeare, as far as heroes are concerned, only with imbeciles and madmen. Immense vistas open up to the German cinema. It will find in the history of the Empire—five centuries of world domination—themes big enough for it.

When I meet the heads of other Germanic peoples, I'm particularly well placed—by reason of my origin—to discuss with them. I can remind them, in fact, that my country was for five centuries a mighty empire, with a capital like Vienna, and that nevertheless I did not hesitate to sacrifice my country to the idea of the Reich.

I've always been convinced of the necessity of welcoming into the Party only truly sturdy fellows, without taking heed of numbers, and excluding the lukewarm. In the same way as regards the new Reich, wherever there are-wholesome Germanic elements in the world, we shall try to recover them. And this Reich will be so sturdy that nobody will ever be able to attempt anything against it.

[323] The legend of William Tell.

5th February 1942, midday
A raid on the Brown House—The Munich putsch—Imprisoned Ministers

One day the police made a raid on the Brown House. I had in my strong-box some documents of the highest importance. One of the keys I had on me, and I happened to be in Berlin. The other was in Hess's possession. The police demanded that he should open the strong-box. He excused himself for not being able to do so, pleading that I was absent and it was I who had the key. The police therefore had to content themselves with putting seals on the box and waiting for my return. Hess had informed me by telephone of this search.

Two days later, he told me I could return. The fact was, he had noticed that it was possible to unscrew the handles on which the seals had been placed. Very cleverly, Hess had himself performed this operation, had opened the box with his own key, and had shut it again (replacing the seals), after having emptied it of compromising documents.

On my return, the police presented themselves for the opening of the strong-box. I protested very energetically, in order to induce them to threaten me that they'd resort to force. I then decided to unlock the box. The lid was opened, the box contained nothing. Their discomfited expressions were a pleasure to behold. On another occasion, I was present when the police took the Brown House by storm. The crowd in the street hurled insults at the policemen who were straddling over the railings. At the windows of the Nuncio's palace, on the other side of the street, where one never saw anyone, there were gloating faces of fat ecclesiastics. The search, which was unfruitful, went on until the middle of the night.

What a struggle there was before we could obtain the right to hoist our flag over the Brown House! The police were against it but they were not themselves in agreement on the subject, and they even brought us in to be present at their disputes. For once, our luck lay in the immeasurable stupidity of the lawyers.

Our skill triumphed over their arguments. This detail shows that one should in no circumstances put one's trust in lawyers. They certainly won't defend our regime any better than they defended its predecessor. Little by little, there was a revulsion in our favour. Now and then a policeman would come and whisper into our ears that he was at heart on our side.

More and more we could count on genuine supporters amongst them, who did not hesitate to compromise themselves for the Party, and through whom we learnt whatever was afoot. A particularly repulsive individual was Hermann in 1923. He was one of the chiefs of the criminal police. Believing in our success, he put himself at our disposal as soon as we had proceeded to the arrest of members of the Government, offering us his help in laying our hands on those who'd escaped our net. When the affair had turned out badly, we knew that he'd be one of the chief witnesses for the prosecution, and we were very curious to see how he would behave.

We were ready, according to what he said, to shut his mouth by saying to him: "Wasn't it you, Hermann, who handed Wutzelhofer over to us?" But he was as dumb as a carp.

It was Weber who opened up for us, unknown to the proprietor, the *Villa Lehmann,* in which we locked up the members of the Government. We had threatened them that if a single one of them attempted to flee, we would shoot them all. Their panic was so great that they remained shut up for two days, though the revolution had come to an end long before. When Lehmann returned to his house, he was quite surprised to discover this brilliant assemblage.

A few days later, Lehmann even had the surprise of receiving a visit from a daughter of one of the Ministers. She'd come to fetch a signet-ring that her father claimed to have forgotten between the pages of a book he had taken from the library. Instead of a signet-ring, what she was looking for was a pile of foreign bank-notes that the father had slipped into a book by the poet Storm!

5th February 1942, evening
Excursions with Baroness Abegg—The fake Donatello—A dubious Murillo

I would find no pleasure in living all the time on the banks of the Königssee. It's too depressing. None of our lakes is so reminiscent of the Norwegian fjords. By contrast, it gives one an impression as of fairyland to arrive there after having come along the Chiemsee, whose blurred tints are so restful to the eye.

I've made innumerable excursions on the mountain, led by the Baroness Abegg. (Without her, I would probably never have been on the summit of the Jenner. She was indefatigable and could climb like a goat.)

All that was arranged by Eckart, who didn't care for walking and could thus remain in peace at the boarding-house. Dietrich Eckart used to say that she was the most intelligent woman he'd ever known.

I would have been willing to accept the intelligence, if it hadn't been accompanied by the most spiteful tongue imaginable. The woman was a real scorpion.

She was as blonde as flax, with blue eyes and excessively long canine teeth, like an Englishwoman.

I admit she was remarkably intelligent. A woman in the class of Frau Bruckmann.[324] She had travelled a lot, all over the world. She was always in one or other of two extreme states. The first kept her at home in a state of almost complete collapse. She would sprawl on her veranda, like a run-down battery, whilst everybody around her was kept busy attending to her. The second state was one of incredible petulance—she'd fly into a rage, sweep out like a whirlwind, climb up somewhere and come rushing torrentially down again.

In my opinion, the most attractive thing about her was the famous bust by Donatello. She valued it at a hundred and fifty thousand marks in gold. In the event of sale, half the money was to go to the Party funds—which would have enabled us to solve all the difficulties caused by the inflation.

Unfortunately, nobody believed in the authenticity of this Donatello. When I saw her for the first time, my instinct immediately told me it was a fake. She claimed that the stucco-worker in whose house she'd bought it had no knowledge of its value. At the best, it could only be a bad copy.

The Baroness's husband had thrown himself into the Königssee. As can well be understood! In his place, I would have done the same. Of the two faithful admirers whom she was known to have, one died, and the other went mad.

That story reminds me of the story of Simon Eckart's Murillo. The picture contained a fault in design that could not have escaped Murillo's attention. If it had done so, there were people in his entourage who would have called it to his attention. These great painters used often to work in collaboration. One of them would paint the Madonna, another the flowers, etc. I intended to write a play on the subject of this Murillo. A man who was furious was the banker Simon Eckart. What a difference between the two Eckarts! A whole world separated them. Dietrich was a writer full of idealism. Simon was a man deeply immersed in the realities of nature.

---

[324] Elsa Bruckmann (1865–1946), born to royalty in Romania and the wife of Hugo Bruckmann, Munich publisher for Houston Stewart Chamberlain.

6th February 1942, evening
Britain must make peace—Common sense and the French—
Consequences of Japan's entry into the war—Turkey and the Narrows

If there appeared amongst the English, at the last moment, a man capable of any lucidity of mind, he'd immediately try to make peace, in order to save what can yet be saved.

The Empire is not sufficiently profitable to support simultaneously the world's largest navy and a powerful land army. The English are in a situation comparable to that of an industrial enterprise that, in order to keep some of its factories working, is forced to shut down the others. The same thing is true of the Americans, as far as their interior economy is concerned.

Every country, I realise, is capable of moments of collective madness—but, at the secret depths of each entity, reason retains its imprescriptible rights.

Daladier, Pétain,[325] the average Frenchman were for peace. It was quite a small gang that succeeded, by surprise, in precipitating the country into war. And it was the same in England. Some were pacifists on principle, others for religious reasons, others again for reasons of an economic nature. Why, therefore, shouldn't reason reclaim its rights? In France, the reaction occurred with the speed of a flash of lightning. Pétain's first declaration had a blinding clarity.

As for the English, all they lack is the power to make up their minds. Somebody should get up in Parliament and say to Churchill: "So that we may at last have some good news for the Empire, have the kindness to disappear!"

No parliamentarian has the courage to do that, because everyone reflects that, if the affair ends badly, his name will remain attached to the memory of a disaster. And yet no English parliamentarian any longer believes in victory, and each of them expects discomfiture.

All the secret sessions of Parliament are favourable to us, because they undermine Churchill's prestige. But he won't fall until his successor has given us an inkling. That's what happened with the French. Their tergiversation[326] was possible only on the basis of our armistice proposals. They began by saying no, then they realised that our conditions were not so terrible.

---

[325] Henri Philippe Pétain (1856–1951), French Army Marshall, World War I hero and leader of Vichy France, that area of France not under German occupation.
[326] The making of make conflicting or evasive statements; equivocate.

A day will come, during a secret session, when Churchill will be accused of betraying the interests of the Empire. Each blow we deliver towards the East will bring that moment nearer. But we must prevent Churchill from attempting a successful diversion. With the fall of Singapore, the curtain falls on the Far East. The hope that the Russian winter would destroy us is in the process of disappearing. Churchill invites public debates because he's depending on the patriotism of the English people, and because he counts on it that nobody who has an independent opinion will risk attacking him from the front. But already several of his opponents are letting slip various disobliging remarks. The influence of events in the Far East is making itself felt on the banks. At present several of them have to be supported to protect them from bankruptcy.

In any case, one thing is clear: the importance of a nation's fortune is a small matter to it if one compares it with the volume of business done in the course of a year. Supposing a nation could import without limit for five consecutive years, and without exporting in exchange, this would suffice for that nation to be utterly ruined. Let's go further and imagine that for six months a people produces absolutely nothing—by the end of that period its fortune will be scattered to the winds.

I don't believe in idealism, I don't believe that a people is prepared to pay for ever for the stupidity of its rulers. As soon as everybody in England is convinced that the war can only be run at a loss, it's certain that there won't be anyone left there who feels inclined to carry on with it.

I've examined this problem in all its aspects, turned it round in all directions. If I add up the results we've already achieved, I consider that we are in an exceptionally favourable situation. For the first time, we have on our side a first-rate military Power, Japan. We must therefore never abandon the Japanese alliance, for Japan is a Power upon which one can rely.

I can well imagine that Japan would put no obstacle in the way of peace, on condition that the Far East were handed over to her. She's not capable of digesting India, and I doubt whether she has any interest in occupying Australia and New Zealand. If we preserve our connections with her, Japan will derive from this a great sense of security, and will feel that she has nothing more to fear from anybody at all.

This alliance is also an essential guarantee of tranquillity for us—in particular, in the event of our being able to rely on a lasting friendship with France.

265

There's one thing that Japan and Germany have absolutely in common—that both of us need fifty to a hundred years for purposes of digestion: we for Russia, they for the Far East.

The English will have got nothing out of the affair but a bitter lesson and a black eye. If in future they make less whisky, that won't do any harm to anybody—beginning with themselves. Let's not forget, after all, that they owe all that's happening to them to one man, Churchill.

The English are behaving as if they were stupid. The reality will end by calling them to order, by compelling them to open their eyes.

Japan's entry into the war is an event that will help to modify our strategic situation.

Whether via Spain or via Turkey, we shall gain access to the Near East. It will be enough for us to inform Turkey that we are renewing the Montreux agreement,[327] and that we are enabling her to fortify the Straits. Thus we can avoid having to maintain an important fleet in the Black Sea, which is merely a frog-pond. A few small ships will be enough, if we have on the Dardanelles a sturdy guardian to whom we supply the guns. That requires no more guns than are needed for the armament of a single battleship. This is the solution most to our advantage.

It seems to me that the attitude of the Turks towards the English has changed, that they're blowing cold on them.

7th February 1942, evening
SPECIAL GUESTS: DR. TODT AND MINISTER SPEER
Younger children and the birth-rate—America's technology was founded by Germans

A people rapidly increases its population when all the younger members of a family are in a position to set up establishments. The peasant needs a numerous labour-force, and it is obviously to his interest to be able to employ his children until the age when they become adult. If the latter can set up establishments in their turn, they don't remain a charge on their father—but it's quite different when the father is obliged to feed them from his own land, and for all their lives. In that case, of course, the birth-rate falls.

---

[327] The 1936 Montreux Convention, signed between World War One's Allied Powers and Turkey's post-Ottoman government, agreed to return the Dardanelles strait, the Sea of Marmara, and the Bosporus strait to Turkish military control and to allow that nation to close the straits to all warships in times of war and to permit merchant ships free passage.

The people in the United States who were originally responsible for the development of engineering were nearly all of German stock (from Swabia and Württemberg).

What luck that everything's in process of taking shape on the Eastern front! At last the German people is about to regain its freedom of movement.

8th February 1942, midday
SPECIAL GUESTS: SPEER AND HIMMLER
Once more about Justice—Penalties in war-time—The solution of the religious problem

Our judicial system is not yet supple enough. It doesn't realise the danger that threatens us at this moment by reason of the recrudescence of criminality. It has again been brought to my attention that very many burglaries, committed by recidivists, are punished by terms of penal servitude. If we tolerate it that assaults may be made with the help of the black-out, in less than a year we shall arrive at a state of security which will be most dangerous for the whole population. England is already in this situation, and the English are beginning to demand that recourse should be had to the German methods (which, for my part, I find insufficiently draconic for the period). In some parts of England, the proportion of merchandise stolen is estimated at 40 per cent.

During the Great War, a deserter was punished by fortress-arrest and reduction in rank. But what about the courageous soldier? What had he to put up with?

The citizen who traded on the black-market in the rear came out of it very nicely. Either he was acquitted, or he had a magnificent time of it reserved for him in prison.

The victims of the thefts had no choice but to earn again, by the sweat of their brow, whatever had been stolen from them, whilst the thief could spend his time causing the product of his thefts to multiply. In every regiment there were likewise scoundrels whose misdeeds were punished by three or four years' imprisonment at the most. That's what embittered the troops.

It's a scandal that, at a time when an honest man's life is so fragile, these black sheep should be supported at the expense of the community.

After ten years of penal servitude, a man is lost to the community. When he's done his time, who'd be willing to give him work? Creatures of that sort should either be sent to a concentration camp for life or

267

suffer the death penalty. In time of war, the latter penalty would be appropriate, if only to set an example. For a similar reason, second-rate criminals should be treated in the same fashion.

Instead of behaving in this radical manner, our judicial system bends lovingly over individual cases, amuses itself by weighing the pros and cons and in finding extenuating circumstances—all in accordance with the rites of peace-time. We must have done with such practices. The lawyer doesn't consider the practical repercussions of the application of the law. He persists in seeing each case in itself. The criminal, in his turn, is perfectly familiar with the procedures of the system, and benefits by his familiarity with it in the manner in which he commits a crime. He knows, for example, that for a theft committed on a train one is punished with a maximum of so many years of penal servitude. He can tell himself that, if things turn out badly, he'll be out of it for a few years leading a well-organised existence, sheltered from want, and under the protection of the Minister of Justice. He has still other advantages. He isn't sent to the front, and, in the event of defeat, he has chances of rising to the highest offices. In the event of victory, finally, he can reckon on an amnesty. In such cases, the judges should exercise the discretion which is at their disposal. But not all of them understand this.

The evil that's gnawing our vitals is our priests, of both creeds. I can't at present give them the answer they've been asking for, but it will cost them nothing to wait. It's all written down in my big book. The time will come when I'll settle my account with them, and I'll go straight to the point. I don't know which should be considered the more dangerous: the minister of religion who play-acts at patriotism, or the man who openly opposes the State. The fact remains that it's their manoeuvres that have led me to my decision. They've only got to keep at it, they'll hear from me, all right. I shan't let myself be hampered by juridical scruples. Only necessity has legal force. In less than ten years from now, things will have quite another look, I can promise them.

We shan't be able to go on evading the religious problem much longer. If anyone thinks it's really essential to build the life of human society on a foundation of lies, well, in my estimation, such a society is not worth preserving.

If, on the other hand, one believes that truth is the indispensable foundation, then conscience bids one intervene in the name of truth, and exterminate the lie. Periods that have endured such affronts without protesting will be condemned by people of the coming generations. Just as the pyres for heretics have been suppressed, so all these by-products of ignorance and bad faith will have to be eliminated in their turn.

8th February 1942, evening
SPECIAL GUESTS: HIMMLER AND SPEER
On the forms of Government in Europe and the United States

The United States of America were born as a republic. That's what distinguishes that country from the European nations. Amongst the latter, the republican form has been a successor to the monarchical form. In Great Britain, the Head of the State is merely a symbol.

In fact, it's the Prime Minister who governs. In Europe, only Germany has a form of State that approximates to that of the United States. In America, the Chamber of Electors does not play a permanent role. As for the Supreme Court, it cannot reverse the President's decisions unless they are anti-constitutional or unless they infringe upon the prerogatives of Congress. The President of the United States has a much wider power than the Kaiser had, for *he* depended on parliament.

In Germany, if things had remained normal, the monarchy would more and more have approximated to the English form. The King, in Great Britain, is merely the guardian of the constitution, and it's only by directly influencing people that he can exercise an influence (provided, moreover, that he's clever enough) on the political level.

The House of Lords, which is practically without influence, is a House of benefice-holders. It acts as a means of side-tracking men in politics whose talent is becoming dangerous.

With us, a man who controlled a majority in the Reichstag could govern against the President. To avoid the crisis that might arise from this duality, I've united in one and the same function the role of the Chancellor, who's responsible to parliament, and that of the Head of the State. But I'm not of the opinion that the Führer is appointed for life. At the end of a certain time, the Head of the State must give way to a successor.

9th February 1942, midday
SPECIAL GUEST: SPEER
The farce of gas-masks—The economics of the cults—Obersalzberg

The spectacle of the publicity to which the gas-masks have been exposed in England convinces me that this is a piece of commercial exploitation in which the top men are mixed up.

To make a few hundred thousand pounds, nobody minds putting on fancy-dress airs and going about with a mask slung over one's shoulder—the more so as the case might contain a satisfactory supply of cigars. One must clearly see into all that, in order to appreciate properly the significance of the exclamation made by the Roosevelt woman,[328] speaking of ourselves: "It's a world in which we could not conceivably live!" Just like the throne and the altar in former times, so now the Jews and the political profiteers form a silent association for the common exploitation of the democratic milch cow.

If, instead of giving five hundred millions to the Church, we made grants to some archbishops, allowing them full freedom to share out as they chose the sums put at their disposal, it's certain that the number of their collaborators would be reduced to the minimum.

They'd try to keep the greater part of the money for themselves, and they'd burst themselves in the attempt to be useful to us. With a tenth part of our budget for religion, we would thus have a Church devoted to the State and of unshakeable loyalty. We must have done with these out-of-date forms. The little sects, which receive only a few hundred thousand marks, are devoted to us body and soul.

Let's abolish the control on money given to the Churches, in accordance with that strictly Christian principle: "Let not thy left hand know what thy right hand doeth." This mania for controls should be regarded as an offence against these just men. Let them fill their own pockets, and give us a bit of peace!

Those rainy days at Berchtesgaden, what a blessing they were! No violent exercise, no excursions, no sun-baths—a little repose! There's nothing lovelier in the world than a mountain landscape. There was a time when I could have wept for grief on having to leave Berchtesgaden. As far as possible, one must avoid ruining landscapes with networks of high-tension wires, telpher railways and machines of that sort.

I'm in favour of roads, when needs must—but what's uglier than a funicular? On New Year's Day I was obliged to go down to Berchtesgaden to telephone, because at Obersalzberg the telephone wasn't working. The fact was, it was my yearly custom to give sacks of gunpowder to our village shots. They fired them off to their hearts' content, playing havoc everywhere with their old rifles and sixteenth-century arquebuses—to the extent of damaging the telephone wires!

---

[328] Anna Eleanor Roosevelt (1884–1962), wife of Franklin Delano Roosevelt.

9th February 1942, evening
British "Fair Play"—Successful air raids—The technological war—
Revelations on the Narvik landing

The last thing these English know is how to practise *fair play*. They're very bad at accepting their defeats.

If I had a bomber capable of flying at more than seven hundred and fifty (kilometres) an hour, I would have supremacy everywhere. This aircraft wouldn't have to be armed, for it would be faster than the fastest fighters. In our manufacturing schedules, therefore, we should first attack the problem of bombers, instead of giving priority to fighters, where production can catch up quickly. We ought to make such a leap ahead that we could put a great distance between ourselves and our opponents. A bomber flying at a height of fourteen thousand metres would provide the same safety—but the snag is, it's difficult to aim from so high.

Ten thousand bombs dropped at random on a city are not as effective as a single bomb aimed with certainty at a powerhouse or a water-works on which the water supply depends. On the day when the *gentry* were deprived of their hydrotherapy, they'd certainly lose some of their conceit.

The problem of bombardment should be considered logically. What are the targets to aim for by preference? A bomb of five hundred kilogrammes on a power-house undoubtedly produces the required effect. That's what's decisive.

With two hundred bombers fulfilling these conditions, and continuing to fly for six months, I'll annihilate the enemy—for it would be impossible for him to catch up with his loss of production during the period.

What I've learnt from Oshima concerning the Japanese submarine war has filled me both with satisfaction and with anger. The fact is that the pocket submarine, with only two men aboard, has been suggested to us several times.

With what an air of superiority our specialists rejected it! In the technological war, it's the side which arrives at a given point with the necessary weapon that wins the battle. If we succeed this year in getting our new tanks into the line in the proportion of twelve per division, we'll crushingly outclass all our opponents' tanks. It's enough to give Rommel twenty-four of them to guarantee him the advantage. If the Americans arrive with their tanks, he'll bowl them over like rabbits.

What's important is to have the technical superiority in every case at a decisive point. I know that; I'm mad on technique. We must meet the enemy with novelties that take him by surprise, so as continually to keep the initiative. If the three transports that we wanted to send to Narvik had arrived safely, our warships would not have been sunk, and history would have taken a different course.

Supposing I would known the exact situation, I would immediately have recalled my men, for lack of audacity. Praise and thanks to the cretin who carried negligence to the point of not informing us that our transports couldn't get through. The fact that our enterprise was nevertheless successful, that was a real defiance of fate—for we had no reasonable chance of succeeding.

It's likewise an event unique in history that we charged to attack a port, believing it to be fortified, and therefore hoping that we could use it as a base—and this all the more inasmuch as we had, from the former Minister for War of the nation concerned, information that later proved to be false.

A savoury detail is that Churchill at once sent his son to Norway—an urchin like that!—to trumpet the arrival of the British liberators. Our good luck was that the English surprised some of our ships, especially the one that was carrying the Flak. Contrary to the orders I would given, the men of this unit were wearing their uniform. The English returned whence they had come, long enough to ask for instructions—and it's to this chance circumstance we owed our ability to be the first to land.

The best proof that these swine wanted to try something that time is that they're in a state of fury. The fact is, we frustrated their intentions by having our information published in the Norwegian and Danish press. What a *post-mortem* they must have held to find out how we were informed! As for their Sicilian intrigues, they've been nipped in the bud by Kesselring's arrival.

10th February 1942, evening
SPECIAL GUEST: HIMMLER
Motor cars and their drivers

Adolf Müller's the man to whom I owe the fact that I understand the art of driving a car. Müller had very much vexed me by saying that my car was not a car but a saucepan, that my drivers drove like dummies, and that if I went on as I was doing, it wouldn't last long. "When a car loses one of its wheels," he said (this is what had just happened to mine), "it's ready for the scrap-heap, and so is its driver." Thus Müller.

Since he was going to Würzburg to buy a rotary press, Müller suggested I should come with him. He arrived at our rendezvous very oddly attired, and his knickerbockers were only a detail in this rig-out. When he told me he would himself drive his car, my first reaction was to inform him that I wouldn't come with him. "Get in," he told me, "and you'll learn what it is to drive a car." I must honestly confess that the journey was a revelation to me. Unlike most people, I'm always ready to learn.

The car itself, first of all, was a sixteen-horse Benz, and it was in absolutely impeccable condition. By comparison, I saw at once all the faults of my own car. And I must add that Müller drove wonderfully well. Secondly, Müller opened my eyes to an infinite number of small details that escape most drivers. Every pedestrian who is installed behind a wheel at once loses his sense of the consideration to which he is convinced he is entitled whilst he is a pedestrian. Now, Müller never stopped thinking of the people on the road. He drove very carefully through built-up areas.

He believed that anyone who runs over a child should be put in prison at once. He didn't skirt the edge of the road, as many people do, but instead he stuck rather to the top of the camber, always mindful of the child who might unexpectedly emerge.

When he wanted to pass a car, he first of all made sure that the driver of the car in front of him had taken cognisance of his intention. He took his curves cleverly, without making his rear wheels skid, and without sudden spurts of acceleration—all gently and flexibly. I realised that driving was something quite different from what I would hitherto supposed, and I was a little ashamed at the comparisons that forced themselves into my mind.

During that journey I took two decisions: I would buy a Benz, and I would teach my drivers to drive. I went to the Benz works, and thus made Werlin's acquaintance. I told him I wanted to buy a sixteen-h.p. "You'll decide for yourself in the end," he said. "I would advise you to try a ten-h.p., to begin with, to get your hand in: it does only eighty kilometres an hour, but it's better to arrive at your destination at eighty than to smash yourself up at a hundred and ten." These were so many dagger-thrusts at my pride.

Theoretical and practical knowledge are one thing and presence of mind at the moment of danger is something else. Schreck had them both to the same degree. He was as strong as a buffalo, and cold-blood-edly fearless. He used his car as a weapon for charging at Communists.

Kempka has been my driver for nearly ten years, and I have nothing but praise for him. Moreover, he impeccably manages the collection of cars for which he's responsible.

When I ask him, in September, if he has his stock of oil for the winter and his snow-chains, I know he's ready equipped. If I need to know the time, I can rely on the clock on the instrument-panel. All the instruments are in perfect working order. I've never had a more conscientious driver. In utterly critical situations, he wouldn't have the same calmness as Schreck. He's entirely wrapped up in his driving. When I had Schreck beside me, it was the old war-time comrade who sat at the wheel.

One day I had to be in Hanover with all speed in order to catch the night train for Munich. I would been lent a car with a Saxon driver. Since we could see nothing, I suggested that he should switch on his headlights.

"They're switched on," he said, "but the battery's flat." A moment later, it was a tyre that gave up the ghost. I saw my Saxon becoming very busy with his car, and I asked him whether he hadn't a spare wheel. "I have one, all right," he said, "but it's been flat for some days." It suddenly occurred to me that Lutze must be behind us. Sure enough, he arrived—at the wheel of an Opel, the first of the eighteen-h.p., four-cylinder models, the most wretched car that ever came out of the Opel works.

So I continued my journey with Lutze, and I asked him whether there was any chance of arriving in time for my train. He's an optimist, like all drivers. The unlucky thing for Lutze is that he has only one eye and is a poor judge of distances. He lost no time in going astray at a fork, and suddenly we found ourselves confronted by a ditch. We finally got out of it by using the reverse gear. I didn't worry—I was already resigned to missing the train! Lutze drove through Hanover at a crazy speed. Another five minutes, another two minutes to go. We arrived in the station. I had just time to leap into the train.

I've had some queer drivers in my time. Göring made a point of always driving on the left-hand side of the road. In moments of danger, he used to blow his horn. His confidence was unfailing, but it was of a somewhat mystic nature.

Killinger[329] was also an ace at the wheel! Once I saw Bastian[330] get down peacefully from his car, knock out some fools who'd jeered at him, take the wheel again and move off in complete calm. One day I was a passenger in a car that was taking me back from Mainz. Schreck was driving behind us in a car equipped with a siren. We arrived in the middle of a bunch of cyclists. They were Reds and began to hurl insults at us. But when they heard Schreck's siren, they left their bicycles on the road and scattered into the fields. Schreck went by quite calmly, crushing the bicycles. The Reds were taken aback, wondering how a police car could behave like that. When they realised their mistake, they began to abuse us again in their choicest terms.

"Murderers, bandits, Hitlerites!" They recognised me, and I take that fact as my badge of rank. We often had very painful incidents of this kind. It was no joke, at that time, to find oneself at grips with a mob of opponents. When one has been driven for years by the same men, one no longer sees them as drivers, but as Party comrades.

17th February 1942, midday
SPECIAL GUEST: HIMMLER

Fascists and aristocrats—Roatta the rat—The Duce should sacrifice the monarchy—The Jews and the natural order—The unhealthy intellectuals of Europe—If the German professor ruled the world

The genuine Fascists are friendly to Germany, but the court circles, the clique of aristocrats, detest everything German.

At Florence, the Duce said to me: "My soldiers are brave fellows, but I can't have any confidence in my officers." The last time I met Mussolini, his accents were still more tragic.

I learnt, with Pfeffer, that when men acquire the habit of a certain type of behaviour, and make the gestures corresponding to it, it ends by becoming second nature to them. Words lose their meaning, the best-established notions create new events. With them, pride becomes transformed into vanity, egotism becomes confused with idealism. It's difficult to conceive that a genuine officer can be a sneaking spy. Now, that was just what Roatta was. He sabotaged the plan of attack by Italian troops along the valley of the Rhine, in June 1940. Until the Duce succeeds in getting rid of this aristocratic Mafia, he won't be able to

---

[329] Manfred Freiherr von Killinger (1886–1944), later German Ambassador to Romania.

[330] Max Bastian (1883–1958), a Navy Admiral who later served as President of the Reich Military Court.

appoint a genuine elite to the highest posts. This Mafia is every bit as base as the German underworld.

It's composed of cretins, who, however, are not so cretinous as not to have a sense of what gives other people their superiority. Their activities, although purely negative, are nonetheless effective, for these are the people who prevent the best men from gaining access to the highest posts. And this conspiracy is what paralyses the Duce's efforts.

Things won't improve in Italy until the Duce has sacrificed the monarchy and taken effective control of an authoritarian State. This form of government can last for centuries.

The Republic of Venice lasted for nine hundred and sixty years. It ruled the eastern Mediterranean throughout that period, and that thanks to the authority conferred upon the Doge. Under the monarchic form, that would not have been possible. Venice couldn't have claimed more—but whatever she coveted, and whatever lay within the scope of her ambition, she got. The example of the Hanseatic cities likewise proves the quality of this system. All that *they* lacked was the Imperial power.

It's not possible that six thousand families can have, on the one hand, maintained perpetual dominion over three hundred and forty thousand Helots, and, on the other hand, reigned over Asia Minor and Sicily. The fact that they succeeded in doing so for several centuries is a proof of the greatness of this race.

The sensational event of the ancient world was the mobilisation of the underworld against the established order. This enterprise of Christianity had no more to do with religion than Marxist socialism has to do with the solution of the social problem. The notions represented by Jewish Christianity were strictly unthinkable to Roman brains. The ancient world had a liking for clarity. Scientific research was encouraged there.

The gods, for the Romans, were familiar images. It is somewhat difficult to know whether they had any exact idea of the Beyond. For them, eternal life was personified in living beings, and it consisted in a perpetual renewal.

Those were conceptions fairly close to those which were current amongst the Japanese and Chinese at the time when the Swastika made its appearance amongst them.

It was necessary for the Jew to appear on the scene and introduce that mad conception of a life that continues into an alleged Beyond! It enables one to regard life as a thing that is negligible here below—since it will flourish later, when it no longer exists. Under cover of a religion, the Jew has introduced intolerance in a sphere in which tolerance formerly prevailed.

Amongst the Romans, the cult of the sovereign intelligence was associated with the modesty of a humanity that knew its limits, to the point of consecrating altars to the unknown god.

The Jew who fraudulently introduced Christianity into the ancient world—in order to ruin it—re-opened the same breach in modern times, this time taking as his pretext the social question. It's the same sleight-of-hand as before. Just as Saul was changed into St. Paul, Mordechai became Karl Marx.

Peace can result only from a natural order. The condition of this order is that there is a hierarchy amongst nations. The most capable nations must necessarily take the lead. In this order, the subordinate nations get the greater profit, being protected by the more capable nations.

It is Jewry that always destroys this order. It constantly provokes the revolt of the weak against the strong, of bestiality against intelligence, of quantity against quality.

It took fourteen centuries for Christianity to reach the peak of savagery and stupidity. We would therefore be wrong to sin by excess of confidence and proclaim our definite victory over Bolshevism.

The more we render the Jew incapable of harming us, the more we shall protect ourselves from this danger. The Jew plays in nature the role of a catalysing element. A people that is rid of its Jews returns spontaneously to the natural order.

In 1925 I wrote in *Mein Kampf* (and also in an unpublished work[331]) that world Jewry saw in Japan an opponent beyond its reach. The racial instinct is so developed amongst the Japanese that the Jew realises he cannot attack Japan from within. He is therefore compelled to act from outside. It would be to the considered interests of England and the United States to come to an understanding with Japan, but the Jew will strive to prevent such an understanding. I gave this warning in vain. A question arises. Does the Jew act consciously and by calculation, or is he driven on by his instinct? I cannot answer that question. The intel-

---

[331] The book now commonly known as "Hitler's Second Book," actually deals with German foreign policy and the question of South Tyrol. It was never published during Hitler's lifetime.

lectual elite of Europe (whether professors of faculties, high officials, or whatever else) never understood anything of this problem. The elite has been stuffed with false ideas, and on these it lives. It propagates a science that causes the greatest possible damage. Stunted men have the philosophy of stunted men. They love neither strength nor health, and they regard weakness and sickness as supreme values.

Since it's the function that creates the organ, entrust the world for a few centuries to a German professor—and you'll soon have a mankind of cretins, made up of men with big heads set upon meagre bodies.

17th February 1942, evening
Big properties in Hungary—The birthplaces of great men—Books for young people—Folk-dancing—Leather shorts

The magnates of Hungary used to be noted for their hospitality. On their country estates they used to receive up to seventy guests at a time. The wines were better than in Austria, but the country-houses were not so beautiful. For most of the time these noblemen led delightful lives in Paris or in the gambling-resorts of the Côte d'Azur. One of them, Esterhazy, at least had it greatly to his credit that Haydn didn't end up like Mozart in a communal grave—which is what happened in Vienna, the homeland of music.

It's my view that, simply for the sake of their beauty, the great noblemen's estates should be preserved. But they must retain their size, otherwise only the State would be capable of maintaining them as private country-houses. And the ideal thing is that they should remain not only in private hands, but also in the family that has traditionally lived in them—else they lose their character. Thus these great monuments of the past, which have retained their character as living organisms, are also centres of culture. But when the country house is occupied by a caretaker acting as a guide, a little State official with a Bavarian or Saxon accent, who ingenuously recites his unvarying piece of claptrap, things no longer have a soul—the soul is gone.

Wahnfried, as in Wagner's lifetime, is a lived-in house. It still has all its brilliance, and continues to give the effect of a lover. Goethe's house gives the impression of a dead thing.

And how one understands that in the room where he died he should have asked for light—always more light! Schiller's house can still move one by the picture it gives of the penury in which the poet lived. All these thoughts occurred to me whilst I was reflecting what might become of my house at Obersalzberg. I can already see the guide from

Berchtesgaden showing visitors over the rooms of my house: "This is where he had breakfast. . ." I can also imagine a Saxon giving his avaricious instructions: "Don't touch the articles, don't wear out the parquet, stay between the ropes. . . " In short, if one hadn't a family to bequeath one's house to, the best thing would be to be burnt in it with all its contents—a magnificent funeral pyre!

I've just been reading a very fine article on Karl May.[332] I found it delightful. It would be nice if his work were republished. I owe him my first notions of geography, and the fact that he opened my eyes on the world. I used to read him by candle-light, or by moonlight with the help of a huge magnifying-glass. The first thing I read of that kind was *The Last of the Mohicans*. But Fritz Seidl told me at once: "Fenimore Cooper is nothing; you must read Karl May." The first book of his I read was *The Ride through the Desert*. I was carried away by it. And I went on to devour at once the other books by the same author. The immediate result was a falling-off in my school reports.

Apart from the Bible, *Don Quixote* and *Robinson Crusoe* are the two most often read books in the world. Cervantes' book is the world's most brilliant parody of a society that was in process of becoming extinct. At bottom, the Spaniards' habits of life have scarcely changed since then. Daniel Defoe's book gathers together in one man the history of all mankind. It has often been imitated, but none of these desert-island stories can compete with the original. One Christmas I was given a beautiful illustrated edition. Cervantes' book has been illustrated by Gustave Doré in a style of real genius.

The third of these universal works is *Uncle Tom's Cabin*. *I* could also mention *Gulliver's Travels*. Each of these works contains a great basic idea. Unfortunately, we have nothing of the kind in our literature.

In Germany, besides Karl May, Jules Verne and Félix Dohn are essential. All those reach a fairly high level.

When I was a young man, there was a book that had an extraordinary success. Its title was *Old Heidelberg*. Such works can contribute enormously to the publicity of a city or a region. Bremen and Spessart had the same thing happen to them. But it's a disaster when a city-dwelling poet sets himself to sing of the beauties of mountains. People who really belong to them don't lend themselves to dramatic

---

[332] Karl May (1842–1912), a German author best known for novels of fictitious travels and adventures, set in the American Old West, the Orient, the Middle East, Latin America, and China.

presentation. Their songs are heard amongst themselves. What other people sing doesn't really belong to our folk-lore. At one time I bore a severe grudge against Hagenbeck for having made fun of our customs.

The dance we call *Schuhplattler* is the most virile imaginable. It has nothing to do with the dance that our trumpery mountaineers perform under that name. It's really a pity we haven't succeeded in popularising it by means of the theatre.

The Americans have devised a dance with clappers that's really worthy of the stage. It's a dance that owes nothing to Africa, but everything to Scotland. We, for our part, have only been able to make fun *of Schuhplattler,* and for that we have idiots to thank.

It goes without saying that the North Germans can't assimilate our folk-lore. Do you know anything more ridiculous than a Berliner in leather shorts? A Scotsman can be received in London, in the best society, dressed in his national costume—but anyone in Berlin who put on a Tyrol costume would give the impression that he was going to Carnival. It was with great reluctance that I had definitely to give up wearing leather shorts. It was too much of a complication for me to have to change my clothes several times a day, like a mannequin, to adapt myself to the psychology of my visitors. In such dress, I couldn't have been taken seriously by Germans from north of Coburg.

Throughout my youth, even in winter, I never wore anything else. I first of all adopted the kind of costume that goes with riding-boots, then I fell back on the bourgeois pair of trousers. Indeed, as soon as one gives up the most comfortable clothes, why should one take to the most uncomfortable in exchange? But it's rather sad to see the old costumes gradually dying out. I suggested to Himmler that he might dress two or three guards units in leather shorts. Obviously they would have to be handsome chaps, and not necessarily all from the South. I can quite well imagine a soldier with a Hamburg accent displaying sunburnt knees.

Apart from all that, leather shorts have the advantage that one's not afraid of getting them dirty. On the contrary, they're ennobled by stains, like a Stradivarius by age. In Germany nowadays all the young men are wearing leather shorts.

There are two things that I find charming when worn by young people—short trousers and skiing trousers. To think that there are idiots who wanted to make them wear boots! The habit of skiing can never be too much encouraged—because of Russia.

18th February 1942, evening
SPECIAL GUEST: GENERAL ROMMEL
Portrait of Churchill

Churchill is the very type of a corrupt journalist. There's not a worse prostitute in politics. He himself has written that it's unimaginable what can be done in war with the help of lies. He's an utterly amoral, repulsive creature. I'm convinced that he has his place of refuge ready beyond the Atlantic. He obviously won't seek sanctuary in Canada. In Canada he'd be beaten up. He'll go to his friends the Yankees.

As soon as this damnable winter is over, we'll remedy all that.

19th February 1942, evening
SPECIAL GUESTS: MINISTER SPEER AND FIELD-MARSHAL MILCH

A presentiment about the Russian winter

I've always detested snow; Bormann, you know, I've always hated it. Now I know why. It was a presentiment.

Night of 19th–20th February 1942
Colonising methods—The perversity of education—Regrets for the help given to Spain—The theatre in Germany—Enriching the Museums.

No sooner do we land in a colony than we install children's crèches, hospitals for the natives. All that fills me with rage. White women degrading themselves in the service of the blacks. On top of that we have the shavelings shoving their oar in, with their mania for making angels! Instead of making the natives love us, all that inappropriate care makes them hate us. From their point of view, all these manifestations are the peak of indiscretion. They don't understand the reasons for our behaviour, and regard us as intolerable pedants who enjoy wielding the policeman's truncheon.

The Russians don't grow old. They scarcely get beyond fifty or sixty. What a ridiculous idea to vaccinate them. In this matter, we must resolutely push aside our lawyers and hygienic experts. No vaccination for the Russians, and no soap to get the dirt off them. But let them have all the spirits and tobacco they want. Anyway, some serious scientists are against vaccination. Dirt shows on black people only when the missionaries, to teach them modesty, oblige them to put on clothes. In the state of nature, negroes are very clean. To a missionary, the smell of dirt is agreeable. From this point of view, they themselves are the dirtiest swine of all. They have a horror of water.

281

And those repulsive priests, when they question a child of seven in the confessional, it's they themselves who incite it to sin, by opening its eyes to sin. And it's the same thing when they turn on the natives.

In 1911, in the clerical citadel of Breslau, a Bavarian was condemned to a fortnight's imprisonment for going out in the city in leather shorts. At the time, this attire created scandal.

Nowadays everybody goes to the mixed baths without its arousing the slightest *arrière-pensée*[333] in anyone. In Rome there are priests who spend their time in measuring the length of women's sleeves and skirts and in checking whether these women have head-dresses.

If God cared about such trifles, he'd have created man already dressed! The idea of nakedness torments only the priests, for the education they undergo makes them perverts.

If there hadn't been the danger of the Red peril overwhelming Europe, I would not have intervened in the revolution in Spain. The clergy would have been exterminated. If these people regained power in Germany, Europe would founder again in the darkness of the Middle Ages.

There are not enough theatres in Germany. A lot of them were built in the 'seventies, it's true, but the number is no longer related to the importance of our population.

A hundred years ago Munich had three thousand five hundred seats for a population of fifty thousand inhabitants. The *Residenztheater,* the National and the *Volkstheater* at the gate on the Isar, were already in existence. Today, for a population of nearly nine hundred thousand inhabitants, Munich has seats for only five thousand spectators. So my plans for Linz are not exaggerated. Berlin has three operas, but should have four or five for its four million inhabitants. Dresden, with its six hundred thousand inhabitants, supports a very fine opera.

There's a lot of marvellous comedy acting in Berlin. In the first place, at the *Deutsche Theater.* The first show I went to after the Great War was *Peer Gynt,* which I saw with Dietrich Eckart, at the *Staatliche Schauspielhaus.* In Berlin the play was always given in Eckart's translation. At Munich, on the other hand, it was in a Jewish translation. I can't give an opinion on the value of the theatre at Munich, for I'm prejudiced on the subject. Whenever I go there, I have a feeling of apprehension. It's possible that I may be unjust. In fact, I'm told on all sides that I should go once to the *Staatliche Schauspielhaus,* which, it appears, has consid-

---

[333] A concealed thought or intention; an ulterior motive.

erably improved under Golling's direction. I'll decide, perhaps, when peace is back again. I've just been reading that the *Kammerspiele* have had a brilliant success with *Othello*.

What sort of concert-hall should Berlin have, if one remembers that Leipzig, with its six hundred thousand inhabitants, possesses the *Gewandhaus*. One realises that a small city can have an intense cultural life if somebody concerns himself intelligently with the matter. Only quite exceptional pieces are reserved solely for the capital.

I could live very well in a city like Weimar or Bayreuth. A big city is very ungrateful. Its inhabitants are like children. They hurl themselves frantically upon everything new, and they lose interest in things with the same facility. A man who wants to make a real career as a singer certainly gets more satisfaction in the provinces.

It's a pity that we haven't a *Gauleiter* in Dresden who loves the arts. After Krauss and Furtwängler, Busch[334] would have become the greatest German conductor, but Mutschmann wanted to force on him old Party comrades for his orchestra, so that this orchestra should be inspired by a good National-Socialist spirit! I must not forget to set up a museum of German masters at Trondheim. Museums like those of Dresden, Munich, Vienna or Berlin ought to have at least two millions a year to make new purchases.

Wilhelm Bode managed things in his own way. He had an extraordinary gift for making use of rich people. He got huge subsidies from them, and in exchange persuaded the Kaiser to ennoble them. That's another sphere in which I intend to introduce some order. It's essential that the director of a museum should be able, without administrative juggleries, to buy a work of value quickly and before it runs the risk of falling into the hands of the dealers.

Night of 20th–21st February 1942

The spirit in peril—The observatory at Linz—The fight against falsehood, superstition and intolerance—Science is not dogmatic—The works of Hörbiger—Pave the way for men of talent

The biretta![335] The mere sight of one of these abortions in cassocks[336] makes me wild! Man has been given his brain to think with. But if he

---

[334] Fritz Busch (1890–1951), left Germany after being dismissed from his post as director of the Dresden Opera in 1933, and spend the rest of his life and career in exile.

[335] A square cap with three flat projections, worn by Roman Catholic clergymen.

[336] Monks.

has the misfortune to make use of it, he finds a swarm of black bugs on his heels. The mind is doomed to the *auto-da-fé*.[337] The observatory I'll have built at Linz, on the Pöstlingberg, I can see it in my mind. A façade of quite classical purity. I'll have the pagan temple razed to the ground, and the observatory will take its place. Thus, in future, thousands of excursionists will make a pilgrimage there every Sunday. They'll thus have access to the greatness of our universe. The pediment will bear this motto: "The heavens proclaim the glory of the everlasting". It will be our way of giving men a religious spirit, of teaching them humility— but without the priests.

Man seizes hold, here and there, of a few scraps of truth, but he couldn't rule nature. He must know that, on the contrary, he is dependent on Creation. And this attitude leads further than the superstitions maintained by the Church.

Christianity is the worst of the regressions that mankind can ever have undergone, and it's the Jew who, thanks to this diabolic invention, has thrown him back fifteen centuries. The only thing that would be still worse would be victory for the Jew through Bolshevism. If Bolshevism triumphed, mankind would lose the gift of laughter and joy. It would become merely a shapeless mass, doomed to greyness and despair.

The priests of antiquity were closer to nature, and they sought modestly for the meaning of things. Instead of that, Christianity promulgates its inconsistent dogmas and imposes them by force. Such a religion carries within it intolerance and persecution. It's the bloodiest conceivable.

The building of my observatory will cost about twelve millions. The great planetarium by itself is worth two millions.

Ptolemy's one is less expensive. For Ptolemy, the earth was the centre of the world. That changed with Copernicus. Today we know that our solar system is merely a solar system amongst many others. What could we do better than allow the greatest possible number of people like us to become aware of these marvels?

In any case, we can be grateful to Providence, which causes us to live today rather than three hundred years ago. At every street-corner, in those days, there was a blazing stake. What a debt we owe to the

---

[337] The "auto-da-fé" (Spanish for an "act of faith") was the ceremony during the time of the Spanish Inquisition where the sentences were read out before guilty parties were executed.

men who had the courage—the first to do so—to rebel against lies and intolerance.

The admirable thing is that amongst them were Jesuit Fathers. In their fight against the Church, the Russians are purely negative. We, on the other hand, should practise the cult of the heroes who enabled humanity to pull itself out of the rut of error. Kepler lived at Linz, and that's why I chose Linz as the place for our observatory. His mother was accused of witchcraft and was tortured several times by the Inquisition.

To open the eyes of simple people, there's no better method of instruction than the picture. Put a small telescope in a village, and you destroy a world of superstitions. One must destroy the priest's argument that science is changeable because faith does not change, since, when presented in this form, the statement is dishonest.

Of course, poverty of spirit is a precious safeguard for the Church. The initiation of the people must be performed slowly. Instruction can simplify reality, but it has not the right deliberately to falsify it. What one teaches the lower level must not be invalidated by what is said a stage higher. In any case, science must not take on a dogmatic air, and it must always avoid running away when faced with difficulties. The contradictions are only apparent. When they exist, this is not the fault of science, but because men have not yet carried their enquiry far enough.

It was a great step forward, in the days of Ptolemy, to say that the earth was a sphere and that the stars gravitated around it. Since then there has been continual progress along the same path. Copernicus first. Copernicus, in his turn, has been largely left behind, and things will always be so. In our time, Hörbiger has made another step forward.

The universities make me think of the direction of the *Wehrmacht*'s technical service. Our technicians pass by many discoveries, and when by chance they again meet one they disregarded a few years before, they take good care not to remind anyone of their mistake.

At present, science claims that the moon is a projection into space of a fragment of the earth, and that the earth is an emanation of the sun. The real question is whether the earth came from the sun or whether it has a tendency to approach it.

For me there is no doubt that the satellite planets are attracted by the planets, just as the latter are themselves attracted by a fixed point, the sun. Since there is no such thing as a vacuum, it is possible that the planets' speed of rotation and movement may grow slower. Thus it is not impossible, for example, that Mars may one day be a satellite of the

Earth. Hörbiger considers a point of detail in all this. He declares that the element which we call water is in reality merely melted ice (instead of ice's being frozen water): what is found in the universe is ice, and not water. This theory amounted to a revolution, and everybody rebelled against Hörbiger. Science has a lot of difficulty in imposing its views, because it is constantly grappling with the spirit of routine. The fact is, men do not *wish* to know. In the last few years, the situation of science has improved.

It's a piece of luck when men are found at the head of a State who are inclined to favour bold researches—for these latter are rarely supported and encouraged by official science.

There's no greater privilege, in my view, than to play the part of a patron of the arts or the sciences. Men would certainly have regarded it as a vast honour to be allowed to encourage the career of a man like Richard Wagner. Well, it's already a great deal gained that people like him are no longer burned alive!

One sometimes hears it regretted that our period does not provide geniuses of the same stature as those of bygone times. That's a mistake. These geniuses exist; it would be enough to encourage them. For my part, when I know that a scientist wishes to devote himself to new researches, I help him. I shall not cease to think that the most precious possession a country can have is its great men. If I think of Bismarck, I realise that only those who have lived through 1918 could fully appreciate his worth. One sees by such examples how much it would mean if we could make the road smooth for men of talent.

It's only in the realm of music that I can find no satisfaction. The same thing is happening to music as is happening to beauty in a world dominated by the shavelings—the Christian religion is an enemy to beauty. The Jew has brought off the same trick upon music. He has created a new inversion of values and replaced the loveliness of music by noises. Surely the Athenian, when he entered the Parthenon to contemplate the image of Zeus, must have had another impression than the Christian who must resign himself to contemplating the grimacing face of a man crucified. Since my fourteenth year I have felt liberated from the superstition that the priests used to teach. Apart from a few Holy Joes, I can say that none of my comrades went on believing in the miracle of the eucharist. The only difference between then and now is that in those days I was convinced one must blow up the whole show with dynamite.

21st February 1942
A rich Jewish couple

I'm thinking of the wife of Consul Scharrer.[338] She had hands laden with rings which were so big that she couldn't move her fingers. She was the sort of Jewess one sees in caricatures. He was a great devotee of the turf. His wife and his horses were his only preoccupations.

One day Werlin showed me Scharrer's car. Its radiator was plated, not in nickel, but in gold. It furthermore contained a thousand little articles of everyday use, starting with a lavatory, all in gold. I can still see Consul Scharrer when he used to arrive in a top-hat, with his cheeks more puffed out than those of Christian Weber, for the Sunday concert on the avenue. On their property at Bernried they had white peacocks. Although he received Prussian princes in his house, in the depths of his heart Scharrer was a Bavarian autonomist. A parrot of genius one day made the unforgivable blunder of crying, amidst this brilliant assembly: "Prussian swine!"

Unfortunately for him, Scharrer had a flame. His wife was furious, and threw him out of the house. He died in poverty. She, the wife, was a daughter of the big brewer, Busch, who had made his fortune in the United States. He must have been some worthy Bavarian, who by chance married a Jewess.

As regards Frau Scharrer,[339] she looked like a ball. Nobody ever checked up whether she was wider or taller. When she was sitting in her carriage, her arms necessarily followed the shape of her body, and her hands hung down at the sides. There are Jewesses like that in Tunis. They are shut up in cages until they put on weight. She finally offered herself to a young lover. It's a painful situation for a husband to be so dependent on a wife as rich as Croesus.

22nd February 1942, evening
A SPECIAL GUEST: A DANISH STURMBANNFÜHRER SS (MAJOR) OF THE VIKING DIVISION[340]

In praise of Dr. Porsche—Defence of the European peninsula—The Russian masses against the individual—Nations must fuse—Europe saved in 1933

---

[338] Eduard Scharrer (1880–1932), a businessman and early NSDAP supporter.
[339] Wilhelmina Busch (1884–1952). She left Germany for Switzerland in 1939, and only returned in 1946. Her Bernried estate is today a national park in Bavaria.
[340] The Danish SS man is likely Christian von Schalburg (1906–1942), later leader of the SS Wiking Division.

Although one wouldn't think it seeing him so modest and self-effacing, Dr. Porsche is the greatest engineering genius in Germany today. He has the courage to give his ideas time to ripen, although the capitalists are always urging him on to produce for quick profit. His experiments made during the war concerning the resistance of materials will enable us continually to improve our Volkswagen. In future, mobilisation will no longer be a problem of transport for us. We'll still have the problem of petrol, but that we'll solve.

Not long ago, at a time when there were still a few acres of land to be shared out in the Far East, everybody went rushing there. Nowadays, we have the Russian spaces. They're less attractive and rougher, but they're worth more to us. We'll get our hands on the finest land, and we'll guarantee for ourselves the control of the vital points.

We'll know how to keep the population in order. There won't be any question of our arriving there with kid gloves and dancing-masters.

Asia didn't succeed, in the course of the centuries, in dislodging us from our peninsula—and all they now have in the way of civilisation, they've got from us. Now we're going to see which side has the real strength.

The Russian, as an individual fighting man, has always been our inferior. Russians exist only *en masse,* and that explains their brutality. I've always rebelled against the idea that Europe had reached the end of its mission, and that the hour of Russia or the United States had come.

It was the Continent that civilised Great Britain, and this is what enabled her to colonise vast spaces in the rest of the world.

Without Europe, America is not conceivable. Why shouldn't we have the strength necessary to become one of the world's centres of attraction? A hundred and twenty million people of Germanic stock, when they've consolidated their positions—that's a force against which nobody in the world will be able to do anything.

The countries that make up the Germanic world will stand only to gain. I see it in my own case. My native land is one of the most beautiful countries in the Reich, but what can it do when left to itself? What could I undertake as an Austrian? There's no way of developing one's talents in countries like Austria or Saxony, Denmark or Switzerland.

The foundation is missing. So it's lucky that once again potential new spaces are opening up before the Germanic peoples.

I understand that it may be hard for a young Dutchman or a young Norwegian to find himself called upon to form a common unit, within the framework of the Reich, together with men of other Germanic connections. But what is asked of them is no harder than what was asked of the Germanic tribes at the time of the great migrations. In those days, bitterness was so great that the chief of the Germanic tribes was assassinated by members of his own family. What was asked of the countries that have formed the Second Reich is similar to what we are asking now, and to what we recently asked of the Austrians.

If Germany hadn't had the good fortune to let me take power in 1933, Europe today would no longer exist. The fact is that since I've been in power, I've had only a single idea: to re-arm. That's how I was able, last summer, to decide to attack Russia.

Confronted with the innumerable populations of the East, we cannot exist except on condition that all Germanics are united. They must compose the nucleus around which Europe will federate. On the day when we've solidly organised Europe, we shall be able to look towards Africa. And, who knows? Perhaps one day we shall be able to entertain other ambitions.

There are three ways of settling the social question. The privileged class rules the people. The insurgent proletariat exterminates the possessing class. Or else a third formula gives each man the opportunity to develop himself according to his talents. When a man is competent, it matters little to me if he's the son of a caretaker.

And, by the way, I'm not stopping the descendants of our military heroes from going once more through the same tests. I wouldn't feel I had the right to demand of each man the supreme sacrifice, if I hadn't myself gone through the whole 1914–18 war in the front line.

Turning towards the Danish guest, the Führer commented: For you, things are easier than they were for us. Our past helps you. Our beginnings were wretched. And if I would disappeared before we were successful, everything would at once have returned into oblivion.

22nd February 1942, evening
SPECIAL GUESTS: HIMMLER AND A DANISH
STURMBANNFÜHRER OF THE VIKING DIVISION
Party organisation—The National Socialist press—Diverting the Jewish virus

It's unbelievable what the Party owes Schwarz.[341] It was thanks to the good order in which he kept our finances that we were able to de-

---

[341] Franz Schwarz.

velop so rapidly and wipe out the other parties. For me, it's marvellous. I don't concern myself with these matters, so to speak, and Schwarz only reports to me once a year. It's an immense relief for a man whose business is to breathe life into a movement not to have to bother about affairs of administration. I appreciate the privilege that has been mine, throughout my existence, to meet men who had the liking for responsibilities and the talent necessary to accomplish independently the work that was entrusted to them.

Amann is one of the oldest of my companions. He was infinitely valuable to me, for I had no notion of what double-entry book-keeping was.

My first treasurer was a former poacher who had lost an arm in the exercise of his talents. His name was Meier. The arm that was left to him was very useful for ringing the bell we used at our meetings. He lived in a cabin which one entered by a ladder designed for fowls.

At that time the Party had a total strength of thirty, and Jegg[342] was already one of our chaps. Meier was the very type of proletarian, in the good sense of the word. The fact that he was one-armed, moreover, earned him respect. As for his role of treasurer, the inflation finally took away all its importance. He was succeeded by Singer. He was a very fine man, a small Bavarian official, exactly what suited us at that time. My supporters all had little jobs. Singer, for example, was a guardian at the Bavarian National Museum. He looked after his old mother in a touching manner.

Whilst I was in Landsberg, the Party having been dissolved, Schwarz turned up. He'd begun by looking after the treasury of the Popular Block. One day Esser[343] came to visit me, to announce that he'd discovered the *rara avis* and to advise me to use him in the new Party. I sent for the man, and it was Schwarz. He told me he was fed up with working with a lot of parsons, and that he'd be delighted to work for me. I was not slow to perceive his qualities. As usual, the man had been stifled by the mediocrities for whom he worked.

Schwarz organised, in model fashion, everything that gradually became the Party's gigantic administration. He'd be quite capable of ad-

---

[342] The details of the man named "Jegg" have been lost. The original manuscript used the words "papa Jegg" (that is, *dad*, or *daddy* Jegg) in this place, but this is either a stenographer error or an unknown nickname.

[343] Hermann Esser (1900–1981), editor of the *Völkischer Beobachter*, State Secretary for Tourism in the Ministry of Public Enlightenment and Propaganda.

ministering the finances of Berlin, and would succeed marvellously as the mayor of a big city. He had the fault—and what luck that was!—of not being a lawyer, and nobody had more practical good sense than he had. He knew admirably how to economise on small things—with the result that we always had what we needed for important matters. It was Schwarz who enabled me to administer the Party without our having to rely on the petty cash.

In this way, unexpected assets are like manna. Schwarz centralised the administration of the Party. All subscriptions are sent directly to the central office, which returns to the local and regional branches the percentage that's due to them. When I need information concerning any one—no matter which—of our members, I have only to pick up the telephone, and I get it within two minutes—even if I don't know the member's name, and know him only by his Party number.

I don't know whether there's such a perfect and also such a simple organisation anywhere else in the world. This centralisation carried to an extreme nevertheless fits in with a high degree of decentralisation on another level. Thus the *Gauleiters* enjoy total independence in their sector.

As regards Amann, I can say positively that he's a genius. He's the greatest newspaper proprietor in the world. Despite his great discretion, which explains why it's not generally known, I declare that Rothermere[344] and Beaverbrook[345] are mere dwarfs compared to him. Today the *Central Verlag* owns from 70 per cent to 80 per cent of the German press.

Amann achieved all that without the least ostentation. Who knows, for example, that the *Münchener Neueste* is one of our press organisations? Amann makes a point of preserving the individual personality of each of his newspapers. He's likewise very clever when it's a matter of handing over to others businesses that are not showing a profit.

That's what happened when he gave Sauckel a newspaper. It had belonged to Dinter,[346] and Amann had taken it over for political reasons.

---

[344] Harold Sidney Harmsworth, 1st Viscount Rothermere (1868-1940), owner of Associated Newspapers Ltd., responsible for the *Daily Mail* and the *Daily Mirror*, two large-circulation UK newspapers.

[345] William Maxwell Aitken, 1st Baron Beaverbrook (1879-1964), owner of the *Daily Express*, and later, Winston Churchill's Minister of Aircraft Production.

[346] Artur Dinter (1876-1948), an early NSDAP member who fell out with the party leadership in 1928.

A short time afterwards, I happened to ask Sauckel what Amann's present had brought him in. "Up to date, it has cost me twenty thousand marks," he replied.

Amann had the idea that the profit of the central organisation was made up of the profits made on each separate business. Hence one can conclude that no business which was in the red had, from any point of view, the slightest interest for Amann. That reminds me that Dietrich[347] used to publish in Coburg a magazine entitled *Flamme*, which was even more violent than Streicher's *Stürmer*. And yet I never knew a gentler man than Dietrich.

One must never forget the services rendered by the *Stürmer*. Without it the affair of the Jew Hirsch's perjury, at Nuremberg, would never have come out. And how many other scandals he exposed!

One day a Nazi saw a Jew, in Nuremberg station, impatiently throw a letter into the waste-paper basket. He recovered the letter and, after having read it, took it to the *Stürmer*. It was a blackmailer's letter in which the recipient, the Jew Hirsch, was threatened that the game would be given away if he stopped coughing up. The *Stürmers* revelation provoked an enquiry. It thus became known that a country girl, who had a place in Nuremberg in the household of Herr Hirsch, had brought an action against him for rape. Hirsch got the girl to swear in court that she had never had relations with other men—then he produced numerous witnesses who all claimed to have had relations with her.

The German judges did not understand that Jews have no scruples when it's a question of saving one of their compatriots. They therefore condemned the servant to one and a half years in prison. The letter thrown impatiently away by Hirsch was written by one of the false witnesses suborned by him—which witness considered that he could conveniently add blackmail to perjury. Today everyone's eyes are opened, but at the time people found it difficult to believe that such things could happen. Poor girls who worked in big shops were handed over defenceless to their employers. In such a state of affairs, Streicher rendered immense services. Now that Jews are known for what they are, nobody any longer thinks that Streicher libelled them.

The discovery of the Jewish virus is one of the greatest revolutions that have taken place in the world. The battle in which we are engaged today is of the same sort as the battle waged, during the last century, by

---

[347] Hans Dietrich.

Pasteur and Koch. How many diseases have their origin in the Jewish virus! Japan would have been contaminated, too, if it had stayed open to the Jews. We shall regain our health only by eliminating the Jew. Everything has a cause, nothing comes by chance.

Night of the 22nd–23rd February 1942
The principal newspapers of the Party—Tristan and other pieces at Vienna

The organisation of our press has truly been a success. Our law concerning the press is such that divergences of opinion between members of the Government are no longer an occasion for public exhibitions, which are not the newspapers' business.

We've eliminated that conception of political freedom according to which everybody has the right to say whatever comes into his head. Amann controls more than half of the German press. It's enough for me to send for Lorenz[348] and inform him of my point of view, and I know that next day all the German newspapers will broadcast my ideas. Our little Dr. Dietrich is an extremely clever man. He doesn't write well, but his speeches are often first-rate. I'm proud to be able to think that, with such collaborators at my side, I can make a sheer about turn, as I did on 22nd June last, without anyone's moving a muscle. And that's a thing that's possible in no country but ours.

Our illustrated newspapers have greatly improved. But, to compete abroad with the Anglo-Saxon weeklies, the *Leipziger Illustrierte* should be more eye-catching. The *Berliner,* the *Münchener* and the *Wiener* are well-made illustrated papers—the *JB* still better. The *Kölner* gained the limelight some years ago thanks to the documents it published. On the other hand, we could easily do without the *Deutsche Illustrierte. Das Reich* is a great success. When peace has returned, we shall need, as a pendant to *Das Reich,* a Sunday weekly for people in the country. It should be easy to read, should have a serialised novel—so that young girls should likewise get their share—and should be copiously illustrated. The English newspapers are in a privileged position as regards both the text and the photographic documentation. From all parts of the world, their material reaches them in floods. We ourselves shall be enabled by our new conquests to make progress in that field.

The brilliance, and what's called the charm, of Vienna are explained by a long past. For five centuries Vienna was the capital of an empire.

---

[348] Heinz Lorenz (1913–1985), Deputy Chief Press Secretary.

I was so poor, during the Viennese period of my life, that I had to restrict myself to seeing only the finest spectacles.

Thus I heard *Tristan* thirty or forty times, and always from the best companies. I also heard some Verdi and other works—leaving out the small fry.

24th February 1942, midday
How great artists can serve their country

I've learnt that young Roller[349] has just fallen at the front. If I would known that he'd gone out! But nobody told me. There are hundreds of thousands of men who could serve their country in no better way than by risking their lives for her, but a great artist should find another way. Can fate allow it that the most idiotic Russian should strike down men like that? We have so many men seconded for special duties!

What harm could it do to add to their number the five or six hundred gifted men whom it would be important to save? Roller is irreplaceable. We had only Sievert, Arent and Praetorius—Austria had given us the young Roller. Why didn't Schirach warn me? I saw his *Friedenstag*. What a lovely thing! The young Roller was a brave man. Before the *Anschluss* he would have had to leave Austria. I'm convinced he went out as a volunteer. I could have sent him anywhere at all, for personal reasons, if he hadn't insisted on staying in Vienna.

Night of 24th–25th February 1942
An exemplary officer—A group of merry fellows

The death of Under-Secretary of State Hofmann[350] has deeply grieved me. In 1919 I harangued his battalion at Passau. What a marvellous lot of men we had there! Blazing patriots. To start with, Hofmann trusted me—and yet at that time I stood for so little. Hofmann was already convinced that it was I who would save Germany.

At the time of the Kapp-putsch, Hofmann sent a telegram: "Putting myself under Kapp's orders. What's regiment doing?" There were a lot of officers of that sort in Bavaria. Seeckt[351] got rid of them all. The

---

[349] Ulrich Roller (1911–1941), a NSDAP activist who took part in the failed July 1934 coup against the Austrian dictator Dollfuss. Roller had a successful career as a stage designer and producer at the Wagner Festivals in Bayreuth, at the German Opera in Berlin, and as head of the Vienna State Opera costume department.
[350] Hans Georg Hofmann (1873–1942), chief group leader of the Storm Troopers and Under Secretary of State for Bavaria. He died of a heart attack.
[351] Johannes von Seeckt (1866–1936), Chief of the German General Staff in 1919, and then Chief of the German Army Command from 1920 to 1926.

only ones who were kept were those who never wavered. I know three people who, when they're together, never stop laughing. They're Hoffmann, Amann and Goebbels. When Epp joins them, the whole thing becomes a madhouse.

As a matter of fact, Epp is not particularly quick. When the others are laughing at the third joke, Epp is beginning to catch on to the first, and starts to let out a huge laugh, which goes on and on. Amann, what a jolly chap he is! Already when we were at the front, he used to let joy loose amongst us. In my unit, even at the worst times there was always someone who could find something to say that would make us laugh. I'm very fond of Hoffmann. He's a man who always makes fun of me. He's a "dead-pan" humorist, and he never fails to find a victim.

20th February 1942, midday
Strengthening the German position—The British proletariat and the threat of revolution—The three objectives of revolution—Paradise on earth—The last somersaults of Christianity

In the last few weeks, I've the feeling that our position has got considerably stronger. The little countries are beginning to look on us as a guarantee of order. They'll approach us all the more when they see that England is tying herself up more closely with Bolshevism.

When the masses in England realise their own power, probably they'll make a bloody revolution. One can only hold the masses by habit—or else by force. Nothing stops me from thinking that they're keeping on the island, as a guard against unexpected circumstances, regiments that would be very useful elsewhere. If the Conservative Party lost the support of the Army, the only thing left to it would be to make an alliance with the nine thousand supporters of Mosley. They'd need a Cromwell to save them, a Premier, who would take everything into his own hands. For lack of this solution, the revolution will sweep away everything.

It will be one of National Socialism's merits that it knew how to stop the revolution at the proper moment. It's very nice to see the people arise, but one must be a realist and go further than phrases. Nobody any longer counts the revolutions that have miscarried, or that degenerated for lack of being led. I've not forgotten the difficulties I had to overcome in 1933 and 1934. Revolution opens a sluice-gate, and it's often impossible to curb the masses one has let loose.

A revolution has three main objectives. First of all, it's a matter of breaking down the partitions between classes, so as to enable every man to rise. Secondly, it's a matter of creating a standard of living such that the poorest will be assured of a decent existence. Finally, it's a matter of acting in such a way that the benefits of civilisation become common property.

The people who call themselves democrats blame us for our social policy as if it were a kind of disloyalty: according to them, it imperils the privileges of the owning classes. They regard it as an attack on liberty; for liberty, in their view, is the right of those who have power to continue to exercise it. I understand their reaction very well—but we had no choice. National Socialism is a purely German phenomenon, and we never intended to revolutionise the world. It was enough for us to be given a free hand in Russia and to be offered a few colonies.

And the English could still be leading their comfortable little existence. It's obvious that, in the long run, they couldn't have avoided certain social reforms.

One can't, in fact, bridge the gap that exists between rich and poor merely with the consolations of religion. I realise, for my own part, that if I were offered the choice between nakedness on this earth (with the compensation of supreme happiness in the world beyond) and an earthly paradise, I certainly wouldn't choose to sing Hallelujahs until the end of time.

In virtue of what law, divine or otherwise, should the rich alone have the right to govern? The world is passing at this moment through one of the most important revolutions in human history. We are witnessing the final somersaults of Christianity. It began with the Lutheran revolution. The revolutionary nature of that rebellion lies in the fact that until then there had been only one authority, on both the spiritual and the temporal level, that of the Pope—for it was he who delegated temporal power. Dogma cannot resist the ceaselessly renewed attacks of the spirit of free enquiry. One cannot teach at ten o'clock in the morning truths which one destroys in the eleven o'clock lesson.

What is ruining Christianity today is what once ruined the ancient world. The pantheistic mythology would no longer suit the social conditions of the period. As soon as the idea was introduced that all men were equal before God, that world was bound to collapse.

What is tragic for the world at present in gestation is that it is itself exposed to the danger of fixing itself in its turn upon a dogma. If Frederick the Great had lived fifty years longer, and had been present as a simple spectator at the evolution of society, he'd have ceaselessly used his baton in sheer anger. Men fortunately have had this piece of luck, that life is taken away from them at the moment when they would have an opportunity to take part in the destruction of the values on which they'd built.

26th February 1942, evening
SPECIAL GUESTS: HIMMLER AND STURMBANNFÜHRER
(MAJOR) KUMM[352]

Fears for Antonescu—The objectionable King Michael—A corrupt ruling class—Erzberger, trafficker in land—Roads—German minorities in the Balkans—Importance of the Danube

If something happened to Antonescu, I would tremble for Romania. Who'd succeed him? King Michael. He didn't even help his mother to get down from her carriage! Did he think it would injure his royal dignity? I saw he was choked with rage when he noticed I would put his mother on my right, the place due to the king. I know very well it wasn't according to protocol—but one can't go on maintaining these obsolete customs. The Romanian peasantry are merely wretched cattle. As for the ruling class, it's rotten to the marrow. In the film *Stadt Anatol*,[353] those Balkan regions, turned upside down by black gold, are admirably rendered. These people for whom chance has suddenly put a petroleum well under their feet, and who all at once become fabulously rich, it's contrary to the whole natural order! A town like Bucharest grows only as a result of speculation.

I was once able to prove Erzberger[354] guilty of illicit dealing—a squalid deal in real estate. As a result of an indiscretion, he'd learnt of a development scheme between Pankow and Berlin. In association with a *monsignore*, he'd bought for a hundred thousand marks or so some land that was later sold for three million seven hundred thousand marks. That's why we inserted in the Party programme a clause concerning speculation in real estate. I don't object to legitimate landowners making a small profit on such occasions, but one must discourage these usurers' enterprises.

For the construction of *autobahnen*, I've made a law by the terms of which the indemnities due to the expropriated persons are fixed by

---

[352] Otto Kumm (1909–2004), SS Brigade Leader and Waffen SS Major General.
[353] The "City of Anatol" was a 1936 German based on a eponymous 1932 novel by Bernhard Kellermann which deals with a town in the Balkans where oil is found.
[354] Matthias Erzberger (1875–1921), a politician for the *Zentrumpartei* (Center Party) and German Minister of Finance from 1919 to 1920.

the State. All strategic roads were built by tyrants—for the Romans, the Prussians or the French. They go straight across country. The other roads wind like processions and waste everybody's time.

The people love to be ruled. That's why it's sensitive to the loss of certain chiefs. We saw it when Todt died. The sorrow was universal. The people love to have the best man in command.

I'm in favour of our building roads everywhere, but it's not essential always to proceed in a uniform manner. The landscape of Flanders doesn't call for roads like ours. These regions should each keep its own character. Let's not kill the picturesque in the world.

The Hungarians are better governed than the Romanians.

What a pity they can't install Croats instead of Romanians! The Hungarians are wildly nationalist. They assimilate the Germans at extraordinary speed, and they know how to select the best of them for posts of command. We shan't succeed in preserving the German minorities in Hungary except by taking over control of the State—or else we shall have to withdraw our minorities from Hungary.

Apart from those in Transylvania, the German minorities in Hungary have a tendency to degenerate. I realised this at Nuremberg, when I saw their delegations march past. In our plans for colonisation in Russia, we'll find room for these minorities. It's not profitable for us to repatriate minorities, but if I settle them on territories that don't cost me anything, that's quite different. A government must have a lot of authority to succeed in such an operation. Anyway, I suppose that if we want to practise a sincere friendship with Hungary, we shall have to withdraw our minorities from the country.

Obviously, if we want to convert the Danube into a German river, our policy will have to be different. In that case, we would have to settle all our minorities from the Balkans on the banks of the river. But we would be obliged to give the Germans of the Banat,[355] for example, a land as fertile as the Banat.

It's clear that the Hungarians and Romanians will never be reconciled, even if they regard Germany as a common enemy.

If I settle the fifteen hundred thousand Germans of our minorities in the Eastern territories, I'll build an *autobahn* fifteen hundred kilometres long, dotted at intervals of fifty to a hundred kilometres with

---

[355] The Banat is a historical region in central eastern Europe now comprising parts of southern Hungary, western Romania and northeastern Serbia. The region's German inhabitants were deported in 1945.

298

German agglomerations, including some important towns. That's a tentative solution, but the Danube remains the Danube. We should establish a strong foothold at the Iron Gates. Unfortunately it's an unprepossessing region and won't attract our colonists. It will always be possible to populate the region by the exploitation of the copper-mines. That will be an excellent way of procuring the copper we need, and there will be all the more reason for it if we're not on good terms with the Yugoslavs.

The Danube is also the link with Turkey. And it's only when one's lines of communication are safe that one can build a world empire.

Night of 26th–27th February 1942
Relief in Russia—The fate of Napoleon—GHQ, Wolfsschanze[356]—Death blow to the petit bourgeois ideal

Sunday will be the 1st March. Boys, you can't imagine what that means to me—how much the last three months have worn out my strength, tested my nervous resistance. I can tell you now that during the first two weeks of December we lost a thousand tanks and had two thousand locomotives out of operation. As a result of the general lack of material, I seemed to be a liar, and yet I wasn't lying. I told the front that trains were arriving, but the locomotives were always broken down. I told the front that tanks were arriving, but they arrived in what a state! Now, when I send something to the southern sector, I know that it will reach its destination. We have nothing more to fear from climatic mishaps. Now that January and February are past, our enemies can give up the hope of our suffering the fate of Napoleon. They've lost nothing by waiting. Now we're about to switch over to squaring the account. What a relief! I've noticed, on the occasion of such events, that when everybody loses his nerves, I'm the only one who keeps calm.

It was the same thing at the time of the struggle for power, but at that time I had the luck to be only thirty, whilst my opponents were twenty or thirty years older.

Here in the *Wolfsschanze*, I feel like a prisoner in these dugouts, and my spirit can't escape. In my youth I dreamed constantly of vast spaces, and life has enabled me to give the dream reality. Ah, if we were at least in Berlin! Space lends wings to my imagination. Often I go at night to the card-room, and there I pace to and fro. In that way I get ideas.

---

[356] The "Wolf's Lair" was Hitler's Eastern Front military headquarters located in the Masurian woods near the East Prussian town of Rastenburg (now Kętrzyn in Poland).

My finest headquarters, when all is said, was *Felsennest*. At the *Wolfschlucht*, the place wasn't very safe, and I had constant eye-ache because of the caustic emanations given off by the fireproofed wood of which the barracks had been built. The third of our headquarters was quite simple, but very agreeable. Unfortunately, it was so damp there that we would all have ended by falling sick if we would stayed there. The fourth, which was intended to be our genuine headquarters, I saw only in a photograph. They made exactly what I didn't want, a castle— and that's the main reason why I refused to settle there.

When peace has returned, I'll begin by spending three months without doing anything. Our soldiers themselves should have a holiday. I'll immediately resign the command of the *Wehrmacht*. I'll at once send for Speer again.

All our war-time administrative services will be reduced to their simplest terms. Even the Four Year Plan will be reduced to a more modest scope of activity. I'll pass it over to the Ministry of Economics, by the way. What counts is to organise the work properly, and to see that everywhere we have *the right man in the right place*.

I shall be glad to know that the *petit bourgeois* ideal of a nation squeezed between the Elbe and the Weser is receiving its death-blow. A new youth is there, avid to make the world's acquaintance, ready to carry on.

27th February 1942, midday

Laws, man-made and natural—God and the religions—Force and torture impose belief—The true religion—Truth will triumph—Towards a new conception of the world

I believe that Providence gives the victory to the man who knows how to use the brains nature has given him. The notions of law invented by the jurists have little to do with natural laws. The wisdom of nations sometimes expresses truths as old as the world, that perfectly reproduce nature's intentions. "God helps him who helps himself!" It's obvious that man forgets his own destiny. One day I explained to Eltz[357] that what is conventionally called creation is probably an immovable thing, that only man's conception of it is subject to variations. Why doesn't God give everybody the possibility of understanding truth? Every man of average culture knows that at this precise moment the Catholic religion is of interest to just one tenth of the population of the

---

[357] Peter Paul Freiherr von Eltz-Rübenach (1875–1943), Minister of Posts and Transport between 1932 and 1937.

globe. He's astonished, too, that Providence, which has willed all that, can allow so many religions, all true from the point of view of those who practise them, to compete for the faith of the faithful. He knows, too, thanks to the view in depth that history enables him to take, that the Christian religion interests only those living in a tiny period of the life of mankind.

God made men. But thanks to original sin we are men in the image of our world, earning our bread in the sweat of our brow.

For five hundred thousand years, God impassively contemplated the spectacle of which He is the author. Then one day He decided to send upon earth His only son. You remember the details of that complicated story! Those who don't believe should, it seems, have faith imposed on them by force. If God is truly interested in men being enlightened, one wonders why He resorts to torture for that purpose.

While we're on the subject, let's add that, even amongst those who claim to be good Catholics, very few really believe in this humbug. Only old women, who have given up everything because life has already withdrawn from them, go regularly to church. All that's dead wood—and one shouldn't waste one's time in concerning oneself with such brains.

In the trade union formed by the Church, many of the members have tangible interests to defend, and see no further.

A given set of grimaces, certain people identify them with true religion. After that, let's express surprise that these cynical exploiters of God are the true purveyors of atheism.

Why should men fight to make their point of view triumph, if prayer should be enough? In the Spanish struggle, the clergy should have said: "We defend ourselves by the power of prayer." But they deemed it safer to finance a lot of heathens, so that Holy Church could save her skin.

If I'm a poor devil and die without having had time to repent, I'm all right. But if, as a preliminary, I can dispose of ten marks to the Church's benefit, my affairs appear in a more favourable light. And is that what God would have wanted? That little country girls and simple working men should be set dancing to that tune, that's a thing that can be explained. But that intelligent men should make themselves accomplices to such superstitions, and that it's because of these superstitions, and in the name of love, that hundreds of thousands of human beings have been exterminated in the course of history—that is something I cannot admit. I shall never believe that what is founded on lies can endure forever. I believe in truth. I'm sure that, in the long run, truth must be victorious. It's probable that, as regards religion, we are about to enter an era of tolerance. Everybody will be allowed to seek his own salvation in the way that suits him best. The ancient world knew this climate of tolerance. Nobody took to proselytising.

If I enter a church, it's not with the idea of overturning idols. It's to look for, and perhaps to find, beauties in which I'm interested. It would always be disagreeable for me to go down to posterity as a man who made concessions in this field. I realise that man, in his imperfection, can commit innumerable errors—but to devote myself deliberately to error, that is something I cannot do. I shall never come personally to terms with the Christian lie. In acting as I do, I'm very far from the wish to scandalise. But I rebel when I see the very idea of Providence flouted in this fashion. It's a great satisfaction for me to feel myself totally foreign to that world. But I shall feel I'm in my proper place if, after my death, I find myself, together with people like me, on some sort of Olympus. I shall be in the company of the most enlightened spirits of all times. I adopted a definite attitude on the 21st March 1933 when I refused to take part in the religious services, organised at Potsdam by the two Churches, for the inauguration of the new Reichstag.

I've never concerned myself, in the Party, with learning to which Church the men around me belonged, or did not belong. But if I were to die today, it would shock me to know that there's a single "sky-pilot" within a radius of ten kilometres around me. The idea that one of these fellows could bring me the slightest help would by itself make me despair of Providence. As far as I'm concerned, I act according to my convictions. I don't prevent anyone from praying silently, but I rebel against all blasphemy. So let nobody waste prayers on me that I shall not have asked for. If my presence on earth is providential, I owe it to a superior will. But I owe nothing to the Church that traffics in the salvation of souls, and I find it really too cruel. I admit that one cannot impose one's will by force, but I have a horror of people who enjoy inflicting sufferings on others' bodies and tyranny upon others' souls.

Our epoch will certainly see the end of the disease of Christianity. It will last another hundred years, two hundred years perhaps. My regret will have been that I couldn't, like whoever the prophet was, behold the promised land from afar. We are entering into a conception of the world that will be a sunny era, an era of tolerance. Man must be put in a position to develop freely the talents that God has given him. What is important above all is that we should prevent a greater lie from replacing the lie that is disappearing. The world of Judaeo-Bolshevism must collapse.

27th February 1942, evening
A Governor for Belgium—The Dutch and Germanic solidarity—Dislike of monarchs—A second French Government—Slogans for the British

In Holland, Denmark and Norway there are movements whose leaders have preferred to nourish an ambition to be one day, thanks to us, Presidents of the Council, rather than to be, without us, merely retired majors, or something similar.

I need a man for Belgium. The difficulty is to choose the man. No question of sending there a North German, somebody brutal, a martinet. I need an extraordinarily clever man, as supple as an eel, amiable— and at the same time thick-skinned and tough. For Holland, I have in Seyss-Inquart[358] a man who has these qualities. I must surrender to the evidence that I'm again going to have to fall back upon my Austrian compatriots. When I try to decide who, amongst my *Gauleiters*, would carry enough guns, I always come back to Jury.[359] He's clever, intelligent, conciliatory—but intractable in the essential things. My *Gauleiter* from Styria would be perfect, too, but he's still a little young.

How would it be to send men like Seyss and Jury to Russia? It would be better to send bulls! But one must not confuse suppleness and weakness—and both of them would cut a good figure there. Schirach has done his job very well, and he's now in the running for any important task.

Seyss has succeeded in encouraging in Holland a movement that is numbering more and more adherents, and is waging war against Wilhelmina without our having to put a shoulder to the wheel. The idea of Germanic solidarity is making more and more impression on the minds of the Dutch.

As regards the monarchs, the worst nuisances are those who've grown old in harness. They become, in a sort of way, taboo. You scarcely touch them, and everybody begins to howl. Franz Josef, for example, was much less intelligent than his successor, but a revolution against

---

[358] Arthur Seyss-Inquart (1892–1946), an Austrian NSDAP loyalist who served briefly in the administration of Austria after the *Anschluss* and thereafter as Deputy Governor-General of the General Government of Occupied Poland before taking over the post of *Reichskommissar* of the Netherlands.

[359] Hugo Jury (1887–1945), Gauleiter of the region of Lower Austria.

him was not possible. What a lot of affronts he swallowed in the course of his interminable life! Finally he acquired the style of a Buddha! For more than half a century he witnessed events without reacting to them.

If the Dane goes about it like the old Swede (who does nothing but gather his strength by playing tennis), he'll reach the age of Methuselah. Gustav V was telling me that he had an excellent constitution, for if his absence from the country lasted more than four weeks, he had to be replaced. It's by dint of doing nothing that these puppets become impudently old. In Denmark, we already have the successor. That's Clausen.[360] When we've reached that point, we'll have three men who'll have sinned so much that they'll be obliged to remain allied to us whatever happens. We can count on Clausen, and likewise on Mussert.

In Belgium, there's this damned king! If only he'd cleared out like the others. I would have allowed his pretty girl-friend to go and join him.

In Paris, we'll probably have a second French government. Abetz is too exclusively keen on collaboration, to my taste. Unfortunately, I can't tell him precisely what my objects are, for he has a wife. The fact is, I know of a man who talks in his sleep, and I sometimes wonder whether Abetz doesn't do the same. But he's intelligent at organising resistance in Paris against Vichy, and in this respect his wife is useful to him. Thus things take on a more innocent character.

If we succeeded in forming a second French government in Paris, the opposition in Vichy would have only one wish, that we should stay—for fear that it should be discovered how many of them are paid by us.

My opinion is that the longer we stay in Paris, the better worthwhile it will be. In any case, I shall never have any difficulty in finding occupants for Paris, and there's no risk that one day a unit of the *Wehrmacht* may mutiny, saying: "We don't want to stay in France anymore!"

I've explained to Himmler that, if I would been an emperor of the Holy Empire, I would have put him in disgrace. I very well understand the emperors who were not tempted by the conquest of the East. These spaces had no roads, and no means of heating. Winter there lasted all the year round. It's easy to say: "Blood and soil." But for the particularism of the German princes, we would have succeeded in Germanising the whole of Northern Italy. Racially, the West is to a great extent Germanic.

---

[360] Frits Clausen (1893–1947), leader of the National Socialist Workers' Party of Denmark (DNSAP).

Himmler's theory needs serious consideration. We pay far too much honour to Heinrich the Lion, for he helped in frustrating the policy of Barbarossa and Heinrich VI. If everyone had supported the emperors' policy, what would we not have achieved? Supposing the expansion to the West had been pursued logically, we would have a great Germanic empire stretching from Denmark to the Loire—and England would not have acquired the importance that is hers today.

The moment has come when propaganda can play an important role in our favour. It's not a matter of attacking each Englishman individually to induce him to such and such a particular action. It's a matter of a propaganda that sets forth undeniable facts, and consequently slogans that fall upon a soil well prepared to receive them. For example: "The British Empire is becoming more and more a colony of American Jews."

On the organ of Westminster Abbey, the *Internationale* was played after the service. What can that mean, if not the fall of Christianity? It's enough to compare the statements now being made in London with those issuing a year ago from Lisbon, to realise the change in the situation. It's a turning-point in history.

Night of 27th–28th February 1942
Financial organisation of the Party press

Amann's great idea was to guarantee the financial existence of the newspaper by the profits realised on the Party editions. These profits accumulated so quickly that the newspaper quickly stopped being exposed to any risks.

Amann realised what a *tour de force* it was to maintain the house of publication during my incarceration in Landsberg. For once, the juggleries of the lawyers were useful to us. The publishing house was a limited company, and the law required the unanimous agreement of its members for its dissolution.

By chance, one of the members, Herr von Sebottendorff, was always abroad (in Turkey, I think), and of course Amann could never succeed in getting hold of him. At the time, I owned a part of the capital (Gutberlet had made me a present of a share of five thousand marks, and I had bought other shares).

The firm had existed for thirty or forty years under the name of Franz Eher Publishing Co. I retained for the newspaper the name of *Völkischer Beobachter.* Dietrich Eckart was furious. "What's the meaning of that word, *Beobachter?*[361] he would say. "I could understand something like 'the chain-smasher'!"

Very intelligently, for reasons of camouflage, Amann created on the side the *Hoheneichen* Publishing Co., whose name covered certain publications. And he left the press to Adolf Müller so as not to have to bring action against Party comrades for payment of their bills.

28th February 1942, evening
Housing crisis—new constructions

To put an end to the housing crisis, we shall build, as soon as the war is over, a million dwellings a year, and that for five consecutive years. The time necessary to build a house should not exceed three months. In this field, the achievements of modern technology must be used in their entirety. The mistress of the house must be set free from all the minor chores that make her waste her time.

Not only must the children's play-gardens be near the houses, but the mother must not even be compelled to take her children there herself. All she should have to do is to press a button for the woman in charge to appear immediately. No more refuse to take downstairs, no more fuel to carry up. In the morning, the works of the alarm-clock must even switch on the mechanism that boils the water. All these little inventions that lighten the burden of life must be set to work.

I have a man, Robert Ley, to whom it will be enough for me to entrust this mission. A nod from me, and he'll set everything humming. Every dwelling should carry the right to a garage, and there's no question of this garage costing forty or fifty marks a month. It ought to cost a tenth of that. If we haven't reached that point today, it's once again those damned lawyers we have to thank. I've been told that these maniacs of the Civil Service have found nothing better to do than to compose a file in which all possible accidents, imaginable or unimaginable, have been foreseen.

And they've used this as a foundation on which to base their regulations. Thus they make such demands that building costs become impossibly high. In many cases, they're based on technical peculiarities that became obsolete twenty years ago.

For example, there is a regulation limiting the angle of the stairs to a certain number of degrees. This regulation, if it's applied, entails enormous expenses: time wasted, room wasted, materials wasted.

[361] "Observer." The NSDAP newspaper, *Völkischer Beobachter* translates as "Folkish Observer."

What's more, it's necessary to standardise the necessary components for the construction of interiors. Don't ask where to begin! If
we succeed in sparing the five million families who'll inhabit the new
apartments the useless expense usually involved in a move to a new
dwelling, this will already be progress. Everything must have a beginning. Let's begin at once!

Night of 28th February–1st March 1942
*The Bayreuth Festival 1925—Bayreuth and National Socialism—Role of
Cosima Wagner—Siegfried Wagner*

In 1925, the Bechsteins had invited me to stay with them in Bayreuth. They lived in a villa in the Liszt Strasse (I think this was the
name of the street), within a few yards of Wahnfried. I had hesitated to
go there, for I was afraid of thus increasing the difficulties of Siegfried
Wagner, who was somewhat in the hands of the Jews.

I arrived in Bayreuth towards eleven o'clock in the evening. Lotte
Bechstein was still up, but her relatives were in bed.

Next morning, Cosima Wagner came and brought me some flowers.
What a bustle there was in Bayreuth for the Festival! There exist a few
photographs of that period, in which I figure, taken by Lotte Bechstein.

I used to spend the day in leather shorts. In the evening, I would put
on a dinner-jacket or tails to go to the opera. We made excursions by
car into the Fichtelgebirge and into Franconian mountains. From all
points of view, those were marvellous days.

When I went to the cabaret of the *Chouette,* I found myself immediately in sympathy with the artistes. I was not yet celebrated enough
for my fame to interfere with my peacefulness. Dietrich Eckart, who
had been a critic in Bayreuth, had always told me of the extraordinary
atmosphere prevailing there. He told me that one morning they had
broken into the *Chouette,* and had gone, in company with the artistes,
into the meadow behind the theatre, to play the *Miracle of Good Friday*
there.

At the first performance of *Parsifal* that I attended at Bayreuth,
Cleving was still singing. What a stature, and what a magnificent voice!
I would already been present at performances of *Parsifal* in Munich.
That same year, I was also present at the *Ring* and the *Meistersinger.*
The fact that the Jew Schorr was allowed to sing the role of Wotan had
the effect of a profanation on me. Why couldn't they have got Rode
from Munich? But there was Braun, an artiste of exceptional quality.
For years I was unable to attend the Festival, and I would been very dis-

tressed about it. Gosima Wagner also lamented my absence. She often urged me to come, by letter or by telephone. But I never passed through Bayreuth without paying her a visit.

It's Gosima Wagner's merit to have created the link between Bayreuth and National Socialism. Siegfried was a personal friend of mine, but he was a political neutral. He couldn't have been anything else, or the Jews would have ruined him. Now the spell is broken. Siegfried has regained his independence, and one again hears works by him. Those dirty Yids had succeeded in demolishing him! I heard, in my youth, his *Bärenhäuter*. It's said that the *Schmied von Marienburg* is his best work. I still have a lot of things to see and hear! In Berlin, I've been present at a performance of a work of Richard Wagner's youth, *The Novice of Palermo*, containing themes that are still reminiscent of Mozart. Only, here and there, a few new themes make their appearance, the first-fruits of a new style.

1st March 1942, midday
SPECIAL GUEST: HIMMLER
A picturesque personality, the Party printer

It was through Dietrich Eckart that I got to know Müller. Our first encounter was not favourable, and I was astonished that Eckart should have put me in touch with such an individual.

"I agree that he's as black as the devil," Eckart replied, "and more cunning than the cunningest peasant, but he's the best printer I've known in my life, and also the most generous man." That happened well before I had the *Völkischer Beobachter*. Müller was wedged in his arm-chair with the self-assurance of a plutocrat. His first words were: "To prevent any misunderstanding from arising, let it be clearly understood that, where there's no payment, there's no printing, either." When one visited him, Müller never ceased to groan. Nevertheless he grew fatter and fatter. He printed more and more. He constantly bought new machines, but his *leitmotiv* was: "I can't get along on these rates, I'm ruining myself."

"To see you so fat, one wouldn't believe it!"

"I've so many worries that I drink a little to drown them, and that swells you up!"

His press is equipped in the most modern style. He's a real genius in the Party. Cunning, nobody could be more so, but he was an employer with a sense of social responsibility. He paid his workers well, and when he took them on an outing, he paid no attention to expense. For a firm of that size, in any case, that meant less than nothing. And the *Völkischer Beobachter* was always there to cough up! I never made a journey with Müller without his having to pay a visit to some woman by whom he had a child. At the birth of each of his bastards, he would open an account for them at the Savings Bank, with a first payment of five thousand marks. I actually know four illegitimate children of his. I wonder how such an ugly blighter manages to have such lovely children! I must add that Müller adores children.

Every week, he spends two days with Ida on the Tegernsee, although he's divorced from her. He had married her simply so that his children should have a respectable name. He likewise spends two days with his legitimate wife, at Munich, and lastly two days at his business. The rest of the time he devotes to shooting.

That Müller's really quite a fellow.

1st March 1942, evening
SPECIAL GUEST: HIMMLER

Jealousy of women—Disproportion between men and women—
Polygamy and the Thirty Years' War—Hypocrites of the upper classes—
The bourgeois marriage—Social prejudices on their way out

In the eyes of a woman, the finest of dresses at once loses its charm—if she sees another woman wearing one like it. I've seen a woman suddenly leave the opera at the sight of a rival who had entered a box wearing the same dress as herself.

"What cheek!" she said. "I'm going!"

In the pleasure a woman takes in rigging herself out, there is always an admixture of some trouble-making element, something treacherous—to awaken another woman's jealousy by displaying something that the latter doesn't possess. Women have the talent, which is unknown to us males, for giving a kiss to a woman-friend and at the same time piercing her heart with a well-sharpened stiletto.

To wish to change women in this respect would be ingenuous: women are what they are. Let's come to terms with their little weaknesses. And if women really only need satisfactions of that sort to keep them happy, let them not deprive themselves, by any means!

For my part, I prefer to see them thus occupied than devoting themselves to metaphysics. There's no worse disaster than to see them grappling with ideas. In that respect, the point of disaster is reached by women painters, who attach no importance to beauty—when it's a question of themselves! Other women are extremely careful of their appearance, but not beyond the moment when they've found a husband.

They're obsessed by their outlines, they weigh themselves on exact scales—the least gramme counts! Then you marry them, and they put on weight by the kilo! Without doubt, when we mock at women's artifices, they could pay us back by pointing out our own coquetry—our poor, male coquetry. It's true that we shave, that we get our hair cut, that we, too, try to correct the mistakes of nature! When I was a child, only actors and priests had shaven faces.

At Leonding, the only civilian whose face was beardless was regarded as the most extreme of eccentrics. The beard gives character to some faces, but it's easier to descry the true personality of a shaven man. By the way, the evolution that has taken place in the sense of sobriety seems to accord with the laws of nature. Hasn't man gradually, through the ages, cleared away some of his hair?

In the countries where women are more numerous than men, the female has recourse to all kinds of methods to dispossess her rivals. It's a form of the spirit of conservation, a law of the species. The gentlest woman is transformed into a wild beast when another woman tries to take away her man. The bigger the element of femininity in a woman, the further is this instinct developed.

Must one regard this innate savagery as a fault? Is it not rather a virtue? The state of society in which woman was regarded merely as a slave (as is still the case in certain tribes) would be, if we returned to it, a clear regression for humanity. But it's not the only possible state. In prehistoric times, matriarchy was certainly a fairly widely spread form of social organisation.

When all is said, a people never dies out for lack of men. Let's remember that after the Thirty Years' War polygamy was tolerated, so that it was thanks to the illegitimate child that the nation recovered its strength. Such particular situations cannot give rise to a legal regulation—but as long as we have in Germany two and a half million women vowed to celibacy, we shall be forbidden to despise the child born out of wedlock.

Social prejudices are in the process of disappearing. More and more, nature is reclaiming her rights. We're moving in the proper direction. I've much more respect for the woman who has an illegitimate child than for an old maid. I've often been told of unmarried women who had children and brought these children up in a truly touching manner. It often happens amongst women servants, notably. The women who have no children finally go off their heads.

It's somewhat striking to observe that in the majority of peoples the number of women exceeds that of men. What harm is there, then, in every woman's fulfilling her destiny? I love to see this display of health around me. The opposite thing would make me misanthropic. And I would become really so, if all I had to look at where the spectacle of the ten thousand so-called elite.

Luckily for me, I've always retained contacts with the people.

Amongst the people, moral health is obligatory. It goes so far that in the country one never reproaches a priest for having a liaison with his servant. People even regard it as a kind of guarantee: the women and girls of the village need not protect themselves. In any case, women of the people are full of understanding; they admit that a young priest can't sweat his sperm out through his brain.

The hypocrites are to be found amongst the ten-thousand strong elite. That's where one meets the Puritan who can reproach his neighbour for his adventures, forgetting that he has himself married a divorcée.

Everybody should draw from his own experience the reasons to show himself indulgent towards others. Marriage, as it is practised in bourgeoisie society, is generally a thing against nature. But a meeting between two beings who complete one another, who are made for one another, borders already, in my conception, upon a miracle.

I often think of those women who people the convents—because they haven't met the man with whom they would have wished to share their lives. With the exception of those who were promised to God by their parents, most of them, in fact, are women cheated by life. Human beings are made to suffer passively. Rare are the beings capable of coming to grips with existence.

3rd March 1942, midday
The road to independence—The British Tories are right—No German schoolmasters for the Eastern territories—Ideas on a curriculum for schools

If ever we allowed a country conquered by us to have its own Army, that would be the end of our rights over that country—for autonomy is the way to independence.

It's not possible to retain by democratic methods what one has conquered by force. In that respect, I share the point of view of the English

Tories. To subjugate an independent country, with the idea of later giving it back its freedom, that's not logical. The blood that has been shed confers a right of ownership.

If the English give India back her liberty, within twenty years India will have lost her liberty again. There are Englishmen who reproach themselves with having governed the country badly. Why? Because the Indians show no enthusiasm for their rule. I claim that the English have governed India very well, but their error is to expect enthusiasm from the people they administer.

If it's true that the English have exploited India, it's also true that India has drawn a profit from English domination. Without the English, India would certainly not have a population of three hundred and eighty million inhabitants. Above all, nobody must let loose the German schoolmaster on the Eastern territories! That would be a sure way to lose at once the pupils he'd be given, and the parents of these pupils.

The ideal solution would be to teach this people an elementary kind of mimicry. One asks less of them than one does of the deaf and dumb. No special books for them! The radio will be enough to give them the essential information. Of music, they can have as much as they want. They can practise listening to the tap running. I'm against entrusting them with any work that calls for the least mental effort.

Just tell me how Russia has requited Europe for the European culture she has imported! They used it to invent anarchism. The more they're allowed to loll in peace, the happier these people are. Any other attitude will have the result of awakening ferocious enemies against us.

The logic of our pedagogues would entail the building of a university at Kiev. That will be their first discovery. In any case, I don't believe there's any sense in teaching men anything, in a general way, beyond what they need to know.

One overloads them without interesting either them or anybody else. It's better to awaken men's instinct for beauty. That was what the Greeks considered the essential thing. Today people persist in cramming children with a host of unrelated ideas.

School training should form a foundation on which it would subsequently be possible to build, if there is room for it, a specialised instruction. In any case, instruction must be adapted to things as they are. What counts today, more than the trivial details, is the history of the Reich. It's a waste of children's time, and a useless cumbering of their minds, to delay while one teaches them item by item all that concerns the village, the region and the country. Let's not forget that the events which we are in the process of witnessing will one day be recited by heart in all the schools of the Reich. The brain of a little peasant-boy can't take in everything.

Moreover, where's the sense in teaching a child in an elementary school a foreign language in addition to German?

Eighty per cent of the children will never go further. Of what use will the rudiments of a foreign language be to them? Let's rather give them some general knowledge.

Thus, instead of teaching them French for four years, at the rate of three hours a week, why not wait until the last year? And even during this last year, let's give them only one hour's French a week. That's quite enough to give a good start to those who intend to continue their studies.

Do you see the necessity for teaching geometry, physics and chemistry to a young man who means to devote himself to music? Unless he has a special gift for these branches of study, what will he have left over of them later? I find it absolutely ridiculous, this mania for making young people swallow so many fragmentary notions that they can't assimilate.

In my day, pupils were not only compelled to achieve a given average, but also in certain branches their reports must not fall below a minimum level. If a pupil is particularly brilliant in his speciality, why embarrass him in his studies by obliging him to assimilate notions that are beyond his powers of assimilation?

Wouldn't it be better to help him further in the direction that comes naturally to him? Forty years ago, the teaching of history was restricted to a dry listing of dates. There was a total absence of principles. What happened when the teacher, into the bargain, lacked the necessary gift for giving these dead things a soul? Such teaching was a real torture.

I had a teacher of French whose whole preoccupation was to catch us out in a mistake. He was a hair-splitter and a bully. When I think of the men who were my teachers, I realise that most of them were slightly mad.

The men who could be regarded as good teachers were exceptional. It's tragic to think that such people have the power to bar a young man's way. Some children have so much vitality that they can't sit still, and won't and can't concentrate their attention. It seems to me useless to try to force them.

I understand, of course, that such an attitude annoys the teachers. But is it just to deprive a child of the possibilities that life offers him, simply because he's unruly?

I remember that on the average I spent a tenth of the time my comrades spent in doing my prep. My selected branch was history. I felt sorry for those of my comrades who never had a minute for play. Some children begin their school careers as excellent book-learners.

They pass the barrage of examinations brilliantly. In their own eyes, everything is at their feet. So what a surprise it is for them when they see a comrade succeeding who is cleverer than they are, but whom they used to regard as a dunce!

7th March 1942, midday

Peculiarities of the German language—Abuse of consonants—Borrowed words—Licence accorded only to great writers

If one compares the German language with English, and then with Italian, a few remarks at once occur to the mind. The English language lacks the ability to express thoughts that surpass the order of concrete things. It's because the German language has this ability that Germany is the country of thinkers.

The Italian language is the language of a nation of musicians. I was convinced of this one day at Obersalzberg, where I heard a speech by an Italian blinded in the war. When his speech was translated, nothing was left—a vacuum.

We Germans are not inclined to talk for the sake of talking. We don't become intoxicated with sounds. When we open our mouth, it's to say something. But our language is poor in vowel-sounds, and we must combat this tendency. Today Germany lacks poets, and our literature tries to make up for this deficiency by stylistic researches. We must take care not to attach too much importance to words. The form is only a means. The essential thing, always, is the inspiration.

If we let our language-reformers have their way, German would end by losing all its music. We're already restricted, unfortunately, to vowels a, e and i. Moreover, we have far too many sibilants. When I say *Kurzchriftler* instead of *Stenograf,*[362] I have the feeling that I'm talking Polish.

As it happens, the word itself is silly. Why not stick to the baptismal name given by the author? The linguists who recommend these

---

[362] Both words mean stenographer.

Germanisations are deadly enemies of the German language. If we followed them in that path, we would soon be unable to express our thoughts with precision, and our language would be poorer and poorer in vowels. It would end—I scarcely dare to say it—by being like Japanese: such a cackling and cawing! How would it be imaginable that one could actually sing in a language like that?

Let's be glad we have a vocabulary rich enough to introduce infinite gradations into our thought. And let's gratefully accept the foreign words that have entered our language, if only for their sonorousness.

What would happen if we expelled from the German language all the words of foreign origin that it has assimilated? First of all, we wouldn't know exactly where to stop. Secondly, we would be stupidly sacrificing the extra enrichments we owe to our predecessors.

Logic would bid us, whilst we're giving up a word, also to give up the thing this word signifies. It wouldn't be honest to retain the thing whilst repudiating the word. We would suppress, for example, the word "theatre"[363]—and we would try to pretend that it was we who invented the theatre (now re-baptised by us!) Enough of such childishness.

Only writers of genius can have the right to modify the language. In the past generation, I can think of practically nobody but Schopenhauer who could have dared to do such a thing. As long as a language evolves, as long as it's alive, it remains a proper medium for expressing new thoughts and notions.

I could wish that, when we take a word from a foreign language, the German spelling would correspond to the pronunciation, so that everybody can pronounce the word in the same way. The example of the English in this respect is not a good one to follow. As long as a language has a letter for every different sound, it's not proper that the exact pronunciation of a word should depend on a knowledge of the language in which the word originates. A word should be written as it is pronounced.

Night of 10th–11th March 1942

Feminine jealousy is a defensive reaction—Some stories about women

In woman, jealousy is a defensive reaction. It surely has an ancestral origin, and must go back to the time when woman simply couldn't do without the protection of a man. First of all, it's the reaction of a pregnant woman, who as such has all the more need of protection. She feels

---

[363] In German, "*Theater.*"

so weak in those circumstances, so timid—for herself and for the child she's carrying. And this child itself, how many years will it take to gain its independence!

Without the protection of a man, woman would feel exposed to all perils. So it's natural that she should be quite particularly attached to the hero, to the man who gives her the most security. Once this security is obtained, it's comprehensible that she should bitterly defend her property—hence the origin of jealousy.

Man is inspired by a similar feeling towards the woman he loves, but the realm of feminine jealousy is infinitely vaster. A mother is jealous of her daughter-in-law, a sister of her sister-in-law.

I was present one day at a scene that Eva Chamberlain[364] made at the expense of her brother, Siegfried Wagner. It was absolutely incredible, the more so as they were both married.

Siegfried's young wife, Winifred, was, so to speak, tolerated by her sisters-in-law. Nevertheless, on the day of the catastrophe, her presence was thought particularly opportune. She was a woman of irreproachable behaviour. Siegfried owes her four handsome children, all of them obviously his—all of them Wagners!

One day I detected an unexpected reaction even in Frau Bruckmann. She had invited to her house, at the same time as myself, a very pretty woman of Munich society.

As we were taking our leave, Frau Bruckmann perceived in her female guest's manner a sign of an interest that she doubtless deemed untimely. The consequence was that she never again invited us both at once. As I've said, the woman was beautiful, and perhaps she felt some interest in me—nothing more. I knew a woman whose voice became raucous with emotion when I spoke in her presence to another woman.

Man's universe is vast compared with that of woman. Man is taken up with his ideas, his preoccupations. It's only incidental if he devotes all his thoughts to a woman.

A woman's universe, on the other hand, is man. She sees nothing else, so to speak, and that's why she's capable of loving so deeply. Intelligence, in a woman, is not an essential thing. My mother, for example, would have cut a poor figure in the society of our cultivated women. She lived strictly for her husband and children. They were her entire universe. But she gave a son to Germany.

[364] Eva Chamberlain, (1867–1942), the daughter of Richard and Cosima Wagner, and the wife of Houston Stewart Chamberlain.

Marriages that originate only in sensual infatuation are usually somewhat shaky. Such bonds are easily untied. Separations are particularly painful when there has been a genuine comradeship between man and wife.

I think it improper that a woman should be liable to be called upon to give evidence in Court on intimate matters. I've had that abolished. I detest prying and espionage. That reminds me of a characteristic of Frederick the Great. He was complaining one day to his Chief of Police that he was the worst informed monarch in Europe concerning what went on inside his kingdom. "Nothing would be easier, Sire. Put at my disposal the methods that my colleagues have use of, and I shall certainly do as well as they."

"At that price," said the King, "I won't take it."

I myself never used such methods, and I shall never give audience to a sneak. There's something utterly repugnant about such a person. As for female spies, let's not speak of them! Not only are these women prostitutes, but they make the man whom they are preparing to betray the victim of the obscenest sort of play-acting.

In the days of my youth, I was something of a solitary, and I got along very easily without society. I've changed a lot, for nowadays I can no longer bear solitude. What I like best is to dine with a pretty woman. And rather than be left at home by myself, I would go and dine at the *Osteria*.

I never read a novel. That kind of reading annoys me.

The *Augsburger Abendzeitung* is the oldest newspaper in Europe. It's a good thing that Amann let it go on existing. But it's a pity that the *Fliegende Blätter* have disappeared, and that the *Jugend* has degenerated. When one cannot keep two enterprises alive at once, I'm in favour of suppressing the newer and keeping the older.

Night of 11th–12th March 1942
The evils of smoking—Three farthings a day—Berlin, capital of the world

I made the acquaintance in Bayreuth of a business man, a certain Möckel, who invited me to visit him in Nuremberg. There was a notice above his door: "Smokers not admitted." For my part, I have no notice above my door, but smokers aren't admitted. Some time ago I asked Göring if he really thought it a good idea to be photographed with a pipe in his mouth. And I added, "What would you think of a sculptor who immortalised you with a cigar between your teeth?"

It's entirely false to suppose that the soldier wouldn't endure life at the front if he were deprived of tobacco. It's a mistake to be written on the debit side of the High Command, that from the beginning of the war it allotted the soldier a daily ration of cigarettes. Of course, there's no question now of going into reverse. But as soon as peace has returned, I shall abolish the ration. We can make better use of our foreign currency than squandering it on imports of poison. I shall start the necessary re-education with the young. I'll tell them: "Don't follow the example of your elders."

I experienced such poverty in Vienna. I spent long months without ever having the smallest hot meal. I lived on milk and dry bread. But I spent thirty kreuzers a day on my cigarettes. I smoked between twenty-five and forty of them a day. Well, at that time a kreuzer meant more to me than ten thousand marks do today. One day I reflected that with five kreuzers I could buy some butter to put on my bread. I threw my cigarettes into the Danube, and since that day I've never smoked again.

I'm convinced that, if I had continued to be a smoker, I would not have held out against the life of incessant worry that has for so long been mine. Perhaps it's to this insignificant detail that the German people owes my having been spared to them. So many men whom I've known have died of excessive use of tobacco. My father, first of all. Then Dietrich Eckart, Troost. Soon it'll be your turn, Hoffmann.

Berlin, as a world capital, can make one think only of ancient Egypt, it can be compared only to Babylon or Rome. In comparison with this capital, what will London stand for, or Paris?

24th March 1942, at dinner

Information at the enemy's disposal—Better use of manpower in the Wehrmacht—Protection of private property—Limits of private ownership—The rights of the State—The ethics of lotteries and gambling—Industrial power monopolies—Capitalist interests

In spite of their inclination to criticise all we do, the democracies miss no opportunity of imitating us when we take measures designed to simplify our organisation.

That's why it will be better in future to give no press publicity to our innovations in this field, for by so doing we are giving useful information to the enemy nations and enabling them to profit from our own experiences. Even in dealing with facts of this nature, silence is nowadays obligatory.

As regards the use of manpower, General Jodl observed that there had been a clear improvement in the Wehrmacht, as compared with the Army of the Great War—in which a fisherman was transformed into an Alpine Light Infantryman, and a butcher into an office clerk, under the pretext of training the soldier. Nowadays, on the other hand, every effort was taken to make the best use of each man's talents, to the greatest benefit of the community. Hitler interrupted: We must not look at things from the narrow standpoint of the *Wehrmacht,* but from the standpoint of the nation as a whole.

I'll take the case of a Reserve officer. I'll suppose that in civil life he holds an important post, even from the standpoint of the conduct of the war. Very naturally this man will be tempted to leave his job and offer his services to the Army—either from patriotism or for fear of being regarded as a draft-dodger.

Thus the *Wehrmacht* will take the man and put him in an office, thus swelling an already plethoric administration, and the man will be lost to the activity in which he'd have been most useful to us. Wouldn't it be simpler to put a uniform on his back and mobilise him at his job? I absolutely insist on protecting private property.

It is natural and salutary that the individual should be inspired by the wish to devote a part of the income from his work to building up and expanding a family estate. Suppose the estate consists of a factory. I regard it as axiomatic, in the ordinary way, that this factory will be better run by one of the members of the family than it would be by a State functionary providing, of course, that the family remains healthy. In this sense, we must encourage private initiative.

On the other hand, I'm distinctly opposed to property in the form of anonymous participation in societies of shareholders. This sort of shareholder produces no other effort but that of investing his money, and thus he becomes the chief beneficiary of other people's effort: the workers' zest for their job, the ideas of an engineer of genius, the skill of an experienced administrator. It's enough for this capitalist to entrust his money to a few well-run firms, and he's betting on a certainty. The dividends he draws are so high that they can compensate for any loss that one of these firms might perhaps cause him. I have therefore always been opposed to incomes that are purely speculative and entail no effort on the part of those who live on them. Such gains belong by right to the nation, which alone can draw a legitimate profit from them.

In this way, at least, those who create these profits—the engineers and workers—are entitled to be the beneficiaries. In my view, joint-stock companies should pass in their entirety under the control of the State. There's nothing to prevent the latter from replacing these shares that bring in a variable interest by debentures which it guarantees and which produce a fixed interest, in a manner useful to private people who wish to invest their savings. I see no better method of suppressing the immoral form of income, based only on speculation, of which England today provides the most perfect example.

This attitude towards stocks and shares entails, by way of compensation on our part, the obligation to maintain the value of money, no matter what happens, and to prevent any boom in products of prime necessity.

A man who, within the framework of such an organisation, consented to pay a thousand marks for a Persian rug that's worth only eight hundred, would prove that he's an imbecile, but there's no way of stopping him. In the same way, one can't stop a gambler from losing his money at gambling, or from taking his own life when he has lost his money. One might relevantly wonder whether the State, which is the main beneficiary of gambling, should not make itself responsible for the cost of the suicide's funeral! We should bear in mind, in fact, that more than half of the profits of gambling—whether lotteries or games of chance played in the casinos—goes into the coffers of the State.

In addition to the material profit the State derives from them, I think I can say that, from a purely philosophic point of view, lotteries have their good side. Tangible realities are not enough to ensure men's happiness. It's not a bad idea to keep alive in them the taste for illusions, and most of them live on hopes which to a great extent cannot become reality. It seems to me, therefore, that the best part of a lottery is not the list immediately proclaiming the winners. On the contrary, the results should be dragged out, for a year if possible—a year in which the gambler has leisure to nourish his illusions and forge his dreams of happiness. The Austrian State knew about this, and used the system very intelligently. This explains why, even in the most difficult times, there were always so many happy people in that country.

The origin of the lottery goes back doubtless to the beginning of the eighteenth century, when an astute minister wondered why the profits of gambling should not go into the State's coffers instead of going to swell private purses. When the State uses the money it wins thus for some good purpose—to build hospitals, for example—the affair takes on a colouring of idealism. Gambling first of all sustains the gambler's hopes. When chance has given its verdict, and if the gambler is thereafter comparable to a man who has made an unlucky bet, he still has a consolation, that of having contributed to a good work.

I studied the question of gambling, as regards Wiesbaden, with *Gauleiter* Wagner. What gives the lottery its pleasant character is not to be found, unfortunately, in roulette and other games of chance played in the casinos. But if we had withdrawn the authorisation for gambling at Wiesbaden, that would have done a considerable wrong to that thermal resort without any profit to the inveterate gamblers, whom this measure would obviously not have amended. They'd simply have gone and gambled somewhere else, on the other side of the frontier—to the profit, that's to say, of the French. Speaking of that, I enquired how much foreign currency the gambling at Wiesbaden might bring us in, and I told myself that even a hundred thousand marks in foreign money (it's not much, when one has it) is quite a sum when one is poor. I drew the conclusion from all this that gamblers can be useful to the State, by losing their money—and especially foreign gamblers, when they lose in their own currency.

Experience proved that, in retaining gambling in a few casinos, we made a sound calculation. In addition to the foreign currencies we thus collected, it enabled us to retain resorts like Wiesbaden for the German community. It goes without saying that the institution of gambling, which produces great profits simply because it's a monopoly and because it entails no payment of labour in exchange, must go to enrich the State and not private people.

Bormann commented that this principle should be equally true as regards industrial power production. Hitler went on: It's obvious that the power monopoly must be vested in the State. That does not exclude the participation of private capital. The State would offer its securities for investment by the public, which would thus be interested in the exploitation of the monopoly, or, rather, in the favourable progress of State business. The fact is that, when State affairs are not prospering, the holders of certificates can put a cross through their unearned incomes—for the various affairs in which the State is interested cannot be dissociated. The advantage of our formula would be to enable everyone to feel closely linked with State affairs. Today, unfortunately, most people are not clear-sighted enough to realise the closeness of this link.

What is true of the power industry is equally true of all the essential primary materials—that is to say, it applies also to petroleum, coal, steel and water-power. Capitalist interests will have to be excluded from this sort of business. We do not, of course, contemplate preventing a private person from using the energy of the tiny stream that powers his small works.

Here's a typical fact, and one that proves the dishonesty of the commercial procedures to which the joint-stock companies resort. It's the case of the former Bavarian Minister Schweyer,[365] who owed his Ministerial appointment only to his remarkable imbecility—and on that everyone was unanimous!

He received from Bavaria Electricity, of which he was chairman, a yearly pension of thirty-eight thousand marks. Despite all the legal obstacles, I managed to have this pension suppressed, since this man had not supplied any services to an equivalent value—far from it! The present law allows the Chancellor of the Reich a pension of thirty-four thousand marks, and this comparison enables one to realise the scandalous enormity of privileges like Schweyer's.

The problem of monopolies handed over to capitalist interests interested me even in my boyhood. I would been struck by the example of the Danube Shipping Company, which received an annual subsidy of four millions, a quarter of which was at once shared out amongst its twelve directors.

Each of the big parties was represented in this august college by at least two of its members, each of them pocketing about eighty million kronen yearly!

One may feel sure that these mandarins saw to it that the comrades voted punctually for the renewal of the subsidy! But the Socialists were acquiring more and more importance, and it happened that none of their lot was on the board. That's why the scandal broke.

The Company was attacked in the Parliament and in the press. Threatened with being deprived of the subsidy, it replied by abolishing the passenger-service. And since the politicians on the board had already taken care that no railway should be built along the Danube, the riverside populations were the chief victims of these arbitrary measures. A solution of the conflict was found quite rapidly—and you can imagine which! Quite simply, the number of members of the board was

---

[365] Franz Schweyer (1868–1935), conservative politician and Bavarian Minister of the Interior from 1921 to 1924.

increased to fourteen, and the two new seats were offered to two well-known Socialists—who hastened to accept them.

What makes England so fragile is that her whole economic system is founded on similar practices.

From the moment of our seizure of power, having my own set ideas on the subject, I took the precaution of forbidding every director of a company to be a member of the Reichstag. Since men who have interests in a private company cannot be objective on a great number of questions, I likewise forbade office-holders in the Party to take part in business of a capitalist complexion. The same prohibition applies, by the way, to all servants of the State. I therefore cannot allow an official, whether he belongs to the Army or to the civil administration, to invest his savings in industry, except in companies controlled by the State.

27th March 1942, midday

Influence of Stafford Cripps[366]—British Conservatives and German middle classes—Labour Party needs a Cromwell—Unrest in India— Jewish influence on German art—Painting in Germany—Women in politics—Madame Chiang Kai-shek[367]—Lola Montez[368]

One thing is indisputable: in Stafford Cripps, and as a counterpart to Churchill, England has found a statesman whose influence is not negligible. It's a symptom, to say the least, that the English trade unions have been able recently to draw up a programme for the nationalisation of the land, to propose a law on the ownership of buildings and another on an organic reform of industry and transport. All that must have a repercussion on the country's internal situation. We have always found it difficult to believe that such reforms can be put through from one day to the next, and that reasonable Englishmen should think this possible.

Let's not forget that it took the Russians more than ten years to carry the experiment through to the end. There is, doubtless, a state of crisis in England, and we must reckon with it. The economy is deficient, the organisation of the Civil Service is deplorable, the English middle class has to submit to dietary restrictions, and there are military setbacks. In the long run, all that ends by having an effect on a nation's morale.

---

[366] Richard Stafford Cripps (1889–1952), Leader of the British House of Commons and later Minister of Aircraft Production.

[367] Soong Mei-ling (1898–2003), wife of President Chiang Kai-shek of the Republic of China.

[368] Eliza Gilbert (1821–1861), who under the stage name of Lola Montez, became famous as a mistress of King Ludwig I of Bavaria.

Let us always take care not to exaggerate the importance of these signs. If the King has no real influence on the orientation of English politics, that doesn't prevent him from being an important political factor—in so far as the Army retains its strength and integrity. For the British Army is monarchist in spirit, and is, so to speak, entirely recruited amongst the aristocracy and the Conservative world. Now, these people are not at present showing any inclination to make the slightest concessions to the people. It's enough to glance through an English illustrated periodical to be convinced of that. One sees only photos of men belonging to the aristocracy, and two thirds of them are photographed in uniform.

One cannot compare the English Conservatives to the old German bourgeoisie that formed the nationalist parties before 1933. The English Conservatives identify themselves with the Empire, they represent traditions and a solidly established form of society—and it's difficult to see them capitulating to the people, like the French aristocracy in 1789. Quite the contrary, they're striving, by means of a gigantic organisation, to propagate their own ideas amongst the people, trying to fill it with the patriotic fanaticism that inspires its airmen and sailors.

To establish himself against the Conservatives, it would take a Cromwell at the head of the Labour Party, for the Conservatives will not yield without a fight. Now, although Cripps (who has Stalin's confidence) has succeeded in sowing Socialist ideas in England, I don't think he carries enough guns for this role. From my point of view, a Red (and therefore fallen) England would be much less favourable than an England of Conservatives.

In fact, a Socialist England, and therefore an England tainted with Sovietism, would be a permanent danger in the European space, for she would founder in such poverty that the territory of the British Isles would prove too small for thirty million inhabitants to be able to keep alive there.

I hope, therefore, that Cripps will be sunk by the fiasco of his mission to India—the most difficult mission with which an Englishman can now be charged. If he isn't, it would become more and more difficult to avoid civil war on British soil. But the mobilisation of the masses, on which the Labour Party's propaganda is working, and which would be the result of the execution of the trade unions' new programme, should be regarded as a very serious threat. Between Churchill and Cripps I have no hesitation in choosing.

I prefer a hundred times the undisciplined swine who is drunk eight hours of every twenty-four, to the Puritan. A man who spends extravagantly, an elderly man who drinks and smokes without moderation, is obviously less to be feared than the drawing-room Bolshevist who leads the life of an ascetic. From Churchill one may finally expect that in a moment of lucidity—it's not impossible—he'll realise that the Empire's going inescapably to its ruin, if the war lasts another two or three years.

Cripps, a man without roots, a demagogue and a liar, would pursue his sick fancies although the Empire were to crack at every corner. Moreover, this theoretician devoid of humanity lacks contact with the mass that's grouped behind the Labour Party, and he'll never succeed in understanding the problems that occupy the minds of the lower classes.

To judge Cripps accurately, and to appreciate the dangers he represents, one must not forget that the Tories have always been the props of the Empire, and that Cripps's gaining control would mean the end of the Empire. With his hypocritical social programmes, he'd be sure to dig a pit between the mother-country and the Dominions, especially the Catholic Canadians, Australia and South Africa.

One must therefore eagerly hope for the failure of his mission to India. It is questionable, by the way, whether Cripps will get any hearing from the Indian people. The Indian world has already been so disturbed by the presence of the Japanese on its frontiers, and by the fall of Singapore, that the man of compromise, Nehru,[369] has been eclipsed by Bose.[370]

If today Cripps endeavours, with the help of blackmail or begging, to induce the Indians to resist the Japanese, I doubt whether Nehru, however much he would like to, would be able to help him effectively. Nehru's fate will be like that of the Socialists in 1918 who were swept away by the masses. I'm thinking of Ebert—who had come to the meet-

---

[369] Jawaharlal Nehru (1889–1964), Indian nationalist who later became the first Prime Minister of an independent India.

[370] Subhas Chandra Bose (1897–1945), a famous Indian nationalist who instigated the creation of the Legion Freies Indien ("Free India Legion"), a Waffen-SS unit raised from Indian prisoners of war and expatriates in Europe. The unit was intended to be deployed against the British in India, but only a few actually made it that far, and most of the 4,5000 men in the unit fought in Western Europe against the Allies. The survivors were repatriated to India after 1945, where they were not prosecuted. Bose is still held in high regard in India, and the Netaji Subhash Chandra Bose International Airport in Kolkata, West Bengal, is named after him.

ing in the Treptow Park with the intention of opposing the munitions strike. He began by making a few concessions to the crowd, in the hope of getting himself heard—but he was quickly overcome by the crowd's enthusiasm, with the result that he himself had to preach the very strike he had intended to torpedo.

In an affair of this nature, every negotiator, every speaker runs the same danger. I've experienced it myself at Weimar in 1926, and I've seen with what precautions, and how artfully, one must proceed when one intends to tell the public the opposite of what it expects from you.

As for the Indian masses, in any case one thing is certain, that it doesn't want to have anything more to do with the English.

I've often had occasion, during recent years, to immerse myself in collections of the review *Die Kunst.*[371] It's striking to observe that in 1910, our artistic level was still extraordinarily high. Since that time, alas! our decadence has merely become accentuated. In the field of painting, for example, it's enough to recall the lamentable daubs that people have tried to foist, in the name of art, on the German people.

This was quite especially the case during the Weimar Republic, and that clearly demonstrated the disastrous influence of the Jews in matters of art. The cream of the jest was the incredible impudence with which the Jew set about it! With the help of phony art critics, and with one Jew bidding against another, they finally suggested to the people—which naturally believes everything that's printed—a conception of art according to which the worst rubbish in painting became the expression of the height of artistic accomplishment. The ten thousand of the elite themselves, despite their pretensions on the intellectual level, let themselves be diddled, and swallowed all the humbug.

The culminating hoax—and we now have proof of it, thanks to the seizure of Jewish property—is that, with the money they fraudulently acquired by selling trash, the Jews were able to buy, at wretched prices, the works of value they had so cleverly depreciated. Every time an inventory catches my eye of a requisition carried out on an important Jew, I see that genuine artistic treasures are listed there. It's a blessing of Providence that National Socialism, by seizing power in 1933, was able to put an end to this imposture.

When I visit an exhibition, I never fail to have all the daubs[372] pitilessly withdrawn from it. It will be admitted that whoever visits the

---

[371] "The Art," a journal published by the Bruckmann Verlag from 1899 to 1945.
[372] A *daub* in this sense is someone that produces an unskilled or crude painting.

House of German Art today will not find any work there that isn't worthy of its place. Everything that hasn't an undeniable value has been sieved out.

I never hesitated, even when it was a question of works by painters given prizes by the Academy of Prussia, to ban these works from the House of German Art whenever they were worthless. It's a pity that the Academy is not up to its task, and that its members played amongst themselves the game of you-scratch-my-back-and-I'll scratch-yours.

The latest victim was our Minister of Religious Affairs, who knows as much about art as a hippopotamus. He fell into the most obvious traps and gave official rewards to genuine ordure. The Jews had succeeded in lulling him to sleep by using on him the same methods as had already enabled them to trick the whole German people.

On the subject of these daubs, people assert that it isn't easy to understand them and that, to penetrate their depth and significance, one must be able to immerse oneself entirely in the image represented—and other idiocies from the same mill. In the years 1905–1906, when I entered the Vienna Academy, these hollow phrases were already being used—to give publicity to innumerable daubs, under the pretext of artistic experiment.

In a general way, the academies have nothing to tell me that's worth listening to. In fact, the professors who are active there are either failures, or else artists of talent (but who cannot devote more than two hours a day to their teaching), or else weary old men who therefore have nothing more to give.

Genuine artists develop only by contact with other artists. Like the Old Masters, they began by working in a studio. Let's remember that men like Rembrandt, Rubens and others hired assistants to help them to complete all their commissions.

Amongst these assistants, only those reached the rank of apprentice who displayed the necessary gifts as regards technique and adroitness—and of whom it could be supposed that they would in their turn be capable of producing works of value. It's ridiculous to claim, as it's claimed in the academies, that right from the start the artist of genius can do what he likes.

Such a man must begin, like everyone else, by learning, and it's only by working without relaxation that he succeeds in achieving what he wants. If he doesn't know the art of mixing colours to perfection—if he cannot set a background-if anatomy still has secrets for him—it's certain he won't go very far! I can imagine the number of sketches it took an artist as gifted as Menzel before he set himself to paint the *Flute Concert at Sans-Souci.*

It would be good if artists today, like those of olden days, had the training afforded by the Masters' studios and could thus steep themselves in the great pictorial traditions.

If, when we look at the pictures of Rembrandt and Rubens, for example, it is often difficult to make out what the Master has painted himself and what is his pupils' share, that's due to the fact that gradually the disciples themselves became masters.

What a disaster it was, the day when the State began to interfere with the training of painters! As far as Germany is concerned, I believe that two academies would suffice: in Düsseldorf and Munich. Or perhaps three in all, if we add Vienna to the list. Obviously there's no question, for the moment, of abolishing any of our academies. But that doesn't prevent one from regretting that the tradition of the studios has been lost.

If, after the war, I can realise my great building programme—and I intend to devote thousands of millions to it—only genuine artists will be called on to collaborate. The others may wait until doomsday, even if they're equipped with the most brilliant recommendations.

Numerous examples taken from history prove that woman—however intelligent she may be—is not capable of dissociating reason from feeling, in matters of a political nature. And the formidable thing in this field is the hatred of which women are capable.

I've been told that after the occupation of the province of Shanghai, the Japanese offered Chiang Kai-shek's Government to withdraw their troops from Chinese territory, on condition:

(a) of being able to maintain a garrison in Shanghai's international concession;

(b) of obtaining advantageous terms on the conclusion of a trade treaty.

It seems that all the generals approved of this proposal and encouraged Chiang Kai-shek to accept it.

But when Mme Chiang Kai-shek had spoken—urged on by her measureless hatred of Japan—the majority of the generals reversed their decisions, and thus it was that Japan's offer, although a very generous one, was rejected. One might speak likewise of the influence of Lola Montez over Ludwig I of Bavaria. The latter was, by nature, a reasonable and understanding king. But that woman completely drove him from his course.

28th March 1942, at dinner
Commercial honesty in the Middle Ages—Five hundred years of honesty—Legal juggling—Reforms in the magistrature—Three good lawyers

The Führer had alluded to the respect enjoyed by merchants and princes during the Middle Ages. In the discredit now attached to them, he saw the work of the Jews.

The Hanseatic League should not be regarded solely as an instrument of political power. It also personified, on the level of relations between individuals, a conception of justice. For example, it never agreed to carry a consignment unless it was provided with a sure guarantee of the weight and quality of the goods. Equipped with the Hansa's seal, the goods thereby enjoyed a high reputation, both in the interior of the country and abroad.

A case is cited of some cloth merchants who had employed the Hanseatic agency in Lübeck to send a bale of linen to Bergen. Now, this merchandise did not correspond to the Hansa's specifications, with the result that, by way of a sanction, the guilty city was excluded for a period of ten years from the traffic of the League. What is important to notice is that the decision was not taken as the result of a complaint by the addressee, but simply as the result of a check-up held at the outset. It was observed that the merchandise did not correspond to the specifications, a few threads of flax were absent in the weaving of the linen.

It was not one of the Hansa's least merits to have stabilised the notion of commercial probity, as it is still honoured in some houses in Bremen and Hamburg.

It was thanks to very severe sanctions, and even to barbarous punishments, that gradually this conception of probity in trade was established. When the Hansa refused its seal to a merchant, for the latter, in view of the League's prestige and the extent of its relations, this meant the first-fruits of ruin.

The example of the Hansa inspired all commercial and industrial activity of the Middle Ages. That's how the price of bread could be kept the same for four hundred years, that of barley—and, consequently, that of beer—for more than five hundred years; and this in spite of all the changes of money. The notion of probity was not implanted solely in commercial relations. It was the basis of the small crafts; the guilds and corporations always took care that this tradition should be maintained. A baker, for example, who cheated on the quality of the flour intended for the manufacture of rolls, was ducked several times in a basin filled with water, and in such a way that he escaped only by a hair from drowning.

As soon as the Jews were allowed to stick their noses out of the ghetto, the sense of honour and loyalty in trade began to melt away. In fact, Judaism, this form of mental deprivation that must at all costs be abolished, has made the fixing of prices depend on the laws of supply and demand-factors, that is to say, which have nothing to do with the intrinsic value of an article. By creating the system *of caveat emptor,* the Jew has established a juridical basis for his rogueries. And thus it is that during the last two centuries, and with rare exceptions, our commerce has been dragged down to such a level that it has become absolutely necessary to apply a remedy. One first condition is necessary: to do away with the Jews.

There was a time when I suffered from fistulas, and this affliction seemed to me more serious than it actually was. Having thought of the possibility of cancer, I one day settled down at my table to write, on official paper, a holograph will. As you know, this task demands a quite special effort on my part, since for years I've had the habit of writing directly on the machine or dictating what I have to say. My will hadn't had time to grow old when I learnt of a decision by the Court of Appeal that declared an old woman's will null and void simply because mention of the place was printed on the paper instead of being written by her hand. I took my head in both hands and wondered what the law was coming to, if the will of the Chancellor of the Reich in person did not satisfy the legal formalities.

I came to the conclusion that such juggleries are simply a mockery, and scarcely the sort of thing that gets Justice respected.

So I sent for Gürtner, the Minister of Justice, and requested him to have this idiocy put right. Well, it took nothing less than a Decree to achieve this result. I was equally struck by another stupidity. It often happens that people leave me legacies. In principle I refuse these, only permitting the NSV[373] to benefit by them. Now, so that such a declaration may be valid, my signature must be authenticated by a notary. So it seems, according to our worthy jurists, that the signature of the Ger-

---

[373] The *Nationalsozialistische Volkswohlfahrt,* or NSV, ("National Socialist People's Welfare"); the NSDAP's party welfare organization.

man Chancellor, accompanied by the Seal of the Reich, is worth less than that of a notary! A merely reasonable being could not conceive of such a thing. That's only a small example, but I suggest in principle that it's impossible for a normal intelligence to understand any part of the edifices built up by the jurists, and I can explain this mental distortion only by the influence of the Jews.

In a nutshell, I regard the whole of our present jurisprudence as a systematisation of the method that consists in saddling other people with one's own obligations. I shall therefore do everything in my power to make the study of law utterly contemptible, if it is to be guided by such notions. I understand, of course, that University studies should turn out men who are fitted for life and capable of ensuring for the State the preservation of natural law. But the studies to which I am referring merely cultivate the liking for irresponsibility in those who devote themselves to them.

I'll see to it that the administration of justice shall be cleared of all judges who don't constitute a genuine elite. Let their number be reduced to a tenth, if necessary! The comedy of courts with a jury must come to an end.

I wish once and for all to prevent a judge from being able to shake off this responsibility by claiming that he has been outvoted by the jurymen, or by invoking other excuses of that nature. I desire only judges who have the requisite personality—but in that case they must be very generously reimbursed. I need men for judges who are deeply convinced that the law ought not to guarantee the interests of the individual against those of the State, that their duty is to see to it, above all, that Germany does not perish.

Gtirtner has not succeeded in forming judges of this type. He has himself had a lot of difficulty in getting rid of his legal superstitions. Threatened by some and despised by others, he has succeeded only slowly in adopting more reasonable attitudes, spurred on by the necessity of bringing justice into harmony with the imperatives of action.

If anyone were to think I chose Gürtner as Minister of Justice because once upon a time, in his capacity as judge, he must have treated me with particular understanding, that wouldn't at all correspond to the facts. It was I who had to make an effort of objectivity—and a great effort, too—to call to the Ministry of Justice the man who had me imprisoned. But when I had to choose amongst the men who were in the running, I couldn't find anyone better. Freisler[374] was nothing but a Bolshevik. As for the other (Schlegelberger[375]), his face could not deceive me. It was enough to have seen him once.

I've had an ample harvest of experiences with the lawyers. In 1920, when I organised my first big assemblies in Munich, a certain Councillor Wagner put himself at my disposal as a speaker. That was a period when I was in search of starched collars, in the hope that they'd help me to reach the intellectual class. So what a blessing I thought this man's offer, and what a bait to win over the lawyers!

It's true that, before giving him a chance to speak before a big gathering, I had the prudence to try him out before twenty or so faithful followers gathered at the Sternecker beer-hall. What faces they pulled when they heard the worthy soul, with trembling hands and waggling head, recommending the reconstruction of a State in which "the clan was based on the family, the stock upon the clan, and the common mother upon the stock".

Since then I've always been distrustful in my dealings with the jurists. In that respect, I know only three exceptions: von der Pfordten,[376] Pöhner and Frick. Von der Pfordten, quite the contrary of Gürtner, was a man of revolutionary tendency.

As for Pöhner, I still remember his statement during our trial for high treason: "Above all, I'm a German, and after that I'm an official. As an official, I've never been a whore. You can take that as admitted. If you think that my activity against the usurpers constitutes a case of high treason, then let me tell you that, as a German, I have for six years considered it a duty to wage the struggle against the usurpers, and thus to commit—if you really cling to this expression—the crime of high treason!"

---

[374] Roland Freisler (1893–1945), the infamous Nazi jurist and judge who served as the State Secretary of the Reich Ministry of Justice from 1934 to 1942 and as President of the People's Court from 1942 to 1945. The allegation that he was originally a Marxist was likely true: when taken prisoner by the Russian Army in October 1915 during the First World War, he was given the job of Prisoner of War "Commissar" for his detention camp. During his early NSDAP days, Freisler was firmly part of the party's "left wing social-nationalists" under the Strasser brothers.

[375] Franz Schlegelberger (1876–1970) Minister of Justice from 1941 to 1942. The reason for Hitler's disparaging remark is unknown.

[376] Theodor von der Pfordten (1873–1923), a judge at the Bavarian Supreme Regional Court who was one of those killed while marching with Hitler during the November 1923 Putsch.

Frick, too, conducted himself admirably at that time. As adjutant to the Chief of Police, he was able to supply us with all kinds of information, which enabled the Party rapidly to expand its activity. He never missed an opportunity to help us and protect us. I can even add that without him I would never have got out of prison. But as it is . . .

There exists, unfortunately, a particular type of National Socialist who at a certain moment did great things for the Party, but who is never capable of doing still better. When our activities spread beyond the framework of what he has been able to grasp, and of what corresponds to his own ideas, he takes fright, for lack of being able to take into account the logic of the facts and that certain acts inescapably demand certain consequences. Dietrich Eckart always judged the world of jurists with the greatest clear-sightedness, the more so as he had himself studied law for several terms. According to his own evidence, he decided to break off these studies "so as not to become a perfect imbecile".

Dietrich Eckart, by the way, is the man who had the brilliant idea of nailing the present juridical doctrines to the pillory and publishing the result in a form easily accessible to the German people. For myself, I supposed it was enough to say these things in an abbreviated form. It's only with time that I've come to realise my mistake. Thus today I can declare without circumlocution that every jurist must be regarded as a man deficient by nature, or else deformed by usage. When I go over the names of the lawyers I've known in my life, and especially the advocates, I cannot help recognising by contrast how morally wholesome, honourable and rooted in the best traditions were the men with whom Dietrich Eckart and I began our struggle in Bavaria.

31st March 1942, at dinner

Attempted assassination of Papen at Ankara—Confidence in the Turks— Distrust of Bulgarians—German eastern policy—Charlemagne "slayer of Saxons" and Hitler "slayer of Austrians"—The work of Charlemagne— From Chancellor to Führer—The First Consul should not have allowed himself to become an Emperor—Frederick the Great a greater man than Napoleon—The best man should be Head of the State—Examples of the Vatican and the Venetian Republic—The Future German Constitution— Need of separation of powers

The conversation was on the attempted assassination of Papen,[377] *ambassador in Ankara.*

---

[377] The Soviet secret police attempted to kill Germany's ambassador to Turkey, Franz van Papen, with a bomb attack on 24 February 1942.

This attempted assassination is revealing as it concerns the mentality of the Russian organisers. With other peoples, supposing such an attempt was judged necessary for political reasons, an attempt would be made to save the man who was given the job of carrying it out. The Russians, on the other hand, for all their cleverness, arranged the action in such a way that it should cost the performer his skin. The setting was well designed.

The poor wretch had an apparatus that enabled him, once the murder was committed, to produce an artificial fog thanks to which he could try to escape. But what he had not been told was that, as soon as he set the machine working, he would himself detonate the explosive charge that was destined to pulverise him. The only traces of him discovered were one of his shoes and his revolver! The assassin's accomplices were so disgusted by their masters' villainy that they decided to reveal all they knew of the plot.

As Allies, I prefer the Turks to the Bulgarians. That's why I'm ready to conclude a trade treaty with Turkey, by which we would supply her with arms and ammunition. In addition, I would be ready to guarantee the inviolability of the Straits and the integrity of their frontiers, if the Turks had any wish for an alliance with us.

Our advantage would be as follows: thanks to the arms we would have delivered, the Turks would be able to defend the Straits, a defence in which we, too, shall have an interest as holders of territory on the Black Sea. In this way, the authoritarian regime in Turkey would be consolidated—and I think that this consequence, on the level of internal politics, couldn't be a matter of indifference to the Turkish patriots who wish to support Atatürk's successor.

In Bulgaria, on the other hand, everything is uncertain. Thus, I was struck to learn that after the conclusion of the Tripartite Pact the President of the Bulgarian Council was scarcely acclaimed by the population of Sofia, despite the major importance of this pact to Bulgaria. And I was not less struck to know that at the same time the population of Sofia was enthusiastically welcoming a Russian football team. The fact is that Bulgaria is strongly affected by Panslavism, both on the political and on the sentimental level. She's attracted by Russia, even if Sovietised. I recognise that the King of Bulgaria is a very intelligent, even cunning, man, but he doesn't seem to be capable of guaranteeing the stability of his regime. He himself confessed that he couldn't change a single Minister or relieve a general of his command without endangering his crown. He has to act very cautiously, he says, beginning with granting sick-leaves and then retaining these men's attachment with the help of numerous favours.

To sum up, as regards Bulgaria and Turkey, it's certain that conditions have scarcely changed since the Great War. From our point of view, Bulgaria can be regarded as reliable only in so far as we're allies of Turkey. On the political and sentimental level, there's no obstacle to an alliance between Turkey and the Reich. By reason of her attachment to Islam, Turkey has a completely clear-cut religious policy. The same is not true of Bulgaria, which, since it practises the Greek Orthodox religion, finds in it new reasons to feel friendly towards Russia.

A reflection of Bormann's on Heinrich I,[378] led the Führer to speak of German policy on her Eastern frontiers.

As regards the East, our present policy has no precedents in history. Whereas it is true that, on several occasions already, combats, sometimes even of a certain size, have taken place on the Eastern frontiers of the Reich, it must be agreed that it was then a matter of tribes that came carrying war to our frontiers.

And the Reich found itself confronted with the alternatives of accepting combat or disappearing. These old-time struggles cannot therefore be regarded as the expression of a German policy in the East. The historians who attributed the idea of such a policy to Heinrich I were in error. What drove Heinrich I in that direction was merely the fact that only in the East could he hew himself out a kingdom.

Throughout the Imperial period, it's not possible to discern any sign that the Reich was interested in the East, or that it followed any coherent policy concerning the colonisation of the Eastern territories for example. The racial policy of the Empire was firmly fixed, it aimed only towards the South. The East—with its population totally different in respect of race, scarcely marked by a Germanic contribution to the higher strata—remained foreign to them. The South, on the other hand, and Lombardy, in particular, had all the special characteristics necessary to make it part of the Roman-Germanic Holy Empire. Thus it was always one of the essential preoccupations of Imperial policy. To what an extent the political ideas of the time were governed by the notion of race is shown by the fact that as late as the fourteenth century an Imperial German party continued to exist in Florence. Who knows

---

[378] Heinrich I, also called Henry the Fowler (*Heinrich der Vogler*) lived from 876 to 936 AD and was founder of the Saxon dynasty.

whether Lombardy would not still be in our hands today if prince-vassals like Heinrich the Lion had not broken their oaths of fealty, counteracted the policy of the Reich and compelled the Emperor suddenly to interrupt his campaigns in the South in order to extinguish the blaze that had broken out in his own house. The policy of the Reich can be successful only if it is characterised by unity of action.

In this respect, the Swabians especially deserve our esteem, for they always realised the meaning of the Imperial idea and never ceased to prove their loyalty to the Reich. We are certainly wrong to glorify princes like Heinrich the Lion because of their nonconformism. These are men who clearly conducted a policy against the interests of the Reich. That's why I've drawn Rosenberg's attention to the fact that one must not let the great German Emperors be relegated to the background, to the benefit of perjurers, and that it was improper to call a hero like Charlemagne by the name "killer of Saxons".[379] History must be interpreted in terms of the necessities of the time.

It's possible that, in a thousand years—supposing that, for one reason or another, the Reich is again obliged to pursue a policy directed against the South—some pedagogue may be found who will claim that "Hitler's Eastern policy was certainly well-intentioned", but that it was nevertheless crack-brained, since "he should have aimed at the South".

Perhaps even some caviller of this type will go so far as to call me "the killer of Austrians", on the grounds that, on my return from Austria to Germany, I locked up all those who had tried to thwart the enterprise! Without compulsion, we would never have united all the various German families with these thick-headed, parochially minded fellows—either in Charlemagne's time or today. If the German people is the child of ancient philosophy and Christianity, it is so less by reason of a free choice than by reason of a compulsion exercised upon it by these triumphant forces. In the same way, in Imperial times, it was under the empire of compulsion that the German people engineered its fusion beneath a Christianity represented by a universal church—in the image of ancient Rome, which also inclined to universality. It is certain that a man like Charlemagne was not inspired merely by a desire for political power, but sought, in faithfulness to the ancient idea, for an expression of civilisation.

---

[379] Charlemagne's well-known massacres of pagans in Germany and his enforced Christianization of that country made him a highly unpopular figure among anti-Christians.

Now, the example of the ancient world proves that civilisation can flourish only in States that are solidly organised. What would happen to a factory given over to anarchy, in which the employees came to their work only when the fancy took them? Without organisation—that is to say, without compulsion—and, consequently, without sacrifice on the part of individuals, nothing can work properly. Organised life offers the spectacle of a perpetual renunciation by individuals of a part of their liberty. The more exalted a situation a man occupies, the easier this renunciation should appear to him. Since his field of vision is wider, he should be able all the better to admit the necessity for self-compulsion. In a healthy State, this is what distinguishes the elite from the men who remain mingled with the great masses. The man who rises must grow with his task, his understanding must expand simultaneously with his functions.

If a street-sweeper is unable or unwilling to sacrifice his tobacco or his beer, then I think: "Very well, my good man, that's precisely why you're a street-sweeper and not one of the ruling personalities of the State!" It's just as well, by the way, that things *are* like that, for the nation, collectively, has just as much need of its street-sweepers.

Guided by these rules, which are quite simple and quite natural, Charlemagne gathered the Germans into a well-cemented community and created an empire that continued to deserve the name long after his death. The fact was that this empire was made of the best stuff of the ancient Roman Empire—so much so that for centuries the peoples of Europe have regarded it as the successor to the universal empire of the Caesars.

The fact that this German empire was named "the Holy Roman Empire" has nothing whatsoever to do with the Church, and has no religious significance. Unlike the idea attached to the word "Reich", the idea of the "Chancellor of the Reich" has unfortunately lost its significance in the course of the centuries. On a single occasion a giant gave it its full glory, and then it came to signify abortions like Wirth, Brüning,[380] etc. At present, in view of the authoritarian form we have given the State, that has no importance. One can even declare that this title is not a suitable designation for the Head of the State. Historically, as a matter of fact, it is connected with the mental picture, according to which, above the Chancellor, there is yet another person who repre-

---

[380] Heinrich Brüning (1885–1970), the *Zentrumpartei* ("Centre Party") chancellor from 1930 to 1932.

sents the State as its supreme chief—and it little matters whether he is called Emperor, President, or by some quite different name.

In the National Socialist form of State, the title "Führer" is the most suitable. It implies, amongst other things, the idea that the Head of the State has been chosen by the German people. Although it sometimes produces superfluities and overlappings—when one reads beneath a photograph, for example: "At the Führer's side, the Oberführer so-and-so", that has no importance, at least while I'm still alive. But when I'm no longer there, it will be necessary to alter that and to give the notion of "Führer" a uniform meaning.

In any case it would be inopportune to change the title of the Head of the State, since this title is associated with the very form of the State itself. In addition to being a display of family pride in political matters, it was Napoleon's greatest error, and at the same time a proof of bad taste on his part, to have renounced the title of "First Consul" in order to have himself called "Emperor".

As a matter of fact, it was under the title of "First Consul" that the Revolution—the one that shook the world—carried him to power above the *Directoire* (that public house committee)—him, the Republican General. By giving up this title and having himself called emperor, he denied the Jacobins, his former companions in the struggle, and lost their support.

At the same stroke he alienated, both at home and abroad, countless partisans who saw in him the personification of the moral resurrection that the French Revolution was to bring with it. To understand the effect produced by this wilful action, it's enough to imagine the effect it would have on the people of Munich, and on the rest of the world, if I had myself carried through the streets of Munich in a gilded coach. In any case, Napoleon gained nothing by committing this fault, for the old monarchies did not fail to display the scorn they felt for a self-made man. The only thing he ever got from them was the *Habsbürgertum*,[381] which was foisted upon him and whose arrival irremediably wounded the national pride of the French. In fact, in the eyes of the French, the lovely Josephine, cast off in favour of the *Habsbürgertum,* was the model of the strictly Republican Frenchwoman.

She was esteemed as the woman who, at Napoleon's side, had climbed the rungs leading to the highest post in the State. The stupe-

---

[381] An untranslatable pun based on a combination of the name of the *Habs*burgs and the word *Bürgertum, or* "bourgeoisie."

faction caused in Europe by that title of "Emperor" is well characterised by the gesture of Beethoven, who tore up a symphony he had just dedicated to Napoleon. He trampled on the fragments, exclaiming: "He's not the extraordinary man I believed, he's only a man!"

What's tragic in Napoleon's case is that when he adopted the imperial title, formed a court and instituted a ceremonial, he didn't realise that, by making common cause with degenerates, he was merely putting himself on their level. Personally, I should regard it as an example of pure lunacy if anyone came and offered me, for example, a dukedom. It would be like asking me to recognise bonds of kinship with all the dwarfs who bear the title.

By looking after his relatives' interests as he did, Napoleon furthermore displayed incredible weakness on the purely human level. When a man occupies such a position, he should eliminate all his family feeling. Napoleon, on the contrary, placed his brothers and sisters in posts of command, and retained them in these posts even after they'd given proofs of their incapability. All that was necessary was to throw out all these patently incompetent relatives.

Instead of that, he wore himself out with sending his brothers and sisters, regularly every month, letters containing reprimands and warnings, urging them to do this and not to do that, thinking he could remedy their incompetence by promising them money, or by threatening not to give them any more. Such illogical behaviour can be explained only by the feeling Corsicans have for their families, a feeling in which they resemble the Scots.

By thus giving expression to his family feeling, Napoleon introduced a disruptive principle into his life. Nepotism, in fact, is the most formidable protection imaginable: the protection of the *ego*. But wherever it has appeared in the life of a State—the monarchies are the best proof—it has resulted in weakening and decay. Reason: it puts an end to the principle of effort.

In this respect, Frederick the Great showed himself superior to Napoleon—Frederick who, at the most difficult moments of his life, and when he had to take the hardest decisions, never forgot that things are called upon to endure. In similar cases, Napoleon capitulated. It's therefore obvious that, to bring his life's work to a successful conclusion, Frederick the Great could always rely on sturdier collaborators than Napoleon could. When Napoleon set the interests of his family clique above all, Frederick the Great looked around him for *men*, and, at need, trained them himself. Despite all Napoleon's genius, Frederick the Great was the most outstanding man of the eighteenth century. When seeking to find a solution for essential problems concerning the conduct of affairs of State, he refrained from all illogicality. It must be recognised that in this field his father, Frederick-William, that buffalo of a man, had given him a solid and complete training.

Peter the Great, too, clearly saw the necessity for eliminating the family spirit from public life. In a letter to his son—a letter I was re-reading recently—he informs him very clearly of his intention to disinherit him and exclude him from the succession to the throne. It would be too lamentable, he writes, to set one day at the head of Russia a son who does not prepare himself for State affairs with the utmost energy, who does not harden his will and strengthen himself physically.

Setting the best man at the head of the State—that's the most difficult problem in the world to solve.

In a republic in which the whole people is called upon to elect the chief of the State, it's possible, with money and publicity, to bring the meagrest of puppets to power. In a republic in which the reins of power are in the hands of a clique made up of a few families, the State takes on the aspect of a trust, in which the shareholders have an interest in electing a weakling as President, so that they may play an important part themselves.

A hereditary monarchy is a biological blunder, for a man of action regularly chooses a wife with essentially feminine qualities, and the son inherits his mother's mildness and passive disposition.

In a republic that sets at its head a chief elected for life, there's the risk that he will pursue a policy of personal self-interest. In a republic where the Chief of State changes every five or ten years, the stability of the government is never assured, and the execution of long-term plans, exceeding the duration of a lifetime, is thereby compromised.

If one sets at the head of the State an old man who has withdrawn from all worldly considerations, he is only a puppet, and inevitably it's other men who rule in his name.

Thinking over all that, I've arrived at the following conclusions:

1. The chances of not setting a complete idiot at the head of the State are better under the system of free elections than in the opposite case. The giants who were the elected German Emperors are the best proof of this. There was not one of them of whom it can truly be said that he was an imbecile. In the hereditary monarchies, on the other hand, there

were at least eight kings out of ten who, if they'd been ordinary citizens, would not have been capable of successfully running a grocery.

2. In choosing a Chief of State, one must call upon a personality who, as far as human beings can judge, guarantees a certain stability in the exercise of power for a longish while. This is a necessary condition, not only so that public affairs can be successfully administered, but in order to make possible the realisation of great projects.

3. Care must be taken that the Chief of State will not succumb to the influence of the plutocracy, and cannot be forced to certain decisions by any pressure of that sort. That's why it's important that he should be supported by a political organisation whose strength has its roots in the people, and which can have the upper hand over private interests.

In the course of history, two constitutions have proved themselves:

(*a*) The papacy, despite numerous crises—the gravest of which, as it happens, were settled by German emperors—and although it is based on a literally crazy doctrine. But as an organisation on the material level, the Church is a magnificent edifice.

(*b*) The constitution of Venice, which, thanks to the organisation of its Government, enabled a little city-republic to rule the whole eastern Mediterranean. The constitution of Venice proved itself effective as long as the Venetian Republic endured—that is to say, for nine hundred and sixty years.

The fact that the Head of the Republic of Venice was chosen from amongst the families who composed the framework of the State (numbering between three hundred and five hundred) was not a bad thing. Thus power was allotted to the best man amongst the representatives of those families who were traditionally linked with the State. The difference between this system and that of hereditary monarchy is obvious. In the former, it was impossible for an imbecile or an urchin of twelve to come to power. Only a man who had pretty well proved himself in life had a fair chance of being appointed.

Isn't it ridiculous, by the way, to think that a child of twelve, or even of eighteen, can rule a State? It goes without saying that, if a king is still a minor, power is provisionally gathered in other hands, those of a Council of Regents. But supposing the members of this Council disagree (and the more competent the councillors are, the greater are the risks of disagreement, in view of the complexity of the problems to be solved daily), then the absence is felt of the personality capable of taking a sovereign decision. A youth of eighteen cannot take a decision that requires deep reflection—that's difficult enough for a man who has reached full maturity!

It's enough to imagine where King Michael of Romania would be without the support of a man as remarkable as Field-Marshal Antonescu. As it happens, the young man is stupid. Moreover, he has been rotted by his spoilt child's upbringing, his father having entrusted him entirely to women during the most important period of his development. To sense the tragic nature of this abyss, it's enough to compare the development of any man who's ambitious to do something in life, with that of a prince by inheritance.

Think of the amount of knowledge that a man of normal rank must acquire, of the desperate work he must do, without truce or rest, to succeed in having his own way. There is a tendency to believe, on the contrary, that one can prepare budding kings for the task that awaits them by keeping them amused. A third of their time is devoted to the study of foreign languages, so that they may be able to utter trivialities in several tongues; a second third to the sports of society (riding, tennis, etc.). The study of the political sciences takes only the last place. Moreover, the education they receive has no firmness.

Their tutors are weakness itself. They resist the temptation to distribute the smacks their princely pupils deserve—for fear of calling down the disfavour of a future monarch. The result is obvious. That's how creatures like Michael of Romania and Peter of Yugoslavia were formed. As regards the government of Germany, I've come to the following conclusions:

1. The Retch must be a republic, having at its head an elected chief who shall be endowed with an absolute authority.

2. An agency representing the people must, nevertheless, exist by way of corrective. Its role is to support the Chief of State, but it must be able to intervene in case of need.

3. The task of choosing the Chief shall be entrusted, not to the people's assembly, but to a Senate. It is, however, important that the powers of the Senate shall be limited. Its composition must not be permanent. Moreover, its members shall be appointed with reference to their occupation and not individuals. These Senators must, by their training, be steeped in the idea that power may in no case be delegated to a weakling, and that the elected Führer must always be the best man.

4. The election of the Chief must not take place in public, but *in camera*. On the occasion of the election of a pope, the people do not

know what is happening behind the scenes. A case is reported in which the cardinals exchanged blows. Since then, the cardinals have been deprived of all contact with the outside world, for the duration of the conclave!

This is a principle that is also to be observed for the election of the Führer: all conversations with the electors will be forbidden throughout operations.

5. The Party, the Army and the body of officials must take an oath of allegiance to the new Chief within the three hours following the election.

6. The most rigorous separation between the legislative and executive organs of the State must be the supreme law for the new Chief. Just as, in the Party, the SA and the SS are merely the sword to which is entrusted the carrying-out of the decisions taken by the competent organs, in the same way the executive agents of the State are not to concern themselves with politics. They must confine themselves exclusively to ensuring the application of laws issued by the legislative power, making appeal to the sword, in case of need. Although a State founded on such principles can lay no claim to eternity, it might last for eight to nine centuries.

The thousand-year-old organisation of the Church is a proof of this—and yet this entire organisation is founded on nonsense. What I have said should *a fortiori* be true of an organisation founded on reason.

2nd April 1942, midday
In praise of the Tsar Ferdinand—Boris the Fox of Bulgaria—Political plots—Wisdom of Kemal Atatürk

In my view, King Boris[382] is a somebody. There's nothing surprising about that, for he has been to a good school with his father, the Tsar Ferdinand, the most intelligent monarch I've known. If one can reproach the Tsar Ferdinand[383] with having been more rapacious than a Jew in money-matters, one must nevertheless acknowledge that he was admirable as regards his audacity and decisive spirit. If we had had him on the Imperial throne of Germany instead of William II, we would certainly not have waited until 1914 before unleashing the Great War. We would have acted as long ago as 1905.

---

[382] Boris III (1894–1943), Tsar of the Kingdom of Bulgaria from 1918 until his death from a heart attack in 1943. It was rumoured that he had been poisoned.
[383] Ferdinand (1861–1948), king (tsar) from 1908 until his abdication in 1918.

Just as the cunning fox succeeded, after the collapse in 1918, in preserving the throne for his son, in the same way I think he'd have found some way for Germany to save herself from the disaster. Moreover, he was an extremely cultivated man, very much above the average in all fields of knowledge. For years on end, for example, he was seen regularly at the Bayreuth Festival.

Unlike what other monarchs usually do, the Tsar Ferdinand gave his son Boris a severe education, driving him on at the study of all that had to do with political and military matters. Under the rod of the old fox, son Boris himself became a young fox, who was able to work his way out of the complicated tangle of Balkan affairs.

In 1919 Boris kept his throne by marching on Sofia at the head of a division. And it was always by behaving like a true soldier that he overcame the political crisis of 1934.

While we're on the subject, he himself has told the story of how one night the lights in the barracks at Sofia, which had been put out at ten o'clock, were suddenly relit at eleven o'clock, and were still burning at midnight. From this he concluded that there was a conspiracy against his life. It's a fact that, until then, when an assassination was attempted in the Balkans, the assassins regularly arranged to find the politician who was to be struck at—in his nightshirt.

Boris therefore at once put on his uniform again, and waited for the conspirators sword in hand. He greeted their ring-leader with the words: "You want to kill me! What have you against me? Do you think you can do any better than I can?" Thereupon the conspirators, who were completely put out of countenance, asked leave to retire to their barracks to deliberate.

Boris kept their leader behind, then he told him that he was about to appoint him President of the Council of Ministers, to give him an opportunity of proving his abilities as a politician. It took less than a year, of course, for the experiment to end in the man's failure. As an end to this story, Boris made a very intelligent remark, to the effect that, in a case of this sort, the worst mistake was to warn the police. You prevent the conspirators, he said, from seeing reason and abandoning their plot. On the contrary, you encourage them to persevere with it out of mere feeling.

Alas, we must be on our guard against political assassination as much now as then. That's shown by the attempt on our Ambassador in Turkey, von Papen. The attempt has a lesson for us in the fact that the conspirators realised that they'd been betrayed by the Russians who commissioned them. The principal author of the attempt had been provided—allegedly to facilitate his flight—with a machine which he was told would produce artificial fog. In fact, the machine contained a powerful explosive charge designed to liquidate the assassin himself. When this treachery on their leaders' part was revealed to them, the accomplices had no scruples in telling all they knew about the objects pursued by the Soviets.

For my part, I've never allowed anyone to resort to assassination in our political struggles. The method is generally inopportune, and to be recommended only in exceptional cases. In fact, it cannot lead to any important success, unless it enables one to eliminate the man on whose shoulders rest the whole organisation and power of the enemy. But, even in such a case, I would have refused to use this weapon.

The reason why political assassination continues to be so formidable in the Balkans is that nowadays the population is still impressed by the idea that, by shedding blood, one is avenging oneself. That's why Kemal Pasha[384] acted wisely, immediately after the seizure of power, by proclaiming a new capital. Thus control by the police could be exercised effectively.

2nd April 1942, at dinner
Inelasticity of German protocol—Our eminent visitors get bored—
Graceful customs of the French—Italian Statesmen visit Berlin

What I dislike most about the *Wilhelmstrasse* is the protocol organisation. When an official guest arrives in Berlin, protocol seizes hold of him from six o'clock in the morning until deep into night. They put on *Faust* or a showing of *Tristan* for Balkan types who would enjoy only a farce or an operetta.

Old gentlemen who've come to Berlin to discuss important problems, and who would be the better for half a day's rest, are dragged from receptions to banquets, where they see the same faces everywhere. For the majority of our guests, the constraint imposed by protocol is a genuine martyrdom.

Wouldn't it be better to offer them the company of some pretty women who speak their language fluently? In Berlin, of all cities, we have the luck to number amongst our actresses women like Lili Dagover, Olga Tschechowa and Tiana Lemnitz.

---

[384] Kemal Atatürk declared Ankara to be the capital of Turkey in 1923, moving it away from Istanbul, the traditional seat of the Ottoman Empire.

In this respect, Boris of Bulgaria showed himself to be more of a fox than we knew. When he received the offer of somebody to pilot him through Berlin, he expressed the wish that his stay should be deprived of official character. He didn't want to put anyone out, he said. The fact was, he wanted to escape the martyrdom of protocol. He wasn't present at the showing of *Faust,* or of another opera, but he went and saw *The Poor Student* and then *The Count of Luxembourg,* He had a royal time.

When dealing with Balkan princes, one must bear in mind that they can scarcely leave their country for more than a week, for fear of losing their thrones during their absence.

If one bears in mind the political atmosphere in the Balkans, always heavy with threats of assassination and revolution, one must allow the political figures who come from those countries to enjoy themselves.

We should offer them a show like *The Merry Widow,* for example, instead of those dramas chosen by protocol, almost all of which contain the inevitable scene with the dagger. I know only one oriental prince who could allow himself to stay for more than a week outside his own country—that was the old Shah of Persia. Every year, before the Great War, he made a trip abroad. But he was really an exception.

I also consider that protocol goes off the rails when it thinks fit to drag our guests from one museum to the next, exactly allotting the time allowed them in which to admire each picture. Without bothering about the distinguished guest's personal preferences, the guide strikes the ground with his long, gold-knobbed cane, and this means it's time to pass on to the next masterpiece! As long as protocol shows so little understanding, it will merely poison our guests' lives.

In Paris, the matter is dealt with quite differently. As soon as the guest arrives, the Quai d'Orsay organises a magnificent procession, with soldiers in brilliant uniform, and the whole affair is followed by a reception at the Elysée. During the next six days, the guest's time is at his own disposal. The Parisian press, which is usually so gossipy, is extremely discreet on this occasion—a thing that greatly pleases the visitor. The latter—and all the more so if he's from the Balkans—goes home absolutely delighted with the welcome he had had in Paris, and begins dreaming of the trip he'll make next year. Since some justification has to be found for this trip, the visitor manages to wangle things so that it will be justified, and France has always profited by its way of treating illustrious guests. Before showing off their talents, our diplomats should at least try to put themselves into the skins of their Balkan visitors. The latter spend most of their time in a capital which, to them, acquires the look of a village where everybody knows everybody.

Each of them is like a Hindu prince who since his adolescence has been afflicted with a legitimate wife. Consequently, when he is at last alone, the poor man heaves a sigh of relief to think that, since the discretion of the press is guaranteed, he can make sheep's eyes at a pretty woman without worrying.

That's why, in cities like Berlin and Vienna, it's entirely the proper thing to give our passing guests some liberty. We've everything to gain on the political level—not to speak of the fact that it always brings in a little bundle of foreign currency.

When I went to Rome, I received a most agreeable kind of welcome. The Duce saw to it that I had all the necessary time to look in peace at the works of art that interested me. As a result of that visit, I took care that the Italian political personages who came to see us should be subjected to the minimum of obligations for reason of protocol. The result was stupefying.

One after another, the Italians accepted our hospitality with enthusiasm. That's what gave me the idea of proposing to Göring that he and I should grant each of them perhaps an hour of our time, so as to enable them to justify their trip to Germany. The great Berlin physicians were usually sufficient to justify the rest of their time spent in Berlin!

4th April 1942, midday

*Japanese political philosophy—Jewish origin of religious terrorism—
Jewish influence in Britain—The elite of the future—Rules for a good
education—Cowardice of the German Princes—The Red Flag of
Canterbury—No mercy on the feeble—Nature is better than pedantry—
All climates are alike to the Jews—I like hard, self-opinionated men—
Condemnation of the pessimists—Most Germans are optimists*

The fact that the Japanese have retained their political philosophy, which is one of the essential reasons for their successes, is due to their having been saved in time from the views of Christianity.

Just as in Islam, there is no kind of terrorism in the Japanese State religion, but, on the contrary, a promise of happiness. This terrorism in religion is the product, to put it briefly, of a Jewish dogma, which Christianity has universalised and whose effect is to sow trouble and confusion in men's minds. It's obvious that, in the realm of belief, terrorist teachings have no other object but to distract men from their natural optimism and to develop in them the instinct of cowardice.

As far as we are concerned, we've succeeded in chasing the Jews from our midst and excluding Christianity from our political life. It's therefore in England and America that one can nowadays observe the effects of such an education upon a people's conduct. Our measures against decadent art have enabled us to get rid of the smears of the Jews. But these daubs, which we've banned, are at present fetching the highest prices in England and America. And nobody amongst the bourgeois over yonder dares to protest. One may well exclaim: "Cowardice, thy name is bourgeoisie!" Although the Jew has seized the levers of control in the Anglo-Saxon world (the press, the cinema, the radio, economic life), and although in the United States he is the entire inspiration of the populace, especially of the negroes, the bourgeois of the two countries, with the rope already round their necks, tremble at the idea of rebelling against him, even timidly.

What is happening now in the Anglo-Saxon world is absolutely identical with what we experienced here in 1918. The Jew, in his imprudence, can't even think where he is to interfere next; the priesthood restricts itself to the shameful exploitation of the people; and, to cap it all, a king who's an utter nitwit! The King of England is worth no more than William II, who in 1918 was trembling with fear and incapable of taking the slightest decision, his only idea being to put his flag in his pocket.

Under such a monarch, the Jew can propagate and spread himself in the way he understands, and instil his poison into the mind of the bourgeois world. The cream of it is that today it's exactly the same in the Anglo-Saxon world as it used to be amongst us: these idiotic *petit bourgeois* believe that no economic life is possible without the Jew—for, as they put it, "without the Jew, money doesn't circulate". As if there hadn't been flourishing periods in our economic life before the intrusion of the Jews—in the Middle Ages, for example! I reckon that our future elite must be given a tough upbringing, so that it may be definitely immunised against such cowardice.

I'm in favour of an absolutely strict law of inheritance, declaring that a single child shall inherit everything, and all the others shall be thrown out into life and obliged to ensure their livelihood themselves. The father who truly loves his child bequeaths him a healthy heredity and a good education.

A good education consists in the following: *(a)* forming the child's character by giving him a sense of what is good; *(b)* giving him a background of solid knowledge; *(c)* it must be strict as regards the object to be attained, and firm as regards the methods used.

Furthermore, the father who has a lot of money must take care to give his child as little of it as possible. The man who wishes to bring up his child rightly must not lose sight of the example of nature, which shows no peculiar tenderness. The peasant class has remained healthy in so far as this form of law has been applied to the countryside. One child inherited the estate, the others received nothing, or almost nothing.

That's exactly the practice amongst the English nobility. The title passes to a single one of the descendants, to the exclusion of all the others. By thus ensuring that the bananas don't fall from the trees into the mouths of the young people, one protects them from cowardice and idleness.

I've given instructions that, from now on, estates given to our colonists in the Eastern territories may not be parcelled out. Only the most capable son will be entitled to inherit his family's farm, the other children will have to break a road through life themselves.

Such measures apply to the family as they do to other living things. Every human organism, however small, can recognise only one chief—and it is only in this way that the patrimony acquired by a family has a good chance of being preserved.

As soon as it's admitted that one can't put a human being in a box full of cotton-wool for the whole duration of his life, Bormann is right in regarding the tough education given in our boarding-schools as exemplary. The State can prop itself only on capable and courageous men. Only those who have proved their worth should be summoned to control public affairs. In the lower strata of the population, life itself assumes the task of practising a pitiless selection.

Likewise, when the popular masses find themselves confronted by rulers who are too pusillanimous, they do not hesitate to treat them with the utmost brutality. That's how one can explain that the revolution from below swept away the tottering house-of-cards of the monarchs of 1918. If there had been a single German prince of the stamp of Boris of Bulgaria, who remained at the head of his division, declaring that he did not dream of withdrawing a single step, we would have been spared that lamentable collapse.

At bottom, destiny is indulgent and benevolent rather than the contrary; it dooms to decrepitude only what is already rotten. If only a single shoot remains healthy and strong, destiny allows it to exist. As it turned out, the poor German princes, in their panic fear, didn't retain even the power of judgment that would have enabled them to assume the inaccuracy of such a report as that of the capitulation of the second Guards division! The proof that things are no better in England, that there, too, everything is rotten to the marrow, is that an Archbishop of Canterbury should hang the flag of the Soviets from his throne. No pity must be shown to beings whom destiny has doomed to disappear. If one must rejoice that a creature as weakly as the present King of England should be irresistibly thrust downhill by the Jews, by the clergy and by the cowardice of the bourgeois, we must likewise rejoice that our decayed potentates underwent a similar fate after 1918. It's absolutely ridiculous to take pity on our old princely houses. On the contrary, it's quite fortunate that with them disappeared the chief obstacle that still existed to the realisation of German unity.

In a general way, one must never have pity on those who have lost their vital force. The man who deserves our pity is the soldier at the front, and also the inventor who works honestly amidst the worst difficulties. I would add that, even here, our sympathy should naturally be restricted to the members of our national community.

As in everything, nature is the best instructor, even as regards selection. One couldn't imagine a better activity on nature's part than that which consists in deciding the supremacy of one creature over another by means of a constant struggle. While we're on the subject, it's somewhat interesting to observe that our upper classes, who've never bothered about the hundreds of thousands of German emigrants or their poverty, give way to a feeling of compassion regarding the fate of the Jews whom we claim the right to expel.

Our compatriots forget too easily that the Jews have accomplices all over the world, and that no beings have greater powers of resistance as regards adaptation to climate. Jews can prosper anywhere, even in Lapland and Siberia. All that love and sympathy, since our ruling class is capable of such sentiments, would by rights be applied exclusively—if that class were not corrupt—to the members of our national community. Here Christianity sets the example. What could be more fanatical, more exclusive and more intolerant than this religion which bases everything on the love of the one and only God whom it reveals? The affection that the German ruling class should devote to the good fellow-citizen who faithfully and courageously does his duty to the benefit of the community, why is it not just as fanatical, just as exclusive and just as intolerant?

My attachment and sympathy belong in the first place to the front-line German soldier, who has had to overcome the rigours of the past winter. If there is a question of choosing men to rule us, it must not be forgotten that war is also a manifestation of life, that it is even life's most potent and most characteristic expression. Consequently, I consider that the only men suited to become rulers are those who have valiantly proved themselves in a war.

In my eyes, firmness of character is more precious than any other quality. A well-toughened character can be the characteristic of a man who, in other respects, is quite ignorant. In my view, the men who should be set at the head of an army are the toughest, bravest, boldest, and, above all, the most stubborn and hardest to wear down. The same men are also the best chosen for posts at the head of the State—otherwise the pen ends by rotting away what the sword has conquered. I shall go so far as to say that, in his own sphere, the statesman must be even more courageous than the soldier who leaps from his trench to face the enemy. There are cases, in fact, in which the courageous decision of a single statesman can save the lives of a great number of soldiers. That's why pessimism is a plague amongst statesmen. One should be able to weed out all the pessimists, so that at the decisive moment these men's knowledge may not inhibit their capacity for action.

This last winter was a case in point. It supplied a test for the type of man who has extensive knowledge, for all the bookworms who become preoccupied by a situation's analogies, and are sensitive to the generally disastrous epilogue of the examples they invoke. Agreed, those who were capable of resisting the trend needed a hefty dose of optimism.

One conclusion is inescapable: in times of crisis, the bookworms are too easily inclined to switch from the positive to the negative. They're waverers who find in public opinion additional encouragement for their wavering. By contrast, the courageous and energetic optimist—even although he has no wide knowledge—will always end, guided by his subconscious or by mere common-sense, in finding a way out.

God be praised, in our people the optimists are in a majority. In basing itself upon them, by the way, the Church has given away its whole game. In the last analysis, in fact, the Christian doctrine is addressed to the optimist, with the object of persuading him that the present life will be followed by another life, a much nicer one, on condition that he decides in time for the right creed—I nearly said, for the right side. Compared with the natural objectivity of the male, the true upholders of optimism are women. They discover the most amazing qualities in their offspring within a week of their birth, and they never lose this faith.

5th April 1942, midday
German patents stolen—Protection in the future—Effrontery of the Russians—The future of Finland and Turkey—Opportunities in Russia—The importance of climate—Leningrad is doomed

Addressing Professor Morell: We shall have to see to it that the French don't sell our *Germanine,* which was the product of so much research, under another name, and, what's more, as a French product. In the peace treaty, we shall absolutely have to introduce a clause preventing the French from continuing to exploit the patents we were compelled to hand over to them by the terms of the Versailles *Diktat.*

In a general way, it's crazy to go on informing foreign countries in this matter, through the Patent Office. With the exception of Brazil, a country that has never particularly distinguished itself in the field of inventions, there is no country that doesn't think itself permitted at this moment to cancel the protection associated with patents and to arrogate to itself the right to exploit ours. In future, I want German patents to be kept systematically secret.

One thing has long struck me. Countries like Russia and Japan, for example, which have no notable inventions to protect, are in the habit of applying to America, England and Germany when there are certain products or machines that they want to manufacture themselves. They have a specimen of the article in question—a machine-tool, for example—sent from each of the three countries, they procure if possible the relative blue-prints, and then, from the models they have before their eyes, they set themselves to build a fourth machine, which naturally has a good chance of being the best. A year of collaboration with Russia showed me how far effrontery can go in this field. Exploiting to the utmost the difficult situation in which I found myself, the Soviets went so far as to demand the right to buy from us location instruments intended for artillery, battleships and even entire battle cruisers, with their blueprints. At the time, the situation was such that I had to end by sending them a heavy battleship. Luckily, by temporising on deliveries in detail, I succeeded in not supplying them with the artillery material. That taught me a lesson that will be useful to me all my life. When

Russian experts turned up at a factory to buy a machine, it sometimes happened that, after having seen all that had been shown them, they'd express the wish to examine such-and-such a machine-prototype of which they knew both the existence and the whereabouts. Communism has created a system of espionage which even today functions admirably.

After their first conflict with the Russians, the Finns applied to me, proposing that their country should become a German protectorate. I don't regret having rejected this offer. As a matter of fact, the heroic attitude of this people, which has spent a hundred of the six hundred years of its history in fighting, deserves the greatest respect. It is infinitely better to have this people of heroes as allies than to incorporate it in the Germanic Reich—which, in any case, would not fail to provoke complications in the long run. The Finns cover one of our flanks, Turkey covers the other. That's an ideal solution for me as far as our political protective system is concerned.

Independently of these considerations, the climate of Karelia—not to speak of the other regions—doesn't suit us Germans at all. If I happen to visit our brave soldiers up there, and they ask me what I think of those unproductive lands (which the Russians themselves have not attempted to colonise), I can only share their feeling. It's quite different with Norway, which, thanks to the presence of the Gulf Stream, offers much more favourable climatic conditions.

So the Reichsführer SS must not entertain the hope of replacing the Russian penitentiary colonies on the Murmansk canal[385] by the occupants of his concentration camps. These men's toil will first of all be needed for the building of the armaments factories we shall build in the vast Russian spaces. Besides, as regards the Russian territories that will pass under our sovereignty, the problems are so plentiful that they'll provide us with opportunities for work for several centuries. In the central sector, it will be necessary to cultivate the marshes, which extend further than eye can see, by planting reeds. They'll form a barrier in future to break the extraordinary waves of cold of the Russian winter. In other parts, it will be necessary to set up plantations of cultivated nettles, for, according to the experiments made by a Hamburg firm, the fibres of these nettles enable one to manufacture a cellulose

---

[385] The first of the infamous Soviet "gulags" supplied the labour which built a canal that connects the White Sea, in the Arctic Ocean, with Lake Onega, and from there to the Baltic Sea.

much superior to cotton. Moreover, it's becoming urgently necessary to re-afforest the Ukraine, in order to struggle effectively against the rains which are a real scourge in that region. They really did a good job, those hunters who, in order to satisfy their passion for the chase, took care to reforest 37 per cent of German soil. In the meantime, along the whole periphery of the Mediterranean, people were de-foresting without thinking of the importance of the forest and, consequently, without adopting the policy their action entailed.

Since there is a question of the future of Leningrad, I reply that, for me, Leningrad is doomed to decay. As one of the officers to whom I awarded the Oak Leaves was saying recently, famine has already reduced the population of Leningrad to two millions. If one thinks that, according to the report of the Turkish Ambassador in Russia, the city of the diplomats itself no longer offers anything decent to eat; and if one knows, too, that the Russians are continuing to eat the meat of broken-down horses, it's not difficult to imagine that the population of Leningrad will rapidly diminish. The bombs and artillery fire have contributed their share to the city's destruction.

In future the Neva will have to serve as the frontier between Finland and ourselves. May the ports and naval dockyards of Leningrad decay in their turn! As a matter of fact, there can be only one master in the Baltic, which must be an inland sea of Germany's. That's why we must see to it there's no room for an important port on the periphery of our Reich. The development of our own ports and those of the Baltic countries will amply suffice to cover our maritime needs, so that we shall be well able to dispense with the port of Leningrad, which in any case is blocked by ice for half the year.

5th April 1942, evening

Shall we try to Germanise the French?—The claims of Mussert—Very limited autonomy in the Great German Reich—Example of Austria— Himmler on the Frisians—Germanisation of Holland—The foreign legions on the Eastern front—Fusion of all Germanic races—But no excess Germanisation—Distrust of the Poles—Traitors within— Spontaneous treachery—How Germany should have shown her resistance spirit in 1918—Admiral Darlan's[386] conjuring trick—France will pay for the errors of Versailles

---

[386] Jean Darlan (1881–1942), Admiral and Commander-in-Chief of the French Navy in 1939, and who, after the defeat of France in June 1940, served in Vichy France's government.

During dinner, the Reichsführer SS declared that, in his view, the best way of settling the French problem would be to carry off every year a certain number of racially healthy children, chosen amongst France's Germanic population. It would be necessary to try to settle these children, while still very young, in German boarding-schools, to train them away from their French nationality, which was due to chance, to make them aware of their Germanic blood and thus inculcate into them the notion of their membership of the great group of Germanic peoples. The Führer replied: "Sinister theory!"

For my part, all these attempts at Germanisation don't mean much to me—in so far, at least, as no successful attempt is made to found them on an appropriate conception of the world. As regards France, one must not forget that the military reputation of that country is not due to the people's moral worth, but essentially to the fact that, on the Continent, the French were able to exploit certain military combinations of circumstance that were favourable to them (during the Thirty Years' War, for example). Every time they were confronted by a Germany that was aware of herself, they got a thrashing—under Frederick the Great, for example, in 1940, etc. The fact that they won victories of universal significance under the leadership of that unique military genius, the Corsican Napoleon, makes no difference at all. The mass of the French people has *petit bourgeois* spiritual inclinations, so much so that it would be a triumph to succeed in removing the elements of Germanic origin from the grasp of the country's ruling class.

Thereupon the Reichsführer SS turned the conversation upon his experiences with Mussert, the leader of the Dutch nationalists. "What struck me," he said, "is that Mussert is trying to get back his legion. He tried to explain to me that, to provide a military safeguard for his seizure of power in Holland, he needed the Dutch Legion, which at present is fighting on the Eastern front. I let him have no hopes on that score, pointing out to him, on the contrary, that once the war was over he could have in Holland only the number of soldiers corresponding to the strength of the legionaries at present fighting on the Eastern front. For territorial defence, he has no need of a Federal Dutch Army, since after the war this defence will be exclusively our business. Nor is it necessary to maintain an important Federal Army for show purposes." The Führer then gave his opinion: Mussert expressed himself in a rather curious fashion, in my presence, on the subject of the oath taken by the legionaries. That's why I asked him whether he supposed it was in sheer lightness of heart that

I divided my Austrian homeland into several *Gaue,* in order to remove it from separatist tendencies and incorporate it more easily in the Germanic Reich. Has not in Himmler's entourage, Rost Van Tonningen[387] always worked against Mussert?

Austria, too, her own history—secular five times over—a history that truly is not devoid of highlights? Obviously, in discussing these problems one must remain very careful, when confronted by Dutch and Norwegians. One must never forget that in 1871 Bavaria would never have agreed to become part of Prussia. Bismarck persuaded her only to agree to become part of a great association linked by kinship—that is to say, Germany.

Nor did I, in 1938, tell the Austrians that I wanted to incorporate them in Germany, but I insisted on the fact that Germany and Austria ought to unite to form the Greater German Reich. Similarly, when speaking to the Germanics of the North-west and North, one must always make it plain that what we're building is the Germanic Reich, or simply the Reich, with Germany constituting merely her most powerful source of strength, as much from the ideological as from the military point of view.

The Reichsführer SS underlined these last words of the Führer's, emphasising that amongst the various populations assembled in Holland there was no real sense of belonging to one community: "It's observed, for example, that the Dutch Frisians don't feel attracted, as far as kinship is concerned, towards the other Dutch; nor does one find in them a Dutch national sentiment founded on a solid idea of the State. It seems the Dutch Frisians would much prefer to be united with the Frisians from the other side of the Ems,[388] to whom they're akin by blood."

Field-Marshal Keitel supported this point of view on the grounds of his own experience. He estimated that the Frisians beyond the Ems desire only one thing, namely, to be united with the Frisians on the near side of the Ems, in a single administrative unit. The Führer, after taking time for reflection, said that, if this were so, the best thing would be to join the Frisians on both sides of the Ems in a single province, and that he would mention the matter to Seyss-Inquart when occasion arose.

The Reichsführer SS then spoke of the creation in Holland of boarding

---

[387] Meinoud Marinus Rost van Tonningen (1894–1945), parliamentary leader of the National Socialist Movement (NSB) in the Netherlands.

[388] The Ems River is still the border between the Lower Saxon area of East Friesland in Germany and the province of Groningen in the Netherlands.

schools for the political education of the young, two for boys and one for girls, to be called "Reich Schools"—a title approved by the Führer. A third of the pupils would be Dutch and two-thirds German. After a certain period, the Dutch pupils would have to visit in turn a similar school in Germany. The Reichsführer SS explained that, to guarantee that instruction would be given in accordance with the purposes of the Germanic Reich, he had refused a financial contribution from Holland and had asked Schwarz to set aside a specific sum exclusively for the financing of these schools. There was a project for the creation of similar schools in Norway. They, too, would be financed solely by the Reich Party treasurer. "If we want to prevent Germanic blood from penetrating into the ruling class of the peoples whom we dominate, and subsequently turning against us, we shall have gradually to subject all the precious Germanic elements to the influence of this instruction." The Führer approved of this point of view.

In any case, we must not commit the mistake of enlisting in the German Army foreigners who seem to us to be worthwhile fellows, unless they can prove that they're utterly steeped in the idea of the Germanic Reich. While we're on the subject, I'm sceptical about the participation of all these foreign legions in our struggle on the Eastern front.

One must not forget that, unless he is convinced of his racial membership of the Germanic Reich, the foreign legionary is bound to feel that he's betraying his country. The fall of the Habsburg monarch clearly shows the full size of this danger. On that occasion, too, it was thought the other peoples could be won over—Poles, Czechs, etc.—by giving them a military formation in the Austrian Army. Yet at the decisive moment it became obvious that precisely these men were the standard-bearers of rebellion. That's why it's no longer appropriate to build the Germanic Reich under the standard of the old Germany. It's not possible to unite the Germanic peoples under the folds of the black-white-and-red flag of the old German Empire—for the same reason as prevented the Bavarians from entering the German Reich, in 1871, under the flag of Prussia. It's the reason why I began by giving the National Socialist Party, as a symbol of the union of all Germanics, a new rallying-sign which was valid also inside our own national community—the swastika flag.

Let's avoid attempting the Germanisation of our vital space on too great a scale. Let's be cautious, especially with the Czechs and the Poles. According to Himmler, history proves that the Poles have their nationality tattooed on their bodies.

They must therefore be kept under control by giving them the strongest possible stiffening of German officers and N.C.O.s, and by trying to have them outnumbered by the German elements. It was agreed with Frank,[389] the Governor-General of occupied Poland, that the Cracow district (with its purely German capital) and also the Lublin district should be peopled by Germans. Once these two weak spots have been strengthened, it should be possible to drive the Poles slowly back.

I don't believe it's necessary to proceed with much circumspection in this field, for we would be condemning ourselves to renew an experience we already had after the divisions of Poland. The soul of Poland remained lively because, on the one hand, the Poles hadn't to take the Russian domination seriously, and, on the other hand, they'd succeeded in putting themselves politically in a strong position with the Germans, being helped in this by their allegiance to a Catholicism deeply tinged with politics (one can even say that the Poles played a decisive role in German home policy).

It's very important for the future that the Germans don't mingle with the Poles, so that the new Germanic blood may not be transmitted to the Polish ruling class.

Himmler is right when he says that the Polish generals who genuinely put up a serious resistance in 1939 were, so to speak, exclusively of German descent. It's an accepted fact that it's precisely the best elements of our race who, as they lose awareness of their origin, add themselves to the ruling class of the country that has welcomed them. As for the elements of less value, they retain the characteristics of their ethnic group and remain faithful to their Germanic origin.

The same caution is necessary towards the Czechs. They're skilled at not awakening the distrust of their occupiers, and are wonderful at playing the role of subjects. It's true they've had five centuries' experience of it! I saw them at work in Vienna during my youth. Arriving penniless and dragging their worn-out shoes over the streets of the city, they quickly acquired the Viennese accent—and one fine day one was quite surprised to see them installed in the key positions.

We shall not win the peace, on the racial level, unless the Reich knows how to maintain a certain stature. Confronted with the United

---

[389] Hans Frank (1900–1946), Hitler's personal legal adviser and party lawyer. He was later appointed to the second Hitler Cabinet without portfolio, and then served as Governor-General of the occupied Polish territories.

States, whose population is scarcely greater than ours, our strength lies in the fact that four-fifths of our people are of Germanic race.

The attitude of our rulers after the collapse of 1918 was truly inconceivable. Numerous industrialists had at that time tried to conceal a portion of our weapons from the enemy—and these weapons were the more precious in that they represented the result of the efforts due to the patience and perseverance of our searchers. Far from supporting and encouraging these industrialists in their activity, our governors created a thousand difficulties for them, going so far as to accuse them of betraying the interests of the country. And yet it wasn't difficult to evade, to a certain point, the conditions of the Versailles diktat! The controls were not so easy to carry out, and who'd have detected, in the course of a check-up, that there were only thirty thousand guns instead of the expected fifty thousand? There were, in fact, thirty thousand! There's no doubt that at this moment the spirit of treachery was rampant in Germany.

Why didn't our rulers all treat the traitors as Pöhner and Frick did in Munich? As a matter of fact, thanks to the microphones installed in the seats of the enemy disarmament commissions, they sometimes succeeded in catching the traitors at work. When they did so, they at once had them hauled in by officials of the criminal police (who passed themselves off as French), and at once arrested them.

If there had been any desire seriously to oppose the disarmament of Germany, the Treaty of Versailles itself offered us the possibility of doing so. Nothing was stopping us from building a great number of fast motor boats, since the building of units of that tonnage was not forbidden to us. As for warships, we could have set their tonnage well above the officially admitted figures.

Have you heard it said that it has been observed that my heavy cruisers do not at all correspond to the official measurements, particularly as regards their draught? With a little know-how, one could have turned that army of a hundred thousand men into a genuine school for officers and N.C.O.s.

By fixing the duration of military service at a small number of years, it would have been possible to train enough men to dispose, in case of need, of eight to nine hundred thousand men. Obviously such responsibilities could not be entrusted to cowards. The first time I gave the order to resume the building of 21-cm guns, some timid fellow recorded my order as being for six guns, instead of the sixty I was ordering. I had to make these gentlemen understand that, as soon as one exceeded the stipulations of the treaty, it mattered little whether one did so by small or by great percentages. In the same way, it would have been possible to build concrete forts along the Franco-German frontier and camouflage them as caves for children's homes, hospitals, etc. Thus, in the event of conflict with France, we would have had a system of fortifications comparable to our West Wall.

Nowadays it's the duty of our High Command to make sure that the French aren't playing this game on us. I was struck by a formula used by Admiral Darlan in an appeal to the French. Side by side with matters of no consequence, he spoke of "precautions for the future", as if he were referring to one of the objects of his policy.

Unfortunately I haven't had an opportunity of asking him to explain this mysterious statement.

In any case, I could have drawn his attention to the fact that he seems to be hatching certain ideas that were not unfamiliar to me at the time of my struggle. And I would have added that the tricks of a small conjurer cannot deceive a master-conjurer.

It will be France's fate to atone for the error of Versailles—for the next fifty years.

6th April 1942, midday
German representatives abroad—Necessity of changing our methods—
Follow the example of Britain—Honorary distinctions

The *Wilhelmstrasse* is certainly not happy in its choice of consuls. They're almost always honorary consuls entrusted with the defence of German interests abroad, men who've wangled an honorific title and are solely preoccupied with their own business, not with the problems that interest us, nor with the protection of our nationals resident in foreign countries.

After the war we shall have completely to transform these categories and in practice give up the system of consuls who have not made the consular service their career. Even if it costs more, we must follow the example of the English and send abroad diplomatic missions composed of men of genuine worth and paid accordingly.

The result will be worth it. In the country to which he's sent, the diplomat's task consists in suitably representing German interests. Furthermore, he must exactly inform his government, with the help of circumstantial reports, on all advisable measures. If our missions abroad fulfilled their duty, it would enable us considerably to lighten the services of the central administration. Fewer people at the *Wilhelmstrasse*, and their activities would be more effective.

Passing to another idea, the Führer speculated whether conferring honorific distinctions on foreigners brought good results. Ambassador Hewel replied that, subject to certain reservations) it did so.

The Führer continued: I've often thought about that problem. Instead of offering gold cigarette-cases, as we have done hitherto, it is in our interest to offer decorations. These latter, unless they're decorated with diamonds, represent an expenditure of from two marks fifty to twenty-five marks, whereas a gold case costs us about seventy marks. Seeing the success we have with the award of decorations, there's no need to hesitate. The fact is that just as men are on the look-out for titles, so they run after decorations.

To tell the truth, I don't much like that sort of traffic. I cannot see myself proclaiming that for a hundred thousand marks one becomes a vice-consul, for five hundred thousand a consul, and for a million a consul-general.

Yet that's how Imperial Germany obtained supplementary resources for herself. She was especially given to turning the title of *Kommerzienrat* (trade councillor) into cash. It's proper to act cautiously in this matter—otherwise titles and decorations lose their value. I think that "old Fritz"[390] would give the Prussian State Council a piece of his mind-that miserable attempt at resurrection—if he were able to see that assembly of do-nothings at work.

7th April 1942, at dinner

The great riots of 1918–19—A clique of evil doers—Our duty to German idealists—What the clergy costs the German State—How to economise on the Church Budget—Put difficulties in the way of recruitment of clergy—The Reich Bishop—Pastor Niemöller[391]—Petty intriguers

When one attentively studies the revolution of 1918-19, one discovers that it was in no way the manifestation of a great idea. It was a vast riot, inspired above all by a scum that had only recently left the prisons and penitentiaries. Read the reports on the spread of the revolution in Cologne, Hamburg or any other town, and you'll realise that this so-called popular rising was characterised above all by lootings and

---

[390] "Alte Fritz"— Frederick the Great

[391] Martin Niemöller (1892–1984), an early supporter of the NSDAP who later turned against Hitler after he was overlooked for the office of *Reichsbischof* ("Reich Bishop").

extortions. One can therefore feel only scorn for the cowards who fled before that gang. If the slightest attempt at a riot were to break out at this moment anywhere in the whole Reich, I would take immediate measures against it. Here's what I would do: *(a)* on the same day, all the leaders of the opposition, including the leaders of the Catholic party, would be arrested and executed; *(b)* all the occupants of the concentration camps would be shot within three days; *(c)* all the criminals on our lists—and it would make little difference whether they were in prison or at liberty—would be shot within the same period.

The extermination of these few hundreds or thousands of men would make other measures superfluous, for the riot would be aborted for lack of ringleaders and accomplices. As for the justification of these summary executions, I've only to think of the German idealists who are risking their lives in front of the enemy or showing their devotion in a war factory, whatever their job may be, and employing all their efforts for the victory of the fatherland.

It's a real scandal that we must give the German Churches such extraordinarily high subsidies. It isn't like that anywhere else, even in the most fundamentally Catholic countries, with the exception of Spain. Unless I'm mistaken, our Churches are still at present receiving nine hundred million marks a year. Now, the priests' chief activity consists in undermining National Socialist policy. The habit of exploiting the State goes back a long way. In periods of national tension, the Catholic Church always tried to occupy positions of temporal power, and always at the expense of the German community. The difficulties of our emperors never provided the priests with a chance to prove their German feelings. On the contrary, it's a tradition amongst them to profit by every circumstance to indulge in their egoistic activities. Thus one can never regret too much that such a powerful personality as Luther found only feeble successors.

Otherwise it would never have been possible, in Germany, to restore the Catholic Church on a sufficiently solid foundation to enable it to last until the present. Instead of squandering all these millions on the Church, I wonder seriously whether we wouldn't be doing better to devote the greater part of the money to building farms for our soldier peasants.

Himmler has told me that each of these farms works out at approximately twenty-three thousand marks, including the necessary fittings. Thus there are more than three thousand farms that we could offer every year, clear of all debt, to those of our soldiers who wished, after twelve years' service, to devote themselves to agriculture. It would be necessary, of course, to urge these men not to marry anyone but country girls. It would be necessary, too, to send them off, during their twelfth year of service, to a school of agriculture in the region where they're about to settle, so as to give them a suitable training. It will be essential, in the service of this project, to create a large number of these schools. In view of the variety of working conditions in the future Reich, these schools, in order to be really useful, will have to take account of the peculiarities of the region in which they'll be installed.

On reflection, it seems to be that an annual grant of fifty millions should be enough for the Catholic Church. It would be paid directly to the princes of the Church, who would be responsible for the sharing out. Thus we could have the "official" guarantee (since it would be a Church matter) of a "just" distribution of the money. These fifty millions would certainly bring us in more than the nine hundred million now squandered every year. You can bet anything, if one relies on historical precedents, that the princes of the Church would lick my boots for the value of the money, the more so if they could do what they liked with it. Therefore, if it's possible to buy the high dignitaries of the Church with money, let's do it! And if one of them wanted to enjoy his life, and for this purpose put his hand into the till, for the love of Heaven let him be left in peace! The ones we have to fear are the ascetics with rings under their eyes, and the fanatics.

After this war, I'll take the necessary steps to make the recruiting of priests extraordinarily difficult. In particular, I'll no longer allow children, from the age of ten and upwards, to devote their lives to the Church, when they've absolutely no notion what they're undertaking— in accepting celibacy, for example. Only the man who has passed his twenty-fourth year, and has finished his Labour Service and his military service, will be able to embrace an ecclesiastical career. At that age, then, if anyone is ready to vow himself to celibacy—well, let him become a priest, with God's help!

In parenthesis, that reminds me that some idiots made me the fatuous proposal that chiefs of the Party should be celibate!

While I'm on the subject, it's interesting to know how they've hitherto succeeded in filling the convents and monasteries. With the women, it's generally reasons of a sentimental nature that constitute the chief motive. With the men, on the other hand, it's usually not either the feelings or the reason that play a decisive part, but more earthy motives, such as material distress, for example.

In the course of the law-suits brought against the monasteries, it was discovered that, in numerous cases, poverty had driven the unemployed to turn into monks. The men who tried to recover their liberty were caught by the priests and fetched back. Thus one must rejoice that the closing of the monasteries enables us to restore to the life of society many men who are capable of rendering services to the community and wishful to work.

This measure does not entail great difficulties. The fact is, the monasteries are generally corporations, and consequently can be dissolved by means of private agreements made with the Prior. Let the Prior receive a monthly payment of five hundred marks, and his direct collaborators allowances of from a hundred to two hundred marks, and most of them will be quite ready to renounce their cloistered lives. In the old days nearly a thousand monasteries and convents were closed in this fashion in Austria.

It is a pity that, in its conflict with the Catholic Church, the Evangelical Church cannot be regarded as an adversary of any stature. This fact is expressed even in material details, and it was a thing that struck me during a diplomatic reception. In their magnificent vestments, the Nuncio and the bishop who accompanied him had so much style that one couldn't have claimed the Catholic Church wasn't worthily represented.

Opposite them, the representatives of the Evangelical Church wore starched collars of doubtful cleanliness and greasy frock-coats. Their attire was so out of place in that setting that I proposed to them that I should put suitable garments at their disposal for the next diplomatic reception. These representatives of the Evangelical Church are such *petit bourgeois* that they tried to discredit the Protestant Bishop of the Reich in my eyes by reporting to me that he had spent fourteen hundred marks on the purchase of new suites for a bedroom and a waiting-room. I retorted to the gentlemen that if they had asked me for a subsidy of thirty thousand marks for this bishop (in his capacity of Pope of the Evangelical Church), I would at once have had it granted by the State; but that, in addressing themselves to me as they had done, they had pronounced their own condemnation.

Men of that sort have not the stature that would enable the Evangelical Church to match itself effectively against the Catholic Church.

The limit of it is that these people aren't even honest. For example, at the moment when the struggle about the dismissal of the Bishop of the Reich had been joined, Marshal Göring was able to record a telephone call[392] from Pastor Niemöller to somebody else. Niemöller, referring to a conversation with Hindenburg, was boasting as follows: "We gave the old man an Extreme Unction, and we pulled his leg so hard that he's ready definitely to sack that whoremaster of a bishop!"

That same day, Niemöller was pleading this case in front of me, in the most unctuous style interspersed with biblical quotations, to persuade me to take action against the Bishop of the Reich. I thereupon asked Göring to read out the monitoring note of the telephone conversation. If you'd seen the fright of Niemöller and the delegates of the Evangelical Church! They literally collapsed, to the point of becoming dumb and invisible. Sometime later, I told Hindenburg of the incident. He dismissed the whole affair, merely remarking: "The fact is, the most insignificant of these intriguers seems to take himself for a Pope!"

8th April 1942, midday
*Cowardice of the middle classes—The Nazi Party wins over the
workers—Nuremberg, the citadel of Marxism—German workers and
their Jewish masters*

Since the beginning of my political activity, I have made it a rule not to curry favour with the bourgeoisie. The political attitude of that class is marked by the sign of cowardice. It concerns itself exclusively with order and tranquillity, and we know in what sense to understand *that*. I aimed, instead, to awaken the enthusiasm of the working-class world for my ideas.

The first years of my struggle were therefore concentrated on the object: win over the worker to the National Socialist Party. Here's how I set about it:

1. I followed the example of the Marxist parties by putting up posters in the most striking red.

2. I used propaganda trucks that were literally carpeted with posters of a flaming red, equipped with equally red flags and occupied by thundering loud-speakers.

3. I saw to it that all the initiates of the movement came to meetings without stiff collars and without ties, adopting the free-and-easy style so as to get the workers into their confidence.

---

[392] Hermann Göring had created the Secret State Police (*Geheime Staatspolizei*, or Gestapo) in 1933 in his state of East Prussia.

4. As for the bourgeois elements who, without being real fanatics, wanted to join the ranks of the National Socialist Party, I did everything to put them off—resorting to bawled-out propaganda, dishevelled clothes, etc. My object was to rid myself right from the beginning of the revolutionaries in rabbit's pelts.

5. I ordered our protective service to treat our opponents roughly and chuck them out of our meetings with so little mildness that the enemy press—which otherwise would have ignored our gatherings—used to make much of the blows and wounds they give rise to, and thus called attention to them.

6. I sent a few of our own people to take a course in public speaking in the schools organised by the other parties. Thanks to this, we obtained a good insight into the arguments which would be used by those sent to heckle at our meetings, and we were thus in a position to silence them the moment they opened their mouths. I dealt with the women from the Marxist camp who took part in the discussions by making them look ridiculous, by drawing attention either to the holes in their stockings or to the fact that their children were filthy. To convince women by reasoned argument is always impossible; to have had them roughly handled by the ushers of the meeting would have aroused public indignation, and so our best plan was to have recourse to ridicule, and this produced excellent results.

7. At all my meetings I always spoke extempore. I had, however, a number of Party members in the audience, with orders to interrupt along lines carefully prepared to give the impression of a spontaneous expression of public opinion, and these interruptions greatly strengthened the force of my own arguments.

8. If the police intervened, women of our Party were given the task of drawing their attention either to opponents or to completely unknown people who happened to find themselves near the entrance to the hall. In cases like this, the police invariably go about their job quite blindly, like a pack of hounds, and we found that this method was most efficacious, both for ridding ourselves of undesirable elements of the audience and for getting rid of the police themselves.

9. I disorganised the meetings of other Parties by sending members of our Party in the guise of ushers to maintain order, but in reality with instructions to riot and break up the meeting.

By judicious use of all the above methods, I succeeded in winning the support of such large numbers of the better elements of the working classes that, in the last elections that took place before our assumption of power, I was able to organise no fewer than a hundred and eighty thousand Party meetings.

Julius Streicher rendered particularly valuable service in our struggle to gain the support of the working classes. And now it is he whom we must thank for the capture of Nuremberg, that one-time stronghold of Marxism. The population of that city—in so far as they were interested in any way in politics, and with the exception of the Jewish colony—was made up of working men who were members either of the Socialist Party or of the Communist Party.

By his unrelenting attacks on the Jews, Streicher succeeded in alienating the workmen from their Jewish masters. Even so, the workers of Nuremberg, engaged for the most part in the metal trades, were by no means an unintelligent lot, and they were most stubborn adherents of Marxism. Streicher's success, then, is all the more meritorious, and he showed himself to be a master of tactics in the handling of a meeting. Not only did he annihilate the shop stewards with a torrent of ridicule, but he deprived them of any means of retaliation, and made use of their discomfiture as an additional weapon with which to convince the workers.

9th April 1942, midday

Economic and military errors we must not repeat—The example of the American motor industry—Mass production and limited number of models—A unique engine, cooled by air—Our debt of gratitude to Dino Alfieri[393]—Cut out the word "if"—Criteria when judging a politician— The Italian débâcle in Albania—How to restore order in an army in flight

This war, like the Great War, has led to a very large measure of standardisation in our technical production. But we must not repeat the mistakes we made at the end of 1918; we must make sure that our war-time achievements and experiences, economic as well as military, are not lost sight of in the days of peace ahead.

In the economic field we can learn much from the United States. The motor industry of the United States, by standardisation of types and mass-production, has reduced the cost of a motor-car to such an extent that every workman over there can afford to keep and run a car. Our own procedure has been exactly the reverse. We are constantly bringing out new models and modifying and improving existing ones.

---

[393] Dino Alfieri (1886–1966), Italian ambassador to Germany, and earlier, Mussolini's press and propaganda minister.

The result is that we have to produce an immense number and variety of spare parts, for the parts of a different model of the same make of car are never interchangeable. Nothing like this occurs in America.

After the war, we must, for military reasons, limit the German motor industry to the production of a dozen models, and the primary objective of the industry should be the simplification of the engine. Higher power must be achieved by increasing the number of standard cylinders rather than by the introduction of a variety of new cylinders. The dashboard, too, must be simplified. But the most important task will be the design of one single engine which can be used just as well for a field kitchen as for an ambulance, a reconnaissance car, road haulage or a heavy artillery tractor.

The twenty-eight-horsepower engine of the Volkswagen should be able to meet all these military requirements. This war has proved that great speeds are of no particular military use, and we must get away from this craze for "performance". Provided that the military vehicles mentioned above can attain a speed of between ten and twenty kilometres an hour, they will be perfectly adequate.

The ideal standard engine which I envisage must possess two characteristics: *(a)* It must be air-cooled; *(b)* It must be easy and swift to dismantle and change.

This latter characteristic is particularly important, because, as this war has shown, it is more difficult to get spare parts than to get a complete engine unit. Obviously, too, there must be a great measure of standardisation and simplification in the manufacture of the engine envisaged.

In reply to a remark by Ambassador Hewel that doubts were being voiced in Berlin about the abilities of the Italian Ambassador, Signor Alfieri, the Führer said: The exceptional services rendered by Alfieri to the cause of German-Italian friendship far outweigh any little weaknesses he may now show. I shall never forget that at the time of the Austrian National Socialist *coup d'etat* in 1934, which led Mussolini to make the one political mistake of his life,[394] Alfieri was among those who came out on the side of Germany. Great credit is due to that small band of men who put Mussolini on his guard against the intrigues and false

---

[394] Mussolini had threatened to deploy Italian troops into Austria should Germany intervene on the side of the Austrian Nazis in the chaos which followed the abortive 1934 coup attempt. This occurred before Italy and Germany became allies.

friendship of the French and thus saved him from further grave political errors. In this, Alfieri did a great service, not only to his own country, but also to Germany. The unarmed Germany of the time would have emerged from a struggle against the combined forces of France, Italy and Great Britain in a state of ruin and desolation comparable only to the situation at the end of the Thirty Years' War.

The criteria by which a politician should be judged are, firstly, the positive virtues he possesses, and, secondly, the actual services he has rendered to his country. In politics facts alone are of value, and any juggling with possible hypotheses is quite futile. It is, for example, perfectly true, but of no importance, to say that had the Romans been defeated by the Huns on the Catalaunian Fields the growth of western culture would have been impossible and the civilisation of the time would have been destroyed—as indeed our own civilisation today will be destroyed if the Soviets are victorious in this war.

In politics, the use of that little word "if" must be avoided. Where should we be today *if* the Czechs had had a little imagination, or *if* the Poles had been realists and had gone about their affairs with a little more honesty? It is precisely the fact that the Pole is a dreamer and the Czech is an out-and-out realist which has enabled us swiftly and successfully to establish the new order in the territories formerly known as Czechoslovakia and Poland.

It is equally impossible to imagine what might have happened *if* the Italian front had not been stabilised in Albania, thanks to Mussolini. The whole of the Balkans would have been set alight at a moment when our advance towards the south-east was still in its early stages.

The most serious aspect of the situation was the fact that we could place no confidence in Russian protestations of friendship. It is even quite probable that we should never have received permission from the King of Bulgaria for the entry into his country of German Commandos in disguise, charged with the mission of preparing for the entry of our troops.

In actual fact Boris is by temperament a fox rather than a wolf, and would have exposed himself to so great a danger only with the utmost reluctance. The fox, as we all know, prefers to pursue a course which will allow him, if danger threatens, to eliminate all trace of his passing.

At the time of the Italian difficulties on the Albanian front, I pondered for some time over the best thing to do if an army started to retreat without orders and could not be brought to make a stand; and the conclusion I reached was that summary executions by shooting would be the only remedy. But it is not the little infantryman who should be shot, the poor, wretched little devil who bears the brunt of war, the pangs of hunger and the plague of fleas. The man to shoot is the commander of the unit in retreat, regardless of who he may be.

9th April 1942, at dinner

The God of the Christians protects the Japanese pagans—Japanese religion and the cult of hero-worship—The unhealthy character of Christianity—Superstition—Brutality of the Catholic Church—The maintenance of morale without the aid of the Church

It is very curious that devout Christians like the British and the Americans should, despite their constant and fervent prayers, receive such a series of hidings from the pagan Japanese! It rather looks as if the real God takes no notice of the prayers offered day and night by the British and the Americans, but reserves His mercies for the heroes of Japan.

It is not surprising that this should be so, for the religion of the Japanese is above all a cult of heroism, and its heroes are those who do not hesitate to sacrifice their lives for the glory and safety of their country.

The Christians, on the other hand, prefer to honour the Saints, that is to say, a man who succeeds in standing on one leg for years at a time, or one who prefers to lie on a bed of thorns rather than to respond to the smiles of inviting maidens. There is something very unhealthy about Christianity.

Another peculiarity of the Christian faith, as it is taught by the Catholic Church, is that it is a school of pessimism rather than of optimism. The Japanese religion, on the contrary, rouses men to enthusiasm by the promise it holds of the rewards in the Hereafter, while the unfortunate Christian has no prospect before him but the torments of Hell.Such pessimism has a marked effect. Even a child of three can be made to acquire a terror of mind which will remain with him for the whole of his life. We all know many grown-up people who are nervous in the dark, simply because they had been told in their childhood that a bogey-man, a robber or the like lurked in the shadows.

It is no less difficult to eradicate these childish inhibitions than it is to free the human soul of that haunting terror of Hell which the Catholic Church impresses on it with such vigour during its most tender years. A man possessed of a minimum of intelligence who takes the trouble to ponder over these questions has no difficulty in realising how nonsensical these doctrines of the Church are. For how, he must ask himself, can a man possibly be put on a spit, be roasted and tortured in a hundred other ways when, in the nature of things, his body has no part in the resurrection?

And what nonsense it is to aspire to a Heaven to which, according to the Church's own teaching, only those have entry who have made a complete failure of life on earth!

It won't be much fun, surely, to have to meet again there all those whose stupidity, in spite of the biblical tag "blessed are the humble of heart", has already infuriated one beyond endurance on this earth! Imagine, too, how tremendously attractive a Heaven will be to a man, which contains only women of indifferent appearance and faded intellect! Only those, we are told, with the minimum of sin shall enter through the gates of Heaven; now, in spite of the fact that the burden of sin must inevitably grow heavier with each successive year, I have yet to meet a priest anxious to leave this life as quickly, and therefore with as light a burden, as possible! But I could name many a Cardinal of sixty and over who clings most tenaciously to life on this sinful earth.

When one examines the Catholic religion closely, one cannot fail to realise that it is an almost incredibly cunning mixture of hypocrisy and business acumen, which trades with consummate skill on the deeply engrained affection of mankind for the beliefs and superstitions he holds. It is inconceivable that an educated priest should really believe all the nonsense that the Church pours out; a proof there, to my mind, is the fact that the priests themselves always try to confuse the issue on the subject of the swindle of dispensations, and avoid whenever possible any discussion of the subject.

In spite of these obvious faults and weaknesses, there are nevertheless a large number of intelligent people who preserve their faith in the Church. They believe that man requires some species of brake on his activities and that, in spite of its many shortcomings, the Church represents the best deterrent that at present exists.

The pity is that people who reason in this manner appear to forget that the Church does not strive to propagate its teaching by reason and gentle persuasion, but by force and threat.

This is certainly not my idea of education. It is moreover obvious that, had the Church followed solely the laws of Love, and had she preached Love alone as the means of instilling her moral precepts, she would not have survived for very long.

She has therefore always remained faithful to the ancient maxim that the right hand must not know what the left hand does, and has bowed to the necessity of imposing her moral principles by means of the utmost brutality, not hesitating even to burn in their thousands men and women of merit and virtue.

We ourselves are today much more humane than the Church.

We obey the Commandment: "Thou shalt not kill", by catching and executing a murderer; but the Church, when the executive power lay in her hands, crucified, quartered and did him to death with indescribable torture.

Maintenance of the nation's morale is a task which the statesman can accomplish just as well as any Church. All he has to do is to incorporate in the law of the land all the moral beliefs of the healthy elements of the people and then to support those laws uncompromisingly with the authority of force.

10th April 1942
Foreign students at German universities

Hitler has just been studying the list of the new Bulgarian Ministers.

There are a large number of Bulgarians who have studied engineering or taken their degrees in Germany. It would be a good policy to facilitate the taking of degrees by foreigners at our universities, and we shall make friends for life of men who spent some of their youth in this fashion. The Universities of Erlangen, Giessen and even Würzburg, which all have difficulty in keeping going, should take special pains to attract foreigners, while Heidelberg, which enjoys so great a reputation in the Anglo-Saxon world, should ensure that everything possible is done to ensure the well-being of foreign students.

10th April 1942, evening
Methods of external broadcasting—Give the facts without comment

Propaganda destined for abroad must not in any way be based on that used for home consumption. Broadcasts to Britain, for example, must contain plenty of music of the kind that is popular among Britons. In this way, when their own transmitting stations starve them of music, they will acquire the habit of listening-in more and more to the concerts we broadcast for them.

As regards news-bulletins to Britain, we should confine ourselves to plain statements of facts, without comment on their value or importance. News about British high finance, its interests in certain sections of the armament industry, in the leadership and conduct of the war should be given without comment, but couched in such a way that the British listeners will themselves draw their own conclusions. As the old saying has it, little drops of water will gradually wear the stone away.

For our own people we must broadcast not only the facts but also copious and precise commentaries on their importance and significance. Good propaganda must be stimulating. Our stations must therefore go on talking about the drunkard Churchill and the criminal Roosevelt on every possible occasion.

11th April 1942, at dinner

Rosenberg and "The Myth of the Twentieth Century"—An unorthodox book from the Party point of view—It has the Catholics to thank for its success—Civilisation and individual liberty—The spirit of solidarity is imposed by force—German policy in the Eastern territories—Faults to avoid—Our attitude towards the local inhabitants—Creation of a network of communication—No arms for natives

I must insist that Rosenberg's "The Myth of the Twentieth Century" is not to be regarded as an expression of the official doctrine of the Party. The moment the book appeared, I deliberately refrained from recognising it as any such thing. In the first place, its title gives a completely false impression. There is, indeed, no question of confronting the conceptions of the nineteenth century with the so-called myth of the twentieth.

A National Socialist should affirm that to the myth of the nineteenth century he opposes the faith and science of our times.

It is interesting to note that comparatively few of the older members of the Party are to be found among the readers of Rosenberg's book, and that the publishers had, in fact, great difficulty in disposing of the first edition. It was only when the book was mentioned in a Pastoral Letter that the sales began to go up and the first ten thousand were sold. In short, the second edition was launched by Cardinal Faulhaber of Munich, who was maladroit enough to attack Rosenberg at a Synod of Bishops and to cite quotations from his book.

The resultant placing of the book on the index, as a work of heresy on the Party's part, merely gave additional fillip to its sale; and when the Church had finally published all its commentaries in refutation of Rosenberg's ideas, "The Myth of the Twentieth Century" sold its two hundred thousandth copy. It gives me considerable pleasure to realise that the book has been closely studied only by our opponents. Like most of the *Gauleiters*, I have myself merely glanced cursorily at it. It is in any case written in much too abstruse a style, in my opinion.

A very large measure of individual liberty is not necessarily the sign of a high degree of civilisation. On the contrary, it is the limitation of this liberty, within the framework of an organisation which incorporates men of the same race, which is the real pointer to the degree of civilisation attained.

If men were given complete liberty of action, they would immediately behave like apes. No one of them could bear his neighbour to earn more than he did himself, and the more they lived as a community, the sharper their animosities would become.

Slacken the reins of authority, give more liberty to the individual, and you are driving the people along the road to decadence.

The eternal mouthings about the communal spirit which brings men together of their own free will, make me smile. In my own little homeland, when the lads of the village met in the local tavern, their social instincts rapidly degenerated, under the influence of alcohol, into brawling, and not infrequently finished up in a real fight with knives. It was only the arrival of the local policeman which recalled them to the realisation that they were all fellow-members of a human community.

The idea of human solidarity was imposed on men by force, and can be maintained only by the same means. For this reason it is unjust to condemn Charlemagne because, in what he considered to be the best interests of the German people, he built up the whole organisation of the State on a basis of constraint.

Stalin, equally, has during these last few years applied to the Russian people measures very similar to those of Charlemagne, because he, too, has taken into consideration the very low level of culture among the Russians. He realised the imperative necessity of uniting the Russian people in a completely rigid political organisation; had he not done so, he could not possibly have ensured a livelihood for the heterogeneous masses which make up the USSR, nor could he have extended to them those benefits of civilisation, such as medical care, the value of which they cannot appreciate.

In order to retain our domination over the people in the territories we have conquered to the east of the Reich, we must therefore meet, to the best of our ability, any and every desire for individual liberty which they may express, and by so doing deprive them of any form of State organisation and consequently keep them on as low a cultural level as possible. Our guiding principle must be that these people have but one justification for existence—to be of use to us economically.

We must concentrate on extracting from these territories everything that it is possible to extract. As an incentive to them to deliver their agricultural produce to us, and to work in our mines and armament factories, we will open shops all over the country at which they will be able to purchase such manufactured articles as they want.

If we started bothering about the well-being of each individual, we should have to set up a State organisation on the lines of our own State administration—and all we should achieve would be to earn the hatred of the masses. In reality, the more primitive a people is, the more it resents as an intolerable restraint any limitation of the liberty of the individual.

The other great disadvantage of an organised society is, from our point of view, that it would fuse them into a single entity and would give them a cohesive power which they would use against us. As an administrative organisation, the most we can concede to them is a form of communal administration, and that only in so far as it may be necessary for the maintenance of the labour potential, that is to say for the maintenance of the elementary basic needs of the individual.

Even these village communities must be organised in a manner which precludes any possibility of fusion with neighbouring communities; for example, we must avoid having one solitary church to satisfy the religious needs of large districts, and each village must be made into an independent sect, worshipping God in its own fashion.

If some villages as a result wish to practise black magic, after the fashion of negroes or Indians, we should do nothing to hinder them. In short, our policy in the wide Russian spaces should be to encourage any and every form of dissension and schism.

It will be the duty of our Commissars alone to supervise and direct the economy of the captured territories, and what I have just said applies equally to every form of organisation. Above all, we don't want a horde of schoolmasters to descend suddenly on these territories and force education down the throats of subject races.

To teach the Russians, the Ukrainians and the Kirghiz to read and write will eventually be to our own disadvantage; education will give the more intelligent among them an opportunity to study history, to acquire an historical sense and hence to develop political ideas which cannot but be harmful to our interests. A loud-speaker should be installed in each village, to provide them with odd items of news and, above all, to afford distraction. What possible use to them would a knowledge of politics or economics be? There is also no point in broadcasting any stories of their past history—all the villagers require is music, music and plenty of it. Cheerful music is a great incentive to hard work; give them plenty of opportunities to dance, and the villagers will be grateful to us. The soundness of these views is proved by our experience at home during the time of the Weimar Republic.

One thing which it is essential to organise in the Russian territories is an efficient system of communications, which is vital both to the rational economic exploitation of the country and to the maintenance of control and order. The local inhabitants must therefore be taught our highway code, but beyond that I really do not see the need for any further instruction. In the field of public health there is no need whatsoever to extend to the subject races the benefits of our own knowledge. This would result only in an enormous increase in local populations, and I absolutely forbid the organisation of any sort of hygiene or cleanliness crusades in these territories.

Compulsory vaccination will be confined to Germans alone, and the doctors in the German colonies will be there solely for the purpose of looking after the German colonists. It is stupid to thrust happiness upon people against their wishes. Dentistry, too, should remain a closed book to them; but in all these things prudence and common-sense must be the deciding factors, and if some local inhabitant has a violent tooth-ache and insists on seeing a dentist—well, an exception must be made in his particular case!

The most foolish mistake we could possibly make would be to allow the subject races to possess arms. History shows that all conquerors who have allowed their subject races to carry arms have prepared their own downfall by so doing.

Indeed, I would go so far as to say that the supply of arms to the underdogs is a *sine qua non* for the overthrow of any sovereignty. So let's not have any native militia or native police. German troops alone will bear the sole responsibility for the maintenance of law and order throughout the occupied Russian territories, and a system of military strong-points must be evolved to cover the entire occupied country.

All Germans living in the eastern territories must remain in personal contact with these strong-points. The whole must be most carefully organised to conform with the long-term policy of German colonisation, and our colonising penetration must be constantly progressive, until it reaches the stage where our own colonists far outnumber the local inhabitants.

12th April 1942, midday

The Olympic Games in Berlin—What they cost and what they earned— If you must spend, spend regally—Schacht and our war budget—No economy when victory is at stake—The breed of schoolmasters— Greasy collars and unkempt beards—A proletariat denuded of all independence—School mistresses for the elementary schools—The role of the Hitler Jugend—Victory of Prussia in the war of 1866—Standard of culture among school-teachers in Bismarck's time—British Public Schools and Reich schools—Thirty-three gold medals for German athletes

At the time when it was decided that the Olympic Games should be held in Germany, the Ministry of the Interior submitted plans to me for the construction of an appropriate stadium. There were two alternative designs, the one costing eleven hundred thousand and the other fourteen hundred thousand marks. None of the people concerned seems to have taken into consideration the fact that the Olympic Games afforded us a unique opportunity to amass foreign credits, and at the same time a splendid chance of enhancing our prestige abroad. I can still see the faces of my colleagues when I said that I proposed to make a preliminary grant of twenty-eight million marks for the construction of the Berlin stadium! In actual fact, the stadium cost us seventy-seven million marks—but it brought in over half a milliard marks in foreign currency!

This is a good example of the tendency of Germans to do things on a niggardly scale. On occasions of this sort one must aim at the greatest success possible, and the proper solution of the problem demands thinking on a grand scale. When Wallenstein was ordered to raise an army of five thousand men, he was quite right to refuse to have anything to do with an army of less than fifty thousand. It would, indeed, be ridiculous to spend a single pfennig on any army which, when the need arose, would be too weak to fight and to win.

In the prosecution of any war it is essential that armament in peacetime should conform to the envisaged war requirements and thus be capable of attaining the desired results. Unfortunately a man like Schacht completely ignored this vital aspect, and he complicated my task very considerably when we came to our own rearmament. Schacht returned again and again to the charge, assuring me that German economy could afford at the most one and a half milliards for the war budget, if it were to avoid the danger of complete collapse. In the event, I demanded a hundred times this sum, and our national economy still continues to function perfectly! Particularly in the case of this war, one must never forget that if we lose it, we lose everything. There can therefore be but one slogan: Victory! If we win, the milliards we have spent will weigh nothing in the scales. The reserves of minerals which we have acquired in Russia are alone enough to repay us amply.

Those who become schoolmasters invariably belong to a type of man who has no chance of success in the independent professions.

Those who feel themselves capable of achieving success by their own unaided efforts do not become teachers—or at any rate, not teachers in primary schools. I must say, I have the most unpleasant recollections of the masters who taught me. Their external appearance exuded un-cleanliness; their collars were filthy and greasy, and their beards were unkempt.

During the interregnum between the two Reichs, they were the spoilt darlings of the Social Democrats, who cherished them, gave them a veneer of culture and left them with a presumptuous arrogance for which there was not the least justification.

One has but to read their literary outpourings, to listen to their po-litical opinions and to hear their eternal complaints to realise that they were the product of a proletariat denuded of all personal independence of thought, distinguished by unparalleled ignorance and most admi-rably fitted to become the pillars of an effete system of government which, thank God, is now a thing of the past.

When these people had the effrontery to complain that they were not being sufficiently well paid by the State, the only possible answer was that any ordinary corporal in the *Wehrmacht* was doing a better job, from the point of view of education, than they were.

It really is no great accomplishment to teach the alphabet to a lot of little boys and girls. I must say, I find it astonishing that these primary schoolteachers can bear it all their lives, condemned as they are year af-ter year to teach the same dull rudiments to a never-ending succession of new classes.

Physically and psychologically a woman is more fitted for this type of work. A mother accepts quite naturally the burden of bringing a succession of infants into the world, and of occupying herself with the upbringing of each one in turn.

378

The shorthand-typist has a purely mechanical task, which she repeats day after day. By nature, a woman is better fitted than a man to teach the alphabet to young children, and I think therefore we should do well to consider whether we could not profitably employ some of the surplus two million women who, in the nature of things, are condemned to celibacy. Such employment would certainly provide them with an outlet for their maternal instincts.

A few years ago the teachers approached me with a request. They had, they suggested, an educational mission which should not be confined to the school-room, but should also participate in the upbringing of the youth of the nation.

When I now look at the success of the Hitler Youth movement, I must say I congratulate myself on having had the sense to reject their kind offer! Teachers in primary schools, with very few exceptions, are not endowed with the authority which the upbringing of youth demands, and in my own opinion we ought to form a corps of teachers for advanced primary education from the ranks of our re-enlisted soldiers.

As all these passed through both the Hitler Youth and the Labour Service before entering the army, they will all have the background appropriate to the educative task we would confer upon them. It should be quite sufficient if, during the last two years of their colour service, they were sent to do a course at a teachers' training establishment. In this way, if recruitment proved adequate for our needs, we should have at our disposal as primary school-teachers a body of men seasoned by twelve years of military service, who would be real men and not stuffed jackanapes.

The teachers tried to enhance their importance by claiming that the Prussian victory in the war of 1866 was due to them. Such a claim is, of course, ridiculous. Prussia won that war thanks, primarily, to the superiority of the new pin-firing rifle and, subsequently, to other elements which had nothing whatsoever to do with the school-teachers.

What is true, however, is that during the last century the standard of education among German school-teachers was exceptionally high in comparison with that of teachers abroad, and it would be unjust of me not to admit it.

Those who contest this and claim superiority for the educational system of the British Public Schools of the period must not forget that there is one essential difference between the two; for, whereas the British Public Schools were open only to the children of the upper classes, our own schools were open to everybody, regardless of social distinction.

The British colleges were in a position to be extremely selective, and their results were therefore naturally better than ours.

But once we have reformed our educational system we shall have no difficulty in surpassing the British Public Schools in every way. I have already briefly indicated the lines which we must follow; we must in the future create institutions inspired with the principles of National Socialism and endowed with the title "Reich School".

The pupils of these schools will consist of a selection of the best elements from the boys and girls of all classes in the German Reich. I aim at forming a *corps d'élite*, of fine physique, well-formed character and supple intelligence, and I shall rely on my new body of instructors to achieve the desired standard. These latter will themselves take part in all the activities, however arduous, of their pupils, including parachute-jumping and motorised manoeuvres.

The results we obtained at the Olympic Games has shown me that these Reich Schools will be able to raise the standard of German youth to an exceptionally high level.

The British, notwithstanding the advantages of their college system of education, were only able to win eight gold medals. The young sportsmen of the Reich took thirty-three!

Think, then, what will happen when the youth of the whole Reich will receive its upbringing, including intensive sports training, in the new Reich Schools!

12th April 1942, at dinner
Caution in giving information to our allies—The loquacity of the British Press—Russian camouflage in the Finnish war, in 1940

I think we must exercise the greatest caution in deciding what information we pass on to our allies. I regret to say that I have myself seen that the Italians are not sufficiently discreet over any matter which does not concern their own immediate interests.

Not infrequently the Italian press has light-heartedly alluded to certain plans of our own. I have decided, therefore, to confine myself in future to giving them only the minimum essential information—and even that only at the last possible moment. I shall do my best to sidestep any requests for precise details, and I shall always give them evasive answers.

In this, the British give us a good object lesson in how not to do things. There is, I think, no press in the world which, with its constant references to "well-informed circles", babbles more freely than the British press.

I don't think it is any exaggeration to say that it was public opinion, animated by the outpourings of the press, which made the British Government decide to undertake the Norwegian campaign, which certainly had no place in the plans of the British General Staff. I must admit that the Russians are much more cunning in this respect: not only do they keep their press in complete ignorance of all their plans, but they also systematically camouflage everything which has anything to do with their army.

The war against Finland in 1940, for instance, was nothing but a great piece of camouflage on their part, for even then Russia possessed armed forces which placed her among the first of the Powers, on a par with Germany and Japan.

22nd April 1942, midday

Problem of German re-armament in 1933—A man of stature at the head of the Reichsbank, Schacht—The scruples of Schwerin-Krosigk[395]— The stupidity of General Blomberg[396]—And the evasions it forced upon me—Schacht rebels—Mobilisation of our foreign credits—Our stock of raw materials—The Metropolitan Opera House in New York closes its doors—The Americans have no great artistes.

It was with Dr. Luther,[397] the then President of the Reichsbank, that I had, in 1933, one of my first discussions on the subject of our rearmament. In view of the deficit in the Reich budget, which then stood at about three milliard marks, and of the financial state of the *Länder*,[398] which was not much better, it was impossible to make even the smallest effort towards rearmament without the collaboration of the Reichsbank. In the course of this conversation I impressed upon Dr. Luther that, unless she regained her military power, Germany was doomed to

---

[395] Johann Ludwig Schwerin von Krosigk (1887–1977), a career civil servant who was also Minister of Finance from 1932 to 1945.

[396] Fritz von Blomberg (1878–1946), Minister of Defence from 1933 to 1935 and Wehrmacht Commander-in-Chief from 1935 to 1938. He was forced to resign after pornographic photographs of his wife emerged.

[397] Hans Luther (1879–1962), right wing politician, Chancellor from 1925 to 1926, President of the Reichsbank from 1930 to 1933, and German Ambassador to the United States from 1933 to 1937.

[398] The "states" or regions of Germany.

strangulation. Luther listened to me for two hours, at the end of which he assured me of his profoundly nationalist sympathies and promised me all the help he could give me. He then mentioned a precise figure, telling me that he would put a hundred million marks at my disposal! For a moment I thought I must have misunderstood him, for I did not think it possible that a financier should have so little knowledge of the vast expense involved in a policy of rearmament.

But when I asked him to repeat what he had said, Luther again gave me the figure of one hundred million. Further comment was obviously superfluous, so I simply asked the President of the Reich to remove the man from his office.

This, however, was not possible without further ado, as the Reichsbank was still an international organisation. I was then compelled to try to reach an amicable agreement. I told Luther that any collaboration between us was impossible, that he might perhaps have some legal means of retaining his position, but that I had now assumed office, that I would brook no argument from him, and that, if the interests of the country demanded it, I should not even hesitate to break him; and then—and this was the idea that Meissner had suggested as a solution—I offered him the post of Ambassador to Washington, if he would voluntarily resign his present position. This he declared himself ready to accept, provided I would add an allowance of fifty thousand marks a year to his pension. I can see him still, his eyes modestly downcast, assuring me that it was pure patriotism which caused him to fall in with my suggestions!

So I had to pay good money to open the way for the appointment of a man of international reputation to the Presidency of the Reichsbank—Dr. Schacht. Schacht understood at once that it would be ridiculous to think of launching any rearmament programme unless we were prepared to vote many milliards for its implementation. In this manner I was able to extract a sum of eight milliards, though the announcement of the figure caused Schwerin-Krosigk, the then Minister of Finance, many grave misgivings.

At this moment General Blomberg was unfortunately stupid enough to disclose that, apart from these eight milliards, a further supplementary sum of twelve milliards would be required to carry out the preliminary phase of the rearmament programme. I reproached Blomberg bitterly for his indiscretion. After all, seeing that the whole gang of financiers is a bunch of crooks, what possible point was there in being scrupulously honest with them? By far the best thing was to state our needs bit by bit as they arose. This method was also to the advantage of the financial experts themselves; for if things should go wrong, they would then be in a position to justify themselves in the public eye by claiming that they had not been told the truth.

It is characteristic of Schacht that, from the first eight milliard marks, he retained five hundred million as interest! He is a man of quite astonishing ability and is unsurpassed in the art of getting the better of the other party.

But it was just his consummate skill in swindling other people which made him indispensable at the time. Before each meeting of the International Bank at Basle, half the world was anxious to know whether Schacht would attend or not, and it was only after receipt of the assurance that he would be there that the Jew bankers of the entire world packed their bags and prepared to attend. I must say that the tricks Schacht succeeded in playing on them proves that even in the field of sharp finance a really intelligent Aryan is more than a match for his Jewish counterpart.

It is Schacht who was the instigator of the plan, subsequently put into practice, of devaluing German shares held abroad. Most of these represented reparations held in the form of shares; these shares were then later purchased in the open market by intermediaries on our behalf at prices varying from 12 per cent to 18 per cent of their real value, after which German industry was compelled to redeem from us at par value. In this way, thanks to a profit of 80 per cent and over, we were able to organise an export dumping campaign which brought in three-quarters of a milliard marks in foreign currency.

It is greatly to Schacht's credit that he remained completely silent on the existence of this foreign currency. There were several occasions on which, had the existence of these funds been known, the most determined efforts would have been made to deprive us of them. I am thinking particularly of the time when we did not know where to lay our hands on the money for the salaries of our officials, and of the moment when we were faced with a complete lack of rubber.

It was only in 1938, when war was obviously inevitable, that I made publicly known the existence of these reserves. It was clear that the future belligerents would, like ourselves, make the most strenuous efforts to buy up any and everything in the way of raw materials that the world's markets had to offer. Speed, therefore, was essential if we wished to avoid seeing our gold and foreign currency reserves transformed suddenly into paper and metal of no value.

It was to Funk that I entrusted the task of buying our share of raw materials. In spite of his ability, I felt I could not quite trust Schacht in this matter, for I had often seen how his face lit up when he succeeded in swindling somebody out of a hundred-mark note, and I feared that in the face of such temptation he would quite probably try his Freemason's tricks on me!

It is reported that the Metropolitan Opera House in New York is to be closed; but the reasons given for its closing are certainly false. The Americans do not lack money; what they lack is the artistes required to maintain the activities of the greatest of their lyrical theatres.

One requires but little knowledge to know that the most famous operas are all of either German, Italian or French origin, and that among the artistes who perform them the Germans and the Italians are the most celebrated.

Deprived of the services of the artistes from these two countries, the management has preferred to close its doors rather than expose the inadequacy of American artistes.

Our newspapers must not miss this opportunity! Copious comment should be made on this illuminating pointer to the cultural standard of the United States.

23rd April 1942, midday

How to refresh the blood-stream of effete peoples—The role of the SS— Build bonny babies—A people of soldiers—War and love go arm in arm—The use of foreign manpower—Servility of the Czechs—British rebuffs in India—The history of Germany starts with Arminius—The personality of Rudolf von Habsburg

Reichsführer SS Himmler mentioned the order he had given two years ago on the duty of healthy members of the SS to perpetuate their species. In view of the heavy losses suffered in this war by the SS, particularly among the younger and unmarried members, Himmler was very pleased now that he had given the order when he did. The fie blood of these men who were gone would not be wholly lost, but was being perpetuated in their children. The Führer expressed himself as follows: At Berchtesgaden we owe a great deal to the infusion of SS blood, for the local population there was of specially poor and mixed stock. I noticed this particularly while the Berghof was being built, and I was most anxious to do something to improve it.

Today, thanks to the presence of a regiment of the *Leibstandarte*,[399] the countryside is abounding with jolly and healthy young children. It is a practice which must be followed; to those districts in which a tendency towards degeneracy is apparent we must send a body of elite troops, and in ten or twenty years time the bloodstock will be improved out of all recognition. I rejoice to know, therefore, that our soldiers regard it as a duty to their country to persuade the young women to bear healthy children. Especially at this moment, when the most precious of our blood is being shed in such quantities, the maintenance of our race is of vital importance. First-class troops should, I think, also be stationed in the East Prussian lake districts and in the forests of Bavaria.

If, in the exigencies of war, industry makes too great a demand on our man-power, then we must use the man-power of the territories which we have occupied. To deserve its place in history, our people must be above all a people of warriors.

This implies both privileges and obligations, the obligation of submitting to a most rigorous upbringing and the privilege of the healthy enjoyment of life. If a German soldier is expected to be ready to sacrifice his life without demur, then he is entitled to love freely and without restriction. In life, battle and love go hand in hand, and the inhibited little bourgeois must be content with the crumbs which remain. But if the warrior is to be kept in fighting trim, he must not be pestered with religious precepts which ordain abstinence of the flesh. A healthy-minded man simply smiles when a saint of the Catholic Church like St. Anthony bids him eschew the greatest joy that life has to give, and offers him the solace of self-mortification and castigation in its place.

If we wish to preserve the military power of the German people, we must be careful not to give arms to the peoples of the countries we have conquered or occupied. One of the secrets of the might of ancient Rome was that throughout the Empire only Roman citizens were entitled to carry arms. One realises the extent to which the bearing of arms contributes to a man's pride and bearing when one compares the Czechs of 1938 with those incarnations of servility whom one finds in the country today!

If Britain has really reached an impasse in India, it is due to the fact that she is no longer strong enough to act as a dominant race. The British have over-estimated the power of their prestige during the last

---

[399] The *Leibstandarte SS Adolf Hitler* (LSSAH), Hitler's personal bodyguard unit which eventually grew into an elite Panzer division of the Waffen-SS.

few decades; and now they are reaping the rewards of their weakness and paying the penalty for failing to remain faithful to those wise principles which characterised the epoch of their greatest glory. Just as the Americans give the impression of being rather vulgar upstarts when they start boasting about their history, so the British look like puffed-up poodles when, in the course of referring to the three hundred years during which they dominated the world, they look disdainfully at the German Reich with its thousand years of living history.

Our history goes back to the days of Arminius and King Theodoric, and among the German Kaisers there have been men of the most outstanding quality; in them they bore the germ of German unity. This fact is too often forgotten, because since the fifteenth century it is only in Austria that the history of ancient Germania has been taught. In other places this history has been sacrificed for the sake of the histories of the various dynasties which fought each other for the possession of our land. It is the duty of our historians to teach our people the story of the German Kaisers, to make the drama of their lives come alive again for us, and above all to portray the greatness of their struggle against Popery.

I am thinking, for example, of the extraordinary personality of Rudolf of Habsburg. His electors placed him on the throne because they thought he would be a feeble monarch. It was he who won the sympathy of the Church by aiding a priest to mount his horse—a splendid little piece of propaganda! But once he was assured of election, with what firmness and energy he defended the interests of the Reich and opposed the intrigues of the Church, without fear or hesitation! First of all he made sure of his hereditary rights to certain territories, which he regarded as his base; then he compelled Ottokar of Bohemia to see reason; and finally he reunited the German Reich.

The Church was equally at fault in its assessment of the Sicilian Frederick, who, as an Emperor at the age of twenty-one, conquered the German Reich.

23rd April 1942, at dinner

My opinion of the Duce—The man who best understood the Bolshevik menace—The fate awaiting Europe—The Duce's difficulties with the Italian aristocracy—In praise of Edda Mussolini[400]

It will give me very great pleasure to see the Duce again and to discuss with him all the military and political problems of the day. I hold

---

[400] Edda Ciano, née Mussolini (1910–1995), the Italian dictator's daughter.

the Duce in the highest esteem, because I regard him as an incomparable statesman. On the ruins of a ravished Italy he has succeeded in building a new State which is a rallying point for the whole of his people. The struggles of the Fascists bear a close resemblance to our own struggles. Did they not have, for example, six thousand six hundred dead at Verona? The Duce is one of the people who appreciated the full measure of the Bolshevik menace, and for this reason he has sent to our Eastern front divisions of real military merit.

He told me himself that he had no illusions as to the fate of Europe if the motorised hordes of the Russian armies were allowed to sweep unchecked over the Continent, and he is quite convinced that, but for my intervention, the hour of decline was approaching for western Europe.

It is always painful to me, when I meet the Duce in Italy, to see him relegated to the rear rank whenever any of the Court entourage are about. The joy is always taken out of the reception he arranges for me by the fact that I am compelled to submit to contact with the arrogant idlers of the aristocracy.

On one occasion these morons tried to ruin my pleasure at the spectacle of a dance given by the most lovely young maids from the Florence Academy, by criticising the dancing in most contemptuous terms. I rounded on them with such fury, however, that I was left to enjoy the rest of the programme in peace!

It was certainly no pleasure to me to find myself continually in the company of the Court hangers-on, particularly as I could not forget all the difficulties which the King's entourage had put in the Duce's way from the very beginning. And now they think they are being tremendously cunning in flirting with Britain!

Nothing, to my mind, is more typical of the ineptitude of these aristocratic loafers than the fact that not once did the Crown Princess of Italy succeed in offering me a hot and decently cooked meal! When a German hostess offers me hospitality she makes it a point of honour, however humble she may be, not only to give me an excellent meal but also to see that it is decently hot. These degenerates of the Italian aristocracy give proof of their futility in even the most elementary things in life. What a pleasure it was, in contrast, to talk to an intelligent and charming woman like Edda Mussolini! A woman of this kind shows the stuff she is made of by volunteering to be a nurse with the divisions serving on the Eastern front—and that is just what she is doing at the present moment.

24th April 1942, midday
Decisive hours of this war—Importance of the occupation of Norway—
Weakness of German High Command in 1914–18—Lack of popular
interest in the Navy—And how we roused it

The two decisive events of the war up to the present have been the Norwegian campaign in 1940 and our defensive struggle in the East during last winter. I attach this measure of importance to the occupation of Norway because I cannot understand, even in retrospect, how it was that the powerful British Navy did not succeed in defeating, or at least in hindering, an operation which did not have even the support of the very modest German naval forces. If the Norwegian campaign had failed, we should not have been able to create the conditions which were a pre-requisite for the success of our submarines.

Without the coast of Norway at our disposal, we should not have been able to launch our attacks against the ports of the Midlands and Northern Britain, and operations in the Arctic waters would also have been impracticable. The advantages which our Norwegian success have given us allow us, by comparison, to see how unimaginative and un-enterprising the German High Command was during the Great War.

It seems incredible, to our eyes today, that the main engagement of that war should have been the battle of Jutland-that little peninsula which nowadays is merely a protuberance in the midst of the home waters which we control.

I am not at all sure that the inadequacies of our High Command in 1914–18 have not their origins in the indifference of the whole German people towards naval warfare. I well remember how difficult it was in 1912, in a town like Munich, to buy a book on the Navy or the colonies. It was for this reason that, when I gave orders for the construction of the first of our new warships immediately after my assumption of power, I supported my action with wide publicity and propaganda.

As a result, our little Navy became an extremely popular service, and this helped me greatly when I came to replace with new ships the old battleships which had been salvaged round about 1920 from the naval cemetery.

Our new units have been built in accordance with the most modern precepts of naval construction, and their crews have been recruited not only from coastal districts but from all over Germany. Proud milestones along the magnificent trail we have blazed are the construction of the *Emden*, twelve ultra-modern torpedo-boats, then three cruisers of the K Class *(Koeln, Karlsruhe, Königsberg)*. Next came the construction of the units of the Deutschland Class, and finally those that composed the High Seas Fleet.

24th April 1942, at dinner

Marriage and the child problem—German soldiers marrying women of the occupied countries—The unmarried mothers of former Austria—The educative role of the Schools of the Reich—The wives of our leaders

This conversation took place during a journey from Führer Head Quarters to Berlin. The subject under discussion was marriage and children. The Führer said: The history of the German Princes proves, generally speaking, that the most successful marriages are not those which are founded solely on reasons of expediency. In all human activities only that which is true has any chance of survival, and it is therefore only natural that a marriage inspired by sincere mutual love should be the union with the best chance of happy success. Such a marriage constitutes a guarantee for the manner in which the children will be brought up, and this is a guarantee of inestimable value for the future of the German people.

I do not think, therefore, that we should sanction, except in isolated cases, marriage between our soldiers and foreign women. The request may often be based on sound reasons, but all the same it should be refused. Most of these cases, obviously, result from a sexual experience which the applicant desires to continue—and the number of requests submitted to me is enormous.

It suffices, however, to glance at the photographs of most of the candidates to realise that in the majority of cases the union is not desirable. Most of the women concerned are either malformed or ugly, and from the racial point of view the results could not be satisfactory. I am sure, too, that such marriages would not stand the test of time. A really happy marriage can only be attained by people deeply attracted to each other. All in all, then, I think it is far better that we should turn a blind eye to certain little irregularities rather than give permission for a legal union which will certainly come to grief in the future.

Where marriage itself is concerned it is, of course, essential that both parties should be absolutely healthy and racially beyond reproach. How decisive the influence of real attachment between the parents is on the children of a marriage is brought home to me when I think of the number of men of outstanding ability who originate from the Orphans' Homes during that period of history when people really in love were so often precluded from marrying for reasons of social expediency. These Orphans' Homes, I think, were most valuable institutions. To the unmarried mother, in danger of social ostracism for herself and her child, they offered a safe haven in which she could discreetly and confidently deposit her infant, with the sure knowledge that it would be well and truly cared for. It was thanks to the moral hypocrisy of the nineteenth century that these invaluable institutions, a blessing from the Middle Ages, disappeared and that the unmarried mothers, many of whom had the excuse of a veritable and noble love, were henceforth exposed to obloquy and shame.

As far as we are concerned, our schools are in a position to deal adequately with the problem. In the National Socialist centres of education, combined with the boarding-schools, all necessary arrangements have been made for the reception of racially healthy illegitimate children and the giving to them of an education appropriate to their talents.

These Schools of the Reich are also an ideal refuge for the children of marriages which have gone wrong; it is far better that they should be removed from the atmosphere of a disrupted home, which leaves its mark on a man for the rest of his life. I grant you, it is a most laudable thing that parents who no longer love each other try to maintain the semblance of a happy marriage for the sake of their children; but it is an effort that very seldom succeeds.

I have seen so many cases among members of our Party, whose wives have not been able to keep pace with their husbands' rise in life. Grasping their opportunities, these latter have seen their talents blossom and expand in the execution of the tasks I have confided to them; burdened with wives who have ceased to be worthy of them, and exposed to unending petty domestic squabbles, they gradually come to accept as inevitable the idea of separation.

To my mind, it is obvious that a man should seek in his wife qualities which are complementary to his own as the path towards a full and ideal life. But one cannot make hard and fast rules, and there are many exceptions. I have now been enumerating cases in which one's sympathies lie with the man, but there are many cases in which it would be unjust in the extreme to demand of a woman that she should systematically sacrifice herself on the altar of matrimony. I have no sympathy whatever for the man who maltreats his wife, and who subjects her either to moral torture or material burdens.

Reich Chancellery, 25th April 1942, midday

The escape of General Giraud[401]—What France really feels towards us—
We will retain strong-points in France—Meat and the vegetarian diet—
Importance of raw food

The Führer replies to a question by Minister Frick regarding the recent escape of General Giraud: We must do everything possible to recapture this man. As far as I know, he is a General of great ability and energy, who might well join the opposition forces of de Gaulle and even take command of them. History shows again and again that it is not only the younger men in their early thirties who are capable of brilliant exploits—some have shone even earlier in life, as, for example, Napoleon and Alexander, who was but twenty years of age—but that very often it is in their sixties and even their seventies that many men accomplish their greatest achievements.

For my part, I see in the escape of this General, to whom every possible facility had been granted to alleviate the burden of captivity, a significant pointer to the real attitude of the French towards us. We must therefore keep a very cool head in our dealings with them, both now during the armistice period and later when the peace treaty is formulated; and we must bear in mind all historical precedents and take decisions in which sentiment plays no part.

We must not be content with the control of the Atlantic Islands. If we are to ensure the hegemony of the Continent, we must also retain strong-points on what was formerly the French Atlantic coast. We must further not forget that the old Kingdom of Burgundy played a prominent role in German history and that it is from time immemorial German soil, which the French grabbed at the time of our weakness.

Dr. Goebbels asked whether a pound of potatoes had the same nutritive value as a pound of meat.

The Führer replied: As far as we know, the food of the soldiers of ancient Rome consisted principally of fruit and cereals. The Roman soldier had a horror of meat, and meat, apparently, was included in the normal rations only when the difficulty of obtaining other supplies made it inevitable.

---

[401] Henri Giraud (1879–1949), the French General captured by German forces in May 1940. Imprisoned at the high-security Prisoner of War (POW) Königstein Castle near Dresden, he escaped using a 150 foot-long rope to lower himself down the castle's cliff face and, using various disguises, reached Switzerland by train and on foot.

From numerous pictures and sculptures it seems that the Romans had magnificent teeth, and this seems to contradict the contention that only carnivorous animals have good teeth. The intervening centuries do not appear to have caused any changes. Travellers in Italy have noticed that the masses still feed on the same things, and that they still have excellent teeth.

One has only to keep one's eyes open to notice what an extraordinary antipathy young children have to meat. It is also an interesting fact that among the negroes the children of those tribes which are primarily vegetarian develop more harmoniously than those of the tribes in which it is customary for the mother to feed her infant up to the age of four or five.

As regards animals, the dog, which is carnivorous, cannot compare in performance with the horse, which is vegetarian. In the same way, the lion shows signs of fatigue after covering two or three kilometres, while the camel marches for six or seven days before even his tongue begins to hang out. Speaking generally, the experts do not take facts sufficiently into consideration. It has been proved that a vegetarian diet—and particularly a diet of potato peelings and raw potatoes—will cure beriberi[402] within a week. Those who adopt a vegetarian diet must remember that it is in their raw state that vegetables have their greatest nutritive value. The fly feeds on fresh leaves, the frog swallows the fly as it is, and the stork eats the living frog.

Nature thus teaches us that a rational diet should be based on eating things in their raw state. Science has proved, too, that cooking destroys the vitamins, which are the most valuable part of our food. It has not yet been established beyond doubt whether cooking destroys merely certain chemical particles or whether it also destroys the essential fermentive juices.

Our children today are much healthier than those of the Imperial and Weimar Republic periods because mothers now realise that they contribute far more to the health of their children if they give them raw vegetables and roots to chew than if they give them boiled milk.

Reich Chancellery, 26th April 1942, midday
Artistes and politics

While lunching hurriedly at the Chancellery before attending a session of the Reichstag, Dr. Goebbels told the Führer of some of his experiences

---

[402] Beriberi is a neurological disease affecting people deficient in vitamin B1.

with artistes in politics. He said that recently he had had to protest again to Jannings[403] about making remarks hostile to the regime. It was with reluctance that Jannings eventually admitted that, in his love of animated conversation, he may have said things which could be misconstrued and enlarged upon to the detriment of the prestige of the State.

The Führer replied: I have long realised that actors and artistes often have such fantastic ideas that one is compelled from time to time to shake an admonitory finger at them and bring them back to earth.

Berlin, 28th April 1942, at dinner

The artistic patrimony of towns—Policy as regards works of art—The claims of Vienna—Budapest and Linz—Fighting the false science of the Church—Plans for a new Linz—Repay the Hungarians in their own coin

Gauleiter Forster turned the conversation to the question of works of art which were the property of Danzig but which were actually at the moment in Cracow, and asked whether these should now be returned to Danzig. The Führer replied: I must say that in principle I am against the idea. If we once start that sort of thing, we shall never end; we should spend all our time examining claims, every town in the place will claim some picture or other, and they will all amuse themselves by trying to prove some connection between themselves and some work of art.

After the French campaign and the occupation of Serbia and the Russian territories, Liebel, the Mayor of Nuremberg, approached me and requested the return to Nuremberg of all the works of art to which he could possibly stake a claim.

If one granted all these requests, the Museums in which the works in question now are would become valueless; not only t hat, but many pictures would find themselves divorced from the environment in which the artist had wished to place them and would thus lose significance.

When I went to see the works of art which had belonged to collections sequestrated from the Jews in Vienna, I insisted that they should remain in Vienna, because their places were earmarked for them in the museums of that city. Contrary to the suggestions made to me, I even insisted that certain other works should be re-assembled in places where they would form the nucleus of new collections—for example, the works of Franz Hals to Linz, and the Tyrolese landscapes to Innsbruck.

---

[403] Emil Jannings was the screen name of the Swiss-born German actor Theodor Emil Janenz (1884–1950). Best known for this 1930 film *Der blaue Engel* ("The Blue Angel") which also starred Marlene Dietrich.

Although my decision was not to the liking of my dear Viennese, I was all the more insistent because I knew that in the course of the five centuries of their reign the Habsburgs had collected in the cellars and store-rooms of Vienna enough works of art to fill three new museums. Of Gobelin tapestries alone there are in the Viennese store-rooms no less than three thousand examples, all worked entirely by hand and all equally magnificent, which the public have never seen.

I know my Viennese inside out! The moment we start to consider a Rembrandt or two taken from the Jews, they will at once start to try, in that gentle, naïve way of theirs, to persuade me to leave all the works of Great Masters in Vienna, arguing that the works of lesser painters will be quite good enough to ensure the happiness of the museums of Linz or Innsbruck.

And what a fuss they made when I announced my decision that any masterpieces which were not required to fill an actual void in the Vienna museums were to be distributed among the museums of the other Alpine and Danubian provinces!

The Führer turns to Speer: Budapest is by far the most beautiful city on the Danube. But I am determined to make of Linz a German town on the Danube which surpasses it, and by so doing to prove that the artistic sense of the Germans is superior to that of the Magyars. Not only shall I have the bank of the river built up in a magnificent fashion, but also I intend to build a number of dwelling houses which will be models of their kind. On the banks of the Danube there will be a great hotel reserved for the "Strength through Joy" organisation, municipal buildings designed by Professor Giesler, a Party House designed by the architect Fick, a building for Army Headquarters, an Olympic Stadium and many other things. As regards bridges, I intend, in contradistinction to Budapest, to have one suspension bridge at Linz.

On the opposite bank I shall construct, as a counter to the pseudo-science of the Catholic Church, an observatory in which will be represented the three great cosmological conceptions of history—those of Ptolemy, of Copernicus and of Hörbiger. The cupola of this edifice will contain a planetarium which will not only satisfy the thirst for knowledge of the visitors but will also be available for purposes of scientific research. The interior decoration will be inspired largely by the ideas of Professor Troost.

In this connection, there was a rather amusing little contretemps. I had amused myself by roughing out some designs for this interior decoration, using for the purpose the red, blue and green pencils I have in my office, and by mistake I sent this very sketch to Frau Troost instead of the birthday card I would done for her! As regards the Party House and the Provincial Parliament, *Reichsleiter* Bormann made a handsome offer which delighted me. As soon as he heard that the plans had been completed, he volunteered to provide the money for the projects. As the Party Treasurer has already undertaken to defray these expenses, I did not feel justified in accepting Bormann's offer; but I am none the less grateful to him.

Ten years after the end of the war Linz must have become the new metropolis of the Danube. I become daily more enthusiastic about this beautifying of Linz, and I think it is the reaction of the artistic sense in me. This city possesses something which no architecture, however magnificent, could give her—a unique natural situation. In spite of the bonds of affection which tie me to Linz, I can honestly say that it is its wonderful position which alone impels me to carry out the project.

The Viennese would be quite wrong to worry that this might prove harmful to their monopoly, or to the cultural interests of the Alpine and Danubian Provinces. Far be it from me to lessen the importance of Vienna, so long as she remains on a sound and solid foundation.

But when one thinks of the truly unique position of Linz, it is impossible, simply out of consideration for the feelings of the Viennese, to give up the idea of making Linz the metropolis of the Danube. It would be a crime. Further, if only to infuriate the Hungarians, everything must be done to embellish and to add to the beauties of Vienna itself. We shall only be repaying the Hungarians in their own coin, once the war is over, for having everywhere and so promptly taken advantage of circumstances and pulled their chestnuts out of the fire.

Munich, 29th April 1942, midday
The value of the Eastern territories—The construction of a gigantic net-work of road and rail communications—Secondary importance of waterways

The Führer discussed with Professor Giesler[404] and Minister Esser the problem of the communication system for the Eastern territories.

In these regions there will have to be a very considerable extension of existing railway lines, but they must not be planned on a local basis. Rapid communication with Constantinople[405] is just as important to

---

[404] Paul Giesler (1895–1945), architect and Minister of the Interior
[405] Constantinople was officially renamed as Istanbul in 1930.

us as is rapid and easy communication between Upper Silesia and the Donetz basin. I envisage through-trains covering the distances at an average speed of two hundred kilometres an hour, and our present rolling-stock is obviously unsuitable for the purpose. Larger carriages will be required—probably double-deckers, which will give the passengers on the upper deck an opportunity of admiring the landscape.

This will presumably entail the construction of a very much broader-gauge permanent way than that at present in use, and the number of lines must be doubled in order to be able to cope with any intensification of traffic. Two of these auxiliary lines in each direction will be reserved for goods traffic. We must plan on a large scale from the beginning, and I envisage for our principal line of communication—that to the Donetz basin—a four-line system. This alone will enable us to realise our plans for the exploitation of the Eastern territories.

I need not say that in the execution of this vast plan we shall meet with many difficulties, but we must not let them discourage us. All the talk about the development of an inland waterway is, in my opinion, just nonsense; in the East there are seven months of winter in the year, and the construction of any inland waterway of practical value is out of the question.

Berghof, 30th April 1942, at dinner

German tenors—A policy for our Operas—The horror of Bruno Walter[406] and Knappertsbusch[407]—Furtwängler,[408] the only real conductor

I am very sorry that Germany at the moment possesses only two really first-class tenors, for these two unfortunates are forced to tear round and round the country singing in town after town with neither rest nor respite. The fault lies with the directors of the Operas and the conductors, who are not at sufficient pains to seek and recruit new talent. As a result of this lack of interest, new-comers are forced to appear solely in the provinces, and the more talent they possess the more extended becomes their repertoire. This is a pity, for no young singer, however talented, can undertake a diversity of roles without harming his voice. Far from being able to develop their talent and improve their

---

[406] Bruno Walter, born Bruno Schlesinger (1876–1962), a German-born Jewish musician who fled Germany in 1933.

[407] Hans Knappertsbusch (1888–1965), a German conductor best known for Wagner, Bruckner and Strauss performances.

[408] Gustav Furtwängler (1886–1954), the German conductor still widely regarded as one of the greatest symphonic and operatic conductors of the 20th century.

voices, they overstrain and ruin them prematurely. These considerations have caused me to order the Director of the Munich Opera to select and train, in a rational way, a troupe of artistes destined for the future Opera of Linz.

I have directed him to proceed with the utmost care and to take as much time—two to five years if necessary—as he thinks fit. I have chosen this method because I think it will permit talented artistes to develop their gifts to their maximum, instead of having to seek their livelihood singing any old thing any old where. During their period of training I will gladly pay allowances to the selected artistes and think it money well spent if, at the end, I am given a company of artistes worthy of the roles they are destined to play.

I hope that the directors of other Operas will follow this example, and that we shall have at our disposal in a few years' time the artistes of whom the German stage has need.

In this connection I would emphasise that the mere possession of a good voice is not enough; these artistes must be taught to act and must be, men and women alike, of good appearance. The eye must also participate in the pleasures of the opera; otherwise one might as well not play the piece at all, but just let the artistes sing their parts.

Above all, the meretricious system of inviting "guest artistes" for particular performances must cease. Why sacrifice the regular artistes instead of giving them an opportunity of showing their talent? The right policy is to encourage those artistes who are accredited to the theatre, and then to hold on at all costs to those who show more than average ability and make it worth their while to refrain from going to Berlin or elsewhere, where all they will get will be a job as an understudy.

Great conductors are as important as great singers. Had there been a sufficiency of good conductors during the time of the Weimar Republic, we should have been saved the ridiculous spectacle of the rise to eminence of a man like Bruno Walter, who in Vienna was regarded as a complete nonentity. It was the Jewish press of Munich, which was echoed by its Viennese counterpart, that drew attention to the man and suddenly proclaimed him to be the greatest conductor in Germany. But the last laugh was against Vienna; for when he was engaged as conductor of the superb Viennese Orchestra, all he could produce was beerhall music. He was dismissed, of course, and with his dismissal Vienna began to realise what a dearth there was of good conductors, and sent for Knappertsbusch.

He, with his blond hair and blue eyes, was certainly a German, but unfortunately he believed that, even with no ear, he could, with his temperament, still produce good music. To attend the Opera when he was conducting was a real penance; the orchestra played too loud, the violins were blanketed by the brass, and the voices of the singers were stifled. Instead of melody one was treated to a series of intermittent shrieks, and the wretched soloists looked just like a lot of tadpoles; the conductor himself indulged in such an extravaganza of gesture that it was better to avoid looking at him at all.

The only conductor whose gestures do not appear ridiculous is Furtwängler. His movements are inspired from the depths of his being. In spite of the very meagre financial support he received, he succeeded in turning the Berlin Philharmonic Orchestra into an ensemble far superior to that of Vienna, and that is greatly to his credit. Some people attribute this superiority to the fact that Berlin possesses a number of genuine Stradivarius, but this explanation must be accepted with reserve. The truth is—and this, to my mind, is much more important—that Berlin enjoys the services of two quite exceptional soloists. One is twenty-three years old, and the second is only nineteen. When one succumbs to the charm of their crystal-clear execution, one realises that the bow of a twenty year-old is bound to have more lightness than that of an old violinist of sixty. With the intention of finding a man of outstanding ability, to become the Director of Music of the future at Linz, I have instructed Klemens Kraus[409] to seek out and train a musician who will prove worthy of this honour.

Berghof, 1st May 1942, midday
Architectural problems—Our architects must plan on a grand scale—
Bayreuth, Weimar and Dresden—The humanities in these towns—
Development of cultural life

I am very grateful to Professor Giesler for having so successfully transformed the Schloss Kiessheim, which is to be our Guest House for distinguished visitors and which was opened in its new role by a visit from the Duce. The general lay-out, which corresponds so closely to my own ideas of spaciousness, pleases me particularly. There is nothing niggardly or trashy, such as one sees in the houses of some of the minor potentates. Schloss Kiessheim is the Guest House of a great nation. Giesler has planned on a grand scale. He has succeeded in leaving vast

---

[409] Clemens Krauss (1893–1954), an Austrian conductor known for his Strauss and Wagner productions.

spaces between the portals and the staircase, and between the staircase and the entrance to the reception halls.

A sense of spaciousness is important, and I am delighted to see our architects planning on broad and spacious lines. Only thus shall we avoid the springing up of more towns in which the houses are cluttered up almost on top of each other, as one sees in Zwickau, Gelsenkirchen and so on.

If I were banished to a town of this kind, devoid of all beauty, I should lose heart and happiness just as surely as if I had been banished from my fatherland. I am therefore determined that some measure of culture and beauty shall penetrate even into the humblest of our towns, and that, step by step, the amenities of all our towns will reach a higher level. There is a lot of truth in the assertion that the culture of a town is dependent upon its traditions. Bayreuth, Weimar and Dresden afford classic examples. It may well be that it is impossible for any city to achieve an appearance which is pleasing to our sense of culture, unless at some time or other some great man has breathed his inspiration into its walls. But we must at least see to it that from the ranks of our Party plenipotentiaries even the smallest little hamlet is given a worthy bearer not only of the torch of National Socialist supremacy, but also of its cultural way of life. If it is not always possible to find the right man in the person of every Kreisleiter, then with the help of the Party and its organisation we must ensure at least that the Kreisleiter becomes the central point of a measure of civilised amenity.

Once this is accomplished, the way is open for a further progress along the path of civilisation and culture. It is not sufficient that a town should have a museum which the students occasionally visit; our representative must see to it that the men of the Labour Service and the *Wehrmacht* find it worthy of visit, and that gradually in this way the interest in, and the appreciation of, art will be aroused throughout the masses of the nation. The eye of the children must be weaned from the niggardly and trained on the grandiose, for only thus will they learn to appreciate both the ensemble and the finer points of any work of art.

3rd May 1942, midday
The Bürgerbrau plot—A Swiss tries his hand at assassination—Measures against assassins—Some unavoidable risks

In the two really dangerous attempts made to assassinate me I owe my life not to the police, but to pure chance. On 9th November 1939, I left the Bürgerbrau ten minutes before the appointed time because of an urgent conference in Berlin which it was imperative that I should attend.

In the other attempt my life was saved because the would-be killer, a Swiss,[410] who stalked me for three months in the neighbourhood of the Berghof, regularly missed me when I went out, and when he tried to continue his stalking in Munich, he was discovered by a railway official. The man apparently had travelled beyond Munich with a ticket from Berchtesgaden to Munich, and the railway official in question asked for an explanation. The story that he had been in Berchtesgaden for several months, trying to deliver a letter to me, aroused the suspicions of the railwayman, who caused him to be held for interrogation. When the man was searched a sealed envelope addressed personally to me was found on him, but the envelope was empty, a circumstance which led to a full confession.

The confessions of this Swiss interested me in so far as they confirmed my conviction that not a soul could cope with an assassin who, for idealistic reasons, was prepared quite ruthlessly to hazard his own life in the execution of his object.

I quite understand why 90 per cent of the historic assassinations have been successful. The only preventive measure one can take is to live irregularly—to walk, to drive and to travel at irregular times and unexpectedly. But that, after all, is merely normal caution, and not prevention.

As far as is possible, whenever I go anywhere by car I go off unexpectedly and without warning the police. I also have given Ratenhuber, the commander of my personal Security Squad, and Kempka, my chauffeur, the strictest orders to maintain absolute secrecy about my comings and goings, and have further impressed on them that this order must still be obeyed even when the highest officials in the land make enquiries.

As soon as the police get to hear that I am going somewhere, they abandon all normal procedure and adopt emergency measures, which, to say the least of it, are most alarming to normal people, and yet they never seem to realise that it is just these emergency antics which are conspicuous and draw attention where no attention is desired. I had

---

[410] Maurice Bavaud (1916–1941), a Swiss catholic theology student purchased a pistol and unsuccessfully stalked Hitler's house in November 1938. When he ran out of money, he tried to stow away on a train to Paris but was arrested in Munich. Convicted of attempted murder, he was executed in 1941.

a splendid example of this sort of thing when, at the time of the *Anschluss*, I went to Vienna and Pressburg.

The police raised the alarm along the whole route both from Vienna to Nicolsburg and on to Pressburg—an action which was all the more dangerous because they simply did not have the necessary forces at their disposal to guard the roads.

Apart from this, the Gestapo plain-clothes men dressed themselves in such an astonishing collection of clothes—rough woollen mackintosh coats, ostler's capes[411] and so forth—that I, and indeed any moron, could recognise them for what they were at a glance. When I gave orders that we were to follow a route other than the one agreed upon and were to stop, like any other citizen, at the traffic lights in the villages, I was able to continue my journey unnoticed and unmolested. Police protection is of great importance only on those occasions when the date, time and place have been precisely fixed. Even on these occasions the activities of the police have a disturbing effect, cause crowds to collect and lead to endless difficulties.

These things, however, must be accepted with good grace on occasions like the First of May, the Ninth of November, the Harvest Festival of Bückeburg, where seven hundred thousand people foregather, and my own birthday. In the midst of such crowds it is easy for some fanatic armed with a telescopic-sighted firearm to take a shot at me from some corner or other; any likely hole or corner, therefore, must be kept under careful observation. During the hours of darkness police searchlights must be so sited that their rays light up these danger-spots and are not, as happened to me in Hamburg, concentrated all the time on my own car.

Narrow streets should, as far as possible, be avoided on official occasions; the five-metre-wide lane leading to the Kroll Opera in Berlin, for example, is potentially one of the most dangerous bits of road I know.

As there can never be absolute security against fanatics and idealists on official occasions, I always make a point of standing quietly upright in my car, and this method has again and again proved the truth of the proverb that the world belongs to the brave. If some fanatic wishes to shoot me or kill me with a bomb, I am no safer sitting down than standing up; and in any case the number of fanatics who seek my life on idealistic grounds is getting much smaller.

---

[411] An "ostler" was someone employed to look after the horses of people staying at an inn, in the era before motor vehicles.

Among the bourgeoisie and the Marxists it would be hard to find a would-be assassin ready to risk his own life, if necessary. The only really dangerous elements are either those fanatics who have been goaded to action by dastardly priests, or nationalistically minded patriots from one of the countries we have occupied; and my many years of experience make things fairly difficult even for such as these.

When I am travelling by night in my car, for instance, I do not think it is any longer possible for any one following us in another car to take a shot at either myself or my chauffeur from the apparently easy position when we are rounding a bend, because, having learned a lesson from the Rathenau plot,[412] I have now installed a searchlight in the back of the car, which allows me to blind the driver of any following car at will.

3rd May 1942, at dinner

Respect for a dead man's Will—The case of Ludendorff—Artistic treasures and the community—Difficulties with the Ministry of Education—Privileges to be respected—The status of Brunswick— Roman schools—Berlin must not monopolise the resources of the Reich—Safeguard the museums of the provinces—Berlin bureaucracy— Administration and decentralisation—Berlin is not an artistic city—The choice of Nuremberg

I must insist that there should be no interference with the last will and testament of the individual, provided, of course, that it does not blatantly run counter to the interests of the State or the nation. If the State gets mixed up in interpreting the last wishes of a deceased, if may well find itself more heavily involved than it expected.

I realised this when Ludendorff died. He expressly stated in his will that he did not wish to be buried either in the Invaliden-Cemetery in Berlin or in the crypt of the Tannenberg Memorial, but at Tutzing. Although this desire was a great disappointment to me, I did not wish to create a precedent, and so I respected the wish of this great soldier.

For the same reasons, it is my firm conviction that the property rights, held in the name of the people by legally constituted bodies such as municipalities, *Gaue* and *Länder,* must be unconditionally respected. Any tampering with them would eliminate one of the most vital

---

[412] Walther Rathenau (1867–1922), a German-born Jew who served as Foreign Minister in 1922. He was assassinated by a right wing group following his assent to the Treaty of Rapallo, which allowed trade with the Soviet Union. The assassination was carried out by armed men in a vehicle which approached Rathenau's from behind.

incentives to human activity and would jeopardise future endeavour.

Take, for example, the case of a community which gathers together a collection of artistic works; if, in the absence of title-deeds assuring possession to the community as such for all time, some strong man comes along and sells and scatters the treasures in all directions, the effect on the public sense of justice will be appalling, and public bodies which otherwise would spend a portion of their resources on the collection of works of art will certainly refrain from doing so.

Unfortunately our Minister of Education, who is responsible for the cultural life of the country, has little understanding for that sort of thing. He quite light-heartedly suggested to me recently that the Academy of Mines at Leoben should be closed, with a view to its subsequent transfer to the future Academy of Technical Sciences at Linz.

The good man seems to have given no thought to the fact that his plan would not only bring ruin to the town of Leoben, which is largely dependent on the Academy for its prosperity, but also that, in and around Linz, mines, which are an elementary essential to the functioning of the Academy, are simply non-existent. It is an act of equally crass stupidity on the part of the Ministry of the Interior to suggest, from the heights of its bureaucratic detachment, that the town of Lindau should be deprived of its status as a county town. Lindau is the cultural centre of the Lake Constance district, and must remain so.

Even a town like Brunswick would be ruined if it were deprived of its status of seat of local government, without being given some equivalent distinction, and I have impressed most emphatically on Göring that, should anything happen to me, he must on no account allow himself to be persuaded by long-winded argument to permit any alteration in the present status of that town.

The Ministry of the Interior is too systematically hide-bound in its outlook. Its jurists overlook the fact that although a town of twenty-five thousand inhabitants may be a simple agricultural centre, easily within the direct administrative competence of the central authority, it may equally well be a centre of tradition and culture with particular administrative needs of its own, which can satisfactorily be met only by an independent municipal administration. In this respect, too, we can learn a lot from the Romans.

They followed the principle of concentration of power in a few hands in time of crisis, but decentralisation of authority in normal times. In the organisation and administration of towns, they allowed themselves to be guided by the needs of the moment, without, however, ever losing sight of the political and cultural aspects of the case. We, too, should be well advised to examine most meticulously all relevant factors before we embark on any large measures of regional reform.

For this reason I have, through *Reichsleiter* Bormann, forbidden, until after the war, any suppression or fusion of the various districts as they at present exist.

I have also taken steps to ensure that Berlin should not take advantage of war conditions and shortages to seize for itself all available building material and the like, at the expense of other towns. The bigger a town is, the more it is tempted to play the role of metropolis, in every sense of the word, and to try to grab everything for itself. This is exactly what Vienna did for centuries; it gathered within its walls all the works of art it could lay its hands on, bleeding white the Alpine and Danubian provinces and leaving them destitute of any sort of cultural or artistic existence. We must see to it that the same thing does not happen at Linz, when we put into execution our plans for the development of that city. There is no point, for example, in emptying the museums of Munich in order to fill those of Linz. As a matter of fact I was a little worried lest this very thing might happen, and it is for this reason that I have started buying in the open market the art treasures that will eventually be destined for the Linz museums. I do not wish to see the museums of one town flourish at the expense of those of other towns.

Suppose we made an exception in the case of Linz and proceeded to pillage all the smaller provincial museums with the object of making one perfect collection at Linz—what would be the result? In the first place we should offend the legal basis on which the ownership of these works is founded; and then there would be no end to the possibilities. We should, in justice, have to accede to the claims of Liebel, the Mayor of Nuremberg, for the return to Nuremberg of all works of art created by the artists of that city, and we should start a scramble for possession of masterpieces which would have neither end nor limits.

In any case, it is absurd to say that a work of art must remain in the place of its origin. A masterpiece knows no local boundaries, and wherever it goes it brings fame and glory both to the artist and to the town which was his home. Mussolini realised this clearly, and it was with this in mind that he made me a present of the famous Discus Thrower.[413]

---

[413] The *Discobolus* ("The Discus Thrower") is a sculpture depicting a discus throw-

The greatest danger which confronts our artistic centres is, to my mind, an increase in the bureaucratic control that the Berlin Ministries already exercise over them. The Berlin bureaucracies confuse central administration, whose proper task is to indicate broad lines and to intervene when help is required, with a species of Unitarianism, which lays a cold and lethal hand on activity throughout the country.

The danger is a very real one, because during the last twenty years the Ministerial bureaucracies have grown and expanded exclusively within the orbit of their own circle; thus, for example, we see a man of extreme mediocrity like Suren promoted to the rank of Under-Secretary of State simply because he has served a stated number of years in the Ministry of the Interior, and quite regardless of the fact that in all his activities he has generally done more harm than good. As a counter-poise to the bureaucrats of the administration we must, therefore, recruit really efficient men in large numbers for the local administrative bodies. Such men, however, must be given the opportunity of proving their mettle in independent administrative jobs. The more decentralised the administration of the Reich becomes, the easier it will be to find efficient people for the key-posts of the central organisation, endowed with the ability to give the necessary broad instructions and the sense to know when their intervention is really necessary.

If we allow the bureaucrats to continue in their present ways, in a few years we shall find that the nation has lost all faith in the administration. Efficient men with both feet planted firmly on the ground will not tolerate that the work they have prepared as, say, mayors, during years of long and anxious endeavour should be rejected or destroyed by the decision of some miserable little jack-in-office in Berlin.

In any case, when the officials of the central administration do intervene in local affairs, they are very seldom in agreement with the local authorities, who have studied the problem in question on the spot and who know quite well what decision ought to be arrived at.

The officials of our Ministries are men of petty minds, for they have proceeded step by step from minor, pettifogging positions to positions of what, to them, seems great importance and responsibility, but to men of real ability seem ridiculous. Do you think that a really capable man in the theatrical business, for example, would accept the

---

er is described in surviving accounts from Antiquity. Hitler acquired the best preserved antique version from Mussolini in 1938. This version, known as the "Lancellotti Discobolus" is now in the National Museum in Rome.

post of Theatrical Adviser to the Ministry of Propaganda—at the seven or eight hundred-mark salary which Government Advisers are paid? These bureaucrats live in the tiny world of their own egoism, and the rest passes them by.

When I think of Bayreuth, I am invariably worried by the thought that one day we may have to appeal to the State for financial aid for the maintenance of its cultural institutions and surrender the administrative control of the city into the hands of the ministerial bureaucrats. This is one of the reasons why I am so interested in the two sons of Frau Winifred Wagner. I hope very much that they will prove capable of carrying on the great work of their parents. As long as I live, I shall always do everything in my power to maintain the prestige of Richard Wagner's city.

I see no better method of safeguarding cultural centres than to confide them to the safe-keeping of the cities which contain them.

Brilliant city though Berlin undoubtedly is, I doubt whether we can make of it a metropolis of the Arts. As a metropolis of political and military power, it is ideal, as I realised on the occasion of the procession organised for my last birthday. But the atmosphere of Berlin is not the atmosphere of an artistic city.

We have no reason for allowing any other town to attain the stature of Berlin. The Reich can be well content with one town of five million inhabitants, Berlin, two towns—Vienna and Hamburg—of a couple of millions, and quite a number which approach the million mark. It would be extremely stupid further to enlarge our great cities and to canalise all cultural activity towards them.

I said one day to Christian Weber that it would be ridiculous to incorporate Starnberg into Munich. To preserve its own character, Munich must remain as it now is. Had I so wished I could have arranged for the Party Congress to take place in Munich. But as I wished as many towns as possible—big, medium and little—to participate and to become centres of German cultural life, I suggested to the Party Committee that we should chose Nuremberg for our Rallies, and our annual gathering there must, I think, give the city for ten days the atmosphere of the Olympic Games Festivals of ancient days.

For the same reasons I refused to remove the Supreme Court of the Reich from Leipzig, but I welcome the suggestion that a Supreme Tribunal for Administrative Affairs should be set up in Vienna. When the war is over, I must discuss with Himmler the question of our Faculties of Medicine and of medical research. It is obviously undesirable that the medical profession should be split up into numberless groups—Army Medical Corps, SS Medical Service, private practice and so on.

4th May 1942, at dinner

Recouping war expenses—Integration of twenty million foreign workers into German industry—No people is ever ruined by its debts

I have already said that the payment of the debts contracted during the war presents no problem. In the first place, the territories which we have conquered by force of arms represent an increase in national wealth which far exceeds the cost of the war; in the second place, the integration of twenty million foreign workers at cheap rates into the German industrial system represents a saving which, again, is greatly in excess of the debts contracted by the State.

A simple calculation, which curiously enough seems to have escaped the notice of the majority of our economic experts, will show the correctness of this contention; the foreign worker earns approximately a thousand marks a year, in comparison with the average yearly earning of two thousand marks by German workers. Work out what this comes to *in toto*, and you will see that the final gain is enormous.

In the assessment of the national wealth I had to explain even to Funk, who, after all, is Economic Minister of the Reich, how the standard of living of the German people had been very considerably raised by the system of employing foreign labour which we had introduced.

One has only to compare the cost of local labour with that of German labour abroad to see that this must be so.

History shows that no country has ever been ruined on account of its debts. You may take it from me that our economists can sleep comfortably and regard the problem of war costs and debts with the utmost optimism.

5th May 1942, midday

Wallonia and Northern France are really German provinces.

The Führer said jokingly that he had read last night with the greatest interest the book by Petri, lent to him by the journalist Frentz and entitled: "Germanisches Volkserbe in Wallonien und Nordfrankreich."[414]

He continued: This work, published in 1937, further strengthens my conviction that Wallonia and northern France are in reality German

---

[414] "German National Inheritance in Wallonia and Northern France," by Franz Petri, Bonn:Röhrscheid, 1937.

407

lands. The abundance of German-sounding name places, the widespread customs of Germanic origin, the forms of idiom which have persisted—all these prove, to my mind, that these territories have been systematically detached, not to say snatched, from the Germanic territories. If there are territories anywhere which we have every right to reclaim, then it is these.

8 May 1942

Frequent changes in the Duce's entourage—Lack of efficient and trustworthy colleagues—Do not move a man who is doing a good job of work—Baldur von Schirach, Axmann,[415] Lauterbacher[416] and Terboven—Lammers a lawyer with common-sense—Importance of efficient collaboration

Bormann remarked that each time the Duce paid us a visit, we found him surrounded by new faces, from which he gathered that the Duce was constantly changing his collaborators. The Führer retorted: If the Duce acts in this manner, then it is undoubtedly because he has no option, for he knows as well as I do that, for the execution of a long-term project, one must be able to count on the continuous collaboration of men in key positions.

The reasons, as I see them, for these constant changes the Duce makes, must be: firstly, that he has not sufficient first-class men at his disposal, and must therefore be constantly weeding out those who do not come up to standard, and secondly that the most capable men among the Fascists are invariably proposed for nomination as Prefects—if they were not, the King, who has the monopoly of nomination, would seize the opportunity of affronting Mussolini by appointing non-Fascists.

I know only too well how difficult it is to find the right man for the more important posts. One is compelled again and again to appeal to the same individuals. When I came to selecting our Commissars for the occupied Eastern territories, I kept on coming back to the names of my old *Gauleiters*; Lohse[417] and Koch,[418] for instance, leapt straight to my mind. I do my best, however, to keep men in those positions in which they have proved themselves, for thus I ensure a really fruitful collaboration. Bormann is quite right when he says that a temporary

---

[415] Artur Axmann (1913–1996), leader of the Hitler Youth from 1940 to 1945.
[416] Hartmann Lauterbacher (1909–1988), Gauleiter of South Hanover-Brunswick.
[417] Hinrich Lohse (1896–1964), Gauleiter in Schleswig-Holstein.
[418] Erich Koch (1896–1986), Gauleiter of East Prussia.

job gives no one the chance to show his capabilities. If a *Gauleiter* has not the assurance of a long term of office, his projects will inevitably suffer, and he will be functioning under a grave handicap. He will perforce ask himself a number of questions—what will my successor think of the work I have undertaken? Will he finish the projects I have started? Will he say that I have chosen my construction sites badly? That I have wasted money with no benefit to the community? And so on.

Although I have succeeded in finding men for the key posts, the SS, the NSKK[419] and the RAD[420]—and in them I have men of the highest capabilities—I have not been able to find the right man to place at the head of the SA. This shows you how rare are men of real merit. As regards the SA, which formed our shock troops before our assumption of power, it has now tended to become a force which often either fails to realise in time which way its duty lies, or bungles the execution of it. When I think of this degeneration of the SA, I cannot help congratulating myself on having found in Schirach the ideal man for the leadership of the National Socialist Youth Movement. To Schirach undoubtedly belongs the credit for having founded and organised on a most solid basis the most important youth movement in the world. Schirach came to me as a very young man, but one who had already distinguished himself among his fellow students.

What splendid young men his collaborators and successors are—Axmann and Lauterbacher! I know exactly what Bormann means when he refers to the outstanding work done by Lauterbacher as *Gauleiter* of Hanover, and I am glad to be able to agree with him, when he expresses appreciation of Lauterbacher as President. Axmann, whom the young people always regarded as a great idealist, is now more admired than ever by them, since he came back from the front so grievously but so gloriously wounded; in the eyes of the Hitler Youth, Axmann is the personification of all the military virtues.

In Terboven I am pleased to have found a man capable of assuming control of Norway, the most difficult Commissarship of the Reich. As he himself told me this very day, if he relaxes his authority for a single instant, he feels as though he were standing on quick-sands. He was, for instance, compelled to arrest a number of Norwegian teachers, who had seen fit to try to sabotage certain measures taken by the German

---

[419] The *Nationalsozialistisches Kraftfahrkorps* ("National Socialist Mechanised Corps"), the NSDAP's motorised transport unit.

[420] The *Reichsarbeitsdienst* ("Reich Labour Service").

High Command—and he is now employing them in building fortifications.

I only regret that the traditional German benevolence of the naval authorities charged with the transportation of these people was once more carried to stupid lengths; the embarkation authorities at first refused to carry these passengers, on the grounds that sufficient life-belts for them were not available! Surely these Norwegians would have been delighted if they had been torpedoed by their beloved British and sent to the bottom of the sea!

Not the least important of the reasons why I have succeeded in filling the key posts with men capable of performing their duties is the fact that they were recruited not on the grounds of having had a juridical training, but because they had successfully passed through the school of life.

The only jurist among my collaborators who is worth a damn is Lammers. Lammers knows that he is there to find legal foundations to fit State requirements, and he does not confuse practical necessity and legal theory. In spite of his legal training, he has a deep knowledge of human nature.

Without the help of these efficient and enthusiastic colleagues, I should certainly not have achieved the political successes which have fallen to me. To those among them who, in their enthusiasm for the regeneration of our nation, go too far and hail me as a Prophet, a second Mahommed or a second Messiah, I can only retort that I can find no trace of any resemblance in myself to a Messiah.

6th May 1942
Infiltration of the Jews into the press and the film world—Their influence on Hugenberg[421] and Rothermere—Independence of the National Socialist press—The financial resources of the Party—How Schwarz got money—Organisation of the Völkischer Beobachter—Amann a shrewd business man

According to a communiqué from Ankara, the Turkish Information Agency is stated to have dismissed a considerable number of Jews from its employment. The Führer remarked that public opinion was formed by the Jews in all the countries actually at war with Germany, and that this had

---

[421] The Hugenberg Group was a media group which controlled advertising and news agencies, press services, press publishers and film companies. Founded by Alfred Hugenberg (1865–1951), it was slowly taken over by the state until it was finally completely absorbed in 1943.

*been the case in Germany, too, even in the days of the Weimar Republic.
He continued:* From time immemorial the Jews have always succeeded
in insinuating themselves into positions from which it was possible to
influence public opinion; they hold, for example, many key positions
both in the press and in the cinema industry. But they are not content
to exercise a direct, open influence; they know that they will attain their
ends more expeditiously if they bring their influence to bear through
the so-called Agencies and by other devious methods.

The most dangerous weapon is the Jewish advertising agency, for,
by cutting off advertising revenue, they can reduce even the greatest
newspapers to the verge of ruin. I myself found it singularly significant
to see how both Hugenberg and Lord Rothermere were compelled to
abandon their attempts to support a reasoned national policy, because
the Jews threatened to cut off their advertising revenue.

Lord Rothermere, who at the time had just published two articles
in support of the Mosley movement, himself described to me at the
Berghof how the Jews went to work, and how it was quite impossible
at short notice to take any effective counter-measures. It has been from
the beginning one of my most potent sources of strength that I made
all the newspapers of the NSDAP, unlike all the other newspapers of
similar importance, completely independent of the Jewish advertising
agencies and thus impervious to economic pressure of this nature.

This happy success with the press of the Party encouraged me to set
about making the whole Party, in every branch of its activities, economically impregnable. I was all the more readily able to accomplish this as
I found in the person of Schwarz, the then Treasurer of the Reich, a
colleague so skilled in the management of the revenues of the Party derived front subscriptions, collections and the like, that our movement
was able to launch the decisive campaign of 1932 from its own financial
resources. Apart from Mutschmann,[422] it was Dr. Ley who collected the
most money for the Party. By describing me as a genuine monster, he
made the industrialists and their ladies so curious to see me that they
were willing to pay anything up to two hundred marks for a seat at one
of my meetings. Unfortunately, a great deal of the money thus collected
was later lost in Ley's subsequent activities in the newspaper industry,
for he failed to realise that the printing-presses owned by the Party
were bringing ruin to the newspapers of the Party.

---

[422] Martin Mutschmann (1879–1947), Gauleiter of Saxony.

For all our propaganda tours, the Party-owned presses had to print all the pamphlets without any guarantee of expenses. A man like Müller, who ran the printing-presses for the *Völkischer Beobachter* in his own name, and for his own profit, was never victimised in this way. He would only accept orders for pamphlets against cash payment, and he always refused any dubious orders by saying that his workmen fed themselves not on political convictions, but on the pay he gave them. Our local chiefs, on the other hand, went on the theory that idealism should replace payment as far as the Party printing-presses were concerned—a theory so economically unsound that it threatened to ruin the presses in question.

The fact that I was able to keep the *Völkischer Beobachter* on its feet throughout the period of our struggle—and in spite of the three failures it had suffered before I took it over—I owe first and foremost to the collaboration of *Reichsleiter* Amann.

He, as an intelligent business man, refused to accept responsibility for an enterprise if it did not possess the economic prerequisites of potential success. Thanks to this rule of his, the publishing firm of Eher, the proprietors of the *Völkischer Beobachter,* developed into one of the most powerful newspaper trusts in the world, beside which the American Press Lords appeared like pygmies.

This success is all the more remarkable when one realises that, when I took it over, the *Völkischer Beobachter* had no more than seven thousand subscribers, not a single advertising contract in its pocket, and not a penny in the till for the purchase of the paper it was printed on! If I had not had all these worries with the Party press, I should probably have remained ignorant of business methods, but this experience was a good school.

My most tragic moment was in 1932, when I had to sign all sorts of contracts in order to finance our electoral campaign. I signed these contracts in the name of the Party, but all the time with the feeling that, if we did not win, all would be forever lost.

In the same way, I today sign contracts in the name of the Reich, quite confident in our ultimate success, but equally conscious of the fact that, if the war is lost, then the German people is inevitably and irretrievably lost with it.

No expense, therefore, is too great provided that it contributes to the assurance of our final victory.

7th May 1942, at dinner
Loss of the British cruiser Edinburgh—*British hypocrisy—German respect for the truth*

A Reuter telegram had just announced the loss of a British cruiser of ten thousand tons, H.M.S. "Edinburgh".

I think we can claim to have extorted this bit of information very cleverly from the British. As the commander of the submarine which was responsible was not able to see the actual sinking, he contented himself with reporting that the *Edinburgh* had been hit by a torpedo. Our official communiqué, therefore, had to be couched in cautious terms. The detailed report left us in little doubt that the vessel had, indeed, been sunk, and in subsequent official news bulletins allusion was occasionally made to the sinking. In this way we have forced the British to admit their loss.

There are two lessons to be learned from this episode: 1. Germany is scrupulous about the truth. But she must not be too pedantic where truth is concerned. I am frequently receiving reports from the front to the effect that the troops, reading the cautious and carefully weighed phrases of the official communiqué, often feel that the full extent of their efforts has not been appreciated at Headquarters. 2. Once one is convinced of a fact—be it of a political or a military nature—one must proclaim it throughout the world. This is the only way in which such consummate hypocrites as the British can be made to confess the truth.

8th May 1942, midday
The role of Crete—No German fleet in the Mediterranean

I do not intend to make Crete into a German strong-point. If I did, I should have to keep a German fleet in the Mediterranean, and that would create a perpetual danger of conflict with Turkey. Our retention of Crete, in the eyes of the Turks, would be merely the opening gambit in a struggle for the control of the Dardanelles. In the circumstances, the most we shall do in Crete after the war will be to maintain a centre for our Strength through Joy organisation.

8th May 1942, evening
Secret Sessions of the British Parliament

The Führer drew attention to the fact that the British Parliament had already held about twenty Secret Sessions. He added: Up to the moment we have not heard a word about what occurred at these Sessions. This is a powerful tribute to the solidarity which unites the British people.

11th May 1942, at dinner
A national sanctuary for our great men—The German sense of family—
Production of honey

It is perfectly natural that a people should have the wish to see the great men of the nation reposing in some sort of national sanctuary. In accordance with the wishes he expressed, Ludendorff has been buried in Tutzing, but I hope that one day his wife will consent to the transfer of his remains to the *Soldatenhalle* in Berlin. I doubt, though, whether she will give this consent unless she has the assurance that she will be allowed to rest beside him when the time comes.

In a like manner, the Hindenburg family have accepted a tomb for the "Old Gentleman" in the Tannenberg monument, on condition that a place is reserved there for his wife. These sentiments are in harmony with the German sense of family, and they must be meticulously respected. For many of our great men, their wives have been the ideal companions of their whole lives, their comrades faithful unto death, their unbreakable shield through all vicissitudes and their inexhaustible sources of strength.

German apiarists could increase their honey production tenfold. Honey was the principal sweetener of the ancient and Middle Ages, and was used even to sweeten wine. The old German drink, Meth, which in my youth was sold at all the Fairs, also had a honey basis. The first cakes we ever exported were the honey-cakes of Nuremberg.

12th May 1942, at dinner
Sound economic principles—Problem of fats and whale oil—Prussian
colonisation mistakes—One hundred million Germans in the Eastern
territories—Work of prisoners of war—German migration eastwards—
Justification of use of force—Lesson from the French in Alsace—Problem
of Alsace-Lorraine—A policy of prudence—Jews with blue eyes and
blond hair—Racial regeneration and moral issues—Marriage by trial—
Nostalgia and poetic sense of Nordic races—"Moral cannibalism"

If we are satisfactorily to solve the problems of the Food Plan and the Industrial Plan, we must get back to sane economic principles. These, unfortunately, disappeared from the moment that our economists began to influence our politicians.

Take fats, for example. Our position now would have been very different if, at the opportune moment, we had paid proper attention to the whale-fishing industry and its rational exploitation. Whale oil not only possesses anti-rickets virtues, but also has the advantage that it can be stored indefinitely. We have today various processes which enable us to make good use of 88 per cent of a whale; apart from the oil, the meat can be preserved, leather can be made from the skin, and the fin-coverings furnish the basis for a material to all intents and purposes indestructible. The organisation of our whale-fishing industry is therefore for us a problem of the most pressing significance.

Gauleiter Forster recalled that in 1830 the population of the town of Thorn[423] *was predominantly German, but that by 1939 the German element had dwindled to quite insignificant proportions. This elicited the following reflections from the Führer:* The fault lies with the policy pursued by Prussia during the last hundred and fifty years. During that period, the Prussian Government transformed the German eastern territories into a veritable punitive colony, sending only such teachers, Government officials and officers as had for some reason or other fallen from grace, or whom it was desired to remove from the functions they had been exercising.

We must make good the mistakes committed by Prussia, and we must do it in the next ten years. At the end of that period I shall expect my *Gauleiters* to be in a position to inform me that these regions have become once again German.

Forster agreed that this might be achieved in the Danzig-West Prussian province. To succeed, it would be necessary, he thought, to appeal to the best elements of the old Reich and to restrict recruitment to men under fifty. To men above that age one could well apply the adage: "Old trees cannot be transplanted".

I agree. For the re-population of our Eastern territories it is to the younger generation, obviously, that we must turn in the first instance. We must imbue them with a feeling of pride in Being invited to go to a country where they will not find their bed nicely made for them, but will be compelled, on the contrary, to create from the beginning—and we must make them understand that we expect them to build up something truly magnificent.

One attraction which will certainly appeal to the young is that by emigrating in this fashion they will find opportunities for promotion infinitely more rapid than those of their less enterprising comrades who remain quietly at home, content to follow the beaten track. My long-term policy aims at having eventually a hundred million Germans

---

[423] The town of Thorn was located in West Prussia on the bank of the Vistula River. In the present-day, it is called Torun and is in Poland.

settled in these territories. It is therefore essential to set up machinery which will ensure constant progression, and will see to it that, million by million, German penetration expands. In ten years' time we must be in a position to announce that twenty million Germans have been settled in the territories already incorporated in the Reich and in those which our troops are at present occupying.

Of what can be done for the inhabitants of these regions in the way of civilised amenities we can get some idea from the Poles, who themselves have succeeded in laying out in the heart of the town of Gotenhafen[424] a series of broad and beautiful arterial roads.

Gauleiter Forster intervened. Even in war-time, he claimed, there were certain cultural aspects which should not be neglected. Turning to the example of Gotenhafen, he remarked that the town possessed three small cinemas but not one large one. The result was that, when warships came into the port to rest, the sailors—whose delight it is to go ashore— were unable to find those distractions they eagerly desired. The materials necessary for the construction of a large entertainment hall, which could later be equipped as a cinema, were certainly available on the spot. The construction could not be undertaken, because the necessary labour, which could easily be furnished by sixty Russian prisoners of war, had been refused.[425] *The Führer continued:* In a case like this we must use common sense; and an undertaking which is so obviously desirable, must not be allowed to lapse simply for want of temporary prisoner-of-war labour. If *Gauleiter* Forster has the necessary material at his disposal, then we must forthwith give him the prisoners he needs for the completion of the construction.

Generally speaking, I am of the opinion that in cases like this practical considerations should be regarded as the determining factor, and particularly so when it is a question of construction to be undertaken in the Eastern territories. One must resolutely turn a blind eye to the counsels of moderation emanating from a tea-table conference in Berlin. The mistakes made by the Prussian Government in these territories which we are trying to resuscitate are too numerous for us to be hidebound by theoretical edicts.

---

[424] Known in Polish as the city of Gdynia.

[425] A note inserted by Martin Bormann in the original manuscript at this point reads "These pages contain many inaccuracies. In the notes taken of a conversation of considerable length, Dr. Picker fails to indicate precisely who were the speakers and who uttered the various opinions expressed."

From the cursory research made into the causes of the diminution of population of Germanic origin in the regions, two appear to stand out. They are: the nobility and the clergy.

We know quite well to what degree the Roman Catholic Church made common cause with Poland in the political struggles. What is less known is the fact that in these regions the German nobility was entirely indifferent and took no pains at all to put German interests before all others. On the contrary, with these gentry, the question of caste was of primary consideration, even when it was a question of Polish nobles. *Gauleiter* Forster is perfectly right when he says that this tendency was greatly fostered by common keenness on shooting and hunting, which constituted a species of open-air freemasonry.

Everything possible was done to dispossess the small German landowner and to replace German agricultural labourers by Poles. Indeed, it is no exaggeration to say that the German nobility struck a mortal blow at the Germanic conception and undermined all the efforts that were made to maintain it.

The Prussian Government, by failing to take measures to counteract these tendencies, gave proof of its total ignorance of historic values. The German Emperors obviously had very good reasons when they applied themselves to the task of forming and maintaining in these South-eastern territories a number of small Germanic colonies. It was done deliberately, and it was the aim of their policy that there should live and develop in these marches of the Reich a population of Germanic origin as dense as possible. If we wish to correct the mistakes of the last century in this respect, we must act decisively. We must remember the example set by the knights of the Germanic Orders, who were by no means kid-gloved. They held the Bible in one hand and their sword in the other. In the same way our soldiers in the East must be animated by the National Socialist faith and must not hesitate to use force to gain their ends, if need be.

We can even learn a lesson from the way the French behaved in Alsace. Without the slightest regard for the generations of men who would have to suffer in consequence, they set to work to eradicate from Alsace every vestige and trace of German influence, thrusting brutally the customs and the culture of France down the throats of the inhabitants. Acting in the same way we will mercilessly wipe out bilingualism in these territories, and the radical methods to which we shall have recourse will themselves prove their efficiency, even on the population hostile to Germanisation. We shall rapidly achieve a clear-cut situation, so that, by the second generation, or at latest by the third, these regions will have been completely pacified.

As regards Alsace and Lorraine, if we want to re-make these into authentic German provinces, then we must drive out all those who do not voluntarily accept the fact that they are Germans. *Gauleiter* Burckel has already taken severe measures in this sense—but we shall still have to get rid of a further quarter of a million of "frenchified" Alsatians. Should we send them to France, or should we send them to colonise the Eastern territories? From the point of view of principle, this is of no great importance. It is just a question of opportunity. And to fill the void left by their departure presents no problem at all.

Baden alone can provide innumerable peasant sons willing to settle in Alsace and Lorraine, particularly as there is little room for them to remain in their own homeland. Actually, the farms in Baden are too small to allow a German family to rear on them a family of more than two children.

As regards the Germanisation of the Eastern territories, we shall not succeed except by the application of the most severe measures. Nevertheless I am convinced that these territories will bear a profound Germanic imprint after fifty years of National Socialist history!

Gauleiter Forster quoted the problems raised by numerous special cases. He quoted the case of a Polish workman employed in the theatre at Graudenz, who wished to become a German national and stated in support of his claim that he had a German grandmother. Should an application of this kind be rejected out of hand? One thing was certain— no German would wish to do the work that this Pole was doing in the Graudenz theatre. There were, added Forster, the problems of the Catholic Sisters of Charity, who were doing splendid work among victims of contagious diseases, and of the Polish women working in the household of a badly wounded German. In Forster's opinion, if any Pole desired to acquire German nationality, the decision should depend upon the general impression made by the candidate. Even in cases where it was not possible to trace exactly the antecedents of the individual, there were nevertheless certain ethnical characteristics, which, taken in conjunction with character and standard of intelligence, gave sure guidance.

According to Forster, it would appear that Professor Günther,[426] a specialist in these matters, was quite right when he asserts, after a tour of

---

[426] Hans F. K. Günther (1891–1968), Germany's foremost racial scientist.

ten-odd days through the province of Danzig, that four-fifths of the Poles living in the north of that province could be Germanised. When called upon to make decisions in such cases one should not forget, added Forster, that real life is always stronger than theory, and that therefore one should Germanise wherever possible, bearing in mind past experience and relying on one's common sense. In the southern and south-eastern parts of the province, it would be better to start by establishing garrisons, with the object of "resuscitating" the population, and only later to examine the possibilities of Germanisation. The thing to be avoided in all these regions and throughout the intermediary period was the introduction of German priests. It would be far better to support the Polish clergy.

Polish priests, with the pressure that could be put on them, would prove more malleable. One could count on their going each Saturday to the Governor and asking what should be the subject of their sermon for the next day.

Even better would be to persuade the Polish Bishop to remain in close touch with the German Gauleiter, and thus to ensure the transmission, through him, of all the instructions thought desirable to the priests under him.[427] *"In this way, Forster concluded, it would be possible to maintain order in the country, even during the transition period.*

The views of Gauleiter Forster met with strong opposition, especially from Reichsleiter Bormann. The latter admitted the necessarily empirical character of some of the decisions to be taken, but maintained that, as regards the Poles, care should be exercised not to Germanise them on too wide a scale, for fear they might inoculate the German population with too strong a dose of their blood, which could have dangerous consequences.

At this point the Führer spoke again: It is not possible to generalise on the extent to which the Slav races are susceptible to the Germanic imprint. In point of fact, Tsarist Russia, within the framework of her pan-Slav policy, propagated the qualification Slav and imposed it on a large diversity of people, who had no connection with the Slavonic race. For example, to label the Bulgarians as Slavs is pure nonsense; originally they were Turkomans.

The same applies to the Czechs. It is enough for a Czech to grow a moustache for anyone to see, from the way the thing droops, that his origin is Mongolian. Among the so-called Slavs of the South the Dinars

---

[427] Note by Bormann in margin reads: "According to Forster's opinion, which is quite wrong."

are predominant. Turning to the Croats, I must say I think it is highly desirable, from the ethnical point of view, that they should be German-ised. There are, however, political reasons which completely preclude any such measures.

There is one cardinal principle. This question of the Germanisation of certain peoples must not be examined in the light of abstract ideas and theory. We must examine each particular case. The only problem is to make sure whether the offspring of any race will mingle well with the German population and will improve it, or whether, on the contrary (as is the case when Jew blood is mixed with German blood), negative results will arise.

Unless one is completely convinced that the foreigners whom one proposes to introduce into the German community will have a benefi-cial effect, well, I think it's better to abstain, however strong the senti-mental reasons may be which urge such a course on us. There are plen-ty of Jews with blue eyes and blond hair, and not a few of them have the appearance which strikingly supports the idea of the Germanisation of their kind. It has, however, been indisputably established that, in the case of Jews, if the physical characteristics of the race are sometimes absent for a generation or two, they will inevitably reappear in the next generation.

One thing struck me when I visited the arsenal at Graz.[428] It is that among the thousand suits of armour to be seen there, not one could be worn by a present-day Styrian—for they are all too small. To me, that is a proof that the representatives of the Germanic tribes who settled formerly in Styria not only infused new strength into the indigenous blood-stream, but also, by virtue of their own more vigorous blood, imposed their own attributes on the natives, and thus created a new racial type. This encourages me to station troops who are ethnically healthy in those regions where the race is of poor quality and thus to improve the blood-stock of the population.

You may object that such a practice might well undermine the mor-al sense of the German people. My answer to that is that it is just the sort of horrified objection one would expect from the moral hypocrite and the pretentious upper ten thousand. These people are shocked at the idea that a Turk may have four legitimate wives, but they admit that the Prussian Princes had forty, and often more, mistresses in the course

---

[428] The Styrian Armoury in Graz, located at the Joanneum Universal Museum, was founded in 1811 and is the largest historic armoury in the world.

of their lives. Such hypocrisy drives me to fury. The Prussian Prince, as he gets bored with his successive mistresses, can pack them off like bits of refuse of no importance, and we have here among us blackguards who regard them as men of honour.

And these same renegades heap sarcasm on the honest German citizen who, with complete disregard of caste, marries the girl by whom he has had a child! It is these hypocrites who are responsible for mass abortions and for the existence of all those healthy women deprived of a man, simply as the result of reigning prejudice. Is there a more lovely consecration of love, pray, than the birth of a handsome babe, glowing with health?

Although it is obvious to the eyes of any reasonable person that nature blesses the love of two beings by giving them a child, these sinister degenerates claim, if you please, that the status of a man or a woman depends on a sealed document given by the State—as if that were of any importance in comparison with the ties which unite two people in love!

To my way of thinking, the real ideal is that two beings should unite for life and that their love should be sanctified by the presence of children. If our farms have remained often for centuries, in some cases for as long as seven hundred years, in the possession of the same family, it is for the most part because marriages were arranged only when an infant was on the way.

And for centuries, the Catholic Church bowed to this custom and tolerated what was called "the trial". When the birth of the infant was imminent, the priest would remind the future father of his duty to marry. Unfortunately the Protestant Church has broken with these healthy customs and has prepared the way, with the aid of laws written or unwritten, for a hypocrisy whose object it is to stigmatise as something shameful a marriage which has been provoked by the arrival of a child. And don't let us forget, if we are going to be completely truthful, that a large part of the Prussian nobility owes its existence to a *faux pas* on the part of one of the girls of the bourgeoisie.

Moreover, these prejudices only operate in reverse, and logic has no bearing on the trend of our desires—for the admissibility of the dissolution of marriage on account of incompatibility is legally recognised. If it is contrary to the law of nature to insist on the maintenance of a union in which the partners are unable to agree, it is no less wrong to put obstacles in the way of a marriage justifiable on the grounds of perfect reciprocal unity. My age saves me from the suspicion that I am perhaps pleading *pro domo,* and so I am able to invite attention to the importance of this problem.

I shall have no peace of mind until I have succeeded in planting a seed of Nordic blood wherever the population stand in need of regeneration. If at the time of the migrations, while the great racial currents were exercising their influence, our people received so varied a share of attributes, these latter blossomed to their full value only because of the presence of the Nordic racial nucleus.

Thus it is that we have acquired a sense of poetry, a tendency to nostalgia, which finds its expression in music. But it is thanks to those attributes that are peculiar to our race and which have been preserved in Lower Saxony that we have been able harmoniously to absorb extraneous characteristics—for we possess one faculty which embraces all the others, and that is, the imperial outlook, the power to reason and to build dispassionately.

In the notes in which the ideas of Frederick the Great were jotted down, I was pleased to find again and again opinions similar to those I have just expressed. For instance, when *der alte Fritz* stigmatises as "moral cannibalism" the opposition to his healthy racial policy, which was on all fours with our own, and when he comes out in favour of marriage based on the presence of an illegitimate child, then I have nothing but approval.

13th May 1942, at dinner
Political instability of Vichy—France's alternatives—Inadequacy of Pétain—Mistrust of Laval[429]—Dangers of a phantom Government—What Germany will keep

The thing that strikes me above all in the present-day policy of the French is the fact that, because they were anxious to sit on every chair at the same time, they have not succeeded in sitting firmly on any one of them. The explanation is that the soul of the country has been torn asunder.

In the Vichy Government alone a whole heap of tendencies is apparent—anti-Semitic nationalism, clerical pro-Semitism, royalism, the spirit of revolution and so on. And as a final misery, if an energetic man make a mistake, there seems to be no provision in the political plan whereby a swift and clear-cut decision can be reached. There are never-

---

[429] Pierre Laval (1883–1945), Prime Minister of France from 1931 to 1932, and from 1935 to 1936. He again held the post in Vichy France from 1940 to 1944.

theless only two possible courses which French policy can pursue, and France must choose one of the following:

(a) She must renounce her metropolitan territory, transfer her seat of Government to North Africa and continue the war against us with all the resources of her African colonial empire, or

(b) She must join the Axis Powers, and thus save the greater part of her territory. She must intervene in Central Africa and ensure for herself possessions there, which will compensate her for the loss of the territories which she will inevitably have to cede, when the peace treaty is signed, to Germany, Italy and Spain.

If she adopts the second alternative, France will not only have a chance of participating actively in the war against Britain and the United States, and thus of realising her ambitions in Africa, but she will also win the good-will of the Axis Powers. If France makes this decision, our communications to North Africa will be child's play. Further, such a decision would accelerate the entry of Spain into the war, and the French fleet would immediately become an important factor in the current military operations. Her fortunes, then, would all be staked on one card. If she comes in with us, however, she must clearly understand that it is essential for us to retain the strategic positions which we at present occupy on the Channel coast. At the same time she must resign herself to the idea of satisfying the territorial demands of Germany, Italy and Spain, both in Europe and in Tunisia. She will be able to compensate herself by conquests in Central Africa.

On the other hand, if she adopts the first solution, or if she persists in her present equivocal attitude, then she must expect to lose all along the line. Somehow or other the Americans will get a grip on Martinique; while Britain will not only never dream of giving up Madagascar, but will also certainly do her best to recoup her Far Eastern losses by thrusting towards southern and western Africa, with the object of founding new dominions there. Spain will not withdraw her demands—nor will Italy. And Japan certainly has no intention of restoring Indo-China to France, where the latter now has nothing more than a caricature of a Government.

A country whose future depends on so tragic an alternative requires at its head a man capable of coldly facing the consequences of the situation. Marshal Pétain is not the man. It is true that he has extraordinary authority over the French, but he owes this primarily to the prestige conferred on him by his great age. When it is a question of taking decisions upon which everything, absolutely everything, depends for the future of his country, I think that the experience of a man of that age is of itself a handicap. For myself, I admit that I now think twice before giving a decision in a case where, ten years or so ago, I should have jumped without hesitation.

Such being the situation, I feel that any meeting with Marshal Pétain would be devoid of interest, in spite of the respect in which I hold this upright man, who, when he was in Spain, always maintained courteous relations with our ambassador and who, moreover, has never ceased to advise his Government to come to terms with Germany. To make a comparison, I would say it would be like giving the principal part in an opera to some famous old singer covered with glory, and then, when faced with a deplorable result, consoling oneself by saying that twenty or thirty years ago, anyway, he had a throat of gold.

It is a great pity that among Pétain's colleagues there is not one capable of taking the decisive action required. Laval, for example, is nothing but a parliamentary hack. The net result is that the Vichy Government has no real power. A phantom Government is always a source of danger. If France is at the moment safe from disintegration, protected against the threat of a *coup de main* or a civil war, she owes it all to the presence of our occupation troops, who constitute the only real power in the country.

During an inspection I was making of the Atlantic Wall constructions, I was accosted by one of the workmen. "Mein Führer," he said, "I hope we're never going away from here. After all this tremendous work, that would be a pity." There is a wealth of wisdom in the man's remark, for it shows that a man hates to abandon a place on which he has worked so hard. I need scarcely say that nothing on earth would persuade us to abandon such safe positions as those on the Channel coast, captured during the campaign in France and consolidated by the Organisation Todt, and retire into the narrow confines of the North Sea!

In the same way, we must organise the Crimea in such a manner that, even in the dim future, we should never be constrained to leave to others the benefits of the work we have done there. We shall have to modernise the ports of the Crimea and establish strong fortifications on the narrows which command the approaches to the peninsula. These fortifications will have to be so strong that the workmen who constructed them will themselves be convinced that here we have an impregnable position. It will be sufficient to have just one such base in the Crimea, for the Black Sea has for us an interest that is purely economic. And, as we have no interests in the Mediterranean, this should give us, after the war, a chance of establishing really amicable relations with Turkey.

14th May 1942, at dinner

Rise of the Völkischer Beobachter—*"Freedom of the Press"—The National Socialist journalist—Role of a national Press—The lure of authority—The task of command*

If the *Völkischer Beobachter*, which originally had merely a few thousand subscribers, has now become a gigantic enterprise, in which reckoning is by the million, we owe it first and foremost to the exemplary industry of *Reichsleiter* Amann. Thanks to a quite military discipline, he has succeeded in getting the very best out of his colleagues, suppressing particularly all contact between the editorial and the administrative staffs. I don't know how often Amann, when telling me of the great financial development of the newspaper, begged me to make no mention of the fact in front of Rosenberg, the editor-in-chief, or of the other members of the editorial staff. Otherwise, he used to say, they would plague him for higher salaries. What discipline, with the severity that is proper to it, Amann succeeded in imposing on all his colleagues! He behaved as if the editorial staff and the editors were nothing but a necessary evil.

And yet—what a task of immense educational value he has thus accomplished! He has moulded exactly the type of journalist that we need in a National Socialist State. We want men who, when they develop a theme, do not first of all think of the success the article will bring them or of the material benefits it will give them; as formers of public opinion, we want men who are conscious of the fact that they have a mission and who bear themselves as good servants of the State.

As a supporter of this viewpoint, I have tried, since I came into power, to bring the whole of the German press into line. To do so, I have not hesitated, when necessary, to take radical measures. It was evident to my eyes that a State which had at its disposal an inspired press and journalists devoted to its cause possessed therein the greatest power that one could possibly imagine.

Wherever it may be, this fetish of the liberty of the press constitutes a mortal danger *par excellence.* Moreover, what is called the liberty of the press does not in the least mean that the press is free, but simply that certain potentates are at liberty to direct it as they wish, in support of their particular interests and, if need be, in opposition to the interests of the State.

It is not easy, at the beginning, to explain all this to the journalists and to make them understand that, as members of a corporate entity, they had certain obligations to the community as a whole. And endless repetitions were necessary before I could make them see that, if the press failed to grasp this idea, it would end only in harming itself.

Take the case of a town with, say, a dozen newspapers; each one of them reports the various items in its own way, and in the end the reader can only come to the conclusion that he is dealing with a gang of opium-smokers.

In this way the press gradually loses its influence on public opinion and all contact with the man in the street. The British press affords so excellent an example that it has become quite impossible to gauge British public opinion by reading the British newspapers. This has been carried to such a pass, that as often as not the press bears no relation whatsoever to the lines of thought of the people.

That is exactly what happened in Vienna before 1914, in the time of Burgomeister Lueger. In spite of the fact that the entire Viennese press was in the hands of Jewry and in the pay of the Liberals, Lueger, the leader of the Christian Social Party, regularly obtained a handsome majority—a fact which showed all too clearly the hiatus existing between the press of Vienna and public opinion.

As, in the military sphere, the aircraft has now become a combat weapon, so the press has become a similar weapon in the sphere of thought. We have frequently found ourselves compelled to reverse the engine and to change, in the course of a couple of days, the whole trend of imparted news, sometimes with a complete *volte face*. Such agility would have been quite impossible, if we had not had firmly in our grasp that extra-ordinary instrument of power which we call the press—and known how to make use of it.

A year before, when the Russo-German Pact was signed, we had the task of converting to a completely reverse opinion those whom we had originally made into fanatical opponents of Russia—a manoeuvre that must have appeared to be a rare old muddle to the older National Socialists.

Fortunately, the spirit of Party solidarity held firm, and our sudden about-turn was accepted by all without misgiving. Then, on 22nd

June 1941, again: "About turn!" Out shot the order one fine morning without the slightest warning! Success in an operation of this nature can only be achieved if you possess the press and know how to make tactical use of it. When you regard the role of the press from this angle, you will realise at once that the profession of the journalist now is very different from that of the journalist of yore. There was, indeed, a time when the profession of journalism was one without any real importance, for rarely had the individual journalist any opportunity to give proof of personal character. Today, the journalist knows that he is no mere scribbler, but a man with the sacred mission of defending the highest interests of the State.

This evolution has been in progress throughout the years following our taking power, and today the journalist is conscious of his responsibilities, and his profession appears to him in a new light. Viewed in this way, the role of the press must be guided by certain principles, which must be rigorously applied.

For example, when there are problems, over which men of eminence are scratching their heads without being able to find the solution, it is unwise in the extreme to air them in public; much better wait till the thing is settled.

Before a military operation, no one would dream of communicating the orders to the troops, so that the rank and file could discuss them among themselves and express their opinion of the best way of carrying out the operation. To act in such a manner would be tantamount to a surrender of all sense of responsibility, all sense of authority, and a negation of all reason. In the same way, when a choice between two models of tanks is under consideration, it is not the rank and file who are asked to decide which shall be put into production.

Whatever the sphere of activity, when the experts are in doubt, higher, authority alone must make the decision. A nation desires leadership, and once it sees that its Chiefs are hesitant about what should be done, then all authority goes by the board. For those in whom authority is vested it is an honour to have to take decisions and to accept the responsibility for the results thereof. The people will more readily forgive the mistakes made by a Government—which, as often as not, by the way, escape their notice—than any evidence of hesitancy or lack of assurance. When the leaders recoil from the responsibility of taking a decision, the people become uneasy. Obviously, then, those in authority must never permit their decisions to be criticised by those subordinate to them. The people themselves have never claimed such a right. Only an inveterate tub-thumper would think of such a thing. A people submits thus voluntarily to authority primarily because its instincts are of a feminine rather than a dominant nature. In the married state a woman will sometimes perhaps reconnoitre a bit, to see whether she could impose her will, but deep within her she has no desire at all to wear the trousers.

It's the same thing with the people. Sticking to military simile, a company does not expect its commander to consult it on all points. This explains how the populace came to cut off the head of a being so pusillanimous as Louis XVI—for the attitude of this King towards the people was far less severe than that of Napoleon; but in the latter the people had recognised a leader—and a man worthy of their veneration.

In short, the people expect not only that their leaders should govern them, but also that they should look after them. For the same reason the officer wielding the greatest authority is he who succeeds in deserving the confidence of his men by paying attention to their well-being. Let him but fuss about their food, their sleeping-quarters and their little family worries, and his men will go through fire for him, even though in other respects he may be an exceptionally severe and hard taskmaster. The whole gamut of human conduct depends on simple ideas such as these; it is only the scale that varies.

During the showing of a film of Tibet, *Reichsleiter* Dietrich was struck with the way in which the wild horses of the high Tibetan plains followed the stallion who was guiding them. And what is true of wild horses applies equally to every community of creatures desirous of safeguarding its survival. If the ram leader is not in his place, the flock of sheep disintegrates. This undoubtedly explains why monkeys put to death any members of their community who show a desire to live apart. And what the apes do, men do, too, in their own manner.

Bismarck was perfectly right when he said that any human society which suppressed the death penalty, the ultimate expression of human defence against the a-social, merely from fear of a possible error of justice, was simply destroying itself.

However one lives, whatever one does or undertakes, one is invariably exposed to the danger of making mistakes. And so, what, indeed, would become of the individual and of the community, if those in whom authority was vested were paralysed by fear of a possible error, and refused to take the decisions that were called for?

15th May 1942, midday
Relations between home and front—Comparison with 1914-18—Ludendorff blackmailed by Jewish Press—The narrow-mindedness of the bourgeoisie—Settling accounts with the Jewish thieves—German honorary titles—Honours to foreigners—A new German Order

The attitude of the German people towards the soldiers at the front is today very different from that which obtained generally during the Great War. Today, men working in industry accept without demur a fourteen-hour stretch of labour without pause for rest. Such a thing would have been regarded as out of the question in the Great War— otherwise it would have been possible, in 1917–18, to manufacture the number of armoured vehicles that were required. In those days a quite exaggerated consideration was shown not only to deserters, but also to profiteers in the rear. Their misdeeds were noted with scandalous indifference, and this attitude contributed directly to the disintegration of the country. The collections (which nowadays are made by the Party) were in those days made by companies whose primary preoccupation was to publish a list of the materials collected—metals, winter clothing, footwear and so on. And these companies did not hesitate to sell to the State at twenty to twenty-four marks a kilo scrap metal, which they themselves had purchased for less than a couple of marks a kilo.

Not only that; these companies—for the collection of metals, for the collection of leather, etc.—were such a splendid hide-out for the draft-dodgers, that in 1917, General Ludendorff was compelled to order a new census of available manhood. He had in this connection the misfortune to come up against the *Frankfurter Rettung*. The state of disintegration was by then such that he was not in a position to overcome the intrigues of that newspaper.

The *Frankfurter Rettung* (or rather the Jews who pulled the strings of the paper) actually threatened to withdraw its support of a new war loan, and even to advise industrial circles not to subscribe to it, if the new census threatened by Ludendorff were in fact made.

And Ludendorff, of course, had not the power to have these Jews brought to Berlin and hanged in public. And it is these same Jews, experts in the stab-in-the-back game, over whom our bourgeoisie now sheds tears when we ship them off somewhere to the east! It is curious, all the same, that our soft-hearted bourgeoisie has never shed any tears over the two or three hundred thousand Germans, who, each year, were compelled to leave their homeland, nor over those among them who elected to go to Australia, and of whom 75 per cent used to die *en route*.

In the political field there is no stupider a class than the bourgeoisie. It is sufficient for an end to be put to some individual's activities, on the score that he is a public menace, and, for reasons of security, for him to be arrested, tried, condemned and put to death, and immediately these tender souls set up a howl and denounce us as brutes.

But that the Jew, by means of his juridical trickery and sleight-of-hand, makes it impossible for innumerable Germans to earn a living, that he should rob a peasant of his land and hearth, disperse his family and oblige him to leave his country, that these German emigrants should lose their lives attempting to seek their fortune abroad—that, of course, is quite different!

And the bourgeois actually regards as legal a State which permits it, simply because these tragedies have as a pretext some measure of juridical justification and are covered by some article or other of some Code!

It does not occur to any of those who howl when we transport a few Jews to the east that the Jew is a parasite and as such is the only human being capable of adapting himself to any climate and of earning a living just as well in Lapland as in the tropics. Among our petty bourgeois there are not a few who pride themselves on reading their Bible; but they don't seem to know that, according to the Old Testament, the Jew survives with equal ease a sojourn in the desert and a crossing of the Red Sea. Frequently during the course of history, the Jew has become too presumptuous and has exploited to excess the country into which he has insinuated himself. And the countries concerned, victims of his plundering, have one after the other borne witness to the damage they have suffered at the hands of Jewry; each country has then tried, in its own way and when the opportunity arose, to solve the problems arising from the presence of the Jews. And the telegram which we have just read shows with what speed the Turks, for their part, are in process of solving the problem.

Facts show that we are cheapening our German decorations by awarding them to foreigners. That is why I think twice before decorating a foreigner with the Iron Cross. It is actually the most beautiful of our decorations (it was designed by Schinkel); and it is furthermore a military distinction of high international repute. To award it for exploits which are not military exploits in the true sense cannot therefore but diminish its lustre. I am, of course, fully aware of the advantages which may accrue from the decoration of foreigners. There are everywhere, and among the diplomats in particular, vain men, whose pro-German sentiments can be greatly increased by giving them an impressive German decoration. So, to satisfy their needs, I have created a special Order, and in this way those decorations of ours which are designed to be rewards of valour will still retain all their original value. Incidentally, this new decoration will be a lot cheaper than the gold or silver cigarette cases which the Reich was formerly wont to present to foreigners whom it wished to honour. The most magnificent of these insignia will cost at the most twenty marks. We are therefore pretty sure to get value for our money, even when the distinction is awarded for the most mediocre service.

My real problem has been to find a way of adequately rewarding cases of exceptional merit and unique exploits. It seemed to me that to meet such cases, and as the expression of the appreciation of the nation, it would be better to create a new Order, to which, of course, no foreigner, under any circumstances, would be admitted.

The death of Minister Todt has made the solution of this problem one of particular urgency, for there is a man who has incomparable claims to the nation's gratitude. In the field of military activity, and thanks to the fortifications in the West, he has saved innumerable German lives. On the civil side, we have to thank him for our *autobahnen*.

The Order which I created on the death of Minister Todt, and of which, posthumously, he is the first recipient, is designed to reward the most outstanding services that a man can render to the Reich. To avoid too wide a distribution, I have decided that recipients shall be grouped into a Chapter, as was done in the case of the Orders of Chivalry of the Middle Ages.

This Chapter shall also have a Senate, with powers to decide admissions and exclusions and limitation of the number of Members of the Chapter.

16th May 1942, at dinner

Handling of arms and a virile education—No armies for the occupied countries—Experiences with the Czechs—Diplomatic activities—Geneva and the League of Nations—The Wilhelmstrasse distinguishes itself

To teach a nation the handling of arms is to give it a virile education. If the Romans had not recruited Germans in their armies, the latter would never have had the opportunity of becoming soldiers and, eventually, of annihilating their former instructors. The most striking example is that of Arminius, who became Commander of the Third Roman Legion. The Romans instructed the Third in the arts of war, and Arminius afterwards used it to defeat his instructors. At the time of the revolt against Rome, the most daring of Arminius' brothers-in-arms were all Germanics who had served some time or other in the Roman legions.

We must, therefore, give a categorical no in reply to the Czech aspirations for the creation of a national army, even for an army in embryo. Servile for as long as he is unarmed, the Czech becomes dangerously arrogant when he is allowed to don uniform.

We have had plenty of time to see that for ourselves during the twenty years in which Czechoslovakia enjoyed political independence. Instead of directing her diplomacy towards the forging of those ties with Germany which alone would have constituted a reasonable policy, the Czech State tried to turn Prague—admittedly one of the most important cities in Europe—into a sort of hub of the universe.

The Czechs took their importance most seriously and they tried to have their finger in every pie. And not one of their statesmen had the sense to see that a Czech diplomat, installed, say, in Copenhagen, was destined to a life of ease, having nothing to do but every fortnight to put in a report made up of press cuttings snipped out for him by his press attaché. Oh! and an occasional telephone call to Prague for the latest news on the trend of Czech policy!

For a little country nothing is more flattering than to have a capital in which, apparently, there is intense diplomatic activity, and to give hospitality to the more or less decadent society who adorn these activities. If you wish to please a little country, transform your Legation there into an Embassy and you've hit the bull's eye. During the period of the League of Nations, the importance in foreign affairs which these little countries arrogated to themselves was very apparent.

They could think of nothing better to do, as members of this hierarchy, than to vote against Germany. In my opinion it would have been more to the point if they had paid their subscriptions! And today they seem quite astonished to find that we have not forgotten their previous behaviour! I must confess that the delegates at Geneva were a pretty exceptional bunch of nincompoops.

Their principal preoccupations were to draw their allowances most punctually, to eat and drink well and last, but by no means least, to throw themselves body and soul into amorous adventures! Following the example set by the Council of Constance, where fifteen hundred "merry maidens" hastened to afford distraction to the high dignitaries of the Church, each session of the Geneva Assembly saw a veritable horde of courtesans descend on the city.

Speaking generally, professional diplomats of every country run true to type. As far as the *Wilhelmstrasse* is concerned, I was forced quite literally to compel them to carry out our decision to withdraw from the League of Nations; and six months later, there were still German diplomats loafing about Geneva, not, apparently, having been recalled!

In 1936 this same Ministry distinguished itself by designing, for the use of diplomats, a colonial uniform adorned with the most enormous insignia I have ever seen! I was a little consoled when I made the acquaintance of the utter blockheads whom the United States were pleased to send us as their representatives, and later by the apparition of Sir Rumbold, the Ambassador of Great Britain, wrapped permanently in the haze of intoxication. This latter was succeeded by a complete thug, Sir Phipps. In this gallery of valorous diplomats it is Sir Henderson, the last of the British Ambassadors, who left the most favourable impression on me.

I recently had occasion to point out more than once the degree to which diplomats are estranged from reality and their abysmal ignorance of political affairs. They tried to persuade me to address a proclamation to the Arabs, completely disregarding the fact that, until our troops were in Mosul, such a proclamation would be stupid, for the British were quite prepared to shoot any and every Arab who rose to support our actions.

17th May 1942, at dinner
The alleged Yellow peril—Usefulness of alliance with Japan

There are certain foreign journalists who try to create an impression by talking about the Yellow peril and by drawing our attention to the fact that our alliance with Japan is a species of betrayal of our own racial principles. One could retort to these oafs that during the Great War it was the British who appealed to the Japanese, in order to give us the *coup de grâce.*

Without going any further it is perhaps sufficient to reply to these short-sighted spirits that the present conflict is one of life or death, and that the essential is to win—and to that end we are quite ready to make an alliance with the Devil himself.

Taking a more objective view, it is obvious that the Japanese alliance has been of exceptional value to us, if only because of the date chosen by Japan for her entry into the war. It was, in effect, at the moment when the surprises of the Russian winter were pressing most heavily on the morale of our people, and when everybody in Germany was oppressed by the certainty that, sooner or later, the United States would come into the conflict. Japanese intervention, therefore, was, from our point of view, most opportune. Apart from that, the way in which Japan interprets her obligations under the terms of our alliance does her the greatest credit and is having a happy influence on the German people.

18th May 1942, midday
Two German diplomats worthy of honour

I must pay tribute to the merits of our last Charge d'Affaires at Washington, the Councillor of the Embassy, Thomson, and also to those of Bötticher, our Military Attaché. These two men showed them over there that they were diplomats who could not be bluffed. The reports which they sent us must be regarded as models of their kind, for they invariably gave us a perfectly clear picture of the situation. I intend not only to give immediate proof of my particular appreciation of these two men, but also, once the war is over, to confide to them missions worthy of their capabilities. I shall hold Thomson, in particular, for a post of exceptional difficulty.

18th May 1942, at dinner
The inevitable characteristics of war with Russia

Nothing demonstrates so clearly as the unfolding of our conflict with Russia how essential it is that the Head of a State must be capable of swift, decisive action on his own responsibility, when a war seems to him to be inevitable.

In a letter which we found on Stalin's son[430] written by a friend, stands the following phrase: "I hope to be able to see my Anuschka once more before the promenade to Berlin."

If, in accordance with their plan, the Russians had been able to foresee our actions, it is, probable that nothing would have been able to stop their armoured units, for the highly developed road system of central Europe would greatly have favoured their advance. In any case, I take credit for the fact that we succeeded in making the Russians hold off right up to the moment when we launched our attack, and that we did

---

[430] Yakov Dzhugashvili (1907–1943), captured on 16 July 1941 at Smolensk.

so by entering into agreements which were favourable to their interests.

Suppose for example that, when the Russians marched into Romania, we had not been able to limit their conquests to Bessarabia, they would in one swoop have grabbed all the oilfields of the country, and we should have found ourselves, from the spring of that very year, completely frustrated as regards our supplies of petrol.

20th May 1942, midday
*National Socialism not for export—Effects of National Socialist
education—Workmen who are grands seigneurs—The new Man—The
cement of the Great German Reich—Vast programmes of construction—
Abolition of social inequalities—President Hácha and the Czech problem*

I am firmly opposed to any attempt to export National Socialism. If other countries are determined to preserve their democratic systems and thus rush to their ruin, so much the better for us. And all the more so, because during this same period, thanks to National Socialism, we shall be transforming ourselves, slowly but surely, into the most solid popular community that it is possible to imagine.

The youth of today, which in ten years, in twenty years from now will be the personification of the National Socialist idea, will have known no other conception of the world, and they will be the product of an education which will make of them men well-disciplined and sure of themselves. We see already how the apprentice guilds have been completely changed.

The apprentice of the past was the recipient of buffets and the plaything of the caprices of the workmen and the master. Today, only six months after enrolment, he is put in charge of work which is within his competence to do and so acquires a measure of self-confidence compatible with his abilities.

The same progress has been made with the girls, who have received an education in accordance with the principles of National Socialism. They are moulding themselves perfectly to the necessities of the modern epoch, working in the war factories, the offices, the hospitals, the fields and so on. Basing our view on current experience, we may assume that if our methods of education can be applied for a hundred years, the German people will then have become the most unified bloc that has ever existed in Europe.

For the education of the young male, let us not forget that the work with the widest horizons and the work that offers the ideal of manual labour is in the high-pressure furnaces, the steelworks, the armoured

435

vehicle factories—in short, all the factories in which steel is worked and arms or machines are manufactured. Every time I visit the Krupp Works at Essen, the truth of this strikes me anew. By their appearance and their conduct, these workmen give me the impression of being veritable *seigneurs*.

I felt the same at the launching of the *Tirpitz* at Wilhelmshaven. The shipyard workmen, who had assisted in this vast construction now ready for launching, were for the most part handsome types, proud of bearing and stamped with the hall-mark of nobility. When I visited some of the other shipyards of the town, I saw a large number of foreign workmen, and I could not help being struck by the difference between them and our men.

What is true of the metal-industry workers is true also of the miners. Our miners are and remain the elite of the German labour world. Physically and morally, these men are moulded by the practice of a profession which today still holds many risks. Only men of stamina, determined and ready to face the risks to which their work exposes them, are capable of manning the mines. And so, no opportunity must be lost of manifesting the appreciation of the nation to our miners. When peace returns, the amelioration of the standard of life of these men, who more than most contribute to the maintenance of the country's potential, must be a matter for our particular concern.

This very afternoon a ceremony will take place in the Mosaic Hall of the *Reichskanzelei*,[431] at which expression will be given to the gratitude due from the nation to its workers. On this occasion, a hundred crosses of the *Kriegsverdienstorden*[432] will be awarded to workmen, and one Knight's Cross of the same Order to the foreman of an armoured fighting vehicle factory.

These decorations will be presented by a soldier holding the *Ritterkreuz*,[433] a corporal returned from the front who, serving his anti-tank gun single-handed, destroyed thirteen Russian tanks. It was a delight for me yesterday to receive a visit from this non-commissioned officer, a typical example of National Socialist youth. Although he has the ap-

---

[431] Reich Chancellery building in Berlin.

[432] The "War Services' Order" or "War Merit Cross" was the highest war decoration for civilians or the military personnel not involved in hostilities.

[433] The *Ritterkreuz*, or "Knight's Cross" (proper name *Ritterkreuz des Eisernen Kreuze*, "Knight's Cross of the Iron Cross") was the highest possible award in Nazi Germany

pearance of a youngster of seventeen, he possesses the assurance of a man whom nothing can daunt.

Once the war is over, and I am less absorbed in military problems, I shall make it my particular business to develop in our youth this type of man—wide-awake, intelligent, self-assured—on the model of this young corporal. This will allow me to oppose foreigners, whose manhood appears to be composed either of degenerates or of brute beasts or some such sort of extremes, with fine lads of the kind that defended Narvik and Cholm.

Exactly in the same way as the war of 1870–71[434] was the melting-pot of the old Reich, the battlefields of this war will be the cement which will bind into one indissoluble whole all the races of the Greater German Reich. Not one of them will come into the confederation feeling like a whipped hound, for each and every one of them will come with the pride born of the knowledge that each and every one has shed his blood and played his part in the greatest struggle for freedom in the history of the German race.

As I expect everyone to give of his best, I shall adhere to the principle that all Germans, whatever their origin, must be represented in the Party Chancellery at Munich. In the same way, when it is a question of major undertakings such as buildings, *autobahnen*, canals, or indeed anything which calls for a determined effort on the part of the whole nation, I wish everyone to play their part.

Dispersal of effort spells merely dissipation of force. Just as intervention in great numbers by the Air Arm is decisive in an operation in war, to know how to concentrate the efforts of the entire nation on the important objective is the decisive factor in great undertakings in times of peace. Munich, for example, can only acquire the great central railway station which it requires, if the power of the whole Reich is behind the undertaking. For the future, therefore, reasoned planning by the German Government is essential; plans must be drawn up for the undertaking, year by year, of some great enterprise, and these plans must be attacked and brought to fruition at all costs.

This sort of collective harnessing of the efforts of the entire German people cannot but have its influence on the individual participant. He will come to feel that nothing is impossible and, as the young Briton of today serves his apprenticeship in India, the young German will learn

---

[434] The Franco-Prussian War which heralded the unification of Germany.

his lessons, looking round the most easterly territories of the Reich, in Norway, or on some other frontier of our land. He will realise, too, thanks to his personal experiences, that, although some sort of hierarchy is necessary in the homeland, abroad there must be no differences at all between German and German. To the last man, too, the Germans must have the conviction as a matter of course that the youngest of German apprentices, the most humble of German mechanics, stands closer to him than the most important British Lord.

The measure of the importance of the revolution we have accomplished in the abolition of social differences can be well gauged if one recalls that German princes in the old days preferred to go off and play the Nabob in some tin pot Balkan State, rather than remain and earn their living in their own country, in however humble a manner—even as a crossing sweeper.

If only we can succeed in inculcating into the German people, and above all into the German youth, both a fanatical team spirit and a fanatical devotion to the Reich, then the German Reich will once again become the most powerful State in Europe, as it was a thousand years after the collapse of the Roman Empire. Such a spirit would be a guarantee, once and for all, that never again would the German Reich split up into a number of little States, with mutual diplomatic representatives, and each with its diplomats abroad, stirring up trouble for German unity—as did, not so very long ago, a certain French Ambassador to Munich.

A Reich whose component entities are moulded in fanatic solidarity will soon find, too, a solution to the Czech problem—as Hácha himself well knows. As a lawyer of the old Austrian State he must feel that the setting up of an independent Czech State was a mistake; for never in the course of history have the Czechs shown themselves capable of solving their own political problems, and even in their cultural development leant heavily on the German culture of the Habsburg State. The right, and, indeed, for the German Reich the obvious, policy is firstly to purge the country of all dangerous elements, and then to treat the Czechs with friendly consideration.

If we pursue a policy of this sort, all the Czechs will follow the lead of President Hácha. In any case, a certain feeling of guilt, coupled with the fear of being compelled to evacuate their homes, as the result of the transfer of population we are undertaking, will persuade them that it will be in their best interests to emerge as zealous co-operators of the

Reich. It is this fear which besets them that explains why the Czechs at the moment—and particularly in the war factories—are working to our complete satisfaction, doing their utmost under the slogan: "Everything for our Führer, Adolf Hitler!"

20th May 1942, at dinner
Results of National Socialist policy—Effects of National Socialist education—Ignominious status of theatre artistes—Encouragement of prostitution

Since we took over power, we National Socialists have completed a vast number of tasks, of which no mention whatever has been made in public. We wasted no breath, for example, in telling the world how tens of thousands of beings who, under the Weimar Republic, were forced to earn their living in most dubious ways, have now been given by us the chance of leading a decent existence. Of primary importance were the measures we took to ensure a living wage for working women, such as secretaries, shop girls, artistes and the like.

By insisting that they receive a regular wage in accordance with their qualifications—instead of the sort of pocket-money they formerly received—we have delivered them from the doleful necessity of being dependent on an *ami* for their existence.

What formerly infuriated me more than anything else was the way in which dancers were treated. While so-called "comedians"—mostly Jews—earned three or four thousand marks a month in theatres like the Berliner Metropol for fifteen minutes of smut, the dancers were paid as little as seventy or eighty marks; and that, mind you, in return not for fifteen minutes, but—if they were to keep themselves up to the mark—for practically a whole day's work of training, practice and so on. Such discrepancies are contemptible.

They left these poor creatures no alternative but to go on the streets, and turned the theatre into a euphemism for brothels. Without making any fuss about it, I made sure that the pay of these dancers was raised to a hundred and eighty or two hundred marks, and thus gave them the chance of devoting themselves entirely to their art.

This also had considerable effect on the theatre itself; firstly, it allowed them to engage really good-looking girls for the stage; secondly, it enabled the theatre to retain them and train them in the further perfection of their art; and thirdly, it meant that the theatre could foster their general education and thus fit them, at the latest at the age of thirty-five or so, to leave the stage, marry and settle down.

21st May 1942, after dinner

The assumption of power—Negotiations with Papen—Intrigues of Schleicher[435]—My demand for the Chancellorship and new elections— Refusal to assume office except by legal means—Danger of military dictatorship and a military putsch—General Hammerstein[436] tries intimidation—Political greed of German Nationalist Party—Hindenburg sides with me—Blomberg neutralises the Wehrmacht—Only two Nazis in the first Cabinet—The tortuous role of Papen—Initial difficulties—My relations with Hindenburg become more close—Hindenburg rebuffs the King of Sweden

When I roundly refused to consider any compromise and accept the Vice-Chancellorship in a von Papen Cabinet, and after the vain and treacherous attempts of General Schleicher, supported by Gregor Strasser, had failed to split the solid unity of the Party, political tension reached its zenith.

Not only did Schleicher fail to win over a log-rolling majority in the Reichstag, but as a result of his go-slow policy as regards national economy, the number of unemployed rose, during the first fifteen days of his regime, by no less than a quarter of a million.

In January 1933—one month, that is, after his assumption of office—Schleicher saw no other alternative but to dissolve the Reichstag and form a military Cabinet, upheld solely by the support of the President of the Reich. But the idea of a military dictatorship, in spite of his great personal confidence in General Schleicher, filled old von Hindenburg with the liveliest apprehension. For in his heart of hearts the Old Gentleman was opposed to soldiers meddling in politics; besides that, he was not prepared to go further in the delegation of political plenipotentiary power than he felt himself able to do in accordance with his constitutional oath.

Faced with this situation of extreme political tension, von Hindenburg, through the intermediary of von Papen, approached me, and in the famous Cologne conversations explored the ground. For myself, I had the impression that all was going well for me. I made it quite clear, therefore, that I would not hear of any compromise, and threw myself, heart and soul, personally into the Lippe electoral campaign.

---

[435] Kurt von Schleicher (1882–1934), a World War One general who served as chancellor from 1932 to 1933. He was assassinated outside his home in 1934.
[436] Kurt von Hammerstein-Equord (1878–1943), Commander-in-Chief of the German Army (*Reichswehr*) during the Weimar Republic.

After the electoral victory at Lippe—a success whose importance it is not possible to over-estimate[437]—the advisers of the Old Gentleman approached me once more. A meeting was arranged at Ribbentrop's house with Hindenburg's son and Herr von Papen. At this meeting I gave an unequivocal description of my reading of the political situation, and declared without mincing words that every week of hesitation was a week irretrievably wasted. The situation, I said, could be saved only by an amalgamation of all parties, omitting, of course, those fragmentary bourgeois parties which were of no importance and which, in any case, would not join us. Such an amalgamation, I added, could be successfully assured only with myself as Reichs Chancellor.

At this juncture I deliberately neglected my work within the Party in order to take part in these negotiations, because I considered it of the highest importance that I should legitimately take over the Chancellorship with the blessing of the Old Gentleman. For it was only as constitutionally elected Chancellor, obviously, and before undertaking any measures of reconstruction, that I could overcome the opposition of all the other political parties, and avoid finding myself in constant conflict with the *Wehrmacht*. My decision to attain power constitutionally was influenced primarily by my knowledge of the attitude of the *Wehrmacht vis-à-vis* the Chancellorship.

If I had seized power illegally, the *Wehrmacht* would have constituted a dangerous breeding place for a *coup d'etat* in the nature of the Röhm putsch; by acting constitutionally, on the other hand, I was in a position to restrict the activities of the *Wehrmacht* to its legal and strictly limited military function—at least until such a time as I was able to introduce conscription. Once that was accomplished, the influx into the *Wehrmacht* of the masses of the people, together with the spirit of National Socialism and with the ever-growing power of the National Socialist movement, would, I was sure, allow me to overcome all opposition among the armed forces, and in particular in the corps of officers.

On 24th January 1933—the day after the SA assault on the Karl Liebknecht-Haus[438] in Berlin had resulted in a tremendous loss of

---

[437] The 1929 Lippe state election returned 0 seats for the NSDAP after it polled only 3.35% of the vote. In the next election—the one referred to above, held on 15 January 1933, Hitler's party came first with 9 seats.

[438] The Karl-Liebknecht-Haus was the headquarters of the *Kommunistische Partei Deutschlands* ("Communist Party of Germany," or KPD), named after that party's

prestige for the Communist Party and caused great indignation in Berlin—I was again invited by von Papen to a conference. Von Papen told me at once that Schleicher had formally asked the Old Gentleman for plenipotentiary powers to set up a military dictatorship, but that the latter had refused and had stated that he proposed inviting Adolf Hitler, in the role of leader of a national front, to accept the Chancellorship and to form a Government, with the *proviso* that von Papen should be nominated Vice-Chancellor.

I replied that I took cognisance of the offer, and, without permitting any discussion of detail, stated the conditions under which I was prepared to accept. These were the immediate dissolution of the Reichstag and the organisation of new elections. Under the pretext that I should be away from Berlin, I avoided a tentative suggestion that I should have a ten-minute talk with the Old Gentleman. Mindful of the experiences of the previous year, I was anxious to avoid giving rise to any undue optimism within the Party, such as was invariably the case whenever I was received by the Old Gentleman. I took the opportunity in this conversation with Herr von Papen of pressing home my advantage and carrying a step further the negotiations started by Göring for the tentative formation of a Government. It was with the German Nationalists that the negotiations proved most difficult, for *Geheimrat*[439] Hugenberg displayed a greed for portfolios out of all proportion to the strength of his party, and, because he feared that he would probably lose a great number of votes in any new elections, he would not hear of an early dissolution of the Reichstag. On 27th January, after a short absence from Berlin, I had a personal conference with Hugenberg, but we were unable to agree.

The negotiations for the formation of a Government were further complicated by General Schleicher and his clique, who did all in their power to wreck them. General von Hammerstein, Schleicher's most trusted colleague and Commander-in-Chief of the Army, was even stupid enough to have the impertinence to ring me up and tell me that

---

leader who had been assassinated in 1919. In the present day, the same building, which still has the same name, is the headquarters of the KPD's successor party, *Die Linke* ("The Left").

[439] The *Geheimrat*, or "Secret Council" was a body of trusted advisors dating from the time of the Holy Roman Empire who could be expected to "keep the secrets" of the emperor while advising him. An English equivalent would be "Privy Councillor."

"under no circumstances would the *Wehrmacht* sanction my acceptance of the Chancellorship"!

If Herr Schleicher and his friends really imagined they could shake my determination with puerilities of this sort, they were grievously mistaken. My only reaction was to impress emphatically on Göring to accept as Minister of the Reichswehr only a General who enjoyed my confidence, such as General von Blomberg, who had been recommended to me by my friends in East Prussia.

On 28th January the Weimar Republic finally collapsed. Schleicher resigned, and von Papen was instructed to sound the various parties with a view to the formation of a new Government.

For my own part, I at once declared that any half measures were now unacceptable to me. The 29th, naturally, was buzzing with conferences, in the course of which I succeeded in obtaining Hugenberg's agreement to the dissolution of the Reichstag in return for the promise to give him the number of seats in the new Government which he had originally demanded for his Party, convincing him that with the Reichstag in its present form, it would be impossible to achieve anything.

The next afternoon Göring brought me the news that on the morrow the Old Gentleman proposed officially to invite me to accept the Chancellorship and the task of forming the Government.

Late in the afternoon, we were surprised by a completely insane action by Schleicher and his clique. According to information received from Lieut.-Colonel von Alvensleben,[440] General von Hammerstein had put the Potsdam garrison on an alarm footing; the Old Gentleman was to be bundled off to East Prussia to prevent his interference, and the *Wehrmacht* was to be mobilised to stop by force the assumption of power by the NSDAP. My immediate counter-action to this planned putsch was to send for the Commander of the Berlin SA, Graf Helldorf, and through him to alert the whole SA of Berlin. At the same time I instructed Major Wecke of the Police, whom I knew I could trust, to prepare for a sudden seizure of the *Wilhelmstrasse* by six police battalions.

Through Herr von Papen, I informed the Old Gentleman of the Schleicher clique's intentions. Finally I instructed General von Blomberg (who had been selected as Reichswehr Minister elect) to proceed at once, on arrival in Berlin at 8 a.m. on 30th January, direct to the Old Gentleman to be sworn in, and thus to be in a position, as Command-

---

[440] Joachim Martin, Count von Alvensleben-Schönborn (1877–1969), a senior officer in the Reichswehr.

er-in-Chief of the Reichswehr, to suppress any possible attempts at a *coup d'etat*.

By eleven o'clock on the morning of 30th January, I was able to inform the Old Gentleman that the new Cabinet had been formed, and that the majority in the Reichstag required by constitution to enable it to function had been acquired. Shortly afterwards I received at the hands of the Old Gentleman my appointment as Chancellor of the German Reich.

At the beginning my task as the head of this Cabinet was the reverse of simple. With the exception of Frick, I had initially not one single National Socialist member of the Cabinet.

It is true that some of the others, like Blomberg and Neurath, had promised me their support, but the remainder were quite determined to go their own way.

Gereke,[441] the Commissioner for Labour, who a little later was arrested and found guilty of embezzlement, was from the beginning my most persistent opponent. I was therefore very pleased when Seldte came and declared that the die was cast, and that in future his party would do nothing that might hinder my efforts.

Apart from the difficulties inherent in the formation of a Government, I very quickly realised that the Old Gentleman had called upon me to accept the Chancellorship only because he could see no other constitutional way out of the political *impasse*. This was obvious from the number of conditions he imposed. He informed me, for instance, that all questions connected with the Reichswehr, the Foreign Office and overseas appointments remained in his hands.

He further decided that von Papen must be present whenever he received me officially; and it was only after much hesitation and the intervention of Meissner, that the Old Gentleman was pleased to sign the order for the dissolution of the Reichstag, which I had managed to rattle through during the session of 31st January.

Within a week or so, however, my relations with Hindenburg began to improve. One day, when he wanted to see me about something or other, I invited his attention to the custom he himself had established—namely, that I could not visit him except in the company of von Papen—and pointed out that the latter was at the moment away from Berlin.

---

[441] Günther Gereke (1893–1970), was convicted of having misused political donations and sentenced to two years and six months in prison.

The Old Gentleman replied that he wished to see me alone, and that in future the presence of von Papen could be regarded as unnecessary.

Within three weeks we had progressed so far that his attitude towards me became affectionate and paternal. Talking of the elections fixed for the 3rd March, he said, "What are we going to do if you fail to get a majority? We shall have the same difficulties all over again."

When later the first results of the elections began to come in, our relations had attained such a degree of frank cordiality, that the Old Gentleman exclaimed in a voice charged with real satisfaction: "Hitler wins!"[442]

And when the overwhelming victory of the National Socialists was confirmed, he told me straight out that he had always been averse to the parliamentary game and was delighted that the comedy of elections was now done with, once and for all.

That the Old Gentleman, in spite of his advanced age, still remained a great man was well demonstrated by the way he handled a situation arising out of a report on the disarmaments negotiations from Ambassador Nadolny.[443] Nadolny proposed to acquiesce in a proposal that Germany should at once proceed with her disarmament, and that that of the remaining Powers should follow—in a few years' time. After I had rejected this proposal out of hand and had informed the Old Gentleman of my action, Nadolny, without consulting me, begged audience of Hindenburg.

The Old Gentleman flung him out and told me afterwards that he had not been in the least taken in by Nadolny's arguments, but had indeed dismissed him with a brusque: "You're pro-Moscow! Very well—you'd better push off!" This incident is a typical example of the way in which the Old Gentleman reduced every problem to its simplest denominator.

He had completely succeeded in unravelling the tangled intrigues woven against us at Geneva—which were tantamount simply to our

---

[442] The March 1934 elections saw the NSDAP win over 17.2 million votes, the Social Democratic Party win 7.1 million votes, the Communists win 4.8 million, and the Centre Party win 4.4 million votes. The German National People's Party (DNVP), in alliance with the NSDAP, won 3.1 million votes, and the smaller Bavarian People's Party won 1 million votes. Together with the DNVP, the NSDAP had 340 seats. 324 were required for a majority.

[443] Rudolf Nadolny (1873–1953), German Ambassador to Turkey from 1924 to 1933, the Soviet Union from 1933 to 1934, and head of the German delegation at the World Disarmament Conference from 1932 to 1933.

binding ourselves to obligations which the others had not the slightest intention of honouring. In the same direct manner, within a few minutes of MacDonald's[444] handing to Germany the demands made of her in the League of Nations, he sanctioned the release to the world's press by Funk, the Reich Press Chief, of the news that Germany was withdrawing from the League. When the German people with a huge 95 per cent majority expressed approval of the decision and, incidentally, of my policy, the Old Gentleman was delighted.

The Old Gentleman was wonderful, too, in his appreciation of the situation as regards the re-occupation of the demilitarised zone of the Rhineland, and carried his point by sheer forceful personality. The various Ministers, on the contrary, had to be won over, one by one, to the idea of the entry of the *Wehrmacht* into this zone. Von Papen was even filled with anxiety, lest the French should take retaliatory measures of occupation.

I myself, however, stuck to my opinion that the French could be allowed to occupy Mainz, provided that we recaptured our liberty of action and were in a position to do what we liked in the rest of the Reich, and were, first and foremost, in a position to re-arm. Subsequent events proved that I was right.

It is true that, in order to set the minds of the people at rest, I went personally to the Rhineland. But the German people, by giving me a 99 per cent majority in the elections to the Reichstag on 5th March 1936, proved conclusively that they both understood and approved my policy.

It was by no means easy to convince the Old Gentleman, but once one had done so, he always gave his fullest support to whatever it might be. For instance, at first he would not hear of any anti-Semitic measures. But when, at a dinner at the Swedish Legation, at which both were present, the King of Sweden expressed certain criticisms of the German policy towards the Jews, the Old Gentleman refuted them, saying in his deep, sonorous, bass voice that this was a purely domestic German affair, with which the German Chancellor alone was competent to deal.

I had some difficulty, also, in persuading the Old Gentleman of the necessity of curtailing the liberty of the press. On this occasion I played a little trick on him and addressed him not as a civilian with "Mr. President", but as a soldier with "Field Marshal", and developed the argument

---

[444] James McDonald (1886–1964) was chairman of the League of Nations' "High Commission for Refugees (Jewish and Others)."

that in the Army criticism from below was never permitted—only the reverse, for what would happen if the N.C.O. passed judgment on the orders of the captain, the captain on those of the general and so on? This the Old Gentleman admitted and without further ado approved of my policy, saying: "You are quite right, only superiors have the right to criticise!" And with these words the freedom of the press was doomed.

For the fact that the Old Gentleman so faithfully followed my lead and always did his utmost to understand my intentions, I am deeply grateful. To what extent he had to free himself from old ideas in the process is shown by his remarks on the appointment of *Gauleiter* Hildebrandt[445] to the post of *Reichsstatthalter.*

The Old Gentleman signed the appointment, growling as he did so: "The fellow was only a farm labourer. Isn't he content with having been made a member of the Reichstag and being given the opportunity of spending the rest of his life in peace and quiet there!"

Once I had won him over to my side, the Old Gentleman's solicitude towards me was truly touching. Again and again he said that he had a Chancellor who was sacrificing himself for his country, and that often he could not sleep at night for thinking of "his Chancellor flying from one part of the Reich to another in the service of the people". What an eternal shame it was, he added, that such a man must belong to one Party.

22nd May 1942, midday
Recruiting spies—The need for barbarous methods against blackout criminals—Weaknesses of the judges—Habit encourages crime

Spies nowadays are recruited from two classes of society: the so-called upper classes and the proletariat. The middle classes are too serious-minded to indulge in such activity. The most efficient way of combating espionage is to convince those who are tempted to dabble in it that, if they are caught, they will most certainly lose their lives. In the same way I am of the opinion that one should proceed with the utmost severity against other contemptible forms of crime which have sprung up under war conditions—for instance, theft under cover of the black-out. For, except by truly barbaric methods, how can one suppress such crimes, under cover of the black-out, as bag-snatching, assaults on women, housebreaking when the cellar door is left open and so on?

---

[445] Friedrich Hildebrandt (1898–1948) was elected to the Reichstag in 1930, and made *Reichsstatthalter* ("Reich Governor") of the Free State of Mecklenburg-Schwerin in 1933.

For all such crimes there must be one penalty alone—the death penalty, whether the evil-doer is seventy or seventeen years of age.

Unless in war-time one punishes crime in the homeland with the utmost severity, two dangers will arise: *(a)* The numbers of the criminal classes will increase and become uncontrollable; *(b)* One will have the anachronism of the decent man losing his life at the front, while the criminal at home gets away with it, because he knows full well that for such and such a crime he can, under paragraph so-and-so, only be imprisoned for a specified period.

One must clearly understand that in wartime the population divides itself into three categories: the out-and-out idealist; the out-and-out egotist; and the betwixt and betweens.

If we permit the blackguard to be treated with mercy at home, while the idealists are dying in large numbers in the field, then we are paving the way for a reverse process of selectivity, and showing that we have forgotten the lessons of the world war in 1917–18. I maintain therefore that there is no alternative. The man at the front *may* die, the blackguard at home *must* die. Any State which is not prepared to accept this principle has not the right to expose its idealists to death in the field.

The judges of today have no clear notion of their duties. For the most part they were appointed before we took power and, like the priesthood, have succeeded in maintaining their corporate entity in spite of changes of regime, and have therefore conserved all their liberal tendencies.

I feel myself constrained in the circumstances to intervene, and I shall not hesitate to dismiss ruthlessly any judge who consistently gives judgment harmful to the good of the people and contrary to the national outlook; for I feel that it is my personal responsibility to see that there does not spring up a race of rascals on the home front, such as we had in 1918, while our men die heroically on the battlefield.

Discipline at the front demands rules of iron, and it would be an injustice to the front line to allow mercy to hold sway at home.

Also as regards young people, the methods employed in wartime must be different from those applied in times of peace, and among them leniency finds no place. In peace-time, of course, with a young fifteen-or seventeen-year-old delinquent one can substitute a damn good hiding for a period of imprisonment, because, if he has an ounce of decency in him, he will feel that prison has sullied his whole life, and, apart from that, he may well pick up all sorts of criminal tricks from the old lags. A young man named Seefeldt,[446] for example, was once condemned for offences against public decency, and while in prison learnt from other criminals how to distil a poison which left no trace whatever twenty minutes after use.

As I believed that this young criminal had committed many more crimes than those to which he confessed in court, I caused him to be handed over to the Gestapo. After twelve hours in a super-heated cell without water, he not only confessed to one hundred and seven more murders, but also showed the officials the places where all the bodies were buried.

Experience shows that unnatural offenders generally turn into homicidal maniacs; they must be rendered harmless, however young they may be. I have therefore always been in favour of the strongest possible punishment of these anti-social elements.

29th May 1942, midday
Lola Montez and Ludwig I of Bavaria—Hostility of the Church—
Personality of Ludwig I—Respect for racial characteristics

On a proposal by Dr. Goebbels to produce a film of Lola Montez.

I welcome the idea, but you must take care that neither the fate of this woman nor the personality of King Ludwig I of Bavaria is in any way distorted. Lola Montez had nothing in common with the dancers of our times, strip-tease artists, but was a woman of exceptional intelligence with wide experience of the world. She was, too, a woman of character, as is shown by the way she resisted the Catholic Church and, in spite of enormous pressure, refused to kow-tow to it.

As regards the personality of Ludwig I, you must be careful, too, not to portray him as first and foremost a *Schürzenjäger.*[447] He was in every sense a great man, and was the finest architect of his time in Europe. The idea and execution of the Walhalla Building[448] alone show him to have been a monarch whose vision stretched far beyond the confines of his own petty State and embraced the whole pan-German panorama.

---

[446] Adolf Seefeldt (1870–1936), a homosexual serial killer who preyed on young boys. He spent 24 years in prison on various convictions for child molestation, where he apparently learned how to concoct a home made poison of wild plants and fungi. He was arrested in 1936, convicted and executed.

[447] "Skirt-chaser."

[448] The Walhalla Hall is a building based on the Parthenon in Greece, built by orders of Ludwig I in 1842, and located near Regensburg, Bavaria. It contains busts of all famous Germans who have contributed to German history and culture.

Apart from that, we have to thank him for having given, in the city of Munich, a magnificent art centre to the German nation.

That he is nevertheless one of the most controversial figures among the Kings of Bavaria is attributable to the fact that the Church never ceased to harry him. The attacks of the latter on Lola Montez were only a pretext, and it was in reality the strong liberal tendencies of the King at which the attacks were aimed. You must not, therefore, represent Ludwig I as a King of the Viennese charm school, something after the style of Paul Hörbiger, but rather as a worthy monarch, and I think Kayssler is the best man for the role.

While respecting their racial characteristics, I have, in the interests of the Reich, divided my Austrian homeland into a series of Alpine and Danubian provinces. I have decided to act in the same way as regards other portions of the Reich. I shall not, for example, permit that West Friesland continue to form part of Holland, for these West Frieslanders are of exactly the same race as the people of East Friesland and must, therefore, be united with them within a single Province.

30th May 1942, midday
Painters and sculptors—Influence of the epoch on painters—The role of Vienna—Death of Mozart—Artists should be supported before they die!

I consider Bruckmann's *Art Review* to be inferior to those published by Professor Hoffmann and the Minister of Propaganda.

As regards the sculptors Kolbe[449] and Klimsch,[450] I think the work of the former—an admitted Master—tends to deteriorate as he grows older, while that of Klimsch, on the other hand, seems with the years to become more and more finished and significant. But it is obviously unfair to reproach an artist because the work of his old age does not show the perfection of his earlier and greatest creations.

With age, eyes grow feeble, and the sculptor in particular is dependent on his sight. When, as sometimes happens, sculptors surpass themselves in their old age, it is probably because they were previously short-sighted and, with the lengthening of sight that accompanies advancing age, had then become normal.

Speaking generally, it would be unjust to reproach an artist—be he sculptor or singer—because his talents fade with age. Rather than emphasise the many faults that are to be found in the later works of Lovis

---

[449] Georg Kolbe (1877–1947) was a leading figure in the modern simplified classical style.

[450] Fritz Klimsch (1870–1960), the younger brother of the painter Paul Klimsch.

Corinth,[451] we should remember with delight the truly magnificent youth pictures of his earlier days.

It should be the task of any reasonable culture policy to discover talent early, to encourage and foster it, and so give it the opportunity of reaching its highest fruition for the benefit of both the present and posterity.

During the last few centuries, the Viennese, who always used to set such store by the cultural standards of their city, have neglected this most important principle of cultural policy in an almost insanely irresponsible fashion.

For example, they actually allowed a genius like Mozart to starve. He was even buried in a pauper's grave, they say, and now no one knows where he lies. Like him, too, Bruckner and Haydn would have been allowed to die of hunger, if they had not found patrons in the Bishop of Linz and the Prince von Esterhazy respectively.

These examples show that the Viennese, like the people of Munich, owe their accumulation of artistic wealth solely to their rulers. Between the Viennese and the people of Munich, however, there is this vital difference, that the latter do show a measure of appreciation to their living artists, while the former wait until an artist has been dead for perhaps centuries and has acquired an international reputation before giving their approval. Our own cultural policy can learn a lesson from this. It is, that artists who do good work must be assured of recognition in good time. It is for this reason that I have caused to be organised the arts exhibition in the House of German Art in Munich, and not merely because I wished to give the already famous a chance to exhibit, where their works will be seen by the whole world.

By far the most important object of this exhibition is to seek out the best of German creative art, and to put on exhibition, and so before potential purchasers, works honestly recognised by experts as meritorious, even when the artist is still unknown outside a narrow circle. At the same time it will afford to purchasers a guarantee that anything they have bought at this exhibition is worth having.

Professor Hoffmann's proposal that competition between artists should be stimulated by the award of gold and silver medals bearing a picture of the House of German Art is in complete accord with this object and should be adopted.

---

[451] Lovis Corinth (1858–1925), a painter who in his later days tended towards impressionism away from his earlier realism.

31st May 1942, at dinner
Kaiser Wilhelm II, an ignoble monarch

The behaviour of Wilhelm II in society was unworthy of a monarch. Not only did he consistently ridicule the members of his immediate entourage, but also fired a constant stream of ironic remarks at his guests for the amusement of the remainder. His bad taste and familiarity with other monarchs—backslapping and the like—robbed Germany of much sympathy.

A monarch must learn that self-restraint and dignity must be observed in everyday life. The example of Wilhelm II shows how one bad monarch can destroy a dynasty. In the same way, those who wish to play their parts in history must understand that one single bad generation can cause the ruin of a whole people.

2nd June 1942, at dinner
Application of the laws of nature to aircraft and naval construction— Fish, birds and the design of aircraft and ships—New fields of research— Tradition the enemy of invention

An animated conversation with Admiral Krancke[452] on the principles governing the construction of means of transport. The Führer speaks: One must start by accepting the principle that nature herself gives all the necessary indications, and that therefore one must follow the rules that she has laid down.

Take the example of the bicycle; it suffices for me to remove in imagination the rims and the tyres from the wheels, to see that the movements of the spokes are exactly those of a man walking.

In aviation, too, we see that the natural laws retain all their original value. The Zeppelin was on this account a completely artificial construction. Nature, obviously, has rejected the "lighter-than-air" principle; she has provided no bird with any sort of balloon, as she has done in the case of the fish. As far as I myself am concerned, I shall never consent to go up in a dirigible, but I have no shadow of anxiety in an aeroplane, even when flying through the worst storms.

The current design of ships certainly does not conform to the laws of nature; if it did, then we should find fish furnished with some sort of propulsive element at the rear, instead of the lateral fins with which they are endowed. Nature would also have given the fish a stream-lined

---

[452] Theodor Krancke (1893–1973), an Admiral famous for his command of the battleship *Admiral Scheer* which, during a five-month-long cruise, sank 13 merchant ships, one armed merchant cruiser, and capturing three more.

head, instead of that shape which corresponds more or less exactly to a globule of water.

One of the most doubtful blessings bestowed upon us by early Christian seafarers is the abandoning of the fish shape and the adoption, in theory and practice, of the principle—which still governs the construction of even our latest vessels of the *Nelson* class—of pointed forward and blunt aft. In ship design, surely, it is most necessary to imitate the ideas of nature and to adopt the design of a falling drop of water. For by thickening the prow you greatly reduce the pressure produced from in front on a pointed bow. It is only quite recently, too, that it has been realised that a pointed spade is not the best spade.

Seeing that we have departed from the natural in the shape of our ships, it is not to be wondered at that we have found also a form of propulsion which is contrary to the example given us in nature by the fish. The screw fixed in the rear acts by suction, and the resultant vacuum acts as a brake on the ship's progress, while this brake effect is augmented by the resistance offered by the mass of water piling up at the bows. In nature exactly the reverse happens—in front suction by vacuum, at the back an inert mass of water tending to further the forward thrust. The fish moves forward by the action of its fins and by the propulsion of water through its gills. Happily these principles have been remembered in the construction of aeroplanes, and the screws have been placed in front, where by producing suction they pull the plane forwards.

You cannot deny that the design and method of propulsion of the present-day ship are out of date. With warships we have already come to the point where an addition of driving power does not lead to a corresponding increase of efficiency. You find that a battleship of over 45,000 tons with 136,000 horsepower engines steams at 30 knots, while an aircraft carrier of half the size with 200,000 horse-power engines raises only 35 knots! Something, obviously, is wrong with the mathematics of it. It is quite absurd that the addition of 75,000 horse-power to a ship of half the tonnage should give a speed increase of only 5 knots, and I can only hope that our naval experts will at last allow themselves to be persuaded that their current methods of ship design and construction are out of date.

That we have made appreciably greater progress in the field of aviation and have attained an enormous increase in speed simply by modifying the shape of the fuselage is due principally to the work of Professor Junker, who has made a profound study of the laws of aerodynamics—in other words, of the laws of nature. It is therefore incomprehensible that the Navy should condemn as idiots such inventors as Fulton and Russell, who broke new ground, simply because these new methods might have entailed a revolution in the art of seafaring.

I have therefore ordered that the Sachsen ship, with its motive-power in front, should forthwith be built and given practical tests. I have further directed that tests be made of the practicability of propelling a ship by means of lateral screws—after the manner of fish-fins—a system which may well give a ship greater powers of manoeuvre and enable it to put about on a pivot.

These ideas of mine have been inspired by the thought that, whenever man is brought to a standstill in any technical field, then a free hand should be given to new inventors in their search for the way ahead. In the case of the microscope, for example, the time is approaching when it will not be possible further to increase the number of lenses integrated, for each additional lens absorbs a little more light. Progress in this field therefore will be attained only by means of some revolutionary invention. Unfortunately it is difficult in the extreme to secure acceptance for new inventions, for rare indeed are the men with minds sufficiently open and possessed of the strength of character to discard the work of a lifetime in favour of some new idea, especially when the latter may well emanate from some outsider.

We all know with what immense difficulty the theory of Copernicus triumphed over that of Ptolemy, and what great effects it had on the life of the world. For with the Ptolemaic theory collapsed a world upon which the whole philosophy of the Church was founded. At the time, it required great courage to declare oneself in favour of the Copernican theory and to take the consequences, for the Church defended itself without mercy.

Which is understandable, of course, for the more bigoted a man or an organisation is, the more shattering becomes the impact of the revelation of their errors and, with it, the destruction of the whole basis of their thought. History shows that inventors have met much the same fate.

The postmaster who made the epoch-making discovery that it was possible to place a vehicle on rails and propel it by steam was, at the time, uproariously ridiculed by the postal directors—that is, by the experts. The tragedy is that it is always an inventor's fate to attack something which is already established and which has therefore come to be regarded by the people as immutable. In addition, the initial effect of a new invention is invariably to create disorder. War, which gives added impetus to every form of activity, is therefore undoubtedly the most favourable atmosphere for invention. Aviation, for instance, made more progress in three and a half years of war than in thirty years of peace. One has only to recollect that in 1906 it was taken as axiomatic that the aeroplane was valueless unless it could attain a speed of twenty-five miles an hour.

3rd June 1942, at dinner
Technological warfare—The elephants of Hannibal

It is astonishing to note to what a degree the ancients succeeded in adapting technology to the needs of war. The victories of Hannibal without his elephants, or of Alexander without his chariots, his cavalry and the technique of his archers are impossible to conceive. In war, the best soldier—that is to say, the soldier who achieves the greatest success—is the one who has the most modern technical means at his disposal, not only in battle itself, but also in the field of communications and supply.

In time of war, to face oneself with the dilemma—shall we have a soldier or a technical expert?—is the greatest mistake one can possibly make. A sound strategy, therefore, must be one which succeeds in moulding the technical means at its disposal in such a manner as to meet one's needs with the maximum of efficiency.

4th June 1942, at dinner
Murder in Prague—Heydrich's imprudence and rashness
The Führer comments on the assassination of Heydrich.[453]

I shall forthwith give an absolute order that in future our men who are particularly exposed to danger must implicitly obey the regulations laid down to ensure their safety.

Since it is the opportunity which makes not only the thief but also the assassin, such heroic gestures as driving in an open, unarmoured vehicle or walking about the streets of Prague unguarded are just damned

---

[453] Reinhard Heydrich had been particularly successful in gaining the support for Germany from the Czech population, and the Czech government in exile in London, aware of the danger this posed to their future, had arranged for an assassination squad—trained by the British Special Operations Executive (SOE)—to be parachuted into Czechoslovakia in December 1941. They carried out their mission on May 27, 1942, with Heydrich dying of infection from the wounds he sustained in the attack on his open car as it slowed down to take a bend in Prague.

stupidity, which serves the country not one whit. That a man as irreplaceable as Heydrich should expose himself to unnecessary danger, I can only condemn as stupid and idiotic. Men of importance like Heydrich should know that they are eternally being stalked like game, and that there are any number of people just waiting for the chance to kill them.

The police alone, with the means of information at their disposal, cannot guarantee security. When a car collides with a tree, for example, it takes them goodness knows how long to decide whether there has, in fact, been any foul play.

If a driver is shot, and the car crashes, the passengers cannot really know what has happened, for when one is travelling at sixty miles an hour a bullet reaches its mark long before the sound of its discharge is heard. So long as conditions in our territories remain unstable, and until the German people has been completely purged of the foreign rabble, our public men must exercise the greatest care for their safety. That is in the interest of the nation.

5th June 1942, midday
Pre-disposition of the Finns to mental diseases—Effects of study of the Bible thereon—Religious mania—Germans must avoid spiritual sickness

The topic of conversation was the exceptionally large number of cases of mental disease in Finland. Among the causes put forward as possible explanations of the vulnerability of the Finns to these types of diseases were—the Aurora Borealis and the strong inclination prevalent among Finns to worry unduly over religious problems. In Finland the farms are often as much as thirty to fifty miles apart, and the inhabitants, condemned, particularly in winter, to a comparatively isolated existence, feel the need of mental exercise; an exceptionally strong tendency to religious surmise is therefore understandable.

The Führer expressed himself as follows: It is a great pity that this tendency towards religious thought can find no better outlet than the Jewish pettifoggery of the Old Testament. For religious people who, in the solitude of winter, continually seek ultimate light on their religious problems with the assistance of the Bible, must eventually become spiritually deformed.

The wretched people strive to extract truths from these Jewish chicaneries, where in fact no truths exist. As a result they become embedded in some rut of thought or other and, unless they possess an exceptionally common-sense mind, degenerate into religious maniacs.

It is deplorable that the Bible should have been translated into German, and that the whole of the German people should have thus become exposed to the whole of this Jewish mumbo-jumbo.

So long as the wisdom, particularly of the Old Testament, remained exclusively in the Latin of the Church, there was little danger that sensible people would become the victims of illusions as the result of studying the Bible.

But since the Bible became common property, a whole heap of people have found opened to them lines of religious thought which—particularly in conjunction with the German characteristic of persistent and somewhat melancholy meditation—as often as not turned them into religious maniacs. When one recollects further that the Catholic Church has elevated to the status of Saints a whole number of madmen, one realises why movements such as that of the Flagellants[454] came inevitably into existence in the Middle Ages in Germany.

As a sane German, one is flabbergasted to think that German human beings could have let themselves be brought to such a pass by Jewish filth and priestly twaddle, that they were little different from the howling dervish of the Turks and the negroes, at whom we laugh so scornfully.

It angers one to think that, while in other parts of the globe religious teaching like that of Confucius, Buddha and Mohammed offers an undeniably broad basis for the religious-minded, Germans should have been duped by a theological exposition devoid of all honest depth.

When one seeks reasons for these phenomena, one is immediately struck by the extent to which the human brain reacts to external influence.

A child, for example, who in its very early years has been frightened with the threat of the bogey-man in the dark, will frequently retain throughout all the years of its development a fear of entering a dark room, a cellar or the like; among women a fear of this nature inculcated in early youth often persists for a lifetime.

On the other hand, there are dangers which, not ever having come to his notice, a man completely ignores. A child living in an area exposed to bombing and to whom the dangers of a bombardment have

---

[454] Flagellants emerged in Christian Europe in the 14th Century, where religious people took to beating themselves in public as "repentance" for sins which they though God had sent them in the form of war, famine, and plague. Some small groups, mainly Catholics, continue the practice to the present day.

not been explained, will regard an enemy air attack as a noisy firework display, and will not as a rule show the slightest sign of fear.

The essential conclusion to which these considerations leads me is that we must do everything humanly possible to protect for all time any further sections of the German people from the danger of mental deformity, regardless of whether it be religious mania or any other type of cerebral derangement. For this reason I have directed that every town of any importance shall have an observatory, for astronomy has been shown by experience to be one of the best means at man's disposal for increasing his knowledge of the universe, and thus saving him from any tendency towards mental aberration.

5th June 1942, at dinner
A Saint is promoted to the rank of General!

A report was submitted to the Führer, according to which the Caudillo[455] *had decided, in a decree dated 22nd September 1941, to award the full honours of a Field-Marshal to Saint Funicisla, the patron saint of Segovia, in recognition of the miracle she performed five years ago, whereby three thousand nationalist soldiers under the command of de Volera, the Minister for War at the time, were enabled successfully to defend that city against an assault by fifteen thousand Reds. He was told also of another case in which a saint was appointed General because, when a bomb penetrated the church of which she was the patron saint, she prevented it from exploding.*

The Führer intervened as follows: I have the gravest possible doubts that any good can come of nonsense of this kind. I am following the development of Spain with the greatest scepticism, and I've already made up my mind that, though eventually I may visit every other European country, I shall never go to Spain.

7th June 1942, midday
Monarchical tendencies in Spain supported by the Church—Same old tactics for the seizing of power—A new revolution in Spain would spell ruin—Two "little requests" from Admiral Horthy[456]—*The river Tisza is the Hungarian Rhine—Horthy's son—Inter-allied Military Commissions in 1925—Treason among Germans—The émigrés of 1933—Views on the crime of treason—All traitors should be shot—Conscientious objectors—Settling with "Bible students"*

---

[455] "Caudillo": In Spain, a military or political leader. In this case, Francisco Franco
[456] Miklós Horthy (1868–1957), Hungarian admiral who served as regent of the Kingdom of Hungary from 1920 to 1944.

During discussion about the Blue Division—the Spanish Division serving on the Eastern front—the conversation turned once more to the internal situation in Spain. Reichsleiter Bormann remarked that the increasing swing in favour of a monarchy received more than a little encouragement from the clergy. The Führer agreed, and continued: The activities of the Church in Spain are no different from those of the Catholic Church in our own country, or indeed from those of most Churches in any other country. Any Church, provided it is in a position to exert influence on the civil regime, will, as a matter of principle, support or tolerate only such a regime as knows and recognises no form of popular organisation other than one under the aegis of the Church, and is therefore dependent, for purposes of general administration, solely on the Church, as the only organised leadership of the people.

Unless it is prepared to renounce that striving for power, which is inherent in every Church participating in politics, the Church in Spain cannot recognise the present regime, which has created in the Falange an organisation of its own for the direction of the Spanish people. There is therefore only one thing the Falange can do to establish definite relations with the Church, and that is to limit the intervention of the latter to religious—that is, supernatural—affairs. If one once allows the Church to exercise the slightest influence on the governing of the people and the upbringing of the younger generation, it will strive to become omnipotent, and one makes a great mistake if one thinks that one can make a collaborator of the Church by accepting a compromise.

The whole international outlook and political interest of the Catholic Church in Spain render inevitable conflict between the Church and the Franco regime, and a new revolution thus comes within the bounds of possibility. Spain may well have to pay with her blood, in the not too distant future, for her failure to carry through a truly national revolution, as was done in Germany and Italy.

Kállay,[457] the new Prime Minister of Hungary, came to me with two "little requests" from Regent Horthy—namely, that firstly the Lord God and secondly I myself should turn a benevolent blind eye if the Hungarians started a fight with the Romanians. From the Hungarian point of view, said Kállay, such a fight would be a struggle against Asia, for the frontier between Europe and Asia was, in Hungarian eyes, the line where the Orthodox Church ceased to hold sway. It was, after all, he

---

[457] Miklós Kállay (1887–1967), Prime Minister of Hungary from 1942 to 1944.

said, only the countries on this side of that frontier which had played their part in European cultural development and all its great accomplishments, such as the Reformation, the Renaissance and the like. It was for this reason that Hungary had always been hostile to Russia and had at the time been at a loss to understand the policy of the Third Reich when it made its pact with Russia.

Kállay went on to point out that the river Tisza held the same significance for the Hungarians as did the Rhine for Germans. The Rhine, in German eyes, was a German river; in the same way the Tisza to Hungarians was not an international frontier but a national waterway. In the field of domestic politics, Kállay mentioned the necessity for a Land Reform Act in Hungary. Such a reform, he thought, should, however, confine itself simply to increasing the size of the very smallest holdings.

Kállay then spoke of Horthy's son, whom he described as a great thruster and whom, he asserted, the Hungarian troops fighting on our Eastern front regarded as a great hero. This I can well believe, for I know that his father, the Regent, is a man of exceptional courage.

I must say I think Horthy has worked out a very neat plan. For, if his son wins his spurs fighting for the Germans, then the latter can hardly raise any objections if the Hungarians appoint him deputy to his father and eventually grace him with the glory of the crown of St. Stephen.[458] Equally Horthy's Hungarian political opponents can take no possible exception to the activities of Horthy junior, since he has proved himself in the struggle against Bolshevism.

Under the Weimar Republic treason assumed such proportions that even military secrets were published in the press and bandied about in open session in the Reichstag. When the foreign military commissions quit Germany in 1925, they left behind them an organised Intelligence Service and spy-ring, which not only rendered their further presence redundant but, in the opinion of the military attachés accredited to Berlin, has also functioned to their complete satisfaction ever since.

I was again and again infuriated by the state of moral degeneracy which alone made possible the setting up of this gigantic spy-ring in Germany and which found expression in the most blatant and shameless form of treason. Even today I remember a case, where a Member of the Reichstag asked, in open session, whether the Government was

---

[458] Stephen I (975–1038) was the first King of Hungary in 1000. His crown is still in existence and is a national symbol of that nation, even though the monarchy was abolished in 1918.

aware of the fact that in *X Street* a section of four tanks of the German Reichswehr had been seen, whose specifications were obviously
contrary to the conditions imposed by the Versailles Treaty, and what
action did the Government propose to take in the matter?

Alas, at that time I could do no more than cause a list to be drawn
up of all these traitorous elements, so as to be in a position, after the
assumption of power by the National Socialist Party, at least to punish
these blackguards as they deserved.

That we got rid of the majority of this riff-raff in 1933 without having to do much about it, is due to the fact that no fewer than 65,000
citizens of the State fled the country as soon as we came into power. I
admit we did not know exactly what misdemeanour each individual
had committed, but we were pretty safe in assuming that in most cases
it was the dictates of their own consciences which caused them to flee
abroad.

A little later quite a number of them thought better of it and showed
an inclination to return to Germany. We quickly dammed this flow-
back of undesirable elements by announcing that all who returned
would, as a matter of principle, have to pass through the concentration
camps, and that any against whom crimes were proved would be liable to be shot. In this way the Reich was freed of many thousands of
anti-social elements, whom it would otherwise have been difficult to
catch or fling out.

Heydrich and his *Sicherheitsdienst*[459] very soon broke up the rest—a
service that was all the more valuable because the Department of Justice proved quite incapable of the task. Our Department of Justice frequently enraged me by its handling of crimes of treason. For instance,
on one occasion they recommended a traitor to mercy on the grounds
that he was "primarily employed as a smuggler and should therefore be
dealt with as such"!

It was only with the greatest difficulty that I was able to persuade Dr.
Gürtner, the Minister for Justice, of the absolute necessity of exercising
the utmost severity in cases of treason. When details of fortifications
in East Prussia were betrayed, Gürtner went so far as to recommend a
mild punishment, because, after all, the damage done was of a minor

---

[459] The *Sicherheitsdienst des Reichsführers-SS* (Security Service of the Reichsführ-
er-SS), or SD, was the SS's own intelligence agency. It was established in 1931
and in 1939 was transferred over to the state *Reichssicherheitshauptamt* (Reich
Security Main Office).

nature! I told Gürtner pretty straight that it was quite impossible to judge what damage had been done. How could one tell whether, one day, one of these betrayed strong-points would not be occupied in war by a Divisional Commander and his Staff and be destroyed? Such an event might have a decisive effect on operations. Was that damage "of a minor nature"?

Eventually I had to tell Gürtner of my implacable resolve to have traitors, who had been too leniently treated by the normal courts, handed over to an SS Commando and shot. For treason is an offence revealing a criminal lack of conscience,[460] and every traitor must be executed regardless of the amount of damage he has done. Initially, the People's Court,[461] set up under the aegis of the Department of Justice, did not, in my opinion, carry out its task with that measure of severity which I thought desirable. It was also by no means easy to make the Legislature adapt itself to the obvious needs of the State, because the jurist members of the Cabinet agreed only after much hesitation to accept treason as a crime revealing a hostile mind.

In all the discussions on this subject I found myself repeatedly compelled to say that such a thing as treason on idealistic grounds did not exist. The only type of treason which one might possibly regard as springing from certain moral inhibitions is a refusal to join the armed forces on grounds of religious conviction.

But we should not fail to point out to these elements which refuse to fight on religious grounds that they obviously still want to eat the things others are fighting to get for them, that this was quite contrary to the spirit of a higher justice, and that we must therefore leave them to starve.

I regard it as an act of exceptional clemency that I did not, in fact, carry out this threat, but contented myself with shooting one hundred and thirty of these self-styled *Bible Students*.

Incidentally, the execution of these hundred and thirty cleared the air, just like a thunderstorm does. When the news of the shootings was made public, many thousands of similarly minded people who proposed to avoid military service on the score of some religious scruple or other lost their courage and changed their minds. If you wish to wage war successfully or to lead a people successfully through a dif-

---

[460] The original German is *ein Gesinnungsdelikt*, literally, "a conscience delict."
[461] The *Volksgerichtshof* (People's Court) was established in 1934 to have jurisdiction over a political offenses.

ficult period of its history, you must have no doubts whatever on one point—namely, any individual who in such times tries, either actively or passively, to exclude himself from the activities of the community, must be destroyed. Anyone who for false reasons of mercy deviates from this clear principle is aiding, willingly or unwillingly, the dissolution of the State. We can see the beginnings of this process today in a country like Sweden.

7th June 1942, at dinner

A Procession at Barcelona—Harassing the Falange—My distrust of Serrano Suñer—Superior resistance of Italians to Church heresies— German Emperors and the Church—A Requiem Mass for the Protector of Bohemia and Moravia

The Führer was informed that on the occasion of the Corpus Christi procession in Barcelona, the Governor of the town forbade by edict the people taking part in the procession to wear the uniform either of the Falange, the Falangist Militia or any part of them. A solitary exception was made in favour of the regional Chief of the Falange and his suite. It appears from the report that this prohibition was obtained by the Nationalists through the medium of the Church authorities. In this connection it will be recalled that some weeks ago incidents occurred between the Nationalists and the members of the Falange, who nevertheless represent the official State Party. It is further significant that the Madrid newspaper Arriba *attacks this ban and states roundly that the wearing of the blue shirt is a duty to which the Falangists are in honour bound, and that all those who oppose them are despicable creatures.*

The Führer's opinion follows: One sees only too clearly from this sort of thing how the Spanish State is rushing towards fresh disaster. The priests and the monarchists—the same mortal enemies who opposed the resurgence of our own people—have joined together to seize power in Spain.

If a new civil war breaks out, I should not be surprised to see the Falangists compelled to make common cause with the Reds to rid themselves of the clerico-monarchical muck. What a pity it is that the bloodshed in common by the Falangists, the Fascists and the National Socialists during the war has not brought better results! But in Spain, unfortunately, someone will always be found willing to serve the political interests of the Church.

Serrano Suñer, the present Minister for Foreign Affairs, is one of them. From my first meeting with him I was conscious of a feeling of revulsion, in spite of the fact that our Ambassador, with abysmal ignorance of the facts, introduced him to me as the most ardent Germanophile in Spain.

That the Fascists were spared a second civil war is due to the fact that the movement, initiated in Rome, succeeded in uniting the Italian nation in spite of the opposition of the Church. Further, Fascism clearly defined the position as regards what things fell within the sphere of the Church and what things fell within the sphere of the State.

When the Church refused to recognise the law for the formation of the Fascist Youth Organisation, the Fascists retaliated by ruthlessly breaking up every religious procession from Rome right down to the South of Italy. The result was that within three days the Church had come to heel.

Speaking generally, the history of Italy shows that the Italian people adopt a very much more realistic attitude towards the Church than do the Spaniards or, alas, not a few Germans! Is it not a sad thought that each time the Italians flung out some Pope or other, there was always a German Kaiser ready and willing to restore order in the Vatican? I must be honest and confess that I myself have not been guiltless in this respect.

By creating a Bishop of the Reich I tried to bring a little clarity into the equivocal situation in the Evangelical Church. When I see what is happening today in Spain, I congratulate myself on the failure of my efforts. Once more Providence prevented me from committing a mistake I was on the point of making. Who, indeed, is prepared to give me a guarantee that one fine day the Protestant Bishop of the Reich will not make common cause against me with the Pope!

The established religions, and particularly the Catholic Church, are adepts at presenting an innocent mien and in flattering the man in power. I myself experienced this when, shortly after assuming power, I received a visit from the Bishop Bertram.[462] He brought me the good wishes and the homage of the Catholic clergy with such unction that, had I not known differently from bitter personal experience, I would not have believed it possible that a single National Socialist could have been excluded from the Church on account of his convictions, or could have been persecuted, and even execrated after death. It is with such semblance of humility that the Church has always wormed its way into

---

[462] Adolf Bertram (1859–1945), Catholic archbishop of Breslau (now Wroclaw in Poland) from 1914 to 1945.

power and succeeded in winning its way by flattery into the good graces of the German Emperors, from Charlemagne onwards.

It is the same technique as that employed by sophisticated women, who at first exude charm in order to gain a man's confidence, and then gradually tighten the strings, until they hold them so firmly that the man dances like a puppet to their whims. With a little diplomatic *savoir faire* such women manage even to persuade their husbands—exactly as in the case of the Church and the German Emperors—that it is they who rule the roost, and this in spite of the nose ring on which they are so obviously being led!

Quite recently the Church tried to pull off a new one of this kind. The Bishop of Bohemia and Moravia begged permission to be allowed to hold a Requiem Mass with chimes for *SS Obergruppenführer* Heydrich. I told the gentleman bluntly that he would have been much better employed if he had previously offered prayers for the safety and welfare of the Reich Protector!

8th June 1942, at dinner

The role of coming generations—Extension of the Germanic idea—A new name for the Reich capital—Youth should lead youth—Ridiculous anomalies in religious divergence—Influence of the National Socialist youth within the family—Penurious inadequacy of school-teachers—Propaganda—The role of the Press in national education

During dinner photographs were passed round, showing the Reich Youth Leader in the company of Youth Group Leaders, male and female, from Norway, Denmark, Holland, etc. The Führer expressed himself as follows: It is an excellent thing that Axmann has been at the front as a soldier. The loss of an arm in battle will undoubtedly enhance his prestige with the youths, not only of Germany, but also of the other countries. I am very pleased, too, to welcome Axmann's efforts, and to see how he strives continuously to bind the youth of the German lands with ever closer bonds to National Socialism and to the German way of thought.

For once youth has been won over to an idea, an action like that of yeast sets in. Youth effervesces and goes on working and working for an idea, regardless of anything that the older generation can do to stop them. Even in Denmark, the opposition of the older generations will not prevent the youth from adopting in ever-increasing numbers the German way of thought, for they feel they spring from the same racial origins.

By methodically supporting the development of this movement I am cutting the ground from under the feet of the old King of Denmark and drawing his people away from him, in exactly the same way as I succeeded at the time in estranging the people of Austria slowly but surely from the Dollfuss-Schuschnigg regime.

Following the example of Bismarck, who never ceased to preach the pan-Germanic idea to the Bavarians, the Prussians, etc., we must systematically draw all the Germanic peoples of continental Europe into the German channel of thought.

I really believe that by re-naming Berlin the capital of our Reich "Germania", we would give very considerable impetus to the movement. The name Germania for the capital of the Reich in its new representative form would be very appropriate, for it would give to every member of the German community, however far away from the capital he may be, a feeling of unity and closer membership. There would be no technical difficulty about re-naming Berlin, as we can see from the Germanisation of Gdynia into Gotenhafen and the changing of the name of Lodz into Litzmannstadt.

In the same way as the press, the school also must be used as an instrument for the education of the people, and must therefore be organised and directed without any regard for private interests.

The school alone, however, as the instrument for the education of youth, does not suffice, because it is too prone to give priority of interest to purely academic achievement. It is for this reason that I have formed the supplementary organisation of the Hitlerjugend and endowed it with the bold motto "youth must be led by youth."[463]

In this way I have set up, in their very early years, a process of selectivity amongst young people, whereby the little group leaders soon select themselves. To the judgment of the schoolmaster, who normally confines himself to exact scholastic attainments, is thus added by the Hitler Youth the judgment of the youth leaders, which lays primary value on character—that is, on sense of comradeship, endurance, courage and qualities of leadership.

The effective value of the school and the Hitler Youth as instruments of education depends on the quality of the instructors. In the choice of leaders for the Hitler Youth and of teachers for the Department of Education, our first principle must be to ensure that these instructors of both kinds are chosen from men who will remain as an example to

[463] "Jugend soll durch Jugend geführt werden."

youth for the rest of their lives, exactly as the instructors in the gymnasia of Ancient Greece set the example of bodily and spiritual perfection to the youth submitted to their charge. It is between the ages of ten and seventeen, that youth exhibits both the greatest enthusiasm and the greatest idealism, and it is for this period of their lives that we must provide them with the best possible instructors and leaders, for only the very best will guarantee the high standard of education at which we uniformly aim.

The criminal follies committed under the Weimar Republic in the field of education were most clearly demonstrated to me by a report on the conditions obtaining in Baden at the time of our assumption of power. The factional splitting of youth education in Baden had been carried to such a pitch that there were actually separate water-closets for Protestant and Catholic children! The Government of the time was apparently blissfully ignorant of the corrosive poison which such a partition of the educational system injected into the soul of youth.

It is also during these years of adolescent development that a child's sensibility is at its strongest. How many of our leading Party members were originally brought into the National Socialist movement by the influence of their own children! Again and again young people, filled with enthusiasm for National Socialism, have succeeded first in persuading their mother, and then, with her help, in winning over the father for the NSDAP.

It is therefore most important that a proper appreciation of the requirements of youth should be inculcated and' strengthened among the teachers in schools. For the ensuring of a continuous supply of school-teachers, we must not overlook the claims of those who, from their environment or as a result of their professional activities, are particularly suited to the purpose. I am thinking primarily, in this respect, of the women and the time-expired soldiers.

In my opinion, women teachers and ex-soldiers are ideal for the elementary schools. There is no need to give these teachers any exaggerated form of training or to stuff their heads till they become stupid with mental indigestion; all that is required is to equip them with just the knowledge that is essential for the elementary schools. A teacher who is destined to spend his life in a village has no need of high academic learning.

This does not *at* all mean that teachers who prove exceptionally efficient should be deprived of the opportunity of promotion. One does not keep a keen officer for ever drilling recruits; if one did, he'd probably hang himself!

In the same way, the best of our teachers must be given the chance of advancement into the higher branches of their profession, and not be condemned to teach for ever in the elementary schools. And in particular, we must make it easy for them to be promoted from elementary to intermediate schools.

Reichsleiter Bormann has just told us that there is such a dearth of teachers in the Warthegau, that it has been necessary to reduce the period of preparatory training even below that obtaining in Austria. Personally, I don't think that matters very much. Those who feel within themselves the urge to higher things will use their free time in seeking the necessary knowledge.

The important thing is that all those who feel that they are worthy of an intermediate or higher education should know that the State will pave their way as regards both instruction and study.

Conversation then turned to questions of administration, the complexities of its organisation and the duplication of effort which not infrequently ensued. The Führer said: In my opinion, it is a mistake to set up a propaganda department in each Ministry, and even in some of the higher administrative departments.

The Ministry of Propaganda and the Press Service of the Reich are there to meet all needs. I have myself set an example in the Chancellery, by refraining from setting up any special propaganda or press department, and I do not find that this in any way hinders the immediate fulfilment of any press or propaganda instructions I issue.

When I am travelling, I can stop at any railway station, give any instructions I consider necessary, and be sure that, through the medium of the press and the radio, by the next morning public opinion will be properly prepared for any political announcement I may have to make—even a Russo-German pact!

It is only by means of the concentration of the whole machinery of press and propaganda in one single organisation that a unified direction of the press can be assured.

And a unified press is a prerequisite, if the press is to enjoy the confidence of the people and thus also to become effective as an instrument of popular education. For only a unified press is free from those contradictions of news items, of political, cultural and such-like communications, which make it laughable in the eyes of the public, rob it of any prestige as a purveyor of truth and of any value as an instrument for the education of public opinion.

How little this was understood in the circle of the so-called national press was brought home to me in 1920 in the course of an altercation with the Reverend Traub,[464] the editor of *Eiserne Blätter*.

When I told the reverend gentleman as bluntly as I could that a free press must give way to a unified and controlled press, because the former was nothing more nor less than a free forum for the dissemination of Jewish impertinences, he crumpled entirely. The mentality of the so-called Nationalists of the type of the Reverend Traub was very correctly assessed by Dietrich Eckart, when he declared that the *Eiserne Blätter*[465] should more properly be called *Blecherne Blätter*.[466] What an enormously important instrument for the education of public opinion the press could become was never understood by the so-called Nationalists. And yet, what other instrument is so well suited to the purpose? I myself put the press on the same footing as the Department of Education, and in both cases, I maintain, private interests must play no part whatsoever, either in their organisation or in the control of them.

22nd June 1942, midday

Popularity of Rommel and Dietl—Fine British publicity for Rommel—
Motorised warfare in the desert—The triumph of the Volkswagen

Dr. Goebbels turned the conversation to the subject of General Rommel. He stated that Generals like Brauchitsch, Rundstedt and others were far from enjoying a popularity comparable to that of Rommel or Dietl. If the press were suddenly to stop writing about men like Brauchitsch and Rundstedt, the public would soon forget all about them.

Rommel and Dietl, on the other hand, stood so high in popular esteem that their names had become the personification of German military virtues; and this applied even more, perhaps, to Rommel than to Dietl.

The Führer expressed himself as follows: Dietl is popular not only here at home, but also in Finland.

As for Rommel, there are two main reasons which explain why he is the centre of public interest in Germany:

---

[464] Gottfried Traub (1869–1956), a conservative theologian who was a co-founder of the *Deutschnationalen Volkspartei* (German National People's Party, or DNVP) and who edited the magazine *Eiserne Blatter* from 1919 until it was banned in 1939. From 1933 onward he was an outspoken critic of Hitler's.
[465] "The Iron Pages."
[466] "The Lead Pages."

(*a*) The majority of our people now understand enough about the background of this war to rejoice greatly over every individual victory over Britain.

(*b*) The British themselves, as Dr. Goebbels rightly says, have given Rommel enormous publicity, because, by writing up his exceptional military capabilities, they hoped to make more palatable to their own people the defeats suffered at his hands.

Rommel's efficiency, of course, is unquestionable. From the very beginning of the present offensive, he foretold with almost photographic accuracy the advance to the coast and the attack on Tobruk; he then added that the British would certainly fall into the trap he had prepared for them, and would occupy a triangle, which seemed to them to be a favourable position, but in reality was commanded by German flak fire, and would be shot to pieces. Rommel's victories, moreover, have been made possible by our timely recognition of the fact that desert warfare is a battle of machines.

The enemy, on the other hand, had a completely wrong conception of desert warfare, because they had arrived at completely wrong conclusions about the capabilities of motor vehicles in the desert.

How often in the history of war has some General Staff officer or other—unhindered by any practical experience—developed the thesis that motor vehicles in the desert can operate only along the highways— and how often has this thesis been hailed as axiomatic! It has always been my wont to insist that theoretical theses of this sort must be tested practically, and it was on these grounds that I ordered the construction of the Volkswagen. And it was this same Volkswagen, which is now giving so magnificent an account of itself in the desert, that convinced me of the futility of this particular thesis. The Volkswagen—and I think our war experiences justify us in saying so—is the car of the future. One had only to see the way in which these Volkswagen roaring up the Obersalzberg overtook and skipped like mountain goats round my great Mercedes, to be tremendously impressed.

After the war, when all the modifications dictated by war experience have been incorporated in it, the Volkswagen will become the car *par excellence* for the whole of Europe, particularly in view of the fact that it is air-cooled, and so unaffected by any winter conditions. I should not be surprised to see the annual output reach anything from a million to a million and a half.[467]

[467] Although built by Dr. Ferdinand Porsche, the basic shape of the Volkswagen

23rd June 1942, midday
Minimum restrictions for the people—The fear of the policeman—Black Market—Understanding for the peasants—Middle-men—Transportation chaos

Gauleiter Forster said that the cafés in Danzig were literally packed in the afternoons. As they had observed that there were a large number of women, heavily made-up and apparently with nothing to do, the police had asked Förster's permission to take these cafés under control. He himself was disinclined to give this permission. The Führer intervened: Quite right! With very few exceptions indeed, everybody in the Reich today has been integrated into the general plan of work—including the women. If the police dog every step of the citizens, we shall turn Germany into a hard-labour prison.

The duty of the police is to keep the really anti-social elements under surveillance and to render them harmless. But this does not necessitate the surveillance of places of public entertainment.

Actually, women who are carrying on relations with some foreigner do not chose a café for a rendezvous, but invite them, rather, to their so-called *salons*. As for the women who frequent the cafés, they are for the most part workers—postal employees, teachers, nurses and the like—off duty and enjoying a moment of repose. There are also a number of housewives, who, deprived of all home life at the moment, but having to work much harder than ever they worked in peace-time, have a right to seek a little distraction. For the rest, if you keep all the somewhat flighty women out of the cafés, the first people to suffer in consequence will be the lads on leave from the front.

For goodness' sake, don't let us rush to the police every time some small peccadillo raises its head. Let us rather stick to educative measures. Don't forget, after all, that it was not by using fear inspired by police methods that we National Socialists won over the people, but rather by trying to show them the light and to educate them.

The same principle applies to food control. The professional black marketeer must be pursued and punished with the utmost rigour, but there is no need to stop trains, hold up motor-cars and badger people because they have bought a couple of eggs "off the record". And the

---

Beetle was designed by Hitler on a paper napkin which he gave to Porsche during a luncheon in 1934. Ultimately, over 40 million VW Beetles were to be manufactured worldwide between 1945 and 2003, making it the most successful motor vehicle in history.

peasant who, after having fulfilled the obligations put on him, helps a friend out with a bit from his surplus, need not have the police put on his tracks. The only effect of that would be to make him eat up all his surplus himself.

Those who took the initiative in causing passengers in trains and cars to be searched ought to remember the conditions which obtain in the North, the land of the big properties.

They surely must have forgotten that even in peace-time the humble peasant woman used to go to the town market to sell a few eggs, a few pounds of butter—things which she thought too precious to be eaten at her own table. No—but if one thinks that this sort of little black-market is assuming too large proportions, to a point where it may have some influence on prices, then the State must intervene again, and buy out of hand, but at prices a little above the official market rates, the entire surplus.

In this case we must act warily, not forgetting that a peasant who has fulfilled the obligations put upon him has the right to dispose of his surplus as he pleases. This encourages him to work harder, and it also helps in consolidating the value of money. Actually, while the peasant tends to hoard, the townsman, on the contrary, tends—particularly in troublesome times—to transform his money into goods.

Dr. Goebbels said the Führer's idea of making the State step in as a subsidiary purchaser was a solution after the manner of Columbus and the egg. When the Führer asked how soon it would be possible to draw up adequate regulations, Bormann replied that the necessary steps had been taken and would come into force very soon, and that a system of price control appropriate to the situation had also been evolved.

The Führer continued: It really is enough to make anyone angry, when one thinks that people are being deprived of essential food simply thanks to the pettiness of certain regulations—and that the food all the time is rotting in the store-rooms. I was furious, for example, when I heard that our soldiers were forbidden to purchase anything they liked in the French shops.

The mighty intellects which conceived measures of this kind are obviously incapable of putting themselves in the place of the soldier who wants to send a little parcel home—a few pairs of stockings, a bit of chocolate, etc.—or to appreciate the tremendous joy such a parcel gives in the family. It required Göring's personal intervention to get this stupid rule cancelled.

As regards fruit and vegetables, Forster said he had authorised direct sale from producer to consumer, with the object of preventing the deterioration of perishable goods while passing through the hands of middle-men. Forster thought, for example, that it was ridiculous to try to stop people from buying asparagus and strawberries direct from the producer by threatening them. These criticisms aimed at the inadequacy of the measures introduced by the Ministry of Food met with general agreement, and the Führer declared that they were well-founded.

The gentlemen in the Ministry must be made to understand that this nonsense has got to stop. Such inept conceptions are simply the result of stubborn concentration on the conditions obtaining in North German big business. Surely they must see by this time that it is the manifold diversity of conditions existing in the field of food supply and distribution which themselves make it essential to restrict rules of universal application to an absolute minimum.

Dr. Goebbels expressed the fear that, from the Berlin point of view, the workmen might well be placed at a disadvantage by an unrestricted authorisation of direct purchase by consumer from producer. The effect might be that the wealthy would send their servants, and the idle would go themselves, into the country and buy up all the fruit and vegetables, while the Berlin workman would then find nothing to buy in the fruit and vegetable stalls of the local market. Replying to a question by the Führer, Bormann said that direct purchase was being controlled by the Gauleiters according to local conditions. In certain West German territories, for example, and in Mutschman's area, it was forbidden.

The Führer concluded: It is essential that the continual carting to and fro of fruit and vegetables, with the great loss of perishable goods which ensues, must be stopped. The transportation of potatoes, too, hither and thither all over Germany, as Speer recently proved to me with voluminous graphs, is sheer idiocy.

Speer further told me that beer and cigarettes were also being carted about in the same aimless fashion. This chaos must also come to an end. It is nonsense that cigarettes manufactured in Dresden should be sent to Berlin for distribution, and that then a portion of them, representing the ration for Saxony, should solemnly be sent back to Dresden. We cannot afford the luxury of such futilities.

We must approach this problem of the transportation of supplies with strict logic. Such produce as is not required for local consumption must be sent to the *nearest* district in which there is a deficiency in these particular goods. Industrial towns must be assured of their supplies by help from the neighbouring countryside. We must encourage the setting up of big concerns, for not only are they easier to supervise, but they will also produce many times the volume that would be produced by a number of minor undertakings, occupying the same amount of ground.

We must further ensure a more methodical utilisation of foodstuffs in the great cities, by increasing in them the number of canteens for workers and employees and the number of public kitchens. This will enable the citizens to have a decent meal two or three times a week, and at the same time save ration coupons. The overriding principle must be that everything in the way of agricultural produce that is grown in the territories under German control must be at the disposal of the consumer. If, for example, eggs go bad in the Ukraine for lack of means of transportation, then we must use the immense reserves of straw held in that country for the manufacture of additional fuel for the gas-burning forms of transportation, which could help solve the problem. As Speer rightly said, if we stop carting beer uselessly about the country, we shall have ample refrigerator wagons for other purposes.

24th June 1942, at dinner
The right man in the right place—The choice of leaders—A free hand for regional Chiefs—Decentralisation and unity—Choice of the Head of the State—Emperors by election

From the time I started to organise the Party, I made it a rule never to fill an appointment until I had found the right man for it. I applied this principle to the post of Berlin *Gauleiter*. Even when the older members of the Party bombarded me with complaints over the Party leadership in Berlin, I refrained from coming to their assistance, until I could promise them that in Dr. Goebbels I had found the man I was seeking.

For Dr. Goebbels possesses two attributes, without which no one could master the conditions in Berlin: he has intelligence and the gift of oratory. Further, he is a typical son of the Ruhr—that type which, thanks to its close ties with the iron and steel processes, gives us a man of exceptional value and merit.

When I invited Goebbels to study the organisation of the Party in Berlin, he reported in due course that the weakness lay in the junior leaders, and he asked me for a free hand to make the necessary changes, and purge the Party of all unsatisfactory elements. I have never regretted giving him the powers he asked for. When he started, he found nothing particularly efficient as a political organisation to help him; nevertheless, in the literal sense of the word, he captured Berlin. He worked like an ox, regardless of all the stresses and strains to which the latent opposition of people like Stinnes must have exposed him.[468]

It is no longer possible today to insist on the same *corps d'élite* as leaders of the Party as we were able to find during the years of struggle. For in those days veritable idealists rushed forward, fanatically determined to give their all for the Idea.

Reichsleiter Bormann is quite right when he mentions Major Dincklage[469] in this respect—"the Rucksack Major," as he was called. Night and day Dincklage was on the road, speaking and recruiting for the NSDAP. When he got home, he stayed there for just so long as was needed to pack a little food in his rucksack, and off he went again. And he was typical of very many at the time.

Whenever I ponder over the question of selection of leaders, I often recall what happened in East Prussia. As long as the Party leadership in East Prussia remained in the hands of some nincompoop, the local landowners declared themselves with vigour in favour of the Party. For they regarded these men of ours as mere jacks-in-office, who could easily be swept away when the time came for them to take power into their own hands. But when I put Koch on their backs as *Gauleiter*—and they soon realised that was a very different proposition—then they immediately joined the camp of the opponents of the NSDAP.

The experience I gained while organising the Party during the *Kampfzeit*[470] will stand me in good stead now that I have the organisation of the Reich in my hands. If at the time I made the *Gauleiters* into Kings of their *Gau*, who received from above only the broadest possible instructions, I now intend to give to our *Reichsstatthalter*[471] the same

---

[468] Hugo Stinnes (1870–1924), Reichstag member for the conservative Deutschenationale Volkspartei (German People's Party, DNVP), an industrialist and important conservative newspaper owner of the *Deutsche Allgemeine Zeitung* in Berlin, the *Münchener Neueste Nachrichten* and the *München-Augsburger Zeitung*. As Stinnes died two years before Goebbels was deployed to Berlin for the NSDAP, Hitler is here referring to conservatives in general, who proved to be as much of an opponent of the NSDAP as those from the left.

[469] Karl Dincklage (1874–1930), SA (brownshirts) leader in Hanover.

[470] The "time of struggle", the period from 1925 to 1933 when Hitler fought for political power in the democratic system.

[471] "Reich Governor." The *Reichsstatthalters* were appointed directly by the Minis-

wide freedom, even if this should sometimes bring me into conflict with the Ministry of the Interior. It is only by giving the *Gauleiter* and the *Reichsstatthalter* a free hand that one finds out where real capability lies. Otherwise, there will eventually spring up a stolid, stupid bureaucracy. And it is only by giving the regional leaders responsibility that one will obtain men eager to accept it, and thus form a nucleus from which to chose leaders for the highest posts in the State.

While giving my *Gauleiters* and *Reichsstatthalters* the greatest possible liberty of action, I have at the same time demanded of them the strictest possible discipline in obedience to orders from above, it being understood, of course, that the central government is not concerned with matters of detail, which vary greatly in different parts of the country.

In this connection I want to lay particular emphasis on one point— namely, that there is nothing more harmful to the organisation of a State than over-centralisation and limitation of local power. The lawyers among us hanker constantly for such limitation. But, as Bismarck rightly pointed out in 1871, it was centralisation that had brought about the downfall of France; the petty *Départements,* being vested with no powers at all, were robbed of all initiative and sat dumbly awaiting instructions from Paris.

I can sum up my own views by saying that one should give to local authority the widest possible powers of self-government, but should at the same time ensure strict obedience to orders from above. Wherever superior authority intervenes, its orders must be regarded as final.

Side by side with the integrated legislative body must stand the executive, as the firmly established instrument of the national will; and this executive, with the *Wehrmacht* at its head, then the police, the labour organisation, the youth education, etc., must be in the control of one single man.

Together, these two—legislative body and executive—form the cement that binds the State into a single corporate entity. The State which succeeds in achieving this has nothing to fear. The greatest danger occurs when the executive possesses at the same time supreme legislative powers—or aspires to them. This leads inevitably to those rivalries between component units of the *Wehrmacht*, between provinces and so on, which in the past have caused the downfall of a number of most healthy States.

try of the Interior, and centralised control of all local governments.

As regards the Head of the State, should anything happen to me, it would be as unsound to elect my successor by public vote as it would for, say, the Pope to be elected by suffrage among the faithful, or the Doge of Venice by the vote of the whole population of the city. If the mass of the people were invited to take part in such a vote, the whole thing would degenerate into a propaganda battle, and the propaganda for or against any candidate would tear the people asunder. If the choice is left to a small body—a senate, for instance—and marked differences of opinion should arise in it, I don't think it would matter very much, provided that no hint of these differences was allowed to become public. But once the votes have been cast, then he who receives the majority becomes automatically and forthwith the supreme head of the state. If it is further arranged that the oath of allegiance to the new Head can be administered to the *Wehrmacht*, the Party and all the appropriate officials within three hours of the result of the election, then maintenance of public law and order can be regarded as assured.

I have no illusions, however, that an absolutely outstanding personality will always emerge by this method of selection. But it does at least ensure that the man chosen will be one so much above the average that, as long as the machinery of government is in good order, the State will not be endangered in any way.

The old German method of electing the Emperor was an ideal way of forming a government. It unfortunately broke down, however, because the princely electors were themselves hereditary princes in their own right. As Germany had for centuries been the incarnation of the western world, without ever being seriously menaced from outside, these hereditary sovereigns, preoccupied primarily with the domestic affairs of their own States, considered that they could afford to have the luxury of a weak Emperor—and consequently, a minimum of interference from the centre in their own affairs.

It must therefore be an absolute and fundamental principle of National Socialism that office in neither *Gau*, State nor Party is hereditary Each *Gauleiter*, I consider, should have a deputy. The danger that the latter might intrigue against his chief is precluded by the Party rule that no deputy may succeed his chief as *Gauleiter* in the *Gau* in which he has officiated as deputy.

In this way we National Socialists guard ourselves against a stab in the back. A Deputy *Gauleiter* can, of course, aspire to promotion as *Gauleiter* of a different province, always provided that he has never intrigued to bring about the downfall of his own Chief. The criterion for judging the qualities of a Deputy *Gauleiter* is the degree of prosperity in the *Gau*; for when all is going well in the *Gau*, it is not due solely to the work and the personality of the *Gauleiter*, but to those of his Deputy as well, who also has definite tasks of his own. As a sure safe-guard against a *Gau* ever becoming a hereditary post, I have adopted a system of transfer applicable to those *Gauleiters* who have not of their own efforts succeeded in winning over their *Gau* to National Social-ism. For example, I have transferred the *Gauleiter* of Salzburg to Styria, and have replaced him in Salzburg by a member of the Party who up till now had been doing work of a totally different kind. On the other hand, I would never send to a town like Vienna a man of whom I have high expectations later on in other spheres of activity. In short, there will never be any question of son succeeding father. Can you see me appointing some youngster of seventeen as Chief of the General Staff!

Bormann interposed that normally the son of a mathematics professor was not inclined to follow in father's footsteps.

The Führer concluded: Well, that is not surprising. As a general rule a son inherits the characteristics of his mother, and not those of his father. I know of the son of an industrialist who refused at any price to go into his father's business. Having inherited the idealism of his mother (who had been divorced and remarried), he decided to become a soldier, and a parachutist into the bargain.

27th June 1942, at dinner

Degrelle asserts—Magnificent behaviour of the Flamands—The three phases of the fate of Belgium and Holland-Roman roads and viaducts—Our road net-work in the East—Tobruk: a happy omen—Churchill and Roosevelt confer—Britain in the toils

The Reich Press Chief, Dr. Dietrich, invited the attention of the Führer to a complaint made by Degrelle,[472] the Belgian royalist leader (at present serving as a legionary on the Eastern front), to the effect that in the recent exchanges of prisoners of war there were never any Rexists among the Belgians so exchanged. The Belgian members of the Exchange Committee were, Degrelle maintained, out-and-out reactionaries, who persistently ignored the existence of the Rexists.

The Führer replied: I direct that steps be immediately taken to ensure that Degrelle has the decisive vote in the selection of Belgian prisoners

---

[472] Léon Degrelle (1906–1994), the Belgian Rexist Party (Rex) leader who served in the Waffen SS on the Eastern Front.

to be liberated. It goes without saying that those who are risking their lives for the Europe of tomorrow have prior claim to a sympathetic hearing in Germany. Let me add that I think we have acted far too leniently towards the Belgian reactionaries.

It was a mistake not to have made King Leopold a prisoner, and, out of consideration for his Italian friends who pleaded for him, to have allowed him to live in Belgium. For while this Belgian King is no intellectual luminary, he has an infinite capacity for intrigue and is the centre of attraction for all reactionaries.

As a counter-weight to these reactionary elements we have the magnificent conduct of the Flemish on the Eastern front. The Flamands have indeed shown themselves on the Eastern front to be more pro-German and more ruthless than the Dutch legionaries. This is certainly due to the fact that the Flemish have for centuries been oppressed by the Walloons. The lack of harmony between the Flamands and the Walloons has not escaped the notice of the Duce. When he speaks of the Europe of the future, he is wont to group the Flemish and the Dutch on one side, and the Walloons and the French on the other.

As regards the status of the Walloons, I am inclined to think that the Duce is not quite correct in his appreciation of the problem of North-western Europe. The solution which he is inclined to dangle before the eyes of the small minority of Walloons is hardly practicable within the framework of the Greater Germanic Empire.[473] I am pleased, therefore, that there exists neither in Holland nor in Belgium, any Government with which we should have to negotiate. This will enable us to impose whatever we feel is politically expedient and obviously useful. I propose solving the problems of these small States by means of brief and decisive declarations.

The beginnings of every civilisation express themselves in terms of road construction. Under the direction of Caesar, and during the first two centuries of the Germanic era, it was by means of the construction of roads and tracks that the Romans reclaimed the marshlands and blazed trails through the forests of Germania. Following their example, our first task in Russia will be to construct roads. To start off with the construction of railways would be to put the cart before the horse. In my opinion, the construction of at least seven hundred and fifty to one thousand miles of thoroughfare is required, on military grounds alone.

---

[473] In the original German, "*Das Grossgermanische Reich.*"

For unless we have unexceptional roads at our disposal, we shall not be able either to mop up, militarily, the vast Russian spaces or make them permanently secure. Such labour in the Russian towns and villages as is not required for agriculture and the arms industry, must therefore forthwith be put on to road construction.

When we start choosing the sites for new villages in Russia, we must not confine ourselves to purely military expediency, but must chose with a view to breaking the monotony of the vast, open roads.

The capture of Tobruk is a victory as great as it was inconceivable, and at the moment it comes as a real stroke of fortune for the German people. With the same effect that Japan's entry into the war burst upon us in a critical moment of the Eastern struggle, so Rommel's victory over the British African Expeditionary Force explodes in the midst of the Spanish intrigues.

To give you some idea of these intrigues let me merely tell you that the Spanish Minister for Foreign Affairs, Suñer, has just allowed himself to be "honoured", if you please, by the Pope with the gift of a Rosary.

That the negotiations between Churchill and Roosevelt continued for eight whole days must not be attributed, however, solely to the fact that Rommel has decisively shattered Britain's position in the Mediterranean. When two people are in general agreement, decisions are swiftly taken. My own conversations with the Duce have never lasted more than an hour and a half, the rest of the time being devoted to ceremonies of various kinds. The only time that our conversations lasted for nearly two days was when things were going badly in Albania, and I had to try to restore the Duce's morale. It is easy, therefore, by comparison to imagine how enormous their difficulties must appear to the Allies.

Apart from that, to harness to a common purpose a coalition composed of Great Britain, the United States, Russia and China demands little short of a miracle. If, for instance, Litvinov[474] is constantly invited to attend conversations between Churchill and Roosevelt, it is, obviously, because Russia holds a most potent trump card against Britain as regards India. Now that Britain has lost the Far East, there is no danger more pressing for her than the possibility that Russia, should

---

[474] Maxim Litvinov, born Meir Henoch Wallach (1876–1951), the Lithuanian-born Jewish "People's Commissar for Foreign Affairs" of the Soviet Union from 1930 to 1939, and Soviet Ambassador to the United States until 1943. Thereafter he served as deputy Commissar for Foreign Affairs.

the relations between the two countries deteriorate, might well seek compensation for her losses in Europe at the expense of India. I think it may well be this option which they hold on India that is causing Russia to avoid at all costs a state of war with Japan. That need not worry us, for the very fact that a state of non-belligerence exists between Russia and Japan strengthens our hand *vis-à-vis* India in the game we have to play against Britain.

By far the most interesting problem of the moment is, what is Britain going to do now? She has already made herself look ridiculous in the eyes of the world by declaring war when quite inadequately armed for war, and it is unlikely that she will perform any miracle at this juncture. At the moment, the British are trying to wriggle out of their difficulties by spreading the most varied and contradictory of rumours. To find out what she really intends to do is the task of the *Wilhelmstrasse*.

The best way of accomplishing it would be by means of a little flirtation with Churchill's daughter. But our Foreign Office, and particularly its gentlemanly diplomats, consider such methods beneath their dignity, and they are not prepared to make this agreeable sacrifice, even though success might well save the lives of numberless German officers and men!

28th June 1942, midday
Belgrade and the Danube—The Danube a German stream—Tasks of the future—Bismarck, Holstein and Ludwig of Bavaria

My Viennese compatriots ask continuously whether we shall once more abandon Belgrade? "Now that we've captured the place for the third time," they say, "we ought to stick to it." The Viennese are right in their opinion, at least in so far as we must exercise the greatest care when defining the frontiers in this corner. One thing is quite certain— in no circumstances can we renounce our claim to the so-called Iron Gates.[475]

The Danube is a river that runs deep into the heart of the Continent, and for this reason must, in a new Europe fashioned by us, be regarded as a German stream and be controlled by Germany. The organisation of the whole East-West traffic in this great territory depends on whether the Danube is or is not to be a German waterway. Any canal construction would be superfluous, indeed stupid, if we did not hold unrestricted control of this main channel.

---

[475] A gorge on the Danube, today on the border between Romania and Serbia.

In the handling of the Danubian problems, our generation must remember that not all the questions of rights which arise were successfully answered by the peace treaties.

Any responsible statesman should, indeed must, leave his successor a whole drawer full of somewhat nebulous claims, so that the latter can be in a position, should the need arise, to conjure up these "sacred" rights as the pretext for any conflict which may seem necessary.

Himmler made the remark that "Old Fritz" based his Silesian campaign upon hereditary rights which were by no means well established, and that Louis XIV again and again had recourse to legal titles, no matter whence they were obtained, in support of his policies.

Hitler continued: The Head of a State can give no better proof of his wisdom than the leaving of claims of this kind to his successor in respect of every region in which it is humanly possible to foresee that any national interests may at any possible time become involved.

If the monks of Athos, on the subject of whose morals I have no desire to dilate, wish to name me as successor to the Byzantine Empire, then their document must be most carefully preserved! I do not wish archives of this nature to be kept in the Foreign Office, where they would probably be lost sight of and forgotten; they should be kept in the Chancellery, as personal papers of the Chancellor, and available at any time for the study of his successors.

These reflections of mine are inspired by my own experience with the difficult piece of history to which I have had to put my hand. The generations which follow us will no doubt accept without comment the unification of Europe which we are about to accomplish, in the same way as the majority of our contemporaries regard the foundation of the Bismarckian Empire as a simple fact of history.

The immense labour involved in the welding of northern, western, central and eastern Europe into one entity will be quickly forgotten; and that is why one only appreciates at their full value such accessories as I have just described, when one has the most urgent need of making use of them.

There is one point I must stress in this connection—and I cannot stress it too often or too strongly—and that is, that this welding together of Europe has not been made possible by the efforts of a number of statesmen devoted to the cause of unification, but by *force of arms*. The welding together of Bavaria, Württemberg, Baden and so on with Prussia into the German Reich of Bismarck was not accomplished thanks to the high-minded understanding of the Princes, but by the power of the Prussian pin-firing rifle.

Just think of the means that Count Holstein[476] had to employ to persuade King Ludwig of Bavaria to write his famous letter to Bismarck,[477] in which he proposed that the King of Prussia should re-assume the title and dignity of Emperor, and which represented the last link in the chain of diplomatic negotiations! King Ludwig strove by the most childish tricks to avoid signing the letter; he even went so far as to take to his bed with pretended toothache! And what a piece of luck it was that Holstein was not one of those wretched creatures who sink respectfully to the ground at the sight of a closed kingly door, but, at the decisive moment, marched right up to it and opened it!

30th June 1942, at dinner
War as an inspiration in art—The protection of daubers—Reform of the Art Academies—The German Museum of Art

This war is stimulating the artistic sense much more than the last war. The works of the artists whom I have recalled from the front after a year or two in the field bear the hall-mark of personal experience and are among the most valuable examples of present-day art that our exhibitions can show.

These war paintings establish beyond discussion that the real artist is ripened by his own personal experience of life and not by study in some art academy. Most of the academy professors lack both the insight and the judgment necessary to bring real talent to the fore. Recall, if you please, how the beautiful seascapes of von Bock[478] were refused by the Prussian Academy, although in their wonderful sweep they alone of current paintings gave a true picture of the northern seas.

This same Prussian Academy which rejected these pictures was, however, not ashamed to adorn its walls with absolute muck. Even in my exhibition in the House of German Art they always try to gain ac-

---

[476] Count Maximilian von Holstein (1835 1895), a close confidant of Ludwig II of Bavaria, whose relationship with the Bavarian king ran hot and cold as Hitler describes, even to the extent of the Count serving time in prison at Ludwig's behest.
[477] The "Imperial Letter," known in German as the *Kaiserbrief,* was a message to the various princes of the German states signed by the Bavarian King Ludwig II on 30 November 1870, in which the restoration of a "German Empire" consisting of the "entire German fatherland" be established under the Prussian King Wilhelm. Shortly thereafter, the unification of Germany became reality.
[478] Alexander Friedrich von Bock (1829-1895), a Baltic German sculptor and art professor.

ceptance for the daubs of their own protégés. But when it comes to flinging these confections out, I am exceptionally obstinate! My views on the value of the academies are well known. And under present conditions it is difficult to see how talent, other than that which in practical life is incapable of producing a real picture, can be injected into the art schools as they are now constituted. The alternatives for the selection of teachers for an art academy of the present type are quite simple. Either one appoints capable artists as teachers, thereby losing their services in the field of creative art, or one fills the academies with nonentities and leaves the young artistic idea with nothing on which to model itself.

When one thinks over this problem, the first and foremost question one must ask oneself—and answer—is: whether after all it is not in the best interests of artistic creation that all the daubers should be concentrated in the academies! If, for instance, in an academy like the Film Academy we had not only a Herr Weidemann, but also our really greatest film producers, would not the quality of our film creation degenerate sharply? It is a characteristic of the present-day academies that they invariably try to stifle genius. No sooner does a real genius make his appearance in the circle of these very moderate "big-wigs" of the academies, than up they rise with their whole plumage ruffled in wrath against him.

If we wish to smoothe the way for an incipient genius in the academies and ensure him a practical livelihood in spite of the academies, then we must radically alter the whole structure of the academic world. They must be split up into a series of individual studios, on the lines of the State studios. Then the greatest artists available must be approached and asked if they would care voluntarily to take over one of these studios. Those who agree must be allowed a completely free hand, themselves to chose those pupils whom they consider worthy of further tuition.

If we organise the academies along these lines, then all the nonsense, claptrap and jargon, and all the juggling with mathematical formulae—a nonsense that only the sparrow-like brain of mediocrity could have conceived—will stop. And the great task of the academy will be, first, last and always, to teach the pupil to paint.

I always get angry when I think of how in the teachers' training colleges the future school-teachers are stuffed with an inchoate mass of material, when all they will be called upon to do later is to teach the children the rudiments of the three Rs.

What special knowledge, for goodness' sake, is required to teach six-year-old kiddies to say *a, b, c* correctly! It is equally ridiculous to try to cram children at school with all sorts of things. If you ask them, two or three years after they have left school, you'll find that they have forgotten practically all about them. The curriculum of a school should be drawn up with the object of teaching the children those things which will enable them in after-life to take their places as decent citizens. And keep the children as much as possible in the open air! We shall then have a healthy rising generation, capable of roughing it without falling on their backs.

1st July 1942, midday

Corporate responsibility of the family for the individual member—Japan gives an example—The treason of the Starhembergs—Jewish blood will out—Mixture with the coloured races—Roosevelt the arch-Jew—Collapse of British domination in Egypt—Repercussions on the man in the street—Turkey and the fall of Sebastopol—Two distinguished Ambassadors—Skilful Japanese diplomacy—The mistakes of François-Poncet

General Bodenschatz[479] *informed the Führer that a brother of Prince Starhemberg was serving in the German Air Force. Another brother, he said, who had been serving in the Army, had been dismissed by order of the Führer, on account of his antecedents. The Luftwaffe hesitated to follow the precedent set without further reference to the Führer, because the Starhemberg serving in the Air Force had acquitted himself nobly and had received excellent reports.*

The Führer replied: Families which exercise considerable political influence have also a corporate family political responsibility. If one member abuses the family influence, it is quite reasonable that the whole should bear the consequences. They are always, after all, at liberty to dissociate themselves from the family black sheep.

In Japan the principle of corporate family responsibility is so deeply rooted, that every family exercising influence, whether in the Army or in the political field, considers it a duty, as a matter of course, to prevent any member from doing anything contrary to the national interest. If their efforts are not successful and they feel that the national reputation of the family has been smirched by the erring son, then all the male members commit hari-kiri, to clear the family honour. It is this principle of corporate responsibility that must be applied in the case of the

---

[479] Karl-Heinrich Bodenschatz (1890–1979), Göring's liaison officer to Hitler.

brothers of the traitor Starhemberg, for the family of Prince Starhemberg has for centuries been one of the most influential families in Austria, and should therefore have been fully aware of their duties towards the German community, even during the time of the Weimar Republic.

But don't let us get angry about Starhemberg; let us rather rejoice over the fall of Sebastopol.

Freiherr von Liebig[480] has always been regarded as an ardent nationalist, and it was as such that he was brought to my attention. When I met him, however, I was repelled by the fellow's undeniable Jewish appearance. I was nevertheless repeatedly assured that in the family tree of the Freiherr, which went very far back, there was no vestige of non-Aryan ancestry.

And now, by pure chance, we have found out that one of the Freiherr's ancestors, born at Frankfurt-On-Main in 1616, was a pure, hundred per cent Jew! And so, although more than three hundred years separate the present Freiherr from his Jewish ancestor, and although with this one exception all his ancestors were pure Aryans, he nevertheless has all the unmistakable racial characteristics of the Jew.

This confirms the opinion I have already expressed when speaking about the Englishman, Cripps, that all half-caste families—even if they have but a minute quantity of Jewish blood in their veins—produce regularly, generation by generation, at least one pure Jew. Roosevelt affords the best possible proof of the truth of this opinion.

Roosevelt, who both in his handling of political issues and in his general attitude, behaves like a tortuous, pettifogging Jew, himself boasted recently that he had "noble" Jewish blood in his veins. The completely negroid appearance of his wife is also a clear indication that she, too, is a half-caste. Such examples should open the eyes of all reasonable people and be a warning of the menace that half-castes can be. A complete assimilation of foreign blood is not possible, and the characteristics of the foreign race inevitably continue to reappear.

Our people therefore is only harming itself if it accepts half-castes into the *Wehrmacht*, and thus admits them to a position of equality with pure-blooded Germans. We cannot accept the responsibility of burdening our blood-stream with the addition of further foreign elements. Exceptions in favour of half-castes must therefore be reduced to a minimum.

---

[480] Hans Wilhelm Hermann Freiherr von Liebig (1874–1931), a chemist and noted pan-German writer.

The surest sign of the collapse of British domination in Egypt is the instructions given by the British Ministry of Information to the press to minimise the importance of Alexandria to the British Empire; for the British press is so well-informed and accurately directed, that it is only when, in the opinion of the Government, some Dominion or other portion of the Empire cannot possibly be held any longer, that it starts such tricks in an endeavour to turn public attention to some other portion of the Commonwealth. In the case of Egypt, the press story will have to be made very convincing, for while the loss of Hong Kong and Singapore has hit only the well-to-do classes, Egypt for the man in the street represents one of the most important props of British prosperity. For Churchill and his supporters, therefore, the loss of Egypt must inevitably give rise to fears of a considerable strengthening of the popular opposition.

One must not lose sight of the fact that today there are already twenty-one Members of Parliament who openly oppose Churchill; and even though the discipline of the voting system is invoked to silence them, it is not by methods such as these that Churchill will succeed in remaining in office. Only if he succeeds by skilful handling of public opinion in turning popular attention from Egypt on to, say, India, will he be able to oppose with any chance of success a tremendously increased opposition.

The Führer stated that Gerede,[481] *the Turkish Ambassador to Berlin, had been called to Ankara for consultation with the Turkish Foreign Minister. In this connection the Führer continued:* The fall of Sebastopol has roused the greatest jubilation in Ankara, and the hatred of the Turks for the Russians was given a free rein during the rejoicings. If, as a result, Gerede should be appointed Foreign Minister, we shall have no cause to complain. He is not, admittedly, a militant diplomat, like Oshima, but he is a man who is absolutely convinced that Germany and Turkey must go forward hand in hand.

Oshima and Gerede are without doubt the two ablest foreign diplomats at the moment in Berlin. Oshima is the more assured, because he has in the Japanese Armed Forces an organisation at his back which has both the knowledge and the power to control the political situation to the best advantage of the country.

Gerede lacks any similarly strong support; the Turkish armed forces

---

[481] Hüsrev Gerede (1884–1962), Turkish ambassador to Romania from 1924 to 1926, and Germany from 1939 to 1942.

play no part in politics, and so he must needs further the interests of his country with the subtlety of a foil rather than the force of a sabre. If Gerede should be appointed Foreign Minister, the problem of the Near East will, from our point of view, assume a totally different aspect. The other principal actor in this part of the world, the Grand Mufti,[482] is also a realist rather than a dreamer, where politics are concerned. With his blond hair and blue eyes, he gives one the impression that he is, in spite of his sharp and mouse-like countenance, a man with more than one Aryan among his ancestors and one who may well be descended from the best Roman stock.

In conversation he shows himself to be a pre-eminently sly old fox. To gain time in which to think, he not infrequently has things translated to him first into French and then into Arabic; and sometimes he carries his caution so far that he asks that certain points be committed straight-away to writing. When he does speak, he weighs each word very carefully. His quite exceptional wisdom puts him almost on equal terms with the Japanese.

And what cunning diplomats the Japanese are, is exemplified by a small episode, in the course of which I myself, I must confess, all but fell into a trap. Somebody had apparently put forward a theory some time or other that, because of their susceptibility to some sort of disturbance of the sense of balance, the Japanese could never become first-class air pilots. When the responsible Japanese statesmen discovered that this twaddle was being swallowed whole by the gullible General Staffs in various countries, they did their utmost to foster the idea. And behind this camouflage they proceeded to build up an Air Force, whose successes have astounded the world.

I have myself often successfully applied the principle that when the representatives of a foreign Power reach a conclusion which is faulty in itself, but which it is in our interest that it be accepted as accurate— then, let well alone.

When, after the assumption of power, I made a start with our re-armament programme, I had to reckon with the certainty of counter-measures from the West. The current rumours of differences between the SS and the Reichswehr were, in this rather ticklish situation, of the greatest assistance to me. The French Ambassador, François-Poncet, greedily gobbled up all these rumours, and the more we fed them to him, the more emphatically did he report to Paris that any

[482] Amin al-Husseini (1897–1974), Grand Mufti of Jerusalem from 1921 to 1948.

military intervention by France would be quite unnecessary, as the tension between SS and Reichswehr would undoubtedly develop in its own time into a life-and-death struggle.

In the same way, the Röhm putsch was portrayed in François-Poncet's reports as an internecine breaking of German heads in the hallowed manner of the Middle Ages, which would leave France at liberty to pull the chestnuts out of the fire as she wished. The Röhm putsch was thus of the greatest assistance to us in postponing the taking of any military measures by either France or Britain long enough for the progress of our rearmament to make any intervention by these Powers impossible.

2nd July 1942, at dinner
The Tyrolese in the Crimea—The struggle between State and Church—
Joan of Arc, witch—Patriotism and dynastic interests

I have just read a report by *Gauleiter* Frauenfeld on the South Tyrol. In it he proposes that the South Tyrolese should be transplanted *en masse* to the Crimea, and I think the idea is an excellent one. There are few places on earth in which a race can better succeed in maintaining its integrity for centuries on end than the Crimea. The Tartars and the Goths are the living proof of it. I think, too, that the Crimea will be both climatically and geographically ideal for the South Tyrolese, and in comparison with their present settlements it will be a real land of milk and honey.

Their transfer to the Crimea presents neither physical nor psychological difficulty. All they have to do is to sail down just one German waterway, the Danube, and there they are.

The Führer next addressed Bormann on the subject of some books which the latter had given him to read.

The Führer said: The passages you have marked interest me very much indeed. It would really be most valuable if these books could be made available to all Germans, and particularly to leading men, such as Generals and Admirals. For they do show that, far from being the only one possessed of heretical ideas, I am on the contrary in the excellent company of many of the best of Germans.

When one reads books on the subject of the State and the Church, it is regrettable to see how often Governments are only too ready to sacrifice the true interests of a people to those of some ideology or clique of vested interests. This is the only possible explanation for the fate of so great a heroine in the cause of freedom as Joan of Arc (portrayed, incidentally, much more faithfully by Shaw than by Schiller), who was betrayed, mark you, by the really influential French circles of the times and was burned as a witch.

The attitude adopted in such cases by the Courts of Justice is admirably summed up by Ernst Haugg in his thesis, "The German National Anthem". In it he shows how German Courts, obsessed with the petty interests of their own little States and blind to the vital interests of the German nation as a whole, had the impertinence to stigmatise as "unpatriotic" the songs of freedom written by that great German, Hoffmann von Fallersleben. With such facts before us, we must regard it as an achievement of high merit that the Habsburg monarchy steadfastly upheld the Pan-Germanic ideal even throughout the period when Germany was divided into a number of petty States and torn asunder by conflicting dynastic issues.

2nd July 1942, after dinner
The British Press gets its orders—Egypt's hour of liberation

Dr. Dietrich presented a report which showed that the British Government had, in fact, issued instructions to the British Press along exactly the lines which the Führer had foretold at lunch the day before. The line taken was that while the loss of India would entail the inevitable disintegration of the Empire, the abandonment of Egypt would increase the difficulties of the German High Command rather than those of Great Britain. The destruction of harbours and roads, coupled with the mining of the Suez Canal, would, it was emphasised, so compromise its vital lines of communication and supply, that Egypt might well become a death-trap for the German Afrika Korps.

The Führer remarked: I certainly did not expect Britain to write off Egypt with such celerity! It is now very important that our own propaganda machine should come swiftly into action and trumpet, throughout the world and with ever-increasing stridency, that for Egypt the day of freedom has at last dawned.

If the slogan is skilfully handled, its effect on other countries under British domination, and particularly on those in the Near East, will be tremendous. It is also of great importance that the King of Egypt should be urged to withdraw as quickly as possible from British "protection", secrete himself somewhere or other and wait for us solemnly to invite his return and formally to restore his throne to him. It is the task of the Foreign Office to give the King a hint along these lines.

3rd July 1942, at dinner
Transport by ship and plane—The future belongs to the air

When the Führer came to table, Captain Baur and Admiral Krancke were discussing the relative profits earned by air and maritime transportation. The Führer said: Increasing speeds in the air have already been assured, and in my opinion an increase in profits will be achieved by aviation only through the introduction of the Diesel engine.

Baur remarked that a passenger aircraft required a payload of sixty to one hundred passengers. The Führer continued: You need not worry about that. In a very short time we shall have aircraft big enough to have bathrooms installed in them.

Admiral Krancke said that in spite of all these anticipated developments in aviation, maritime transportation had nothing to fear from air competition. "I cannot believe" he said, "that it will ever be possible to build aircraft big enough to replace cargo-ships as carriers of coal, timber, iron, etc."

Baur retorted: "Not necessary! As it is, the railways have left the carrying of tiles to the ships."

The Führer concluded: One must judge these things in the light of common progress. The bird is one degree in advance of the flying fish, which itself is higher than the ordinary fish; and in the same way, the aircraft is an advance on the ship—and the future belongs to the air.

4th July 1942, at dinner
German Embassy at the Vatican—Interpretations of the Concordat—My relations with the Papal Nuncio—Americans stand no nonsense from the Church—A milliard a year into the pockets of the priests!—The Concordat must be ended—Faulty manoeuvres by the Wilhelmstrasse—I refuse open war with the Church—An account to be settled with Bishop von Galen—The Bishops will soon fawn on the State

Should we decide to recall our present representative from the Vatican, I can see no adequate reason for sending any fresh incumbent to this Embassy. The relations between Germany and the Vatican are based on the Concordat. But this same Concordat is no more than the survival of agreements reached between the Vatican and the different German States, and, with the disappearance of the latter and their incorporation in the German Reich, it has become obsolete.

It is true that it has as its basis these various agreements, but it is a confirmation of past agreements rather than a current agreement in

force. I am therefore of the considered opinion that the juridical consequence of the disappearance of the sovereignty of the individual German States and its incorporation in the sovereignty of the Reich render
the continuation of diplomatic relations with the Vatican redundant.

From military reasons connected with the war I have so far refrained from translating this conception into fact. Equally, however, I
have shown myself unresponsive to the attempts of the Vatican towards
extension of the provisions of the Concordat to embrace the newly acquired territories of the Reich. The Saar, Sudetenland, Bohemia and
Moravia, the *Reichsgau* Danzig-East Prussia, the Warthegau, a large
part of Silesia and Alsace-Lorraine have, in fact, no relations with the
Roman Catholic Church which are supported by formal international
agreement. In these territories, therefore, Church affairs must be settled locally.

If the Papal Nuncio seeks audience of the Foreign Office and tries
through this channel to gain some say in religious developments in the
new territories, his advances must be rejected. He must be told clearly that, in the absence of any particular Concordat, the settlement of
Church affairs in these territories is a matter to be settled exclusively
between the relevant State representative—that is, the *Reichsstatthalter*—and the head of the local ecclesiastical body.

I should, of course, have preferred Minister Lammers to impart this
information to the Papal Nuncio. Unfortunately the *Wilhelmstrasse*,
with its usual greed for fields of fresh authority, has allowed itself to be
imposed upon by the Papal Legate. Well, I shall be interested to see how
these gentlemen get themselves out of the tangle!

Regulations framed to cover the whole Reich cannot but make
more difficult the clarification of relations between State and Church,
at which we are aiming; for the Catholic Church strives always to seek
advantage where we are weakest by demanding the application to the
whole Reich of those of the various Concordats which conform most
closely to its aspirations.

Therefore, as regards future relations between State and Church, it
is very satisfactory from our point of view that in nearly half the Reich
negotiations can now be conducted by the appropriate *Reichsstatthalter*, unfettered by the clauses of the central Concordat. For this means
that in each district the *Gauleiter* can, according to the degree of eman-
cipation acquired by the population of his *Gau*, lead the people forward step by step in the sense that we desire.

Although, in general, I hold no brief for the Americans, I must in this respect take off my hat to them. The American statesmen, by subjecting the Church to the same regulations governing all other associations and institutions, have limited its field of activity to reasonable proportions; and, as the State does not contribute from State Funds one single cent to the Church, the whole clergy cringes and sings hymns in praise of the Government. This is not to be wondered at! The parson, like everyone else, has got to live; what he makes out of the public offertory doesn't amount to much, and so he is more or less dependent on State charity. As he has no legal claim whatever on the State, he therefore takes very good care that his demeanour is always pleasing in the eyes of the State and therefore deserving of the crumbs it cares to toss to him.

Once we cease handing out milliards of marks a year to the Church, our damn parsons will very quickly change their tune and, instead of having the impudence to revile us and attack us in the most shameful manner, will very soon be eating out of our hands. We can make this clerical gang go the way we want, quite easily—and at far less cost than at present.

Contributions should be made to selected individual parsons. If we give some Bishop—for himself and his subordinates—a round million, he will pocket the first three hundred thousand for his own use—otherwise he's no true parson! The distribution of the meagre rest among the parsons of his whole diocese will cause a pretty little uproar among the whole brood—and leave us laughing like hell!

In one respect, however, we must remain absolutely obdurate. Any petitions for State intervention must be rejected out of hand. Justification for such rejection is obvious. On its own showing the Church knows full well that no profane spirits could possibly succeed in mediating in Church affairs as well as the clergy itself. How can you expect some wretched little Government jack-in-office like myself, to whom the light has not been vouchsafed, to tackle so vital and intricate a problem! Agreement as to distribution of funds must, as in other agreements, be left in the hands of the *Reichsstatthalter*.

I don't think we need fear that they will enter upon any commitments which are directed against either the State or its interests. For one thing, the *Gauleiters* are under firm control, and for another, most of the *Reichsstatthalters* are much stricter in these affairs than I am. Once the war is over we will put a swift end to the Concordat. It will give me the greatest personal pleasure to point out to the Church all those occasions on which it has broken the terms of it. One need only recall the close co-operation between the Church and the murderers of Heydrich. Catholic priests not only allowed them to hide in a church on the outskirts of Prague, but even allowed them to entrench themselves in the sanctuary of the altar. The development of relations between State and Church affords a very instructive example of how the carelessness of a single statesman can have after-effects which last for centuries.

When Charlemagne was kneeling at prayer in St. Peter's, Rome, at Christmas in the year 800, the Pope, giving him no time to work out the possible effects of so symbolic an action, suddenly bent down and presto! popped a golden crown on his head! By permitting it, the Emperor delivered himself and his successors into the hands of a power which subjected the German Government and the German people to five hundred years of martyrdom.

Today, as always, there are responsible people to be found who are careless enough to allow a crown of gold to be popped on to their heads, and one cannot exaggerate the enormous effects which such an action, seemingly trifling at the time, can later produce.

Much in the same class and equally stupid is the idea of the *Wilhelmstrasse* that every note from the Vatican must be answered. The very act of answering is tantamount to an admission of the right of the Vatican to interfere in German domestic issues—if only in ecclesiastical issues—and to maintain official correspondence with us.

Not only the history of the past, but also present times afford numberless examples of the very hard-boiled diplomats to be found in the service of the Catholic Church, and of how extremely cautious one must be in dealing with them.

Just after my entry into Vienna I heard a tremendous whistling and cheering under my window and was told that it was for Cardinal Archbishop Innitzer,[483] who was on his way to visit me. I expected to see a wretched little parson, downcast and oppressed with the burden of his sins. Instead of which there appeared a man who addressed me with self-assurance and a beaming countenance, just as if, throughout the

---

[483] Theodor Innitzer (1875–1955), Archbishop of Vienna and a cardinal of the Catholic Church, had previously supported the Schuschnigg dictatorship, but upon the *Anschluss*, endorsed the Nazi takeover and became known as the "Heil Hitler Bishop."

whole period of the Austrian republic, he had never even touched a single hair of the head of any National Socialist! Let me add, however, that once one has come into contact with gentlemen of this type, one soon learns to recognise them on sight.

The Papal Nuncio, on whom, as doyen of the diplomatic corps, falls the duty of delivering the congratulatory address at the New Year's ceremony, invariably tries to use the occasion to turn the conversation to the position of the Catholics in Germany. But I always manage to side-step him, asking him in a most amiable and pressing manner for news of the health of his Holiness and, when this engrossing subject has been dealt with, turning hastily to greet the remainder of the diplomatic corps. Except at this reception, I have on principle always refused to meet the Papal Nuncio, and fob him off on to Lammers instead. I have thus succeeded in withdrawing myself from all personal contact with the Vatican.

During the years of our struggle Rosenberg once submitted to me the draft of a leading article he proposed publishing in reply to the attacks of the Catholic Church. I forbade him to publish it; and I still think it was a great mistake that Rosenberg ever let himself be drawn into a battle of words with the Church. He had absolutely nothing to gain from it; the hesitant Catholics of their own free will regarded the Church with a critical eye, and from the truly devout not only could he expect no fair hearing for his "heretical outpourings", but he must also have realised that the opposition propaganda would condemn him for his meddling in matters of faith and successfully point to him as a man guilty of mortal sin.

The fact that I remain silent in public over Church affairs is not in the least misunderstood by the sly foxes of the Catholic Church, and I am quite sure that a man like the Bishop von Galen knows full well that after the war I shall extract retribution to the last farthing. And, if he does not succeed in getting himself transferred in the meanwhile to the *Collegium Germanicum*[484] in Rome, he may rest assured that in the balancing of our accounts, no "t" will remain uncrossed, no "i" undotted!

The attitude of the Bishop von Galen affords just one more argument in favour of terminating the Concordat after the war, substituting for it regional regulations and immediately withholding from the Church

---

[484] The *Collegium Germanicum* (proper name *Collegium Germanicum et Hungaricum*) is to the present day still a German-speaking seminary for Catholic priests in Rome, founded in 1552.

the financial support at present guaranteed to it by that treaty. I am sure it will give my *Reichsstatthalters* great pleasure to inform some Bishop, who, from the State's point of view, has strayed from the straight and narrow path, that the *Reichsgau*, owing to a temporary lack of funds, is, unfortunately and to his own personal deep regret, compelled temporarily to stop such contributions as it was in the habit of making from time to time!

When once the Concordat and its financial obligations have been repudiated, and the Church becomes dependent on the offertory, it will pocket a bare 3 per cent of the money it at present gets from the State, and all the Bishops will come creeping and begging to the *Reichsstatthalter*.

It will be the duty of the *Reichsstatthalter* to make it quite clear after the war that he will deal with the Church in exactly the same way as he deals with any other national association, and that he will not tolerate the intervention of any foreign influence. The Papal Nuncio can then return happily to Rome, we shall be saved the expense of an embassy at the Vatican, and the only people who will weep tears over the jobs that have been lost will be the Foreign Office!

4th July 1942, at dinner
Two men in advance of their time—Naming battleships—Stronger collaboration from Czechoslovakia—Those who are not for me are against me

I think it is very astonishing that men like Ulrich von Hutten[485] and Goetz von Berlichingen[486] should have been so far in advance of their times and so progressive in their ideas, and it is a great pity that they had behind them in their struggle no strong and concrete doctrine, which would have given them the necessary moral *élan* and perseverance. Their completely German outlook nevertheless entitles them to a high place in the esteem of the German people. I have for this reason suggested that battleships or other large warships at present under construction should be named after them.

I rejected the suggestion that a battleship should be named after myself, because if such a ship has bad luck, the superstitious would regard

---

[485] Ulrich von Hutten (1488–1523) was a knight and scholar, follower of Martin Luther and a strong critic of the Roman Catholic Church.

[486] Gottfried von (1480–1562), a Franconian knight and poet, who fought in numerous military campaigns including the Peasant's War, the first conflict sparked off by Martin Luther's teachings.

it as an unfavourable omen for my own activities. Imagine a battleship named after me having to spend six months in dry dock for repairs! Look, for example, at the very harmful effect the announcement of the destruction of Fort Stalin at Sebastopol had on Russian morale.

In a State which is founded on a concrete political philosophy, prudence must be exercised in the naming of warships. *October Revolution, Marat,* the *Commune of Paris* in the Soviet Navy is an example of what I mean. I have therefore ordered that the battle cruiser *Deutschland*[487] should be re-named, for the loss of a ship of that name would cause greater consternation than the loss of any other ship.

For the same reason I will not allow the names of anyone associated with the National Socialist movement or philosophy to be used for any warships. After a man like Goetz von Berlichingen, on the other hand, you can name as many ships as you like; for such is his popularity among the people that even if any number of ships bearing his name were successively sunk, the christening of a new one with the same name will always be greeted with applause.

The Führer stated that, according to a telegram received, the Government of Bohemia and Moravia had organised a gigantic rally of the Czech people, at which an appeal for complete co-operation with the Greater German Reich was made, and that the appeal had gone on to say that those who in the future held themselves aloof from such co-operation would be branded as traitors to the Czech people.

The Führer's remarks on the subject were: This action was initiated during the course of a conversation I had with President Hácha in the Reich Chancellery, on the occasion of a memorial service for Ober-gruppenFührer Heydrich.

I told Hácha and the members of the Czech Government accompanying him that we would tolerate no further grave acts in the Protectorate prejudicial to the interests of the Reich, and that if any occurred, we should have to consider deporting the whole Czech population. I added that as we had accomplished the migration of several million Germans, such an action would present no difficulty to us. At this, Hácha collapsed like a pricked balloon, as did also his colleagues.

After a pause, they asked whether they might—at least partially and

---

[487] The *Deutschland* pocket battleship was renamed the *Lützow* in 1940. She was scuttled in the damaged in the shallow waters of the East Prussian Kaiserfahrt canal (now the Piast Canal in Poland) in April 1945 after being damaged by British bombers.

with appropriate discretion—make use of this communication in their own country.

As I consider the Czechs to be industrious and intelligent workers and am most anxious to see political stability restored in their country—and particularly in view of the presence therein of two great and most important German armaments factories—I acceded to their request.

The fact that the Government of the Protectorate has carried out its task in a manner that can only be described as 100 per cent pro-German can be attributed, among other things, to the action of Minister of State Meissner. After the conference, the latter took a walk round the Chancellery gardens with the Czechs, in the course of which, in answer to their anxious enquiries, he succeeded in persuading them that, as regards the mass deportation of the Czech population, I certainly meant exactly what I had said.

The Czech gentlemen were left in so little doubt that they decided forthwith to accept, as the basis of their future policy, that all Beneš intrigues and all pro-Beneš individuals must be stamped out, and that in the future struggle for the survival of the Czech people there would be no room for neutrals or anyone who remained lukewarm.

The Czech Government is obviously also relieved that it can at last give the Czech people sound reasons for its action against the Benea party. Hácha and his colleagues have never had so favourable a platform from which to launch the slogan: "Who is not for me is against me", and thus to rid themselves of their opponents.

In any case, I had the firm impression, when they took their leave, that Hácha and his friends were greatly relieved at having been given permission to hint to their people what would be the consequences of an attitude hostile to the interests of the Reich.

5th July 1942, midday
Frugality of the Italians—Professional out-of-works—Maritime sub-soil and chemical fertilisers—The ambitions of Franco—The stupidity of kings

The frugal habits of the southern Italians are quite extraordinary. There must certainly be a million of them who live on fruit, fish and the like, literally from hand to mouth. Towns in southern Italy—at least those near the coast—have certainly never known what it is to be hungry, for the sea provides not only fish, but also shell-fish of every kind and goodness knows what else, in quantities quite sufficient for the needs of this frugal people. Such frugality, however, is not without potentially dangerous consequences. The majority of human beings have a leaning towards *laissez-faire,* and they very quickly lose the zest for endeavour when they find that they can get along very nicely as they are. The ten or fifteen thousand professional loafers who were lounging about Germany at the time of our assumption of power, and who showed no inclination to take a regular job when once German industry had started to function again, have been put into concentration camps. For it is ridiculous to try to deal by ordinary methods with muck of this kind. The fear of being put into a concentration camp has had a most salutary effect, and it greatly facilitated the gearing up of the gigantic industrial activity which our rearmament programme demanded.

That Germany has succeeded in solving this problem, as it has solved many others, is due in no small measure to the fact that the State has progressively assumed more and more control. Only in this way was it possible to defeat private interests and carry national interests triumphantly to their goal.

After the war, equally, we must not let control of the economy of the country slip from our hands. If we do, then once more all the various private interests will concentrate on their own particular objectives. The coastal population, for example, from the view-point of life as they see it, still regard land reclamation by means of dam construction as the last word in wisdom; in point of fact, however, land reclamation by this method is the purest folly, for we have all the land we need in the East. On the other hand, enrichment of the soil is still most important, and it must not be impeded by the interests of industry. When once we are convinced that slime from the sea-bed is, on account of higher nitrogen content, a better fertiliser than any artificial manure, we must transport whole trainloads of it, in spite of the protests of our chemical industry.

As most people are egotists at heart, any efficient functioning of a national economy is not possible without State direction and control. The Venetian Republic affords an excellent example of how successful a State directed economy can be. For five hundred years the price of bread in Venice never varied, and it was left to the Jews with their predatory motto of "Free Trade" to wreck this stability.

The opinion was expressed that the strong pro-monarchist tendencies which had recently been manifest in Spain could perhaps be attributable to the ambition of Franco to obtain, in the event of the restoration of the monarchy, a minor coronet for himself. The Führer disagreed.

I disagree entirely. Franco has, I think, sufficient intelligence to realise that any king—if he stopped at that—would at least dismiss him and his followers on the spot, tarnished as they are with the responsibility for the civil war. Nobody is so monumentally stupid as a king; that I know from my own personal experience.

About a year after the victory of our Party, one of our former potentates, Rupprecht of Bavaria, sent an emissary to me to say that he was sure I would recognise the necessity of restoring the monarchy. The emissary, following his instructions, went on to say quite frankly that I could not, of course, remain as Reich Chancellor in the restored monarchy, because my continued presence would be an obstacle to the unification of the German people.

I should, however, be most generously treated and should be rewarded—with a dukedom! This fellow was so damn stupid that he could not even see that it was just he himself and his fellow Princes who had always been the cause of the disintegration of the German people throughout history, and that never has there been a stronger and more integrated unity of the German races than that which we have achieved under my leadership.

And the idiot imagined that some confounded nincompoop could tempt me to give up the leadership of this great people—by making me a Duke!

5th July 1942, evening

Falsification of war communiqués—Switzerland believes the Jewish lies—No foe in Europe compares with the British—But National Socialist Germany will beat them in the end-Britain in the hands of the Jews—Conservation of our racial integrity—Farcical success of Saint Paul

Commenting on a completely false Soviet war communiqué which had been published in the Swedish and Swiss Press as well as in that of Britain and America, the Führer said: These communiqués are typical Jewish fabrications. Although they do not even give names of places, they are nevertheless published by news agencies all the world over; and the explanation is, of course, that these agencies themselves are for the most part in the hands of Jews.

Unfortunately, this Jewish twaddle is being accepted without question not only in Britain and America, but also in Sweden and Switzerland. The reason why the Jews and their fabrications find such credence becomes apparent if you take a look at a country like Switzerland. In that country, Tom has milk interests, Dick follows the prices of the grain market, and Harry exports watches. In these circumstances, even old Wilhelm Tell himself could not maintain the military spirit at any high level. As a result, military knowledge has been so discounted, that any Swiss officer who shows a true appreciation of the facts of this war is immediately relieved of his command.

In Germany, one of the primary services rendered by the NSDAP is its success in restoring to the people the emphatic conviction that perpetual military training of the rising generations must always continue.

If this spirit is to be maintained, it is essential that those who have distinguished themselves either by great successes in the field or as men of very wide experience in war should be made available as models and instructors for the rising generation.

The Reserve of Officers must be carefully nursed, for in the military training of the individual the Reserve Officers, the living incarnations of the martial spirit of our race, have an incomparable military duty towards the whole people. Apart from this, the schools and other centres of instruction must in all circumstances foster that interest—an interest, by the way, which remained active even during the Weimar Republic—which Germans have always shown in the connection between science and the military art.

I have always been an ardent disciple of the belief that, in a struggle between peoples, the people with the higher average morale must always emerge victorious. In my opinion, that an inferior people should triumph over a strong is a negation of the laws of nature.

The British maintained their position of world domination for three hundred years solely because there was during that period nothing on the Continent comparable in race or intelligence to oppose them. Napoleon himself was no real menace to them, because, in the frenzy of the French Revolution, he had no solid basis on which to found a new order in Europe; and apart from him, there has never been in Europe, since the disintegration of the old German Empire, any State which, in either quantity or quality, could compare with the British.

Thanks to the development of National Socialist Germany, I firmly believe, if only on purely biological grounds, we shall succeed in surpassing the British to such an extent that, with one hundred and fifty to two hundred million Germans, we shall become the undisputed masters of the whole of Europe.

A recrudescence of the problem Rome or Carthage in the new guise of Germany or Great Britain is not, in my opinion, possible. For the result of this war will be that, whereas in Britain each additional million of population will be an additional burden on the island itself, the increasing growth of our own races will have open to them horizons of political and ethnological expansion which are limitless. Further, any alleviation of the overcrowding of towns by a movement back to the land is not possible in Britain, for this would necessitate an immediate revolution of the whole social system of the Kingdom, which, in its turn, would lead to the disintegration of the rest of the Empire.

These very important facts have been largely overlooked in Britain because the country is ruled not by men of intelligence but by Jews, as one must realise when one sees how the intrigues of the Jews in Palestine are accepted in Britain without comment or demur.

One of our most important tasks will be to save future generations from a similar political fate and to maintain for ever watchful in them knowledge of the menace of Jewry. For this reason alone it is vital that the Passion Play be continued at Oberammergau; for never has the menace of Jewry been so convincingly portrayed as in this presentation of what happened in the times of the Romans. There one sees in Pontius Pilate a Roman racially and intellectually so superior, that he stands out like a firm, clean rock in the middle of the whole muck and mire of Jewry. The preservation of our racial purity can be assured only by an awareness of the racial issues involved; our laws, therefore, must be framed with the sole object of protecting our people not only against Jewish, but also against any and every racial infection.

We must do all we can to foster this racial awareness until it attains the same standard as obtained in Rome in the days of her glory. In those days the Roman protected himself subconsciously against any racial adulteration.

The same thing occurred in Greece at the height of her power; according to reports handed down to us, the very market-place itself in Athens shook with laughter when St. Paul spoke there in favour of the Jews.

If nowadays we do not find the same splendid pride of race which distinguished the Grecian and Roman eras, it is because in the fourth century these Jewish-Christians systematically destroyed all the monuments of these ancient civilisations. It was they, too, who destroyed the library at Alexandria.

6th July 1942, at dinner
Relations with the foreign press—Miserly outlook of our Press Chief—
The Nuremberg Rally—Four thousand special trains

When I visited Berlin before we came into power, I used to stay at the Kaiserhof;[488] and as I was always accompanied by a complete General Staff, I generally had to book a whole floor, and our bill for food and lodging usually came to about ten thousand marks a week. I earned enough to defray these costs mostly by means of interviews and articles for the foreign press. Towards the end of the struggle period I was being paid as much as two or three thousand dollars a time for such work.

In placing these articles and arranging interviews I often had rows with my Foreign Press Chief, Hanfstaengl, because, as a business man rather than a politician, he judged everything in terms of cash received. Once, for example, when I told him to get a certain article published in the whole world press just as quickly as it could possibly be done, he lost a lot of valuable time haggling over the best terms obtainable.

On one occasion he came back at me three times in an attempt to gain my consent to the sale of an article to some news agency, finally hoping to persuade me by dangling an offer of a thousand pounds sterling before my eyes.

When I turned on him in fury and shouted: "Get to hell out of this, you and your damned greed! Can't you understand that if I want a certain article to appear at a certain time throughout the world, money just doesn't matter?" He simply shook his head wonderingly, unable to understand how I could possibly let a cool thousand slip through my fingers in this way.

His rapacity and avarice frequently made Hanfstaengl impossible to deal with. On one occasion in some small peasants' tavern he made the whole company look ridiculous by raising a frightful row over the bill for a supper which, mark you, he wasn't being called upon to pay for personally, and on which in any case, there had been an overcharge of only three pence!

He was a mighty consumer of vegetables—but he never ordered any for himself; instead—and this is typical of the man—he kept a sharp eye on the rest of the company, and then would go round the table, gathering up the odds and ends left by the others and muttering in

---

[488] The Hotel Kaiserhof was a luxury hotel in Wilhelmplatz in Berlin. It was destroyed by Allied bombing during the war.

justification: "Vegetables are the most health-giving food in the world!"
In the evenings, in the same way, remarking that cheese was "so nour-
ishing", he would go round scrounging bits of cheese from the whole
company.

On one occasion when we had to undertake a journey in a great
hurry I told Hanfstaengl to get something to eat for everybody before
we left. Although he knew full well that most of us disliked cheese, he
came back with two baskets full of cheese sandwiches—and then with
the greatest aplomb and satisfaction he carted the not inconsiderable
remnants off to his own house!

*Reichsleiter Bormann and General Bodenschatz then told anecdotes
about Hanfstaengl and his miserly avarice which confirmed the description the Führer had painted of him.*

In the course of our many electoral tours my companions and I have
got to know and to love the Reich from Berlin to its uttermost corners. As for the most part I was invited to take my meals *en famille*,[489] I
also got to know intimately Germans all over Germany. There I used to
meet whole families, in which the father would be working in our political section, the mother was a member of the Women's Association,
one brother was in the SS, the other in the Hitler Youth, and the daughter was in the German Girls' League. And so when we all meet once a
year at the Party Rally at Nuremberg, it always gives me the impression
of being just one huge family gathering.

The Party Rally has, however, been not only a quite unique occasion
in the life of the NSDAP but also in many respects a valuable preparation for war. Each Rally requires the organisation of no fewer than
four thousand special trains. As these trains stretched as far as Munich
and Halle, the railway authorities were given first-class practice in the
military problem of handling mass troop transportation.

Nor will the Rally lose its significance in the future. Indeed, I have
given orders that the venue of the Rally is to be enlarged to accommo-
date a minimum of two million for the future—as compared to the
million to a million and a half today.

The German Stadium which has been constructed at Nuremberg,
and of which Horth has drawn two magnificent pictures, accommo-
dates four hundred thousand people and is on a scale which has no
comparison anywhere on earth.

---

[489] French for "informally."

7th July 1942, midday
Our dreamy archaeologists—Deforestation is the precursor of decadence—The antiquity of our towns

People make a tremendous fuss about the excavations carried out in districts inhabited by our forebears of the pre-Christian era. I am afraid I cannot share their enthusiasm, for I cannot help remembering that, while our ancestors were making these vessels of stone and clay, over which our archaeologists rave, the Greeks had already built an Acropolis.

One must be cautious also with any detailed assertions as regards the standard of culture attained by our ancestors during the first Christian millennium. If, for example, some most ancient school primer is discovered in East Prussia, one must not immediately leap to the conclusion that it originated there. In all probability it had come from the south in exchange for a piece of amber.

The real protagonists of culture, both in the thousand years before Christ and in the thousand years after him, were the peoples of the Mediterranean. This may appear improbable to us today, because we are apt to judge these people from present-day appearances. But that is a great mistake. North Africa was once a heavily wooded territory, and Greece, Italy and Spain, too, at the time of the Graeco-Roman era also had many vast forests.

In passing judgment on Egyptian history, too, let me advise caution. Like Greece and Italy, Egypt also during the period of her glory was a most habitable country with a most equable climate.

So when a people begin to cut down their trees without making any provision for reforestation—and thus rob nature's wise irrigation system of its most essential pre-requisite—you may be sure that it is a sign of the beginning of their cultural degeneration.

The many false ideas prevalent among our people as regards the cultural development of our ancestors have been encouraged to no small degree by false premises about the age of our cities. I was myself quite taken aback, for instance, when I found that Nuremberg itself was but seven centuries old.

Nuremberg's reputed antiquity is attributable in some measure to the slyness of the Nurembergers themselves. The Oberbürgermeister Liebel—as he himself confessed to me—allowed the seven hundredth anniversary to pass unheralded, because he did not wish the attention of people, who believed the city to be much older, drawn to the truth of the matter. It has, however, been reasonably firmly established that the origin of Nuremberg was an old Salic castle, round which, little by little, a village grew. Most medieval cities were founded in the same way; hence the large number of towns created during the Middle Ages in Eastern Germany. These fortress castles were of great importance for the protection of the peasantry. Without them, the country folk would never have been able to maintain themselves against the oriental hordes, which even at that time ceaselessly pressed against our frontiers, and sometimes even over-ran our territories.

In Transylvania, where these fortresses were not so numerous, fortifications had to be constructed against, among others, the Turks, and this explains why one frequently finds that even the churches are designed to resist attack.

7th July 1942, at dinner

The changing Spanish scene—Serrano Suñer and the Church—Where Franco's policy differs from National Socialism or Fascism—Spanish Reds are not Russia's vassals—A nincompoop not a hero—The intervention of Heaven in war—and of the skies—a different thing—The first Falange—General Muñoz Grande,[490] a fine soldier—Anti-social elements, female Communists

General Jodl told the Führer of an incident which had occurred at the Spanish frontier on the occasion of the return home of some wounded of the Blue Division. These men were refused places in the South Express, and when they tried to get into the guard's van, a company of infantry intervened on the orders of the Military Governor and ejected them. Marshal Keitel suggested that the Blue Division was in bad odour because of its name, the colour blue being a reminder of the old original Falange, which was not a disciple of the Church. In the new Falange admission could be obtained only with the approval of the local priest.

The Führer said: The Spanish situation is developing in a deplorable fashion. Franco, obviously, has not the personality to face up to the political problems of the country. Even so, he started off from a much more favourable position than either the Duce or myself; for we both had not only to capture the State, but also to win over the armed forces to our side. Franco, on the other hand, had both political power and military force in his own hands.

---

[490] Agustín Muñoz Grandes (1896–1970), Spanish vice-president and commander of the Blue Division, the Spanish volunteers fighting on the Eastern Front against the Soviet Union.

It is obvious that he is incapable of freeing himself from the influence of Serrano Suñer, in spite of the fact that the latter is the personification of the parson in politics and is blatantly playing a dishonest game with the Axis Powers.

In point of fact, these parsons are too stupid for words. They are trying, through Serrano Suñer, to give a reactionary impulse to Spanish politics and to restore the monarchy; all they will succeed in doing, however, is to cause another civil war, which they themselves will certainly never survive.

General Jodl suggested that the British pound might well be behind it all, and that the British hoped in this way to create a second front.

The Führer continued: One must be careful not to put the Franco regime on the same level as National Socialism or Fascism.

Todt, who employs many so-styled "Red" Spaniards in his workshops, tells me repeatedly that these Reds are not *red* in our sense of the word. They regard themselves as revolutionaries in their own right and, as industrious and skilled workers, have greatly distinguished themselves. The best thing we can do is to hold as many of these people as we can, commencing with the forty thousand already in our camps, and keep them as reserves in case a second civil war should break out. Together with the survivors of the old Falange, they will constitute the most trustworthy force at our disposal.

Ambassador Hewel then said that he had seen soldiers without arms or badges of rank working under armed guard in the streets of Madrid. He presumed that they were old soldiers of the Red army and thought that, if they must be employed in this fashion, they should at least be given different clothing. Marshal Keitel said that, in passing judgment on the Spanish army, German criteria were of no value.

"When the Führer met Franco," he continued, *"the Spanish Guard of Honour was deplorable, and their rifles were so rusty that they must have been quite unserviceable. When the meeting was being arranged, Admiral Canaris*[491] *warned me that the Führer would be disillusioned to meet in Franco—not a hero, but a little sausage."*

The Führer continued: Franco and company can consider themselves very lucky to have received the help of Fascist Italy and National Socialist Germany in their first civil war. For, as the Red Spaniards never cease explaining, they had not entered into co-operation with the Soviets on ideological grounds, but had rather been forced into it—and

---

[491] Wilhelm Canaris (1887–1945), *Abwehr* (military intelligence) chief.

thence dragged into a political current not of their own choosing—simply through lack of other support.

One thing is quite certain. People speak of an intervention from Heaven which decided the civil war in favour of Franco; perhaps so—but it was not an intervention on the part of the madam styled the Mother of God, who has recently been honoured with a Field Marshal's baton,[492] but the intervention of the German General von Richthofen[493]and the bombs his squadrons rained from the heavens that decided the issue.

Ambassador Hewel said the upper classes in Spain were both bone idle and quite impervious to adverse criticism.

Hitler continued: Well, thank goodness, the discipline of both the Reds and the Falangists working in the Todt organisation is first class, and the more of them we can recruit, the better.

But the finding of people capable of clearing up the Spanish political situation will be much more difficult. The problems are more of an internal political, than of a military, nature; and the foremost of them—the food crisis—is, in view of the proverbial idleness of the population, about the thorniest of the lot.

Whether a General possesses the political acumen necessary to success, the future alone will show. But in any case, we must promote as much as we can the popularity of General Munoz Grande, who is a man of energy, and as such the most likely one to master the situation. I am very pleased indeed that the intrigues of the Serrano Suñer clique to get this General dismissed from the command of the Blue Division were frustrated at the last moment; for the Blue Division may well once more play a decisive role, when the hour for the overthrow of this parson-ridden regime strikes.

In a report on the disorders in Serbia, it was stated that over 35 per cent of the insurgents taken prisoner were ex-criminals.

The Führer said: I am not in the least surprised to hear it, for it only confirms my own ideas about revolutionaries, based on the experience of 1918–19. If you wish to prevent a revolution by anticipation, the first thing you must do, as soon as the situation becomes critical, is to kill off the whole anti-social rabble; and you can do this only if you have

---

[492] Saint Funicisla. See entry for 5th June 1942.
[493] Wolfram von Richthofen (1895–1945), cousin of Manfred von Richthofen (the "Red Baron" of World War I), commanded the Condor Legion, a Luftwaffe contingent sent to support Franco's Nationalists in the Spanish Civil War.

already gathered them safely together in a concentration camp. The theory that by thus putting them in prison you deprive this anti-social rabble of the benefits of the influence of family life is pure clap-trap. If you allow them the blessings of family life, all you are doing is to build the foundation cells for a further brood of criminals. Children who grow up in the company of subversive-minded parents themselves become rogues, for their mothers are invariably of the same pernicious ilk as their rogue fathers.

Our period of struggle gave me valuable experience of this. At the SS rallies it was the females of the Communist species who were the most despicable. These hags would pelt our men with everything they could lay their hands on, and when our men started to defend themselves, they would hold up their own children, regardless of the danger, as shields to protect themselves. What better proof than that can you have of their complete disregard for the safety and welfare of their children, in which they show themselves to be the complete antithesis of the normal parent and faithful adherents to their own criminal, anti-social instincts?

8th July 1942, midday
Destruction of a British convoy bound for Archangel

To my great delight, our aircraft and submarines have already succeeded in sinking no less than thirty-two ships out of a British convoy of thirty-eight on its way to Archangel. Even yesterday, when a bare two-thirds had been sunk, I urged the drawing of a caricature of Roosevelt in *Kladderadatsch*. Most of the war material in this convoy came from America, and I suggested that Roosevelt should therefore be shown sitting on a high platform and laughingly casting into the sea all the tanks, planes and other material that the American workmen were handing up to him. The caption I suggested was: "We do not fight for gain or gold, but for a better world."

Be that as it may, the owners of naval construction yards in America have certainly veritable gold-mines in their possession!

8th July 1942, at dinner
My dog a vegetarian—The cat and the mouse—Effects of the meat diet

In many ways, my sheepdog Blondi is a vegetarian. There are lots of herbs which she eats with obvious pleasure, and it is interesting to see how she turns to them if her stomach is out of order. It is astonishing to see how wise animals are, and how well they know what is good for them. I once watched how a cat went about eating a mouse. She did not gobble it at once, but first of all played with it, as if giving it the chance to escape. It was only when the mouse was bathed in sweat with all this running hither and thither that the cat gave it the *coup de grâce* and ate it. Obviously it is in this state that the mouse appears most succulent and savoury to the cat.

Keitel said that man also does not normally eat his meat raw, and that the Huns used to put their meat under their saddles, to make it tender.

Hitler continued: Rather on the analogy of letting it stew in its own juice, you mean? Man, too, undergoes considerable change as the result of profuse perspiration engendered by violent physical effort.

Whenever I have to make a speech of great importance I am always soaking wet at the end, and I find I have lost four or six pounds in weight. And in Bavaria, where, in addition to my usual mineral water, local custom insists that I drink two or three bottles of beer, I lose as much as eight pounds.

This loss of weight is not, I think, injurious to health. The only thing that always worried me was the fact that my only uniform was a blue one, and it invariably stained my underclothes! When I later gave up eating meat, I immediately began to perspire much less, and within a fortnight to perspire hardly at all. My thirst, too, decreased considerably, and an occasional sip of water was all I required. Vegetarian diet, therefore, has some obvious advantages. I shall be interested to see whether my dog eventually becomes a complete and confirmed vegetarian.

9th July 1942, midday
Ukrainian harvest—Food problem is a problem of transport

The note issued to the press on the subject of the Ukrainian tour of the Minister for Eastern Territories is a bad one. What is the use of warning the population now against false hopes of a higher ration, based on the Ukrainian harvest? There are always more pessimists among the people than optimists, and in my opinion it shows an irresponsible lack of consideration at this juncture to dash the hopes of an easing of the situation, and so to make life for the people harder than it need be.

In any case, any declaration on the subject is at present premature. As things are, it is impossible to say whether or not the population of the Reich will derive any material benefit from the Ukrainian harvest. The problem is less one of a good or bad harvest than of transport. If we can solve the transport problem, we can raise the rations. But even if all *did* depend on the crop itself, and the crop turns out to be a bad one, public announcement of the fact merely increases the justification for pessimism.

What we must do is to speed up the measures already in hand to increase production in the appropriate agrarian territories and by this means find the way out of the *impasse*. Further, we must at all costs avoid any suggestion that the military units, by accumulating reserves of food and thus decreasing the amount available for home distribution, are in any way responsible or to blame for the current situation. The *Leibstandarte*, for example, have acted perfectly correctly, in my opinion, in collecting for their own use a herd of five hundred pigs and running their own Kolkhoz; as is also Field Marshal Kluge in accumulating many months of food reserves for his Eighth Army. If our troops on the Eastern front get stuck in the mud, and rations cannot be sent up to them, we shall be thankful indeed that they have had the foresight to look after themselves.

9th July 1942, at dinner
Events in Egypt—Italian susceptibility—Churchill's praise of Rommel—The future status of Egypt—German colonists in the Eastern Territories—The role of Italian colonists—Road construction before all else

When we occupy Alexandria or Cairo, the Foreign Office need not even suggest the appointment of a Resident for Egypt. In Rommel we have a Commander-in-Chief who has covered himself with imperishable renown and who must be regarded as one of the outstanding figures of the war; and for the Foreign Office to presume to meddle in his affairs is a palpable absurdity.

I am, moreover, of the opinion that Egypt belongs properly to the Italian sphere of influence. For us the Egyptian sphinx has no particular attraction, but for the Italian Imperium it is of vital importance. The appointment of a Resident might well create an annoying precedent and would justify the Italians in sending a representative to, say, the Caucasus, a region in which we alone are vitally interested. It will suffice if a suitable person is accredited to the Italian Resident in Egypt as the representative of Rommel, as operational Commander-in-Chief.

People frequently ask how it is that Rommel enjoys so great a worldwide reputation. Not a little is due to Churchill's speeches in the House of Commons, in which, for tactical reasons of policy, the British Prime Minister always portrays Rommel as a military genius.

Churchill's reason for doing so, of course, is that he does not wish to admit that the British are getting a damned good hiding from the Italians in Egypt and Libya. He may also hope that by emphasising the super-excellence of Rommel, he may sow seeds of discord between the Italians and ourselves. The Duce, however, is far too clever to be taken in by a trick of that sort. Indeed, he has himself frequently sung Rommel's praises throughout the world. Between them, Churchill and the Duce have caused the name of Rommel to be hallowed among the primitive races of North Africa and the Middle East with a prestige which it is impossible to exaggerate. This shows how dangerous it is for a responsible person to portray his opponent in the manner in which Churchill has portrayed Rommel. The mere name suddenly begins to acquire a value equal to that of several divisions.

Imagine what would happen if we went on lauding Timoshenko[494] to the skies; in the end our own soldiers would come to regard him as a superman.

And when one is dealing with semi-primitive peoples, these considerations carry even more weight. The remark of our General Crüwell [495]when he was captured by the English ran like lightning through the whole Islamic world as far as Ankara; when asked how he liked Shepheard's luxury hotel in Cairo, he replied: "It will make a grand Headquarters for Rommel!"

As regards the future status of Egypt, it is clear that Italy must retain a vital interest therein. Their possessions in Eritrea and Abyssinia alone render it essential that they should receive the Suez Canal; and they can guarantee the security of the Suez Canal only by maintaining garrisons in Egypt. If the Italians wish to establish themselves firmly in Egypt, both politically and militarily, they must guard against the danger of evoking among the local population any feeling of inferiority.

In this they would do well to learn a lesson from the British, who, with centuries of colonial experience behind them, have learned the art of being masters, and of holding the reins so lightly withal, that the natives do not notice the curb. The Italians must also guard against too eager an adaptation of all the local habits. Here Rommel gives them

---

[494] Semyon Timoshenko (1895–1970), a Marshal of the Soviet Union who held several commands throughout the war.
[495] Ludwig Crüwell (1892–1958), an *Afrika Korps* general who was captured after his pilot mistook British troops for Italian soldiers and landed in the middle of a British army position.

a good example. Throughout the campaign, Rommel has never once gone ambling round on a camel, for he knows that he can't ride a camel as well as the natives in the first place, and that secondly by invariably moving at speed in an armoured vehicle he has always made a tremendous impression on them. As far as we are concerned, we, too, must avoid over-enthusiasm in our Eastern territories; we must not try too ardently to impose our own German ideas of personal cleanliness on the local inhabitants and attack them daily with curry comb[496] and polish. It really does not matter to us whether they wash and sweep their houses daily; we are not their overseers, all we are there for is to promote our own interests.

The life of the German colonists must therefore be kept as far separate from that of the local inhabitants as is possible. In the pubs in which the natives spit all over the shop no German must be allowed to enter. The Germans must have their own pubs, from which the natives will be excluded. Then the locals can spit away to their hearts' content.

By leaving the local inhabitants to their own devices and by not interfering with their local customs, we create the most favourable atmosphere for the creation of purely and exclusively German settlements; and the easiest way of preventing any fusion between the German and the native population is to encourage the latter to adhere to their own ways and discourage them from imitating ours.

To return to Egypt, I hope that the Italians, who so far have shown considerable skill in their relations with the Mussulmans, will not tarnish the reputation they have deservedly gained. They should avoid getting involved in matters of minor detail. In the things that matter— irrigation, road construction and the like—I am quite sure that the Italian colonists, who work like bees, will achieve marvels under the leadership of the Duce.

If they had but been given ten years in Ethiopia, the Italian road constructors would have turned it into a model colony. In Egypt, the Italians will have a much easier task, for, except for lack of coal and iron, the country is completely self-supporting.

I cannot repeat too often that, as in Egypt, so in our Eastern territories, road construction is one of the most important tasks. As road maintenance is practically impossible during the winter, the new roads must be so sited and constructed as not to expose them to the dangers

---

[496] A curry comb is a device with serrated ridges, used for removing dirt from a body brush with which a horse is being groomed.

of snowdrifts. They must be constructed for the most part on embankments, which the winds of winter will sweep free of any undue accumulation of snow; and the foundations of the embankment must be particularly solidly constructed, bearing in mind the powerfully disintegrating forces of the thaw period. Where it is available, granite must be used; otherwise the stone which abounds in all river-beds.

17th July 1942, midday
Radio control in Russia—Goebbels fails

In the neighbourhood of our "Werwolf" Headquarters[497] we found that almost every house was provided with a wired-wireless. This shows that the Russians had realised in good time the dangers of a wireless receiving set. For one thing, the wired-wireless has the great advantage that it eliminates all interference, and for another, it permits the State to choose the broadcasts which it considers suitable. In Russia, the Commissar chooses the programmes, and the listeners are therefore completely cut off from the influence of foreign propaganda.

Before the war I myself directed the Minister for Propaganda to introduce wired-wireless in Germany. In this way German listeners would have been able to receive only our own national stations and such foreign broadcasts as we decided to retransmit. I am very sorry that we were not able to apply these measures before the conflict started. It was a bad piece of work on the part of the Ministry of Propaganda, for although Dr. Goebbels has tried to put the blame on to other services, it is he who is responsible for the failure. When the execution of an order demands the co-operation of several services, he who receives the original order must assume the responsibility for the execution of the whole. The desirability of introducing wired-wireless is indisputable. No Government can permit its population to be poisoned by enemy propaganda; otherwise one might as well invite a thousand enemy propagandists to come over and do their work openly.

All measures of this nature should be examined in peacetime with an eye to their probable effects in time of war. For war is a life-and-death struggle, which has its own rules and ignores the normalities of peace. A people which is prepared to accept compulsory military service of three or four years as a preparation for a possible war will not mind the slight inconvenience of a change over from wireless to wired-wireless.

---

[497] *Führerhauptquartier Werwolf* ("Leader Headquarters Werwolf") was Hitler's most easterly headquarters, located north of Vinnytsia in the Ukraine.

17th July 1942, at dinner
Self-satisfaction of the Italians

The Italians have a remarkable aptitude for arrogating to themselves all sorts of virtues, without in reality ever having accomplished any of the exploits which would result from them. This is particularly noticeable in the manner in which, in their *History of Fascism*, they describe the last phases of the Great War. According to it, the Allied victory in 1918 was due to the virile action of the Italians.

The same idea crops up as regards our campaign in 1940, during which, they claim, their attitude of "non-belligerency" tied down at least sixty French Divisions! Now that French official sources disclose that not sixty, but seven French Divisions were holding the Italian frontier during the western campaign, and that, even of these seven, three were withdrawn without any particular difficulty, the Italians are feeling proportionately shamefaced. But they will quickly get over it. They can take hiding after hiding for three unbroken years in succession, and then, if one day they suddenly achieve some minor success, all the buffets are forgotten and the whole peninsula bursts into songs of triumph!

18th July 1942, at dinner
Motor roads going East—The autobahn and the cinema—The autobahn and the shortening of space—Railways and national unity—The economics of the autobahn—Lloyd George, a man of method

Once we have secured our grip on the Eastern territories by means of the construction of a network of *autobahnen*, the problems of distance, which worry us a little today, will cease to exist. Of what importance will the thousand-kilometre stretch to the Crimea be, when we can cover it at eighty kilometres an hour along the *autobahn* and do the whole distance easily in two days!

I am absolutely determined to link up the whole of the Eastern territories behind the East Wall by means of a network of *autobahns* radiating from Berlin. The normal 7.5-metre road, will, however, be inadequate for the purpose. Instead I shall at once construct an 11-metre road, capable of taking three lanes of continuous traffic, slow-moving lorries on the right, normal traffic in the centre and swift-moving traffic on the left.

When one recalls that in pre-war Germany we have built more than two thousand kilometres of motor highway, I am surprised that the film industry has not made a great film out of the story. Unfortunately, however, we, unlike the British and the French, do not make films of our great achievements. The one exception is Vienna, and Vienna figures so often in films that I'm sick and tired of the sight of the place! I know of only one film which has the *autobahn* as its background —a wretched slap-stick affair, in which two lovers chase each other along the highway; and even there, not only is the story and the handling of the film miserable in the extreme, but they did not even select a particularly good section of *autobahn* on which to make it. The film, incidentally, had a terrific success in Upper Bavaria!

When we are able to go from Klagenfurt to Trondheim and from Hamburg to the Crimea along a Reich *autobahn*, we shall have a system of communications which will shorten space to the same degree as the old carriage highways for the conception of their time.

The *autobahn*s have proved immensely valuable from the political as well as from the transportation point of view. One of their greatest services is that they have swept away the internal frontiers of the Reich, and now one goes from one province to another without noticing it.

In the days of the old highways, the numerous toll-gates and the differences in surface made one only too aware of provincial boundaries; once over the Mecklenburg border, for instance, the pot-holes reduced one's speed to ten or fifteen kilometres an hour—and one was very lucky if one escaped without broken springs! The State Railways, too, have of course made their contribution to the process of the unification of the German races.

But in contrast to the *autobahn* on which even the little Volkswagen can skip in three bounds from the Alps to the North Sea, the train, with its innumerable stops, still draws attention to the old boundaries.

Everything combines to remind one that once upon a time there were the Royal Bavarian Railways, the Royal Württemberg Railways and even, as Bormann has just reminded me, the Grand Ducal Friedrich-Franz von Mecklenburg Railway Company! Dynastic interests proved too strong for the railways.

This is just one further confirmation of the fact that it would never have been possible to form a united German Reich if the Princes had not been swept aside. Each of these Princes built and developed his railway system as the spirit moved him. The *autobahn*, on the other hand, where uniformity in all aspects has been the guiding principle, allows anyone to travel anywhere he likes and still feel at home. It is only after passing the frontier of the Reich—and this I would emphasise most strongly—that he may expect to meet the first pot-hole. That no one before me thought of building these *autobahns* is due, probably, to the fact that the central administration never scientifically worked out the financing of the project.

In road construction, the system was prevalent whereby the local authorities in each small locality through which the highway was to run were called upon to defray the costs of construction in the territory under their jurisdiction. With such an idea, no wonder the scheme did not achieve much!

When I studied the financial aspect of the project, I came to the conclusion that a thousand kilometres of *autobahn* should be constructed each year and that the Central Government should contribute a milliard marks annually to finance it. One day I explained to Lloyd George how I proposed to find this money; firstly, I intended to get my labour by mobilising all the unemployed and putting them to work, thus saving some six hundred million marks in dole payments; secondly, I intended to increase the income tax and the tax on petrol to an extent that would bring in an estimated revenue of four hundred million marks. And thus my *autobahn* would cost the State nothing.

During our conversation, that old fox Lloyd George asked me what thickness of concrete I proposed to use? The American motor highways have five or six centimetres of concrete, and Lloyd George could hardly believe me when I told him that ours would have from twenty-five to thirty centimetres. Indeed, Kempka told me later that one day Lloyd George stopped his car, pulled a tape measure out of his pocket and verified the correctness of what I had told him.

The war shows how right I was. Even direct hits from bombs have caused only minor damage on the *autobahns*. But the war, alas, has obliged us to change their appearance, and to paint them black in order to render them invisible to hostile aircraft. Those who know how near to my heart the *autobahns* lie will be able to appreciate how much it hurts me no longer to be able to bowl along those lovely white tracks.

18th July 1942, evening
An interview on the war on the Eastern front—What I shall say about the "Second Front"

To enable me to make some retort to the constant allusions to a Second Front in the British press, I have instructed Dr. Dietrich to arrange an interview for me with a foreign journalist on the subject of the Eastern front.

As each individual picks from an interview of this sort the things which seem to him personally to be the most important, I hope to be able to touch on the subject of the Second Front in an oblique way. I propose to develop the idea that, as the British are children in military affairs, we must, of course, be prepared for anything, however foolish, and that we cannot therefore dismiss out of hand all the twaddle written in the Anglo-Jewish press; but that, in the same way as our preparations allowed us to counter the onslaught of the Russians, we are now taking all the necessary steps to prepare a worthy reception for such unfortunate British soldiers as may be led, by those military nonentities who command them, to attempt a landing on the coast of Europe.

I shall treat the subject of the Second Front in a manner that will come as a cold *douche* to the British. I shall not say that I do not believe in the possibility of a Second Front, for that would jeopardise the whole object of the interview. I shall, on the contrary, emphasise that German military precision and thoroughness ensure that we are prepared for any and every eventuality—including that of a Second Front.

In accordance with Dr. Dietrich's recommendation, I have agreed that this interview should be granted to some foreign journalist who has already shown appreciation of the German press and its work. Whether he be the representative of a country great or small, neutral or friendly, is of no consequence, for—as the Reich Press Chief rightly says—this interview will certainly be reproduced in the whole world press. I could, of course, give my opinions on the Second Front in a public speech; but to make a speech without having a specific reason for it is always a bad practice. The intelligent man will swiftly see through the ruse and recognise the real object behind it; and if this object is too blatantly apparent, the desired effect will be completely ruined.

On the other hand, if the question of the Second Front is introduced obliquely in the course of an interview on the Eastern theatre of operations, I can, I am sure, convey exactly the impression I desire in a few incidental sentences.

19th July 1942, midday
Naval warfare—The advantage of little ships—Sea and superstition

When a battleship is sunk, the loss of life may be as high as two thousand souls. But if we could construct a mass of tiny craft, each fitted with a torpedo tube and manned by a single man, the losses we should suffer would be fractional in comparison, and the successes, from the combat point of view, might well be considerably greater. Many years ago, I once asked Graf Luckner[498] why he always used comparatively small craft for his world sailing tours? Luckner gave me the significant answer that, when anything goes wrong on a big ship, people save themselves by getting into little boats—one might therefore just as well start off at once in the latter and have done with it!

Luckner, of course, was a marvellous spinner of yarns, and I could listen to him for hours on end. One day someone or other explained to me that certain of Luckner's statements were nonsense—and I was as angry with my informant as a child who has been deprived of his Christmas tree!

The Führer then asked Admiral Krancke if he could explain the origin of the terms "a seaman's yarn" and "spinning a yarn"? The Admiral replied that in the old days on long voyages the sailors, bored with the same food and the eternal sea and having but few books to read, passed their spare hours telling each other stories, which grew taller and taller, and at the same time fashioning yarn-nets for fishing and so on—hence the expressions.

The Führer continued: I once had an ex-sailor as a servant. At all hours of the day and night the fellow used to try to spin me yarns which any fool could see were nonsense. In the end I had to tell him that I was quite as good a liar as he was, and that he must not tempt me to try to go one better! As even that did not stop him, we were forced to part company. A thing which always strikes me about sailors' tales is the great part that superstition plays in them. Sailors, apparently, are like actors in this respect. In the lives of both there occur unexpected events which they cannot possibly foresee and with which they cannot cope. The sailor never knows when a storm or even a hurricane will descend on him, and the actor cannot tell whether the audience will receive him with applause or with derisory whistling; and so they are both extremely superstitious. Superstition, I think, is a factor one must take into consideration when assessing human conduct, even though one may rise superior to it oneself and laugh at it. It was for this reason, to give you a concrete example, that I once advised the Duce not to initiate a certain action on the thirteenth of the month. For the same reason I think it is a bad thing to let a ship sail on a Friday, because all old salts know that a Friday sailing is unlucky.

Such things are the imponderables of life, which one cannot afford to neglect, for those who believe in them are quite capable, at a moment

[498] Felix Graf von Luckner (1881–1966), a World War I Navy raider commander.

of crisis, of causing the greatest consternation. Just when the difficulties of the eastern winter campaign in the East had reached their height, some imbecile pointed out that Napoleon, like ourselves, had started his Russian campaign on 22nd June. Thank God, I was able to counter that drive with the authoritative statement of historians of repute that Napoleon's campaign did not, in fact, begin until 23rd June!

The horoscope, in which the Anglo-Saxons in particular have great faith, is another swindle whose significance must not be under-estimated. Just think of the trouble given to the British General Staff by the publication by a well-known astrologer of a horoscope foretelling final victory in this war for Germany! All the newspapers in Britain had to dig out all the false prophecies previously published by this eminent quack and reprint them, before public anxiety could be pacified!

In judging any question connected with superstition, it must be remembered that, although an oracle's prophecies may be wrong a hundred times (when they are promptly forgotten), it suffices for one prophecy to be fortuitously confirmed by subsequent events, for it to be believed, cherished and handed down from generation to generation.

21st July 1942, at dinner
Society in France—A ruling class which retains its powers

It is characteristic of the French that every well-to-do citizen—be he business man, officer, famous artist or prominent politician—always buys himself, generally in the village or district of his origin, a little house with a neat garden. The result is that in almost every French village you find among the mass of nondescript cottages one or more handsome villas, belonging to an advocate, a painter, a cotton-spinner or the like. The French upper classes usually spend two or three months in the country and thus acquire an affection for the land, the political importance of which must not be overlooked. Gradually they get to know each individual villager and thus very quickly become associated with all the joys and sorrows, great and small, of the simplest, and at the same time most solid, class of the population. There is, in State affairs, no finer way of binding the upper classes to the interests of the country.

22nd July 1942, midday
King of England and Duke of Normandy—The Channel Islands and the Frisian Isles—Those who work and those who reap

The inhabitants of the Channel Islands which we occupy consider themselves as members of the British Empire rather than as subjects of the King, whom they still regard, not as King, but as the Duke of

Normandy. If our occupation troops play their cards properly, we shall have no difficulties there.

I do not approve of the suggestion made to me that these islands should be colonised by people from Friesland and the Ems regions; for whereas these latter are primarily marsh-dwellers and cattle-drovers, the inhabitants of the islands themselves are first and foremost small farmers.

If the British had continued to hold these islands, fortifying them and constructing aerodromes on them, they could have been a veritable thorn in our flesh. As it is, we have now firmly established ourselves there, and with the fortifications we have constructed and the permanent garrison of a whole division, we have ensured against the possibility of the islands ever falling again into the hands of the British.

After the war they can be handed over to Ley, for, with their wonderful climate, they constitute a marvellous health resort for the Strength through Joy organisation. The islands are full of hotels as it is, so very little construction will be needed to turn them into ideal rest centres.

The Italians could have got hold of a similar prize, if, on entering the war, they had occupied Cyprus. Unfortunately, however, they restricted their military activities to a declaration that now they regarded themselves as being in a state of war! And that, if you please, after we had shown them in Norway how things should be done. The average Italian of today is a mighty trencherman at the table, but a weedy warrior in war. How very different are the men of the Caucasian tribes, who are about the finest and proudest men to be found between Europe and Asia.

22nd July 1942, at dinner

Lawyers not admitted!—Thief does not rob thief—Crocodile tears for sale, at a fee! Let me issue a word of warning to our legal gentlemen; that they should refrain from attempting to impose their mania for regulations on the administration of our Eastern territories

It is typical of lawyers that, according to their doctrine, while I have the absolute right, as Chancellor of the Reich, to sign and promulgate laws and decrees affecting hundreds of millions of marks, I am not legally allowed to sign a will disposing of, say, ten marks, without having my signature witnessed by a lawyer. I had to make a special law in order to rid us of this pedantry. As long as I am here, there is no great danger to be feared from the lawyers; whenever necessary, I shall ride rough-shod over their formalities. But I am worried about the future.

A little while ago I took steps which enable me to put a stop to their little games, when they become really harmful. I was forced to do so, because up to now these crooks were answerable for their conduct only to their own legal tribunals, in which it was axiomatic that thief does not rob thief. But I soon put a stop to that.

During our period of struggle, I had plenty of personal experience with these gentlemen. I am sometimes told that I am confusing the lawyers who flourished under the Weimar Republic with their successors of today, who are quite different. I disagree absolutely; the very curriculum for the training of a lawyer ensures that the rising generation will be just the same *Smart Alecs* as their predecessors.

How can you describe as honest a profession which, from its beginning to its end, is engaged in defending blackguards? And in which the fervour of their eloquence is in direct ratio to their client's capacity to pay! Look at Lütgebrune![499] He can work himself up to a tempest of tears—provided sufficient pennies are put in the slot!

How can they dare claim that they are furthering the cause of justice when they whisper advice in the ears of criminals and conduct their examinations in the most dubious manner! Whenever I witness the disgusting performance I always feel—here we have the master fox teaching the little fox the way to go.

In olden times it was the strolling player who was buried in the public refuse-heap; today it is the lawyer who should be buried there.

No one stands closer in mentality to the criminal than the lawyer; and if you can see much difference between them, I can't. The only way to clean up this profession is to nationalise it; and I think, incidentally, that it is scandalous that these people should be entitled to call themselves "Doctor".

23nd July 1942, after dinner

Russia's two main weapons—We beat time—Let us admire Stalin—
Adults and infants of the Ukraine—Contraception should be
encouraged—The danger of racial pressure in the Eastern territories—
Local population, the right policy—German administration and the
cockchafer hunters

The Soviets could have become a mortal danger to us, if they had succeeded in undermining the military spirit of our soldiers with the slogan of the German Communist Party: "No more War!" For at the

---

[499] Walter Lütgebrune (1879–1949), a lawyer who defended many NSDAP activists in court.

same time as they were trying by Communist Party terrorism, by strikes, by their press, and by every other means at their disposal to ensure the triumph of pacifism in our country, the Russians were building up an enormous army.

Disregarding the namby-pamby utterances about humanitarianism which they spread so assiduously in Germany, in their own country they drove their workers to an astonishing degree, and the Soviet worker was taught by means of the Stakhanov system[500] to work both harder and longer than his counterpart in either Germany or the capitalist States. The more we see of conditions in Russia, the more thankful we must be that we struck in time. In another ten years there would have sprung up in Russia a mass of industrial centres, inaccessible to attack, which would have produced armaments on an inexhaustible scale, while the rest of Europe would have degenerated into a defenceless plaything of Soviet policy.

It is very stupid to sneer at the Stakhanov system. The arms and equipment of the Russian armies are the best proof of its efficiency in the handling of industrial man-power.

Stalin, too, must command our unconditional respect. In his own way he is a hell of a fellow! He knows his models, Genghiz Khan and the others, very well, and the scope of his industrial planning is exceeded only by our own Four Year Plan. And there is no doubt that he is quite determined that there shall be in Russia no unemployment such as one finds in such capitalist States as the United States of America . . .

Bormann, who has just returned from a tour of inspection of the Kolkhoz in the vicinity of General Headquarters, gave his impressions: "When one looks at the children, it is difficult to realise that sooner or later they, too, will acquire the flat, Slav faces of their parents. Like the inhabitants of the Baltic States, they are fair, with blue eyes, bonny and chubby-faced. In comparison, our children look like tottering little chicks. It really is curious to think that these children will become Ukrainian adults, with their vulgar, inexpressive faces. I was much struck by the fact that in these huge open spaces one saw so many children and so few men. Such prolific breeding may one day give us a knotty problem to solve, for as a race they are much hardier by nature than we are. The men have admirable teeth, and rarely does one see a man wearing glasses. They are well fed

---

[500] The Stakhanovite system was a campaign created by a Russian miner, Alexei Stakhanov (1906–1977), intended to increase worker productivity and to demonstrate the superiority of Communism.

and bursting with good health at all ages. The difficult conditions under which these men have lived for centuries have brought into being a merciless process of selection. If one of us drinks a drop of their water, he all but dies. They on the other hand live in the dirt, drink the muddy stagnant water of their ponds and thrive on it. We fill ourselves with quinine as a safeguard against malaria, while the Ukrainians are so immune, not only to malaria but to scarlet fever as well, that they can live with impunity in surroundings teeming with fleas and ticks. If these people are allowed, under German supervision—that is, under greatly improved conditions—to multiply too quickly, it will be against our interests, for the racial pressures which these damned Ukrainians will exercise, will constitute a real danger. Our interests demand just the reverse—namely, that these territories, hitherto Russian, should in time be populated by a larger number of German colonists than local inhabitants."

Hitler commented: I recently read an article from the pen of some Herr Doktor advocating the prohibition of the sale in the occupied territories of contraceptives. If any criminal lunatic should really try to introduce this measure I would soon have his head off!

In view of the extraordinary fertility of the local inhabitants, we should be only too pleased to encourage the women and the girls to practise the arts of contraception at all times. Far from prohibiting the sale of contraceptives, therefore, we should do our utmost to encourage it. We should call on the Jews for help! With their unrivalled sense of commerce, they are the very people for the job!

In all seriousness, however, there is a very real danger that these local inhabitants will increase too rapidly under our care and domination. Their conditions of life will inevitably improve under our jurisdiction, and we must take all the measures necessary to ensure that the non-German population does not increase at an excessive rate. In these circumstances, it would be sheer folly to place at their disposal a health service such as we know it in Germany; and so—no inoculations and other preventative measures for the natives!

We must even try to stifle any desire for such things, by persuading them that vaccination and the like are really most dangerous! It is, furthermore, essential to avoid doing anything which might give rise to a feeling of superiority or of racial pride among the natives. This is of the utmost importance, for it is only by the creation of the very reverse state of mind that we shall be able to prepare the ground for the accomplishment of our plans. For these reasons, the local population must be given no facilities for higher education. A failure on our part in this respect would simply plant the seeds of future opposition to our rule. Schools, of course, they must have—and they must pay for their tuition. But there is no need to teach them much more than, say, the meaning of the various road-signs. Instruction in geography can be restricted to one single sentence: The Capital of the Reich is Berlin, a city which everyone should try to visit once in his lifetime. Finally, elementary instruction in reading and writing in German will complete the course. Mathematics and such like are quite unnecessary.

In setting up the educational system, the same principles apply to both Eastern territories and any other colonies. We do not want any of this enlightenment nonsense propagated by an advance guard of parsons! What is the use of talking about progress to people like that? Jodl is quite right when he says that notices in the Ukrainian language "Beware of the Trains" are superfluous; what on earth does it matter if one or two more locals get run over by the trains? I am in favour of teaching a little German in the schools simply because this will facilitate our administration.

Otherwise every time some German instruction is disobeyed, the local inhabitant will come along with the excuse that he "didn't understand". For the same reason, the Russian script must be replaced by the Latin. The greatest possible mistake we could make would be to take the local population too much under the wing of the State; and to avoid all danger of our own people becoming too soft-hearted and too humane towards them, we must keep the German colonies strictly separated from the local inhabitants.

Germans will in no circumstances live in a Ukrainian town.

If essential, it will be better to put Germans in barracks outside a town than to allow them to live inside it. Otherwise, sooner or later, the process of cleaning up and improving the town will inevitably start; and Russian and Ukrainian towns are not in any circumstances to be improved or made more habitable.

It is not our mission to lead the local inhabitants to a higher standard of life; and our ultimate object must be to build towns and villages exclusively for Germans and absolutely separate from Russian or Ukrainian towns. The houses to be constructed for the Germans must in no respect resemble those of the Russians, and lime-plaster and thatched roofs will not be used. In pre-war Germany everything was too meticulous and too stylised. One reason for this is that we Germans were compelled to cluster in such close proximity, that the police had no option but from time to time to issue regulations for the conduct of communal life. This craze for regimentation, however, carried with it this danger, that when any German found himself settled abroad—in a British Dominion, for example—he would sigh with relief at his freedom of action and movement and very soon become estranged from his German fatherland.

We must in no circumstances repeat the mistakes of excessive regimentation in the Eastern territories. If we wish to avoid antagonising the local population we must restrict our interference with their local habits and customs to the minimum compatible with our interests.

In pre-war Germany things had got to such a state that Berlin wanted a finger in the pie whenever the mayor of any town was being elected. They even wanted to forbid dog breeding, and I had personally to intervene in order to restore permission to the dog fanciers. The unfortunate Cockchafer[501] Associations *(Maikaefer-Vereine)* were overwhelmed by a deluge of regulations from Berlin, with paragraphs governing the administration, finances, audit, and God knows what else, and holding the president of the Association personally responsible for compliance!

As regards the Eastern territories, therefore, I wish only broad instructions to be issued from Berlin; the settlement of day-today issues can safely be left in the hands of the respective regional Commissars.

I propose further to reduce the danger of regimentation in the Eastern territories by reducing the German administrative machine in them to an absolute minimum, and seeing that the regional Commissar deals with and through the local mayors. I do not, of course, intend that out of this should grow anything in the nature of a Ukrainian Civil Service!

24th July 1942, at dinner

What to expect from the Dutch—A poor people that tolerated Wilhelm II—The husbands of Wilhelmina and Juliana—The popularity of the Duce—Claims on Europe's gratitude—Italy, land of internal struggles—Sabotage against the Duce

When people tell me that the Dutch will not make good SS-men, I always remember the cartoons of Spitzweg,[502] who represented the

---

[501] The cockchafer, colloquially called the "Maybug" is the name given to any of the European beetles of the *genus* Melolontha.

[502] Carl Spitzweg (1808–1885), a Bavarian romanticist painter who often portrayed comical scenes and characters.

German soldiers of the South German States sitting and knitting socks. But twenty years of instruction have put a very different complexion on the matter. A race like the Dutch, which has shown itself capable of organising a magnificent Far Eastern air service and which produces a host of first-class seamen, can easily be taught to assimilate the military spirit. One must not lose faith in the essential soundness of the race, for sound it certainly is.

I well remember how completely staggered I was when an industrialist of the stature of Kirdorf,[503] while promising me his full support for our Movement, declared that there was only one thing I must not ask of him—namely, belief in the success of our campaign; a people, he said, who tamely put up with a Kaiser like Wilhelm II was, in his opinion, too inherently lazy to be capable of any renaissance.

That Kirdorf was too pessimistic in his assessment of our people is shown by the fact that the ex-monarchs and the members of the former ruling houses have been completely forgotten by the nation even during their lifetime. Who cares a rap, for instance, for Rupprecht of Bavaria! Kingship possesses but little wisdom, and the boundary between the throne and the mad-house is a slender one.

If we can succeed in getting rid of the King of Belgium by giving him a pension of half a million or so and thus ensuring for him a gilded exile, I for one shall be heartily thankful.

In Holland, thank goodness, things are much easier, for in Prince von Lippe-Biesterfeld we have an absolute imbecile oaf on the throne. When, before his marriage, he came to pay me a farewell visit, he cringed and scraped like a gigolo. A couple of days later he declared in the Dutch press that in his heart he had always felt himself a Dutchman! The late Prince Consort of Queen Wilhelmina was also a typical royal idiot. He even had the impertinence to approach me, shortly after our assumption of power, for a loan of seven and a half million guilders, in return for his assurance that he would then do all in his power to increase German influence in Holland!

Not only among crowned heads but also among the so-called upper ten thousand, stupidity and pride are proverbial. Again and again I have had to defend the Duce in certain circles of society, pointing out to them that, without him, Italy would certainly have become a Com-

---

[503] Emil Kirdorf (1847–1938), the German industrialist who was awarded the *Verdienstorden vom Deutschen Adler* (the "Order of the German Eagle") on his 90th birthday in 1937 for his support to the NSDAP in the 1920s.

munist State. And again and again these same circles have dismissed him as a broken man and a spent force.

Bormann is quite right when, on the authority of his collection of photographs, he declares that the Duce enjoys an immense popularity. I have myself seen in a dozen different episodes in Italy how very popular the Duce is with the majority of the people; and there is no denying the unparalleled achievements of this man and of Fascism—the innumerable new factories, the construction of new houses and schools and hospitals, the great colonial enterprise and many more; when one recalls the deplorable state of Italy at the time of the Duce's assumption of power, one realises the magnitude of his achievements.

Over and above all this he overcame Bolshevism, not by military force, but by superior intellect, and it is him we have to thank for showing for the first time, by his decisive defeat of the inner power of Bolshevism, that even in this twentieth century it is possible to recall a people to a sense of purely national pride.

There he has rendered us all a great service—much as, in the years to come, my own greatest service to humanity will be thought to be my success in saving Europe from the Asiatic onslaught.

The Duce's political activity is considerably impeded by royal prerogative; it is, for example, all but impossible to assume the leadership of a country if the armed forces thereof owe allegiance to another. No business firm could be efficiently run by the managing director, if some other shareholder held a majority of shares, and was thus in a position to alter or cancel orders at will. Unless legislative and administrative power are in one hand, endless difficulties will arise.

When we Germans pass judgment on the Duce, we must bear all these considerations well in mind, not forgetting that, when all is said and done, it is the Duce we have to thank for the fact that Italy is not in the war on the side of the Allies.

When some aspects of our alliance with Italy appear irksome to us, let us not forget that the King and his Court have much too far-reaching powers of intervention both in military matters and in affairs of State. Even the Prefects are appointed by the Crown, The Duce, I know, says that does not worry him; because he had guarded against the danger of a few Prefects intriguing against him by seeing to it that some of his most stalwart and trustworthy Fascists are always put on the Prefectorial nomination list. But he has to act as swift as lightning and be ready with his recommendation the very second a Prefecture falls vacant; if he is in the least tardy, the post is immediately filled by some Court sycophant, and what that means I have myself seen in Rome.

I could scarcely believe my eyes when I saw how shamelessly the Queen behaved towards the Duce, and how the Court clique was always pressed to the fore. Never have I seen the necessity for a militia better demonstrated. When I said this to the Duce, he laughed and said that under present circumstances even he could not carry on with only the executive power of the police behind him.

The upper ten thousand of Italy, instead of realising that a victory for Communism would mean their own immediate annihilation, and instead therefore of giving him all the support they could, placed difficulty after difficulty in his way in the struggle against the Bolsheviks. They were as little conscious of the tremendous assistance they were giving the Bolsheviks as the stupid calf, of which it is said: "The stupid calf chooses its own butcher."

26th July 1942, midday
Oilfields in the Caucasus and elsewhere—Russian methods—The value of gas propellants

The presence of oil in the Caucasus, in the vicinity of Vienna and in the Harz leads one to suspect the existence of an oilfield of whose magnitude and importance one had not the least idea.

This is not in the least surprising. As in the case of mineral wealth, the trusts would immediately buy up any newly discovered oil-bearing territories, with the intention of restricting their development to a degree compatible with their other interests; in this, their primary object would be to prevent exploitation by others.

One must give the Russians their due and admit that, in this respect, they have succeeded in limiting the power of monopolies and eliminating private interests. As a result, they are now in a position to prospect throughout their territory for oil, whose position and probable extension are studied by experts with the assistance of very large-scale maps.

In this way, they have not only been able to trace the course of the oil-veins, but have also verified their facts and extended their knowledge by test borings carried out at the expense of the State. There is a lot we can learn from them.

There is no limit to what we could have extracted from the sources in the vicinity of Vienna, if the State had undertaken the necessary exploitation in time. This, added to the oil-wells of the Caucasus and Romania, would have saved us from all anxiety for the future. One must not, however, forget that oil wells are not inexhaustible; and that is why I am still in favour of gas-driven public vehicles, and particularly of gas-driven vehicles for the Party.

I advocate this not only as a precaution for the future, but also as a means of reducing the cost of transportation. For twelve pfennig one can cover the same distance in a gas-driven car as one can with a litre of petrol in an ordinary car, and petrol costs forty pfennig a litre. In the northern countries, and particularly in Finland, charcoal is plentiful; in Germany we have lignite in abundance, and in the Ukraine there are the briquettes made from the limitless straw which yearly rots on its own.

26th July 1942, after dinner
Do's and Don'ts for Civil Servants—The temptations to corruption—
Caesar's wife—The old State servant and private business—A few
swindlers

The Führer asked Bormann whether the necessary steps had been taken to make it illegal for any member of the Reichstag to sit on the Board of Directors of any private concern. Bormann replied that the matter had been deferred until the end of the war and suggested that Lammers should be asked to give a detailed explanation in his next report.

The Führer was horrified at this reply, and said: No servant of the State must be a shareholder. No *Gauleiter*, no Member of the Reichstag and, in general, no Party leader must be a member of any board of directors, regardless of whether the appointment is honorary or paid; for even if the individual were actuated solely by the interests of the State, and even if he possessed the integrity of Cato himself, the public would lose faith in him.

In capitalist States, it is essential for a great enterprise to have in its employ men of influence—hence the large number of members of Parliament and high officials who figure on boards of directors. The amounts disbursed to these personages in directors' fees, share of profits and so on is more than recouped by one or two fat Government contracts which they are in a position to secure for their company.

The Danube Shipping Company, for example, paid out eighty thousand kronen a year to each of the dozen Members of Parliament who sat on its board of directors. But it recouped itself many times over for this expenditure through the influence these men were able to exercise in its favour. All competition was eliminated and a virtual monopoly was gained—all to the detriment of the State, or, in other words, of the community. It must therefore be accepted as an absolute principle that no Member of the Reichstag, no civil servant and no Party leader must be in any way connected with business of this nature.

The common people have a remarkable flair for anything of this kind. When I decided to buy a property, my choice lay between the Berghof and a property at Steingaden. Fortunately, I chose the Berghof. If I had taken the Steingaden place, I should have been compelled to become a producer of the famous Steingaden cheese, in order to keep the place up.

Suppose, then, that for some reason or other the price of cheese went up. Everybody would immediately say: Of course! The Führer is himself personally interested in the price of cheese.

This viewpoint of the Führer was supported by Field Marshal Keitel, who told the following story. The former Food Minister, Hugenberg, had energetically encouraged the campaign undertaken by the State to promote the consumption of milk. When his own lorries, carrying milk from his own properties, passed through the streets, plastered with posters of the official campaign, everybody said that the real object of the exercise was to bolster the sales of the Minister's milk business!

The Führer continued: When an official retires from State service, he should not be allowed to enter a line of business with which he previously had official dealings. For one may be quite sure that any firm would gladly employ him—not on account of the services he could render, but for the connections which he undoubtedly would have. If this were not so, then directors would not earn fees amounting to thirty-six thousand marks a year—and more.

Further, it is a scandal that men of this kind should usurp the positions to which others have a prior claim, namely, those who have passed their whole lives in the service of an enterprise and have risen, step by step, to the top. This one characteristic is alone sufficient to demonstrate the immorality of the whole system. Big business is as hot on the trail of such connections as the Devil after the soul of a Jew.

⋅ If once one permit a *Gauleiter* to become a shareholder or a director in some industrial undertaking, one will not be able to prevent the Kreisleiter, the Mayor and other junior officials from doing the same; and that would spell the beginning of corruption.

For all these reasons, we must see to it that any State official who has invested all his money in shares should forthwith invest it in State loans instead. This—as the Field Marshal rightly remarks—was the practice in the old Army; in the old Imperial Army, an officer was not allowed to invest either his own fortune or the dowry of his wife in a private industrial concern, but was expected to subscribe to State loans recommended and guaranteed by the State. This was a good system, for it guaranteed that the private interests of the officer, like those of the State official, were bound indissolubly to the interests of the State. After all, the State does not exist in order to raise a man to a high social level and give him the best of everything, only to see him later slip away from under its aegis.

Admiral Krancke asked what the attitude of the State would be towards an employee who made some invention?

The Führer replied: If the invention is of an epoch-making nature, it will be taken over by the State, and the inventor will receive an appropriate remuneration in State bonds.

The Admiral then asked whether an officer retiring voluntarily from the service should also be precluded from entering private business?

The Führer replied; I very much doubt if a retired Major has the ability to fill any post in business, even that of accountant. We had enough trouble at the end of the first war in finding uses for the demobilised officer. One must further draw a sharp distinction between those who retire from State service with the object of entering business, and those who are permitted to retire on account of their inefficiency.

To discourage State officials from constantly bearing in mind the possibility of a switch-over to private business, the State must make sure that in its agreements with large undertakings it never grants a monopoly. Whenever there is a question of a large contract, it must always be split up between three or four of the firms competing for it.

Only in this way can one prevent commercially minded civil servants from building for themselves "golden bridges" to certain firms. Further, the granting of big contracts must be made by a committee, the members of which are constantly being changed. Purchasing commissions on behalf of the army should always be composed of select officers recalled from the front for the purpose and having no connections whatever with the industries concerned. If there is any sign that they are being tempted—especially with invitations to shooting-parties—they must be relieved instantly.

I say shooting-parties, because shooting and hunting have the same effect on officers as jewels have on women. The industrialists are experts in all these arts of corruption, and their skill is the result of many years of experience! This explains the cool audacity with which they pursue their aims.

On one occasion they even approached me and tried to get my support for something or other, in which the Führer's signature would have raked in a packet of capital for them—and they dangled before me a bunch of shares—to be given, of course, to any charity I cared to select!! The alchemist Tausend,[504] by making skilful use of the name of Ludendorff (who had fallen into the trap), extorted four million marks from a small group of industrialists—nine hundred thousand from Mannesmann alone—to finance his further experiments.

If an officer of Ludendorff's high qualities can become the dupe of a swindler, all the more reason to see that other, more ordinary folk, like officers allowed to retire for reasons of inefficiency, are prevented from entering business. That officers are unsuited for business activities is shown by Ludendorff's failure when he tried, with Captain Weiss, to found a newspaper.

Even the most capable business man is sometimes caught by the swindler. I am thinking of Roselius, who extracted the caffeine from coffee and sold it at a high price as a medicine, and then sold his processed coffee at a price above that of normal coffee.

Well, even this astute Roselius was caught by a crook who claimed to be able to transform dirty water into pure water. Shortly after I came into power, Roselius forced my hand and I consented to receive this eminent person. I only had to hear this great "inventor" speak for a moment, to discover that he was a complete crook.

Then the Minister for Church Affairs, or course, had to fall into the hands of another *soi-disant*[505] inventor, who claimed to be able to extract petrol from coal by means of a process with water![506] Even Keppler allowed himself to be led by the nose for nearly a year by the same sharper, who really did produce petrol for his dupes' inspection—but it was petrol procured from other sources! When things at last got too hot for this particular swindler, he tried to get a safe-conduct out of the country.

---

[504] Franz Tausend (1884–1942), a chemist who claimed to be able to extract gold from base metals. He raised millions from gullible investors, and spent most of the money on funding an extravagant lifestyle for himself and his partners. He was imprisoned twice for fraud, once in 1929 and again in 1937.

[505] Self-styled, or so-called.

[506] The swindler Heinrich "Heinz" Kurschildgen.

But Himmler, who originally had believed in him, gave him instead a *carte d'entrée* for one of the concentration camps, where he was able to continue his experiments in peace!

"*If such swindles are possible here in this country,*" said Bormann, "*what must it be like in a place like the United States!*"

The Führer continued: Germany's strength lies in the fact that the men of the Party, the State and the armed forces take no part in business; and those of them who still have any connection with business must now make their final decision: either they must abandon all such connections, or they must resign from their official positions.

27th July 1942, at dinner
Russia's floating population—The lure of the South—German bureaucracy and the nomads

Ambassador Hewel reported that the Commissar of a neighbouring town had told him that a large number of Russians were applying for laissez-passer,[507] *apparently to go to the Crimea. Most of these applicants came, with wives and families, from Leningrad.*

The Führer said: But that is ridiculous! Here am I trying to empty the Crimea in order to make way for our own colonists, and our command posts issue *laissez-passer* to any and every Russian who applies for one! And it is only by chance that it comes to my knowledge! Has anyone, I wonder, taken the trouble to think why these Russians wish to emigrate?

Primarily, of course, it is the attraction of the south; they all know that the climate of the Crimea is more temperate, their stock of warm clothing is meagre in the extreme, and last winter was a particularly severe one. The Russians have not that love of homeland which is characteristic of the German peasant; even in the time of the Tsars, millions used to emigrate, and the hope of being able to avoid taxes was not the least of their motives, for the mass emigration period usually coincided with the arrival of the Imperial tax collectors.

Correctly to appreciate the mentality of these people, one must realise that they are nomadic. The wanderlust is as inherent in them as it is in a herd of beasts; when they have denuded one district they wander on in search of fresh pastures. This explains why Russians are always ready to abandon even a valuable possession like a wagon, if it impedes their move onwards.

---

[507] French for a document allowing the holder to pass or a permit.

I cannot help grinning when I think what a heaven-sent field of activity these people constitute for our bureaucrats! I can already see in my mind's eye some of the measures they will introduce: first of all, a sort of journey book, to be duly stamped on departure from each pasturage; then a ban on certain routes—with the routes not so banned made compulsory! And the tit-bit will be the battle of the bureaucrats to decide who shall have the right to administer these gipsies. Will it be the military authorities or the Ministry of Internal Affairs? Might it not even be the Ministry for Foreign Affairs? They surely will stake a claim on the grounds that some of these nomads might, one fine day, wish to go beyond even the far-flung frontiers of the German Reich of the future!

28th July 1942, midday
The transport of grain

The question under discussion was whether a hundred thousand tons of grain captured at Morosovskaya should be transferred to Germany. It represented two million sacks, or forty million seven-pound loaves. The Führer gave his opinion as follows: A hundred thousand tons! That rings a bell in my memory. It was exactly the amount that I had to find, fighting like a lion, so that the Swabian should not be deprived of their beloved *Spätzle*.[508] I do not believe in the theory that all foodstuffs must be distributed equally throughout the Reich.

Common sense dictates that the Swabians should have their Spätzle and Munich should get its beer, Vienna a little more coffee and white bread, and for the Berliners an extra ration of *charcuterie!*[509] For there is no doubt about it, the morale of the people is dependent to quite a considerable degree on a sympathetic understanding of, and catering for, the little things that make life more pleasant for them.

This grain from Morosovskaya should, I think, be sent to Germany and distributed among the workers in heavy industry.

29th July 1942, midday
Men and machines

During the first war we had to wait until 1918 before the Army consented to release forty thousand workmen needed urgently for the construction of submarines. In 1917, the military authorities refused to make available the men required for the manufacture of tanks. In

---

[508] Egg noodles typically served as a side for meat dishes with gravy.

[509] Charcuterie: French for *chair*, "flesh", and *cuit*, "cooked"; a term for cooking devoted to processed meats.

535

this the High Command committed a fatal error, sacrificing a potentially tremendous improvement in war technique in order to avoid a decrease in their available man-power. For the decisive factor in any war is the possession of the technically superior weapons.

Our main preoccupation today must be to maintain the lead we have already gained in this respect, which has been the foundation of our great victories up to date. If we do, we shall be able to wage—and win—this war at a third of the cost, in casualties, which we inflict on our foes. It would therefore be the height of folly to insist in retaining in the army specialists in submarine construction.

The net result would be that the British would be able to blast their way through to Archangel with a convoy carrying a thousand tanks and as many aircraft; and then the Army and the Air Force would have to destroy them all in bloody and single combat, and with losses many times greater than the number of men demanded from the *Wehrmacht* for the construction of submarines.

If during the first war, five hundred thousand technicians had been released from the army at the appropriate moment—say, after the battle of Cambrai—for the construction of armoured fighting vehicles, and particularly of tanks, then instead of our two million casualties our total would certainly not have exceeded a million.

In this connection, too, it must be remembered that death comes in a flash, while the technician can spend three hundred and sixty days a year fashioning the most perfect armaments of the age and saving the soldiers untold loss of life. Of equal importance is the construction of minesweepers; for without them, supplies of iron ore from Sweden cannot be maintained, since the British mine the fairway with an absolutely devilish persistence.

The results of any lack of minesweepers are manifold; firstly, weapon production would decrease through lack of iron ore, and casualties at the front would therefore increase through lack of armaments; secondly, the absence of minesweepers would allow the British to mine the fairways essential to our submarines, thus both jeopardising their efficiency and increasing their losses. Construction of submarines and minesweepers and the release from the armed forces of technicians required for the task are therefore of primary and equal importance. The more submarines we have in service, the larger will be our requirements for maintenance and repairs; and this must also be borne in mind when deciding the numbers of technicians to be released.

29th July 1942, at dinner
The sculptor Kreis—German art and the Jews—Twelve hundred masterpieces at Munich—The artist's dilemma

The monument erected at Laboe to the memory of the submarine service is, with its distorted bows, a singularly pernicious piece of art. I am only thankful, therefore, that we now have in Professor Kreis[510] an artist in stone capable of the most magnificent designs for all future war memorials.

Bormann then showed the Führer some photos of the pictures exhibited at the biennial exhibition in Venice.

The Führer commented: To my mind the complete lack of technique in these incredible daubs represents the ultimate prostitution of art.

Public reception, according to reports I have received, throws a significant light on the value of this exhibition; when they saw the pictures, the public, apparently, simply burst out laughing. Such a thing could not happen at an exhibition in the House of German Art in Munich.

The twelve hundred works accepted for the Munich exhibition, out of some ten or twelve thousand submitted, were, without exception, first-class works of art.

The meticulousness of the selection was assured, because it was not carried out by artists themselves, but by men of the calibre of Professor Hoffmann and Director Kolb. Artists as selectors are somewhat prone to select for exhibition a certain number of mediocre works, which then serve as an excellent foil for their own pictures.

The value of the Munich exhibition is twofold. It ensures that the purchaser of any picture can safely hang it in his home with pride, and it contributes greatly to the education of the artist.

I have inexorably adhered to the following principle: If some self-styled artist submits trash for the Munich exhibition, then he is either a swindler, in which case he should be put in prison; or he is a madman, in which case he should be in an asylum; or he is a degenerate, in which case he must be sent to a concentration camp to be "re-educated" and taught the dignity of honest labour. In this way I have ensured that the Munich exhibition is avoided like the plague by the inefficient.

The approval of my viewpoint by the German people, expressed in the terms of the millions who visit the exhibition, is a source of the keenest satisfaction to me.

---

[510] Wilhelm Kreis (1873–1955), a professor of architecture, active from 1896 to his retirement after the war.

1st August 1942, evening
American credulity—Reticence in British public opinion—British lies—A comparison with America—Swine in a model piggery—The Church's cunning wisdom—The evolution of knowledge and good faith—Exit the Pope—Hatred of the clergy in Spain—Serrano Suñer, the grave-digger of modern Spain

Conversation turned to a book entitled "Juan in America" which Bormann had recently lent to the Führer. In it the author paints a picture of the unbelievable conditions which reigned in the intellectual and political circles of the United States, and of the astonishing credulity of the American citizen. Hewel stated that this credulity was not an exclusively American characteristic, and that in Britain, too, the people swallowed everything they were told.

Hitler said: This reminds me of the Hausser reunion which I attended in Stuttgart, where exactly the same sort of thing occurred. The fellow, who was either an idiot, a madman or a first-class swindler, heaped a torrent of abuse on his audience, calling them swine, oxen, beasts and so forth, although, in point of fact, the majority were very respectable people. Once, in some election in Munich, this fellow Hausser got twenty-nine thousand votes, because the voters confused the name and thought that the Hausser party represented the interests of the householders! In the same election Streseman, the Chancellor of the Reich, obtained only twenty-seven thousand votes!

Field Marshal Keitel expressed the opinion that we had much the same situation now with the Bible Students.

Hitler replied: That sort of thing must be stamped out. If society surrenders to anti-social tendencies of this kind, it will disintegrate. We must not tolerate it. Even by the law of the jungle, the antisocial elements among the beasts are annihilated. If they are not, we might well have a repetition of our experiences in 1918, and see these elements, in a moment of national weakness, usurp power! During the Great War major operations generally came to an end about the end of November or the beginning of December, and the front became comparatively quiet. I remember well that we had some very hard fighting at the end of October 1918, and then on the 27th down came the rain, and everything was washed out.

Since then, however, we have had some pretty rigorous experiences on the Eastern front in this war, of which our western enemies can have no idea. Why, I wonder, did the British spend the whole of March talking about "the Spring Offensive"? For March, in England, is the spring. Thanks to the riches of their colonial Empire, the British have naturally become a nation of rulers—and oh! the beauty of their country seats and the grandeur of their estates!

It is perfectly true that the British swallow everything they are told. At the moment, nevertheless, there is a certain amount of murmuring over faked reports. To justify their bluff, those at the head of affairs are reduced to telling the discontented that these false reports are being spread in order to deceive the enemy. A large portion of intelligent Britons say: "We are waging this war by bluff, and it's the only way we can wage it!" Whether they believe that they are really bluffing us, is a very different matter. In the autumn of 1939 they declared that there were already a million Britons in France! Even I estimated their strength at between thirty-five and forty divisions, whereas in reality they had twelve or fifteen—a mere 350,000 men! I cannot imagine the publication of a deliberate lie in the German official communiqué; but they don't mind how many they publish in their reports, and one realises now the extent to which they are hoodwinking their own people.

According to the Americans themselves, America has the finest, biggest and most efficient of everything in the wide world; and when one then reads a book like this about them, one sees that they have the brains of a hen! Well, the disillusionment will be all the more severe, and the consternation, when this house of cards collapses, will be enormous.

This has already occurred as far as the Far East is concerned. Why should a people of that sort fight—they've got everything they want! Anyway, the ardour for battle will soon wane when the individual finds himself called upon to endure a further curtailment of the amenities of life! It is very difficult to argue with Americans.

They immediately shout: "Say, take a look at what our workers earn!" True, but let us take a look at the shady side as well. The industrial worker earns his eighty dollars; but the man who is not in industry gets absolutely nothing. At one time they had no less than thirteen million unemployed. I have seen pictures of shelters built out of old kerosene tins which the unemployed had erected for themselves and which remind me of the holes of misery to be found in the Bolshevik industrial cities. I grant you that our standard of life is lower. But the German Reich has two hundred and seventy opera houses—a standard of cultural existence of which they over there have no conception.

They have clothes, food, cars and a badly constructed house but with a refrigerator! This sort of thing does not impress us.

I might, with as much reason, judge the cultural level of the sixteenth century by the appearance of the water-closets of the time—an apartment which was not then regarded as of particular importance! A few days ago I read another book—about Spain. Spaniards and Americans simply cannot understand each other. Those things which the Spaniard venerates most highly mean nothing to the American, and to the Spaniard the American way of life is a closed book.

To sum it up, the Americans live like sows—in a most luxurious sty!

Reichsleiter Bormann drew attention to the gifts which France made almost every day to the Church, and on which the power of the Church was thriving mightily.

The Führer continues: It was exactly the same in Bavaria! Held[511] restored to the Church forest lands to the value of thirty or forty million marks, lands which by expropriation belonged to the State!

The Church has succeeded in striking a very pretty balance between life on earth and in the Hereafter. On earth, they say, the poor must remain poor and blessed, for in Heaven the earthly rich will get nothing; and the unfortunate poor on earth believe them! It is only by keeping the masses ignorant that the existing social order of things can be maintained; in the eyes of the faithful, this is the justification for supreme Papal authority.

Cramer-Klett[512] told me one day that he had become a Catholic because he realised that Luther with his Reformation had completely destroyed authority as such. Possibly—but I cannot help thinking that man has been endowed with a brain which he is intended to make use of, and that anything which is founded on a premise unacceptable to the human intellect cannot endure forever. It is not possible to hold fast for very long to tenets which the progress of knowledge have proved to be false.

I should be wrong if I condemned as a liar a man who believed firmly in the Aristotelian or Ptolemaic world, when he had no other alternative to choose from. But a man who still believes in this old conception of the world today certainly is a liar. No science remains stationary.

In my eyes the ability of mankind to reject a proven untruth is one of its virtues. By the Church the Unknown is described and explained

---

[511] Heinrich Held (1868–1938), Minister President of Bavaria from 1924 to 1933.
[512] Theodor von Cramer-Klett (1874–1938), a Bavarian industrialist.

with precision, and if she advances with the times, the ground must inevitably be cut from under her feet. For this reason she is opposed to all progress. It adds little to our knowledge of the Creator when some parson presents to us an indifferent copy of a man as his conception of the Deity. In this respect, at least, the Mohammedan is more enlightened, when he says: to form a conception of Allah is not vouchsafed to man.

The most pressing danger, as I see it, is that Christianity, by adhering to a conception of the Beyond which is constantly exposed to the attacks of unceasing progress, and by binding it so closely to many of the trivialities of life which may at any moment collapse, is ripening mankind for conversion to materialistic Bolshevism. And that is a terrible tragedy. Man will lose all sense of proportion, and once he considers himself to be the lord of the universe, it will be the end of everything. And if the Church in Spain continues in the way it is doing, it will end on the refuse-heap.

The rapidity with which Mustapha Kemal Atatürk rid himself of his parsons makes one of the most remarkable chapters in history. He hanged thirty-nine of them out of hand, the rest he flung out, and St. Sophia in Constantinople is now a museum![513]

In Venice, in 1934, the Duce once said to me: "One of these days the Pope will have to leave Italy; there is not room for two Masters!"

In the Spanish people there is a mixture of Gothic, Frankish and Moorish blood. One can speak of the Spaniard as one would speak of a brave anarchist.

The Arabian epoch—the Arabs look down on the Turks as they do on dogs—was the most cultured, the most intellectual and in every way best and happiest epoch in Spanish history. It was followed by the period of the persecutions with its unceasing atrocities.

The Russian priest was not hated; he was merely despised for the parasite he was, hanging on at all costs to his job for what it would bring him. The Russian Princes, unlike the German and Spanish, were never slaves of the Church. In Spain the clergy is hated and will very soon be wiped out! All who have watched Franco's progress say that he is heading for another revolution. The rest of the world cannot be separated from Spain by a Chinese wall. Sooner or later the explosion must come.

Here, too, we see a fundamental truth: The parasites, in their avarice, do not realise that they are destroying the very ground which is their

[513] The Haga Sophia in Istanbul.

foundation. The Church of today is nothing more than a hereditary joint stock company for the exploitation of human stupidity. If I had not decided in 1936 to send him the first of our Junker aircraft, Franco would never have survived. Today, his salvation is attributed to Saint Isabella! Isabella the Catholic—the greatest harlot in history, who was decorated by the Pope with the Rose of Virtue about the same time as our Ludwig of Bavaria was all but crucified on account of Lola Montez!

The real tragedy for Spain was the death of Mola;[514] there was the real brain, the real leader. Franco came to the top like Pontius in the Creed.[515] The most evil spirit is undoubtedly Serrano Suñer, whose task it is to prepare the way for the Latin Union. In reality he is the grave-digger of modern Spain!

3rd August 1942, evening
Bees and ants—Intelligence and instinct—Weak and strong

Here is one of the most curious things in nature. There is a certain species of ant, in which the whole race dies when the queen ant dies. If a queen bee is ill, the whole hive is uneasy.

There is another species of ant which cultivates mushrooms on which to raise lice. The ants look after the lice, carry them out into the sunshine and then back into the mushroom box. Then they make a special brew of them, on which the queen ant is constantly fed.

The question occurs to me—where does natural instinct end and human reason begin? One must draw distinctions. A bitch has puppies. Bitches get no training, but they all tend their young with uniform efficiency. That is basic instinct, which most not be confused with reason, which takes its decisions according to certain definite facts. The most primitive of instincts, to which all forms of life respond, are those of feeding and reproduction of the species.

In my youth I had every opportunity to study bees, for my old father was a keen apiarist. Unfortunately I was frequently so badly stung that I all but died! To be stung by a bee in our family was an ordinary, every-

---

[514] Emilio Mola (1887–1937), one of the three leaders of the Nationalist coup of July 1936 which started the Spanish Civil War. He died in an aircraft crash.

[515] The Nicene Creed is the doctrinal statement of correct belief among most mainstream Christians, in which they profess their articles of faith. Apart from Jesus Christ, the only other person named in the Creed is, strangely and unexpectedly—given his role in the story of Jesus —Pontius Pilate. The reason for the inclusion of his name in the Creed is a still-debated mystery, and it is to this fact that Hitler is here making about Franco's emergence as a leader.

day occurrence. My mother often pulled out as many as forty-five or fifty stings from the old gentleman when he returned from clearing the hives. He never protected himself in any way; all he did was to smoke all the time—in other words, a good excuse for another cigar!

The weakling has always in history gathered to himself the smallest following. This was the case in Russia. The last Tsar, who was a man of no personality, had no following. It is the bloodhounds that the people follow. Things are no different in the West. We can only gain our ends by merciless and continual perseverance. That is contrary to the opinion of many of our upper ten thousand who are always the telephone lines, the harbingers of weakness. How often have I heard the objection: with your brutal methods, you will achieve nothing! With any other methods I would certainly have achieved nothing. The soldier, too, is for the most part devoted to the leader who is stern but just. If a man is a real leader, the people will follow him.

4th August 1942, midday
Memories of the first war—The lace workers of Belgium—Ypres and Lübeck

When we went into the line in 1916, to the south of Bapaume, the heat was intolerable. As we marched through the streets, there was not a house, not a tree to be seen; everything had been destroyed, and even the grass had been burnt. It was a veritable wilderness.

In the present campaign I got my greatest surprise when I revisited Arras. In the old days it was just a mound of earth. And now—! Fields filled with blossom and waving corn, while on Vimy Ridge the scars are much as they were, shell holes and all. I believe it is much the same in the Champagne.

The soldier has a boundless affection for the ground on which he has shed his blood. If we could arrange the transport, we should have a million people pouring into France to revisit the scenes of their former struggle.

Marching along the roads was a misery for us poor old infantrymen; again and again we were driven off the road by the bloody gunners, and again and again we had to dive into the swamps to save our skins! All the thanks we got was a torrent of curses—"Bloody So-and-Sos" was the mildest expression hurled at us.

My first impression of Ypres was—towers, so near that I could all but touch them. But the little infantryman in his hole in the ground has a very small field of vision.

I shall send our people who have been given the task of rebuilding Lübeck to Ypres before they start work. Fifty different shades of tiles, from salmon-pink, through gold to deep violet! The new Ypres is a city out of fairyland! In those days the girls making lace always sat working outside the houses, surrounded, of course, by a horde of soldiery. But at least they were able to buy and send home genuine Flemish lace and the embroidery of Brabant.

If a soldier in France buys chocolate or a pair of stockings for his wife, I agree absolutely with the Reichsmarshall; we did not start the war, and if the French population have got nothing, what the blazes does it matter to us! I wish to goodness we could buy something here. But here there is nothing but mud.

4th August 1942, evening
American military courts in Britain—Invasion from the West

Speaking to Dr. Dietrich, the Führer said: If I were you, I should treat this business—the introduction of American courts of law for American soldiers in Britain—in the following way: The Turks have abolished extra-territoriality, and Britain has stepped into Turkey's shoes; swift decline of Britain to a second-class Power! They can only make a landing in the West by throwing in the finest of their units—nothing less has a hope of success. But that means staking their all on one card.

As regards the Air Arm, their experts will probably say to themselves, "Germany is in a position to increase her forces at will and with lightning speed, and to attack in three or four places at the same time. We simply haven't the requisite forces!"

I think that the soldiers will fight tooth and nail to avoid having to shoulder the responsibility, particularly as they well know how cautious the politicians can be! So, the Generals write memoranda to show that the thing is not possible; the politicians retort that, on the other hand, only operations conceived on the largest possible scale stand a chance of success—but they will say so in a way which will permit them, in case of failure, to turn round and exclaim: "There! What did I tell you!"

And the soldier's only reply can be: "There's no going back now! If things go wrong, all is lost!"

Even so—think of the declaration of war in 1939! They had no armaments at all—and yet they declared war! In those days they had, I believe, six divisions. It's quite possible that they will again let themselves be hoodwinked by fairy tales from the *émigrés*. The soldiers, I know, were against war. But there are people over there who don't give a damn if Britain does collapse—yes, I mean the Jews! There are others who say: "If the Russians are beaten, then we shall be the war criminals—there will be trials, and we shall end up in the Tower."

The soldiers will defend themselves by saying that they had given full warning of the danger Britain ran in accepting the risks of undertaking an invasion. But for the politicians who declared war and the Jews who drove them to it, there is no defence! And these latter are quite capable of risking a second attempt. On the other hand, they may say to themselves: we are taking on an opponent who has so far knocked the teeth out of everybody who has opposed him.

In 1940 they had beside them one hundred and thirty-eight French divisions, eighteen Dutch and thirty-three or thirty-four Belgian divisions. With the ten divisions or so at their disposal now, they can do nothing! If, thanks to the measures we are now taking, we can succeed in increasing their reluctance to face so great an enterprise, so much the better! By next spring the build-up of our fortifications will have reached a point where even an attack against one of our submarine bases will be out of the question. Little by little, the Atlantic Wall is acquiring all the characteristics of the West Wall.

I can well imagine the furious activity, behind the scenes, of the opponents of Roosevelt!

5th August 1942, midday

Importance of food supply—The rascally clan of chefs—The gluttony of the Swiss—The heroic period of German colonisation—The experiences of the Prince von Ahrenberg

The number of courses served at an official banquet is monstrous! I think there is something rather degrading in laying such store by food. And the most disagreeable feature is that these banquets always last for hours, and one always sits next to someone with whom one has nothing in common.

My own particular tragedy is that, as Head of the State, I always have the most worthy ladies as my dinner partners! I would far rather go on board the *Robert Ley*[516] and pick out some pretty little typist or sales-girl as my partner! The whole of this banquet business is a racket, invented by that rascally band, the cooks! These Kings of the Cooking-pots are all ridiculous idiots, mesmerising the people and

---

[516] The *Robert Ley*, named after the head of the Labour Front, was a *Kraft durch Freude* ("Strength Through Joy") cruise ship, one of a fleet used to provide German workers with inexpensive international holidays.

intoxicating themselves with a mass of meaningless phrases and obscure names, which no one understands in the least. Where is the good old one-dish meal of the past? Nothing so vulgar exists any more—it has disappeared, like the good old honest soup! It is all so beautifully mixed—food and phraseology—that nowadays one has not the faintest idea what one is eating.

It was the same thing before the war; every festive occasion demanded a twelve-course banquet! In 1923, I was in Switzerland, and I remember a meal in Zurich at which the number of courses completely flabbergasted me. What sort of mentality has this little people, pray?

In Austria we have now acquired mountain country of such wonderful beauty, that no one will dream of going to Switzerland until the Swiss themselves crawl on their knees and beg to be taken under the wing of the Third Reich!

Turning to Dr. Dietrich: It seems, from reading their press, that the Swiss have become a little less bombastic? They are a little less contemptible than before. They attained the depth of ignominy at the time of our occupation of Yugoslavia; now, they thought, we have had it! And they exposed all the pettiness of their miserable little souls! "Thieves! Robbers of other people's lands!" they shrieked at our frontier guards.

I was quite astonished recently at the amount of drink the Finns put away; it seems that the further North one goes, the more drink people can carry.

Aden, I suppose, is the most infernal heat cauldron on earth. I have quite made up my mind that nothing will induce me to travel through the Red Sea—I should die of heart failure! Prince Arenberg,[517] one of our earliest adherents, has told me many interesting tales of pioneering days in our colonies. He was once sentenced to twelve years' penal servitude—and served six of them—for having killed a negro who had attacked him! The answer to people who asserted that we were not good colonisers, he said, was that with the methods we tried to employ we could not get any colonies at all! And his opinion was based on a very considerable amount of thought.

Arenberg used to drive one of the oldest Benz cars I have ever seen; and in it he once insisted in driving me to Kempten, when I was on my way to Switzerland. On the level the old car ran reasonably well; but at the slightest sign of a hill it blew its head off, and we were in grave

---

[517] Engelbert-Maria von Arenberg (1872–1949), Ninth Duke of the House of Arenberg.

danger of sticking fast. He had to change gear all the time, and so we trundled along hour after hour. At last we came to the downhill part of the journey, and there the car flew along at at least thirty miles an hour!

And the man was a multi-millionaire; but in this respect he was as obstinate as a mule!

In the East it will be all over once we have cut their communications to the south and to Murmansk. Without oil they are finished! In the West it will be all over when once we are able to transfer even half of our forces to France. And that we shall be able to do as soon as we have smashed the armament-and food producing centres in Russia.

5th August 1942, evening
SPECIAL GUEST: FIELD MARSHAL KESSELRING [518]

Balbo's[519] tragic death—National Socialism and Fascism—The disadvantages of monarchy—Britain commands respect

The Italians are first-class colonisers. Given ten years of Italian rule, Addis Ababa would have become a most beautiful city.

The death of Balbo was a great tragedy; there was a worthy successor of the Duce, a man who had something of the *condottiere,*[520] of the Renaissance in him! A man whose name alone was worth something!

I must admit that the Italians infuriate me with their continual running away, but purely from the point of view of a world philosophy, they are the only people on earth with whom we can see eye to eye. When I read the *History of Fascism,* I feel as if I am reading the history of our movement; the same cowardly and lazy bourgeoisie, which believed in nothing, avoided any sort of conflict and lived in perpetual fear of irritating the Reds!

The first time I wished to go to Ingolstadt, I was told it was fifteen years since a meeting of such a nature had been held there, and that the proletariat would certainly regard it as an act of provocation! The main difference between Italy and Germany is that in the former the Duce has not been made the supreme Dictator of the State; as a result, there

---

[518] Albert Kesselring (1885–1960), a Luftwaffe officer who served in every theater of war, ending his career commanding a skilful fighting retreat in Italy.

[519] Italo Balbo (1896–1940), the Italian fascist Blackshirt leader, Marshal of the Air Force, and Governor-General of Libya and Commander-in-Chief of Italian North Africa. He died when his aircraft was shot down by Italian anti-aircraft batteries after being misidentified over Tobruk.

[520] The *condottieri* were Italian captains in command of mercenary companies widely used in Europe from the Middle Ages onward.

are always ways and means of circumventing his orders. If, for example, he calls for a particularly valiant effort, the corps of officers immediately appeals to the King!

Such a state of affairs must be maddening to a man of the Duce's personality. But I must, however, quite frankly confess that in 1920, if the monarchy had been restored after the Kapp putsch, we should have supported it. It was only later that we gradually realised that a monarchy had outlived its times. Schönerer is the only one who attacked the monarchy, and with unparalleled mercilessness—but his attack was directed against the House of Habsburg; and this did not prevent him from supporting the House of Prussia.

The Duce dare not absent himself very long from Rome. If he does that nest of intrigue immediately sets to work. Balbo had the great advantage that he had equal influence with both Party and Armed Forces, and it is an ironic fate that he should have been shot down by Italian anti-aircraft guns.

As long as ships sail, aircraft fly and soldiers march, the problem of the ideal form of command will continue to exist. Should one have one centralised, unified command, or should the various services of the Armed Forces each have its own separate command organisation? In many cases a sole, unified command is preferable.

We shall only have complete control of Norway when the railway reaches Kirkenes. In North Africa, the British were incredibly stupid; they never for a moment believed that the Italians would gain possession of their railway system. If we wish to deal them a real low blow, we ought to spread the rumour that Rommel postponed his offensive until the British had completed the construction of their line as far as Tobruk! We must at all costs advance into the plains of Mesopotamia and take the Mosul oil-fields from the British. If we succeed here, the whole war will come to an end, for the British have now only Haifa as their sole loading port for oil.

As regards oil, statistics show that the Russians until quite recently obtained 92 per cent of their oil from the Caucasus. The people in the vicinity of these headquarters are all excellently nourished. I cannot help feeling that the Soviet State is being completely hoodwinked by the peasants, in spite of its most strenuous efforts. But conditions in the Ural districts and in Siberia must be terrible—as they must be, also, in the big cities. Let us hope that our Ministry for Eastern Territories will not, in conjunction with the Ministry of the Interior, introduce here our laws against contraception. There are plenty of other things with which our busybody officials can occupy their time; and thank God I shall not live to see them at it. If I did, I might regret ever having captured the country! In this respect the British are our superiors. They, too, are the most frightful bureaucrats; but at least they have the sense not to exercise their bureaucracy in occupied territory to the advantage of the local inhabitant and the detriment of their own country! They have a genius for keeping others at a distance and in winning and preserving respect. Here, perhaps, we have the worst possible example of our methods—de-lousing infuriates the local inhabitants, as does our fanatical desire to civilise them.

The net result is that they say to themselves: "These people aren't really our superiors—it's only the way they're made"!

6th August 1942, midday
The grandeur of the open spaces—Flemish and Dutch peasants—
Ukrainian markets

How small Germany looks from here! The British—and the Russians—possess that self-assurance which is born of vast spaces. I hope that in time we, too, shall acquire it.

Somebody ought immediately to write a book: "The Ideal State of the Future—a Problem of Diet and Education". And in it one should advocate that the citizen should be fed on grass in order to increase his docility and amenity to discipline! It is a fact that tuberculosis is more prevalent among cattle kept in stables than in cattle out at pasture.

In my part of the world the peasants maintain that big windows and plenty of light reduce the milk output. In North Germany, where the cattle live almost entirely in the open, there is practically no tuberculosis at all. In wooded territories, on the other hand, the cattle are kept in stalls throughout almost the whole year, and it is only recently that the veterinary surgeons have realised how dangerous that can be. Most of the properties there are so small that they cannot afford to keep oxen, and harness their cows to the carts.

In Germany we have some districts which are deplorable—part of the Bavarian forest land, the western part of the Hessian mountains, the Waldviertel, and parts of the Swabian Alps. The life of the peasants in these territories is a real hell on earth. If all the work and endeavour used there could be applied to this part of the world, we should increase production five times over. When I was young lad, the whole of my homeland was strewn with boulders; it must originally have been at the bottom of a glacier into which the rocks of the moraines were thrust. Gradually the peasants blasted the rock-masses away. But the same conditions continue all the way down to Lower Austria. And somehow, it makes the landscape seem very friendly and attractive.

In the German Reich we have only one district that can compare with the Ukraine—the Moravian plains northwards from Vienna, eastwards from Brunn and south-eastwards from Olmutz; and that is a land of unbelievable fertility.

One of the things which astonished me most at the beginning of the first war was the amazing industriousness of the Flemish farmer. You would hardly credit the things I saw! Nothing is wasted. When a mounted column passed through, the children would be on the alert, and the moment it had passed, out they would come and pounce on any manure that might have fallen. Every square yard is utilised to the utmost, exactly as in Holland.

There is, however, a dangerous side to this tendency. Such people are apt to lose the broad view, which, after all, is the most important. The man who possesses the wide spaces must show himself to be the master of the others, even if he restricts his activities to the colonisation of his own country.

When the rest of the world was engaged in seizing the open spaces, Germany was in the throes of religious warfare.

The foundation of St. Petersburg by Peter the Great was a fatal event in the history of Europe; and St. Petersburg must therefore disappear utterly from the earth's surface. Moscow, too. Then the Russians will retire into Siberia.

It is not by taking over the miserable Russian hovels that we shall establish ourselves as masters in the East. The German colonies must be organised on an altogether higher plane.

We have never before driven forward into empty spaces. The German people have absorbed both northern and southern Austria, and the original inhabitants are still there; but they were Sorb-Wends, members of basic European stock, with nothing in common with the Slavs.

As for the ridiculous hundred million Slavs, we will mould the best of them to the shape that suits us, and we will isolate the rest of them in their own pig-sties; and anyone who talks about cherishing the local inhabitant and civilising him, goes straight off into a concentration camp! At harvest time we will set up markets at all the centres of any importance. There we will buy up all the cereals and fruit, and sell the more trashy products of our own manufacture. In this way we shall receive for these goods of ours a return considerably greater than their intrinsic value. The profit will be pocketed by the Reich to defray the price of the campaign.

Our agricultural machinery factories, our transport companies, our manufacturers of household goods and so forth will find there an enormous market for their goods. It will also be a splendid market for cheap cotton goods—the more brightly coloured the better. Why should we thwart the longing of these people for bright colours? My one fear is that the Ministry for Eastern Territories will try to civilise the Ukrainian women. These girls, bursting with health, would introduce a welcome strain into the race, for many of them are obviously of sound Germanic origin—otherwise, whence the fair, blue-eyed children? The best among them we will gradually assimilate and take into the Reich; the rest can remain here.

6th August 1942, evening
Income tax and the peasant—Taxation in kind—The peasant and the beauties of nature

Our peasants always lack ready money because the ground at their disposal is too small for their needs. I have often wondered whether it would not be a good idea to re-introduce some sort of tithe system, under which the peasant could pay his taxes in kind. As things are, the middle-man gets for his potatoes, for instance, three or four times what he pays the peasant for them.

It would therefore be to the peasant's advantage to be able to pay his taxes in potatoes rather than in money. The advantages accruing to the State would counteract the loss of revenue from taxation.

In most professions income can be judged in terms of money, but this does not hold in the case of the small farmer. German agriculture will benefit greatly if we introduce new regulations to govern farming based on the potential revenue of the property. In Württemberg and Baden the situation is particularly bad.

As a result of the never-ending process of division among heirs, the properties are becoming smaller and smaller. I shall not mind at all if I am compelled to eject four or five thousand peasants from Alsace; I can replace them with the greatest ease with men from Baden and Württemberg. In the Middle Ages a hide of land sufficed. But now the introduction of the triple crop system demands much more space.

Our country today is over-populated, and the numbers emigrating to America are incredible. How I wish we had the German-Americans with us still! In so far as there are any decent people in America, they are all of German origin.

In Britain they have the sound law that only the eldest son of a peer can inherit the title; in our country we have nobles by the score, who cannot make a living and who will not die. This calls for reform in the future. The whole social structure of the State must be built up on cold, logical lines.

Once we are in a position to start colonising in the East, most of our difficulties will disappear. When the first few hundred are comfortably settled, the rest will soon follow. It is the earth that attracts the peasant. Several hundreds of thousands have emigrated from Salzburg and Upper Austria to East Prussia.

It is only in the pictures of the Court artists that one sees peasants gazing at the stars in heaven. The real peasant keeps his eye firmly on the land, and he lives by the plough. The beauties of the woods were discovered, not by the peasant, but by the professor. Wherever good-quality land is to be found, there one also finds the best type of peasant. It is not, however, the good earth that has improved the peasant stock, but rather that the best type of peasant always finds and takes possession of the best land.

The peasantry therefore is the solid backbone of the nation, for husbandry is the most chancy occupation on earth. What, think you, would happen if the work of a city worker or an official depended on chance? Work on the land is a schooling which teaches energy, self-confidence and a readiness to make swift decisions; the town-dweller, on the contrary, must have everything exactly mapped out for him, and does all he can to eliminate the slightest chance of any risk. As a last resort he takes out an insurance policy—and the insurance company which issues it to him re-insures itself into the bargain!

France, which has 59 per cent of its population on the land, is still fundamentally sound. It is a great tragedy when once a nation loses the solid foundation of its peasantry. The great British landowners have not the faintest idea of practical agriculture—quite apart from the time and money they waste on their celebrated lawns! The Italians have a splendid foundation of peasantry. Once when I was travelling to Florence, I thought, as I passed through it, what a paradise this land of southern France is! But when I reached Italy—then I realised what a paradise on earth can really be! Herein lies one of the Duce's main sources of strength. He once said to me: "Führer, thank goodness! Only a very small percentage of my population are town-dwellers!"

7th August 1942, evening

Reclamation of the Pontine marshes—The gentle art of negotiation

The Pontine marshes[521] can now be put under cultivation, thanks solely to quinine. All previous attempts to drain them had been defeated by malaria, and malaria has now in its turn been defeated by quinine. The work itself has been simple; all that was required was the construction of canals leading to the sea. It is the same scheme that Julius Caesar outlined and that many Popes later tried to put into practice. The cities in the marshy area have been built on sober, colonial lines, but are of excellent quality. Once the war is over, the Duce will be able, over a period of ten or fifteen years, to build up an immense colonial activity in these regions.

The Russian colossus is being destroyed by his own immobility. The British Empire is dying because of the small size of its motherland. Moreover, the British have stubbornly adhered to a fixed policy, in spite of a complete revolution in conditions. If Churchill goes to see Stalin, the latter will tear the hide *off* him! He'll say to Churchill: "I've lost ten million men, thanks to your Mr. Cripps! If he had kept his mouth shut, the Germans would never have attacked!"

To allow negotiations to be conducted by a man endowed with plenipotentiary powers to take decisions is always a grave mistake, for it enormously enhances the difficulties of repudiation, if such should become desirable. It is a mistake I never make. I always send a representative, with precise instructions to stop as soon as difficulties arise and to come back and consult me. The Duce follows the same principle.

8th August 1942, evening

SPECIAL GUEST: REICHSARBEITSFÜHRER HIERL[522]

The Goths in the Crimea—Bringing order in the East—The gold myth

It is the Goths who have succeeded in maintaining themselves longest in the Crimea. As recently as the eighteenth century, there was once a court case in which the litigants could only speak Gothic! No power on earth will eject us! Some of our Army Groups there have already organised themselves into complete, self-supporting entities in every

---

[521] The Pontine Marshes are located in central Italy, southeast of Rome.

[522] Konstantin Hierl (1875–1955), head of the Labour Service.

way. The struggle we are waging there against the Partisans resembles very much the struggle in North America against the Red Indians. Victory will go to the strong, and strength is on our side. At all costs we will establish law and order there.

I am of the opinion that the use of the present currency in this district should be discontinued in the near future and be replaced by a new currency. This autumn, we must organise markets—rather on the lines of the big German Fairs—in the vicinity of railway junctions, and beside them we must construct silos for the reception of grain. In these markets we must display for sale all the trivialities which our commerce and industry produce.

Saxony, for example, will enjoy an unprecedented trade boom, and we shall create for her a most profitable export market, which it will be the task of Saxon inventive genius to develop. In former times it was Saxony which supplied the colonies with glass beads, trinkets and other baubles, while Thuringia provided the toys, and both made a notable contribution to our trade balance.

In the Bulgarians we have an ally on whom we can rely against the Turks. The Finns have but one desire—to keep East Karelia, and to see St. Petersburg disappear from the face of the earth. Whoever occupies St. Petersburg controls the Baltic. The presence of a second Great Power in the Baltic would be intolerable for us, too, for it would enable it to swamp the whole sea with mines.

In this case we must revert to the practice of ancient days, and St. Petersburg must be razed to the ground. I was furious when the Air Force were reluctant to attack the place from their bases in Kiev. One day, it has got to be done, otherwise the Russians will return and try to set up a Government there.

We shall soon win the peasantry completely to our side. Already they begin to breathe freely, and for the first time someone has paid them something for their wares! For the most part, these peasants are first-class stock. The remnants of the old Goths are still there, for though a language may disappear, the blood remains! The Americans are still delighted so long as they can amass more gold; they do not seem to realise that the stuff has no intrinsic value at all.

You may say what you like about our pub-strategists, but in comparison with the British speakers on military affairs, they are veritable von Moltkes! They have quite convinced me on one point—you cannot exist in the colonies without Scotch whisky!

9th August 1942, midday
SPECIAL GUESTS: REICH MINISTERS VON RIBBENTROP AND
DR. LAMMERS; REICHSFÜHRER SS HIMMLER; GAULEITERS
BÜRCKEL,[523] SIMON,[524] ROBERT WAGNER [525]

*Britons have no rights in Europe—The Great German Reich—The
granary of the East*

The British are nothing but a twig from the German tree. They have
no claim whatever to a share in the responsibility for the security of
Europe. For that Germany is prepared to accept full and sole responsibility. By harsh rule we must bring law and order to the Continent. The
Balkans we will leave alone for the moment, so that we can continue to
export arms to them.

If the Hungarians go to war with the Romanians, then, unless I am
much mistaken, Antonescu will knock hell out of them! The day will
come when the Viennese idea will be proved to be right. In the ten
thousand cafés of Vienna, this is how the Hungarian problem is envisaged: "Hungary belongs to us, and the people in Berlin know nothing about it. It was we who liberated the Hungarians from the Turks,
and order will not be restored in Hungary until we liberate the country
again. So why on earth don't we take it over and have done with it! And
the Slovenes? It is no doubt fine that they should be independent; but
after all they, too, belong to us!"

Vienna is becoming more pan-Germanic than the Germans themselves! They are inspired by the feeling that they have a mission to fulfil—and we might just as well egg them on a little. Belgrade used to
be a miserable little collection of hovels; it was Prince Eugene[526] who
brought fame to the city. From the East we shall get between ten and
twelve million tons of grain annually; I think we ought to build spa-
ghetti factories on the spot; all the prerequisites are there. This will enable us to give a little extra to those western territories which are rich
in industry, but badly off as regards foodstuffs. There is one thing about
which we must be quite clear; anyone here who gets ideas above his
station and beyond the confines of his farm must be sharply jumped
upon.

---

[523] Joseph Bürckel (1895–1944), *Gauleiter* in Westmark and Vienna.

[524] Gustav Simon (1900–1945), *Gauleiter* of Moselland (1931–1945).

[525] Robert Wagner (1895–1946), *Gauleiter* and *Reichsstatthalter* of Baden.

[526] Prince Eugene Francis of Savoy (1663–1736), the French-born military commander who served as a field marshal in the army of the Holy Roman Empire.

9th August 1942, evening
SPECIAL GUESTS: GAULEITERS BÜRCKEL, ROBERT WAGNER
AND SIMON

Riches of the Ukraine—The giant Stalin

There are here a million tons of wheat in reserve from last year's harvest. Just think what it will be like when we get things properly organised, and the oil-wells are in our possession!

The Ukraine produces thirteen or fourteen million tons a year. Even if we show ourselves to be half as successful as organisers as the Russians—there's a cool six million for us! Next year, after the next harvest, we must organise thoroughly and work at full speed!

One thing which we have so far not taken into account is the fact that every three days there is a thunderstorm. This country is a regular forcing-house; fifty degrees of heat one moment, then a torrent of rain, and then the heat again!

Had it not been for the mud and rain last October, we should have been in Moscow in no time. We have now learnt that the moment the rain comes, we must stop everything.

When the war ends, the German people need not bother its head about what it is going to do during the next fifty years! We shall become the most self-supporting State, in every respect, including cotton, in the world. The only thing we shall not have will be a coffee plantation—but we'll find a coffee-growing colony somewhere or other!

Timber we shall have in abundance, iron in limitless quantity, the greatest manganese ore mines in the world, oil—we shall swim in it! And to handle it all, the whole strength of the entire German man-power! By God! how right the peasant is to put his trust solely in the earth! What's the use of talking about scenic beauty, when the earth is oozing with wealth! In the future, it will be a pleasure to work!

Stalin is half beast, half giant. To the social side of life he is utterly indifferent. The people can rot, for all he cares. If we had given him another ten years, Europe would have been swept away, as it was at the time of the Huns.

Without the German *Wehrmacht*, it would have been all up with Europe even now. The doors of the Continent would have been flung open for him by the idiocy of the masses.

The worst of our winters is now behind us. In a hundred years' time there will be millions of German peasants living here.

11th August 1942, evening
SPECIAL GUESTS: REICH MINISTER SPEER, GENERAL REINECKE
Reichsmark and Ost-Mark—Peace with Britain—The finest colony in the world—Fabulous inventions of a gang of epileptic Jews

The German Reichsmark must be made unassailable and must become the most stable currency in the world.

Here, in the East, there exists in reality only one currency—the produce of the soil. For local usage we will create an Ost-Mark. We will fix the rate of exchange at five Ost-Marks to the Reichsmark. But tourists coming here will be given only one hundred Ost-Marks for their hundred Reichsmarks, for with that he can get as much value here as he can with a hundred Reichsmarks in Germany. The difference will be pocketed by the State.

Prices here and at home are quite different, and they must remain so, in favour of the Reich; this will give us the wherewithal with which to pay for the war. Our goal must be to reduce the war debt by from ten to twenty milliard marks a year and thus become the only belligerent of this war to be free of war debts within ten years, and be in a position to concentrate, broadly speaking, on the colonisation of the territories acquired.

Any substantial war indemnity from our enemies, I think, will not be obtainable. From the British we shall certainly get nothing. If the British were to come to me tomorrow and say that they would like to make peace on the basis that each bears his own costs, I should most probably agree. In actual fact, we have already been paid.

The real profiteers of this war are ourselves, and out of it we shall come bursting with fat! We will give back nothing and will take everything we can make use of. And if the others protest, I don't care a damn! We have the richest and best colonies in the world; in the first place, they are next door to us; in the second, they are inhabited by healthy peoples, and in the third, they produce in abundance everything we require except coffee. Within ten years, the colonies of the other countries will have lost their value. The greatest boon we could get would be peace as soon as we can have it.

The great ambition of the parson clique is, and always has been, to undermine the power of the State. And for as long as we suffer these parsons in our midst, it serves us right! Every country gets the type of parson it deserves, at the moment I can do nothing about it, and so I continue to keep them happy.

But one of these days I shall bring this conflict, as old as German history itself, to an abrupt and decisive conclusion. I'll make these damned parsons feel the power of the State in a way they would never have dreamed possible! For the moment I am just keeping my eye on them; if I ever have the slightest suspicion that they are getting dangerous, I will shoot the lot of them.

This filthy reptile raises its head wherever there is a sign of weakness in the State, and therefore it must be stamped on whenever it does so. We have no sort of use for a fairy story invented by the Jews. The fate of a few filthy, lousy Jews and epileptics is not worth bothering about. The foulest of the carrion are those who come clothed in the cloak of humility, and the foulest of the foul is Count Preysing! What a beast! The Popish inquisitor is a humane being in comparison. Vileness and hypocrisy walk arm in arm; both must be extirpated. The uselessness of the parson is nowhere better illustrated than here at the front. Here we have enemies who are dying by the million—and without a single one of these liars. The Catholic Church has but one desire, and that is to see us destroyed.

When Eckart was in Landsberg, the prison parson came and said to him: "Eckart, if anything should happen to you—which God forbid!—have you given a serious thought to the future?"

"I have given the question of the Hereafter much more serious consideration than ever you have done, my good sir," replied Eckart. "And if the Hereafter is in reality what you believe it to be, then, take it from me, I can be of more help to you than you can be to me!" Dripping hypocrisy with the swift and poisoned arrow behind it!

12th August 1942, midday
Marriage customs—German Nationalists in 1921—Admiral Schröder—The Marines

I have never attended a wedding which was conducted with becoming solemnity. Marriage is a holy act, the binding into one of two human beings of different sex; less moving, perhaps, for a man than for a woman, but still a most solemn occasion. And what do most of the guests do but make pointed jokes at the expense of the bride and bridegroom! I attended one wedding—that of Thiersch[527]—at which every guest made a short and suggestive speech; and this was regarded as the height of wit! I wonder why it is?

[527] Frieda Thiersch (1889–1947), a Munich-based graphic artist, book cover designer and bookbinder at the Bremen Press.

As regards superficiality, we are as children in comparison with the British. It is quite astonishing how trumpery trash and good taste exist cheek by jowl in Britain. I once had a book on British masterpieces of architecture—and what magnificent conceptions it contained! In London the Government buildings may be redolent with history, but history is made in the great castles of the countryside.

The National Club in Berlin! I was taken there one day in 1921 by Gansser. The people had absolutely no idea whatsoever of how the German problem should be solved. One of the good gentlemen told me solemnly that all Germany's hopes rested on Kahr! The further away from Bavaria one went the greater the stature that Kahr seemed to acquire in the people's eye! And in a nonentity like that they placed their hopes of salvation! It was there that I met the old Admiral Schröder,[528] our first supporter.

Next day I went to the Officers' Club in the Pariser Platz. Of them all, it was Schröder who made the best impression on me. A grand old bull of a man, charged with energy!

My 1921–22 programme had filled most citizens with consternation. They were even terrified lest people should know they had even heard of it! The purging of all foreign elements in Germany, introduction of compulsory military service, re-constitution of the German Army, abolition of the freedom of the press, suppression of provincial governments! Good heavens! Such ideas were pure blasphemy! People swore solemn oaths that they had never lent an ear to such things!

But old Schröder, that most energetic of men, that uncompromising fanatic, accepted the whole thing without further ado. He was to the Navy what Lützow[529] was to the Army. Hutier,[530] too, was a national figure, and a fine one at that! But he had, I think, a tiny streak of the Catholic in him. When I discover a man like Schröder, I grab him at once. Schröder had already retired, when, during the war, he received the order to join up and raise corps of Marines. What we accomplish today is child's play in comparison with the efforts we were called upon to make then. Schröder had absolutely nothing! But in no time he was leading his corps to battle. I myself saw these Marines in action for the first time at the battle of the Somme; and compared with them, we felt

---

[528] Ludwig von Schröder (1854–1933), a First World War Navy Admiral.

[529] Ludwig von Lützow (1782–1834), a Prussian general famous for his ""Lützow Freikorps" during the Napoleonic Wars.

[530] Oskar von Hutier (1857–1934), a First World War Army General.

we were the rawest of recruits. We then received orders to march to Ostend for a test. The Regiment arrived there in a most deplorable state. Any Russian regiment, after a five-hundred-mile retreat, would have looked like the Brigade of Guards in comparison. While in Ostend I had the chance of going for a short trip on a submarine, and the sailors, smart, efficient, turned out always as if for a review, were magnificent! It made one ashamed to be seen in their company.

Turning to Admiral Krancke: I suppose this accounts for the slight inferiority complex which the land forces feel in the presence of the Navy. We had to cut up our great-coats in order to make puttees, and we looked like a bunch of tatterdemalion[531] ballet-dancers! They, on the other hand, looked frightfully smart in their belts and gaiters; and we were not sorry when we escaped to the decent obscurity of our trenches once more.

12th August 1942; isolated remarks
Fats—Dancing and the artistic sense—Bavarian national costume

With this war-time soap I can wash my hands as often as I like without fear of cracked skin. I do wash my hands very frequently, on account of the dog. But with the old peace-time soap, I became very sore. Why is that? The experiment of extracting fats from coal has not been a success. It was the *Reichsmarschall* who pressed for it; I myself was against it. It seems rather absurd to use vegetable oil for soap-making—and eat fats extracted from coal!

In the future, small arms must consist of machine-guns and automatic rifles only; and every weapon must have a telescopic sight, if accuracy is to be deadly.

Dancing was the first method of artistic expression employed by man. The most beautiful dance in the world is without doubt the waltz, a perfect harmony of movement and music. After it I should place the *Schuhplattler* dance of Upper Bavaria, which, thanks to its austere and dignified style, never makes a man look ridiculous. But the ballroom dancing of today! It's nothing but a series of simian posturings! In a film one sometimes sees people dancing without music. It is one of the most ridiculous things I've ever seen!

Let me make a rather curious remark. The two professions in which one most readily reaches ripe old age are those of the actor and the officer. It is not really surprising, for these are the two professions in which one remains in perpetual contact with youth.

---

[531] Tattered or dilapidated.

It is not correct to say that life in the mountains is good for everybody. I am thinking of Frau Endres[532] and of my own sister Elli,[533] who came to us from Austria. If Elli spends six weeks on end in Obersalzberg, she has to go to Nauheim for a cure! There are some people who will climb up to the summit of the Göll in boots, and, if it happens to be raining, wrapped in a heavy coat. That seems to me to be an astonishing thing to do! Boots, of themselves, are unhealthy things, for they allow of no ventilation. Moccasins are a very different proposition. The healthiest clothing, without any doubt, is leather shorts, shoes and stockings. Having to change into long trousers was always a misery to me. Even with a temperature of ten below zero I used to go about in leather shorts. The feeling of freedom they give you is wonderful. Abandoning my shorts was one of the biggest sacrifices I had to make. I only did it for the sake of North Germany. Anything up to five degrees below zero I don't even notice.

Quite a number of the young people of today already wear shorts all the year round; it is just a question of habit. In the future I shall have an SS Highland Brigade in leather shorts! We have made the uniforms of the *Wehrmacht* much more comfortable and practical. Engineers, for example, now work in bathing-shorts. Attention to minor detail of this sort gives the men the feeling that they are being commanded by men of intelligence. If subordinates once get the idea that their superiors are lacking in intelligence, it is a very bad thing. Nowadays the officers and men are united in one and the same entity.

One still sees in Russia quite a number of handsome costumes. The owners must have kept them hidden. In my opinion, we should make a German Mediterranean of the Baltic sea.

16th August 1942, midday
The Tsar Ferdinand—And some diplomats—Ways and means between Russia and Britain

I always hope for the best and prepare for the worst.

Draganov has copied the features and the gestures of Ferdinand to perfection! Anyone would mistake him for the old man, if only he

---

[532] Elsa Endres was a cook at Hitler's favourite Munich restaurant the "Osteria Bavaria," and from 1935, worked at Hitler's house, the Berghof.

[533] This is surely a transcription error. Hitler had no sisters named or nick-named "Elli." His full sister was named Paula, and his half-sister was named Angela. It is likely that he was here referring to his niece, Elfriede Raubal (sister of the more famous Geli Raubal) and that the note-taker of this conversation made an error.

would eat a little more, put on a small tummy, and dress appropriately. He said to me: "I have no idea what to do when I get to Madrid. But I'll do my best for Germany."

History is a most untrustworthy guide. The Bulgarians are now behaving as if the developments in the Balkans were all the results of their own decisive action. In reality, Boris, caught between his cupidity on the one side and his cowardice on the other, was so hesitant that the strongest intervention on our part was necessary to make him do anything at all. Old Ferdinand wrote some very straight letters, too, pointing out that the hour of Bulgaria's destiny had struck. These Balkan people are quite extraordinary, and they have an astonishing gift for languages.

There were some curious characters among the diplomats accredited to Berlin. The Dutchman, who had a young and beautiful wife, was concerned chiefly with fussing and watching over his ewe-lamb, and he was in a fever if any man spoke to her!

The Romanian, on the other hand, was, to say the least of it, most open-minded in this respect! He seemed to adopt the attitude that one little peccadillo more or less doesn't make much odds. His lady slept sixteen hours a day and retained an astonishingly youthful appearance. One day she introduced me to a middle-aged lady—her daughter! Then there was a Royal Highness, a Princess from Iran; she was a real baggage! She was taking lessons in painting and had a new master every week! If ever there were a man who repelled me, it was the Belgian. He was a real hard-bitten scoundrel and a sly and cunning fox.

Well, now we have him exactly where we want him; but at the time, in 1940, we committed a silly mistake, for which my own personal stupidity is responsible. We should, of course, have treated him as a prisoner of war. On the other hand, one must remember that his sister is the Crown Princess of Italy—the one charming and delightful woman in the whole Italian Court, and one who, alas, has been grossly maltreated there from the psychological point of view! Stalin is an anarchist educated in an ecclesiastical college!

Our newspapers ought to ask whether he and Churchill sang psalms together in Moscow! I cannot help connecting in my mind Churchill's visit to Moscow with the affair of the last convoy. I think Churchill was expecting some important development and went to Moscow hoping to return with the prestige of a great feat accomplished. That they had some big project in view, I am convinced; otherwise, why should they have sent the Mediterranean Fleet to sea? If they had seized Crete, that would have been a grievous blow, for the possession of Crete is vital to the holding of the North African coast—as they themselves admit. Their project, whatever it was, was abandoned, I think because of the slight damage sustained by the three aircraft-carriers, for without adequate air cover, any big operation is not feasible. I am not at all sure that it would not be a good idea to publish a report that they had intended to attack Crete!

I have a hunch that that was the intention. If they were carrying troops, we could be sure of it, for they have no need of troops in Malta. If it is true that they lost a battleship, that explains their hesitation. In Northern Norway we did not have any idea of their real intentions. It was before the Norwegian campaign—at the time of the *Altmark* outrage[534]—that dear old Chamberlain said that I had missed the bus! There are today a lot of very superstitious people in Britain, who consider that the case of the Duke of Windsor[535] was a bad omen; for the King personifies the Empire.

16th August 1942, evening

Britain prepares for war—Hats off to the French worker—Wehrmacht estimates—My struggle for success—Obstruction by Wehrmacht Chiefs and Schacht—Absorbing the unemployed—Conscription once more—Germany can tolerate even me!

Churchill and his friends decided on war against us some years before 1939. I had this information from Lady Mitford;[536] she and her sisters were very much in the know, thanks to their relationship with influential people. One day she suddenly exclaimed that in the whole of London there were only three anti-aircraft guns! Her sister,[537] who was present, stared at her stonily and then said slowly: "I do not know whether Mosley is the right man, or even if he is in a position, to pre-

---

[534] The *Altmark* incident occurred in February 1940 when British forces illegally seized control of a German ship in neutral Norwegian waters.
[535] Edward VIII (1894–1972), King of Britain from January 1936 until his abdication that December following his marriage to American divorcee Wallis Simpson.
[536] Diana Freeman Mitford (1910–2003), one of the famous "Mitford sisters" of the aristocratic English family of the same name. She was married to British Union of Fascists leader Oswald Mosley.
[537] Unity Valkyrie Freeman-Mitford (1914–1948) who was more pro-Hitler than even her sister. She was in Germany when war was declared, and tried to commit suicide rather than see Britain and Germany at war. Her suicide attempt was unsuccessful, and she suffered severe brain damage.

vent a war between Britain and Germany." Once conscription was introduced into Britain, the die was cast—and not in our favour. Happily the rascals had not the patience to wait. If they had held on for three or four years, they would have had an army of thirty or forty divisions, which they could have sent to Europe.

The French workman is an exceptionally skilled craftsman. Their factories and machinery are certainly out of date, but the workmanship is first class, and they carry out repairs with incredible rapidity. We, I think, lose a great deal of time by working so slowly on repairing damage.

As regards rearmament, it was my principle to outline the plan for one year at a time, for a man invariably rises to the occasion that circumstances impose on him. For the year 1933–34 I allotted three milliard marks to the *Wehrmacht*, for 1934–35, the amount rose to five milliards, and by the time war was declared ninety-two milliard marks had been expended on the armed forces. Such figures are wholly without precedent.

Before the first war, the defence budget called for about one milliard! No one can say that he was prevented from carrying out a task of national importance by lack of funds! The Reichstag was never consulted on the subject of money; the decision on what was to be done and what was not to be done was mine, and mine alone.

From the moment that I abandoned the gold standard, and while I still had large numbers of unemployed at my disposal, I had no financial problems. I had to support seven million whole-time and four million part-time unemployed. This necessitated a budget of five milliards. We should have saved many milliards of overseas expenditure if the *Wehrmacht* had from the beginning been content to accept our own synthetic and supplementary raw materials instead of insisting on importing from abroad. I declared that we must put our economy on a war footing, but the *Wehrmacht* refused to follow my lead until compelled to do so by the pressure of war.

You would not believe the lengths to which they went in order to thwart me! When I called for the construction of warships, they retorted by demanding copper to the tune of one eighth of the annual production of the whole world! When the Great War started we had at our disposal the accumulated reserves of thirty years. But in 1939 we had nothing. I cannot tell you with what fury and anger I had to work in order to get what I wanted. Even with good old Fritsch I had a battle royal on the day I re-introduced conscription. "Thirty-six divisions will be raised," I ordered, "and don't think you can turn me from my purpose by telling me that we have not the requisite arms and equipment!"

The Führer turns to Jodl: You say you had to fight tooth and nail for every single thing and that even so you were frequently compelled to reduce your demands by 40 per cent, 60 per cent, and even as much as 80 per cent. Well, you can thank Blomberg for that! I had nothing to do with it.

To the *Wehrmacht* I allotted more in money and kind than it could possibly make use of. Again and again I had to protest that such and such an order had not been passed on, and quarrels on this subject were a weekly event. The invariable reply given to me was: "The *Wehrmacht* doesn't want it." There was a mass of people working against me behind my back and systematically sabotaging my efforts. And yet—what on earth did it matter if expenditure exceeded budgetary estimate? The Air Force regularly over-spent about two milliards annually.

A crisis could only have arisen after all the unemployed labour had been absorbed, and this did not happen until late 1937 or early 1938. Up till then the only difficulties we had to face were those of foreign exchange. Schacht had told me that we had at our disposal a credit of fifteen hundred million marks abroad, and it was on this basis that I planned my Four Year Plan, which never caused me the slightest anxiety. Göring, by the way, was given very wide powers in this field. And that is how things are today, and we never find ourselves blocked for want of money.

I always protested against the homoeopathic-like quantities which the *Wehrmacht* demanded! The industrialists were always complaining to me about this niggardly procedure to-day an order for ten howitzers, tomorrow for two mortars, and so on. And that when one knows that production lines require four to eight months before they can set to work!

In the end I had to step in and order mass production—and mass production without limit. Had it not been for these restrictive practices, our Navy would today have had four more battleships than it actually possesses; craftsmen, steel—we had everything we needed. My political economy has always been aimed at obtaining the maximum return for expenditure. I have invariably been opposed to certain practices, as, for instance, the financing of a factory destined to produce material for the *Wehrmacht*.

The Four Year Plan made such practices impossible, for under it, the money voted to the *Wehrmacht* had to be spent exclusively on the purchase of material. To give an order for five hundred thousand haversacks, and then to advance to industry the money to build a factory for their manufacture, is sheer stupidity!

As for the Navy, they never once made any demands on their own behalf; it was always I who had to do it for them, and then, if you please, the Navy themselves would whittle down the programme I proposed for them!

The Army were no better; here again it was I who had to urge the adoption of a programme of real expansion, and it was the Army which countered with hesitancy and evasions. I was so frustrated that in the end I was compelled to withdraw their prerogatives from the Army and assume them myself.

I can give you dozens of examples; the best one is the West Wall itself. Then Heligoland; the Navy declared that defences there were quite unnecessary, and it was only when war had been actually declared that they agreed to the fortification of the island.

Tanks, I was told, were of no value unless they were both light and fast; again after a hard struggle, I imposed my will and ordered the manufacture of heavy tanks. I ordered the installation of wired-wireless throughout Germany; the Ministry of Propaganda evaded the execution of my order on the grounds that the Ministry of Posts and Telegraph had declared that the project was not yet technically sufficiently advanced.

But the Ministry had never suffered from lack of funds with which to perfect the technique! Before the war, when I saw that the Army could not be induced to take any steps as regards motorisation, I went myself to Krupps and arranged that the SS units should be equipped with Panzer Mark IV. Hardly had war been declared, when the Army shrieked to high heaven that these tanks be allotted to them!

Immediately after the re-introduction of conscription in 1936 I demanded that the whole country should forthwith be put in a state of defence. The negative results were puerile. The Army, it is true, submitted a scheme, to be spread over several years (and to be completed in 1952!), the net result of which would have been the construction of a few strong-points. There was no question of any lack of funds; it was just that the General Staff wanted it that way. So it was that I was always compelled to use my overriding powers to get my own way. It is much the same even now; but now there is no excuse. We have a Reich War Minister whose sole duty it is to come to me and say: "We require this and that." It was for this sole purpose that he was appointed! During all these years I have never allowed the slightest discussion with the finance branch. I have never had a conference with Schacht to discover what means were at our disposal.

I restricted myself to saying simply: "This is what I require, and this is what I must have." I would add: "Has the mark so far suffered any harm? Is it not retaining its full value, thanks to the authority of the State and its economic principles? You are not here to tell me that such-and-such a project is impracticable; your job is to provide me with the means to make it practicable!"

Schacht always opposed me on principle. His negative attitude produced so devastating an effect on his audience that on one occasion at the end of a conference Stülpnagel cried: "Poor old Germany!"

But I was more than a match for Herr Schacht. These financiers seemed to have no idea of the real efficiency of our economic principles. One day when Krosigk[538] came to me full of objections, I said to him: "My dear Herr Krosigk, you are quite wrong. The thing has got to be done. No State has ever gone bankrupt for economic reasons—but only as the result of losing a war!"

The most able of our financiers was my Party colleague Reinhardt.[539] His estimate of our revenue from income tax was most accurate, and thanks to him we were able to raise our revenue from this source from five milliards to eighty milliards without increasing the cost of living and without suffering any of the devaluation which one sees in other countries.

My attention was recently drawn to the fact that all the laws which we submit are systematically rejected by three Ministers—Schacht, Stanislaus and Neurath. The rest are always in agreement. And the infuriating thing is that most of these laws are no concern of the Ministers mentioned, who, in any case, are not members of the Cabinet! The best method is always to settle the thing directly with the Minister concerned, and thus avoid tedious discussion, in which one will argue from the legal point of view, while another quotes principles of financial orthodoxy. That sort of thing drives me to fury. One day I said to one of these gentlemen: "The German nation has survived the period

---

[538] Johann von Krosigk (1887–1977), Minister of Finance from 1932 to 1945.
[539] Friedrich Reinhardt.

of the great migrations, the wars with the Romans, the onslaughts of the Huns, the Magyars and the Mongols, the Thirty Years' War, the campaigns of Frederick the Great and Napoleon—and it will no doubt survive even my rule!"

16th August 1942

An invention of the lawyers—Sabotaging the nation's morale

Major Engel reported that at Königsberg Air Port one of the Port offi-cials had seized from a plane some foodstuffs brought in by the pilots and destined for the black market.

The Führer was very angry and said: That is the sort of thing which one would expect from enemies of the State and which would infuriate our soldiers beyond all control, if they knew of it. So that's the thanks they get from the Home Front! Sabotage of the people's will to resist! I'll get to the bottom of this affair; I don't care whether the culprit is in the *Wehrmacht* or the Customs, I'll have him in prison, and I shall employ the utmost savagery to put an end to such practices. What can one bring back from the East—works of art? There are none. Only odds and ends of food, and one cannot do better than distribute that among German families.

It is perfectly true that the soldier lives better at the front than he does at home on leave. The instigator of this sorry practice is without doubt a lawyer—probably the Minister of Finance himself! What a pity Bormann was not there!

20th August 1942, midday

SPECIAL GUESTS: DR. LAMMERS, DR. THIERACK[540] AND DR. ROTHENBERGER[541]

Crimes big and little—The punishment fits the crime—Judges and the nation's morale—I am not by nature a brutal man—No mercy on traitors—An anti-Semitic Jew—The hero of a hundred murders—Legislators and Magistrates—The education of judges—The lawyer as a Civil Servant

I have just read that a man has been sentenced to three months' imprisonment for having ill-treated an animal; apparently he kicked a hen which had strayed into his garden. Well, I do not approve. In my opinion shooting hares is a far greater horror of cruelty. Every sports-man who shoots an animal without killing it should, in my opinion, receive at least a like sentence. The nation must not get the idea that

---

[540] Otto Georg Thierack (1889–1946), Reich Minister of Justice from 1942 to 1945.
[541] Curt Ferdinand Rothenberger (1896–1959), State Secretary, Justice Ministry.

one type of sadist is applauded and the other put in prison. The sports-man shoots game to satisfy his lust for murder. The man who kicked the hen simply did so to guard his garden from damage, and had no murderous intention. I know how irritating it can be when a hen gets in your garden, and every time you chase it out, back it comes again! When I was a child my parents had a little garden in Leonding. Our neighbour insisted on letting her hens forage in our garden. One day I loaded a shot-gun and blazed off at them. Since then I have learnt that the legal remedy is for the hens to be confiscated and returned only after damages have been paid. All that palaver over a hen pecking in a neighbour's garden! The case of the persistent poacher who steals a hen is quite different. Here, I would say, his activities constitute an offence against public austerity in time of war.

I think justice in cases like these must take motive, which is by no means constant, into consideration. I have had a good deal to do with the law and have been behind the bars for quite a time. At Landsberg, the Great Pundit[542] once told me quite solemnly that he could not make up his mind whether punishment should be administered as revenge, as a means of prevention, or as a method of correction! My retort was that as far as the man at the receiving end was concerned, it didn't make a damn of difference! Seriously, I do not think one can lay down hard-and-fast rules in these matters. For example, if some youth of eighteen snatches a woman's handbag in peace-time, I would not condemn him to death. But now we are at war; we have the blackout.

A large majority of the women have been incorporated into indus-try, and we are obliged to take severe precautions for their protection. In Berlin at one time the criminals became so bold that women did not dare to go out alone after dark. If they are not checked, crimes of this sort can develop into an epidemic of rape, robbery with violence, etc. A timely intervention is therefore very necessary; the spark must be put out before it bursts into flame.

Take, for example, the robberies from cellars. These are very serious, particularly at a time like this, when we are compelled to break down the walls between the cellars of various dwelling houses.

When the thieves begin to take advantage of this state of affairs, we must either take active steps against them or see the whole of our air-raid shelter system—and with it the morale of the population—put in

---

[542] It is unknown who exactly the "Great Pundit" at Landsberg was, but it is likely to have been Hitler's Chief Warder Franz Hemmrich.

jeopardy. One single bomb falling in the midst of a row of houses may cause two thousand deaths, and the man who risks his life at the front might with justice become bitter against a State which expects this sacrifice from him, and at the same time does not trouble to safeguard his family at home. Harsh and brutal lines of distinction must therefore be drawn.

If a man hits a hen over the head, it is not a crime that is likely to initiate a crime wave; but when some blackguard systematically robs from gardens and takes away the few miserable vegetables the owner is trying to produce, then, I say, he's a criminal of the most ignominious type, for whom no punishment is too severe. Those sort of crimes must be strangled at birth.

Measures must be introduced—and must be made clear to all—to ensure the repression of any breach of public law and order, and to make certain, too, that the inevitable cheapening of life at the front is not counterbalanced by a proportionate over-valuation of the lives of the less worthy elements on the Home Front.

The morale of a people depends to a large extent on the activity of their judges. Every war gives rise to a species of selectivity in reverse; the finest and fittest perish by the thousand.

Even among the brave the choice of arm of the services constitutes a sort of super-selective process, the bravest of the brave going for Air Force and the submarine service. And then, in all branches of the service the call is continual: "Who volunteers for . . .?" and always gallant men come forward—and die. In time, then, there remains only the rascal living in peace and security. The man who is sent to prison has the certainty that nothing further can befall him. If this process is allowed to continue for three or four years, it will upset the whole equilibrium of the nation.

Prison is no longer a hardship; on the Volkhov front,[543] men lie not on a bunk as in prison, but in the icy water, exposed to the winds, sleepless, often without food or hope of relief.

A people, taken *en masse,* is neither wholly good nor wholly bad. It possesses neither the courage to be wholly admirable nor the wickedness to be wholly evil. It is the extremes at each end of the scale that decide the level of the average. If the good are decimated while the evil are preserved, then it is quite possible, as happened in Germany in 1918, for a handful of a few hundred evil vagabonds to do violence to

[543] The Volkhov River lies to the east of Leningrad (St. Petersburg).

a whole nation. In Berlin itself, eight Party members fall for every one non-Party man killed; and unfortunately it is always the flower of the Party—my SA leaders, my Regional and Group Leaders—who are the first to fall. If I fail to exterminate the vermin as a counter-balance, a dangerous situation would arise.

I am certainly not a brutal man by nature, and consequently it is cold reason that guides my actions. I have risked my own life a thousand times, and I owe my preservation simply to my good fortune. I say, therefore, that sentiment must play no part in these matters; we must apply a rule of iron and admit of no exceptions. This may often pain me personally, and it may well lead to errors which one will later regretfully acknowledge. But any other course of action is out of the question.

At the end of the first war I was far more imbued with humanitarian ideals than was our system of justice. Circumstances alter cases. The main thing is to be honest and logical with one's self. Weakness in wartime is not admissible.

In the case of a traitor, the amount of damage he has done carries little weight; it is the act itself which counts. There are some crimes which, without any shadow of doubt, put him who commits them outside the pale of the community. In the Third Reich no traitor shall commit treason and escape with his life.

It is the least we can do for those who have left their homes and wives to do battle at the front. In such matters I am merciless. And the law should be equally merciless; it should also be capable of appreciating public opinion.

As it is, a poacher kills a hare and goes to prison for three months! I myself should have taken the fellow and put him into one of the guerrilla companies of the SS. I am no admirer of the poacher, particularly as I am a vegetarian; but in him I see the sole element of romance in the so-called sport of shooting.

Incidentally, there is no doubt that we number quite a few poachers among the most stalwart adherents of the Party. When I say all this, do not imagine that I condone the wholesale depredations of poachers among the wild life of the forests. On the contrary, my sympathies are entirely with the gamekeepers.

It is most interesting to note how wisely a people, from children upwards, react to measures taken in the general interest. If a woman sends her man at the front a parcel, and it is stolen on the way, the primary reaction is: "Bloody swine! he should be bumped off!" That is primitive human instinct. The woman deprived herself of something for her man's sake; this bastard grabbed it from her! Kill him! There's nothing sentimental about that. It is just plain, sane herd-instinct.

The community at large derives no benefit or support from the inbred degenerates in its midst. It is nevertheless curious to see how these latter, in certain circumstances, react in much the same manner as ordinary people. I know of a comedian, Pallenberg by name, who was a typical Jew intellectual. He salted his money away in a Jew bank in Holland; now that he has, of course, lost it all, he is violently anti-Semitic![544]

In the case of Seefeldt, I told Gürtner that if the fellow had really committed thirty-six murders, it was essential to find out how he had done so. (At that moment only twelve had been proved against him.) Gürtner was very hesitant, so I suggested that he should allow the Gestapo to try their hand, adding that nothing would happen to the fellow, that at the most he would get a good hiding, that had I myself received in one fell swoop all the thrashings I deserved (and had had) in my life, I should be dead! The net result was that the blackguard confessed to one hundred and seven murders, of which Gürtner would have remained in ignorance but for the Gestapo. According to his confession he had employed unique methods of his own. I quote this example to prove that there are cases in which severity is essential.

The law is not an end in itself. Its function is to maintain public order, without which there can be neither civilisation nor progress. All means used to this end are justifiable. The law must be neither harsh nor lenient. But it must adapt itself to the ends for whose benefit it has been created.

The legislator cannot possibly catalogue and prescribe for every conceivable crime. When a crime is committed for which no provision at law exists, it is the duty of the judge to pass sentence on the merits of the case; for, obviously, the absence of a particular crime from the Statute book does not presuppose that the legislation intended it to go unpunished. An efficient judge will find the means adequately to punish the criminal and to safeguard the public interest.

The Body Judicial must be recruited from the best elements of the nation. The judge must possess a keen sensitivity which permits him to

---

[544] Max Pallenberg, born Max Pollack, (1877–1934). The Dutch bank concerned, the *Amstelbank,* was owned by the Rothschild's *Creditanstalt* banking group.

grasp the intentions of the Legislature, to implement them in spirit as in fact, and to amplify them whenever necessary. It is essential that a judge have the clearest possible picture of the intentions of the Legislature and the goal which this latter pursues. Admittedly, in peace-time a leaven of humanitarianism is admissible. The fact that today the Executive intervenes to some degree in the application of the law must not in any way be regarded as a violation of the judicial prerogative; nor, indeed, is this intervention in any way intolerable.

It is rather an attempt to co-ordinate the desires of the Legislature and the duties of the Body Judicial, both of whom have the same object in view. But the idea that the judge is there to give absolutely irrevocable judgment, even if the world should come to an end as a result, is nonsense. The judge's primary duty, on the contrary, is to secure law and order for the community.

The officers of the law must be the best-paid officials of the State, a *corps d 'elite* whose whole education teaches them not to take cover behind the Legislature, but to have the courage to act on their own responsibility.

This, it might be objected, could be tantamount to turning the Law into the handmaid of political power. Not necessarily; the holders of power are themselves subject to the law! No Body Judicial conscious of its responsibilities and willing to assume them will condone a shameful act. But should the Government act shamefully, the law is in no position to prevent it. Neither Roman law, the law of the Middle Ages nor our present code of justice has ever been, in a position to do that.

If the Government of a State is composed of indifferent individuals, then the Body Judicial can do nothing to correct the mistakes of the legislators; but when the reins are in the hands of an honest and capable legislator, then the law can support him wholeheartedly in his task of strengthening the bonds of national community, and of thus laying the ideal foundation on which a healthy and dignified constitution can be built.

The task of the judge is a mighty one. He must be as ready to accept responsibility as the legislator himself; he must cooperate with him in the closest possible manner, so that together they may protect society from destructive elements and promote the interests of the community by such means as the times and the circumstances may from time to time dictate. If this degree of collaboration is achieved, the Legislature will find itself relieved of the necessity of forever having to promulgate new laws; and no longer will it feel itself called upon to prescribe exact punishments, ranging from imprisonment to penal servitude and from penal servitude to the death penalty.

Its task will be restricted to the drawing up of a general code of justice, under which the judge will have the sole responsibility of deciding the appropriate punishment—from simple imprisonment to the death penalty—for the particular crime committed. As things are, when a court condemns to death and at the same time makes a recommendation for mercy, it places me in an embarrassing position. It is not a situation in which the Legislature should be called upon to intervene. If the code of justice is sound, and the judge is thoroughly conversant with it, then the latter, in a doubtful case, would undoubtedly consult his Ministers before passing sentence. There must be the closest collaboration between the State incarnate and the Body Judicial.

Instruction in the law schools must be drastically revised. In my opinion it is vital that a judge should acquire considerable experience of life before he is called upon to accept the responsibilities of his position. No one, for example, should be appointed as a judge who has not had previous administrative experience in the Party.

A judge must have profound personal experience of the matters in which he will be called upon to pass judgment. Present conditions offer him no opportunity of acquiring the insight which is a pre-requisite to the successful accomplishment of his duties. Another prerequisite is that he should have a general knowledge of the various activities—industrial and others—of society. I have known a motor-car case in which the presiding judge thought that the speedometer was actuated by gas! All he knew about a motor was that, somewhere or other, water, oil and petrol had to be put into it. One has no right to expect a sound verdict from a man in such a position.

The expert whom he calls in to his assistance may well be some old rogue, bent solely on prolonging the period of his employment by abundant use of technical argument and phraseology.

To me it appears very desirable that a host of petty causes should be heard, not by a judge *de carrière*,[545] but by honorary magistrates, versed and experienced in the ordinary ways of life. A very large number of minor cases are dealt with in this way within the Party, and it should not be difficult to find men endowed with sufficient wisdom to deal with these small causes.

---

[545] A career judge.

I think that the lawyer, as well as the judge, should be a servant of the State. I am quite satisfied that a judge weighs the facts placed before him most conscientiously, and I see no reason why a lawyer in advising his client as to his best line of defence should not act in a like manner. I have had considerable experience of the law courts. Two people go to court; they cannot both be right, and the one who has had the better and more well-known lawyer wins his case. The first time I went to court I thought that lawyers were honourable men.

When my lawyer suggested to me that I had been the victim of grievous damage, I, in my innocence, agreed with him; it was only later, when I received his account, that I realised the consequences of my ready acquiescence. Now, am I not right in saying he acted dishonestly? I have known cases in which a peasant has been shamefully exploited by the lawyers, who squeeze the wretched little man like a lemon to the last available drop; and once that has been extracted, the case ends! Such malpractices must cease; the lawyer of the future, like the judge and the physician, must be a servant of the State. For the whole object of the Law is to arrive at the truth.

I once had a lawyer who was so timid that within forty-eight hours I had the feeling that I was the defendant, not the plaintiff! The worst feature of the legal system is trial by jury.

Formerly this was regarded as the ideal, and up to 1918, I myself regarded the jury in a case as men apart. As a matter of fact at that time I held all officials, I think, in similar respect. I reminded myself that my father was a man of honour, a Chairman of the Assizes[546] and a *Justizrat*.[547] I had no idea that a *Justizrat* is a private individual who makes his living by defending scoundrels!

On one occasion I was called as a witness in a case against an army deserter—a first-class swine named Sauper. The *Justizrat* rose and asked me a few questions, to which, like a silly fool, I answered quite frankly. "You have just returned from the front? You have, I see, a wound-stripe and the insignia of the Iron Cross, First Class—what is your opinion of this deserter?"

I told him in unmistakable terms what I thought of the swine.

The *Justizrat* smiled. "I object to this witness on the score of personal prejudice," he declared solemnly. The objection was upheld and the filthy Sauper got off scot-free! When the case ended, an officer who was

---

[546] An court which sat at intervals to administer civil and criminal law.
[547] A person who dispenses legal advice, a lawyer.

in the public gallery came up to me with outstretched hand. "For God's sake, let's get out of here!" he cried.

I have a reputation for driving very slowly through built-up areas. One day, my chauffeur received a summons for having driven through a village near Nuremberg at an excessive speed. I attended the court personally, and the following little dialogue took place:

The Judge. But, Herr Hitler, what is your object in defending this case?

Myself. I am objecting because it is not true that we were doing more than thirty kilometres an hour.

The Judge. In this court everyone charged with exceeding the speed limit is invariably fined; I'm sorry, but I'm afraid I can make no exception in your particular case!

I had engaged a lawyer recommended to me by the insurance company to which our Association paid thousands of marks yearly; to save the man trouble I drove him to and from the court in my own car. Thanks to him, the court fine was reduced from thirty to ten marks. And three weeks later I received a bill from him for over four hundred!

The same jurist should, in my opinion, be available for duty as either a judge or an advocate. As a State servant he can fulfil both roles. He should have the right at law, when defending an incorrigible criminal, to plead extenuating circumstances, but not to defend his innocence with the oratory of an angel! Very far-reaching reforms are required in our judicial system. But they must be introduced gradually, and concurrently with the gradual reorganisation of the whole legal profession.

20th August 1942, evening

Dangers of over-mechanisation of an army—God favours the big battalions—Frederick the Great, an exceptional case—American civilization—Bismarck and Wilhelm II—The ignominious behaviour of the Kaiser—Insignificance of German potentates—Mussolini, air pilot

The opinion is repeatedly expressed that war should, ideally, be waged by a highly trained technical force with the maximum of mechanisation and the minimum of man-power.

These theories, however, are demonstrably false, because practice has shown that any one arm acquires its maximum efficiency only when used in collaboration with other arms. The various weapons are indeed so interdependent that success in war is achieved by the skilful and combined use of all of them. Even in ancient days war was never waged with one arm alone.

The saying that God favours the big battalions is not without significance. Without the requisite force, nothing can be accomplished. To think otherwise is to try to make a virtue out of necessity; if this were not so, the smaller peoples of the world would not have been the victims of oppression throughout history.

It was only because they anticipated war in the West, which would give them the chance swiftly to seize the Baltic States, that the Russians stopped the war with Finland. The history of war can furnish not one single instance in which victory has gone to the markedly weaker of the combatants. The nearest approach to it is the case of Frederick the Great, who had luck in defeating, by superior skill, adversaries who were numerically slightly superior.

It makes me laugh when I think what consternation would be caused among us humans if the news suddenly announced that an inter-planetary ship had landed in America! All our earthly little wars would stop immediately!

American civilisation is of a purely mechanised nature. Without mechanisation, America would disintegrate more swiftly than India. Actually, in America the European has reverted to becoming a nomad. What a pity that the film "The Emperor of America"[548] did not end by pointing the moral lesson!

Trenker has produced two films which are masterpieces of their kind, "Mountains in Flames" and "The Rebel".[549] In these he was beholden to no man; but in his other films he was financed by Catholic interests.

A question which is frequently put to me is, should we now release the film "Bismarck"?[550] I know of no more trenchant criticism of the Kaiser than that given in the third volume of Bismarck's own mem-

---

[548] *The Emperor of America* was a film of the eponymous 1929 novel by English novelist Arthur Ward (writing under the name "Sax Rohmer"), best remembered for this "Dr. Fu Manchu" series.

[549] Luis Trenker, born Alois Trenker (1892–1990) was a South Tyrolean film producer. His 1931 film *Berge in Flammen* ("Mountains in Flames") was based on his own novel of the same title, based on his own experiences during the First World War on the Italian front. His 1932 film *Der Rebell* ("The Rebel") dealt with a rebellion set in 1809 against Napoleonic occupying French forces.

[550] Hitler is here referring to the second (1942) Bismarck film made by the Tobis Film company, titled *Die Entlassung* ("The Dismissal"), which deals with the dismissal of Otto von Bismarck as Chancellor. The first film, just titled *Bismarck*, which deals with his political career, was released in 1940.

oirs. When I read it I was appalled. But even Bismarck's criticism is not as damning as are the speeches of the Kaiser himself. Bismarck shows how the eyes of the whole people were fixed on the Kaiser, and what great things could have been accomplished had there been a monarch endowed with more tact, more human charity and a greater readiness to accept the responsibilities of his exalted position.

Instead, the last of the Kaisers did everything possible, by speeches which were as tactless as they were stupid, to alienate the German Princes, with a complete disregard for the consequences. It was the quintessence of stupidity on his part, as a youthful monarch, to treat all the other Princes as mere vassals; I might as well adopt the same attitude towards Horthy and Tiso![551]

Not content with that, the young fool writes to the "Ruler of the Pacific" and signs himself "The Ruler of the Atlantic"! The acts of an imbecile! Can you ever see me signing myself "The Ruler of Europe"!

Had Wilhelm II been a monarch of character and vision, had he possessed the virtues of his grandfather, he would have kept Bismarck close to his side, he would have won the affection of his people, and Social Democracy could never have become the power it did become in Germany. The dismissal of Bismarck undoubtedly shattered the nation, and not only the fact itself, but the manner in which it was accomplished; for Bismarck, after all, was the symbol of national unity. The irresponsibility of that young man is past comprehension. On the day he dismissed Bismarck he gave a ball; in his whole attitude the heritage of his Jewish ancestry comes out in the completely cynical lack of self-control, which was characteristic of him. A mighty wielder of the bombastic word, but a coward in deed; a sabre-rattler, who never drew sword—though God knows he had opportunities enough! And as vain and as stupid, into the bargain, as the vainest and most stupid peacock!

When I recall the German potentates, I find each one more futile than the other. I make one solitary exception—the Tsar of Bulgaria. He was a man of infinite wisdom, inexhaustible tact and unique force of character.

Had we had a man like Ferdinand on the throne of Germany, the Great War would never have been fought.

I shall never in my life make a present of an aeroplane to anyone. A 'plane is a 'plane, and I detest those people who suddenly go all sport-

[551] Jozef Tiso (1887–1947), the president of the independent state of Slovakia which was created after the dismemberment of Czechoslovakia in 1939.

ing! The ordinary man does not suddenly jump on the concert platform and sing! I hate all that type of bravado; the Duce is very foolish in this respect—he's not the type for bravado! People sometimes ask me why I play no games? The answer is simple—I'm no good at games, and I refuse to make a fool of myself!

Adolf Müller once taught me to drive a car. Then I became involved in politics and landed in gaol, where it would have given the Bavarian Government the greatest joy to keep me permanently. In any case, I cannot see myself driving for twelve hours and making a speech at the end of it. That would be just silly exhibitionism!

I have only to look round the gentlemen of my acquaintance—there's always one of them with a black eye or a broken leg! Furtwängler, for example, suddenly had the wonderful idea of going in for skiing! The man who with his genius as a conductor fascinates thousands of women, suddenly has the desire to shine as a skier! Nothing less than a slalom race will satisfy him; off he starts, and then—crash! and there he lies in a sorry mess!

Famous people must guard against making themselves ridiculous in spheres other than their own. Bismarck, when asked to go swimming, said: "I think I can swim, but from me people would expect something of which I know I am not capable. I would rather not!"

The Duce might well take this to heart. It always makes me nervous when he pilots a 'plane; his job is to steer the Italian ship of State. When I think of the numbers who have lost their lives in this fortuitous fashion! If any and every one could pilot a 'plane, then those who adopt the job as their life's profession are bloody fools! (*Turning to Below*[552]) Tell me, does Kesselring fly himself?

Below: Only a *Storch*[553]—not a big plane.

The Führer: He would do much better to leave all that to proper pilots.

1st August 1942, midday
SPECIAL GUEST: GENERAL GERCKE[554]
The Völkischer Beobachter—The Baltic Barons—The genealogical

---

[552] Gerd-Paul von Below (1892–1953), a General who served in Poland, France, and on the Eastern Front.
[553] The Fieseler Fi 156 *Storch* ("stork") was a light aircraft known for its short take off and landing ability.
[554] Rudolf Gercke (1884–1947), Chief of Field Transport in the High Command of the Army.

maniacs—Princes and grooms—Marriage in the country—The girls of
the Labour Service—The broad-minded Bavarians

Events have shown that journalism demands a style of its own. Real journalistic jargon came into being, I think, in the *Völkischer Beobachter* during our electoral campaign in 1932. Rosenberg feared a landslide. I am quite sure that at the time he despaired of humanity, and his contempt for mankind was only increased when he found that the more he lowered the intellectual level of the journal, the more sales increased! He ought really to have called the paper: *"Münchner Beobachter—Baltic Edition"*![555]

At the beginning, the *Völkischer Beobachter* sailed on so high an intellectual plane that I myself had difficulty in understanding it, and I certainly know no woman who could make head or tail of it! Rosenberg insisted on this extremely high level; at that time, where the leading article now appears, he gave us deeply philosophical treatises written by Professors, and mostly on Central Asia and the Far East.

During the Reichstag fire, I went in the middle of the night to the offices of the *Völkischer Beobachter*. It took half an hour before I could find anyone to let me in. Inside there were a few compositors sitting around, and eventually some sub-editor appeared heavy with sleep. He was quite incapable of grasping what I was telling him, and kept on repeating: "But really! There's no one here at this time of night; I must ask you to come back during business hours!"

"Are you mad!" I cried. "Don't you realise that an event of incalculable importance is actually now taking place!" In the end I got hold of Goebbels, and we worked till dawn preparing the next day's edition.

I often find it difficult to get on with our Baltic families; they seem to possess some negative sort of quality, and at the same time to assume an air of superiority, of being masters of everything, that I have encountered nowhere else. Nevertheless, I was very relieved, in 1941, when we received the lists of German families in the Baltic States, to find included in them all our old friends of the nineteen-twenties. One very lovable trait is their marvellous spirit of solidarity. As they have for centuries been the rulers among an inferior race, they are not unnaturally inclined to behave as if the rest of humanity were composed exclusively of Latvians. Constituting as they do a minority, they were all intimately acquainted with each other and kept themselves rigorously apart.

---

[555] Alfred Rosenberg was a Baltic German, born in what is today Estonia.

For my own part, I know nothing at all about family histories. There were relations of mine, of whose existence I was quite unaware until I became Reich Chancellor. I am a completely non-family man with no sense of the clan spirit; I belong solely to the community of my nation. The Balts are wont to gauge the intelligence of everyone with whom they come in contact by the yardstick of his being the nephew of Count This or Princess That.

I, on the other hand, have to think twice before I can remember my cousins or my aunts; to me the whole thing is uninteresting and futile. One of our Party members was most anxious to show me the results of the laborious investigations he had made into the history of his own family. I cut him very short. "Pfeffer,"[556] I said, "I am just not interested. All that sort of stuff is a matter of pure chance; some families keep family records, others do not." Pfeffer was shocked at this lack of appreciation; and there are people who spend three-quarters of their lives in research of this kind. Pfeffer was, however, most insistent in his desire to show me that his wife, at least, was a descendant of Charlemagne.

"That," I retorted, "must have been the result of a slip! A *faux-pas* which can be traced back to Napoleon would be splendid; but of anything else, the less said the better!"

Really, you know, it is only the women who transgress who deserve any praise; for many a great and ancient family owes its survival to the tender peccadillo of a woman! The original slip is, of course, decently disregarded, particularly as its motive was not to infuse new blood, but was usually the result of an animal attraction for some virile being, who, quite incidentally, became the instrument for restoring new health into the veins of a degenerating family. Think what would have happened to the German Princes if little things like this had not happened!

Sauckel told me a very curious fact. All the girls whom we bring back from the Eastern territories are medically examined; and 25 per cent of them are found to be virgins. That couldn't happen in Upper Bavaria!

Contrary to popular belief, it is wrong to suppose that virginity is a particularly desirable quality; one cannot help suspecting that those who have been spared have nothing particular to offer! And what is popularly said on the subject of Christian virgins, I hesitate to repeat. When in the marriage ceremony the priest mentions virginity and the

---

[556] Franz von Pfeffer (1888–1968), first leader of the SA (Brownshirts) after that organisation's re-establishment in 1925.

holy bond of matrimony, one always sees some of the lads grin and nudge each other; quite a number of them probably know this "Christian virgin" inside out!

In point of fact there is no great harm in this, and it is explained by the rural custom of matrimonial trial. The rural districts are so poor that the hiring of any servants is out of the question and if there are no children, disaster overtakes them; from the age of twelve or thirteen the boys have to work all day. And so the custom of trial has sprung up. It is only when a lad prolongs the period of trial too long that he is looked upon askance, and is expected to marry the girl.

Generally speaking, one must admit that there is no more primitive instinct than love; the unfortunate thing is that the results of these customs are not outstandingly satisfactory. It is in the small towns that one finds the best blood, for it is there that people lead the healthiest lives.

In the country, the peasants are bowed down with work and burdened with a hygienic system that is bad in every way. But at least in the country they have a breath of fresh air; and that blows when the girls of the Labour Service, clad lightly in their sports costumes, descend on the farms as voluntary workers. All this to the great indignation of the gentlemen of the Cloth.

Formerly, the country girls, and particularly the more well-to-do among them, wore at least six petticoats—the more the better—as a sign of a girl of substance. Now there has been a complete transformation, and a healthy wave has swept over the whole countryside.

Munich is a particularly tolerant town in this respect. When I arrived there from Vienna, I was astonished to see officers in shorts taking part in a relay race. Such a thing would never have been tolerated in Vienna.

Incidentally, I have heard of a priest in Bavaria being reproached for having had an affair with his serving-maid. On the contrary, the whole community hugs itself with glee. "He's a young lad, our chaplain is," they chortle; "you can't expect him to sweat it all out of himself by means of his learning alone"! And we should make a great mistake, politically, if we use these normal liaisons between priest and serving-wench as a weapon against them. The people see nothing wrong in it—quite the contrary!

1st August 1942, evening
Necessity and the taking of decisions—Patois and High German—
German replaces Latin as official language—Our shorthand-typists

If one enters a military operation with the mental reservation: "Caution! This may fail," then you may be quite certain that it *will* fail. To force a decision one must enter a battle with a conviction of victory and the determination to achieve it, regardless of the hazards. Just imagine what would have happened if we had undertaken the Crete operations with the idea: "We'll have a crack at it; if it succeeds, so much the better; if it fails, we must pull out!"

A compatriot of mine, Stelzhamer,[557] has written some wonderful poetry, but unfortunately in dialect; otherwise he would have become the literary counterpart of Bruckner. If his contemporary, Adalbert Stifter,[558] had written in dialect, he, too, would not have had more than ten thousand readers. What a great loss this represents!

In the same way I always think it is a great pity when a really first-class comedian is dependent solely on dialect for his humour; he does so limit his audience thereby. Valentin,[559] for example, can only be really appreciated in Upper Bavaria; even in the rest of Bavaria itself, half his wit goes begging, and in Berlin, if he appeared there, he would be a complete failure. If only he had trained himself to play in High German as well, he would have been famous everywhere, long before the arrival of the great American comedians. There is a more serious aspect to all this. A foreigner spends two or three years learning German, and then he comes to Munich. The first thing that greets him is a torrent of unintelligible dialect; for the moment the good burgher of Munich realises that he is dealing with a foreigner, he avoids High German like the plague.

"This fellow," he says to himself, "may be a Prussian—I'll give him what for!" And he persists with the purest dialect he can produce until his wretched victim is completely perplexed and driven from the field. I do my utmost to bring good German to the ears of Danes, Swedes and Finns, and the radio blares forth dialect! I do away with the Gothic script, because I regard it as an obstacle, and people go on spouting dialect! It doesn't make sense.

I remember that one of my companions at the front came from the Allgäu;[560] for the first few days, he might just as well have been a China-

---

[557] The Austrian poet and novelist Franz Stelzhamer (1802–1874).
[558] Adalbert Stifter (1805–1868), an Austrian writer noted for his dramatic novels.
[559] Karl Valentin, born Valentin Fey (1882–1948), an actor, comedian and active performer in the cabarets and beer halls of Munich.
[560] The Allgäu is a region in Swabia in southern Germany.

man. All this may be great fun. Fritz Reuter[561] is a great writer, but only a small minority can read him.

Where should we be if Hoffmann von Fallersleben[562] had written the national anthem in dialect? Everyone should have a deep affection for his place of origin, but that alone does not suffice; his allegiance should stretch beyond the confines of the parish.

Are you not ashamed when you hear a well-educated Czech speak better German than many a German? To set up an Imperial government it was necessary to do violence to a large number of dialects and to introduce an official German language. Before this was done, the official language was Latin; and it probably still would be, but for this drastic measure.

There is a world of difference between chanting a Mass in Latin and receiving an income-tax demand in the same language. The old saying: "We'll soon make you speak proper German", dates from those heroic days. It was the time when the Habsburgs behaved as though they were the Emperors of Germany.

For hours on end, I tried to make Krosigk understand that a shorthand-typist in Lammers' office was not an ordinary stenographer, but a secretary. Krosigk at first stubbornly refused to put these girls on the civil service list, in spite of the fact that the most secret documents passed continually through their hands. Clerks in the *Wehrmacht* are in the same boat—and they are the worst-paid employees we have.

In my opinion, in the grading of appointments, the importance of the duties assigned should be the determining factor. The best secretary in the world is hardly good enough for the tremendous task put upon her; she must be as swift as lightning and as silent as the grave—and all she gets is eighty or a hundred marks a month!

It always infuriates me to think of a court writer, sitting there scribbling slowly, with a greasy bit of paper, in which her cheese was wrapped, beside her. The only time she ever bestirs herself is when she corrects a mistake or crosses something out. When I dictate to Fräulein Gerbeck, I know she does not take in a word of the sense of what she

---

[561] Fritz Reuter (1810–1874), a novelist who wrote in Low German, the dialect still used in northeastern Germany and north Holland.

[562] August Heinrich Hoffmann (1798–1874), who called himself "von Fallersleben" after his home town. He wrote the *Das Lied der Deutschen* ("The Song of the Germans," also known as the "Deutschlandlied"), which has been the German national anthem either wholly in part since 1922.

is noting. Fräulein Stahl,[563] who previously worked in the Ministry of Propaganda, was very different. The moment one made the slightest slip in dictation she would stop, sit still and await the correction.

22nd August 1942, evening

Hungarian bluff—India the school for Britons—British policy in India—Methods of colonisation—The artisan at work—Respect the local customs—Budapest

The Hungarians have always been *poseurs*. In war they are like the British and the Poles; war to them is an affair which concerns the Government and to which they go like oxen to the slaughter. They all wear swords, but have none of the earnest chivalry which the bearing of a sword should imply.

In a book on India which I read recently, it was said that India educated the British and gave them their feeling of superiority. The lesson begins in the street itself; anyone who wastes even a moment's compassion on a beggar is literally torn to pieces by the beggar hordes; anyone who shows a trace of human sentiment is damned forever. From these origins springs that crushing contempt for everything that is not British which is a characteristic of the British race. Hence the reason why the typical Briton marches ahead, superior, disdainful and oblivious to everything around him. If the British are ever driven out of India, the repercussions will be swift and terrible. In the end, the Russians will reap the benefit. However miserably the inhabitants of India may live under the British they will certainly be no better off if the British go. Opium and alcohol bring in twenty-two and a half million sterling to the British Exchequer every year.

Anyone who raises his voice in protest is regarded as a traitor to the State, and dealt with accordingly. We Germans, on the contrary, will all go on smoking our pipes, while at the same time compelling the natives of our colonies to abandon the horrors of nicotine!

Britain does not wish to see India over-populated; it is not in her interest. On the contrary, she would rather see a somewhat sparse population. If we were to occupy India, the very first preoccupation of our administrators would be to set up countless Commissions to enquire into the conditions of every aspect of human activity with a view to their amelioration; our Universities, full of solicitude for the welfare of the natives, would immediately open sister organisations all over the

---

[563] Ilse Stahl (1912–1972), a secretary who worked full time for Goebbels, until the time she married the administrator of Norway, Josef Terboven in 1934.

country; and we should finish up by quickly proving that India has a civilisation older than our own!

The Europeans are all vaccinated and so are immune from the dangers of the various epidemics. The owner of a plantation knows that it is in his own interest to prevent the outbreak of disease among his coolies, but—well, perhaps it is, after all, better to content oneself with a little less profit and not to interfere with the normal course of nature!

I have just been reading some books which every German going abroad should be compelled to read. The first of them is Alsdorf's[564] book, which should be read by every diplomat. According to it, it was not the British who taught Indians evil ways; when the first white men landed in the country they found the walls surrounding many of the towns were constructed of human skulls; equally, it was not Cortez who brought cruelty to the Mexicans—it was there before he arrived.

The Mexicans, indeed, indulged in extensive human sacrifice, and, when the spirit moved them, would sacrifice as many as twenty thousand human beings at a time! In comparison, Cortez was a moderate man. There is no need whatever to go rushing round the world making the native more healthy than the white man.

Some people I know are indignant at the sale of shoddy cotton goods to the natives; what, pray, do they suggest—that we should give them pure silk?

In Russia, we must construct centres for the collection of grain in the vicinity of all railway stations, to facilitate transportation to the west. The Ukrainian Mark must also be tied to the Reichsmark, at a rate of exchange to be fixed later.

Rosenberg wishes to raise the cultural level of the local inhabitants by encouraging their penchant for wood-carving. I disagree. I would like Rosenberg to see what sort of trash is sold in my own countryside to pilgrims! And it's no good saying: "What rubbish!" Saxon industries must also live. I once knew a Saxon woman who sold printed handkerchiefs. In each corner was the picture of a famous man—Hindenburg in one corner, Ludendorff in another, myself in a third, and in the fourth—her own husband!

Every time I visit the Permanent Exhibition of German Crafts, I get angry. In the first place, the furniture exhibited is simply a bad joke;

---

[564] Ludwig Alsdorf (1904–1978), Indologist attached to Humbolt University in Berlin, and an important liaison with the Indian nationalists under Chandra Bose. Hitler is referring to his 1940 book simply titled *Indien* ("India").

as is also the method of indicating the prices. One sees, for example, a label with RM 800 and one assumes, naturally, that it applies to the whole suite. One then finds that the bench, the picture and the curtain are not included; and the last straw is that these trashy articles claim to represent a form of art styled popular—the art of our small independent craftsmen.

In reality the public are not interested. When the man in the street pays twelve hundred marks for something, he expects value for his money, and he does not care a rap whether the nails have been driven in by machine or hand. Honestly, what do we mean when we say the work of a craftsman? Why buy furniture in plain unvarnished wood, when the furniture industry will give you beautiful furniture polished to perfection for the same money? In Stortz's[565] shop, for example, I have seen excellent furniture, which modest people would be delighted to possess. Arts and Crafts? Rubbish! If a negro delights in wearing a pair of cuffs and nothing else, why should we interfere with him?

I have been reading tales of the burning of corpses at Benares.[566] If we were out there, our hygiene experts would rise in their wrath and institute a crusade, backed by the most rigorous penalties, to suppress this evil practice! Every day official chemists would come and analyse the river-water, and in no time a new and gigantic Ministry of Health would be set up! The British, on the other hand, have contented themselves with forbidding the immolation of widows. The Indians can think themselves lucky that we do not rule India. We should make their lives a misery! Just think of it! Two hundred yards downstream of the place where they pitch the half-burned bodies of their dead into the Ganges, they drink the river-water! Nobody ever takes any harm from it. But would we stand for a thing like that?

The inhabitants of Budapest have remained faithful to their river, and are rightly proud of two things—the beautiful monuments and buildings which adorn the surrounding hillsides, and the marvellous bridges which span the Danube. It is a wonderful city, and one of immense wealth. Its background consisted of Croatia, Slovakia, Bosnia and Herzegovina; all the plutocratic magnates poured their wealth into Budapest. After the 1848 revolution all the main thoroughfares of the city were rebuilt, twice the width of those in Vienna.

---

[565] A high-end furniture store in Munich.
[566] Benares (also called Varanasi) is a city on the Ganges River in India famed for its open air riverside cremations according to Hindu customs.

I sent all the Berlin architects to Paris, to seek inspiration there for the improvement of their own city. Three bridges are always cheaper than fifty-five streets. I am only sorry I never saw the new bridge at Cologne. It must have been marvellous!

22nd August 1942, evening

SPECIAL GUESTS: UNDER-SECRETARY OF STATE BACKE[567] AND CAPTAIN TOPP[568]

The Bolshevisation of Europe—Lloyd George, a great Briton— Remorseless warfare

Had he been given the time, Stalin would have made of Russia a super-industrialised monster, completely contrary to the interests of the masses, but justified by demagogic pedantry and designed to raise the standard of life for his own particular partisans. His final objective would have been the absorbing of the whole of Europe into the Bolshevik ring. He is a beast, but he's a beast on the grand scale. He made use of the Jews to eliminate the intelligentsia of the Ukraine, and then exported the Jews by trainloads to Siberia. I think it quite possible that he will go off to China, when he sees no other way of escape open to him.

The Briton who made the deepest impression on me was Lloyd George. Eden speaks a repulsive, affected type of English, but Lloyd George was a pure orator, and a man of tremendous breadth of vision. What he has written on the Treaty of Versailles will endure forever.

He was the first man to declare that this Treaty would lead inevitably to another war. The idea that a people like the German people can be destroyed is madness, he said. Britain, he added, had no alternative but to live on terms of friendship with Germany.

That events have taken a different course is the fault of the *Zentrum* (the Catholic Party). The Social Democrats were opposed to the policy, and thus Scheidemann's hand was forced. We have only ourselves to thank that the British quickly realised in the Great War that war is a day-and-night nonstop affair; we ourselves taught them that. Left to themselves, they would have ordered that all firing should cease punctually at five o'clock. Then, to their indignation, our bloody batteries went on firing! And what batteries we had! One fine day they even succeeded in making the Briton forsake his beloved tea to retaliate, and then, gradually, the evening peace began to be a thing of the past! Then we had other batteries that fired all night, and again they were forced

---

[567] Herbert Backe (1896–1947), Minister of Food and Agriculture.
[568] Erich Topp (1914–2005), U-Boat commander ace who sank 35 Allied ships.

to do likewise, and in this way war soon became a rotten sort of game, and of course it was all our fault!

If five hundred thousand cigarette ends are thrown away in Berlin on a Sunday, one of them will start a fire somewhere. We dropped incendiaries galore on the Westerplatte, and there was not a single fire. In the Reich Chancellery I find the marks of the smoker everywhere on all the carpets and all the furniture.

I wonder why the British have suddenly stopped using incendiaries?

25th August 1942
SPECIAL GUEST: GAULEITER LAUTERBACHER
The work of Schacht—Failure of the British blockade—Misers and monsters

Putting our export trade on a sound footing again was the most valuable service that Schacht has rendered us. When it is a question of a bit of sharp practice, Schacht is a pearl beyond all price. But if he were ever called upon to show strength of character, he always failed.

In these sort of deals one Freemason will swindle another. When I dissolved Freemasonry in Germany, Schacht immediately turned obstructionist.

Thanks to the way in which our soldiers send home the things they amass in the occupied territories, the *Wehrmacht* has become a wonderful distributing agency. If we succeed in raising the ration in October, the British can abandon any hope they had of starving us out. They have always cherished the hope that they would not have much difficulty, as in the Great War, of cutting us off from the rest of the world. But now, after Norway, the Channel Islands, and with their difficulties in the Far East, they have to sing a different tune.

The war leader who takes no risks gains no prize.

In the years immediately following our assumption of power many people were of the opinion that inflation was inevitable. The only ones who appreciated our policy were the workmen. For years I had been telling them: Your wages can only rise in proportion to the increase in your productivity. The less money a man has, the more common-sense he shows. The richest people are the least reasonable, and some are so stupid that they become misers! This tendency is generally corrected by the sons, who fling the money away with both hands. For this reason we must see to it that the gaming-tables are not done away with; casinos are marvellous institutions, and we must say to everyone with too much money: Come on, you people, come and gamble!

The whole of life is one perpetual hazard, and birth is the greatest hazard of them all. Every parent knows that his son is the most intelligent baby born, even after the first week: one tells that, of course, from the child's weight.

26th August 1942, evening
SPECIAL GUEST: GRAND ADMIRAL RAEDER

The fidgety bureaucrats—Italy saps our moral courage—Switzerland a pimple on the face of Europe—The Swedish vermin—Remedies against high blood pressure—Industrialisation of Russia—British strategy—The Peace of Westphalia and the modern Germany—Pride without power— The Dieppe raid—Lines of communication in Russia

Bureaucrats are often prone to take away all the joys of life from the people. When the soldiers bring something home with them from the Eastern front, it means an additional two hundred and fifty or three hundred thousand parcels—a very welcome addition to the home. It is absurd to say they should be stopped. On the contrary, I think every soldier ought to be encouraged to bring something every time he comes home.

I recently spoke at some length on the subject of our system of justice and of the reforms to be introduced regarding the training and activities of legislators. The individual must be given more latitude and be taught to cultivate a sense of responsibility and a readiness to accept it.

There is today no valid reason for making peace with the French. We should never succeed in keeping their army down to a strength from which, within three years, they would not be in a position to smash the Italians; for that matter the Paris police are capable of that, by themselves! And so we must always be on hand to help the Italians.

What neither the campaigns of Poland nor Norway, France, Russia nor the desert have succeeded in doing, the Italians are on the point of accomplishing—they are ruining the nerves of our soldiers.

The greatest victories in the history of the world have always been the result of a mighty effort. Life consists of the overcoming of a series of crises, which one man survives and the other does not. In 1918 victory was as nearly in our grasp as it was in that of our adversaries. It was a battle of nerves. No one has a monopoly of success. Frederick the Great is the nearest thing to an exception. To what should one ascribe his success—foolhardiness or what? Frankly, I do not know. The cards were stacked against him, and Prussia was a miserably poor little State. Nevertheless he ventured forth with incredible temerity; on what, I wonder, did he base his faith in victory? If we compare our present situation with his, the comparison will make us feel ashamed—even if we count the Italians as only half an ally. The war of 1866 was a singularly bold venture. Ranged against her Prussia had not only the other German States, but France as well, and Austria into the bargain—Austria alone a far mightier nation at that time than Prussia! There's one very curious thing to note in all this; it is—that the side on which Italy is, invariably wins!

A State like Switzerland, which is nothing but a pimple on the face of Europe, cannot be allowed to continue.

The touchiness of the Italians comes from an inferiority complex; it is the touchiness of a people with a guilty conscience.

Geographically, we shall never dominate the Mediterranean. But the French will certainly never be given the chance to do so—particularly after the peace treaty which we shall impose on them.

It is to be hoped that one day we shall achieve complete hegemony in Europe. As for the Swedish vermin, they must be swept away like the Danish vermin in 1848! We must not take everything on our own shoulders; if we did, our successors would have nothing to do but to sleep. We must leave them some problems to solve, and the means with which to solve them—namely, a mighty Army and a mighty Air Force; and the Army must be taught that, if some cowardly crew of politicians should come to power, then it is the Army's duty to intervene—as the Army in Japan did.

As a general principle, I think that a peace which lasts for more than twenty-five years is harmful to a nation. Peoples, like individuals, sometimes need regenerating by a little blood-letting. Our ancestors fought duels. Next came the barber and his bleeding-cups—and now we have the safety razor!

Nobody in the Middle Ages suffered from high blood-pressure— their constant brawls were ample safeguard against it; and in Upper Bavaria they practised the custom of Sunday blood-letting. Now, thanks to the safety razor, the world's blood pressure is rising. It fills me with shame when I think that I have lost more blood shaving than on the field of battle.

If Stalin had been given another ten or fifteen years, Russia would have become the mightiest State in the world, and two or three centuries would have been required to bring about a change. It is a unique phenomenon! He has raised the standard of living—of that there is no

doubt; no one in Russia goes hungry any more. They have built factories where a couple of years ago only unknown villages existed—and
factories, mark you, as big as the Hermann Göring Works.[569] They have
built railways that are not yet even on our maps.

In Germany we start quarrelling about fares before we start building
the line! I have read a book on Stalin; I must admit, he is a tremendous
personality, an ascetic who took the whole of that gigantic country
firmly in his iron grasp. But when he claims that Russia is a Socialist
State, he's a liar!

Russia is the very personification of the Capitalist State, and there
is no other Capitalist State in the world like it: a population of two
hundred millions, iron, manganese, nickel, oil, petrol—everything one
could desire, in limitless quantities, and all belonging to the State; and,
at the head of it, a man who says: "Do you think the loss of thirteen million lives is too great a price to pay for the realisation of a great idea?"

Poland would have been overrun, and Germany, too, with her hun-
dred-thousand-man army, in the wink of an eye. In Paris itself they
hoisted the Red Flag.

Europe has got away with it by a miracle—and with a black eye!
Europe has once before had a similar lucky escape; at the battle of Lieg-
nitz, the Hungarians—how, goodness only knows—stopped the Mongol hordes. Whether it was the losses they suffered in the battle or the
death of Genghiz Khan in Mongolia that caused the Mongols to retreat,
we shall never know.

British strategy is founded on hesitancy and fear. If the fools had
but gone on, once they had been cleared out of Greece, they could have
marched straight on to Tripoli and taken the place. Instead, they chose
that very moment to call a halt, without the slightest reason. It is a
classic example of a lack of imagination and orderly thinking. And why
this desperate desire to take Salonika? Was it because they were less
anxious to bomb us, and wanted instead to attack some Italian town
each night? For us things are much more simple, for in most cases we
have no choice.

In the East, if I don't attack, the Russians will gain the initiative. We
have constantly faced the danger of being annihilated. On the third
day of the Russian campaign, the issue hung by a thread. If we had

---

[569] *Reichswerke Hermann Göring* was Germany's largest industrial works, created as part of the Four Year Plan. It included mining operations, heavy steel and
chemical processes, and by 1941 was the largest company in Europe.

not taken the most audacious risks, even to the extent of putting in our paratroopers before even our own artillery had ceased to shell the landing-grounds on which they were to land, the whole campaign might well have been jeopardised. When one knows that there is no alternative but to advance, the problem simplifies itself enormously. In any case, we cannot very well retire out of Europe, can we? To keep the cowardly on the right path, I was compelled to say to him: "If you retire, you will be shot. If you go forward, at least you have a chance of survival." We were obliged to shoot a few hundred conscientious objectors, but, after that example, we had no more.

In 1914, the British faced the mighty Germany and survived. This time they faced, as they thought from the tales of the emigrants, whom they believed, the Germany of the Weimar impotence.

The Germans, too, once possessed that sense of insular security which is such a source of strength to the British. At one time they could with justice claim that all western Europe identified itself with the German State. It was the Peace of Westphalia[570] which was the foundation of the permanent weakness of modern Germany.

I have always said to my supporters: "It is not the Treaty of Versailles we must destroy, but the Treaty of Westphalia." The French, of course, regarded the Versailles Treaty as just a continuation of the Westphalian Peace.

Amour propre,[571] in a general sense, is a source of strength. But pride often goes before a fall. In Spain the Castilians are as proud as kings, even when they go about in rags. That is a completely inverted type of self-esteem which thinking Spaniards have for centuries regarded as ridiculous. The Castilian will deign to fire his rifle, but he considers it quite beneath his dignity to clean it!

All this loud talk about American reserves—it's just nonsense! The only reserves that any capitalist State builds up consists of just what is required for the current year. As I see it, the most important result of the Dieppe raid[572] from our point of view is the immense fillip it has

---

[570] The Peace of Westphalia consisted of two peace treaties signed in October 1648 which ended the Thirty Years' War, which had seen the Habsburgs and their Catholic allies on one side, battling the Protestant powers who were allied with France. The latter nation, though Catholic, became involved in the war because of its hatred of the German Habsburgs, hence Hitler's comments above.

[571] Meaning a sense of one's own worth.

[572] On August 19, 1942, Allied forces attempted to seize and hold the port of Die-

given to our sense of defensive security; it has shown us, above all, that the danger exists, but that we are in a position to counter it. Less important, perhaps, but equally pleasing, is the gift the British have given us of a first-class collection of their latest weapons; never before, I think, has anyone taken the trouble to cross the seas in order to present his adversary with samples of his most modern arms! It is always so much easier to decide on the specifications of a new tank, for example, when one knows beforehand the weapons it will be called upon to face!

Britain enjoys one immense natural advantage: she is completely surrounded by a gigantic anti-tank ditch. Her colonies are far away from the motherland and cannot therefore dissociate themselves from it without exposing themselves to the danger of falling into the grasp of someone else.

Unless we wish to remain dependent upon river traffic, with all the disadvantages that are inherent in it, we must construct a vast railway system in the Eastern territories. We were wrong to have regarded the canal system as a rival of the railway; it never was and never will be. A really first-class network of canals joining us up with the river Don would, nevertheless, be of great value. But even this would have the disadvantage that for six months in the year it would for the most part be icebound.

All in all, there is no doubt—particularly when the immense cost of canal construction is taken into consideration—that a really comprehensive railway system is by far the more advantageous. But the Danube will one day become one of the greatest of our traffic arteries; connected as it is with the Main and the Oder, it will carry goods direct into the heart of the country. Through the Black Sea and up the Danube will come iron, manganese ore, coal, oil, wheat—all in an unending stream. The Black Sea territories open immense potentialities for the future. We must make sure that we do not assume the role of permanent guardians of the peace in the Danube basin, but rather that of permanent referee; and for each decision which we give, we must receive our little fee!

The Viennese regard Belgrade as a species of distant suburb. "Every century," they say, "we have to capture the place at least three times— and each time we give it back again."

---

ppe in northern France in order to test the practical feasibility of a seaborne invasion of Europe. The operation was a failure, as the German counterstrike brought the invasion to a halt in less than six hours.

27th August 1942, midday
The threat of invasion—Spain and the Latin bloc—Naval warfare

It is essential to have a clear understanding both of the economic objective which inspires the launching of an offensive, and of the economic effect it would produce if successful. My primary preoccupation was the possibility of an offensive against the Ruhr, which might have had disastrous consequences for us.

At that time I was always nervous of the occupation of Norway; today that would be of less consequence, for we have alternative sources of supply—the mineral resources of Lorraine and the East are at our disposal, and only the problem of transportation presents itself. In the East, too, we can relieve pressure on home production by the manufacture of munitions in the Donetz basin.

In the same way, we can farm out the manufacture of many things which are not of too technically complicated a nature. The steel-works at Mariopol are at our disposal.

During October the power-stations at Zaporozhye will be repaired, and by the 1st of December will be in full working order.

In Spain there are two movements: the Papists wish to see the monarchy restored and the old close ties with Great Britain renewed. Franco has evil designs on the French North African possessions; the Falangists aspire to Gibraltar and a good slice of the Oran province.

The danger of a pan-Latin bloc disappears owing to the enormous demands which its inauguration would make on France; in the face of them, France will turn to us for protection. I must make the Duce understand that, to meet a possible attempt at invasion by the British, I would much prefer to have a quiet and contented France. Were an attempted invasion to be the sign for a general rising in France, it would greatly complicate matters for us.

The possibility of an Italian offensive with any chance of success does not at the moment exist; the whole of their officers' corps is much too old, and their infantry won't attack. Italy's great value is as a manufacturer of tanks, planes and artillery—and she had better stick to that!

Turning jokingly to Admiral Krancke: In the whole war we have not had a fight between battleships! It never entered my head to give the Navy tasks ashore; the Westerplatte I thought to conquer with the Engineers, and thereby, apparently, I offended the Navy mightily; and so I have raised a few brigades of sailors, and made the Navy responsible for the defence of the islands which they occupy.

The Navy ought really to take over the responsibility for Crete; that would enable me to withdraw the land forces, of which I could make very good use elsewhere!

28th August 1942, midday
Italian susceptibilities—Germany faces the Asiatic hordes—If Charles Martel had been defeated—Horthy and the Habsburgs—Budapest and Vienna—The new capital of the Reich

I see Ciano has again been invited to come and shoot. I shall have to use the soft pedal in expressing my views on sport! What a light-hearted, lucky little nation they are! When they get a hiding, they forget all about it in a couple of days; but when they have a success, they never forget it. That is the most delightful frame of mind one could possibly wish for oneself—forget all failures and magnify all successes! Ciano still speaks no German, but the Duce is making progress.

If we were to write a single article about the Italians in the same style as the Americans write about the British, the fat would be properly in the fire! The Americans are a completely unpredictable crowd. In a tight corner the British are infinitely more courageous than they are—there's no comparison! How they have the nerve to cast aspersions on the British passes my comprehension.

As regards the Russians, their powers of resistance are inimitable, as they proved in the Russo-Japanese War. This is no new characteristic which they have suddenly developed. If anything happens to Stalin, this great Asiatic country will collapse. As it was formed, so it will disintegrate. In German history, the Reich, under the leadership of the Habsburgs, fought an unbelievably bitter war with the Turks. It continued for nearly three hundred years, and had it not been for Russian intervention, the Turks would have been flung out of Europe. That was in the glorious days of Prince Eugene.

Here is a lesson we should do well to learn: if we do not complete the conquest of the East utterly and irrevocably, each successive generation will have war on its hands, in a greater or lesser degree. Even stupid races can accomplish something, given good leadership. Genghiz Khan's genius for organisation was something quite unique.

Only in the Roman Empire and in Spain under Arab domination has culture been a potent factor. Under the latter, the standard of civilisation attained was wholly admirable; to Spain flocked the greatest scientists, thinkers, astronomers and mathematicians of the world, and side by side there flourished a spirit of sweet human tolerance and a sense of the purest chivalry. Then, with the advent of Christianity, came the barbarians. The chivalry of the Castilians has been inherited from the Arabs. Had Charles Martel not been victorious at Poitiers—already, you see, the world had fallen into the hands of the Jews, so gutless a thing was Christianity!—then we should in all probability have been converted to Mohammedanism, that cult which glorifies heroism and which opens the seventh Heaven to the bold warrior alone. Then the Germanic races would have conquered the world. Christianity alone prevented them from doing so.

I have just read a paper according to which the Crimea is the richest country, in mineral wealth, in the whole world. Its foundations are composed of primeval rock, gneiss and granite, and I did not know that there were nickel mines there also. The Russians only completed the conquest of the Crimea in the middle of the last century.

How the Romanians and the Hungarians hate each other! Horthy has some astonishing ideas! Like all Hungarians, he hates the Habsburgs. Taking a wholly dispassionate view, I think it is a great pity that Horthy's son has been killed.

The internal stability of the country would have been much more strongly assured had he survived. The old man himself is animated by a fanatical desire to conserve his own health. He's a bull of a man, and was, without doubt, the bravest man in the Austrian Navy.

The Hungarian aristocracy has predominantly German blood in its veins; all the original aristocracies of Europe belong, fundamentally, to one single international community. I should not be surprised to see Horthy try, thanks to his hatred of the Habsburgs, to re-establish contact with Vienna.

It is a characteristic of old age that, while its memory for past events remains phenomenal, it gradually loses the faculty of creative action.

So close is the fusion between Hungary and Austria, that all the baroque one finds in the former would be equally appropriate in the latter.

Rudolf von Habsburg was a real German Emperor. He had to hold territory in his own right as an indispensable base for the foundation of his power. It is only during the last twenty-five years that Hungary has ceased to form part of the eastern portion of the Austro-Hungarian empire; before that, it was always an integral part of it.

The Reich must get a worthy capital. At the moment, Budapest is the most beautiful town in the world, and there is no town in the whole German Reich that can even compare with it. The Houses of Parliament, the Citadel, the Cathedral and the bridges, seen in the shimmer of the setting sun, present a spectacle of beauty unsurpassed in the world. Vienna, too, is impressive, but it is not on a river. And all these beauties have been built by German architects.

It shows one how important the construction of a capital city can be. In olden days, Buda and Pest were both a conglomeration of peasant hovels. In a single century, Budapest rose from a city of forty thousand inhabitants to a great capital with a million and a quarter citizens. With the exception of the Town Hall, all the buildings in Budapest are twice the size of their equivalents in Vienna.

Berlin must follow suit, and I know we shall make a magnificent city of it. Once we have got rid of the hideous expanse of water which defaces the north side of the city, we shall have a magnificent perspective, stretching from the *Sudbahnhof* to the Triumphal Arch, with the cupola of the People's Palace in the distance.

Madrid, too, they tell me, is marvellously situated.

28th August 1942, evening
*Sky-scrapers—Their vulnerability to air attack—Anti-aircraft defence—
New artillery weapons—Learning while facing the enemy*

Some German towns must be protected at all costs—Weimar, Nuremberg, Stuttgart. Factories can always be rebuilt, but works of art are irreplaceable.

Multi-storey houses are reasonably safe against a direct hit from a bomb, but not against the subsequent blast. A small breeze is enough to make a sky-scraper sway as much as from forty to eighty centimetres.

The depth of the foundations of some sky-scrapers in New York is as much as seventy metres, and the driving of the cement foundation demands a pressure of six or eight thousand hundredweights. An air raid, such as those against London, would have a devastating effect on New York. It would be physically impossible to clear the debris, and it is not possible to build air-raid shelters.

In America, the capitalist conception, based on the gold standard, leads to many absurdities.

If this war continues for ten years, aircraft will all be flying at a height of forty thousand feet, and ocean-going traffic will all be submarine, and the world at large will be free to lead a pleasant existence. Fights will take place, but they will not be visible; Britain will lie in ruins; in Germany every man and every women will belong to an anti-aircraft crew.

With an annual production of six thousand anti-aircraft guns, every little village in Germany will soon have its own battery and its own searchlight section, and the whole Reich will be one single, integrated defence unit. Blinded by the reflection of mirrors, the enemy pilots will be able to see nothing; if a mirror is placed at each corner of a five-hundred-metre square, the desired effect will be obtained.

I wonder what people would have thought if I had spoken of figures of this kind before the war! The Navy has the most efficient anti-aircraft defences. I have seen them, and the shooting was magnificent. Thirteen hits for every hundred shots! This is attributable principally to the fact that the Navy is taught to shoot accurately from continuously moving platforms. As a result, their total of 'planes shot down is colossal.

The best A.A. gun is the 8.8. The 10.5 has the disadvantage that it consumes too much ammunition, and the life of the barrel is very short. *Reichsmarschall* Göring is most anxious to continue producing the 12.8. This double-barrelled 12.8 has a fantastic appearance. When one examines the 8.8 with the eye of a technician, one realises that it is the most beautiful weapon yet fashioned, with the exception of the 12.8.[573]

With a new type of weapon, much often depends on the hands into which it is first delivered. If it comes first into clumsy, incapable hands, we are very liable to write it off.

We had that experience, nearly, with the 34 machine gun.[574] One must never condemn a weapon because one has not got the hang of how to use it. The 34 machine gun fired consistently, even in the greatest cold, as soon as we found the right lubricating oil for it.

The grenade-throwers issued to the Engineers, which were completely noiseless, were rejected time after time for one reason after another; and I must say that, every time I poked my nose into a report on the subject, the reasons given for rejection seemed to me to be, to say the least of it, very thin.

If one restricts instruction to the essentials, one can teach a soldier all he requires to know for all practical purposes in three months. The rest he will learn gradually, with experience.

---

[573] The 8.8 cm Flak (*Fliegerabwehrkanone*, "aircraft-defence cannon") gun is possibly the most recognizable German weapon of the war. The 12.8 cm Flak gun was however one of the most effective anti-aircraft guns of the conflict.

[574] The "machine gun 34" is better known as the MG 34 (shortened from the German *Maschinengewehr 34*), the world's first proper general purpose machine gun.

Under war conditions, a soldier learns more in three months than he learns in a year in peace-time. Instruction acquired in the face of the enemy cannot be bettered.

29th August 1942, evening

Difficulties of the maintenance of organised society—My twenty Protestant Bishops—Do we keep Belgium, France and Norway?— Universal suffrage signed the death warrant of the Austrian Empire— War with the partisans—We must adopt the arrogance of Britain— Education and stuffed heads—The safety-valve of military service—Once we were a people of energy—A fitting job for a woman

There never was a party more badly led than the Social Democratic Party; and yet the masses flocked to join and support it. This, it might be argued, was because they had no alternative choice; but that is not true.

Man is not endowed by nature with the herd instinct, and it is only by the most rigorous methods that he can be induced to join the herd. He has the same urge as the dog, the rabbit and the hare, to couple up with one other being as a separate entity.

The social State as such can be maintained only by a rule of iron; take away the laws, and the fabric falls immediately to pieces.

The easiest people to conquer are those endowed with the most versatility. The Swabians? For years on end the only result of my rallies in Augsburg was ignominious failure; but once I had won them over, my difficulties were gone for good. In other districts I had an immediate initial success, only to find that, a week later, I had to begin all over again.

I had to fight desperately to gain power; but today there are only a few insignificant groups of intellectuals who remain obdurately against me. They are people bereft of logic, and their opinion is of no importance. Generally speaking, the people never question an established regime; they are content to accept things as they are.

History affords three examples where those who have seized power have succeeded in winning over the people—the Roman Empire, the Holy Roman Empire and the British Empire. In India, the British started by dividing the country; one portion consisted of Grown Colonies, and the other was made up of independent princely States, whose rulers became the vassals of the British Grown.

In the Eastern territories, our policy should be to encourage the survival of as many religious sects and communities as possible. If anyone

600

should try to form them into one corporate entity, I shall have plenty to say to him; I should like each petty little district to have its own Pope.

Once only in my life have I been stupid enough to try to unite some twenty different sects under one head; and God, to whom be thanks, endowed my twenty Protestant Bishops with such stupidity that I was saved from my own folly. If I had succeeded, I should now have two Popes on my back! And two blackmailers! I can easily deal with the seventeen Protestant Bishops who still exist—but it is only because I have the absolute power that I can do it.

In this respect the Holy Roman Empire had no success; and yet it survived as a power in the eyes of the world long after it had ceased, in fact, to exercise any power at all.

A principle which must never be forgotten is that a confederation of States can be maintained only by a continuation of the methods used to conquer them and bring them into confederation.

Fundamentally speaking, Belgium, France and Norway are not our natural enemies. I have no desire to incorporate all Frenchmen in the Reich; those who dwell on our borders and with whom we have contact were all Germans four hundred years ago. I admit, if I were to follow the example of the old Germany and ignore completely their origins and environment, then I should have to impose on them the will of the State without mercy or consideration. But the real question one must ask oneself is: Can we absorb them with advantage—do they by blood belong to our own race? And then one must act in accordance with the answer one gives oneself.

There is perhaps a fourth example—the Austrian Empire. What a mosaic, what an astonishing conglomeration it contained! And yet it held together. In a case like this, however, those in power sign their own death-warrant when they introduce universal suffrage. Up to that moment, the German minority had held the power so securely in their own hands that no one has the right to say that minority government is a monopoly of British genius. Then, however, there arose a general feeling that this State, in reality a German State, should not be allowed to continue, for fear that it might lead to complete German domination and eventually to the foundation of a single pan-Germanic Empire.

The Hungarians, too, were most uneasy. Then came 1848; the Hungarians rebelled, but the rebellion was crushed with—most unfortunately—Russian assistance. Yet, in spite of this, mention of the monarchy in Hungary arouses the deepest emotions to this very day, for the Hungarians still consider themselves to be the last survivors of the glorious epoch of Imperial grandeur.

With our eighty-five million Germans, we have in the Reich itself a major part of the population of the Germanic races. No other nation possesses so strong a proportion of these elements. It would then be a sorry business if, with such strength at our disposal, we failed to bring law and order to ancient Europe. We may have a hundred years of struggle before us; if so, all the better—it will prevent us from going to sleep! People sometimes say to me: "Be careful! You will have twenty years of guerrilla warfare on your hands!" I am delighted at the prospect! With a number of small armies we can continue to dominate a large number of peoples. In the future our divisions will not be in dull garrison towns like Lechfeld and Hommerburg, but will be sent to the Caucasus! Our lads have always shouted with joy at the prospect of service abroad, and I shall see to it that in the future they range the four corners of the world. Germany will remain in a state of perpetual alertness.

We will adopt the British attitude of arrogance. In the time of the old German Emperors, let it not be forgotten, the Kings of England were of little more account than the King of Denmark today. In the first war, we found, on going through the pay books of prisoners of war, that many of them had served in the South African War,[575] They had been all over the world, and for them the fatherland was their Regiment! With men like that, nothing is impossible!

For the future it will, I think, be essential to introduce a three-year period of military service; only by so doing can we ensure efficiency in the handling of new technical weapons. A three-year period will be a great advantage to those who later propose to adopt a learned profession, for it will give them ample time to forget all the muck that was jammed into their heads at school; they will have time to discard everything which will not be of future use to them, and that, in itself, is most valuable.

Everybody, for example, learns two or three foreign languages, which is a complete waste of time. The little one learns is not of the slightest use when one goes abroad. Everybody, I agree, should receive a basic education. But the whole method of instruction in secondary and higher schools is just so much nonsense. Instead of receiving a sound basic education, the student finds his head crammed with a

[575] The Second Anglo-Boer War, fought from 1899 to 1902.

mass of useless learning, and in the end is still ill-equipped to face life. Lucky are those who have the happy knack of being able to forget most of what they have been taught. Those who cannot forget are ripe to become professors—a race apart. And that is not intended as a compliment!

In 1933 things were still being taught in the higher educational establishments which had been proven by science to be false as long ago as 1899. The young man who wishes to keep abreast of the times, therefore, had to accept a double load on his unfortunate brain. In a hundred years' time, the number of people wearing spectacles, and the size of the human brain, will both have increased considerably; but the people will be none the more intelligent.

What they will look like, with their enormous, bulging heads, it is better not to try to imagine; they will probably be quite content with their own appearance, but if things continue in the manner predicted by the scientists, I think we can count ourselves lucky that we shall not live to see them!

When I was a schoolboy, I did all I could to get out into the open air as much as possible—my school reports bear witness to that! In spite of this, I grew up into a reasonably intelligent young man, I developed along very normal lines, and I learnt a lot of things of which my schoolfellows learnt nothing. In short, our system of education is the exact opposite of that practised in the gymnasia of ancient days. The Greek of the golden age sought a harmonious education; we succeed only in producing intellectual monsters. Without the introduction of conscription, we should have fallen into complete decadence, and it is thanks to this universal military service that the fatal process has been arrested. This I regard as one of the greatest events in history. When I recall my masters at school, I realise that half of them were abnormal; and the greater the distance from which I look back on them, the stronger is my conviction that I am quite right.

The primary task of education is to train the brain of the young. It is quite impossible to recognise the potential aspirations of a child of ten. In old days teachers strove always to seek out each pupil's weak point, and by exposing and dwelling on it, they successfully killed the child's self-confidence. Had they, on the contrary, striven to find the direction in which each pupil's talents lay, and then concentrated on the development of those talents, they would have furthered education in its true sense. Instead, they sought mass-production by means of endless generalisations. A child who could not solve a mathematical equation, they said, would do no good in life. It is a wonder that they did not prophesy that he would come to a bad and shameful end! Have things changed much today, I wonder? I am not sure, and many of the things I see around me incline me to the opinion that they have not.

I was shown a questionnaire drawn up by the Ministry of the Interior, which it was proposed to put to people whom it was deemed desirable to sterilise. At least three-quarters of the questions asked would have defeated my own good mother. One I recall was: "Why does a ship made of steel float in the water?" If this system had been introduced before my birth, I am pretty sure I should never have been born at all! Let us, for God's sake, throw open the windows and let the fresh air blow away nonsense of this nature! Put the young men into the Army, whence they will return refreshed and cleansed of eight years of scholastic slime!

In the olden days we were an energetic people; but gradually we developed into a people of poets and thinkers. Poets do not matter, for no one takes them seriously; but the world is greatly overburdened with "thinkers". I keep a bust of Scharnhorst on my table; it is he who started our people back on the road to sanity. The world at large welcomed this Germany of poets and thinkers, because it knew how they sapped our virility.

One of the worst pupils of whom I have ever heard was little Fräulein Wagner, who was the *bête noire* of her teachers and who was finally expelled from school.

While nursing at the front, she was seized with the desire to become a doctor. She returned to school, passed all her examinations easily, and is now studying at the higher school of medicine. This is a fine example of perseverance supported by enthusiasm.

It is a mistake to say that youth is stupid; youth follows its instinct, and any little urchin has a very much shrewder knowledge of his teacher than the latter has of him! My dog understands perfectly everything I say to him; I am the one who does not understand.

Still, we have made progress in the field of education, in spite of having a pedant at the head of the Educational Department. With another in control, progress would have been more rapid.

A man worthy of the name does not solemnly re-learn the alphabet each year. With a woman it is different; she is following the laws of nature and is fulfilling her natural function when, having had a child, she starts to have another. But there is no professor who, to my knowledge, has shown creative genius. Yes!—Felix Dahn—but, then, he was no real professor.[576]

A man who spends thirty years teaching the rudiments of the French language comes in the end to believe that his instruction is the foundation of all knowledge. Just think how in the old days a bit of paper could alter the course of one's whole life! Look at my school reports—I got bad marks in German! My disgusting teacher had succeeded in giving me an intense dislike for my mother-tongue! He asserted that I would never be capable of writing a decent letter! If this blundering little fool had given me a grade five, I should have been precluded from becoming a technician!

Now, thank God, we have the Hitler Youth, where the child is judged on all his qualities, and not solely on his scholastic attainments; character is taken into consideration, the talent of leadership is encouraged, and every child has the legal right to show what he can do.

30th August 1942, evening
Brigands of yesterday and today—The Russians and prostitution—
Unseasonable weather

After the Thirty Years' War, brigandage flourished for many decades, and the post had to be escorted by a squadron of cavalry.

It is here in Russia that Communism shows its true face. We must undertake a campaign of cleaning-up, square metre by square metre, and this will compel us to have recourse to summary justice. The struggle with the terrorists will be savage warfare in the real sense. In Estonia and Latvia these bands have all but ceased to be active; but until Jewry, which is the bandits' Intelligence Service, is exterminated, we shall not have accomplished our task.

It is interesting to note the way in which this little Catholic priest who calls himself Tiso sends the Jews into our hands.

Fundamentally, there is a certain moral to be drawn from the Russian attitude towards brothels—it is beneath one's dignity to legislate for such places. In our own country, however, prostitution has to a certain extent been sanctified by the fact that it was the Archbishops and the Bishops who introduced the levying of the harlot's tithe.

The princely Bishop of Mainz drew a large portion of his revenues from this source.

---

[576] Felix Dahn (1834–1912), professor of law and rector of the University of Breslau (today Wroclaw in Poland).

That the Bolsheviks admit the legality of a woman's having children by different men is due, I think, to their desire to bring about a fusion of their various races. It is curious, but it is none the less a fact, that our medical examinations show that 80 to 90 per cent of their unmarried girls up to the age of twenty-five are virgins and have a clean bill of health.

The continuation, week after week, of fine weather is most unusual for this district. Last year, at this time, our advance in the south was painfully slow, because every two or three days we had a thunderstorm. After the terrible winter of 1929, we had a series of fine harvests. I hope we shall now have the same again.

That we have succeeded in converting the Russian railway network to our own use is one of the most astonishing feats of all time.

31st August 1942, evening
Lloyd George and the Treaty of Versailles—The error of Almeria—
Britain, Germany and the Duke of Windsor—Jews spur on the deadly
work of the warmongers—Baldwin and Chamberlain—Churchill gathers
a few crumbs

It is a mistake to think that all Britons are arrogant. It is perfectly true that they have a handful of degenerates at their head, and I must admit that our leaders of 1917–18 shone in comparison. I asked Lloyd George why it was that he had failed to gain his point when negotiations for the peace treaty were in progress? (He was advocating a magnanimous peace treaty.) He explained that Wilson[577] opposed him from the beginning, and that the French never ceased from their witch hunt; it was not his fault, and he had done all that was in his power to do.

When the German Government declared that it would never sign such a treaty, a second draft was drawn up, whereby the Allies would renounce the Corridor, we should keep the Cameroons, and the German Navy would be allowed to retain four battleships and eight other major warships; the claim for reparations was also reduced to approximately twenty-five milliards.

Lloyd George reminded me that at that time the British were hated by the French, and in Paris the old cry of *"perfide Albion"*[578] once more

---

[577] Woodrow Wilson (1856–1924), 28th president of the United States.

[578] "Perfidious Albion," or "deceitful Britain" is a pejorative phrase first used by the French in the 17th century to describe dealings with Britain, based on the latter's alleged duplicity in international affairs. From the Latin *perfidia* (faithlessness, treachery or betrayal) and *Albion*, the earliest-known name for the island of Brit-

gained currency. He also told me that he was surprised and completely taken aback when, at the last minute, the German delegation declared its readiness to sign. As they went out, Clemenceau[579] hissed in his ear: "*Voilà*".

When a nation behaves too disgracefully, it loses all claim to respect. Neither Britain nor France would have been in a position to continue the war in 1919. But in the summer of 1919 the German people had already decided to continue the struggle. A wave of sympathy for Germany swept over Britain as a result of the bombardment of Almeria, and the Eden-Vansittart gang worked for years before they could suppress it. Recently they have announced the internment of eleven thousand Fascist followers of Mosley.

The real reason for the destruction of the Duke of Windsor was, I am sure, his speech at the old veterans' rally in Berlin, at which he declared that it would be the task of his life to effect a reconciliation between Britain and Germany.

That rally in Berlin bore the stamp of sincere and mutual esteem, and the subsequent treatment of the Duke of Windsor was an evil omen; to topple over so fine a pillar of strength was both wicked and foolish.

The campaign of antagonism against Germany was organised by Churchill on the orders of his Jewish paymasters, and with the collaboration of Eden, Vansittart and company. The Jews had already succeeded, step by step, in gaining complete control of the press. To counteract Rothermere, the Jews cut off his complete revenue from advertising, and it was Rothermere himself who told me the story of how he was compelled to toe the line. Any and every nation which fails to exterminate the Jews in its midst will sooner or later finish by being itself devoured by them. In retrospect it is quite impossible to understand how all this happened. Old Baldwin started the rot; he himself had great interests in the arms industry, and rearmament certainly put many hundreds of millions into his pocket. Another with the same interest was Chamberlain. Churchill, the raddled old whore of journalism, picked up a few crumbs. Churchill is an unprincipled swine. A perusal of his memoirs proves it; in them he strips himself naked before the public. God help a nation that accepts the leadership of a thing like that!

---

ain, as used by Greek geographers from the 4th century BC.

[579] Georges Clemenceau (1841–1929), Prime Minister of France from 1906 to 1909 and again from 1917 until 1920.

1st September 1942, evening

Schirach and the charms of Vienna—Vienna before 1918—and after—
Vienna, Munich and Berlin—Churchill's visit to Moscow—Goethe on
smoking

During the two years that he has been in Vienna, Schirach has come more and more under the influence of the city. I myself have never succumbed to the magic of Vienna, because I have been adamantly true to my German sentiments. Before 1914, Vienna was incredibly rich, and she was not burdened with those puffed-up parvenus who were an ornament of Berlin at the time.

The Viennese cuisine was delightful; at breakfast nothing was eaten, at mid-day the little *midinettes*[580] lunched off a cup of coffee and two croissants, and the coffee in the little coffee-shops was as good as that in the famous restaurants. For lunch, even in the fashionable places, only soup, a main dish and dessert were served—there was never an entrée. A menu in French was unknown. The first time I came to Berlin, I was given a menu printed in French; the same custom, I found, was followed up to 1933 in the Chancellery. But I swiftly stopped that, when I got there.

After 1918 the average Viennese found himself reduced to extreme poverty. But before the war it was wonderful; never shall I forget the gracious spectacle of the Vienna Opera, the women sparkling with diadems and fine clothes. In 1922 I was again at the Opera—and what a difference! In the places of the cultured society of old there now sat the Jewish riff-raff; the women stretched out their hands to show off their jewellery—a heart-rending sight! I never once saw the Imperial box occupied. I suppose the Emperor Franz Josef was not musical. I am an implacable enemy of the Habsburgs, but the sight of this mob sprawling to the very edge of the Imperial box was disgusting and repulsive, and it angered me immensely.

I returned to Vienna quite recently. This repellent mob has now disappeared, but Vienna is an impoverished city. In the old days it was quite a sight to see the handsome carriages bowling along the roads, which were for the most part paved with wood. The relations between master and man in old Vienna were charming in the mutual loyalty and affection which characterised them. There is only one town in Ger-

[580] A midinette (from the French *midi* "midday" and *dînette* "light dinner," referring to a short break taken at lunchtime), used in France to describe a young, sometimes vacuous, seamstress or assistant in a Parisian fashion house.

many, Munich, in which social differences were so little marked. I can blame no Viennese for looking back with sad longing to the Vienna of old; my younger sister[581] is filled with this nostalgia.

Berlin, of course, is a city vibrating with energy; it has all the faults of youth, but it will soon learn. In former times, Berlin was a simple and dignified city. Then came the epoch of the nineteen-course dinners, a surfeit of bad food indifferently cooked, the era of Wilhelm II and the bad taste which was its hallmark! A happy hunting-ground for the upstart, a vicious and degenerate Society, and a Court life that was as ridiculous as it was undignified.

A woman like the wife of General Litzmann[582] had not the *entree* to the Court, but any old rich Jewess, or the daughter of any old Chicago pork king, was most welcome.

The old Wilhelm was a *grand seigneur,*[583] but Wilhelm II was a strutting puppet of no character. The most insignificant letter of Bismarck is of more value than the whole life-work of this Kaiser. Parliament was wondrously ornate—but all lath and plaster;[584] the Grand Hall—again lath and plaster and Trieste marble! It is our task to see that the Berlin of the future is worthy of the capital of the world; not a city of feasting and carousing, but a city beauteous and gracious to live in.

Churchill's visit to Moscow has done him a lot of harm, not only in the eyes of the Labour Party but also in those of the Conservatives. It was the most futile stupidity he could have committed, and on his return he was greeted with a most marked frigidity. He had pleased no one—for one side he had gone much too far, for the other he had not gone nearly far enough.

Today I appreciate what Goethe meant when he said that there was no more repulsive habit than smoking. It is admittedly all right for the honest old burgher, and whether he smokes his occasional cigar or not does not matter in the least.

But it is not for people like us, whose brains night and day are on the rack of responsibility. Speaking for myself, it is the nights which I find are a torment; I know that I shall never reach the ripe old age of the

---

[581] Paula Hitler (1896–1960).

[582] Karl Litzmann (1850–1936), NSDAP supporter, World War I general, and senior member of the Prussian State Parliament

[583] French for a great lord or nobleman.

[584] Lath and plaster is a way of building internal walls and ceilings by mailing narrow strips of wood (laths) across spaces and then coating them in plaster.

ordinary citizen. But what would become of me if I led a life like his, smoking and drinking my time away . . .?

2nd September 1942, midday
Justice and injustice—Anomalies and confusions—The case of the poachers—War on the criminals—Habits and customs of the mountaineers—The Gauleiter of Carinthia

A certain butcher had a vicious dog, which one day he deliberately set on a small child. The child was very badly mauled, and died; the Public Prosecutor demanded a sentence of several years of penal servitude, and the court sentenced the man to two and a half years' simple imprisonment. There we have one case; in another, a man gets three months for kicking a chicken!

There was a case which concerned me very closely. A certain blackguard asserted that I had spent the whole of my war service as a cook, that I had then deserted, and that it was only thanks to the revolution that I was reprieved. Naturally I took him to court, where he was fined fifty marks! Very shortly afterwards, the same judge fined our friend Zaeper eighty marks because his dog had barked at a Jew! It is high time that our courts introduced some measure of relative continuity in their judgments; as things are, the judge is far more interested in the soul of the criminal than in that of his victim.

I observe that since the revolution, no sentence of death has been carried out on the young blackguard who murders a girl because she is going to bear him a child. His state of mind, they tell me, must be taken into consideration; Meissner himself explained it all to me as if it were a matter of course. To Gürtner I have always said: "Are you mad, to recommend mercy in cases like these? There is only one thing to be done—carry out the sentence!"

Let me tell you that the hardened criminal is in for a very bad time in Germany in the near future; youngsters, on the other hand, who are guilty of some foolishness, will be arrested, of course; but they will be quickly released, to prevent them from coming into contact with the professional criminals and being subverted by them. But such anomalies as the sentencing of one man to two and a half years' imprisonment because his dog has killed a child, and of another, a poacher, to three years for killing a hare, cannot be tolerated. With poachers, let the punishment fit the crime—enrol them in the pioneer corps and send them to fight against the guerrillas!

That a poacher will sometimes shoot to kill when caught in the act is a heritage from the old days when a peasant was subjected to torture for having killed a hare which was ruining his crops. Personally, I cannot see what possible pleasure can be derived from shooting. Think of the tremendous ceremony that accompanies the slaughter of a deer! And the hare is shot, not sitting, but on the run, to make his end more spectacular. The Society for the Prevention of Cruelty to Animals would do well to turn its attention to the sportsmen themselves. One of the prime causes of peasant revolts against their *seigneurs* has been exasperation at the damage to crops and fields done by the latter in pursuit of their pleasures. Do not think I am pleading the cause of the poacher because I am one myself! I have never fired at a hare in my life. I am neither poacher nor sportsman.

Among mountaineers, shooting has become a passion. A youngster will crawl up a dozen hills during the night in the hope of getting his chamois and particularly the male of the species. One must, of course, remember that meat is very scarce in the mountains, and that game is very often the only meat a mountaineer can obtain. Of course we must suppress the activities of the poachers. But, as I have said, let the punishment fit the crime—send them to fight the guerrillas, make them into a marksman's *corps d 'elite*. After all, the best gamekeepers are retired poachers! In regions like the Styria, Salzburg and the Tyrol, if I excluded poachers from the Party, we should lose the support of entire districts.

Like chamois, girls are rare in the mountains. I must say, I admire those lads who tramp for hours through the night, carrying a heavy ladder and running the risk of being badly bitten by the watch-dog—or of having a bucket of cold water thrown over them for their pains! I have much more sympathy for them than for the type who wanders round the big cities, rattling his five or ten marks in his pocket! On the other hand, there are times when the countryside has its advantages, though none but the brave deserve the fair.

The nights of May, the month of the festival of the Holy Virgin, are wonderful in the country—and afford wonderful opportunities for a tender rendezvous, to say nothing of the various pilgrimages, which offer a good excuse to spend the night anywhere. In Austria it is in Carinthia that these happy practices are most prevalent, and it is there one finds the loveliest maids! I am very glad that I sent Rainer to Carinthia—he comes from those parts. In point of fact all the *Gauleiter* in

Austria are good men. I was deeply grieved to hear that the former *Gauleiter* of the Lower Danube had been killed in action. Leopold[585] was a man of outstanding quality; with his company he used to protect my rallies in Austria with the utmost efficiency. He was a Captain in the Army of the Republic and at the same time chief of his local section of the Party. He was no great orator, but a man of exceptional idealism. I did not even know that he was at the front; had I known of his intentions, I should certainly have stopped his going.

2nd September 1942, evening
A "Museum of the Chase"—Political evolution of Britain—Possibility of a volte face by Churchill—The Tories oppose Churchill—American greed—My contacts with Lord Rothermere

What an absurd monstrosity Christian Weber's Museum of the Chase is![586] In Munich there is an Alpine museum; but it is not the mountaineers who visit it—they are all out on the mountainside.

I said to Weber: "You're a clever fellow in lots of ways, but the one thing of which you know nothing is Art. Not a soul in Munich will put a foot inside your Museum—the sportsmen won't, and the others most certainly will not."

I don't mind sports in their proper place. Let the youngsters go skiing by all means. But God defend me from the stupid old *Gauleiter* or *Reichsleiter* who tries to emulate them.

I do not believe that Britain is going Left; if she did, it would be a catastrophe! For as long as the war lasts, Churchill will remain. But I do not regard it as beyond the realms of possibility that some event, like, perhaps, the fall of Stalingrad, may compel him to make a complete *volte face*.

A leading statesman has, of course, his eye on the possible proceedings the State may take against him, once the game is lost, and this may act as a deterrent. When once the terms we offered to Great Britain are made public there will be an uproar throughout the Kingdom.

If a change of leadership occurs, the first thing the new man should do would be to release all those who have been incarcerated by Churchill. They have already been in prison for three years, and a better preparation of the spirit of revolution does not exist. These people would

---

[585] Josef Leopold (1889–1941), who had served as Gauleiter of the Lower Danube in pre-Anschluss Austria from 1927 to 1933, when the Austrian dictatorship banned the NSDAP.

[586] A hunting museum in Munich.

soon settle accounts with the Jews! It is possible that Moscow is using Churchill as a puppet.

The British hate and despise the Bolsheviks, and one day the break must come, believe me. Stalin is the arch-blackmailer—look at the way he tried to extort things from us! The Americans will certainly take Canada, and they may well have other demands which Britain will not tolerate; the result must be unbroken and intense tension. They are doomed to defeat. Even if they were to defeat Germany, Russia would still be there, south of the Caucasus, and against Russia they can do absolutely nothing. Opinion in the Conservative Party is against Churchill. The man who, in my opinion, may well play a leading part is Beaverbrook. He at least can say: "I told you so!"

The most sensitive part of a man is not his skin, but his purse. The people know that the game is up, and on top of it all, they face the prospect of losing India. If India should suddenly rise, and civil war should break out, they will be terrified lest the Japanese should gain a foothold in the country.

When war was declared, a bare 40 per cent of the Members of Parliament were in their seats; immediately afterwards, on another occasion, two hundred and fifty-four members ostentatiously refrained from voting. Never has Britain waged a war which is such an offence to the intelligence and which was thrust upon her by a small clique. Iceland, too, the Americans will never give up.

The Americans and the British brother nations? So what? The German brotherhood of nations fought the most bitter internecine wars for centuries on end. If only Britain had supported the Southern States in the American Civil War! And what a tragedy that God allowed Germans to put Lincoln firmly in the saddle!

The first time the Princess[587] visited me, she brought a letter from Rothermere. I asked Neurath if he considered it advisable for me to receive her. His reply was that, if we could get Rothermere on our side, it would be a terrific accomplishment; and that, at all costs, I must hear what she had to say. When the scarecrow appeared, I muttered "For God and Fatherland" and braced myself to receive her.

In his letter Rothermere said he would gladly use his Press to further a *rapprochement* between Britain and Germany. We subsequently

---

[587] Stephanie Julianne von Hohenlohe, born Richter (1891–1972), an Austrian princess by her marriage to the diplomat Prince Friedrich Franz von Hohenlohe-Waldenburg-Schillingsfürst.

exchanged a series of letters, one of which was very important. I had written to Rothermere to say that I had no grounds for hostility towards Italy, and that I considered Mussolini to be an outstanding personality; that if the British thought they could ride roughshod over a man like Mussolini, they were greatly mistaken; that he was the incarnation of the spirit of the Italian people (in those days I still had illusions about the Italians); that attempts to strangle Italy were futile; and that Italy, as Germany had done before her, would look after herself; and finally, that Germany could be no party to any action directed against Italy or Italian interests.

Thereupon Rothermere came over to see me, and the Princess accompanied him. I must admit I prefer a friendly little kitchen wench to a politically minded lady! Nevertheless, the fact remains—the attitude of the *Daily Mail* at the time of our re-occupation of the Rhineland was of great assistance to us, as it was also over the question of our naval programme. All the British of the Beaverbrook-Rothermere circle came to me and said: "In the last war we were on the wrong side." Rothermere told me that he and Beaverbrook were in complete agreement that never again should there be war between Britain and Germany.

Later, the Princess sought, by means of a court case, to make use of this correspondence to her own advantage. She had taken photostat copies of all the letters, and sought permission of the court to publish them. The judge—and this shows that, in spite of everything, judges are decent people—said that he had read all the letters, which reflected great credit on both correspondents concerned, but that he could not see that this was a good reason for their publication.

3rd September 1942, midday

Ownership of the soil and its products—Fools to the top of the tree—The press and parliamentary immunity

The soil belongs to the nation, and the individual has only the rights to the loan and the fruits of it. It is therefore the duty of everyone to extract the maximum value from the good earth. When Professor Hoffmann asserts that his property is the most productive in his district, then that, I think, is a good justification for his possession of it. The more he puts into the earth, the more he will get out of it.

I have just read in the *Hoheitsträger*[588] the assertion that the soil of the Ukraine is no more fertile than that of Germany. All I can say is that

---

[588] *Der Hoheitsträger* ("The Standard Bearers") was an internal NSDAP ideological publication distributed only to senior NSDAP officials.

the article must have been written by someone who knows nothing of agriculture. If the same amount of endeavour were exerted here in the Ukraine as is exerted by the farmer in Upper Bavaria, the rich black soil of the former would offer a far greater yield.

The office theorists are invariably men who have had no practical success in life. Herr Wagener, proud holder of honorary degrees, is appointed Agricultural Adviser to the Party—and later we find that he has made a mess of every single thing he ever undertook! It is the same in every branch of the State machine, but particularly in the agricultural branch, that the blockheads are put in authority over the experts.

Whenever anyone writes anonymously, I immediately think: judging from its stupidity, this is probably another article by Kranz! Every article should bear the signature of the author.

During the struggle period, all the newspapers had a permanent editor, either a man who was soft in the head—in which case he stoutly spent as much time in prison as out of it—or a Member of the Reichstag! Then the damn German Nationalist party came along and voted against parliamentary immunity, with the result that when the Reichstag was dissolved, the detectives were outside waiting for their victims. Our own supporters had the most astonishing adventures in escaping their clutches.

I have often thought that, if only we would give up wine, what wonderful fruit we should have.

3rd September 1942, evening
A monument Franco must erect—Never yield an inch to Britain—
No war against the British, but against the clique who rule them—
Cultivating the artistic taste—A few artists

Franco ought to erect a monument to the glory of the Junker 52. It is this aircraft that the Spanish revolution has to thank for its victory. It was a piece of luck that our aircraft were able to fly direct from Stuttgart to Spain.

One thing is quite certain—we should never have got anywhere with the British, if I had given way to them in one single instance. Today, they regard me capable of anything; hence the satisfactory reply to our demand for the immediate cancellation of the order to manacle prisoners of war. We must persist in our assertion that we are waging war, not on the British people, but on the small clique who rule them. It is a slogan which promises good results. If we say we are fighting the British Empire to the death, then obviously we shall drive even the last of them to arms against us; and do not forget that there are very many among them who never wanted war.

If I give Churchill grounds for declaring that Britain is fighting for her survival, then I immediately close the ranks for him—ranks which at the moment are most desperately torn asunder.

What has Britain achieved by her declaration that she will destroy the German people? I'll tell you what she achieved: she has welded the whole German people into one mighty, determined fighting unit. Of one thing I am sure; the people at present at the helm will continue the war until they see that it can no longer be won and—and this is important—are at the same time satisfied that a cessation of hostilities will not mean the destruction of the British Empire. In spite of everything, I therefore think that we are psychologically right in continuing to declare, now and in the future, that we are not fighting against the British people, but against this ruling clique.

Remembering, no doubt, that in olden days the Princes of the German Electorates caused themselves to be crowned by the French, the present Pretender to the French throne addressed me immediately after the armistice, saying that he was prepared to conform in all things to German law. What a spineless fool! There are pictures which the eye of a peasant girl is not capable of appreciating, just as there are peasant lads whom it would be useless to take straight off to a performance of *Tristan*.

One of Britain's great sources of strength is that she does not hesitate to give the people the things they understand and like. In Germany the filthy Jews have succeeded in condemning nearly everything that was healthy in art as junk and trash.

The later canvases of Makart are of no great value, for by that time he was a mentally sick man. The Jews condemned them, but that did not prevent them from praising to the skies equally indifferent works— for the very reason that the creators of them were mentally deranged. The blackguards derided Piloty, Kaulbach and Keller![589]

The first Buerkels[590] I bought cost me about three hundred marks apiece; but Buerkel, of course, was a prolific painter, whose living depended on his brush. The only artists to whom the damn Jews gave any credit were Slevogt and Trübner in his later period—and, of course,

---

[589] Karl von Piloty (1826–1886), Germany's leading realist. Wilhelm von Kaulbach (1805–1874), and Ferdinand Keller (1842–1922) were both realist painters.
[590] Heinrich Buerkel (1802–1869), a humorous landscape painter.

Leibl.[591] I have the best collection of the works of Spitzweg in the world, and they are worth anything from sixty to eighty thousand marks each. I have also paid eighty thousand marks for a Defregger.[592] From one point of view, that is a lot of money, but when one remembers that they were the sole pictures of an epoch which would otherwise have never been perpetuated pictorially, it is nothing. For photography, remember, did not exist at that time. It is German painters who painted the Campagna, not Italian; so it was in the days of Goethe, and so it has always remained.

We must teach the British to appreciate not only the Germany of the Goethe epoch, but also the mighty Germany of today!

4th September 1942, midday

Intelligence and a knowledge of foreign languages—Confession is good for the soul—Folk-dancing—An acrobatic danseuse—People travelling—Crock's grotesque house—Some architectural peculiarities

The speaking of several languages is not necessarily a proof of intelligence. For a child to speak two or three languages as the result of having had an English or a French nurse is an everyday occurrence.

Spanish women, even though they speak several languages, are outstandingly stupid. Franco's wife, for instance, goes to church every day of her life.

I admit confession has its uses; the woman has the satisfaction of absolution and permission to carry on with her little games, and the parson has the pleasure of hearing all about it! But, of course, it must all be paid for!

These Hungarian girls have a terrific temperament! The Tabódy is a devil incarnate, and the very devil of a baggage![593] The Hungarian *Csardas* is a fine dance, comparable to our *Schuhplattler*, and worthy of any man. Our ballroom dancing, on the other hand, is, in my opinion, the essence of effeminacy.

Some years ago I was visited in the Chancellery by one of our youngest artistes, the little Endres, who, at the time, was still a little girl. She came to see me about something—a request for a reduction in the costs

---

[591] Max Slevogt (1868–1932), a German Impressionist painter and illustrator. Wilhelm Trübner (1851–1917), a realist and later, impressionist, painter. Wilhelm Leibl (1844–1900), a realist painter and later, impressionist, painter.

[592] Franz Defregger (1835–1921), an Austrian history painter of Tyrolean scenes.

[593] A reference to the Hungarian actress Klára Tabódy (1915–1986), who toured extensively in Austria and Germany in the 1930s.

of transporting her baggage, I think. And now, I hear, she is the foremost tight-rope actress in Germany.

Recently she petitioned for the release from the Army of her brother, whom she wished to have as her partner in a tour she was undertaking of *Wehrmacht* units. She had been unable to find any other suitable partner, and it seems to me that he would give us more value entertaining the troops than fighting at the front. When I saw her before the war she was an angular, awkward little maid, but even then a great future was being predicted for her as an artiste. I read recently that a whole family of acrobats had fallen to their deaths, and I therefore immediately ordered that no dangerous acrobatic turns should be permitted without a safety-net. It is not right that some brilliant artiste should fall to his death through some tiny miscalculation; and the presence of a safety-net does not lessen public attraction to an act.

I was once present when a fatal accident occurred, and I decided I would never risk it again. My nerves are already exposed to quite enough strain, without fortuitous additions of this sort. The main thing is to give the artiste the chance to exhibit his prowess; failure in a special trick is no reason why he should lose his life. Next time, he will do better! But in variety turns the public expect the artistes to take more and more risks. My greatest pleasure is to see clowns like Grock. Such people are the sounding-board of the human soul. Grock's house on the Riviera was so astonishing that a Hindu pagoda is a sober Prussian dwelling-house in comparison! Only a raving madman of a Saxon could have conceived anything like it.[594]

On the road from Freiburg in Saxony to Dresden I once saw an edifice of the same kind, a real masterpiece of bad taste. We had stopped for a meal at a restaurant beside it, and we were told that the owner had made his fortune in the Far East. And it was in this house that the alchemist Tausend carried out his experiments.

At Berchtesgaden we have succeeded in maintaining a unity of style. I do not think we ought to build Swiss chalets at Grünewald; but in districts like that a broad pent-roof is necessary, otherwise the wind drives the rain, which then runs along the length of the planks and eventually rots the wood. Wind should be given no means of access,

---

[594] Charles Adrien Wettach (1880–1959), using the stage name Grock, was a Swiss-born clown, composer, musician, and is widely regarded as one of the greatest clowns of all time. His 50-room house, Villa Bianca (now called "Villa Grock") still exists in Imperia, Italy.

and the upper storey must be protected against water. In the Erzgebirge it is better to retain the dark-coloured slates. The Rhineland, unfortunately, lacks uniformity. But in the vicinity of the Alps and all the way to the Allgäu, one finds the most beautiful farm-houses with their gaily coloured façades.

5th September 1942, midday
The monastery of Maulbronn—You can't help liking Spain

The monastery of Maulbronn[595] is one of the most beautiful in existence, thanks chiefly to the fact that it ceased to be a monastery in the Middle Ages and has not, like so many others of its kind, been altered or modernised in any way.

The rules of the Order, which I have read, were extremely severe. In winter the monks had but one room heated; this common room was built over a cellar, in which fires were lighted and from which pipes led the hot air into the room above. The Romans employed the same system two thousand years ago, and the remains of their heating installations are still visible in the castle at Saalburg.

Spain is a country for which it is impossible not to entertain feelings of affection. The Spaniards are full of *grandeza,* and, in war, of courage. I do not think there is a German who would not agree with me. One of our principal regional Chiefs has just recently returned from Spain, and he is longing to return there. I do not think I have met anyone who is not filled with admiration for the Spanish.

5th September, 1942
I helped pull down Serrano Suñer—Personality of Alphonse XIII—The race of Princes—The process of selectivity in reverse—The train of the Arch Duke Otto—The art of cultivating idols—Serrano Suñer and the Latin Union

Epp has just submitted a paper on the colonial problem to me. I must say, no colonies which we may obtain elsewhere in the world will compare with those which we hold in the East.

Serrano Suñer, had he been given the chance, would gradually have engineered the annihilation of the Falange and the restoration of the monarchy. His disgrace has certainly been accelerated by my recent declaration that he was an absolute swine! Alfonso XIII[596] was certainly

---

[595] Located in the state of Baden-Württemberg.

[596] Alfonso XIII (1886–1941), King of Spain from 1886 to 1931. In 1923, he supported a coup which installed a dictatorship under Miguel Primo de Rivera (see note below). Alfonso XIII then perceived the dictatorship to be a failure, and

a man, yet he, too, brought ruin on himself. Why, I wonder, did he not keep Primo de Rivera?[597]

I can understand most things, but I shall never understand why, when once one has seized power, one does not hold it with all one's might! Princes constitute a race unique in the world for the depth of their stupidity; they are the classic example of the laws of selectivity working in reverse. If the Habsburgs were to return to Hungary, they are so stupid that their presence would immediately give rise to a crisis without parallel.

There are circumstances in which an attitude of passivity is absolutely untenable. With each generation, the Princes of Europe become a little more degenerate. In Bavaria this process developed into tragedy, for they eventually became insane. When all is said and done, the whole of the European royal families are descended from the old Frankish nobility, which was founded by Charlemagne and has since withered away through inbreeding.

The Austrian Princes had a better chance of survival, for they were allowed to seek their wives amongst commoners.

I cannot but admire the patience of the people who tolerate such fripperies! The practice of kneeling to Royalty had at least this advantage, that it prevented the subjects from contemplating the idiot faces of their rulers!

Efforts for improving the breed of cattle never cease, but in the case of the aristocracy, the reverse obtains. The Hohenzollerns are no exception to the rule; they all have their little idiosyncrasies—not excluding our dear little A.W.[598] There should be a law prohibiting Princes from having any intercourse with anyone, except chauffeurs and grooms!

If the crown of Brazil were offered to the Spanish Pretender, he would accept it unhesitatingly. He would become King of Sweden with

---

withdrew support from Primo de Rivera, forcing his resignation. After the elections of April 1931, which was widely viewed as a referendum on whether Spain should remain a monarchy or not, Alfonso abdicated and left the country for Italy.
[597] Miguel Primo de Rivera (1870–1930), was a military officer who served as dictatorial Prime Minister of Spain from 1923 to 1930. After failing to make any great social reforms, he lost the confidence of the King and the military, and resigned. His son, José Antonio Primo de Rivera (1903–1936), was the founder of Spanish Falange Española ("Spanish Phalanx") and was executed by the Republicans during the first stage of the Spanish Civil War.
[598] Prince August Wilhelm Albert (1887–1949), son of Emperor Wilhelm II. An outspoken NSDAP supporter and member of the Prussian Parliament.

the same enthusiasm! He doesn't care a damn what the country is, as long as he is King of it! Are people like that of any real value?

To browse through the archives of these families is an edifying experience; the Wittelsbachs wanted to exchange Salzach for Belgium, but the whole thing fell through thanks to a disagreement over sixty-eight acres of land, and thanks, also, to a certain degree, to the intervention of Frederick the Great, who did not wish to see the influence of the Habsburgs spread westwards. The negotiations were conducted by the Minister Kreittmeyer, which is why our friend Hanfstaengl insisted on the destruction of Kreittmeyer's statue in Munich. I myself was opposed to it. The men of those days did not possess the national sense, as we understand it today. Ludwig I of Bavaria was the first monarch who thought in terms of the whole German Reich. For the others, dynastic interests were predominant.

The journey of Otto, the son of Zita,[599] to Budapest reads like a novel. His suite consisted of a Hungarian nobleman—and a trumpeter, perched on the engine, who from time to time all but burst his lungs with his trumpetings! Horthy did not even deign to receive him. The whole buffoonery had been organised by Zita; its repulse was the work of Madame Horthy. I leave you to imagine for yourselves the *dénouement* of this grandiose undertaking! The only person whose head it entered to welcome the heroes was the brother of Franz Lehár.

In Vienna, Otto would just about have been fitted to become a *maître d'hôtel*. If the Habsburgs had had an ounce of character they would have defended their heritage or died; as it was, they docilely surrendered their rights—and then tried to recover them by force!

Humanity cannot exist without an idol. The Americans, for instance, must needs put their President on a pedestal—for as long as he remains President. The monarchies have shown themselves singularly adept at setting up this particular type of idol, and there is no doubt that the whole performance has a measure of common sense in it.

It succeeds splendidly, provided always that it is backed by force and power. The Church, for example, possesses nothing but the outer trappings; its troops consist of inoffensive archers, nice fellows with broken arrows! One has only to see them marching in the Corpus Christi procession to understand why the revolutionaries of 1918 left them in

---

[599] Otto von Habsburg (1912–2011), the last crown prince to the former Empire of Austria-Hungary. "Zita" was Zita Maria Agnese (1892–1989), his mother and the last Empress of Austria and Queen of Hungary.

peace! When Franco appears in public, he is always surrounded by his Moorish Guard. He has assimilated all the mannerisms of Royalty, and when the King returns, he will be the ideal stirrup-holder!

I am quite sure that Serrano Suñer was goaded on by the clergy. His plan was to found a Latin Union of France, Italy and Spain, and then to range it at Britain's side—the whole to have the blessing of the Archbishop of Canterbury—and a little spicing of Communism for good measure! I think one of the best things we ever did was to permit a Spanish Legion to fight at our side. On the first opportunity I shall decorate Muñoz Grandes with the Iron Cross with Oak Leaves and Diamonds. It will pay dividends. Soldiers, whoever they may be, are always enthusiastic about a courageous commander. When the time comes for the Legion to return to Spain, we must re-equip it on a regal scale, give it a heap of booty and a handful of Russian Generals as trophies. Then they will have a triumphal entry into Madrid, and their prestige will be unassailable.

Taking it all round, the Spanish press is the best in the world!

6th September 1942, midday
The tenuous thread of Destiny—Russian mistakes at Stalingrad—Racial mixtures—Sailors on leave

It is sobering to think on how thin a thread of fate the history of the world sometimes depends! We lost the 1914–18 war; but we have not the right to say that we did so because the Home Front let us down. Our enemies at the time had some men of the highest quality. It was in 1916, at the battle of the Somme, that tanks made their first appearance; but it was not until 1917 that our industry was switched to their construction, with orders to make an initial quota of six hundred. At the same moment Fuller,[600] supported by Lloyd George and Churchill, succeeded in causing the ban on their production to be lifted, which had been imposed by Haig.[601] It is becoming more and more obvious that a rift in public opinion in Britain is gradually widening, each individual going to the Right or the Left as it suits him.

Of all our allies, it is Antonescu who has the greatest breadth of vision. He is a man of real personality, and he has, moreover, realised

---

[600] John Frederick Charles Fuller (1878–1966), a British army general best known for being one of the earliest proponents of armoured warfare. He was also known as an avid supporter of Hitler.

[601] Douglas Haig (1861–1928), British army Field Marshall who commanded the British Expeditionary Force (BEF) on the Western Front from 1915 to 1918.

that this war gives Romania the chance to become predominant in the Balkans, but at the expense of finding the other Balkan States in alliance against her.

The concentration of effort in the defence of Stalingrad is a grave mistake on the part of the Russians. The victor in war is he who commits the fewest number of mistakes, and who has, also, a blind faith in victory. If the Russians had not decided to make a stand at Stalingrad, they would have done so elsewhere; but it does prove that a name can give to a place a significance which bears no relation to its intrinsic value. For the Bolsheviks it would have been an evil omen to lose Stalingrad—and so they still hold Leningrad!

For this reason I have always refused to allow my name, or that of any of my colleagues, to be given to anything exposed to the hazards of war—be it a town or a battleship. It is precisely in time of war that people become most superstitious.

The Romans, including Julius Caesar, were a superstitious people; although it is quite possible that Caesar was not really superstitious, but simply bowed to public opinion. I myself would never launch an attack on the thirteenth, not because I myself am superstitious, but because others are. Dates play no part in my life. I have frequently had setbacks on days deemed propitious, and successes on days condemned as unlucky. The break-through to Abbeville was an advance of a mere three hundred and fifty kilometres, which is nothing in comparison with distances in the East. There we must pursue ceaselessly and give them no respite.

What a fine race the Dutch are! The girls are splendid and very much to my taste. The blemishes in the Dutch are due to interbreeding with the Malays, and that, in its turn, is the result of sexual urge and the lack of a sufficiency of white women in their colonies. We had much the same thing in our own colonies; a German had the right to marry a negress, provided she was a Catholic, but not a German girl, if she happened to be a Protestant.

Even today, the Catholic priest chatters for months if one of his flock wishes to marry a Protestant. It is not very long ago that, in the country, a marriage between Catholic and Protestant was stigmatised as an insult to the Holy Altar; but nobody bothered their heads about the colour of bastards! In the British Empire, things are very different; but the Church of England is a political, rather than an ecclesiastical, organisation.

Again and again I am asked to sanction marriage between one of our soldiers and a foreign girl; and as often as not the soldier is a splendid young lad and the girl a little trollop. Nothing but catastrophe could come of such unions. The branches of the services most exposed to this danger are the Navy and the anti-aircraft units, because they stay in one place longer than anyone else. It was the same in the first war. The Flemish girls were most attractive, and, had the war had a normal ending, many of them would undoubtedly have married German soldiers.

The Führer turns jestingly to Admiral Krancke: Your sailors have only three hours' liberty ashore each day; can't you give them a bit more? If they must hang about in port, they will be best employed chasing the girls!

6th September 1942, evening
German emigration and the use of chemical fertilisers—Between us and the British—Retaliation—Britain started the air bombing

In the past it was economic pressure which compelled Germans to emigrate *en masse;* this pressure ceased abruptly—almost overnight, one might say—with the introduction of artificial chemical fertilisers, which had a profound effect on our food-production problem. To this must be added the industrialisation of the country as the result of the inventions of the early nineteenth century.

For centuries on end, war was confined to conflicts between States within the Reich. The British, on the other hand, have always waged war against foreigners, and as a consequence have no conception of chivalry in war. For many years we were held up to ridicule in the world press as *der deutsche Michel*;[602] but now the British press treats us more kindly. Gradually they have come to regard us as socially acceptable, because we have shown that we pursue our own way, regardless of everybody.

It is essential that we should give the British as good as we get, an eye for an eye and a tooth for a tooth. We must straightaway declare that from now on pilots descending by parachute will be fired on, that submarines will shell survivors from torpedoed ships, regardless of whether they are soldiers or civilians, women or children! Within a month those cads over there will have realised that they hold the muddy end of the stick, and will act accordingly.

---

[602] *Der Deutscher Michel* ("Michael the German") is a light-hearted stereotype of the Germans in much the way that "John Bull" or "Uncle Sam" is supposed to be of British and Americans.

I make no secret of the fact that in my eyes the life of a single German is worth more than the lives of twenty Britishers, and in this respect we hold the advantage. We hold infinitely more prisoners-of-war than they do, and the great thing is to capture as many "honourables" as possible. The handcuffing of a hundred and thirty officers after the Dieppe raid had a splendid effect. They are completely indifferent to the fate of the ordinary soldier, but the hanging of half a dozen British Generals would shake British society to its very foundations.

Now that Mrs. Churchill goes about arm in arm with Madame Maisky,[603] British prisoners-of-war cannot complain if they are made to live with Russian prisoners.

This would be an excellent measure, to which their only counter would be to make our prisoners live with the Italians! If they were to threaten more drastic reprisals, we will retort by hanging the captains of all ships sunk! The Merchant Navy would then begin to act very differently. The Japanese do this, while we entertain them with coffee and cognac.

The British are realists, devoid of any scruple and as cold as ice; but as soon as we show our teeth, they become propitiatory and almost friendly! It was the British who started air attacks. For four months we patiently—and perhaps erroneously—held our hands.

The German is always restrained by moral scruples, which mean nothing to the British; to the latter such an attitude is merely a sign of weakness and stupidity. In the past we have readjusted the balance only by retorting in the most ruthless and even barbarous manner.

Our gains in the West may add a measure of charm to our possessions and constitute a contribution to our general security, but our Eastern conquests are infinitely more precious, for they are the foundations of our very existence.

7th September 1942, midday
SPECIAL GUESTS: REICH MINISTER SPEER, REICHSKOMMISSAR KOCH, FIELD MARSHAL MILCH

School-day memories—Towards a seasoned system of education

We pupils of the old Austria were brought up to respect old people and women. But on our professors we had no mercy; they were our natural enemies. The majority of them were somewhat mentally deranged, and quite a few ended their days as honest-to-God lunatics!

---

[603] Wife of the Soviet Union's ambassador to London, Ivan Maisky.

Those among them who were good fellows we treated with the utmost affection; but they were very few and far between.

Information about the individual weaknesses of the various masters was handed on from class to class and from generation to generation. In the third form we had a physics master named Koenig. Each form knew that at the beginning of the new scholastic year, the pupils would be divided into two groups—why, I still have no idea.

Koenig would give the following order: "The pupils on the side nearest the window will gather near the window; those on the stove side of the room will gather in the vicinity of the stove!"

Immediately the pupils rushed to do the reverse. The wretched man danced with indignation, exclaiming that the students became more stupid with every year; it never entered his head that the real fool was he himself!

The priest who taught us divinity was a very tubby, portly little man. Before his entry, we used to slant the forms inwards along the gangway through which he had to pass, making it narrower and narrower.

Never did the stupid man realise the trick; solemnly he would walk on until finally, half-way to his desk, he found himself stuck between the benches!

Before the lesson in natural science, we used to strew the floor of the classroom with grass and nutshells, and explain innocently that we had been studying botany.

We had a methodical plan, according to the season of the year, for fomenting riot and chaos in the classroom.

In the spring a very successful trick was to release a swarm of cockchafers in class and then exclaim in unison: "O-Oh, sir! How can we study with all these cockchafers in the room!"

As you may imagine, I was in particularly bad odour with the teachers. I showed not the slightest aptitude for foreign languages—though I might have done, had not the teacher been a congenital idiot. In addition, I could not bear the sight of him, and in honesty I must confess that the feeling was reciprocated. Behind a frosty beard one caught a glimpse of a collar, greasy and yellow with dirt, and he was in every way a most repellent creature; he was furious because I learnt not a word of French. A bright youngster of thirteen or fourteen can always get the better of a teacher dulled by the grind of years of teaching.

Our teachers were absolute tyrants. They had no sympathy with youth; their one object was to stuff our brains and to turn us into erudite apes like themselves. If any pupil showed the slightest trace of originality, they persecuted him relentlessly, and the only model pupils whom I ever got to know have all been failures in after-life.

Good teaching should recognise and develop the personality of the individual pupil. In this respect the foundation of a corps of teachers and the revision of educational methods have brought a very great improvement in modern times.

Among our teachers there was only one who dressed decently; and it is an interesting fact that, when I once visited Klagenfurt, I found him—in the SS! The old gentleman, who was then already on pension, had, it seems, been a member of the illegal SS before the *Anschluss*. I was very much moved to meet him again.

I can readily understand why the youth of ancient Greece sometimes went far afield, in order to study under the teacher of their choice. And it was grouped around their teachers, by the way, that the youth of ancient days went into battle.

There is no enthusiasm greater than that of a young man of thirteen to seventeen years of age. They will gladly let themselves be cut to pieces for the sake of their teacher, if he is a real man. I should very much like to see our youth led into battle by their teachers!

PART THREE
June 1943

13th June 1943, evening
Dangers of over-centralisation of cultural life—The future of technology—The French painters—The great artistic achievements of the nineteenth century were German—Architecture in Berlin and Munich

I am very nervous lest, one day when I am no longer here, someone should get the idea of centralising in Berlin a series of museums for the artistic masterpieces of the Reich, for military trophies and weapons and for examples of German industrial and scientific genius. This would give a completely erroneous conception of the unified state, and the worst of it would be that the initiator would certainly claim that in so doing he was following the conceptions "of our late Führer".

In point of fact we should, on the contrary, pursue a policy of judicious decentralisation. The *Deutsches Museum*[604] in Munich, with its

---

[604] The Deutsches Museum in Munich is still in existence, and is devoted to sci-

twenty-three kilometres of exhibits of all kinds, amply fulfils the purely national need, and it would be disastrous if somebody said we must have a museum in Berlin with forty-five kilometres of exhibits!

In the Military Museum which I intend to found in Linz, I wish to devote one section to the science of fortification, from the earliest times down to the days of the Maginot Line and the West Wall. Exact models will be necessary in order to arouse the interest of young people.

One of the great attractions of the *Deutsches Museum* in Munich is the presence of a large number of perfectly constructed working models, which visitors can manipulate themselves. It is not just by chance that so many of the young people of the inland town of Munich have answered the call of the sea.

We must start from the viewpoint that technical science today stands at the threshold of its development. Motorisation is now only taking its first few hesitant steps. Many centuries passed before human energy was replaced by animal energy, and it will equally be many centuries before motorisation reaches its full perfection.

I cannot make up my mind to buy a picture by a French painter, because I am not sure of the dividing line between what I understand and what I do not understand. I have the same feeling when I look at paintings by Corinth[605] and Trübner—to mention only two of our German artists. These men started by painting pictures of great merit, and then, urged on by pride, they started to produce the most startling and extraordinary works. In literature the Jew has already blazed the same pernicious trail, and artists like Corinth and Trübner have followed them. The result is the frightful daubs with which they now inflict us.

In painting, the Italians were truly great from the fourteenth century to the seventeenth; in the eighteenth century they rested on their laurels, in the nineteenth their light began to wane, and today Italian art is completely degenerate. All this seems quite incomprehensible to me, but I suppose it is the law of averages.

In the nineteenth century the greatest masterpieces in every branch were the works of us Germans. In the same period the French, too, had some good artists, but they all deteriorated in time.

When I think of the Paris Opera House, I cannot help feeling that those of Dresden and Vienna are in a very different category. The de-

ence and technology.
[605] Lovis Corinth (1858–1925), a realist painter who later became influenced by Impressionism.

sign itself of the Paris Opera is a work of genius, but the execution, from the artistic point of view, is very ordinary; and the interior is pretentious, overcrowded with decoration and devoid of all artistic taste. We must make sure that the new Opera House which we intend to build in Munich surpasses everything, in every way, that has ever gone before it.

Munich of the nineteenth century has many characteristics in common with the Berlin of Frederick the Great's days. Conceptions were magnificently wide, but construction could not keep pace, simply because the necessary money was not available.

In Frederick the Great's Berlin they were so short of funds that it was possible to put statues only on the main plinth of a monument. In Munich it is freely admitted that the houses of the period were shoddily built. In the construction of the Prinzregenten-Theater every possible economy was practised, and the cost of construction, apart from interior decoration, was under thirteen hundred thousand marks.

In Berlin, at the same time, the scale was more generous. The Reichstag—monstrosity though it was—cost in all every bit of twenty-eight million marks. But that it was well and truly built was proved at the time of the great fire. The Palace of Justice in Munich is perhaps the most beautiful example of the baroque of recent times. Typical of the epoch of liberalism is the Palais de Justice in Brussels. It is a Cyclops which dominates the whole town; and fancy having the Law Courts, of all things, as the dominating feature of a place!

I am quite sure that a man is never more ready to fight for his country than when it is a question of defending the artistic and intellectual heritage of the nation. We have a fresh proof of it today. The destruction of a national monument has a greater effect on public opinion than the destruction of a factory.

14th June 1943, evening
In defence of Metternich[606]—Metternich and Bismarck, a parallel

Metternich is often misjudged. He did his utmost to infuse new life into a corpse. As Chancellor of Austria, and from the point of view of the Habsburg dynasty, he could not have acted otherwise. He served the Habsburgs, animated by the desire to restore to them their glories of the past. It was this which inspired his superhuman efforts to bring about a renaissance of the old Empire. That he was unscrupulous in the

[606] Klemens Lothar (1773–1859), better known as Prince Metternich, was the Austrian Empire's foreign minister from 1809 and Chancellor from 1821 until 1848.

means he employed to this end is undeniable. But his actions must be judged in the light of the conditions which prevailed at the time.

No one, for example, could have envisaged, in 1830 or 1840, the methods employed by Bismarck. It is not therefore a question of Bismarck or Metternich, but rather a question of an Imperial Chancellery or that heterogeneous conglomeration, Germanic Confederation.

At Frankfurt nothing was accomplished and nothing could have been accomplished; and yet it can truthfully be said that each in his way was pursuing the same object.

Metternich hoped to attain it by re-establishing the authority of the Habsburgs; Bismarck by asserting the predominance of Prussia. Both avoided any parliamentary solution. Bismarck succeeded, Metternich failed. But that is no reason for condemning the latter.

Without the drastically revolutionary step of war in 1866, Bismarck himself would not have succeeded. And had he failed, he would certainly have been crucified. When Metternich was at the helm, the time was not ripe for a decisive solution. For the same reason Bismarck cannot be reproached for not having founded the Greater German Reich of today. In the struggle against Napoleon, Metternich was as enthusiastic as the most devoted of German patriots.

How undecided public opinion was, even after 1866, on the question of whether Austrian or Prussian hegemony should prevail, is clearly demonstrated by the fact that in 1867 the Prussian conservatives took their stand against Bismarck and demanded his resignation.

It is obviously very difficult to do justice retrospectively to a man like Metternich.

15th June 1943, midday
*Intellectual and artistic poverty—Bric-à-brac and chromium plate—
Only decadent art is harmful—Teutonic nostalgia—The need of open
spaces*

The industrialisation of a country invariably provokes an opposite reaction and gives rise to a recrudescence of a certain measure of romanticism, which not infrequently finds expression in a mania for the collection of *bibelots* and somewhat trashy *objets d'art*. It is a phenomenon which recurs with each fresh migration from the land to the town. It is not the museums and the picture-galleries which attract these new-comers, but the vaults which foster the liking for the mysterious, like the blue grotto of the nymphs. The process of readjustment takes fifty or a hundred years.

Unfortunately, the period of economic and industrial progress in Germany coincided with a period of artistic hesitancy and poverty. One cannot, in justice, blame the masses, when one remembers the artistic junk with which the big industrialists filled their houses. But the latter were people of intelligence, and them I blame greatly.

The masses are still attracted by somewhat trashy art, but that has nothing in common with artistic degeneracy. If I am asked whether I am prepared to condone this, my reply is that I will condone anything which does not lead to artistic depravity.

The admiration for what we sometimes call chocolate box beauty is not of itself vicious; it gives evidence, at least, of artistic feeling, which may well become later the basis for real taste. Permanent injury is done only by real depravity in art.

It is perfectly true that we are a people of romantics, quite different from the Americans, for example, who see nothing beyond their sky-scrapers. Our romanticism has its origins in the intense appreciation of nature that is inherent in us Germans. Properly to appreciate such artists as Weber,[607] Ludwig Richter and the other romanticists, one must know Franconian mountains, for that is the background which gives birth to romanticism in both music and painting; and, of course, the stories and legends of our folk-lore also make a potent contribution.

The only romance which stirs the heart of the North American is that of the Redskin; but it is curious to note that the writer who has produced the most vivid Redskin romances is a German.[608]

One thing the Americans have, and which we lack, is the sense of the vast open spaces. Hence the particular characteristics of our own form of nostalgia. There comes a time when this desire for expansion can no longer be contained and must burst into action. It is an irrefutable fact that the Dutch, for example, who occupied the most densely populated portions of the German lands, were driven, centuries ago, by this irresistible desire for expansion to seek ever wider conquest abroad. What, I wonder, would happen to us, if we had not at least the illusion of vast spaces at our disposal?

For me, one of the charms of the Spessart[609] is that one can drive there for hours on end, and never meet a soul. Our *autobahn*s give me

---

[607] Gottlieb Weber (1823-1916), a German painter most famous for his landscape paintings of early northeast America.

[608] Karl May. See footnote 331.

[609] The Spessart is a range of low mountains in north-western Bavaria.

the same feeling; even in the more thickly populated areas they reproduce the atmosphere of the open spaces.

17th June 1943, evening
The great cataclysms of nature—The Fear of the Unknown

I cannot believe that the various ages in the history of the globe lasted as long as the experts would have us believe. In any case, they have no proofs to offer of the correctness of their hypotheses. I have the feeling that in their estimates the fear of the unknown and of natural catastrophe have played their part.

During the recent earthquakes in Württemberg, the principal preoccupation of the press was to reassure the public by insisting that there was no grave danger and no sign of any aggravation of the phenomenon. It is quite extraordinary how many men there are who are incapable of facing reality and who, when face to face with danger, cannot calmly make plans to meet it. Such people are, for the most part, cowards, and the fear of the unknown is ineradicably engrained in them.

19th June 1943, at table
Big battleships—The infantry of the seas

Formerly I planned to construct the most powerful squadron of battleships in the world, and intended to name the two mightiest of them the *Ulrich von Hütten* and the *Goetz von Berlichingen*. I am now very pleased that I abandoned the idea.

For, if we had such a squadron, we should be under a moral obligation to use it. Of what practical assistance could such a squadron be today? It would be condemned to playing the part of "the last of the knights in armour".

Evolution these days has been so swift that it is now the infantry of the sea which assumes the prime importance. Apart from submarines, our greatest need is for little ships—powerful corvettes, destroyers and the like—these are the classes that carry on the fight.

The Japanese today possess the most powerful fleet of battleships in the world, but it is very difficult to use them in action. For them, the greatest danger comes from the air. Remember the *Bismarck*.[610]

24th June 1943, evening
The vibrant pulse of Berlin—Vienna the home of music—Mozart—Slav blood and German blood—Beethoven—For and against Vienna—The

---

[610] The battleship *Bismarck*—one of the largest such ships every built in Europe—was launched in 1939 and was scuttled after being seriously damaged by aircraft strikes during a sea battle in May 1941.

new capital of the Reich—Loyalty at Linz—A remark of Treitschke[611]—
The interests of the Reich are paramount

In Berlin, I think, people work harder than anywhere else. I know of
no other city in which it would have been possible to complete the construction of the Reich Chancellery in nine months. The Berlin workman is unique as a swift and efficient craftsman. There is nothing to
touch him in Munich or Vienna, where the infusion of foreign blood—
Polish, Czech, Slav, Italian—still has an influence.

When one speaks of Vienna and music and proclaims Vienna to
be the most musical city in the world, one must not forget that at the
time of our great composers, Vienna was the Imperial city. She was
an attraction for the whole world, and was thus the city which offered
artists the greatest scope and opportunity. In spite of this, how shabbily
the musicians were treated there! It is not true that either Beethoven or
Haydn had any success there during their lifetime. Mozart's *Don Juan*
was a failure there.

Why then did Mozart go to Vienna? Simply because he hoped to get
a pension from the Emperor, which he never obtained. Mozart's family,
it has been established, came from Augsburg; he was therefore not an
Austrian but a Swabian. The whole blossoming of our music in Vienna
is not due to the town; such things do not spring from their environment, but from the genius of a race.

Really creative music is composed partly of inspiration and partly
of a sense of composition. The inspiration is of Slavonic origin, the art
of composition is of Germanic. It is when these two mingle in one man
that the master of genius appears.

In Bach's music it is the composition which is marvellous, and he
certainly had no drop of Slav blood in his veins. As regards Beethoven,
on the other hand, one glance at his head shows that he comes of a different race. It is not pure chance that the British have never produced a
composer of genius; it is because they are a pure Germanic race.

Do not for a moment imagine that I am hostile to Vienna. I criticise
with equal vigour everything in Berlin which displeases me. My task is
a far greater one, and I do not think in terms of Vienna or Berlin. My
historical sense tells me that things will change in the future, and so I
must needs think of what may happen when I am no longer here. For
Vienna to become the sole centre of attraction for the Austrian portion

---

[611] Heinrich von Treitschke (1834–1896), a prominent German nationalist politician, historian, and writer who served in the first Reichstag.

of our territories would be dangerous for the whole Reich. For this reason I feel impelled to take steps to counteract any such possibility; and for this reason, too, I am anxious to create other centres of culture in Austria. A monopoly of cultural attraction in Vienna would have serious political repercussions.

And these, if we digest the lessons that history has to teach us, are repercussions we cannot tolerate. Munich presents no such dangers, for the radius of its cultural influence does not go beyond the borders of Bavaria. It is my duty to ensure that an evolution does not occur which will inevitably lead to disaster.

I can well appreciate a sentimental affection for Vienna, but when great political decisions have to be taken, they must be taken in the light of logic and cold reason. Therefore, all that Vienna has drained from its neighbouring provinces must be channelled back into the *Gaue*.

Furthermore, I will not tolerate any rivalry between Vienna and Berlin. Berlin is the capital of the Reich, and will remain the capital of the Reich. I once toyed with the idea of moving the capital, and thought of moving it to Lake Müritz in Mecklenburg. But Speer persuaded me to abandon the idea, because the soil there is as bad, from the building point of view, as it is in Berlin.

I shall see to it that Berlin acquires all the characteristics of a great capital. But none of this is based on any sentimental preference. I do not like the Berliners more than I like the Viennese. I feel equally at home anywhere in the Reich, and my love for all Germans is equal, as long as they do not range themselves against the interests of the Reich, of which I am the guardian. In this respect I behave as if I am in the midst of my family. But if I see any province or city trying to make unreasonable claims to its own individual advantage, then I am up in arms at once. Do not tell me that Vienna has made heavy sacrifices in this war and that her sons are dying gallantly on the battlefield. The same can be said of all towns and all their sons throughout Germany. That is but the expression of a clear-cut sense of duty, and is no cause for tears. I should indeed be a bad son of my own country if I did not place her, in this respect, side by side with Germany herself.

No *Gauleiter* may expect more support from me, financial or otherwise, than that dictated by the interests of the Reich. If I make a gift of a building to a *Gau* or a city, it is not a personal gift—for I myself am a poor man—it is a gift from the whole German people. Mark well this fact, for therein lies my great responsibility.

Who can say that I do not hold Vienna in high esteem? Have I not sent there the man whom I consider most suitable, and most capable of directing the affairs of the *Gau*? The Viennese are so touchy, that the simple fact that I have started some building at Linz is enough to upset them. But that does not worry me, and I remain quite impartial as regards all the *Gaue*.

I must, however, say that in Vienna I see a source of potential danger, if that city were to be given special privileges. It is perfectly true that I was received in Vienna with joy and jubilation. But the same thing occurred at Linz, Klagenfurt, Hamburg, Cologne and everywhere else. And in any case I hope I shall not be expected to give preference to any town on account of the fervour of its welcome to me. Their acclamations, it goes without saying, are not personal, but acclamations for the Leader of the German State.

Of course the friendly reception in Vienna delighted me; but that will not prevent me from doing my duty, as I conceive it, in the interests of the whole State. In such things sentiment has no part. I told Eigruber:[612] "Linz owes all it possesses, and all that it will possess, to the Reich. For this reason Linz should become the personification of the Reich, and the façade of every building in the city should bear the inscription: 'Gift of the German Reich.'"

Linz realises it, as this example will show you. I read in the *Linzer Tagespost* that some cabaret artist had maliciously attacked the Berliners. The paper went on to state indignantly that such behaviour towards the capital of the Reich would not be tolerated in Linz. The right to criticise is a common right; but not the right to vilify. The petty rivalries between town and town, district and district, have by no means yet been suppressed; and this is a danger which may reappear after the war.

Now, therefore, is the time to eliminate all cause for rivalry. It is perhaps a blessing in disguise that I was for so long a Stateless person;[613] for it has taught me the tremendous value of a unified Germany.

Treitschke once said: "Germany has cities, but she possesses no capital." To that I will add that she must, and she shall, have one. I shall take care that no town in the Reich can rival the capital. I have examined certain projects for Vienna, but they demand a financial backing from

---

[612] August Eigruber (1907–1947), *Gauleiter* and *Reichsstatthalter* of the Upper Danube *Gau*.

[613] Hitler renounced his Austrian citizenship in 1925, and only became a German national in 1932.

the Reich which I do not consider should be accorded to any city but the capital of the Reich. Any other decision would be wrong. Vienna must, of course, be cleaned up and cleared of slums; and this will be done. I have already cleared the Jews out of the city, but I should like to see the Czechs go, too. Whatever new construction may be undertaken in Vienna, it would be folly for her to try to surpass the existing glorious monuments of the Imperial City.

It would be a criminal act on my part to use the money of the Reich to create a situation which one day might develop into a menace to that same Reich. My sense of history and my political instinct combine to forbid me to act in any way other than as I am doing.

Schirach, it is your duty to see that Vienna retains her high level of culture. My duty is to safeguard the interests of the Reich, and I expect every *Gauleiter* to understand that clearly. To achieve great things, it is necessary to burn many of one's boats behind one—especially those which are laden with personal prejudices. Reason alone must have the last word.

PART FOUR
March to November 1944

1 March 1944, midday
A nursery for film actors—Futility of the art critics—Weber's Freischütz and Bizet's Carmen

It is often said that among our film actors we have none capable of playing certain parts—that, for instance, of the hero. This type of artiste, they say, is non-existent. I have never heard such nonsense. But to find them, you must, of course, look for them.

Producers make the mistake of seeking always in the same old circle—the stage and the theatrical agencies. If they would look elsewhere, they would soon find what they want. One has only to think of the splendid types of manhood to be found even now, after five years of war, in our regiments.

Some years ago, before the war, I passed a camp of the Labour Service at Bergdorf. Immediately my car was surrounded by a crowd of bronzed and laughing young men. I remember remarking to one of my companions: "Why don't our film producers come to places like this in search of talent? In a year or two it would be possible to transform one of these lads into an accomplished actor, even if it were just for one particular part for which they are seeking a star."

In this respect Leni Riefenstahl has the right idea: she scours the villages in search of the peasant types she requires.

In the nature of things, the opinion of an art critic must not be accepted as an irrevocable and unassailable truth. His criticism is, after all, only the expression of his own personal opinion.

When in ten different newspapers ten different critics give their opinion on one and the same work, ten separate personal opinions emerge—unless, of course, they have previously received instructions from interested parties. Has such an opinion any value? I doubt it. We are too prone to forget that the ancients disregarded the art critic. They judged a work on its merits, as they saw them, which, after all, is the natural method of selection.

Art criticism, as it has developed since the beginning of the nineteenth century, means either the death of a work of art, since the critics never cease to tear it to pieces; or the death of the press, since the public could have no faith in a press in which the critic of each individual newspaper gives a completely different story on exactly the same work. If we were to be deprived of art critics, we should not lose very much! One single critique signed with a well-known name may destroy the aspirations of an artist for as long as twenty years.

Examples are not lacking. How many of the artists whom we admire greatly today were previously castigated by the oracles of the times! What is true of painters is true of artists in other fields. Do not forget that a single adverse critique by E. T. A. Hoffmann[614] was sufficient gravely to prejudice the chances of success *of Der Freischütz*. And yet this work, with its deep harmonies, had all the ingredients which should have appealed to the romanticism in Hoffmann.

Think of Wagner and how he was torn to bits for ten years by the critics! Had there been no one who appreciated him, it is questionable whether he would have continued with his work. The same thing happened with *Carmen*.

And now the critics who tore these masterpieces to shreds are completely and utterly forgotten, and the works live on.

---

[614] Ernst Theodor Wilhelm Hoffman (1776–1822), using the name E.T.A. Hoffmann (Ernst Theodor Amadeus Hoffmann, with the Amadeus being taken from his hero Wolfgang Amadeus Mozart), was an author, music critic, and artist who became important in the Romantic Movement.

23rd March 1944, midday
Charm of the Rhineland—And of other parts of Germany—The marvellous countryside of Bohemia and Moravia

I saw the Rhine for the first time in 1914, when I was on my way to the Western Front. The feelings which the sight of this historic stream inspired in me remain forever graven on my heart. The kindness and spontaneity of the Rhinelanders also made a profound impression on me; everywhere they received us and fêted us in a most touching manner.

The evening we reached Aachen, I remember thinking that I should never forget that day for the rest of my life; and indeed the memory of it remains today as vivid as ever, and every time I find myself on the banks of the Rhine I re-live again the wondrous experience of my first sight of it.

This is no doubt one of the main reasons—quite apart from the unrivalled beauty of the countryside—that impels me each year to revisit the Rhineland.

There are other parts of Germany, apart from the Rhineland, which give me intense pleasure to visit—the Kyffhaeuser, the forests of Thuringia, the Harz and the Black Forest. It is most exhilarating to drive for miles through the woods and forests, far away from the throng.

One of my greatest delights has always been to picnic quietly somewhere on the roadside; it was not always easy, for our column of cars would often be pursued by a crowd of motorists, eager to see their Führer off duty, and we had to employ all sorts of ruses to shake off these friendly and well-meaning pursuers; sometimes, for instance, I would drive up a side-turning, leaving the column to continue along the main road.

Our pursuers would then overtake the cars of the column one by one, and, failing to find me, would go ever faster in the hope of overtaking me farther on. In this way we managed occasionally to snatch a few hours of peace and tranquillity.

On one occasion, I remember, a family out gathering mushrooms came suddenly on our picnic party. In a few moments these kindly folk had alerted the neighbouring village and the whole population was surging towards us, filling the air with their shouts of *"Heil."*

It is a great pity that Germans know so little of their own country. Since 1938 the number of beauty spots within the boundaries of the Reich has increased considerably.

In addition to Austria, we have the wonderful countryside of Bohemia and Moravia, which is a closed book to all but a few Germans.

Some of them may have heard of the virgin forests of Bohemia, but how many have ever seen them?

I have a collection of photographs taken in Bohemia, and they remind one of the vast forests of the tropics. To visit all the beauties of his country, a German today would require to take a holiday in a different district each year for the rest of his life.

17th May 1944, evening

Our religious policy—The State misses an opportunity—Modernism

Throughout the course of German history, the State has seldom had the opportunity of exercising any influence on the internal evolution of the Church. Perhaps the greatest opportunity offered was during the Modernist period round about 1907–1909.

It is true that the Modernist movement was in many respects nothing more than a recrudescence of the old Catholic way of life; but in many other respects it was something quite new.

If the State had then had the skill to exploit these aspirations to its own advantage, it would most probably have been in a position to found a German National Church wholly independent of Rome.

It must not be forgotten that the Modernists were most sincere in their desires to reach agreement with the Evangelical Church; the State, then, had a golden opportunity of building a bridge between these two Christian faiths.

But the State was too weak, and missed its chance. It had none of the necessary vision to grasp the opportunity and to make the most of it; and so the game fell easily into the hands of the established Church, which had but to continue to threaten and to excommunicate. For a priest in his fifties and defrocked carries no weight at all.

The Modernists themselves were so tormented with threats that in the end they, too, were compelled to submit.

The wrath of the Church constitutes in life no idle threat; in the face of real crisis, the Church does not limit itself to threats of Hellfire and Purgatory in the Hereafter, but has tangible means of making life a misery for its victims on this earth as well.

The Modernist movement gradually collapsed, and the introduction of the oath of absolute obedience to Church tenets imposed on all newly ordained priests gave it its final death-blow.

16th May 1944, evening
Research and Instruction—State encouragement for free research—The two tasks of research worker and teacher—Kant,[615] *Schopenhauer, Nietzsche—Instruction must be State-directed—My relations with the economists—The economists change their minds*

The theory that independent research and instruction are two fields of activity which must be indissolubly related is false. Each has an entirely different function, each calls for men of a different type, and each must be approached by the State from a different angle.

Research must remain free and unfettered by any State restriction. The facts which it establishes represent Truth, and Truth is never evil. It is the duty of the State to support and further the efforts of research in every way, even when its activities hold no promise of immediate, or even early, advantage from the material or economic point of view. It may well be that its results will be of value, or indeed will represent tremendous progress, only to the generation of the future.

Instruction, on the other hand, should not, in my opinion, enjoy a like liberty of action. Its liberty is limited by the interests of the State, and can therefore never be totally unrestricted; it has not the right to claim that same degree of independence which I most willingly concede to research.

The attributes demanded of a successful teacher and a research worker are fundamentally different, and are seldom to be found together in the single individual. The man of research is by nature extremely cautious; he never ceases to work, to ponder, to weigh and to doubt, and his suspicious nature breeds in him an inclination towards solitude and most rigorous self-criticism.

Of quite a different type is the ideal teacher. He has little or no concern with the endless riddles of the infinite—with something, that is, which is so infinitely greater than himself. He is a man whose task it is to impart knowledge and understanding to men who do not possess them and who, therefore, are generally his intellectual inferiors; and in consequence he is a man who is often inclined to be pedantically dogmatic.

There are many men endowed with a genius for research who are useless as teachers, just as there are brilliant teachers who have no gift whatever for research and creative work; yet all of them, in their re-

---

[615] Immanuel Kant (1724–1804), a Prussian philosopher and one of the foremost Enlightenment thinkers.

spective spheres, make contributions of outstanding value to the sum of human knowledge.

I do not agree with the idea that liberty of research should be restricted solely to the fields of natural science. It should embrace also the domain of thought and philosophy, which, in essence, are themselves but the logical prolongation of scientific research. By taking the data furnished by science and placing them under the microscope of reason, philosophy gives us a logical conception of the universe as it is. The boundary between research and philosophy is nebulous and constantly moving.

In the Great Hall of the Linz Library are the busts of Kant, Schopenhauer and Nietzsche, the greatest of our thinkers, in comparison with whom the British, the French and the Americans have nothing to offer. His complete refutation of the teachings which were a heritage from the Middle Ages, and of the dogmatic philosophy of the Church, is the greatest of the services which Kant has rendered to us.

It is on the foundation of Kant's theory of knowledge that Schopenhauer built the edifice of his philosophy, and it is Schopenhauer who annihilated the pragmatism of Hegel.[616] I carried Schopenhauer's works with me throughout the whole of the Great War. From him I learned a great deal. Schopenhauer's pessimism, which springs partly, I think, from his own line of philosophical thought and partly from subjective feeling and the experiences of his own personal life, has been far surpassed by Nietzsche.

It is the custom in Germany for students to pass from one university to another during the course of their studies—a custom, incidentally, which no other country has. But it would be false to assume that this variety in instruction is a safeguard against uniformity of outlook, for although the professors of the various universities fight among themselves, they are all, fundamentally and at heart, in complete agreement. I came to realise this clearly through my contacts with the economists. This must have been about 1929.

At that time we published a paper on certain aspects of the economic problem. Immediately a whole company of national economists of all sorts, and from a variety of universities, joined forces and signed a circular in which they unanimously condemned our economic proposals. I made one attempt to have a serious discussion with one of the

[616] Georg Hegel (1770–1831), the philosopher widely regarded as one of the most important figures in German idealism.

most renowned of them, and one who was regarded by his colleagues as a revolutionary in economic thought—Zwiedineck.[617] The results were disastrous! At the time the State had floated a loan of two million seven hundred thousand marks for the construction of a road. I told Zwiedineck that I regarded this way of financing a project as foolish in the extreme. The life of the road in question would be some fifteen years; but the amortisation of the capital involved would continue for eighty years.

What the Government was really doing was to evade an immediate financial obligation by transferring the charges to the men of the next generation and, indeed, of the generation after. I insisted that nothing could be more unsound, and that what the Government should really do was to take radical steps to reduce the rate of interest and thus to render capital more fluid.

I next argued that the gold standard, the fixing of rates of exchange and so forth were shibboleths which I had never regarded and never would regard as weighty and immutable principles of economy. Money, to me, was simply a token of exchange for work done, and its value depended absolutely on the value of the work accomplished. Where money did not represent services rendered, I insisted, it had no value at all. Zwiedineck was horrified and very excited. Such ideas, he declared, would upset the accepted economic principles of the entire world, and the putting of them into practice would cause a breakdown of the world's political economy.

When, later, after our assumption of power, I put my theories into practice, the economists were not in the least discountenanced, but calmly set to work to prove by scientific argument that my theories were, indeed, sound economy!

Night of 29th–30th November 1944
Jesus and Saint Paul—Christianity, a Jewish manoeuvre—Christianity and Communism—National Socialism, the implacable enemy of everything Jewish

Jesus was most certainly not a Jew. The Jews would never have handed one of their own people to the Roman courts; they would have condemned Him themselves. It is quite probable that a large number of the descendants of the Roman legionaries, mostly Gauls, were living in Galilee, and Jesus was probably one of them. His mother may well have

---

[617] Otto Wilhelm Helmut von Zwiedineck (1871–1957), professor of economics at the University of Munich.

been a Jewess. Jesus fought against the materialism of His age, and, therefore, against the Jews.

Paul of Tarsus, who was originally one of the most stubborn enemies of the Christians, suddenly realised the immense possibilities of using, intelligently and for other ends, an idea which was exercising such great powers of fascination. He realised that the judicious exploitation of this idea among non-Jews would give him far greater power in the world than would the promise of material profit to the Jews themselves. It was then that the future St. Paul distorted with diabolical cunning the Christian idea. Out of this idea, which was a declaration of war on the golden calf, on the egotism and the materialism of the Jews, he created a rallying point for slaves of all kinds against the elite, the masters and those in dominant authority.

The religion fabricated by Paul of Tarsus, which was later called Christianity, is nothing but the Communism of today.

Bormann intervened. Jewish methods, he said, have never varied in their essentials. Everywhere they have stirred up the plebs against the ruling classes. Everywhere they have fostered discontent against the established power. For these are the seeds which produce the crop they hope later to gather. Everywhere they fan the flames of hatred between peoples of the same blood. It is they who invented class-warfare, and the repudiation of this theory must therefore always be an anti-Jewish measure. In the same way, any doctrine which is anti-Communist, any doctrine which is anti-Christian must, ipso facto, *be anti-Jewish as well.*

The National Socialist doctrine is therefore anti-Jewish in excelsis, *for it is both anti-Communist and anti-Christian. National Socialism is solid to the core, and the whole of its strength is concentrated against the Jews, even in matters which appear to have a purely social aspect and are designed for the furtherance of the social amenities of our own people.*

The Führer concluded: Burgdorf[618] has just given me a paper which deals with the relationship between Communism and Christianity. It is comforting to see how, even in these days, the fatal relationship between the two is daily becoming clearer to the human intelligence.

---

[618] Wilhelm Burgdorf (1895–1945), General and chief adjutant to Adolf Hitler.

Index

A

Abegg, Claire von 194, 262
Abetz, Otto 248, 304
Abortion 82, 99, 201, 202, 283, 337, 421
Aden 546
Africa 81, 102, 152, 154, 156, 157, 160, 280, 289, 423
Afrika Korps 490, 512
Agriculture 12, 58, 140, 363, 480, 551, 552, 615
Ahrenberg, , Engelbert-Maria von 546
Air transport 491
Air warfare 271
Albania 155, 367, 369, 480
Alexander the Great 391, 455
Alfieri, Dino 367, 368, 369
Alfonso XIII 619
Alsace (and Lorraine) 15, 414, 417, 418, 492, 551
Alsdorf, Ludwig 586
Altmark, ship 563
Alvensleben, Joachim Martin 443
Amann, Max 122, 155, 191, 290–293, 295, 305, 306, 317, 410, 412, 425
Ambras treasures 41
American civilization 576
American credulity 538
American military courts in Britain 544
American motor industry 367
Ancient Egypt 505
Ancient Greece 467
Ancient Rome 1
Anglican Church 50
Anglo-Jewish press 518
Anschluss 294, 401, 627
Anti-aircraft defence 598
Antonescu, Ion 26, 27, 41, 42, 57, 58, 106, 159, 198, 297, 342, 555, 622

Archangel 509
Arent, Benno von 233, 294
Arminius (Hermann) 68, 384, 386, 432
Aryan 1, 7, 65, 75, 111, 112, 132, 134, 136, 218, 390, 493, 495
Asia 20, 32, 34, 81, 110, 204, 276, 288, 459, 521, 580
Atatürk, Kemal 198, 204, 334, 343, 541
Atheism 4
Atlantic Wall 424, 545
Auer, Erhard 240
Australia 135, 265, 325, 430
Autobahn 2, 3, 174, 175, 250, 297, 298, 431, 437, 515, 516, 517, 631
Axmann, Artur 408, 409, 465

B

Backe, Herbert 588
Balbo, Italo 547, 548
Baldwin, Stanley 91, 606, 607
Ballerstedt, Otto 233
Baltic States 13, 29, 523, 577, 580
Barcelona 463
Bastian, Max 275
Battle of Coburg 1922 120ff
Battleships vulnerable to air attack 632
Baur, Hans 156, 173, 174, 491
Bavarian national costume 560
Bavarians 580
Bayreuth 10, 214, 215, 216, 250, 253, 283, 307, 308, 317, 344, 398, 399, 406
Beaverbrook, Baron 291, 613, 614
Bechstein family 187, 194, 254, 307
Bees and ants 542
Beethoven, Ludwig 162, 214, 338, 339, 632, 633
Belgium 24, 25, 47, 113, 303, 304, 478, 479, 527, 543, 600, 601, 621
Beneš, Edvard 180, 209, 498

Benghazi 236

Berghof 145, 186, 187, 384, 396, 398, 400, 411, 531

Bergius process 63

Berlichingen, Gottfried von 496, 497, 632

Berlin Philharmonic Orchestra 398

Berlin to be renamed "Germania" 466

Bessarabia 11, 435

Bible 6, 50, 72, 166, 221, 279, 417, 430, 456, 457, 458, 462, 538

Bible is "Jewish mumbo-jumbo" 457

Big battleships 632

Bismarck, Otto 15, 16, 70, 120, 121, 246, 250, 253, 286, 356, 428, 466, 476, 481–483, 576–579, 609, 629, 630, 632

Bismarck, ship 632

Black market 471, 568

Black Sea 36, 45, 266, 334, 425, 594

Blaschke, Hugo 98

Blitzkrieg 152

Blomberg, Fritz von 381, 382, 440, 443, 444, 565

Blondi 509

Blood Order 106

Blue Division 459, 506, 508

Bock, Alexander Friedrich von 483

Bodenschatz, Karl-Heinrich 485, 504

Bolshevik revolution 160

Bolshevisation of Europe 588

Bolshevism 3, 4, 5, 11, 18, 26, 30, 34, 38, 44, 65, 66, 68, 76, 77, 108, 110, 127, 130, 160, 164, 179, 226, 238, 277, 284, 295, 302, 303, 460, 528, 541

Boris III 343, 344, 346, 349, 369, 562

Bormann, Martin 180, 184, 281, 321, 335, 349, 395, 404, 408, 409, 419, 459, 468, 472, 473, 475, 478, 489, 504, 516, 523, 528, 530, 534, 537, 538, 540, 568, 643

Bose, Subhas Chandra 325, 586

Böttcher, Karl 248

Bouhler, Philipp 127

Bourgeoisie 15, 16, 94, 118, 121, 135, 203, 208–210, 311, 324, 338, 348, 365, 402, 421, 429, 430, 547

Brahms 181, 182

Brauchitsch, Walther von 164, 469

Brazil 229, 352, 620

Breker, Arno 62

Britain started the air bombing 624

British Empire 80, 81, 137, 163, 305, 487, 520, 553, 600, 615, 616, 623

British lies 538

British Parliament 413

British policy in India 585

Brown House 261

Bruckmann, Elsa 263, 316, 326, 450

Bruckner, Josef Anton 84, 181, 182, 451, 583

Brüning, Heinrich 240, 337

Budapest 393, 394, 585, 587, 596, 597, 598, 621

Buddha 53, 304, 457

Buerkel, Heinrich 616

Bulgaria 101, 209, 334, 335, 343, 346, 349, 369, 578

Buna rubber 230

Bürckel, Joseph 555, 556

bureaucracy 6, 14, 211, 213, 402, 476, 534, 549

Bureaucracy 14

Burgdorf, Wilhelm 643

Bürgerbrau assassination attempt 399

Busch, Fritz 283

Busch, Wilhelmina 287

C

Caesar, Julius 100, 154, 479, 530, 553, 623

Cameroons 64, 606

Canada 60, 81, 281, 613

Canaris, Wilhelm 507

Cancer 101, 136, 330
Cannae 21
Capitalism 18, 66, 319
Carol II 11
Catholicism 43, 50, 76, 78–80, 96,
    126, 141, 148, 195, 240, 283,
    300, 325, 358, 362–364, 370,
    371, 385, 394, 417, 418, 421,
    449, 457, 459, 464, 467, 492,
    494, 495, 540, 542, 558, 559,
    577, 588, 605, 623, 639
Chamberlain, Eva 316
Chamberlain, Houston Stewart 128
Chamberlain, Neville 91, 162, 163,
    215, 225, 226, 563, 606, 607
Channel Islands 520, 589
Charlemagne 42, 258, 333, 336, 337,
    374, 465, 494, 581, 620
Charles Martel 596
Chemical fertilisers 498, 624
China 85, 158, 162, 423, 480, 588
Christianity 4, 5, 29, 38, 39, 43, 44, 49,
    51, 52, 65, 66, 68, 76, 77, 109,
    110, 127–130, 195, 225, 226,
    232, 233, 258, 276, 277, 284,
    295, 296, 302, 305, 336, 347,
    348, 350, 370, 371, 541, 558,
    597, 642, 643
Christianity and Communism 642
Christ, Jesus 65, 66, 127, 135, 148,
    221, 505, 542, 642, 643
Churchill, Winston 62, 157, 158, 162,
    164, 165, 178, 179, 183, 210,
    226, 236, 245, 246, 264, 265,
    266, 272, 281, 323, 324, 325,
    373, 478, 480, 481, 487, 511,
    512, 553, 562, 563, 606–609,
    612, 613, 616, 622, 625
Ciano, Gian 87, 596
Civil Service 91, 92, 105, 138, 306,
    323, 526, 583, 584
Clausen, Frits 304
Clemenceau, Georges 607
Coal will be replaced by renewable
    energy 185

Coburg 120, 122, 238, 280, 292
Codreanu, Corneliu 57
Colonies 13, 20, 30, 63, 112, 230, 235,
    296, 353, 376, 388, 417, 525,
    546, 550, 554, 557, 585, 594,
    600, 619, 623
Commune 78, 497
Communism 15, 27, 244, 353, 529,
    622, 643
Communism in Saxony 15
Concentration camps 25, 56, 180, 353,
    362, 461, 499, 534
Concordat 49, 50, 491, 492, 493, 495,
    496
Confucius 85, 457
Conscientious objectors 458, 593
Conscription 563, 603
Constantine, emperor 225, 226
Constantinople 395, 541
Contraception 522
Copernicus, Nicolaus 284, 285, 394,
    454
Corinth, Lovis 451, 628
Council of Constance 433
Counter-Reformation 6
Cramer-Klett, Theodor von 540
Crete 2, 180, 413, 563, 583, 596
Crimea 2, 12, 29, 30, 59, 60, 91, 97,
    103, 151, 424, 425, 489, 515,
    516, 534, 553, 597
Cripps, Stafford 323, 324, 325, 486,
    553
Croats 5, 83, 298, 420
Croesus 64, 287
Crüwell, Ludwig 512
Cyprus 2, 521
Czechoslovakia 177, 180, 181, 369,
    432, 496
Czechs 30, 130, 161, 180, 181, 203,
    207–209, 235, 357, 358, 369,
    384, 385, 419, 431, 432, 438,
    439, 498, 636

D

Daladier, Édouard 162, 163, 264

Dancing 278, 288, 301, 387, 560, 617
Dante Alighieri 6, 7
Danube 45, 297, 298, 299, 318, 322,
    394, 395, 481, 489, 530, 587,
    594, 612
Danube Shipping Company 322, 530
Danzig 15, 393, 415, 419, 471, 492
Darlan, Jean 354, 360
Darré, Richard Walther 14
Death penalty 26, 58, 98, 268, 428,
    448, 573, 574
Decadent art 630
Deforestation 96, 505
De Gaulle, Charles 391
Degrelle, Léon 478
Denmark 47, 64, 112, 288, 303, 304,
    305, 465, 466, 602
Destiny 622
Deterding, Henri 229, 230
Deutsche Kolonialgesellschaft 30
Deutsches Museum 627, 628
Dieppe raid 590, 593, 625
Diesel engine 491
Dietl, Eduard 9, 120, 123, 124, 172,
    469
Dietrich, Hans 120, 121, 292
Dietrich, Otto 89, 293, 428, 478, 490,
    517, 518, 544, 546
Dietrich, Sepp (Josef) 120, 121, 125,
    136, 137, 140, 146, 148, 153,
    154, 155, 156, 157, 159, 160,
    174, 186, 187, 188, 189, 193,
    194, 201, 234, 262, 263, 282,
    292, 293, 305, 307, 308, 318,
    333, 393
Difficulties of the maintenance of
    organised society 600
Dincklage, Karl 475
Dinter, Artur 291
Dodd, William 90
Dogs 121, 136, 153, 192, 220, 221, 541
Donetz basin 396
Dorpmueller, Julius 143
Dresden 399

Drexler, Anton 188, 194
Duce, see Mussolini
Duelling 200, 202
Duke of Normandy 520
Duke of Windsor 563, 606, 607
Dutch 13, 17, 21, 29, 81, 112, 129,
    134, 143, 158, 229, 248, 303,
    355–357, 479, 526, 527, 545,
    549, 623, 631
Dutch Legion 355, 479

E

East Karelia 554
East Prussia 21, 198, 443, 461, 475,
    492, 505, 552
Eben Emael 61
Ebert, Friedrich 240, 325
Eckart, Dietrich 125, 136–138, 140,
    153, 186–190, 193–195, 201,
    234, 262, 263, 282, 305, 307,
    308, 318, 333, 469, 558
Economists 640
Eden, Anthony 62, 165, 588
Education 348
Effects of the meat diet 509
Egypt 102, 318, 485, 487, 490, 505,
    511, 512, 513
Eigruber, August 635
Eisner, Kurt 124, 234
Emperors by election 474
Epp, Franz 253, 295, 619
Error of Almeria 606
Esser, Hermann 194, 290, 395
Esthonia 6
Ethiopia 513
Europe must be a federation 289

F

Falangists 141, 463, 508, 595
Fallersleben, Hoffmann von 490, 584
Falsification of war communiqués 500
Farmers 521
Fascism 226, 235, 237, 464, 507, 515,
    528, 547

Fats 560
Fear of the Unknown 632
Felsennest 60, 61, 218, 300
Finland 19, 47, 352, 353, 354, 381, 456, 469, 530, 577
Fischer-Tropsch process 19
Fish, birds and the design of aircraft and ships 452
Flamands 479
Flemish and Dutch peasants 549
Florence 7, 239, 275, 335, 387, 552
Ford, Henry 249
Foreign press 503
Foreign workers 407
Forster, Albert 82, 393, 415–419, 471, 473
Four Year Plan 35, 49, 63, 88, 111, 210, 230, 300, 523, 565, 566
Foxl 206
Franco, Francisco 459, 498, 500, 506, 507, 508, 542, 595, 615, 622
François-Poncet, André 245–248, 485, 488, 489
Franco's policy differs from National Socialism 506
Frank, Hans 358
Franz Josef 303, 608
Frederick II 72, 111
Frederick the Great 11, 27, 54, 56, 69–71, 96, 109, 110, 111, 115, 153, 232, 296, 317, 333, 339, 340, 355, 422, 568, 576, 577, 590, 621, 629
Freedom of the Press 425
Freemasons 110, 252, 384, 589
Free Trade 499
Fricke, Kurt 80, 205
Frick, Wilhelm 92, 138, 332, 333, 359, 391, 444
Fritsch, Werner von 134, 152, 564
Frugality of the Italians 498
Führer, origin of the title 153
Funk, Walther 45, 186, 230, 384, 407, 446

Furtwängler, Gustav 283, 396, 398, 579
Future of technology 627

G

Galen, Clemens von 79, 491, 495
Galilee 66, 642
Galland, Adolf 232
Gambling 144, 278, 318, 320, 321
Gansser, Emil 194, 195, 559
Gas propellants 529
Gause, Alfred 159, 160
German-Americans 552
German colonisation 545
German colonists in the Eastern Territories 511
Germania 466
Germanic races 602
Germanic Reich, as opposed to Germany 353, 356, 357
Germanic tribes 289, 420
Germanisation of certain peoples 420
German Museum of Art 483
German replaces Latin 582
Gestapo 401, 449, 572
Gibraltar 595
Giesler, Paul 394, 395, 398
Gneisenau, August Wilhelm von 95
Goebbels, Josef 17, 78, 140, 200, 295, 391, 392, 449, 469, 470, 472–474, 514, 580
Goethe, Johann 214, 278, 608, 609, 617
Gold myth 553
Goltz, Rüdiger von der 25
Göring, Hermann 146, 149, 151, 161, 173, 178, 181, 182, 190, 211, 230, 243, 274, 317, 347, 365, 403, 442, 443, 472, 565, 592, 599
Goths 5, 83, 489, 553, 554
Grandes, Muñoz 506, 622
Grand Mufti of Jerusalem 488
Greater Germanic State 479

Great German Reich 555
Great War (First World War) 3, 8–10,
    13, 23, 27, 32, 34, 37, 43, 44, 47,
    55, 63, 70, 76, 82, 105, 108, 110,
    130, 131, 148, 152, 177, 178,
    204, 206, 210, 225, 236, 247,
    267, 282, 319, 335, 343, 346,
    367, 388, 429, 433, 515, 538,
    564, 578, 588, 589, 641
Greece 68, 258, 259, 502, 505, 592,
    627
Grock the clown 618
Günther, Hans F. K. 82, 418
Günther, Otto ("Krumel") 1
Gürtner, Franz 83, 107, 116, 117, 256,
    331, 332, 461, 462, 572, 610

H
Habsburg dynasty 338, 629
Habsburg, Otto von 621
Hácha, Emil 180, 181, 208, 233, 235,
    435, 438, 497, 498
Halifax, Earl (Edward Wood) 176, 179
Hanfstaengl, Ernst 220, 503, 504, 621
Hannibal 455
Hanseatic League 329
Harvest Festival of Bückeburg 401
Hasenauer, Baron Karl von 183
Häusser, Ludwig Christian 253
Head of the State 474
Hegel, Georg 641
Hermitage 2, 3, 132, 254
Hess, Rudolf 150, 195, 200, 201, 256,
    257, 261
Hewel, Walther 88, 89, 124, 219, 238,
    361, 368, 507, 508, 534, 538
Heydrich, Reinhard 76, 455, 456, 461,
    465, 494, 497
Hierl, Konstantin 553
Himmler, Henirich 25, 113, 134, 147,
    213, 260, 280, 304, 354, 357,
    358, 362, 384, 406, 482, 534
Hindenburg, Paul von 154, 197, 198,
    365, 414, 440, 441, 444, 445,
    586

Hitler, Adolf,
— childhood memories 166
— enters Austria 401
— memories of the first war 543
— school-day memories 625
— smoked as a young man 318
Hitler, Paula 561, 609
Hitler Youth 212, 379, 409, 465, 466,
    504, 605
Hoare, Samuel 225, 227
Hoffman, E. T. A. 637
Hoffmann, Heinrich 145, 155, 189,
    193, 194, 206, 255, 295, 318,
    450, 451, 490, 537, 584, 614,
    637
Holy Roman Empire 337, 600, 601
Hörbiger, Hans 220, 222, 283, 285,
    286, 394, 450
Hore-Belisha, Leslie 62, 163, 165, 176
Horoscope 520
Horthy, Miklós 28, 458, 459, 460, 578,
    596, 597, 621
Hötzendorf, Conrad von 44
House of German Art 327, 451, 483,
    537
House of Habsburg 30, 31, 110, 130,
    131, 338, 357, 384, 386, 438,
    490, 548, 597, 629
House of Hohenzollern 30, 31
Hugenberg, Alfred 197, 410, 411, 442,
    443, 531
Hungarians 393, 555, 585
Hunting 82, 87, 102, 417, 532, 609
Hydrogen, predicted use as energy
    source 19

I
Iceland 166, 613
IG. Farben 230
Importance of food supply 545
Incas 97
Income tax 551
India 11, 19, 20, 26, 28, 36, 81, 114,
    157, 159, 160, 165, 166, 175,
    176, 179, 183, 184, 210, 235,

265, 312, 323–325, 384, 385,
437, 480, 481, 487, 490, 577,
585, 586, 587, 600, 613
Indian population increase 184
Industrialisation of Russia 590
Inflation 54, 56, 193, 263, 290, 589
Inquisition 257, 285
Intellectual and artistic poverty 630
Intelligence and a knowledge of for-
eign languages 617
Intelligence and instinct 542
Intuition 13, 100
Invasion from the West 544
Iron Cross 105, 430, 575, 622
Islam 5, 110, 335, 347, 512
Istanbul 345, 395, 541

J
Japan 30, 81, 134, 135, 143, 157, 158,
162, 165, 175, 204, 265, 266,
277, 293, 328, 352, 370, 381,
423, 433, 434, 485, 591
Japanese in Australia 135
Jeschonnek, Hans 232
Jesuits 6
Jews 5, 56, 57–59, 62, 65, 66–68, 76,
103–105, 124, 125, 135, 136,
138, 163, 170, 178, 209, 210,
227, 229, 236, 258, 276, 277,
282, 284, 286–288, 290, 292,
293, 305, 307, 308, 323, 326,
327, 329–331, 343, 344, 347–
351, 365, 367, 383, 394, 398,
411, 414, 420, 426, 429–431,
439, 447, 457, 469, 485, 486,
500–503, 518, 524, 531, 532,
537, 545, 557, 558, 568, 569,
572, 588, 597, 605–610, 613,
616, 617, 628, 636, 642, 643
Joan of Arc 489
Jodl, Alfred 87, 213, 319, 506, 507,
525, 565
Julian the Apostate 65, 66, 225, 226
Jurists 91, 114, 117, 212, 233, 300,
330–333, 403

Justice and injustice 610
Justification of use of force 414

K
Kahr, Gustav 102, 244, 255, 559
Kaiser Wilhelm II 452
Kai-shek, Chiang 323, 328
Kállay, Miklos 459, 460
Kant, Immanuel 640, 641
Kapp putsch 548
Kaulbach, Wilhelm von 616
Kautsky 241
Keitel, Wilhelm 86, 90, 155, 162, 356,
506, 507, 510, 531, 538
Kempka, Erich 216, 217, 219, 274,
400, 517
Kepler, Johan 285
Keppler, Wilhelm 112, 230, 533
Kerrl, Hanns 129
Kesselring, Albert 272, 547, 579
Kiel 156
Kiev 2
Killinger, Manfred Freiherr von 274,
275
King Theodoric 386
Kirdorf, Emil 527
Klimsch, Fritz 450
Kluge, Günther von 61, 82, 86, 511
Knight's Cross 105, 106, 436
Koch, Erich 408, 475, 625
Krancke, Theodor 452, 491, 519, 532,
560, 595, 624
Kreis, Wilhelm 537
Krupp Works 436
Kurschildgen, Heinrich 112, 533
Kurusu 146
Kvaternik, Slavko 83

L
Labour Service, see *Reichsarbeitsdienst*
Lammers, Hans 116, 212, 213, 408,
410, 492, 495, 530, 584
Latvia 4, 605
Lauböck, Theodor 187

Lauterbacher, Hartmann 408, 409, 589
Laval, Pierre 422, 424
Lawyers 17, 25, 26, 114, 151, 202, 234, 261, 281, 305, 306, 329, 332, 333, 476, 521, 522, 568, 575
League of Nations 431, 432, 433, 446
Legislators and Magistrates 568
Lehmann, J.F. 204
Leibstandarte SS Adolf Hitler 146, 385, 511
Leningrad 178, 352, 354, 534, 623
Leopold, Josef 612
Ley, Robert 60, 306, 411, 521, 545
Liberalism 3, 175, 629
Libraries of the ancient world 77
Libya 236, 512
Liebel, Friedrich 132, 133, 139, 393, 404, 505
Lines of communication in Russia 590
Linge, Heinz 218
Linz 41, 135–137, 145, 146, 169, 170, 172, 177, 182, 185, 282–285, 393–395, 397, 398, 403, 404, 451, 628, 633, 635, 641
Lipski, Józef 246, 247
Litvinov, Maxim 480
Lloyd George, David 162, 229, 231, 515, 517, 588, 606, 622
Lohse, Hinrich 408
Lossow, Otto von 244, 255
Louis XIV 482
Louis XVI 428
Luckner, Graf 519
Ludendorff, Erich 140, 195, 250, 251, 255, 256, 402, 414, 429, 533, 586
Ludwig I, Emperor of Germany 35
Ludwig I of Bavaria 449, 450
Lueger, Karl 130, 131, 426
Lufthansa 53, 173
Luther, Hans 381
Luther, Martin 6, 7, 152, 195, 362, 381, 382, 540

Lutze, Viktor, junior 149
Lutze, Viktor snr 149
Lützow, Ludwig von 559

M
Maginot Line 628
Makart, Hans 214, 215, 616
Malta 156, 196, 197, 563
March on Rome, 1922 6, 7, 237
Maria Theresa 208
Marriage 78, 79, 90, 144, 168, 194, 218, 219, 309, 311, 389, 390, 414, 421, 422, 527, 558, 580, 581, 623, 624
Martel, Charles 596, 597
Marxism 7, 79, 170, 241, 365, 367
Marxists 276, 365, 366, 402
Marx, Karl 65, 69, 277
Maurice 147, 190, 217, 253
Meat 391
Meissner, Otto 117, 197, 382, 444, 498, 610
Men and machines 535
Mesopotamia 548
Metal industry 436
Meteorological forecasts 53, 54
Methods of colonisation 585
Metternich, Prince 629, 630
Michael, King of Rumania 106, 297, 342
Milch, Erhard 232
Minesweepers 536
Ministry of Foreign Affairs 88, 89
Missionaries 20, 60, 281
Modernists 639
Mola, Emilio 542
Monarchy 11, 30, 107, 130, 269, 275, 276, 340, 459, 490, 500, 507, 547, 548, 595, 601, 619
Montez, Lola 323, 328, 449, 450, 542
Morell, Theo 181, 352
Morell, Theodor 180, 181, 352
Moscow 2, 3, 445, 550, 556, 562, 608, 609, 613

Mosley, Oswald 176, 180, 225, 227, 295, 411, 563, 607
Mother's Cross 105
Motor roads going East 515
Mozart, Wolfgang 182, 214, 278, 308, 450, 451, 632, 633
Mufti, Grand 234, 254, 255, 488
Müller, Adolf 122, 123, 148, 217, 254, 255, 272, 273, 306, 308, 309, 412, 579
Munich Pinakothek 186
Mussert, Anton 134, 304, 354, 355, 356
Mussolini, Benito 6–8, 41, 57, 119, 124, 127, 129, 152, 164, 238–240, 275, 276, 347, 368, 369, 386, 387, 398, 404, 408, 479, 480, 506, 512, 513, 519, 526–528, 529, 541, 547, 548, 553, 576, 579, 595, 596, 614
Mussolini, Edda 386
Mutschmann, Martin 132, 283, 411

N
Nadolny, Rudolf 445
Napoleon I 225, 338, 339, 340, 355, 391, 428, 501, 520, 568, 581, 630
Narvik 271, 272, 437
Narvik landing 272
Nationalisation 323
National Socialism 4, 7, 18, 28, 31, 32, 53, 54, 83, 120, 129, 137, 144, 205, 210, 226, 228, 231, 296, 307, 308, 326, 379, 380, 435, 441, 465, 467, 477, 479, 507, 511, 551
National Socialism and Fascism 547
National Socialism not for export 435
National Socialist education 439
Natural law 4, 44, 331
Naval warfare 518, 595
Neanderthal man 199, 200
Negroes 40, 60, 128, 546, 587

Nehru, Jawaharlal 325
Nero 76, 78
Neurath, Konstantin von 208, 231, 444, 567, 613
New Zealand 210, 265
Nicene Creed 542
Niemöller, Martin 361
Nietzsche, Friedrich 77, 640, 641
Nordic blood 422
North Africa 97, 183, 204, 423, 505, 512, 548
Norway 19, 47, 93, 113, 204, 210, 272, 303, 353, 357, 388, 409, 438, 465, 521, 548, 563, 589, 590, 595, 600, 601
Noske, Gustav 141, 240
Nuremberg 103, 120, 132, 133, 137, 138, 139, 149, 156, 186, 214–216, 241, 246, 254, 292, 298, 317, 365, 367, 393, 402, 404, 406, 414, 503–506, 576, 598
Nursery for film actors 636

O
Odessa 26, 27, 57
Oilfields in the Caucasus 529
Old Fritz (Frederick the Great) 482
Old Testament 430, 456, 457
Olympic Games 215, 377, 380, 406
Organisation Todt 424
Origins of the human race 220, 221
Orphans' Homes 390
Orthodox Church 459
Oshima, Baron 143, 146, 158, 271, 487
Ownership of the soil 614

P
Palestine 502
Pallenberg, Max 572
Pan-Germanism 466
Papen, Franz von 54, 55, 174, 197, 198, 199, 211, 213, 333, 344, 440, 441, 442, 443, 444, 445, 446

Paris 6, 8, 18, 40, 41, 44, 60, 61, 78, 82, 86, 87, 183, 236, 237, 245, 246, 278, 304, 318, 346, 476, 488, 497, 588, 590, 592, 606, 629
Paris Opera House 628
Parliamentary immunity 614
Paul (Saul) of Tarsus 65, 66, 67, 68, 125, 127, 277, 450, 500, 502, 642, 643
Peace of Westphalia and the modern Germany 590
Peace with Britain 557
Penal system 17, 98, 99
Pétain, Henri Philippe 264, 422, 423, 424
Peter the Great 340, 550
Petroleum 2
Pfeffer, Franz von 275, 581
Piloty, Karl von 616
Pleiger, Paul 141
Pöhner, Ernst 250, 251, 255, 256, 332, 359
Poland 21, 25, 62, 71, 358, 369, 417, 590, 592
Polenta 101, 136
Poles 203, 208, 209, 354, 357, 358, 369, 416, 417, 419, 585
Pope 6, 7, 108, 129, 207, 209, 216, 258, 296, 364, 365, 386, 464, 477, 480, 494, 538, 541, 542, 553, 601
Porsche, Dr. Ferdinand 176, 287, 288
Port Arthur 30
Pour le Mérite 38
Primacy of race 71
Primo de Rivera, José Antonio 620
Production of honey 414
Propaganda 372, 465
Protector of Bohemia and Moravia 463
Protestantism 6, 78, 126
Prussia 379, 417
Ptolemy 284, 285, 394, 454
Puttkamer, Robert von 90

R
Racial mixtures 622
Racial pressure in the Eastern territories 522
Racial regeneration 414
Radio control in Russia 514
RAD, see *Reichsarbeitsdienst*
Raeder, Erich 134
Railways and national unity 515
Rainer, Friedrich 203, 611
Ramin, Jürgen von 121
Rathenau, Walther 402
Reclamation of the Pontine marshes 553
Reformation 460, 540
Reichsarbeitsdienst 31, 49, 363, 379, 399, 409, 580, 582, 636
Reichsmark and Ost-Mark 557
Reichsstatthalter 447, 475, 476, 492, 493, 496, 555, 635
Reichstag fire 580
Religious mania 456
Religious policy 639
Renaissance 7, 129, 182, 460, 547
Reparations 55, 383, 606
Republic of Venice 212, 276, 341
Research and Instruction 640
Results of National Socialist policy 439
Reticence in British public opinion 538
Rhineland 55, 231, 259, 446, 614, 619, 638
Ribbentrop, Joachim von 17, 88, 127, 158, 231, 441, 555
Riefenstahl, Leni 225, 637
Rintelen, Enno von 72
Röhm, Ernst 188, 244, 441, 489
Roman Empire 5, 7, 67, 97, 98, 226, 260, 337, 438, 596, 600
Romania 11, 27, 57, 58, 106, 130, 159, 297, 342, 435, 529, 623
Romanians 42, 57, 199, 203, 298, 459, 555, 597

Romans 5, 66–68, 97, 134, 166, 258, 276, 277, 298, 369, 392, 403, 431, 432, 479, 502, 568, 619, 623

Roman tolerance of religions 67

Rome 6–8, 41, 50, 65, 67–71, 76, 78, 86, 98, 102, 109, 110, 164, 166, 209, 226, 235

Rommel, Erwin 146, 152, 156, 157, 159, 160, 271, 469, 470, 480, 511, 512, 513, 548

Roosevelt, Franklin Delano 80, 81, 108, 110, 157, 158, 179, 210, 211, 270, 373, 478, 480, 485, 486, 509, 545

Rosenberg, Alfred 115, 336, 373, 425, 495, 580, 586

Ross, Colin 247, 248

Rost van Tonningen, Meinoud 356

Rothenberger, Curt 568

Rothermere, Lord 291, 410, 411, 607, 612–614

Rotteck, Karl von 76

Rubber 18, 29, 46, 63, 165, 175, 383

Rudolf of Habsburg 386

Rudolf von Habsburg 597

Rumania 11, 57, 58, 106, 130, 159, 297, 342, 435, 529, 623

Rumanians 555

Russia 1, 6, 12, 17, 18, 20, 22, 24, 26–28, 30, 36, 37, 47, 49, 59, 62, 68, 76, 81, 97, 108, 111, 113, 145, 160, 161, 183, 184, 186, 196, 197, 213, 232, 236, 258, 266, 280, 288, 289, 296, 298, 299, 303, 312, 334, 335, 340, 352, 354, 378, 381, 419, 426, 434, 460, 479, 480, 481, 514, 523, 543, 547, 561, 586, 588, 590–592, 605, 613

Russian-Finnish War 380

Russia's floating population 534

S

Saint Funicisla 458

Saint Paul 500, 642

SA *"Sturmabteilung"* (Brownshirts) 146, 148, 149, 235, 237, 241, 343, 409, 441, 443, 571

Sauckel, Ernst 58, 291, 292, 581

Schachleiter, Albanus 79

Schacht, Hjalmar 56, 229, 230, 377, 381–384, 563, 565, 567, 589

Scharnhorst, Gerhard von 95

Schaub, Julius 18, 256

Scheidemann, Philipp 240, 588

Schiller, Friedrich von 182, 214, 260, 278, 490

Schirach, Baldur von 41, 294, 303, 408, 409, 608, 636

Schloss Kiessheim 398

Scholtz-Klink, Gertrud Emma 225

Schönerer, Georg Ritter von 130, 131, 548

School of Fine Arts 85

Schools 377, 389

Schopenhauer, Arthur 75, 77, 315, 640, 641

Schreck, Julius 120, 147, 190, 216, 217, 273–275

Schröder, Ludwig von 558, 559

Schroeder, Christa 4, 144, 219

Schwarz, Franz 166, 167, 168, 169, 212, 252, 289–291, 357, 410, 411

Schweyer, Franz 7, 241, 256, 322

Science 3, 49, 50, 51, 52, 53, 56, 72, 73, 74, 75, 109, 126, 223, 278, 285, 286, 373, 392, 393, 394, 501, 541, 613, 636, 638, 643

Sea transport 491

Sebastopol 485, 486, 487, 497

Second Front 517

Sedan 21, 71

Seefeldt, Adolf 449, 572

Severing, Carl 136, 140, 141, 240

Seyss-Inquart, Arthur 303, 356

Shah of Persia 22, 346

Shakespeare 9, 260

Shaw, Bernard 490

Short pants 561
Singapore 143, 159, 164, 165, 178, 180, 245, 265, 325, 487
Sky-scrapers 598
Slav blood and German blood 632
Slavs 26, 28, 83, 161, 208, 259, 419, 550
Smoking 317
Social Democracy 16, 30, 39, 95, 578
Social Democratic Party 600
Social Democrats 17, 123, 378, 588
Society in France 520
South Africa 325
South Tyrol 489
Spain 28, 109, 141, 145, 257, 266, 281, 282, 362, 423, 424, 458, 459, 463, 464, 499, 505, 508, 538, 540–542, 593, 595, 596, 615, 619, 622
Spanish Civil War 282
Sparta 4, 100, 102
Speer, Albert 62, 72, 300, 394, 473, 474, 634
Spitzweg, Carl 526, 617
SS 10, 23, 91, 93, 127, 146, 147, 148, 153, 203, 204, 238, 343, 384, 407, 409, 462, 488, 489, 504, 509, 526, 561, 566, 571, 627
Stakhanovite system 523
Stalingrad 612, 622, 623
Stalin, Joseph 4, 6, 16, 18, 19, 22, 26, 60, 110, 160, 324, 374, 434, 497, 522, 523, 553, 556, 562, 588, 591, 592, 596, 613
Starhemberg, Ernst von 17, 78, 79, 485, 486
Stelzhamer, Franz 583
Stifter, Adalbert 583
Stoss, Veit 132
St. Paul 65, 66, 67, 68, 125, 127, 277, 502, 643
St. Petersburg 3, 554
Strasser, Gregor 332, 440
Streicher, Julius 136–140, 292, 367

Strength through Joy 394, 413, 521
Stresemann, Gustav 54, 253
Stuttgart 598
Submarines 388, 509, 535, 536, 624, 632
Sudetenland 87, 492
Suez Canal 490, 512
Suñer, Serrano 115, 463, 480, 506–508, 538, 542, 619, 622
Swastika 276, 357
Sweden 19, 23, 24, 47, 232, 440, 446, 462, 463, 500, 536, 620
Switzerland 23, 232, 257, 288, 500, 501, 546, 590, 591

T
Tabódy, Klára 617
Tannenberg 21, 44, 71, 198, 402, 414
Taxes 63, 112, 131, 211, 212, 534, 551
Terboven, Josef 127, 408, 409
Teutoberg forest 21
Teutonic nostalgia 630
Thälmann, Ernst 16, 17, 141
The Myth of the Twentieth Century 373
Theory of evolution 72
Thierack, Otto Georg 568
Thirty Years' War 43, 71, 203, 235, 309, 310, 355, 369, 568, 593, 605
Timoshenko, Semyon 512
Tiso, Jozef 578, 605
Titulescu, Nicolae 209
Tobacco 155, 281, 318, 337
Tobruk 470, 478, 480, 548
Todt, Fritz 58, 60, 106, 298, 424, 431, 507, 508
Topp, Erich 588
Torgler, Ernst 17, 141
Trade Unions 121, 301, 323
Transport of grain 535
Treaty of Versailles 199, 230, 359, 588, 593, 606
Tristan and Isolda 214

Troost, Frau 225
Troost, Paul Ludwig 182, 318, 394, 395
Trotsky, Leon 125
Trübner, Wilhelm 616, 617, 628
Turkey 22, 198, 264, 266, 299, 305, 334, 335, 344, 345, 352, 353, 413, 425, 485, 487, 544

U
Ukraine 11, 12, 24, 29, 32, 40, 46, 58, 59, 60, 81, 97, 101, 113, 354, 474, 522, 530, 550, 556, 588, 614, 615
Ukrainian women 551
Unification of Europe 482
United States of America 45, 81, 146, 166, 197, 229, 267, 269, 277, 287, 288, 348, 358, 367, 384, 423, 433, 434, 480, 523, 534, 538
Universal suffrage 600
Upper Silesia 396
Urals 3
Ustaše 83

V
Valentin, Karl 583
Vandals 97
Vansittart, Robert 246, 607
Vatican 129, 240, 333, 464, 491, 492, 494–496
Vegetarian diet 100, 391, 392
Vegetarianism 100, 110, 180, 205, 391, 392, 509, 510, 571
Versailles 197, 199, 230, 352, 354, 359, 360, 461, 588, 593, 606
Vichy 18, 304, 422, 424
Vichy France 18, 264, 304, 354, 422, 424
Vienna 23, 40, 41, 72, 86, 98, 130, 131, 167, 177, 182–184, 186, 192, 204, 220, 238, 260, 278, 283, 293, 294, 318, 327, 328, 347,

358, 393–395, 397, 401, 404, 406, 426, 450, 478, 494, 516, 529, 535, 550, 555, 582, 587, 596–598, 608, 609, 621, 628, 632–636
Vienna Opera House 183
Vikings 29, 100
Vögler, Albert 229
Völkischer Beobachter 120, 123, 194, 305, 306, 308, 309, 410, 412, 425, 579, 580
Volkswagen 176, 178, 249, 288, 368, 469, 470, 516
Voltaire 72, 73
Von Fallersleben (August Heinrich Hoffmann) 490, 584

W
Wagner, Cosima 214
Wagnerians 215
Wagner, Richard 10, 128, 130–133, 139, 181, 182, 215, 223, 225, 253, 278, 286, 308, 316, 321, 332, 406, 604, 637
Wagner, Robert 555
Wagner, Sigfried 307
Wallonia 407
Walloons 479
War expenses 407
War of the Spanish Succession 71
War with the partisans 600
Waterloo 21
Wavell, Archibald Percival 179
Weak and strong 542
Weber, Christian 187, 188, 189, 262, 287, 406, 612, 636
Weber, Gottlieb 631
Weimar 399, 598
Wesendonck, Mathilde 214
Whale oil will be replaced with vegetable oil 175
White race 36, 135, 143, 160
White Russia 59, 113
Wiedemann, Fritz 150

Witches burned at the stake 257
Wilhelmina 303, 526, 527
Wilson, Woodrow 606
Witzig, Rudolf 61
Wolff, Karl Otto 87
Wolf, Johanna 219
Wolfsschanze 299
World religions all claim to be the
　　　truth 75
Wotanism, impractical to resuscitate
　　　52

Y
Yellow peril 433

Young Plan 54, 55
Yugoslavia 11, 342, 546

Z
Zander, Elsbeth 138
Zeitzler, Kurt 154, 158, 239
Zentrum (Centre, or Catholic Party)
　　　588
Zentz, Eugen 250, 251
Zeppelin 452
Zollverein 47
Zwiedineck, Otto 642

Printed in the USA
CPSIA information can be obtained
at www.ICGtesting.com
LVHW020720251023
762021LV00003B/9